SOUTHEAST ASIAN AFFAIRS 2019

The **ISEAS – Yusof Ishak Institute** (formerly Institute of Southeast Asian Studies) is an autonomous organization established in 1968. It is a regional centre dedicated to the study of socio-political, security, and economic trends and developments in Southeast Asia and its wider geostrategic and economic environment. The Institute's research programmes are grouped under Regional Economic Studies (RES), Regional Strategic and Political Studies (RSPS), and Regional Social and Cultural Studies (RSCS). The Institute is also home to the ASEAN Studies Centre (ASC), the Nalanda-Sriwijaya Centre (NSC) and the Singapore APEC Study Centre.

ISEAS Publishing, an established academic press, has issued more than 2,000 books and journals. It is the largest scholarly publisher of research about Southeast Asia from within the region. ISEAS Publishing works with many other academic and trade publishers and distributors to disseminate important research and analyses from and about Southeast Asia to the rest of the world.

Contents

Introduction vii
Khairulanwar Zaini and Malcolm Cook

THE REGION
Challenges to Southeast Asian Regionalism in 2018 3
Leszek Buszynski

Regional Integration in Asia and the Pacific, and Dealing with Short and Long Term Challenges 21
Jayant Menon

Looking West, Acting East: India's Indo-Pacific Strategy 43
Rohan Mukherjee

An Australian Vision of the Indo-Pacific and What It Means for Southeast Asia 53
Rory Medcalf

The Trump Administration's Free and Open Indo-Pacific Approach 61
Brian Harding

Japan's "Free and Open Indo-Pacific Strategy" and Its Implication for ASEAN 69
Tomohiko Satake

BRUNEI DARUSSALAM
Brunei Darussalam: Making Strides with a Renewed Focus on the Future 85
Mahani Hamdan and Chang-Yau Hoon

CAMBODIA
Cambodia in 2018: A Year of Setbacks and Successes 105
Sorpong Peou

INDONESIA
Indonesia in 2018: The Calm before the Election Storm 123
Natalie Sambhi

Indonesia-China Relations: Coming Full Circle? 145
Dewi Fortuna Anwar

LAOS
Laos on the Path to Socialism? 165
Boike Rehbein

Rent Capitalism and Shifting Plantations in the Mekong Borderlands 177
Yos Santasombat

MALAYSIA
Malaysia in 2018: The Year of Voting Dangerously 195
Geoffrey K. Pakiam

GE14 in East Malaysia: MA63 and Marching to a Different Drum 211
James Chin

MYANMAR
Myanmar in 2018: New Democracy Hangs in the Balance 225
Morten B. Pedersen

Ethnicity, Citizenship and Identity in Post-2016 Myanmar 243
Moe Thuzar and Darren Cheong

THE PHILIPPINES
Toxic Democracy? The Philippines in 2018 261
Nicole Curato

The Rise of China, New Immigrants and Changing Policies on Chinese Overseas: Impact on the Philippines 275
Teresita Ang See and Carmelea Ang See

SINGAPORE
Singapore in 2018: Between Uncharted Waters and Old Ghosts 297
George Wong and Woo Jun Jie

THAILAND
Thailand in 2018: Military Dictatorship under Royal Command 327
Eugénie Mérieau

Competing Logics: Between Thai Sovereignty and the China Model in 2018 341
Gregory V. Raymond

TIMOR-LESTE
Timor-Leste in 2018: An Eventful Year Ends in Tension 361
Michael Leach

VIETNAM
Vietnam in 2018: A Rent-Seeking State on Correction Course 375
Alexander L. Vuving

Vietnam and Mekong Cooperative Mechanisms 395
To Minh Thu and Le Dinh Tinh

Introduction

Khairulanwar Zaini and Malcolm Cook

The year 2018 was an eventful one for Southeast Asia, with many of its developments likely to shape those in 2019 and beyond. In 2018, the United States' policy towards China, and by extension towards the region more broadly, crystallized into one of full-spectrum major power rivalry. The broader Indo-Pacific regional strategic concept is gradually replacing the long-standing Asia-Pacific one. It could well be that 2018 is seen as the year that the post–Cold War Asia-Pacific era ended.

There was better news on the regional economic front. The inelegantly named Comprehensive and Progressive Agreement for Trans-Pacific Partnership (CPTPP) was signed by eleven states and ratified by seven, while the ASEAN-led Regional Comprehensive Economic Partnership (RCEP) negotiations experienced what in diplomatic language is termed "substantial progress".

A number of domestic developments in the eleven states of Southeast Asia also had wider regional implications. The Rohingya crisis in Myanmar demonstrated the limits of the ASEAN Way, as noted by Leszek Buszynski in his chapter on regional security. Malaysia's surprise election result and first change of government by the ballot box countered the narrative about the decline of democracy in Southeast Asia and brought Dr Mahathir back on to the regional scene. In the Philippines, the passage of the Bangsamoro Organic Law offers the best chance of addressing the long-running Moro insurgency in Muslim Mindanao and the safe haven this conflict has provided for local and regional terrorists.

KHAIRULANWAR ZAINI is Research Associate at the ISEAS – Yusof Ishak Institute, Singapore.

MALCOLM COOK is Senior Fellow at the ISEAS – Yusof Ishak Institute, Singapore.

The twenty-four chapters of *Southeast Asia Affairs 2019*, written by twenty-nine authors, reflect the diversity within the eleven countries that make up the region, and they provide timely analysis of the current political, economic and social developments at the regional level and in each country. Four themes in particular connect a large number of these chapters and reflect structural, rather than temporary, factors that will help determine the trajectories of the region as a whole and those of its eleven states for the foreseeable future.

The Indo-Pacific

The regional section of this edition features four shorter pieces looking at the development of the Indo-Pacific regional security concept in the United States, Japan, India and Australia. Brian Harding's contribution on the United States focuses on the role of strategic rivalry with China. Tomohiko Satake for Japan and Rory Medcalf for Australia address directly Southeast Asian and ASEAN's concerns with the Indo-Pacific, particularly the place of ASEAN in the concept. Rohan Mukherjee's contribution on India is organized around the elaboration by Prime Minister Modi of the Indo-Pacific concept in his keynote speech at the 2018 Shangri La Dialogue in Singapore. The four national concepts are overlapping but are far from the same.

Leszek Buszynski presents the Indo-Pacific concept as a major challenge for ASEAN, which has long favoured an Asia-Pacific outlook. Natalie Sambhi's review of Indonesia covers Indonesia's own Indo-Pacific concept, which it has been promoting with limited success within ASEAN since 2013. It is unlikely that the Indonesian version will supplant those of the United States, Japan, India or Australia. How these Indo-Pacific concepts of the United States, Japan, India and Australia develop and deepen strategic cooperation between the four countries, and how China reacts to this, is a major new strategic factor for Southeast Asia, and one that Southeast Asian states have limited ability to affect.

Chinese Economic Penetration into the Region

The strategic rivalry between the United States and China occurs as China's economic activities in Southeast Asia gather pace, especially through its signature Belt and Road Initiative (BRI). For many countries in the region, Chinese investment has proven to be a much-needed economic boon. For instance, Mahani Hamdan and Chang-Yau Hoon describe how "Chinese investments are important to Brunei's economic diversification strategy" as the oil-rich sultanate pursues an economic future less reliant on fossil fuels.

As China deepens its economic penetration into the region, it has increasingly sought to parlay its economic largesse into political influence and geostrategic advantage. Sorpong Peou reveals how this has unfolded in Cambodia, for whom China remains the largest donor and investor. Commenting on the "nineteen new memorandums of understanding and other agreements" signed during Premier Li Keqiang's state visit to Cambodia in January 2018, Peou suggests that this indicates "Cambodia's growing dependence on China, not only for economic development but also for political protection and security". China was also key in defending Prime Minister Hun Sen's electoral victory in July amidst domestic and international accusations of a sham election. In return, Cambodia has adopted a staunchly "pro-China foreign policy", which involves being "a reliable supporter" of China's territorial and maritime claims in the South China Sea and scuppering regional efforts by ASEAN to address the issue. Morten Pedersen also describes how China pursues a similar strategy in Myanmar, with China agreeing to finance various economic initiatives and mega-infrastructure projects while shielding Myanmar from scrutiny at the United Nations over the Rohingya issue.

This is not to say that China has been entirely successful in its efforts to translate its economic influence into regional hegemony. Gregory Raymond charts how China has not merely functioned as a critical economic partner, but also as a potential model of governance for Thailand over the past five years since the 2014 military coup. However, Raymond argues that the imperatives of national identity and sovereignty are gradually prompting Thailand to move away from further embracing the "China Model of marrying political authoritarianism with free market liberalism", and to pursue instead improved relations with Thailand's other strategic partners in order to balance and manage China's dominance. In a similar vein, Boike Rehbein argues that the "return to socialist rhetoric" under the government of Prime Minister Thongloun Sisoulith is an effort to both negotiate the ongoing capitalist and consumerist transformation of Laotian society as well as to manage Chinese economic influence in order to avoid becoming "China's puppet". Alexander Vuving also details Vietnam's cautious approach towards economic opportunities under the BRI, with Vietnamese government officials seeking "to find a way to placate Beijing without increasing its dependence on China".

Furthermore, there remains lingering scepticism in the region towards Chinese economic generosity. The spectre of Hambantota looms large. Chinese offers of infrastructural investment are often underwritten by loans from Chinese state-owned financial institutions, involving sums that are relatively considerable, especially for the smaller economies in the region. In their chapters, Rehbein and Vuving raise the growing domestic anxieties in Cambodia and Vietnam about the possible use of debt diplomacy by the Chinese. These fears are echoed by the authors of the two chapters on the Philippines, especially as President Rodrigo Duterte continues to leverage his administration's friendly relations with China to secure Chinese funding for his infrastructure programme.

The growing Chinese economic presence can also prove to be a domestic liability for some governments in the region. For instance, Geoffrey Pakiam identifies how this issue became "a major flashpoint" during the Malaysian general elections in May, with incumbent prime minister Najib Razak receiving flak for his government's dependence on Chinese money to fund signature infrastructural initiatives. Similarly, Dewi Fortuna Anwar reports that President Joko Widodo, or Jokowi, is coming under "increasing criticism for not sufficiently protecting Indonesia's wider national interests in his pursuit of Chinese foreign investment". According to Natalie Sambhi, this is an especially potent line of attack against Jokowi as he faces re-election in April 2019, with his opponent looking to mount a populist campaign accusing him of "allowing the country's resources to be plundered by foreign forces". Moreover, one significant bugbear for Indonesians, as Sambhi notes, is the influx of Chinese migrant labour as a result of the infrastructural projects. Dewi Fortuna similarly discusses how widespread misapprehensions about Chinese immigration have been manipulated into a "massive black campaign on social media" against Jokowi, accusing him of "being a handmaiden of both China's and local [Chinese Indonesian] interests". In their thematic chapter on the Philippines, Teresita Ang See and Carmelea See also discuss how the prominent presence of Chinese migrants (and their reported involvement with crime) has contributed to societal tensions as well as reinforced public resentment at President Duterte's accommodationist policies with China.

Furthermore, countries in the region may find themselves burdened with the long-lasting environmental repercussions of Chinese economic investment. In his discussion of Chinese-owned banana production in the Mekong riparian regions, Yos Santasombat documents how the system of "shifting plantations" has resulted in health hazards and environmental degradation in one particular Laotian town. As these banana plantations occupy plots of land only on short-term leases, there is also uncertainty about whether the small and medium Chinese investors would assume responsibility for soil depletion upon their departure, especially since the aggressive growth and irrigation techniques in these banana plantations leave the ground barren and unsuitable for re-conversion to rice cultivation. For Santasombat, this will become an increasingly regional concern as Chinese investors seek to replicate the practice of shifting plantations, particularly along the Mekong borderlands of Myanmar, Cambodia and Thailand.

Regime Renewal: Elections

Three countries in the region — Malaysia, Timor-Leste and Cambodia — underwent elections in 2018, with new governing coalitions emerging victorious against the incumbents in Malaysia and Timor-Leste.

Geoffrey Pakiam narrates the developments in Malaysia that preceded the "stunning" electoral victory of the Pakatan Harapan on 9 May. Defeating the UMNO-led Barisan Nasional — which had hitherto been in power in one incarnation or another since Malaysia's independence in 1959 — required a political rapprochement between Mahathir Mohamad and some of his erstwhile foes during his first term in office, including one-time protégé Anwar Ibrahim. Pakiam raises concerns about the Pakatan government's future prospects, especially when it comes to stabilizing its intra-coalitional politics in light of the pending succession of the premiership from Mahathir to Anwar within an agreed-upon two-year time frame.

In a similar vein, James Chin highlights how coalitional politics in Malaysia will have to contend with the growing importance of local political parties in East Malaysia in determining the federal balance of power. This means that any governing coalition relying on the support of East Malaysian federal parliamentarians to maintain their majority must seriously address the pervasive sense of "historical grievance" felt by the residents of Sabah and Sarawak over what they perceive to be the federal government's persistent failure to respect the "special position" of the two states under the Malaysian Agreement of 1963 (MA63). The continued underdevelopment of Sabah and Sarawak, especially relative to the progress in the peninsular states, also engenders public resentment. Despite leading the country in oil and gas production, the East Malaysian states have yet to reap much benefit, since ownership of natural resources is vested by law in the federal government. Hence, as the parties in Sabah and Sarawak follow the lead of public sentiment in becoming more attuned to issues of state nationalism and sovereignty, federal coalitions must be prepared to negotiate with these parties over their demands for greater autonomy and a more equitable share of petroleum revenue, not least to avert the development of outright secessionist or independence movements in the two states.

Coalitional politics also played a significant role in Timor-Leste, although it came with the unprecedented challenge of "cohabitation tensions" between the president and parliament. Michael Leach recounts how the failure of the Fretilin minority government to pass its budget prompted a second election in as many years, leading to the "decisive" victory of the Alliance of Change for Progress (AMP) as it emerged with an outright, if narrow, parliamentary majority — a significant feat under Timor-Leste's proportional electoral system. Two of the parties in the three-party AMP coalition are the National Congress for Timorese Reconstruction (CNRT) and the Popular Liberation Party (PLP), the respective parties of Xanana Gusmão and Taur Matan Ruak — two former presidents of Timor-Leste as well as veteran leaders of the armed resistance group FALINTIL who had been "at loggerheads" during the 2017 elections. Leach characterizes the campaigns of the 2018 election in terms of a "resurgence of the 'history wars' ", with the hustings turning into "a contest between the military front and members of the diplomatic front, who were outside the country during the occupation". However, despite the resounding victory of the AMP, Leach describes how hopes for stability were thwarted by the "first experience of genuine 'cohabitation' in Timor-Leste's semi-presidential system between a Fretilin president and an AMP [parliamentary] government". The AMP government encountered early difficulties as President Francisco Guterres refused to approve certain ministerial appointments, which portends future challenges as the AMP lacks the necessary two-thirds parliamentary majority to override presidential vetoes.

The election results in Cambodia however bucked the trend of deposing incumbents. Sorpong Peou identifies "the beginnings of a one-party state" in Cambodia as the ruling Cambodian People's Party further consolidated its control with a clean sweep of all parliamentary and senatorial seats. This was in large part due to Prime Minister Hun Sen's sustained persecution of the opposition, in particular the Cambodia National Rescue Party (CNRP). Expectations that the CNRP could improve on its electoral performance in 2013 (in which it secured 55 out of 123 seats) were thwarted by the imprisonment of party president Kem Sokha for treason in 2017, the same year that the party itself was dissolved by the Supreme Court and had 118 of its party officials banned from participating in politics for a period of five years.

Meanwhile, forthcoming elections in 2019 drove the political momentum in Indonesia and Thailand. Natalie Sambhi describes the "calm before the storm" in Indonesia as it looks forward to a "rematch of the 2014 presidential race" between Jokowi and Prabowo Subianto. Sambhi discusses the significance of Jokowi's new running mate, describing how the choice of Ma'ruf Amin — spiritual leader of Nahdlatul Ulama and head of the Indonesian Ulama Council — helps to "further boost Jokowi's Islamic credentials" and to counter the support that Prabowo has cultivated among certain Islamic parties and organizations.

In Thailand, the junta prepares to hold the first general election since the May 2014 military coup, which will also be the first to be organized under the new "permanent" constitution promulgated in April 2017. However, Eugénie Mérieau argues that the elections will not herald Thailand's "return" to democracy. This is due to the slew of constitutional, statutory and administrative provisions which effectively guarantee that "the tutelary powers, identified as the monarchy and the army, can veto decisions of elected politicians whenever needed, while allowing some degree of electoral politics to play out". Mérieau also outlines the challenges that a non-military prime ministerial aspirant might face, both in terms of getting elected and of governing in tandem with a Senate fully appointed by the military.

Political developments in Myanmar and Singapore also signalled the incumbents' preoccupations about the prospect of elections in the near future. With elections looming in 2020, Morten Pedersen identifies how the National League for Democracy (NLD) in Myanmar has engaged in a "new reform push" in order to "maintain voter support and consolidate civilian, democratic government", which has included the election of the "more decisive" U Win Myint as the new head of state and the restructuring of the Cabinet economics team with the elevation of U Soe Win as finance minister and U Thaung Tun as investment minister. These changes, according to Pedersen, signal the NLD's pivot towards economic issues, with both State Counsellor Aung San Suu Kyi and the new president reiterating "the need to step up efforts to improve the socio-economic lives of the people" in their speeches following the latter's inauguration.

For Singapore, while Prime Minister Lee Hsien Loong is expected to remain as party leader in the next election (which is not due until April 2021), George Wong and Woo Jun Jie analyse how the ruling People's Action Party (PAP) is assiduously preparing for its "first leadership transition since the passing of Lee Kuan Yew". Wong and Woo describe how members of the fourth-generation (4G) leadership ranks are being accorded more ministerial responsibilities, with the appointment of Finance Minister Heng Swee Keat as the party's 1st Assistant Secretary-General, indicating his status as the frontrunner to succeed to the premiership. For Wong and Woo, the cautious management of this transition belies the PAP's "stance of not throwing caution to the wind" as it approaches the ballot box with its new slate of 4G leaders.

Regime Renewal: Power Consolidation

Regime consolidation was another significant feature in the domestic politics of the region as many governments invested significant effort in entrenching their power and lengthening their longevity through illiberal and authoritarian policies. Sorpong Peou describes how the Hun Sen government in Cambodia has not only used the judiciary to harass and suppress the opposition but has also sought to terminate the work of the Extraordinary Chambers in the Court of Cambodia, the tribunal responsible for prosecuting the former leaders of the Khmer Rouge regime for crimes against humanity and war crimes during their reign of terror. In a similar vein, Nicole Curato depicts the increasingly "toxic character" of Philippine democracy under the administration of President Duterte, arising especially from harassment by his government of online media platform *Rappler* and the ouster of chief justice Maria Lourdes Sereno from the Supreme Court. Curato also draws attention to the "strongman" tendencies of the president, especially in his "iron-fisted" approach to governance and his aversion to public consultation in the shutdown of Boracay and in the rehabilitation of Marawi.

There was also a noticeable tightening of civil society in Laos and Singapore. Boike Rehbein identifies how a recent revision to Decree 115 compels all civil society organizations in Laos to register and seek official approval on an annual basis, which narrows the already-constrained space in which these organizations operate. In Singapore, George Wong and Woo Jun Jie describe "how the PAP government continued to act vigorously against what it regarded as unfounded charges of corruption in government or slurs against the country's judiciary". In 2018, a civil society activist and a opposition politician were found guilty of scandalizing the judiciary with their Facebook posts, while the nephew of the prime minister is currently contesting a similar contempt of court charge.

Alexander Vuving discusses the anti-graft campaign undertaken in Vietnam under the supervision of the Communist Party of Vietnam general secretary Nguyen Phu Trong, which Vuving characterizes as an effort ultimately aimed at staving off "political liberalism". Currently wearing the "dual hat" of party chief and head of state, Trong has sought to dismantle various rent-seeking networks in the government, military and police, and these efforts have resulted in the arrests and imprisonment of a significant number of senior officials. Vuving however highlights the circumspect reach of this anti-corruption programme; Trong has chosen to leave untouched certain officials and their rent-seeking networks in order not to "break the vase when beating the rats". This, Vuving suggests, reflects the "higher goal" of political stability underlying Trong's crusade against corruption.

Identity Politics: Ethnic and Nationalist Revivalism

With the legacy of colonial migration, and national borders reflecting administrative rather than organic boundaries, the management of polyglot societies remains a pre-eminent concern for many of the post-colonial states of Southeast Asia. However, the increasing weaponization of identity politics portends how sectarianism may become an abiding feature of regional politics in the near future. In her chapter on Indonesia, Natalie Sambhi conveys her concerns about the potential "blacksliding in social and religious pluralism" as hard-line groups like the Islamic Defenders Front (FPI) gains ascendancy, especially in the wake of the conviction of then Jakarta governor Basuki Tjahaja Purnama (or Ahok) for blasphemy in May 2017. The Surabaya church bombings in 2018 have also contributed to a more hostile atmosphere for the country's Chinese-Christian minority.

Suspicions of the ethnic Chinese are also rife in the Philippines. Teresita Ang See and Carmelea Ang See describe how local resentment against China and Chinese immigrants has occasionally spilled over into a general animus against local-born Chinese Filipinos, or Tsinoys. The authors also point out that the situation has been aggravated by China's failure to strictly distinguish between Chinese nationals abroad and foreign citizens of Chinese descent in its recent iterations of its diasporic policy.

The two chapters on Myanmar also highlight the centrifugal capacity of ethnic politics, as the military remains "unable to make any substantial progress" with the various ethnic armed organizations (EAOs) under the 21st Century Panglong peace process. While the Tatmadaw expects EAOs to disarm under the National Ceasefire Agreement prior to peace negotiations, many EAOs consider such unilateral disarmament to be a "de facto surrender". Moreover, the situation in Myanmar is also complicated by the persecution of the Rohingya Muslims in Rakhine State. For Moe Thuzar and Darren Cheong, the shared "contextual origin" of the two issues lies in "the entrenchment of Bamar ethnic nationalism", which leads to the "marginalization of Myanmar's minority ethnic populace".

Conclusion

In a presentation on 8 January 2019 at the ISEAS – Yusof Ishak Institute, the Australian diplomat Peter Varghese noted how "trends are like waves. We can see them on the horizon but we do not know exactly when they will break and in what pattern they will reach the shore".[1] Some trends like the major power rivalry between the United States and China became visible at the horizon, while others like the end of UMNO-led rule in Malaysia crashed on to the shore. The scanning of the 2018 horizon contained in this edition of *Southeast Asian Affairs* should help readers to have a better idea of what may appear on the region's horizon in 2019, and on those of its eleven diverse states.

Note

1. Peter Varghese, *The Indo-Pacific and Its Strategic Challenges: An Australian Perspective*, Trends in Southeast Asia 2019, no. 4 (Singapore, ISEAS – Yusof Ishak Institute, 2019), p. 13 <https://www.iseas.edu.sg/images/pdf/TRS4_19.pdf>.

The Region

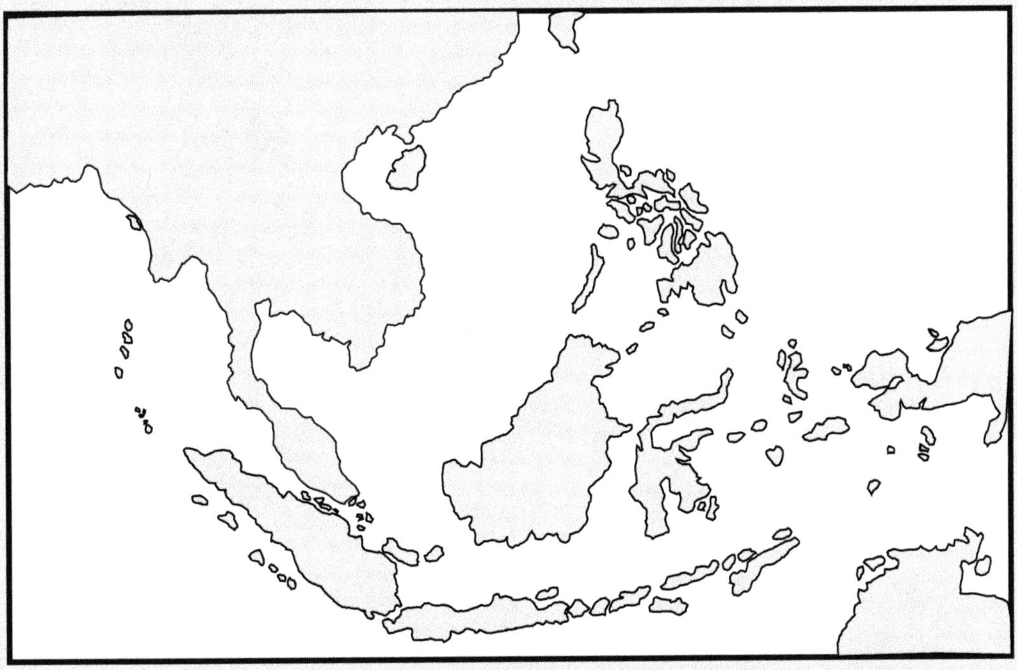

CHALLENGES TO SOUTHEAST ASIAN REGIONALISM IN 2018

Leszek Buszynski

The year 2018 saw various trends and developments that posed challenges to ASEAN and its future. One was the ongoing difficulty the grouping has had in dealing with the Rohingya problem, which reveals the constraints and limitations under which it operates. The Rohingya problem became internationalized as the issue was taken up by international agencies and external governments in the face of ASEAN inaction. Secondly, with regard to the issue of the South China Sea, the United States and China faced off against each other in a way that sidelined ASEAN. ASEAN's relevance to this issue might be ensured in the negotiation of a Code of Conduct (CoC) with China, but 2018 saw little progress on a matter that has been on the table for several decades now. Thirdly, the ASEAN economies were being steadily integrated into a wider region that included its major trading partners and sources of investment. ASEAN's pursuit of broader trade regimes with its external trading partners such as the Regional Comprehensive Economic Partnership (RCEP) and the Trans Pacific Partnership (TPP) pose a major challenge to its centrality. Moreover, the so-called trade war that erupted between the United States under President Donald Trump and China exposed the vulnerabilities of the ASEAN economies, although opportunities were also present. Fourth, the notion of the Indo-Pacific gained currency in 2018, not only amongst ASEAN's external

---

LESZEK BUSZYNSKI is Visiting Fellow with the Strategic and Defence Studies Centre at the Australian National University, Canberra Australia. He has published widely on Asia-Pacific security issues and is the author of "ASEAN, Grand Strategy and the South China Sea; Between China and the United States" in *Great Powers Grand Strategies: The New Game in the South China Sea*, edited by Anders Corr (2018). He was editor of and contributor to *The South China Sea Maritime Dispute: Political, Legal and Regional Perspectives* (2014).

partners but in Indonesia as well. The idea of Southeast Asia that was included in the Bangkok Declaration of August 1967 has been a supporting foundation for ASEAN regionalism, but how this can be reconciled with the notion of the Indo-Pacific will be ASEAN's major challenge.

ASEAN's Rohingya Problem

The Rohingya problem has bedevilled ASEAN for the past three decades. Myanmar's relationship with ASEAN has been troubled ever since the Myanmar military pushed some 250,000 of the Muslim minority from Rakhine State to Bangladesh in 1991 and 1992. The problem has been festering ever since and has demonstrated ASEAN's inability to deal with a member who invokes the non-intervention clause of ASEAN's founding charter, Article 2 of the Treaty of Amity and Cooperation and Article 2(a) of the ASEAN Charter of 2007. The Myanmar military has simply and successfully resisted demands within ASEAN to curb its campaigns against the Rohingya. In August 2017, after the Arakan Rohingya Salvation Army attacked military and police outposts, the Myanmar military launched yet another campaign and, according to the UNHCR, over 720,000 Rohingya were pushed into the Cox's Bazar district of Bangladesh. When the prime minister of Bangladesh Sheikh Hasina addressed the United Nations General Assembly on 28 September 2018, she declared that there were now 1.1 million Rohingya refugees in her country.[1]

ASEAN has had its hands tied by its non-interference charter and the conditions by which members joined. At the ASEAN Summit on 28 April 2018, the chair's statement reported that ASEAN leaders had received a briefing from Myanmar on the humanitarian situation in Rakhine State. The statement also expressed "support for the Myanmar Government in its efforts to bring peace, stability, the rule of law, to promote harmony and reconciliation among the various communities as well as to ensure sustainable and equitable development in Rakhine State".[2] The foreign ministers of ASEAN also met informally on the sidelines of the UN General Assembly in late September to urge Myanmar to form an independent commission of inquiry to investigate the reported abuses. Singapore's foreign minister Vivian Balakrishnan said that the purpose of such an inquiry would be "to hold all those responsible fully accountable".[3] As Balakrishnan explained, ASEAN wanted to facilitate the voluntary repatriation of the Rohingya, which Myanmar has resisted.

Within ASEAN the issue has been advanced by Muslim-majority member states Malaysia and Indonesia, while being resisted by Thailand and Myanmar.

Frustration with ASEAN's muted response over this issue has in the past stimulated calls for a change in its internal decision-making process from one of consensus to some form of majority voting, thus helping to prevent a one-country veto over issues that concerned the majority. Surin Pitsuwan, the Thai foreign minister from 1997 to 2001 and a Muslim from southern Thailand, was distressed by the violence against the Rohingya. Surin had once promoted the notion of "flexible engagement" as a modification to ASEAN's principle of non-interference in each other's domestic affairs. However, any attempt to modify the consensus rule in favour of majority voting was too radical for ASEAN, and any change had to be agreed to by consensus anyway.

Despite the anguish caused by the Rohingya issue amongst the Muslim-majority member states, ASEAN was bound by the rules of its formation and constrained from taking the lead over the issue. In December 2017, Balakrishnan called the Rohingya issue a humanitarian disaster but stressed that consensus was the foundation of ASEAN's unity and that "unity and centrality are key to our survival".[4] The director general of ASEAN cooperation in Indonesia's Foreign Ministry, Jose Tavares, said in November 2017 that members saw little need to change ASEAN's decision-making procedures and that there would be no reforms to strengthen the grouping's institutional capacity.[5] Weeks later, the outspoken Indonesian diplomat in a public forum criticized ASEAN's record on human rights and the little progress it has made since the ASEAN Human Rights Declaration was adopted in November 2012.[6]

Within Malaysia, there were also calls for a firmer position against Myanmar over this issue. The chair of the ASEAN Inter-Parliamentary Myanmar Caucus, Datuk Zaid Ibrahim, wrote that Malaysia should take what he called a case of "genocide" to the International Court of Justice.[7] Similarly, the new Pakatan Harapan government headed by Mahathir which was elected on 9 May 2018 was particularly concerned about the treatment of Muslims, in Myanmar as well as in China. When Mahathir was the leader of Malaysia back in the 1990s, he had agitated against the Myanmar military's campaign against the Rohingya in 1991 and 1992. Nevertheless, Mahathir supported Myanmar's membership of ASEAN in 1997. Now elected once again as Malaysia's premier as head of the Pakatan coalition, Mahathir has expressed his disappointment with Myanmar's state councillor Aung San Suu Kyi for her refusal to condemn the military's campaign against the Rohingya. Describing her as a "changed person", Mahathir revealed that he had lost faith in her.[8] Malaysia's prime-minister-in-waiting Anwar Ibrahim was more outspoken when he declared that he was "appalled" by Aung San Suu Kyi, while also condemning China's treatment of the Muslim Uighurs.[9]

In Jakarta, public protests by Islamic organizations were held outside the Myanmar Embassy. Legislators from Indonesia's House of Representatives called for humanitarian intervention under Chapters VI and VII of the UN Charter. They also anticipate that Indonesia's elevation to the UN Security Council as a non-permanent member over 2019–20 would allow it to press the Myanmar government for action, and possibly even referring the issue to the International Criminal Court (ICC).[10] Indonesia's President Jokowi has adopted a diplomatic approach and he expressed his country's concerns over the issue when he met with Myanmar's new president, Win Myint, before the ASEAN summit in April 2018. Jokowi called for the implementation of the UN-recommended measures to alleviate the humanitarian crisis, which includes allowing humanitarian aid workers into the north of Rakhine state and setting up an independent investigation into the Rohingya issue.[11]

President Duterte of the Philippines has similarly called the Rohingya crisis "genocide" and pledged to accept refugees from Myanmar. However, Duterte himself is facing criticism from human right activists for his policy of extra-judicial killings in the Philippines. Having attacked his foreign critics for "meddling with the Philippines' affairs", Duterte has advised Aung San Suu Kyi to similarly ignore her critics as he does.[12]

In Thailand there was a different picture. Under a democratic government in the 1990s, human rights activists held demonstrations in Bangkok against the Thai government's engagement of Myanmar and its unwillingness to condemn the violence against the Rohingya. The current military government in Thailand has however suppressed all protests against Myanmar, including instructing the police to close a public forum in Bangkok on 10 September 2018 at which various activists had been scheduled to speak on the Rohingya issue. The explanation given for the shutdown was that Thailand's national security and "neighbourly relations" were at stake.[13]

The Rohingya issue has, however, become internationalized and elevated well beyond ASEAN's constrained parameters, as various international agencies have weighed in to express alarm over what has become a humanitarian disaster in a way that has bypassed ASEAN. The Annual Report of the UN High Commissioner for Refugees (UNHCR) and the UN Human Rights Council of 3 July 2018 detailed "grave human rights violations and abuses carried out in a systematic, targeted and deliberate manner by the Myanmar security forces".[14] In their report of 27 August 2018, UN investigators concluded that "criminal investigation and prosecution is warranted, focusing on the top Tatmadaw generals, in relation to the three categories of crimes under international law; genocide, crimes against humanity and war crimes."[15] UN secretary-general Antonio Guterres described the "horrendous persecution" of the Rohingya as a case of "ethnic cleansing".[16] The U.S. State Department also conducted its own investigations of the Rohingya situation based on interviews conducted in refugee camps in Bangladesh in April 2018. While U.S. representative to the UN Nikki Haley declared that the State Department's findings were "consistent" with those of the UN, she avoided using the term "genocide", since the Genocide Convention of 1948 would obligate the United States to impose punitive measures against Myanmar.[17]

Similarly, a UN Human Rights Council mission reported that it had "established consistent patterns of serious human rights violations and abuses", and called for the prosecution of Myanmar's army chief Senior General Min Aung Hlaing and five other top-ranking generals for genocide, war crimes and crimes against humanity.[18] UN investigators, with the support of Sweden's deputy UN ambassador Carl Skau, called for the situation in Myanmar to be brought to the attention of the ICC, which would require a referral by the Security Council.[19] On 18 September 2018, ICC prosecutor Fatou Bensouda declared that the court could exercise jurisdiction over the Rohingya issue on the basis that Bangladesh had signed the Rome Treaty, even though Myanmar had not. The ICC would begin a preliminary investigation of the situation.[20] However, a referral to the ICC would require a Security Council decision, and this is unlikely in view of China's support for Myanmar. In the absence of a referral, the ICC prosecutor can only initiate an investigation and gather information that can be presented to the five permanent members of the Security Council.

China and the South China Sea

The South China Sea has become an arena of confrontation between the United States and China, leaving ASEAN on the sidelines but exposed to its destabilizing consequences. China concluded its construction of military facilities and runways on Subi, Mischief and Fiery Cross reefs, triggering accusations that it was militarizing the South China Sea. In May 2018 it was reported that China had installed cruise and anti-ship missiles on these reefs — the last step in its efforts to fortify them.[21] During his Senate confirmation hearings in April 2018, the commander of the U.S. Indo-Pacific Command, Admiral Philip S. Davidson, claimed that "China is now capable of controlling the South China Sea in all scenarios short of war with the United States".[22] The Trump administration continued with its Freedom of Navigation Operations (FONOPs), with four FONOPs conducted in 2018 — on 23 March, 27 May, 30 September and 26 November. On 30 September there was a near collision between the USS *Decatur* and a Chinese warship in the South China Sea, which may portend a tougher response from the Chinese. However, the United States was not alone on insisting on "freedom of navigation" in the South China Sea, as the amphibious assault ship HMS *Albion* of Britain's Royal Navy sailed close to the Paracel Islands on 31 August. The Japanese submarine *Kuroshio*, helicopter carrier *Kaga* and two destroyers — *Inazuma* and *Suzutsuki* — also conducted an anti-submarine warfare exercise in the South China Sea on 13 September.[23]

ASEAN has struggled to maintain its unity over this dispute, as it is pulled in different directions by members with claims in the South China Sea, such as Vietnam, and non-claimants such as Cambodia and Laos who prioritize their relationships with China. When the ASEAN foreign ministers met on 6 February 2018, they carefully avoided taking sides, while stressing the importance of "non-militarization and self-restraint in the conduct of all activities by claimants and all other states", and the importance of "freedom of navigation in, and overflight above, the South China Sea".[24] ASEAN's concern to maintain good relations with China was reflected in the first ASEAN-China Maritime Field Training Exercise, which was conducted from 22 to 27 October in Zhanjiang. Naval units from China and five ASEAN countries — Brunei, the Philippines, Singapore, Thailand and Vietnam — were involved.[25]

Most urgent for ASEAN is to negotiate a CoC with China. The CoC is meant to govern activities in the South China Sea in order to avoid dangerous incidents that could escalate into conflict. However, the CoC has been under negotiation for over two decades as ASEAN members have pressed for a legally binding agreement with a dispute resolution mechanism — which China resists. On 6 August 2017 the foreign ministers of ASEAN and China met in Manila and agreed on a "framework" for a CoC to pave the way for further negotiations. While the Chinese have joined these negotiations, they have not shown any enthusiasm for concluding them, which indicates that Beijing had not formed a consensus on the issue. At the ASEAN summit in November 2017, Chinese premier Li Keqiang declared that the CoC would be a "stabilizer" for the region, but when pressed by Philippine president Rodrigo Duterte to identify a timetable with a specific date for the conclusion of the negotiations, Li avoided the issue.[26] The respective ASEAN and Chinese foreign ministers met again in March 2018, allowing Singapore's Vivian Balakrishnan to announce the following June that they have agreed on a common "working text" for negotiations that remains as yet confidential.[27] A Chinese foreign ministry official, Yi Xianliang, dampened expectations when he declared that it is impossible to define a timetable for the conclusion of the CoC, suggesting Beijing's continued resistance to the ASEAN demand that the code should be legally binding.[28]

However, at the 33rd ASEAN summit in November 2018, Chinese premier Li Keqiang declared that the CoC should be concluded within three years, stimulating hopes within ASEAN that these negotiations would finally reach a favourable end. Singapore prime minister Lee Hsien Loong expressed his hope that the first reading of the CoC could take place in 2019, with the final document to be agreed upon within three years.[29] Nevertheless, it is unlikely that China would accede to a legally binding code, and it may be the case that Beijing would press for a general statement of principles similar to the November 2002 Declaration on the Conduct of Parties in the South China Sea. Beijing may calculate that ASEAN would rather accept such a version of a CoC than have the negotiations prolonged indefinitely, but whether ASEAN would do so is unclear.

Furthermore, ASEAN was also able to avoid any distressing internal dispute over China as the Philippines under President Duterte continued his close engagement with China. This rapprochement ensured that there was no repeat of the disagreements that erupted during the tenure of his predecessor Benigno Aquino. As president, Aquino not only adopted a hard-line stance against China and its activities in the South China Sea but also tried to enlist the support of ASEAN — a move that drew opposition from Hun Sen's Cambodia. With Duterte currently at the helm in the Philippines, ASEAN could thus maintain some unity in the broadest sense over the issue, although there might be some political cost for Duterte as domestic criticism mounts against what Senate minority leader Franklin Drilon has described as "appeasement".[30] For instance, when Philippine Congress members were alarmed by China's missile deployments in the area of the Spratly Islands, Duterte seemed unperturbed and even claimed that China would "protect" the Philippines. Duterte has also touted the agreement that would allow Filipino fishermen to continue fishing in their traditional fishing areas as a major achievement of his visit to China in October 2016.[31] However, this agreement is not always honoured, and Duterte's spokesman Harry Roque announced that the Chinese Coast Guard had confiscated the catch of Filipino fishermen around Scarborough Shoal.[32]

During Xi Jinping's visit to Manila on 20 November, he signed a memorandum of understanding (MoU) on joint oil and gas exploration with Duterte. The MoU called for a joint intergovernmental steering committee and an inter-entrepreneurial working group to draft a framework for joint exploration. However, the details — including the area earmarked for joint exploration — were kept confidential.[33]

The resort to secrecy in these negotiations has already provoked criticism that the joint exploration will be located in the sea zones claimed by the Philippines, and that such actions would be tantamount to Philippine recognition of rival Chinese claims.

Duterte's close engagement of China was also criticized for not bringing increased levels of Chinese investment into the Philippines as the president had promised. According to the Philippine Central Bank, China had made a US$24 billion commitment to the Philippines (US$15 billion in foreign direct investment and US$9 billion in aid), but to little effect. Philippine commentators have surmised that the huge discrepancy between the declared commitments and the actual investment was a result of Chinese machinations to turn the Philippines away from its alliance with the United States, but there were other reasons such as the existence of bottlenecks in the country. Moreover, much of the Chinese investment flowed into the Philippines from Hong Kong and thus was not attributed to the mainland.[34] On another note, Duterte has health problems that have not been disclosed, and there are some in Manila who think that he may not last his term of office, which expires in 2022. If that were to be the case, his overly accommodating approach to China may be readjusted.

Trade Regimes and ASEAN Centrality

The ASEAN economies will benefit from the trade regimes being negotiated that promise expanded export markets and increased investment. However, ASEAN will struggle to maintain its centrality as newer and broader regional associations are created. As defined by Article 1(15) of the ASEAN Charter, centrality is the notion that ASEAN should be the "primary driving force in its relations and cooperation with external partners". This has worked well with the ASEAN Regional Forum and the East Asia Summit (EAS), as meetings are orchestrated by ASEAN and follow the annual ASEAN summits. However, broadly based trade regimes pose new challenges for ASEAN centrality, since they will embrace ASEAN's major economic partners and investors who will deal with the member states directly. These major partners would make decisions impacting the region, which could reduce the grouping to a passive recipient.

Furthermore, the trade regimes pursued are extraordinarily complex, as the participants are at different levels of development and have conflicting demands. Once negotiations go beyond tariff reductions into services, intellectual property and demands for institutional change, difficulties are encountered and resistance mounts. Singapore may join Australia and Japan in pressing for free trade and liberalization of the trade-related institutions, but those countries with extensive domestic industries and agricultural sectors such as Malaysia will be less enthusiastic. The complexity of the negotiations may result in a considerable reduction of expectations as contentious provisions are filtered out to ensure the agreement's acceptability.

One of Singapore's priorities as it took over the ASEAN chair for 2018 was to promote the RCEP, which includes the ten ASEAN member states plus the six external partners that ASEAN has established free trade agreements with: China, India, Australia, New Zealand, South Korea and Japan.[35] The RCEP was proposed by ASEAN members at the EAS in Phnom Penh in November 2012 as a trade regime that would consolidate ASEAN's various FTAs and maintain the grouping's centrality in response to negotiations over the TPP. The RCEP was intended to be comprehensive, embracing not only tariff reductions and the removal of non-tariff barriers but also cover trade in services, intellectual property, investment, and economic and technical cooperation. At the outset, ASEAN members declared that the RCEP would recognize ASEAN Centrality in the development of economic regionalism, but it remains unclear how ASEAN can control the direction and process of negotiations. In terms of progress, Singapore and China have both been pushing for a speedy agreement on the RCEP, which for Beijing is a means to pre-empt the TPP, which excludes China. The RCEP has also become more important as a process since President Trump withdrew the United States from the TPP negotiations in January 2017. However, negotiations drag on. Trade ministers initially anticipated that negotiations would be concluded by the end of 2015, they however agreed to a new deadline of the end of 2018 when they met again in New Delhi in January 2018.

Singapore's Prime Minister Lee Hsien Loong on 29 August was expressing optimism when he declared that "After a great deal of work, the possibility of substantively concluding the RCEP negotiations is finally in sight."[36] However, there remains a major difficulty with the RCEP, and it is an issue that is beyond ASEAN's ability to rectify, which demonstrates the extent to which the grouping may be marginalized. The problem has to do with India's trade deficit with China and its intention to protect its domestic market against Chinese imports. India's commerce minister, Suresh Prabhu, was responding to intense domestic pressure when he declared that his government wants a twenty-year window to reduce import duties on several products in order to shield domestic industries against Chinese imports.[37] India also demanded differential tariffs for different countries; the upshot is that there would only be minimum tariff concessions to Chinese goods, which would be maintained for some time, whilst imports from other countries are allowed at reduced tariffs. India also demanded that the free movement of professionals and labour be recognized in the negotiations over services, and that goods and services should be linked in the negotiations. For India, it was important to avoid the situation where negotiations on traded goods would leave services behind.[38] As such, by September 2018 Prime Minister Lee admitted that he was unsure whether the RCEP would be concluded in 2018.[39] At the second RCEP summit in Singapore on 14 November, the leaders could not reach an agreement but did promise to "bring RCEP negotiations to a conclusion by next year".[40] Negotiations on the RCEP will thus continue in 2019.

Despite the Trump administration's withdrawal from the TPP in 2017, eleven members agreed at the Tokyo meeting in January 2018 to move forward with negotiations with what is now called the Comprehensive and Progressive Agreement for TPP (CPTPP). The CPTPP is a modification of the original TPP-12 agreement signed in February 2016 that included the United States. In the aftermath of the U.S. withdrawal from the TPP, Japan and Australia continued with negotiations for a TPP-11 agreement in the hopes of enticing the United States back into negotiations.[41]

The TPP was initially mooted by two ASEAN members (Brunei and Singapore) together with Chile and New Zealand in 2005. Later it was expanded to include Malaysia and Vietnam, while Indonesia and Thailand were considering whether to join. The idea of the TPP was not merely a free trade agreement, since it proposed extensive measures to promote institutional reform — a contentious affair that adds to the complexity of the negotiations. Its primary attraction to Asian exporters was the fact of access to the American market, as well as functioning as a stepping stone to a Free Trade Area of the Asia Pacific that would include China. Asian economists also value the promised stimulus to economic reform and change, particularly in countries such as Japan that face structural stagnation. Likewise, Vietnam was set to benefit from the TPP with increased access to the U.S. market for its apparel and footwear. Vietnamese economists also regarded the TPP as a means of reforming an economy in which dominating state-owned enterprises (SOEs) have crowded out the private sector and prevented the country from reaching its full economic potential.

During the TPP-11 negotiations, many of the original provisions of the TPP regarded as excessive were put aside. For instance, both Malaysia and Vietnam opposed the provisions regarding SOEs, while others objected to provisions relating to intellectual property and pharmaceuticals. In total, some twenty-two provisions of the original TPP were suspended, including those that covered intellectual property copyright and pharmaceuticals. The final agreement was signed by the eleven members on 8 March 2018 in Santiago, Chile. Australia was the sixth of eleven members to ratify the CPTPP on 31 October, triggering its entry into force on 30 December. However, the CPTPP divides ASEAN as only four member states are involved and of those four members only Singapore and Vietnam have ratified the agreement, while Malaysia and Brunei have not.

U.S.-China Trade War

Prime Minister Lee Hsien Loong told the ASEAN Summit in April 2018 that the U.S.-China trade war was one of ASEAN's most pressing concerns. At the 33rd ASEAN summit in November, Prime Minister Lee expressed the fear that the trade war might divide ASEAN and compel member states to have to choose between the United States and China. However, the description of a "trade war" is a misnomer as there are deeper resentments motivating President Trump to resort to extensive tariffs in an attempt to readjust the relationship with China. While the immediate concern was the trade deficit with China — which reached US$375 billion in 2017 — this does not capture the real situation, as the design, technology and value-added components of many manufactured goods imported from China are of American origin, and are included in the supply chain. Other motives include the American fear that China's mercantilist trading practices would challenge the U.S.-sponsored open trading system, and that the "made in China 2025" declaration of October 2015 was a plan to achieve Chinese dominance in high-technology industries, which would push out American companies. If the problem was solely limited to America's trade deficit with China, an agreement to resolve the dispute would be possible. However, because deeper issues are involved, no easy resolution can be anticipated, and the dispute will likely be prolonged. The clash between the United States and China over trade at the APEC summit in Port Moresby in November 2018, which resulted in the unprecedented failure to issue a joint communiqué for the summit, may be less of an aberration than expected in future.

How would the trade war affect Southeast Asia? IMF director Christine Legarde predicted that it could trigger vulnerabilities in Asian countries whose supply chains are closely linked to Chinese industry and are dependent on exports to the United States. Already, economic growth in Indonesia, Malaysia, the Philippines, Singapore and Thailand slowed over July–September 2018 in comparison with previous quarters. Vietnam was the exception, registering 6.88 per cent growth over 6.73 per cent the previous quarter. The United States is ASEAN's second-largest export market, absorbing some 11 per cent of its total exports, and ASEAN's third-largest trading partner after the European Union and China. ASEAN trade with the United States reached $233.1 billion in 2017. If American tariffs are extended to the ASEAN countries, their economies could face the prospect of recession. A Trump appointee, Jeffrey T. Gerrish, a deputy trade representative, has called for equivalent market access and a "rebalancing" of trade relations with the ASEAN countries. As justification for this view, he pointed to the $38 billion trade deficit with Vietnam, the $25 billion with Malaysia, the $20 billion with Thailand and $13 billion with Indonesia, although with Singapore the United States enjoys a trade surplus.

However, ASEAN countries may benefit from the trade war, as transnational companies may try to avoid the American tariffs by moving production from China to Southeast Asia and elsewhere. ASEAN countries may emerge as an attractive alternative supply chain base for companies looking to diversify production away from China.[42] For instance, Japanese companies have long complained about the rising costs of production in China and increasing numbers of them have decided to shift production either back to Japan or to Vietnam. Japanese companies have generally regarded Vietnam as a small-scale alternative to China, and it is now an even more attractive option after the U.S. imposition of tariffs on Chinese goods. In addition, as China moves to higher-technology industries, it thus seeks to phase out assembly and lower-level manufacturing processes where returns are minimal. The Chinese company GoerTek, which assembles Apple's Airpods, has announced that it will move its production from China to Vietnam, while Taiwanese enterprises in China are also considering the move, though not just because of the trade war but due to the increasingly tense cross-strait relations. American manufacturers in China face a similar problem. However, as much as they regard the ASEAN countries as possible alternative bases for production, they are faced with the problem of being so deeply embedded in the Chinese system that it might prove to be disruptive for them to move.[43]

Likewise, Malaysia's Robert Kuok has claimed that the trade war would lead to trade growth in Malaysia, Vietnam, Myanmar and Laos. He declared that his firm, Kerry Logistics, will particularly benefit as operations will move back to Malaysia.[44] Similarly, Malaysia's deputy minister of international trade and industry Ong Kian Ming thought that the trade war was an opportunity for Malaysia to attract higher-value-added manufacturing, and for ASEAN to showcase the region's attractiveness to foreign investment. Malaysia could provide an "export platform" for Chinese companies in the Malaysia-China Kuantan Industrial Park (MCKIP).[45]

Indo-Pacific and ASEAN Centrality

The idea of the Indo-Pacific region is a challenge to ASEAN centrality, since it could remove the supporting foundation of a Southeast Asian region. Introduced by Japanese prime minister Shinzo Abe in his address to the Indian parliament in 2007, the notion of the Indo-Pacific has since been endorsed by ASEAN's external partners, the United States and Australia, as well as Japan. For Japan, the Indo-Pacific was a conceptual means to connect India with the United States and Australia in quadrilateral security cooperation, but without the regional countries. Moreover, it was narrowly focused on security.

The Indonesian foreign minister Retno Marsudi has promoted a broader vision of the Indo-Pacific that would detach the notion from its security origins and include both China and India. This particular vision would ensure ASEAN centrality by extending existing ASEAN dialogue and cooperation in maritime security, trade and investment to the wider concept of the Indo-Pacific. Retno Marsudi cast Indonesia as the link between ASEAN and the Indian Ocean Rim Association (IORA), an organization that includes East African as well as some Middle Eastern countries — a very broad field.[46] At the ASEAN foreign ministers retreat in February 2018, Retno explained that in order to preserve ASEAN centrality, existing mechanisms should be utilized and there was no need to create new bodies as the EAS could serve as the main platform for the Indo-Pacific idea.[47] Indonesia then circulated a concept paper to all sixteen EAS members to head off the American "Free and Open Indo-Pacific" initiative, which would downgrade ASEAN's role.[48] In effect, Indonesia was proposing to upgrade the EAS into an Indo-Pacific forum within which ASEAN could assume the key role. However, while ASEAN can provide a platform for the forum through the EAS, ASEAN centrality is dependent on ASEAN unity. Over the security issues that have disturbed the group's external partners, such as the South China Sea, ASEAN unity has been absent. Without that unity, ASEAN members will individually reach out to external partners on a bilateral basis, preventing the group from speaking with one voice.

Indonesia has reached out to ASEAN's main Indo-Pacific partner, India. At the 15th ASEAN-India summit in November 2017, President Jokowi called for closer cooperation with India over maritime security through the IORA. When Indian prime minister Narendra Modi visited Jakarta in May 2018, Jokowi declared that "India is a strategic defence partner" as both countries showed concern about Chinese maritime activities in the South China Sea and Indian Ocean. Modi and Jokowi agreed to develop an Indonesian naval port in the Indian Ocean at the entrance to the Malacca Strait. They also agreed to enhance defence and maritime cooperation, to upgrade regular naval exercises and coordinated patrols in the Indian Ocean, and to develop infrastructure and an economic zone at Sabang, on the tip of Sumatra at the entrance of the Malacca Strait.[49]

Indonesian cooperation with another Indo-Pacific partner, Australia, has also moved forward, surprisingly so in view of past animosities associated with Australia's role in East Timor that rankled Jakarta. Jokowi visited Sydney for the first ASEAN-Australia summit in March 2018 and, when interviewed by the Australian press, said that Australia should play a bigger role in defence and regional security. When asked about the possibility of Australian membership in ASEAN, he replied that "it's a good idea … because our region will be better, stability, economic stability and political stability. Sure it will be better."[50] This comment created a sensation in Australia, as it was the first time a senior ASEAN leader had suggested it. However, membership is not a serious option for Australia, as the Bangkok Declaration of 1967 restricts ASEAN membership to the countries of Southeast Asia, and there is unlikely to be an ASEAN consensus in favour of Australia's admission. The comment is however an indication of the development and upgrading of Indonesia's relationship with Australia and the realization that external partners in the Indo-Pacific were becoming more important to Jakarta. When Australia's prime minister Scott Morrison visited Jakarta in August 2018, an Indonesia-Australia Comprehensive Economic Partnership (IA-CPA) was concluded, as well as a free trade deal that would benefit Australian agricultural exports. The two countries also concluded a $6.92 billion currency agreement to provide Indonesia's rupiah with support against wild currency swings.[51]

Conclusion

The year 2018 saw the development of challenges to Southeast Asian regionalism that will demand an adjustment to ASEAN's role and function. As ASEAN members interact more frequently with external partners and economic groupings, the notion of a regional association limited only to Southeast Asia loses meaning. Already, the Rohingya issue demonstrates ASEAN's inability to deal with a humanitarian problem that concerns its Muslim-majority member states and goes against everything that was attempted in the ASEAN Charter of 2007, which called for "respect for and protection of human rights fundamental freedoms". While ASEAN has been immobilized over this issue, international agencies and governments willing to press the issue against the Myanmar military leaders are increasingly involved. The South China Sea issue has gone well beyond ASEAN's ability to resolve on its own, though it impacts directly upon the group's unity and security. ASEAN has also been pushing for the RCEP, hoping to engage its major trading partners in one large trading group, but, if realized, ASEAN economies would merge into the wider grouping and ASEAN centrality would be undermined. ASEAN also intends to promote a digital economy and e-commerce within this framework, but should payment systems become fully digitized, Southeast Asian banks would be relegated to providing access to digital systems that are global in nature and not limited to any one region. The challenge of the Indo-Pacific is far-reaching, since it may supplant the notion of Southeast Asia as the regional basis behind ASEAN regionalism. Already, Indonesia is reaching out to Indo-Pacific partners in India and Australia in a way that demonstrates the increasing importance of these relationships. To ensure its relevance, ASEAN can provide the Indo-Pacific idea with a platform in the EAS and ensure that the development of the notion is inclusive and not directed against any particular country. Indeed, ASEAN may have to adjust its expectations and its basic assumptions as it faces the future.

Notes

1. "Bangladesh's Leader Accuses Myanmar of Rohingya 'Genocide' ", *South China Morning Post*, 28 September 2018 <http://www.scmp.com/news/asia/southeast-asia/article/2166101/bangladeshs-leader-accuses-myanmar-rohingya-genocide>.
2. Chairman's Statement of the 32nd ASEAN Summit, Singapore, 28 April 2018 <https://asean.org/storage/2018/04/Chairmans-Statement-of-the-32nd-ASEAN-Summit.pdf>.
3. "ASEAN Urges Accountability for Rakhine Violence", *The Star*, 3 October 2018.
4. "Asean Must Continue to Seek Consensus but Cannot Do Nothing on Rakhine Situation: Vivian", *Straits Times*, 5 December 2017.
5. "No Reforms for ASEAN Anytime Soon", *Jakarta Post*, 25 November 2017.
6. "Indonesia Criticises ASEAN for Lax Attitude on Human Rights", *The Star*, 20 January 2018 <http://www.thestar.com.my/news/regional/2018/01/20/indonesia-criticises-asean-for-lax-attitude-on-human-rights/>.
7. Jefferi Hamzah Sendut, "ASEAN Must Not Remain Silent", *The Star*, 20 September 2018; "Take Rohingya Genocide to ICJ", *The Star*, 18 September 2018.
8. "Malaysia No Longer Supports Suu Kyi: Mahathir", *Straits Times*, 2 October 2018.
9. "Anwar 'Appalled by Suu Kyi over Rohingya Issue, Criticises China's Muslim Camps", *Straits Times*, 12 September 2018.
10. "Indonesia Urges Myanmar to Apply UN's Decision on Rohingya", *Tempo*, 4 September 2018 <https://en.tempo.co/read/news/2018/09/04/309921327/Indonesia-Urges-Myanmar-to-Apply-UNs-Decision-on-Rohingya>.
11. Marguerite Afra Sapiie, "Indonesia Wants End to Rohingya Crisis, Jokowi Tells Myint", *Jakarta Post*, 28 April 2018.
12. Alexis Romero, "Philippines to Accept Refugees from Myanmar 'Genocide' ",

Philippine Star, 7 April 2018 <http://www.philstar.com/headlines/2018/04/07/1803600/philippines-accept-refugees-myanmar-genocide#mKswZ3jXmcGWLDR1.99>.

13. "Thai Silence Deafening as World Condemns Myanmar", *The Nation*, 13 September 2018.
14. Oral update of the High Commissioner for Human Rights on Situation of human rights of Rohingya people, Human Rights Council, Thirty-eighth session, 18 June – 6 July 2018, Agenda item 2, Annual report of the United Nations High Commissioner for Human Rights and reports of the Office of the High Commissioner and the Secretary-General.
15. "Myanmar Military Leaders Must Face Genocide Charges – UN Report", *UN News*, 27 August 2018 <https//news.un.org/en/story/2018/08/1017802>.
16. Edith M. Lederer, "UN Chief Urges Accountability for Myanmar Crimes on Rohingya", Associated Press, 28 August 2018.
17. "Haley: US Rohingya Report 'Consistent' with UN Findings", Voice of America, 28 August 2018.
18. "Human Rights Situations that Require the Council's Attention, Report of the Detailed Findings of the Independent International Fact-Finding Mission on Myanmar", United Nations Human Rights Council, Thirty-ninth session, 10–28 September 2018 <https://www.ohchr.org/Documents/HRBodies/HRCouncil/FFM-Myanmar/A_HRC_39_CRP.2.pdf>.
19. Edith M. Lederer, "UN Chief Urges Accountability for Myanmar Crimes on Rohingya", Associated Press, 28 August 2018.
20. "Statement of ICC Prosecutor, Mrs Fatou Bensouda, on Opening a Preliminary Examination Concerning the Alleged Deportation of the Rohingya People from Myanmar to Bangladesh", International Criminal Court, 18 September 2018 <http://www.icc-cpi.int/Pages/item.aspx?name=180918-otp-stat-Rohingya>.
21. "China Installs Cruise Missiles on South China Sea Outposts: CNBC," Reuters, 3 May 2018.
22. Tom O'Connor, "Only 'War' Could Stop China from Controlling South China Sea, U.S. Military Commander Says", *Newsweek*, 20 April 2018.
23. "Royal Navy Ship Sails near Disputed Islands in South China Sea", *Navaltoday.com*, 7 September 2018 <https://navaltoday.com/2018/09/07/royal-navy-ship-sails-near-disputed-islands-in-south-china-sea/>; "Japan Dispatches Submarine Kuroshio to South China Sea ASW Drill", *Navaltoday.com*, 19 September 2018 <https://navaltoday.com/2018/09/19/japan-dispatches-submarine-kuroshio-to-south-china-sea-asw-drill/>.
24. "Press Statement by the Chairman of the ASEAN Foreign Ministers' Retreat", Singapore, 6 February 2018 <https://asean.org/wp-content/uploads/2018/02/Press-Statement-by-the-Chairman-of-the-ASEAN-Foreign-Ministers-Retreat-clean.pdf>.
25. "ASEAN-China Maritime Exercise Concludes in Zhanjiang, China", *Navaltoday.com*, 29 October 2018 <https://navaltoday.com/2018/10/29/asean-china-maritime-exercise-concludes-in-zhanjiang-china/>.

26. James Pomfret and Neil Jerome Morales, "South China Sea Code of Conduct Talks to Be 'Stabilizer' for Region: China Premier", Reuters, 14 November 2017 <https://www.reuters.com/article/us-asean-summit-southchinasea/south-china-sea-code-of-conduct-talks-to-be-stabilizer-for-region-china-premier-idUSKBN1DE05K>.
27. Dian Septiari, "ASEAN, China Debuts COC 'Single Draft' ", *Straits Times*, 2 August 2018.
28. "Unrealistic to Set Timetable for South China Sea Code Says Chinese Official", *The Star*, 10 August 2018.
29. "Asean, China Agree on Early Completion of Sea Code", *Straits Times*, 15 November 2018 <https://www.straitstimes.com/singapore/asean-china-agree-on-early-completion-of-sea-code>.
30. Jefferson Antiporda, "China Policy Not Working – Drilon", *Manila Times*, 23 July 2018.
31. Alexis Romero, "Duterte Defends China amid Missile Deployment Report", *Philstar*, 7 May 2018.
32. "Philippines Demands China Stop Taking Fishermen's Catch", *Jakarta Post*, 11 June 2018.
33. Christina Mendez and Paolo Romero, "Philippines, China Sign MOU on Joint Gas, Oil Development", *Philstar*, 21 November 2018 <https://www.philstar.com/headlines/2018/11/21/1870458/philippines-china-sign-mou-joint-gas-oil-developement#9iiDZBMkqBuur2sw.99>.
34. Alvin Camba, "What Happened to the Billions China Pledged the Philippines? Not What You Think", *South China Morning Post*, 5 August 2018.
35. "Vivian Balakrishnan Sets Out Singapore's Priorities as 2018 ASEAN Chair", *Straits Times*, 5 December 2017.
36. "RCEP Talks Could Be Nearing Finish Line; Integrated ASEAN a More Attractive Economic Partner: PM Lee", *Business Times*, 29 August 2018 <https://www.businesstimes.com.sg/government-economy/rcep-talks-could-be-nearing-finish-line-integrated-asean-a-more-attractive>.
37. "India Wants 20 Years to Cut tariffs under RCEP", *Times of India*, 5 September 2018.
38. Yuthika Bhargava, "Breakthrough Achieved in RCEP Talks, Claims India", *The Hindu*, 5 September 2018 <https://www.thehindu.com/todays-paper/tp-business/breakthrough-achieved-in-rcep-talks-claims-india/article24867580.ece>.
39. "Singapore PM Unsure If China-backed Trade Pact Will Be Finalised This Year", Reuters, 12 September 2018 <https://www.reuters.com/article/us-wef-vietnam-trade/singapore-pm-unsure-if-china-backed-trade-pact-will-be-finalised-this-year-idUSKCN1LS0FA>.
40. "Joint Leaders' Statement on the Regional Comprehensive Economic Partnership (RCEP)", 14 November 2018 <https://dfat.gov.au/trade/agreements/negotiations/rcep/news/Documents/rcep-summit-joint-leaders-statement.pdf>.

41. In January 2018, President Trump indicated to the World Economic Forum in Davos that the United States might return to the TPP, a prospect that was raised by U.S. Treasury Secretary Steven Mnuchin, who said that renegotiating the trade deal was on the table. President Trump campaigned on the basis that trade deals exploited Americans and cost them jobs and that the United States could only return to the negotiations if it could demonstrate to the public that it had made substantial changes to the agreement. Any such American demands would likely meet strong resistance from the TPP-11. "US Mulling Over Rejoining TPP, Says Treasury's Mnuchin", *Straits Times*, 1 March 2018.
42. Saheli Roy Choudhury, "US-China Trade War Could Create Winners in Southeast Asia: Bain & Co", CNBC, 23 November 2018.
43. "US-China Trade Tensions Presents Opportunity for ASEAN", *Straits Times*, 5 July 2018.
44. "Factories Shift Out of China to Avoid Trade War, Boosting Volume for Logistics Firms Like Kerry", *South China Morning Post*, 31 July 2018.
45. "Two Chinese Investors Keen to Set-up Operations in Malaysia-China Kuantan Industrial Park", *Malay Mail*, 11 September 2018 <http://www.malaymail.com/s/1671522/two-chinese-investors-keen-to-set-up-operations-in-malaysia-china-kuantan-i>.
46. Retno Marsudi, "Indonesia: Partner for Peace, Security, Prosperity", *Jakarta Post*, 11 January 2018.
47. "Indonesia Proposes Strengthening Regional Architecture in Indo-Pacific", Antara, 7 February 2018.
48. "ASEAN to Meet Next Month to Further Discuss Indo-Pacific Concept", Kyodo News, 4 August 2018.
49. "Indonesia, India to Develop Strategic Indian Ocean Port", Reuters, 30 May 2018 <https://www.reuters.com/article/indonesia-india/indonesia-india-to-develop-strategic-indian-ocean-port-idUSL3N1T11XL>; "Indonesia, India Agree to Strategic Partnership, Declare Shared Vision on Maritime Cooperation", *Jakarta Globe*, 30 May 2018.
50. Indonesia Wants Australia as Full ASEAN Member", *Jakarta Post*, 16 March 2018.
51. "Indonesia, Australia Sign $6.92B Currency Swap Deal", *Jakarta Globe*, 12 August 2018.

REGIONAL INTEGRATION IN ASIA AND THE PACIFIC, AND DEALING WITH SHORT AND LONG TERM CHALLENGES

Jayant Menon[1]

In the last few decades, Asia and the Pacific has established itself as a formidable economic force that has proven remarkably resilient to difficulties, weathering both the Asian financial crisis in 1997 and the global financial crisis (GFC) in 2008.[2] While countries elsewhere on the globe continue to struggle to shake off the worst effects of the 2008 GFC, Asia and the Pacific has continued to prosper and post gains in economic growth and poverty eradication.

Coming into 2018, the outlook for the region was largely optimistic. Early in the year, the global trade slowdown, which started around 2010, appeared to have begun bottoming out, with East and Southeast Asia in particular leading the recovery. Export growth in the second half of 2017 reached 7.9 per cent in the People's Republic of China (PRC) and 16.5 per cent in the five largest ASEAN economies: Indonesia, Malaysia, the Philippines, Thailand and Vietnam.[3] That Asia and the Pacific managed to achieve this in the midst of growing protectionism elsewhere speaks volumes about the region's commitment to regional and global integration.

Unfortunately, more recent data suggests that the recovery in global trade may have been short-lived. With growth expected to ease in some advanced economies, the growth in world trade is projected to decline slightly from 4.7 per cent in

Jayant Menon is Lead Economist in the Office of the Chief Economist at the Asian Development Bank in Manila, Philippines, where he works on trade, international investment and development issues.

2017 to 4.5 per cent in 2018. In developing countries in Asia and the Pacific, trade volume growth is also projected to ease from the estimated 7.6 per cent in 2017 to 5.5 per cent in 2018.[4]

Moreover, although the economic outlook for the region in 2018 and 2019 remains somewhat favourable, downside risks are on the rise. The Asian Development Bank (ADB) still expects developing countries in the region to hit 6 per cent growth this year, but it has trimmed the forecast for 2019 by 0.1 percentage points to 5.8 per cent.[5]

A number of critical changes are afoot. Many of the favourable conditions that have helped fuel the region's successes may not hold in the short-term, while emerging trends such as population ageing and the fourth industrial revolution (4IR) bring with them new long-term opportunities as well as challenges. The region's ability to evolve amidst these changes will determine whether it can continue to be a powerhouse in the global economy. This chapter examines the role which regional cooperation and integration (RCI) can play in this evolution.

This chapter is divided into six parts. Following this introduction, the next section provides an overview of recent economic progress in Asia and the Pacific and gains made by the region in pursuing RCI. The third section discusses the immediate challenges facing the region's economy as a whole and RCI in particular. The fourth section then takes a broad sweep of two major developments that are likely to affect the region in the medium and long-term: population ageing and the 4IR. The fifth explores what policymakers can do to address these challenges, followed by a conclusion.

Economic Performance and Progress of Asia and the Pacific in RCI

Recent Economic Gains

The economic performance of Asia and the Pacific over the last two decades has been nothing short of impressive. Although the Asian financial crisis in 1997 caused growth to stall in several countries in the region, it also laid the foundation for many critical reforms that allowed the region to withstand the worst of the GFC that hit the globe about a decade later. Sound macroeconomic fundamentals coupled with appropriate policy measures enabled the region to grow at an average rate of 6 per cent per year since the GFC. They also made it possible for Asia and the Pacific to increase its share of global gross domestic product (GDP) from 25 per cent in 2000 to 33 per cent in 2016, as Figure 1 illustrates.[6] The emergence of the PRC as a major economic player accounted for much of this expansion.

FIGURE 1
Asia and the Pacific's Increasing Share of Global GDP

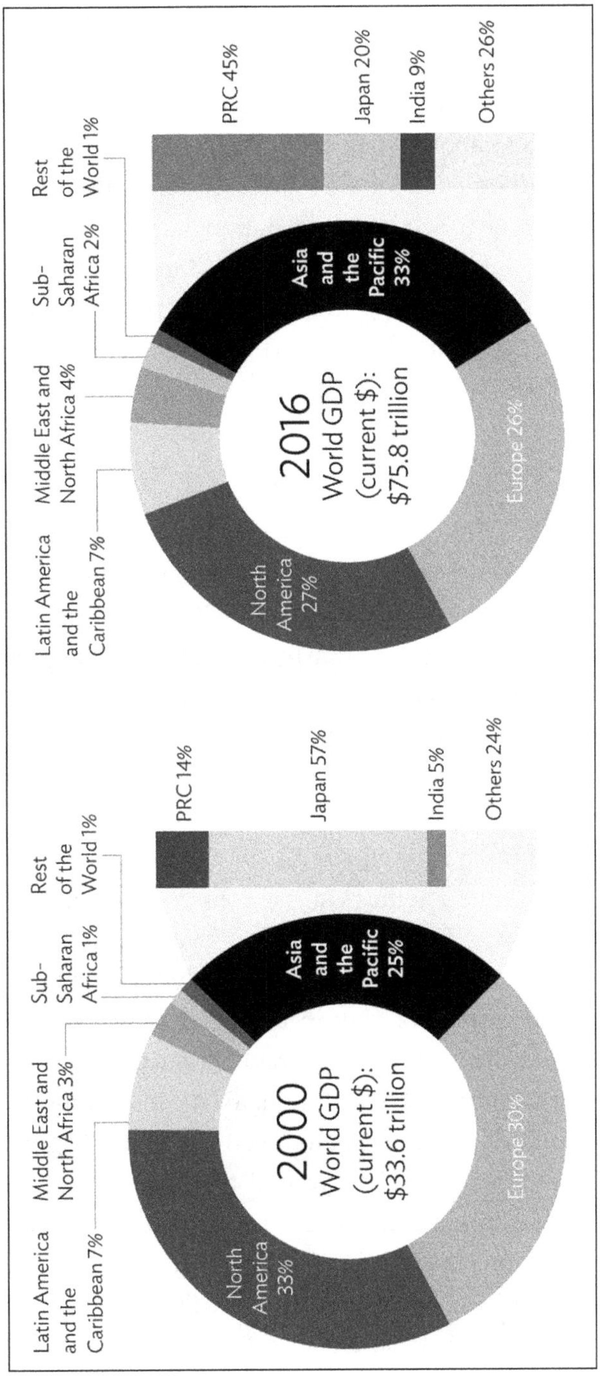

Source: Strategy 2030: Achieving a Prosperous, Inclusive, Resilient, and Sustainable Asia and the Pacific (Manila: ADB, 2018).

Whereas the PRC only accounted for 14 per cent of Asia and the Pacific's GDP in 2000, by 2016 its share had tripled to 45 per cent of regional GDP.

These economic achievements are reflected in continued improvements in social conditions. In the region's developing countries, extreme poverty (as measured by the $1.90/day threshold at 2011 purchasing power parity) has declined from 53 per cent in 1990 to about 9 per cent of the total population in 2013 (Figure 2).

Despite the emergence of downside risks in the short-term (which will be discussed in the next section), the outlook for the region in 2018 and 2019 remains somewhat favourable. The ADB's *Asian Development Outlook 2018 Update* estimates that, excluding high-income economies, the region is expected to grow at 6.0 per cent in 2018. Growth, however, is expected to moderate to 5.8 per cent in 2019.

Progress in RCI

The region's strides in economic growth and living conditions have been associated with increased trade as a result of outward-oriented policies. In East and Southeast Asia, in particular, support for labour-intensive and low-technology export manufacturing has helped transform countries from predominantly agrarian economies into established manufacturing-based ones.

Perhaps due to the remarkable success the region has had with outward-oriented policies, Asia and the Pacific has remained largely open despite the rising tide of protectionism that has come in the wake of the GFC. While other countries have chosen to turn ever more inwards, there have been no similar major policy reversals in Asia and the Pacific. On the contrary, regional integration indicators reveal that interlinkages have grown rather than shrunk since the beginning of the century. Clearly, countries in the region continue to recognize the role that openness and cooperation can play in their economic fortunes.

One piece of evidence for this is the continued rise in free trade agreements (FTAs) involving countries in the region. FTAs in various stages of negotiation and implementation have nearly quintupled since the beginning of the century, from 51 in 2000 to 249 in 2018. Around two thirds of this total are FTAs that are already in effect (Figure 3). The vast majority of these FTAs are bilateral (Figure 4). In addition, the number of proposed FTAs also continues to climb, with a further 90 FTAs being proposed as of 2018.

Trade in Asia and the Pacific also suffered as a result of the 2008 GFC, but by 2017 it seemed as though the region was poised to lead a recovery in world trade. Trade volume growth increased from 2.3 per cent in 2016 to 7.1 per cent

FIGURE 2
Declining Poverty and Vulnerability

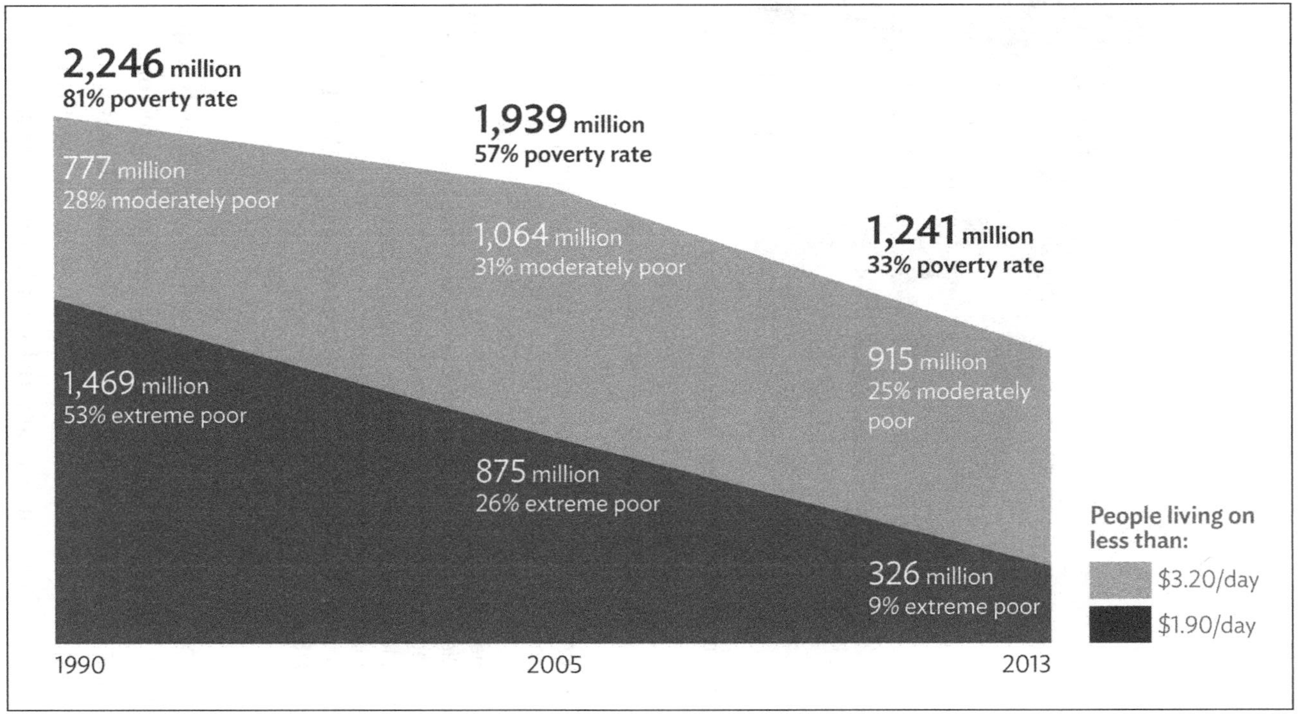

Notes: The latest reference year for poverty estimates is 2013. Poverty lines are expressed in 2011 purchasing power parity. Some figures may not add up due to rounding.
Source: *Strategy 2030: Achieving a Prosperous, Inclusive, Resilient, and Sustainable Asia and the Pacific* (Manila: ADB, 2018).

FIGURE 3
Free Trade Agreements under Negotiation or Implementation, 2000–2018

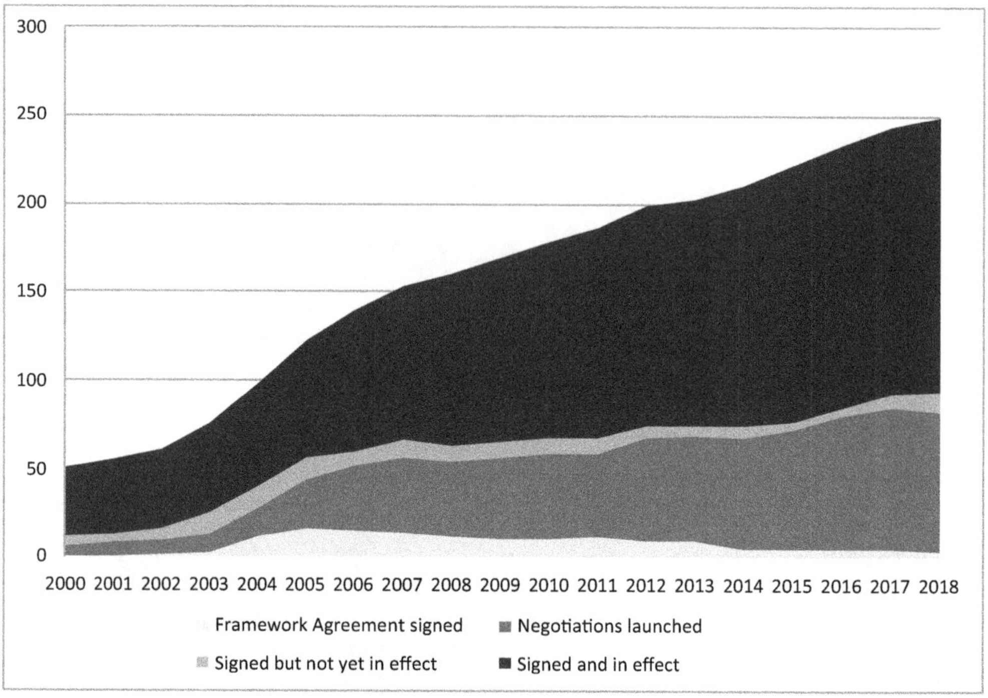

Notes: "Framework Agreement signed" means that the parties have negotiated the contents of an agreement that will serve as a framework for future negotiations. "Negotiations launched" indicates that the parties, through the relevant ministries, have declared the official launch of negotiations or set the date for such, or have started the first round of negotiations. "Signed but not yet in effect" means that the parties have signed the agreement after negotiations have been completed, but the agreement has yet to be implemented. "Signed and in effect" means that the provisions of the FTA have come into force, after legislative or executive ratification.
Source: Data drawn from the Asia Regional Integration Center FTA Database, and correct as of 8 August 2018.

in 2017 (Figure 5), surpassing world trade growth, which only expanded from 1.8 per cent to 4.7 per cent during the same period. The region accounted for nearly 62 per cent of this growth in global trade volume. However, trade expansion of Asia and the Pacific gradually eased in the first seven months of 2018, and as the next section will show, intensifying risks could further undermine the region's trade prospects.

Within certain subregions of Asia and the Pacific, a key driver of trade performance in the last two decades has been the rise in product fragmentation

FIGURE 4
Free Trade Agreements by Scope, 2000–2018

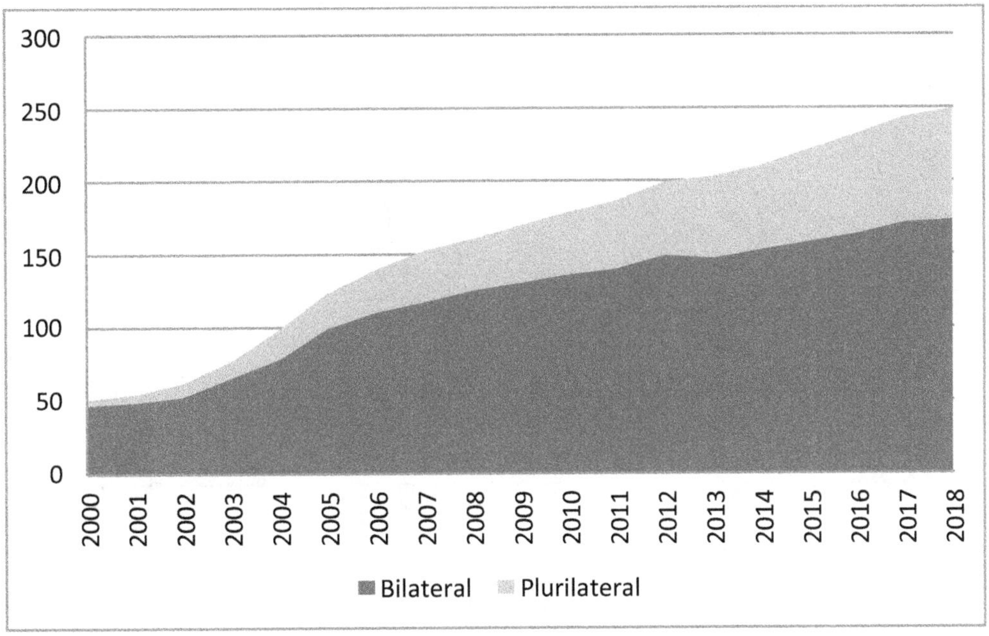

Note: A bilateral FTA refers to a preferential trading arrangement involving only two parties, while a plurilateral one involves more than two parties.
Source: Data drawn from the Asia Regional Integration Center FTA Database, and correct as of 8 August 2018.

trade taking place within global or regional production chains. The share of trade emanating from production networks is much higher in East and Southeast Asia than in more integrated regions of the world, such as the European Union and in North America under the North American Free Trade Agreement.

Asia and the Pacific's participation in regional value chains (RVC) and global value chains (GVC) expanded up until the 2000s, but this growth slowed between 2012 and 2016. The ADB has cited the maturing of value chains as one of the potential causes for this slowdown.[7] Data for 2017, however, shows that the region's participation in RVC and GVC has picked up slightly (Figure 6). It remains unclear, however, whether this expansion will be sustained.

Along with trade, foreign direct investment (FDI) has played a critical role in the economic success of Asia and Pacific. Total inward FDI flows to the region took a huge hit shortly after the 2008 GFC, and although FDI flows have since made a recovery, growth has remained sluggish (Figure 7). Global FDI into the

FIGURE 5
Growth in Trade Volume, 2005–17

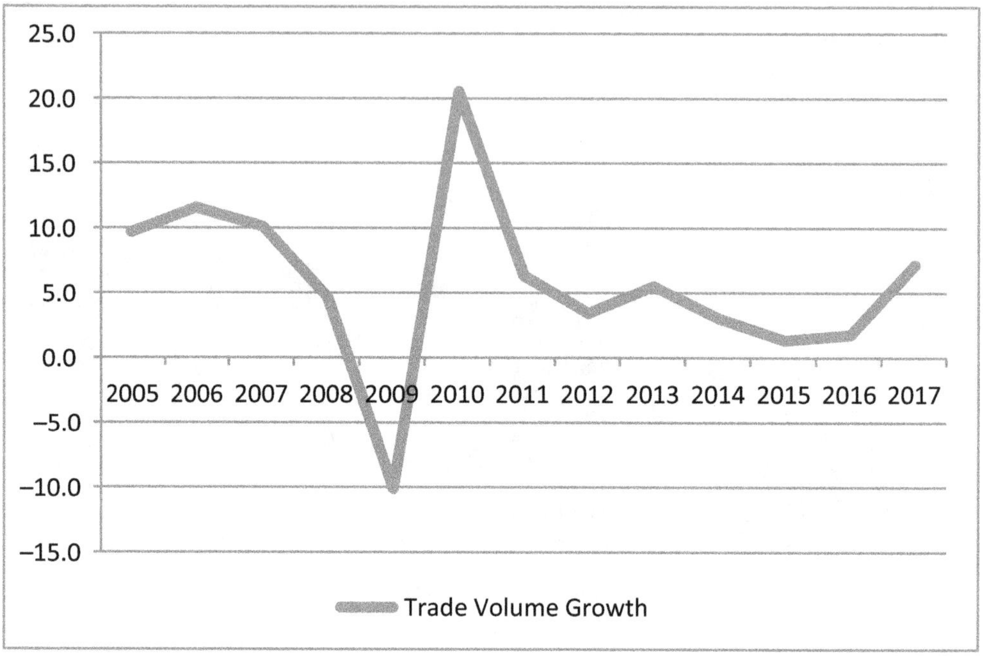

Source: Data from the ADB Asian Regional Integration Center Database.

region actually decreased slightly, from $519.9 billion in 2016 to $517.5 billion in 2017. On the upside, the region's share of global inward FDI increased from 27.8 per cent to 36.2 per cent during the same period.

Far more promising, however, are signs which suggest that integration within the region continues to increase in both goods and factor markets. In 2001, intraregional trade share (measured by value) accounted for only 53 per cent of the total; by 2017, its share had increased to 58 per cent, a little higher than the 56 per cent average during 2010–15. Intraregional investment flows have likewise been rising. Intraregional FDI increased from $254.7 billion in 2016 to $260.0 billion in 2017, while its share of the total increased from 49.0 per cent to 50.2 per cent during the same period. Similar increases have been recorded in the shares of intraregional equity (from 12 per cent to 19 per cent) and debt (from 8 per cent to 16 per cent).

As for tourist flows, the majority of tourists in Asia and the Pacific come from within the region, with the share of intraregional tourism rising from 74 per cent to 78 per cent of the total between 2001 and 2017 (Figures 7 and 8).

FIGURE 6
GVC and RVC Participation Rates, 2014–17

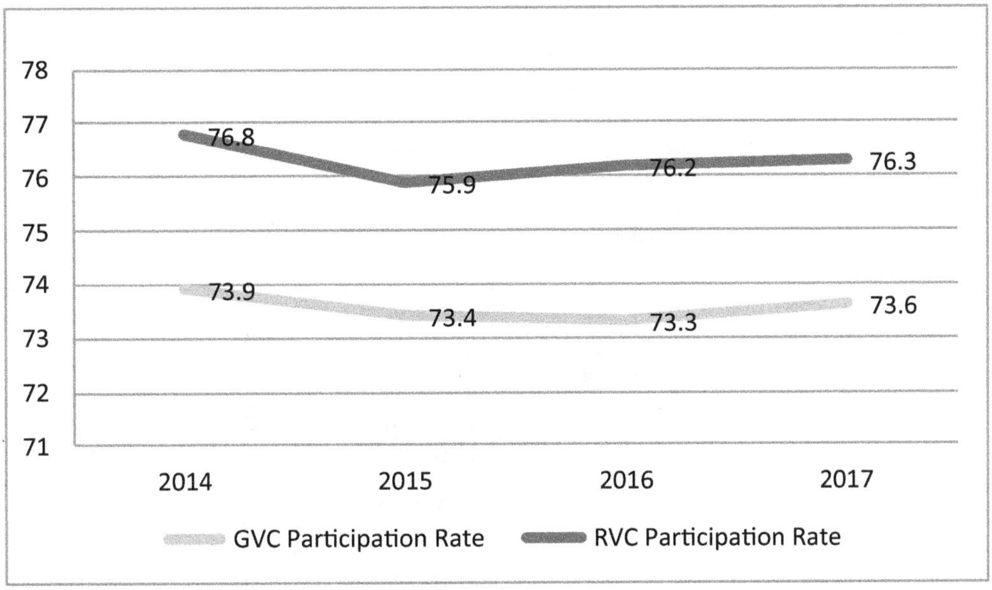

Notes: The participation rate is measured by the share of value-added contents of gross exports used for further processing through cross-border production networks. It is computed as the ratio of value chain components of exports (gross exports less domestic value added in final goods exports data from 2010 to 2017 to gross exports).
Source: Data from ADB Asian Regional Integration Center Database.

Progress in other areas such as trade facilitation and sustained reforms in domestic business environments continue to bode well for Asia and the Pacific's linkages, both within and outside the region. Twenty-three economies in Asia and the Pacific ranked within the top half of the Ease of Doing Business Index for 2017, with a good mix of economies from across the region (Table 1).

Immediate Challenges to Continued Progress

Despite continued progress in RCI, there are a number of immediate challenges that much be addressed.

First, there remain large gaps in performance across subregions in Asia and the Pacific, as well as across integration areas. Within subregions, the degree of trade, investment and capital market integration remains highest in the ASEAN+3, consisting of the ten member countries of the Association of Southeast Nations (ASEAN) and the PRC, Japan and the Republic of Korea. This is largely due to

FIGURE 7
Foreign Direct Investment Inflows, 2005–17

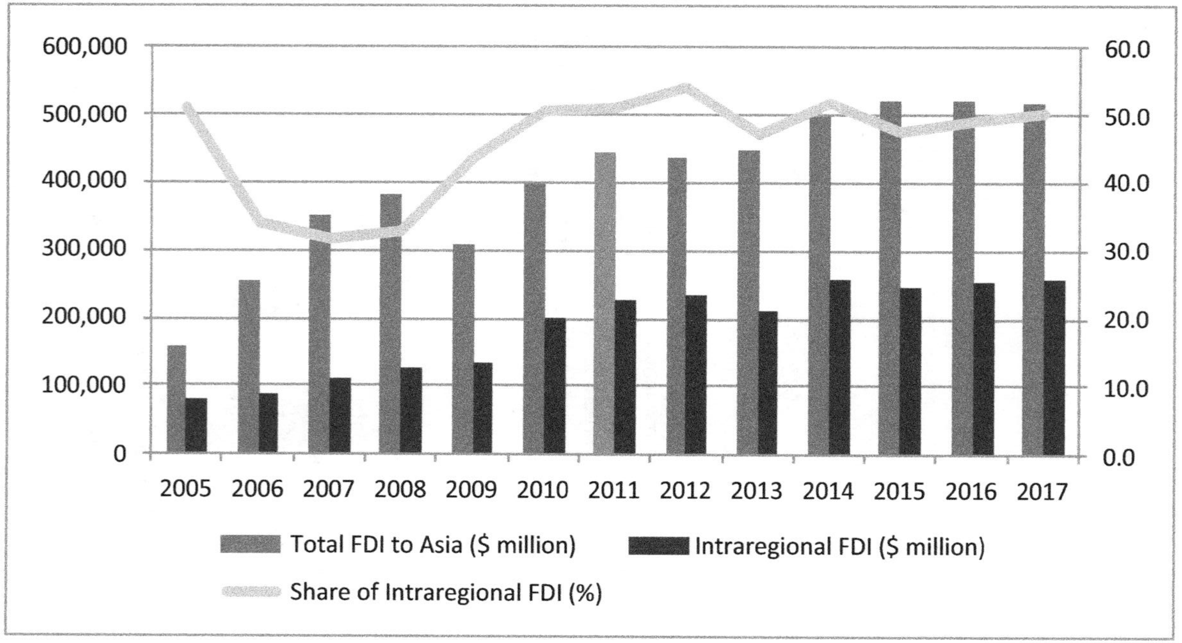

Source: Data from ADB Asian Regional Integration Center Database.

FIGURE 8
Intraregional Integration Shares, 2001 and 2017

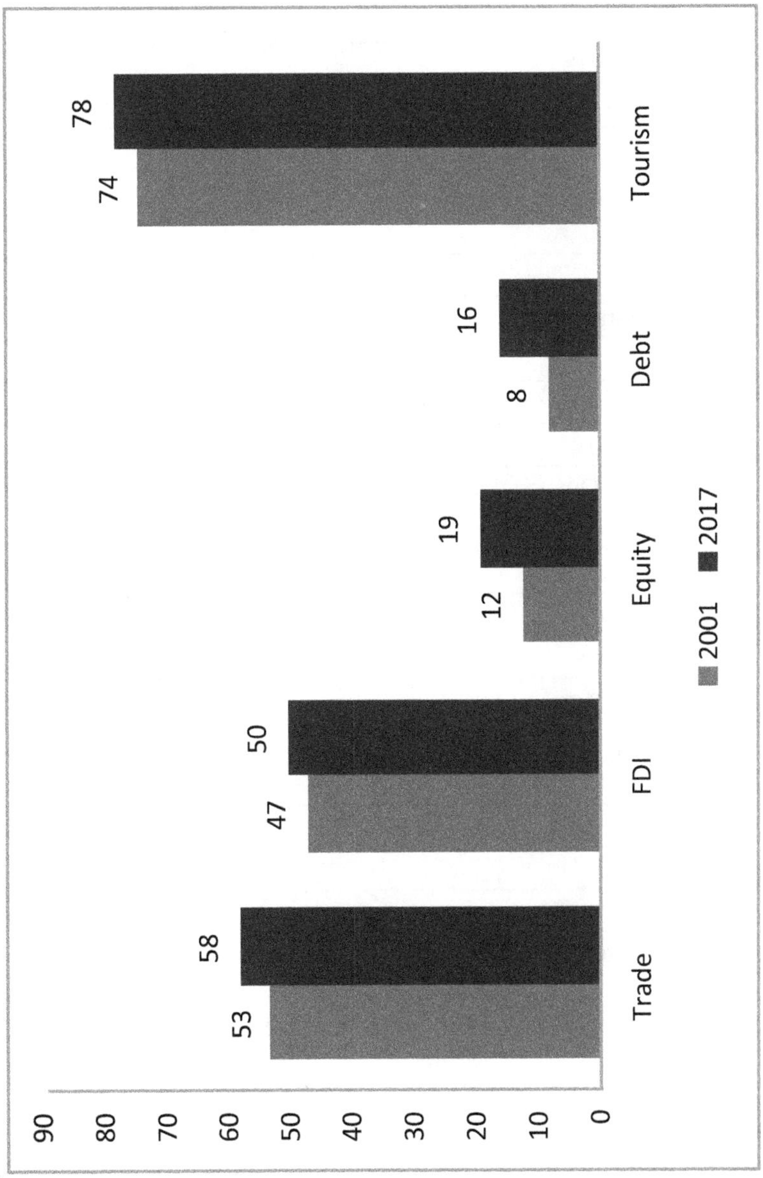

Source: Data from ADB Asian Regional Integration Center Database.

TABLE 1
Asia and the Pacific Economies in the Top 50 per cent of the Ease of Doing Business Rankings, 2017

Economy	*2017 Rank*
New Zealand	1
Singapore	2
Republic of Korea	4
Hong Kong, China	5
Georgia	9
Australia	14
Malaysia	24
Thailand	26
Japan	34
Kazakhstan	36
Armenia	47
Brunei Darussalam	56
Azerbaijan	57
Mongolia	62
Vietnam	68
Indonesia	72
Uzbekistan	74
Bhutan	75
Kyrgyz Republic	77
PRC	78
Samoa	87
Tonga	89
Vanuatu	90

Note: Data unavailable for Cook Islands and Taipei, China.
Source: World Bank World Development Indicators.

the expansion of subregional trade and FDI as a result of plugging into regional and global supply chains. By comparison, subregional integration in these areas is weaker in Central Asia and the Pacific. Integration within Central Asia and the Pacific remains strongest in the movement of people; i.e., tourism in the case of the former and migration in the case of the latter. In terms of linkages across subregions, the Pacific and Southeast Asia come in strongest as far as trade and FDI are concerned. Southeast Asia also has strong linkages with other subregions in capital flows.

As for areas of integration, many of the achievements to date relate to tariff liberalization, investment promotion and other "low hanging fruit" reforms. For the most part, cooperation and integration in finance still lag far behind trade and investment linkages. The region's portfolio investors continue to favour external markets, and intraregional shares of outward equity (debt) investment have remained less than a fifth of the total.

The second immediate challenge to continued progress in RCI comes from the changing environment. The region's successes up until the GFC were largely built on a buoyant global economy, favourable macroeconomic fundamentals and a generally positive view of openness and globalization. But this foundation for success has gradually eroded in recent years.

Although the global economy has experienced an upswing in the past couple of years, global economic growth remains fragile. In its updated *World Economic Outlook* released in October 2018, the International Monetary Fund cut its forecast for global growth from 3.9 to 3.7 per cent for 2018–19 in the face of significant downside risks.

Many developing economies in the region are already grappling with large currency depreciations, rising inflation and financial market volatility due to a combination of higher interest rates in the United States and other advanced economies and rising energy prices. If interest rates climb further, economies in the region holding substantial private debt could face additional financial and economic risks.[8]

With regard to openness, both the appetite and momentum for liberalization reforms have waned. There has been a lack of progress at the WTO, and multilateralism is being replaced by regional and bilateral trade deals that are not very deep. Discontent with globalization has led to rising protectionism, particularly in the West.

But the biggest risk facing both global and regional trade comes from rising trade tensions. Early this year, the ADB estimated that import tariffs imposed globally by the United States in January 2018 had had little impact on growth in the region.[9] However, as of 25 September 2018, tariffs and countermeasures imposed by the United States and the PRC now cover nearly half of the goods and services that the PRC exports to the United States, and nearly 60 per cent of what the United States exports to the PRC. The United States has further threatened to impose tariffs on another $267 billion worth of PRC products. Such

TABLE 2
RCI Performance in 2017

	Movement in Trade and Investment		Movement in Capital		People Movement		
	Trade (%)	FDI (%)	Equity Holdings (%)	Bond Holdings (%)	Migration (%)	Tourism (%)	Remittances (%)
	2017	2017	2017	2017	2017	2016	2017
Within Subregions							
ASEAN+3 (including HKG)[a]	46.8 ▼	50.7 ▼	15.0 ▼	10.7 ▲	38.3 ▼	69.9 ▼	32.6 ▼
Central Asia	7.3 ▲	5.5 ▲	0.0 ▼	0.4 ▲	9.2 ▼	52.5 ▼	6.7 ▲
East Asia	36.3 ▼	48.2 ▼	10.6 ▼	7.5 ▲	33.1 ▼	69.4 ▼	35.5 ▼
South Asia	5.6 ▼	0.2 ▲	0.2 ▼	1.7 ▼	23.4 ▼	23.2 ▲	9.4 ▼
Southeast Asia	22.3 ▼	19.6 ▼	6.4 ▼	7.4 ▼	32.4 ▼	41.7 ▼	12.4 ▼
The Pacific and Oceania	6.2 ▼	7.0 ▲	3.2 ▼	2.1 ▲	56.5 ▲	29.6 ▼	28.9 ▲
Across Subregions							
ASEAN+3 (including HKG)[a]	11.4 ▲	2.4 ▼	3.6 ▼	5.9 ▲	8.6 ▼	10.7 ▲	3.0 ▼
Central Asia	24.1 ▼	12.8 ▼	11.9 ▲	16.3 ▲	0.4 ▼	2.1 ▼	0.7 ▼
East Asia	20.0 ▲	5.2 ▲	3.1 ▼	7.6 ▲	13.9 ▼	10.9 ▲	15.4 ▲
South Asia	34.5 ▲	36.4 ▲	34.9 ▲	7.8 ▼	5.7 ▼	23.9 ▼	5.8 ▲
Southeast Asia	45.8 ▲	32.8 ▼	33.5 ▼	16.2 ▲	14.5 ▼	40.4 ▲	13.8 ▲
The Pacific and Oceania	64.0 ▲	40.7 ▲	11.2 ▲	11.9 ▲	5.6 ▼	39.5 ▲	13.8 ▼

Notes: HKG = Hong Kong, China.
ASEAN+3 includes ASEAN plus Hong Kong, China; Japan; the People's Republic of China; and the Republic of Korea.
Trade: national data unavailable for Bhutan, Kiribati, Nauru, Palau, Timor-Leste, and Tuvalu; no data available on the Cook Islands, the Federated States of Micronesia, and the Marshall Islands.
Equity and Bond holdings: based on investments from Australia; Bangladesh (start from 2013); Hong Kong, China; India; Indonesia; Japan; Kazakhstan; Malaysia; New Zealand; Pakistan; Palau (start from 2015); the Philippines; the Republic of Korea; Singapore; and Thailand. Data start from 2001 unless otherwise stated.
Intraregional share not comparable to previously released issue due to data availability.
Migration: share of migrant stock to total migrants in 2017 (compared with 2015).
Tourism: share of inbound tourists to total tourists in 2016 (compared with 2015).
Remittances: share of inward remittances to total remittances in 2017 (compared with 2016).
Source: ADB Asian Economic Integration Report 2018.

a move would mean roughly all of the PRC's exports to the United States would be subject to new duties.[10]

The ADB continues to expect that measures implemented or proposed by 24 September will have a moderate impact on growth.[11] GDPs in the PRC and the United States are estimated to be lower by only 0.5 percentage points and 0.1 percentage points respectively. However, the ADB cautions that an imposition of 25 per cent tariffs on all bilateral trade between the United States and the PRC would have an impact that would be particularly hard on the PRC, which is estimated to suffer a 1.0 percentage point decrease in GDP (U.S. GDP is only estimated to decrease by 0.2 percentage points).

While the impact on the rest of the region is estimated to be negligible, one cause for worry is the potential second-round effects on global supply chains. Continued uncertainty about future tariff rates and trade policy could also further derail global economic recovery by affecting business confidence and financial conditions.[12] Any further escalation of tensions could also spill over into non-tariff measures, which could raise the stakes considerably.

Medium Term Challenges and their Implications

Apart from the immediate issues facing RCI, in the medium term, two emerging developments — population ageing and the 4IR — bring a raft of new challenges. But there are also some opportunities. These two trends are transforming our social, economic and political systems in often unpredictable ways. Almost every aspect of our lives will be touched: jobs, business models, industrial structures, social interactions, and even systems of governance.

Population Ageing

The region's population is ageing, albeit at different speeds. The demographic transition towards an ageing population is more advanced in developed countries like Japan and in the PRC and the newly industrialized economies (NIEs) — Hong Kong, China; Republic of Korea (Korea); and Singapore. However, many developing countries in the region are on the same demographic path, and they are making the transition at a much faster rate.

Population ageing affects growth through a number of channels. A rapidly ageing population can have adverse effects on economic performance and prospects through a decrease in the labour force, lower saving and investment rates, and spiralling pension and healthcare costs. Japan, the PRC and the NIEs are already wrestling with some, if not all, of these problems.

Not all of Asia and the Pacific is ageing at the same time or at the same speed, however. Populous nations such as India and Indonesia and several countries in the Mekong region have relatively young populations. In these countries, in the near to medium term a bulge in the size of the working age population will occur. Overall dependency rates will fall, and a demographic window will emerge, with the potential for higher employment, savings, investment and economic growth.

Younger economies in the region have the potential to earn significant demographic dividends in the years ahead, but the potential benefits presented by this demographic window will not come automatically. Unless the proper policies and institutions are in place, a diametrically opposite situation could arise, raising the potential for significant levels of unemployment and related social problems. This is a critical issue, since fertility declines and population ageing in developing countries have been proceeding at a much faster rate. Globally, more than half of the elderly were in developed regions up until 1975, but by 2005 this trend had been reversed. This means that many developing countries in the region face the prospect of ageing at low levels of income.

The Fourth Industrial Revolution (4IR)

The 4IR is a set of "disruptive technologies" such as artificial intelligence, robotics, blockchain, and 3D printing that are transforming our social, economic and political systems in often unpredictable ways. These technologies are proving revolutionary, not only because of the breadth of their impact but also the speed at which they are being developed and adopted.

4IR creates both opportunities and challenges for countries in the region. It provides opportunities for developing countries to bypass traditional phases of industrial development by enabling technological leapfrogging. It can expand consumer choice, lower costs and raise the quality of products and services. It will also create new ways for citizens to connect to each other, to trade with each other and to access services that are currently not available.

4IR can be particularly useful in empowering micro, small and medium enterprises (MSMEs), which make up the bulk of enterprises and employment in developing countries. Digital technologies and online services can significantly lower the costs faced by MSMEs, allowing them to participate in regional and global trade, thereby increasing the inclusiveness of growth. 4IR can also create new employment opportunities in emerging technology industries and services.

On the other hand, artificial intelligence and robotics could decrease the competitiveness of low-cost and low-skilled labour, which has thus far played a huge role in the expansion of trade and investment in the region. There are indications that 4IR technologies could lead to a reshoring of production back to industrialized economies.

Increased reliance on artificial intelligence and robotics could also threaten jobs. The immediate threats are to low-skilled, repetitive jobs (such as assembly line workers), but people will still need to man the process. Services jobs are also at risk, and this risk could increase over time. But the fears over automation may be overblown. Research by the OECD shows that when the individual tasks in jobs are considered, only 9 per cent of jobs in OECD economies are at risk of displacement. This outcome could apply to Asia and the Pacific as well.

The transformative impact of 4IR behoves countries to think about their policies and priorities. Many Asian governments are aware of this need and have launched national responses, such as Thailand 4.0, Singapore's Smart Nation initiative and Malaysia's National Industry 4.0 Policy Framework to be launched this year. The more-developed countries are better prepared to deal with the challenges and take advantage of the opportunities introduced by 4IR. The poorer countries need to catch up with preparedness to avoid falling further behind.

What Should Policymakers in the Region Do?

Continue to Be Open and Signal Openness

Asia and the Pacific needs to demonstrate its continued conviction that openness and economic integration will help improve the lives of its citizens. It needs to remain outward looking and continue to demonstrate its commitment to open regionalism.

Strengthen Cooperation in Other Areas

With goods markets largely integrated, boosting efforts of integrating factor markets (capital and labour) could open up new opportunities and generate significant benefits. Thus far, efforts to promote capital market integration have focused mainly on regional surveillance and developing Asian bond markets, particularly in the ASEAN+3 economies. While this is important, it needs to be complemented by broader domestic policy reforms aimed at lowering regulatory barriers and harmonizing standards and regulations.

Support for greater labour mobility will be necessary to overcome remaining sensitivities. In ASEAN, for instance, harmonization and streamlining of employment visas has been an important initiative in reducing barriers to labour mobility. ASEAN economies have signed a number of mutual recognition agreements for skilled jobs, but implementation has been stymied by domestic rules and regulations on employment and licensing requirements.

But removing the barriers to factor mobility will involve more difficult and politically sensitive policy reforms. Pursuing behind-the-border policy reforms and policy harmonization has proved the most difficult. But it is in the region's best interest to continue to seek uniformity in regulatory rules.

Prepare for Population Ageing and 4IR

Policies to address population ageing will differ depending on where a particular country finds itself on the demographic curve. In economies where ageing is more advanced, the biggest challenge will involve sustaining output growth and preventing a decline in standards of living despite a contraction in the labour supply. There are a number of ways that ageing countries can make up for labour shortfalls. Ageing economies could increase labour force participation rates by facilitating the entry of young adults into the labour force; removing barriers to the participation of women; increasing the mandatory retirement age, or scrapping it altogether; and adopting more flexible working arrangements. Improvements in labour productivity will also be necessary, compelling reforms in education and greater investments in technology. The potential to turn to greater automation and other technologies could play a mitigating role.

For the younger and less-developed economies, the biggest challenge lies in adopting policies that will allow them to utilize the demographic window to achieve rapid economic growth, increase per capita incomes and build up human capital. Central to meeting this challenge is providing productive employment and enhancing the skills of the growing labour force. This is particularly critical in light of the impact that 4IR technologies can have on industries and jobs.

Economic interactions are expected to take place among countries that are economically integrated but ageing at different speeds; these interactions can help mitigate many of the negative impacts that ageing will have at the domestic level. Ageing countries could use regional interactions as a way of getting around labour shortages, by allowing greater migration or immigration, or continuing to export capital to countries with a youth bulge.[13] In the immediate future, the second option may prove to be the easier alternative. Countries in the region have made considerable progress in removing restrictions to capital flows, whereas liberalizing labour flows continues to be fraught with controversy.

Cross-border labour flows might play a more important role in the future, but the challenge continues to be overcoming the various political and social barriers that stand in the way of greater labour mobility. In the meantime, more consideration will have to be given to the kind of effects this might have on macroeconomic outcomes, as well as on welfare outcomes, particularly for sending developing countries.

Young developing countries must ensure that their macroeconomic management, investment climate, infrastructure, and legal and administrative systems continue to improve so that they can attract capital from capital-surplus ageing countries. Developing countries also need to increase investment in human capital to improve the quality of their workforce.

4IR will require a fundamental transformation in education. Governments must pursue education reform and promote lifelong learning. Augmenting cognitive skills such as mathematics and sciences will be critical for the transition to a more innovative, knowledge-based economy. There will also be a need to strengthen regional education networks and connect innovation incubators in the region. New and innovative approaches to public-private collaboration are also needed, particularly in areas such as research and development.

Continue and Strengthen Regional Dialogue and Institutions for RCI

Given the emerging challenges facing the region, regional dialogue and institutions for RCI must evolve. RCI platforms need to find a new way of formulating policy and regulation that is flexible, timely, iterative, open and inclusive.

The role of RCI in sustaining peace and stability in the region is often undervalued, if not overlooked. It is easy to see why — war cannot go unnoticed, whilst peace easily can. But the gains of Asia and the Pacific would not have been possible without the key role played by RCI in preserving peace and security in the region. Nowhere is this more evident than in Southeast Asia, where ASEAN was born as a security pact during the Vietnam War. ASEAN is arguably the most durable and successful regional grouping in the developing world. It has contributed greatly to regional harmony and prosperity, and that peace has allowed member economies to grow and prosper. Sustaining dialogue and strengthening avenues for cooperation will be essential to secure continued peace in the region.

Conclusion

The Asia and the Pacific region has witnessed tremendous progress in economic and social conditions over the last couple of decades. While the rest of the world continues to struggle to shake off the worst effects of the 2008 GFC, Asia and the Pacific has prospered and continued to grow and make further inroads into poverty eradication. The gains have increased the resilience of the region, and this will be particularly important as we enter a new age of growing uncertainty. Apart from the short-term uncertainties, there are a number of longer-term challenges that need to be addressed. The two that we have focused on are demographic change and the 4IR. To deal with these challenges, countries in the region will mainly need to respond with national policies. But strengthening regional cooperation, dialogue and institutions must play a complementary role. It is more important now than ever that countries resist the temptation to resort to protectionism and that they continue to remain open and signal clearly their desire to do so. The right combination of national and regional policies will ensure that we realize the Asian Century.

Notes

1. I am grateful to Shujiro Urata and participants at the 20th Anniversary Symposium of the Graduate School of Asia Pacific Studies at Waseda University, Tokyo, on 12 October 2018, for comments and to Anna Cassandra Melendez for excellent research assistance. The views expressed in this chapter are those of the author and do not necessarily reflect the views and policies of the Asian Development Bank, or its Board of Governors or the governments they represent.
2. For purposes of this chapter, Asia and the Pacific consists of the Asian Development Bank's forty-eight regional members: Afghanistan; Armenia; Australia; Azerbaijan; Bangladesh; Bhutan; Brunei Darussalam; Cambodia; China, People's Republic of; Cook Islands; Fiji; Georgia; Hong Kong, China; India; Indonesia; Japan; Kazakhstan; Kiribati; Korea, Republic of; Kyrgyz Republic; Lao People's Democratic Republic; Malaysia; Maldives; Marshall Islands; Micronesia, Federated States of; Mongolia; Myanmar; Nauru; Nepal; New Zealand; Pakistan; Palau; Papua New Guinea; Philippines; Samoa; Singapore; Solomon Islands; Sri Lanka; Taipei, China; Tajikistan; Thailand; Timor-Leste; Tonga; Turkmenistan; Tuvalu; Uzbekistan; Vanuatu; and Vietnam.
3. *Asian Economic Integration Report 2018: Toward Optimal Provision of Regional Public Goods in Asia and the Pacific* (Manila: ADB, 2018).
4. Ibid.
5. *Strategy 2030: Achieving a Prosperous, Inclusive, Resilient, and Sustainable Asia and the Pacific* (Manila: ADB, 2018).

6. In contrast, the shares of North America and Europe contracted during the same period.
7. *Asian Economic Integration Report 2016: What Drives Foreign Direct Investment in Asia and the Pacific?* (Manila: ADB, 2016).
8. *Asian Development Outlook 2018 Update: Maintaining Stability Amid Heightened Uncertainty* (Manila: ADB, 2018).
9. *Asian Development Outlook 2018: How Technology Affects Jobs* (Manila: ADB, 2018).
10. "Fast Facts on Escalating US-China Trade War", Voice of America, 24 September 2018 <https://www.voanews.com/a/fast-facts-us-china-trade-war/4585225.html>.
11. *Asian Development Outlook 2018 Update: Maintaining Stability Amid Heightened Uncertainty* (Manila: ADB, 2018).
12. Ibid.
13. Jayant Menon and Anna Melendez-Nakamura, "Aging in Asia: Trends, Impacts and Responses", ADB Working Paper Series on Regional Economic Integration no. 25, February 2009.

LOOKING WEST, ACTING EAST: India's Indo-Pacific Strategy

Rohan Mukherjee

Ever since the Indo-Pacific re-emerged as a viable strategic concept in 2017 and Asia's four democratic major powers — the United States, Japan, Australia and India — reconvened their quadrilateral security dialogue (the Quad), Southeast Asian countries have been wary of ASEAN losing its centrality in the regional political and economic order.[1] The conceptual linkage of the two oceans and consequent expansion of geopolitical space was bound to have this effect to some extent. Moreover, the combination of four democratic major powers in a region largely home to single-party governments and authoritarian regimes raised the spectre of goals beyond the containment of China, or at least the containment of China through the creation of democratic transitions on its periphery — this was an argument the original boosters of the Quad in Washington had made in 2007.[2] Finally, the overlaying of the Quad on the Indo-Pacific concept gave rise to fears of a return to Cold War–style containment, this time of China, and major-power politics rearing its ugly head yet again in Southeast Asia.[3]

Although these concerns are real and require a response from ASEAN, Southeast Asian countries can expect to find support from an unexpected quarter: India. When the Quad was originally proposed in 2007, diplomatic protest from China had caused India and Australia to roll back their commitments, and the initiative went into stasis after George W. Bush and Shinzo Abe subsequently left office. A decade later, as the Quad returns, Australia's and China's positions have changed but India's remains the same. Canberra is now an enthusiastic supporter

---

ROHAN MUKHERJEE is Assistant Professor of Political Science at Yale-NUS College, with a joint appointment by courtesy at the Lee Kuan Yew School of Public Policy. Previously, he was a Stanton Nuclear Security Fellow at the MIT Security Studies Program, and a non-resident Visiting Fellow at the United Nations University in Tokyo.

— arguably because of China's growing attempts to influence Australian civil society and government — and Beijing is less concerned as its own power has grown by leaps and bounds in the intervening decade. New Delhi, however, is and always has been keen to create significant distance between the concept of the Indo-Pacific and the institutional arrangement that is the Quad.

It was telling, for example, that India's official statement following the Quad's landmark Manila meeting in November 2017 diverged significantly from the statements of the other three powers in choosing to omit any mention of freedom of navigation, respect for international law, and maritime security (though these are causes that India has supported in bilateral and trilateral statements).[4] When Prime Minister Narendra Modi spoke at the Shangri-La Dialogue in Singapore in June 2018, he firmly emphasized the importance of the Indo-Pacific being an *inclusive* region: "India does not see the Indo-Pacific Region as a strategy or as a club of limited members. Nor as a grouping that seeks to dominate. And by no means do we consider it as directed against any country. A geographical definition, as such, cannot be."[5] The writing on the wall was clear for observers across the region. "In short", noted one Japanese scholar, "Modi's references to inclusiveness mean the inclusion of China."[6] Indeed, India's addition of the term "inclusive" to the Japanese formulation of "free and open Indo-Pacific" is now accepted by both Washington and Tokyo — if nothing else, signalling India's pivotal role in the region.[7]

India's Indo-Pacific Strategy

How is it that a democratic major power engaged in a longstanding border dispute with China, competing with China for geopolitical influence in Asia, and assiduously courted by Western powers as a bulwark against Chinese expansionism would choose a China-friendly interpretation of the Indo-Pacific? The reasoning behind India's inclusive approach to the Indo-Pacific can be deduced from India's grand strategy, or the logic by which India seeks to create security for itself.

Broadly speaking, India has three grand-strategic objectives. The first is domestic, to ensure that the Indian economy continues to grow in a manner that improves the lives of the 224 million Indians currently living in poverty.[8] Achieving this goal will require vast sums of development finance channelled towards building and maintaining economic and social infrastructure, as well as a major improvement in state capacity in the long term. India's second objective is to deter serious challenges to its security and territorial integrity from its two powerful and nuclear-armed regional rivals, Pakistan and China, who have a long history of cooperation with each other. To achieve this goal, and because of the weakness of its domestic defence industrial base, India has invested heavily in augmenting its military capabilities through imports. Between 2009 and 2015, India was annually the largest importer of military equipment in the world, being overtaken by Saudi Arabia in 2016.[9] India's third and final objective is to ensure peace and stability in Asia. The motive here is not just security but, more importantly, economic. India depends on sea lanes for 95 per cent of its trade by volume and 68 per cent by value, making the space between the Arabian Sea and the East China Sea one of vital geoeconomic importance to New Delhi.[10]

Given these overarching national objectives, the rational choice for India has increasingly been to rely on the comparative advantage of the West in military power and the East in economic vitality. Although Russia has been a longstanding supplier of military equipment to India since the Cold War, its share of India's total defence imports declined from 65 per cent in 1991 to 56 per cent in 2017, whereas the share of the United States and its allies increased from 34 per cent to 43 per cent during the same period.[11] At the same time, China's share of India's global trade has increased from 0.2 per cent in 1991 to 11.4 per cent in 2017 (and rising to almost 15 per cent if Hong Kong was included). China is India's largest trading partner today.[12] India's economic imperative ensures that it can ill afford to alienate China, and India's security imperative (relating to China and Pakistan) ensures that it will continue to deepen its ties with the United States. New Delhi faces the additional challenge of minor standoffs and skirmishes along the Sino-Indian border escalating into a military conflict. This type of scenario — brought vividly to life via the seventy-three-day Doklam standoff in mid-2017 between the Chinese and Indian militaries — gives pause to Indian strategists who seek not to antagonize China but to manage its rise in a way that can benefit India without compromising India's sovereignty or national interests. If the Indo-Pacific region and associated institutional frameworks begin to take shape as a containment strategy, India is likely to step on the brakes.

Aside from its longstanding strategic objectives, India faces a dynamic challenge from China in the form of the Belt and Road Initiative (BRI), which has spread out across South Asia in the form of large infrastructure loans to India's neighbours, such as Pakistan, Sri Lanka, the Maldives and Nepal. It is questionable just how much non-economic (i.e., foreign policy or security) influence China is able to buy in this manner. Because of a combination of opaque terms, corruption and poor implementation, Chinese development finance has failed to deliver feasible projects, instead provoking protests over the extent of Chinese control and involvement in local economies.[13] Nonetheless, Indian decision-makers are concerned about the growing strategic competition in South Asia that they are being drawn into due to the BRI. In his Shangri-La speech, Modi was careful to state that infrastructure initiatives in the Indo-Pacific "must be based on respect for sovereignty and territorial integrity, consultation, good governance, transparency, viability and sustainability". He added, "They must promote trade, not strategic competition."[14] There is no guarantee that Beijing will accept these terms, leaving Indian strategic planners constrained to devise alternative economic mechanisms by which to compete for regional influence. The inability of any one major power to match Beijing's considerable resources on this front has necessitated cooperation with other Indo-Pacific powers such as the Asia-Africa Growth Corridor launched in 2017 by India and Japan,[15] as well as Washington's recently declared intention of creating a US$60 billion development fund to counter the BRI.[16]

Given the realities that India must contend with in its part of the world, it is unsurprising that India has eschewed containment and embraced inclusivity when it comes to the Indo-Pacific.[17] Modi has emphasized that India's vision of the region is "a positive one" composed of six elements: inclusivity, ASEAN's centrality, rules-based order, equal access to the commons, trade liberalization, and connectivity.[18] A delicate balancing act emerges when these components are considered together. The emphasis on a rules-based order, equal access to the commons, and connectivity constitutes a nod to the other members of the Quad, while the emphasis on inclusivity (i.e., engaging China), ASEAN's centrality, and trade liberalization offers other countries in the region what they seek from the Indo-Pacific: a commitment that it will not devolve into the power politics of the Cold War.

India's position on the Indo-Pacific sets it apart from the United States, which is concerned about losing strategic primacy to China in Asia; from Japan, which is concerned about existential security in connection with its territorial disputes with China; and from Australia, which is concerned about Chinese penetration of Australian society and the decline of U.S. hegemony in Asia. India not only has a major defence relationship and strategic partnership with Russia that makes managing relations with Washington difficult,[19] it seeks to engage China on questions of regional order while also standing firm in the event of a security crisis involving Beijing. In practical terms, this has meant carefully calibrating New Delhi's Indo-Pacific strategy to cooperate with the other Quad members, but not to an extent that might irritate Beijing. For example, India has consistently refused Australia's requests to join the annual Malabar naval exercise, which since 2015 has featured the Indian, U.S. and Japanese navies. New Delhi's most recent refusal to Canberra came on the heels of Modi's highly publicized meeting with Xi Jinping at Wuhan in April 2018, which was seen as finally defusing the tensions surrounding the Doklam crisis of 2017, and contributed to a U.S. analyst decrying India as "the weakest link in the Quad".[20]

Southeast Asia's Role from India's Perspective

India's pronouncements on the Indo-Pacific are often designed for a Western audience, whereas India's actions are often aimed at Eastern audiences, especially those in Southeast Asia. After all, India's primary vehicle for engaging with the Indo-Pacific minus the United States and Australia is its Act East Policy, which has since its inception in 1991 been focused on Southeast Asia and more recently Japan and South Korea.[21] Modi and his senior ministers of external affairs and defence have repeatedly referred to Southeast Asia as "the heart" and "the central pillar" of India's Act East Policy.[22]

In geopolitical terms, it makes sense to think of Southeast Asia as the centre of the Indo-Pacific. More importantly, emphasizing ASEAN's centrality allows India to pursue its vision of a free, open, *and* inclusive Indo-Pacific. There are perhaps few better ways of minimizing the potentially threatening nature of this new strategic concept — to both China and Southeast Asian nations — than opening its membership to all regional states. Diluting the influence of the United States and its allies in this way allows India to continue playing the role of a "swing state"[23] in the region and thereby pursue its grand-strategic objectives in a flexible manner. This approach is, in essence, the result of India's dogged adherence to a foreign policy of strategic autonomy, or the pursuit of "maximum options" in foreign relations in order to "enhance India's strategic space and capacity for independent agency — which in turn will give it maximum options for its own internal development".[24] Strategic autonomy suits India's grand-strategic objectives of creating economic development while warding off threats from Pakistan and China and contributing to a peaceful and stable continent. It allows India to spread the risk of engaging with the United States and its allies on the one hand and China and Russia on the other.

At the same time, India stands to benefit a great deal from economic engagement with Southeast Asia, which has been a consistent theme since the early 1990s across the Look East and Act East policies. India has pursued greater infrastructural connectivity with Southeast Asia, invited Southeast Asian nations to invest in the development of northeastern India, a region with deep cultural and historical ties to the Mekong region, and sought greater foreign direct investment from ASEAN member-states. The India-ASEAN Free Trade Agreement, painstakingly negotiated and completed in 2010, produced a significant bump in trade with the region for India, which nearly doubled between 2009 and 2017 — ASEAN today accounts for almost 11 per cent of India's global trade.[25]

Missing from this picture until recently was deeper political and security engagement between India and Southeast Asia. The Modi government has filled this gap with hectic diplomacy and positive messaging. For example, India and Singapore have built on their longstanding defence relationship through a defence cooperation agreement in 2015, a defence ministers' dialogue in 2016, an access agreement to Changi Naval Base in 2017, and a naval logistics agreement in 2018.[26] Similarly, India's state-owned oil company ONGC Videsh is engaged in offshore drilling in Vietnam's waters in the South China Sea, and India has supplied Vietnam with patrol boats, a line of credit for defence purchases, and access to satellite data for maritime domain awareness.[27]

On the diplomatic front, Modi has travelled to all but two ASEAN countries since becoming prime minister in 2014[28] — the exceptions being Cambodia and Brunei — and in January 2018 unprecedentedly hosted all ten ASEAN heads of state at India's annual Republic Day parade. Previous Indian administrations have not paid comparably close attention to elevating India-ASEAN ties at the symbolic level. For example, following Singaporean Prime Minister Goh Chok Tong's attendance as chief guest for Republic Day in 1994, it took another seventeen years for another Southeast Asian head of state (President Yudhoyono of Indonesia) to be invited in the same capacity.[29] While critics denounce Modi's diplomacy as mere theatrics, India's efforts to build political relations with Southeast Asia have arguably demonstrated New Delhi's willingness to at least diplomatically support countries at the frontline of China's rise, thus playing what former Indian foreign secretary S. Jaishankar has called the role of a "leading power, rather than just a balancing power" in global affairs.[30]

Looking Forward

There are clearly important strategic upsides for Southeast Asia when considering India's view of and role in the Indo-Pacific. New Delhi's eagerness to develop economic ties with the region offers ASEAN member states an entry point into a large and growing market for trade and investment. The Modi government's active diplomacy in the region assuages some concerns about potential counterweights to Chinese influence. However, India's Indo-Pacific strategy — indeed its grand strategy writ large — suffers from an important internal contradiction that might diminish the prospect for a meaningful security commitment to Southeast Asia.

The contradiction is that it will be increasingly difficult for India to follow a policy of strategic autonomy while harbouring great power aspirations. Being a great power entails picking sides and intervening decisively in conflicts around the world to maintain order. Until recently, the United States single-handedly played this role in Southeast Asia, assuring partners and allies that its military power would preclude any major threats to their security and prosperity. ASEAN thrived under this protective umbrella but today seeks alternative security guarantors in an increasingly multipolar and unpredictable world. India, however, is both unable in material terms and unwilling in doctrinal terms to support the United States in the latter's increasingly difficult task of maintaining regional order in the face of China's growing power and assertiveness. The same is probably true of Japan and Australia individually. This is precisely why many analysts in Washington, Tokyo and Canberra see (or wish to see) the Quad as a preliminary step towards aggregating capabilities and coordinating strategy with India in order to deter China. Unfortunately for them, India is not an ally of the United States and will continue to resist becoming one so long as it can benefit materially from Washington's military and economic largesse without significant commitment — indeed, New Delhi's commitment to the Quad has so far been entirely rhetorical.

This state of affairs suggests two possible scenarios in the future: one where India is forced by crises to come out of its shell and engage in power projection across the Indo-Pacific, and another where India retreats further into its shell as the United States and its allies considerably downgrade their willingness to bankroll India's rise indefinitely. One of these outcomes is undeniably better for Southeast Asia. It becomes incumbent on regional leaders to try and shape India's rise in ways that will lead to that outcome.

Notes

1. "ASEAN Crafts Position on US 'Free and Open Indo-Pacific' Strategy", *Nikkei Asian Review*, 2 August 2018.
2. Michael J. Green and Daniel Twining, "Democracy and American Grand Strategy in Asia: The Realist Principles behind an Enduring Idealism", *Contemporary Southeast Asia* 30, no. 1 (2008): 1–28.
3. Malcolm Cook, "Asia is No Longer Pacific", *Straits Times*, 30 November 2017.
4. Ankit Panda, "US, Japan, India, and Australia Hold Working-Level Quadrilateral Meeting on Regional Cooperation", *The Diplomat*, 13 November 2017.
5. Ministry of External Affairs (MEA), Government of India, "Prime Minister's Keynote Address at Shangri La Dialogue", 1 June 2018.

6. Takenori Horimoto, "The Free and Open Indo-Pacific Strategy: India's Wary Response", Nippon.com, 9 October 2018.
7. Press Trust of India, "India Bats for Making Indo-Pacific a Region for Shared Prosperity in First 'JAI' Trilateral Meet", *Economic Times*, 1 December 2018.
8. Press Trust of India, "India Has Highest Number of People Living below Poverty Line: World Bank", *Business Today*, 3 October 2016.
9. Stockholm International Peace Research Institute (SIPRI), "Importer/Exporter TIV Tables" <http://armstrade.sipri.org/armstrade/page/values.php>.
10. Ministry of Shipping, *Annual Report 2016–17* (New Delhi: Government of India, 2017), p. 4.
11. SIPRI Arms Transfer Database.
12. United Nations Comtrade Database <https://comtrade.un.org/data/>.
13. Darren J. Lim and Rohan Mukherjee, "What Money Can't Buy: The Security Externalities of Chinese Economic Statecraft in Post-War Sri Lanka", *Asian Security* (December 2017).
14. MEA, "Prime Minister's Keynote".
15. Jagannath P. Panda, "Asia-Africa Growth Corridor (AAGC): An India-Japan Arch in the Making?" *Focus Asia: Perspective and Analysis*, no. 21 (August 2017): 1–11.
16. Nyshka Chanda, "A Proposed US Initiative Aims to Be a 'Clear Alternative' to Chinese Investment in Asia", CNBC, 7 September 2018.
17. Rahul Roy-Chaudhury and Kate Sullivan de Estrada, "India, the Indo-Pacific and the Quad", *Survival* 60, no. 3 (2018): 181–94.
18. MEA, "Prime Minister's Keynote".
19. Tanvi Madan, "Between a Cold War Ally and an Indo-Pacific Partner: India's U.S.-Russia Balancing Act", *War on the Rocks*, 16 October 2018.
20. Derek Grossman, "India is the Weakest Link in the Quad", *Foreign Policy*, 23 July 2018.
21. Shankari Sundararaman, "India-ASEAN Relations: 'Acting' East in the Indo-Pacific", *International Studies* 54, nos. 1–4 (2018): 62–81.
22. "ASEAN is Central Pillar of India's Act East Policy: Sitharaman", *The Statesman*, 24 October 2017; Ministry of External Affairs, Government of India, "Keynote Address by External Affairs Minister at the Delhi Dialogue IX (Charting the Course for India–ASEAN Relations for the Next 25 Years)", 4 July 2017.
23. Richard Fontaine and Daniel M. Kliman, "International Order and Global Swing States", *Washington Quarterly* 36, no. 1 (Winter 2013): 93–109.
24. Sunil Khilnani, Rajiv Kumar, Pratap Bhanu Mehta, Prakash Menon, Nandan Nilekani, Srinath Raghavan, Shyam Saran, and Siddharth Varadarajan, *Nonalignment 2.0: A Foreign and Strategic Policy for India in the Twenty First Century* (New Delhi: Centre for Policy Research, 2012), p. 6.
25. Calculated using data from the World Bank's World Integrated Trade Solution (WITS) database <https://wits.worldbank.org/>.

26. Prashanth Parameswaran, "India-Singapore Relations and the Indo-Pacific: The Security Dimension", *The Diplomat*, 27 November 2018.
27. Rahul Roy-Chaudhury, "Debate: India's 'Inclusive' Indo-Pacific Policy Seeks to Balance US, China", *The Wire*, 5 July 2018.
28. Suyash Desai, "Revisiting ASEAN-India Relations", *The Diplomat*, 18 November 2017.
29. Rohan Mukherjee, "East by Southeast: Three Challenges for India's 'Act East' Policy", *Business Standard*, 23 January 2018.
30. Ministry of External Affairs, Government of India, "IISS Fullerton Lecture by Dr. S. Jaishankar, Foreign Secretary in Singapore", 20 July 2015.

AN AUSTRALIAN VISION OF THE INDO-PACIFIC AND WHAT IT MEANS FOR SOUTHEAST ASIA

Rory Medcalf

The concept of the Indo-Pacific plays a role of growing importance in the way the world is coming to terms with China's power and assertiveness. This concept serves two related purposes: an objective definition of an Asia-centric strategic and economic system, spanning a two-ocean region and replacing the late-twentieth-century idea of the Asia-Pacific, and the foundation for a strategy of incorporating and diluting Chinese power within a multipolar order reflecting respect for rules and equal sovereignty.[1] No one country or strategic thinker can lay claim to the rapid emergence of this concept. In fact, the Indo-Pacific is not such a new idea, with precursors of pan-Asian maritime connectivity going back to pre-colonial times. Moreover, a sense of this revived regional construct emerged through a process of interaction among policy establishments and strategic thinkers in a number of nations, including Australia, India, Japan, the United States and Indonesia, in the first two decades of the twenty-first century.

It is notable, however, that Australia has been the most prominent and active proponent of this concept. Australia was the first country to formally introduce the Indo-Pacific as the official definition of its strategic environment in 2013. This has consistently been reaffirmed since, and elaborated in the 2017 Foreign Policy White Paper that provides a vision for Australia's international relations. It is fair to say that the Indo-Pacific is now bipartisan orthodoxy in Australia. A likely change to a Labor government in 2019 is unlikely to shift this perspective.

Professor Rory Medcalf is Head of the National Security College at the Australian National University. His career has spanned diplomacy, intelligence analysis, think tanks, academia and journalism. He is internationally recognized as a thought leader on the emerging concept of the Indo-Pacific. His forthcoming book on the Indo-Pacific concept will be published by Black Inc. (Melbourne).

Some critics of the Indo-Pacific idea assume that it is essentially a "made-in-America" concept designed with the principal purpose of containing or at least balancing Chinese power. In fact, a closer look at Canberra's version of the Indo-Pacific, most formally articulated in the Foreign Policy White Paper, suggests it has some authentically Australian characteristics, such as its encouragement of agency and cooperation among smaller and middle powers. This places it within the tradition of Asian engagement and creative middle power diplomacy as espoused by Australian Labor governments in decades past. Moreover, such a reading of Australia's "new" Indo-Pacific strategy makes it suited for convergence with the imperatives of partner countries in Southeast Asia, and indeed with the Association of Southeast Asian Nations (ASEAN) as a whole. Diplomatic developments in 2018 have reinforced the potential for Australia and ASEAN to work together on an inclusive Indo-Pacific concept that provides an alternative to both China-centric and U.S.-led versions of regional order.

Understanding the Indo-Pacific Idea

What is the Indo-Pacific? It treats as a single strategic system what were hitherto seen as two very separate Asian regions: East Asia, centred on China and lapped by the Pacific Ocean, and South Asia, centred on India and abutting the Indian Ocean. A strategic system can be understood as a set of geopolitical power relationships among nations where major changes in one part of the system affects what happens in the others. In this sense, the Indo-Pacific can be understood as a maritime "super-region" with its geographical centre in Southeast Asia. None of this should be mistaken as some kind of effort to reduce the centrality of Asia in regional conceptions. The Indo-Pacific is a region with maritime Asia at its core. The Indo-Pacific concept underscores the fact that the Indian Ocean has replaced the Atlantic as the globe's busiest and most strategically significant trade corridor. The powerhouse economies of East Asia depend acutely on oil imports across the Indian Ocean from the Middle East and Africa.

The reality of an Indo-Pacific region has been brought about by a confluence of economic and strategic factors. A principal driver has been the rise of China and India back to their pre-colonial status as great trading economies and powers that have become increasingly outward-looking in their economic and military affairs. The Indo-Pacific power narrative is however not only about China and India. The region involves the intersecting interests of at least four major powers — China, India, Japan and the United States — as well as many significant middle players, including Australia, South Korea, the Southeast Asian countries, and more distant stakeholders such as from Europe. Furthermore, the interests of

Japan, which relies even more acutely than does China on energy supplies across the Indian Ocean, need to be taken into account. Indeed, in 2016 Prime Minister Abe declared that Japan would pursue a so-called "Free and Open Indo-Pacific strategy", encompassing development, connectivity, investment and security issues stretching to Africa.

Australia's Two-Ocean Strategy

The most active power, however, in advocating the Indo-Pacific idea has been Australia. Canberra has a unique role here in multiple ways: it is a middle power in the gathering Indo-Pacific strategic game. These include its relative diplomatic influence, its unusual two-ocean geography, its proximity to and advanced surveillance of the crucial sea lanes connecting the Indian Ocean and the Pacific, and its status as a state that — despite being a close U.S. ally — is diversifying and deepening economic, societal and security relations with multiple Asian powers. Moreover, Australia has long grappled with its singular status as neither an Asian nor a Western power, perceived as both integral to yet separate from both the Western world and the Asian region. All of this helps to explain why Australia has been at the forefront of driving an Indo-Pacific understanding of the region. This was reinforced in Australia's recent defence and foreign policy White Papers, in 2016 and 2017 respectively.[2]

Notably, the Australian version of the Indo-Pacific is somewhat more pragmatic and objective than the "Free and Open Indo-Pacific" championed by Japan and the United States. There is obvious overlap and complementarity of these concepts; however, the Australian conception — like the more recent 2018 Indonesian policy — allows more scope for cooperation with diverse partners holding distinct interests and priorities. Like Japan and the United States, Australia recognizes the utility of the Indo-Pacific as a basis for a strategy to balance China. However, the Australian approach is also grounded in the reality that the Indo-Pacific is the most logical and objective geographic basis for a coherent worldview: it is quite literally where Australia finds itself to be. The same could be said of Indonesia, Singapore, Malaysia and Thailand — four countries with their own two-ocean geography.

Some Features of the Indo-Pacific

There are some other significant features of the Indo-Pacific that suit the interests of the small and medium maritime states that comprise ASEAN. The Indo-Pacific is a *multipolar* system, in which the fate of regional order, or disorder, will not be determined by one or even two powers — the United States and China — but also by the interests and choices of others. It is also a *maritime* system, where the interests of and interactions of countries at sea tend to overshadow the continental, land-based elements of their relations with each other.

The Indo-Pacific matters as a maritime region, but given the emphasis on competing port access and infrastructure in the unfolding great game, perhaps it is the connection of the sea to the land that defines what is strategically important. The Indo-Pacific is thus better understood as a complement, not merely an alternative, to continental conceptions of connectivity in Eurasia. Or more accurately, Eurasia is the complement to the Indo-Pacific, given that that the sea outweighs the land for ease of power projection and cheapness of transportation. The Indo-Pacific is about Asia but also more than Asia. It is regional *and* global: the Indo-Pacific is the main highway for commerce and energy between Asia, Africa, Europe, Oceania and the Americas.

Australian Conceptions of the Indo-Pacific

The Indo-Pacific had been an occasional point of reference in Australian commentary and analysis since 2005, when it featured both in an internal government document and early academic reflection on the emerging East Asia Summit. In official policy publications, it began to feature from 2012 onwards, when the Labor government's "Asian Century" White Paper explored the topic as an alternative to the Asia-Pacific. More definitively, the early 2013 Defence White Paper, also by Julia Gillard's Labor government, identified the Indo-Pacific as Australia's region of strategic interest. This then became bipartisan orthodoxy under the conservative Abbott, Turnbull and Morrison governments.

The November 2017 Foreign Affairs White Paper consolidates this view that Australia's region had fundamentally changed, and that, moreover, the Indo-Pacific is a useful framing principle for strategic and foreign policy. The idea of the Asia-Pacific — largely excluding India and the Indian Ocean — was a convenient construct for our interests and regional dynamics in the late twentieth century. The Indo-Pacific suits Australia even better, and is here for the indefinite future. This is because all the powers that matter to Australia are either resident or deeply enmeshed in the Indo-Pacific: in a sense it is the global region and is defined by its fundamental quality of multipolarity (which also makes it the natural setting for balancing a rising power). And those countries — China, the United States, Japan, India and more — are now striving to shape the region and to define their Indo-Pacific strategies for doing so. Even the Chinese rejection of the rhetoric of the Indo-Pacific confirms the balancing utility of the term as well as the irony of the situation: through the so-called Belt and Road geoeconomic initiative and its growing naval footprint in the Indian Ocean, Beijing is already executing its own Indo-Pacific strategy with Chinese characteristics.

The 2017 White Paper thus begins with defining the contours of diplomatic policy settings under the framework of this geopolitical construct. It states that as uncertainties deepen about America under Trump, the Australia-U.S. alliance is embedded in a wider set of regional partnerships and "smaller groupings", which is code for an emerging mini-lateralism of self-selecting trilateral arrangements and more. It illuminates the need for a layered approach to a regional strategy. This includes key bilateral relations, with continued emphasis on the U.S. alliance but without relying on that alliance alone. A key line in the White Paper emphasizes that the Australian government will "lift the ambition of our engagement with major Indo-Pacific democracies", including Japan, India and Indonesia.

Although the Trump administration has identified the Indo-Pacific as the framework for its engagement with Asia (and competition vis-à-vis China), it is important to note that Australia's Indo-Pacific strategy is to a large degree about diversifying its partnerships beyond America. The White Paper is not especially explicit about the reborn quadrilateral dialogue of Australia, India, Japan and the United States, although it rightly emphasizes the role these new arrangements or "smaller groupings" can play in bolstering a "regional balance favourable to our interests" and to "promote an open, inclusive and rules-based region". This captures Australia's diplomatic activism in building not only the Quad but also other three-way arrangements involving, variously, India, Japan, Indonesia and France. Australia is also strengthening the longstanding trilateral strategic dialogue with Washington and Tokyo, as well as an array of bilateral engagements with countries — like Singapore and Vietnam — increasingly uncomfortable with Chinese power. Australia's emerging Indo-Pacific strategy — of which the White Paper sketched a beginning — will also likely involve greater use of established multilateral bodies centred on ASEAN, like the East Asia Summit, to dilute and moderate Chinese power.

Charting a New Course with ASEAN

All these offer substantial opportunities for ASEAN. Indeed, in March 2018 a special Australia-ASEAN diplomatic summit in Sydney reflected the enduring centrality of ASEAN in a stable, peaceful and prosperous regional order. Southeast Asian governments should see in the Indo-Pacific not a threat but an opportunity.

From an Australian perspective, the following features of an Indo-Pacific strategy lend themselves to closer cooperation with ASEAN in 2019 and beyond:

- An emphasis on inclusive multilateralism: Australia is increasingly active and creative in using ASEAN-centric mechanisms as part of its wider approach to moderate Chinese power and great power tensions through bodies such as the East Asia Summit, ADMM+ and the ASEAN Regional Forum.
- A focus on rules, values and equal sovereignty: Although Australia has not been active in unilateral or (with the U.S.) bilateral Freedom of Navigation Operations in the South China Sea, it remains a critic of China's unilateral affronts to international law in that location. There remains scope for Australia, ASEAN and others to undertake diplomatic initiatives to preserve the internationalization of the South China Sea issue, for instance on reporting of incidents or monitoring declining fish stocks.[3]
- Multipolarity of the Indo-Pacific: There is a quiet recognition that the multipolar dynamic of the Indo-Pacific means that countries have to manage uncertainties regarding the Trump administration as well as concerns about Chinese ambitions to dominate the region.
- Non-military instruments of engagement: There is scope for further cooperation through capacity-building and development assistance. Australia is increasingly active in geoeconomics, for instance in helping craft regional arrangements for infrastructure, investment, development assistance, standards and governance that complement — or compete with — the China-centric efforts of the so-called Belt and Road. This is of salience given recent concerns about China's expanding influence and security presence in Australia's South Pacific neighbourhood, a sub-region where Australia would welcome a wider range of players. A logical next step in Australia's Indo-Pacific strategy would be to step up capacity building with ASEAN partners in areas like civil maritime security and environmental monitoring.

To Australian policymakers, the Indo-Pacific is about shaping a regional order in which China is not the only Asian power that matters. This will elevate the importance of ASEAN.

To be sure, the term Indo-Pacific has not yet entered into the standard ASEAN diplomatic lexicon, which has long identified the bloc of ten Southeast Asian nations as the leading institution across the Asia-Pacific. That late twentieth-century construct was ambivalent about India and marginalized the Indian Ocean. Yet, regardless of choice of words, the animating idea of the Indo-Pacific may be precisely what ASEAN needs to sustain and revitalize its place in the geopolitics and institutions of a maritime Asia that is becoming the global centre of strategic and economic gravity. As a contemporary version of Asia, the Indo-Pacific recognizes the continuing political centrality of ASEAN in regional organizations. Indeed, the big diplomatic institutions that are of ASEAN born — such as the East Asia Summit and the ASEAN Regional Forum — are already Indo-Pacific in character, with a membership that is inclusive of India, Australia, the United States and other partners beyond East Asia. This has been essential to ensure such institutions are dominated by no single power. Unlike the old Asia-Pacific, the Indo-Pacific also recognizes Southeast Asia as the geographic as well as the political heart of the region.

Of course, the Indo-Pacific neatly defines the region so that Australia automatically belongs. But it equally suits Indonesia, Singapore, Malaysia and Thailand — countries at the strategic boundary of the two oceans. Indonesia in particular seems to recognize that this two-ocean worldview could help turn Southeast Asia's sense of a geographic vulnerability into an advantage, with Indonesian leaders becoming bolder with their own Indo-Pacific designs. Early in 2018, President Joko Widodo declared Indonesia's ambition for an Indo-Pacific diplomatic architecture based on openness, transparency and inclusion. Public indications were that he and his foreign ministry had sustained this idea throughout the year, advocating for an ASEAN version of the Indo-Pacific throughout various regional diplomatic forums. This culminated in the chair's statement at the November 2018 East Asia Summit in Singapore giving the Indo-Pacific careful but constructive attention. This leaves the way open for ASEAN states to evolve their pragmatic region-wide diplomacy — a tradition ever since Lee Kuan Yew first engaged India — in ways that reflect an inclusive two-ocean worldview.

Notes

1. These definitions are expanded elsewhere by the author, notably in Rory Medcalf, "Pivoting the Map: Australia's Indo-Pacific System", *The Centre of Gravity Series* 1 (Canberra: ANU Strategic and Defence Studies Centre, 2012); Rory Medcalf, "The Indo-Pacific: What's in a Name?" *The American Interest* 9 no. 2 (2013): 58–66; and Rory Medcalf, "Mapping Our Indo-Pacific Future: Towards an Indo-Pacific Strategy for Australia", speech at the National Security College, Australian National University, 21 May 2018 <https://nsc.crawford.anu.edu.au/news-events/news/12677/mapping-our-indo-pacific-future-rory-medcalfs-public-lecture>.
2. Australian Government, Defence White Paper 2013 <http://www.defence.gov.au/whitepaper/2013/>; Australian Government, Defence White Paper 2016 <http://

www.defence.gov.au/WhitePaper/Docs/2016-Defence-White-Paper.pdf>; Australian Government, Foreign Policy White Paper 2017 <https://www.fpwhitepaper.gov.au/foreign-policy-white-paper>.

3. See, for instance, Marina Tsirbas, "Saving the South China Sea Fishery: Time to Internationalise", National Security College Policy Options Paper No. 3 (2017) <https://nsc.crawford.anu.edu.au/department-news/10725/saving-south-china-sea-fishery-time-internationalise>.

THE TRUMP ADMINISTRATION'S FREE AND OPEN INDO-PACIFIC APPROACH

Brian Harding

After nearly two years, the Trump administration's approach to the Indo-Pacific region has finally taken shape. Its objectives are a "Free and Open Indo-Pacific", in line with decades of U.S. policy in the region, but in a new context of outright strategic competition with China. Its means include familiar tools of U.S. engagement, with some modest improvements for the times. But in Donald Trump's America, actions often do not support stated goals and, in the case of policy in the Indo-Pacific, President Trump's personal instincts, in particular his dogmatic approach to trade, have undermined his administration's best efforts in the region.

Early Days

Over the course of two years, a series of formal speeches and documents have articulated in increasing detail the administration's Indo-Pacific approach. Throughout this period, the administration has also faced frequent criticism for the slow pace of policy formulation and in appointing key Asia policymaking officials. To understand why policy formulation has been so slow, it is important to go back to Trump's unconventional presidential campaign and presidential transition.

While all major U.S. presidential campaigns in recent memory have been supported by networks of public policy professionals helping the nominees and

---

BRIAN HARDING is Deputy Director and Fellow at the Southeast Asia Program at the Center for Strategic and International Studies (CSIS) in Washington DC.

crafting policy agendas for the event the candidate is elected, Donald Trump's presidential campaign was different. In stark contrast to Hillary Clinton's 2016 campaign — with an enormous team of unpaid foreign policy advisors working to develop a potential presidential agenda, including a strategy for Asia — Trump had almost no foreign policy advisors. During the 2016 Republican primary season, leading Republican foreign policy hands supported a range of candidates, but almost none signed up to support candidate Donald Trump. Instead, many leading Republican experts actively opposed Trump's candidacy.[1] Furthermore, soon after the election, Trump disbanded his small presidential transition office, depleting any preparatory work that had been done.

Without a coherent foreign policy framework and with little expertise on Asia within its ranks, the early Trump administration's approach to Asia became highly reactionary, guided by a deep scepticism of China and the reality that North Korea presented an increasingly untenable threat to the U.S. homeland. In particular, the North Korea threat forced the administration to focus considerable attention on Asia in its first few months with a flurry of meetings with Asian leaders. Within months, Japanese Prime Minister Shinzo Abe, Chinese President Xi Jinping, South Korean President Moon Jae-In, Vietnamese Prime Minister Nguyen Xuan Phuc, Malaysian Prime Minister Najib Razak, Thai Prime Minister Prayuth Chan-Ocha, and Singaporean Prime Minister Lee Hsien Loong all visited the United States to meet with President Trump, with North Korea and the president's focus on bilateral trade deficits dominating discussions.

2017: A Free and Open Indo-Pacific Strategy Emerges

While the early Trump administration's attention to Asia was primarily focused on North Korea, an ancillary result of this intensive engagement was that it quickly became clear to senior officials that the administration needed a broader Asia strategy. Trump's strong interest in taking a harder line on China, largely due to his contention that China has taken advantage of the United States economically, also drove his team to develop a broader approach in line with this objective. As the administration cast around for a broader vision distinct from Obama's "rebalance" or "pivot", it landed on the concept of a "Free and Open Indo-Pacific", a vision and name which is heavily influenced by the close interaction between key senior Trump officials and their Japanese counterparts at a time when the latter were rolling out the Japanese concept of a "Free and Open Indo-Pacific". Japan's interest in deepening quadrilateral cooperation including India and Australia also resonated with Trump administration officials.

The administration's first major speech to rely heavily on the terminology of "Indo-Pacific" took place in October 2017 and was delivered by then secretary of state Rex Tillerson at the Center for Strategic and International Studies in Washington DC.[2] While the speech largely focused on U.S.-India relations, he foreshadowed language that would appear in later, more comprehensive, descriptions of the Free and Open Indo-Pacific strategy, stating, "India and the United States must foster greater prosperity and security with the aim of a free and open Indo-Pacific".

A month later, at the Asia-Pacific Economic Cooperation (APEC) leaders summit in Da Nang, Vietnam, in a speech often cited by Trump officials as the unveiling of the Free and Open Indo-Pacific strategy, the president described "a free and open Indo-Pacific" as "a place where sovereign and independent nations, with diverse cultures and many different dreams, can all prosper side-by side and thrive in freedom and in peace".[3] However, despite the lofty rhetoric, the speech included scant details about his agenda for the region, with much of it focused on "fair and reciprocal trade" and lacking a vision for a broad U.S. economic agenda for the region.

Finally, in December 2017, the U.S. National Security Strategy (NSS) clearly described the administration's vision, including the crucial context of competition with China, stating that a "geopolitical competition between free and repressive visions of world order is taking place in the Indo-Pacific".[4] The NSS identifies how "China seeks to displace the United States in the Indo-Pacific region, expand the reaches of its state-driven economic model, and reorder the region in its favor." While President Trump has made little mention of the NSS, the document authoritatively represents the policy outlook of senior appointees at the White House, State Department and Pentagon.

2018: "Flesh on the Bones"

With the vision finally set by the end of 2017, 2018 became the year of "putting flesh on the bones", which included adjusting the vision in response to regional critiques, such as Southeast Asian concerns about the place of ASEAN in U.S. policy.

In June 2018, at the Shangri-La Dialogue, Secretary of Defense James Mattis presented details for the defence aspect of the FOIP strategy in a speech that sought to draw a sharp contrast between the approaches to regional affairs by the United States and China, including the South China Sea.[5] Mattis outlined that increasing time and attention had been focused on maritime issues, interoperability, the rule of law, and economic development led by the private sector. Importantly, in recognition of Southeast Asian concerns about the place of ASEAN in the U.S. strategy amid attention to quadrilateral efforts, he repeatedly stressed continued U.S. support for ASEAN centrality and established multilateral mechanisms.

In July 2018, a full eighteen months into the administration, Secretary of State Mike Pompeo spoke at the U.S. Chamber of Commerce's Indo-Pacific Business Forum to lay out the economic components of the FOIP vision and he gave the clearest explanation of the strategy to date.[6] First, he clearly defined the geographic scope, defining the region as stretching from the west coast of the United States to the west coast of India. He then outlined what the administration means by "free and open":

> When we say 'free' Indo-Pacific, it means we all want all nations … to be able to protect their sovereignty from coercion … at the national level, 'free' means good governance and the assurance that citizens can enjoy their fundamental rights.… When we say 'open' in the Indo-Pacific, it means we want all nations to enjoy open access to seas and airways … peaceful resolution of territorial and maritime disputes.… Economically, 'open' means fair and reciprocal trade, open investment environments, transparent agreements between nations, and improved connectivity…

Pompeo also announced modest new initiatives intended to put flesh on the bones of the strategy, including US$113 million in support for initiatives on the digital economy, energy and infrastructure, a figure which was however panned in many circles when contrasted with the hundreds of billions of dollars associated with China's Belt and Road Initiative.

By November 2018, when Vice President Mike Pence travelled to Singapore and Papua New Guinea to attend the East Asia Summit and APEC meetings in place of President Trump, the United States' FOIP vision and some new tools were well in place. Most notably, Pence was able to tout the recently passed Better Utilization of Investment Leading to Development (BUILD) Act, which reforms U.S. development finance and provides new tools and resources to incentivize U.S. businesses to take part in infrastructure development (although whether these resources will be substantially directed towards Asia remains an open question). He also announced initiatives on cyber security, smart cities and transparency that sought to demonstrate U.S. commitment to open and responsible governance, in contrast to China. And Pence went out of his way, too, to declare that "ASEAN is at the center of our Indo-Pacific strategy".[7]

Continuity and Change

While the Trump administration's development of its Free and Open Indo-Pacific strategy took the better part of its first two years in office to outline and flesh out, the objectives of the strategy largely represent a continuity with decades of U.S. Asia policy: open markets, free societies, rule of law, sovereignty for all, and American leadership. In the end, rather than an abrupt break from the past, centred on an "America First" doctrine, it outlines familiar objectives. As John Lee has eloquently written in an ISEAS article, "The Free and Open Indo-Pacific is a reaffirmation of the security and economic rules-based order which has existed since after the Second World War."[8]

Even the geographic scope of the concept — the Indo-Pacific — is not especially novel. Both the George W. Bush and Barack Obama administrations focused on building stronger ties with India and bringing India more fully into the strategic fold in East Asia. More broadly, below the headlines, there has also been a great deal of continuity with U.S. policy around the region — increasingly close, practical alliance cooperation with Japan, South Korea and Australia and the steady building of bilateral relations with most Southeast Asian nations and with ASEAN as a bloc. In terms of tools and resources, little has changed either. U.S. engagement continues to be well resourced on the defence side, with diplomacy under-resourced and economic engagement lacking focus.

However, despite the continuity in articulated ends and presented through the various government programmes and policies, three personal inclinations of President Trump have muddled the U.S. Indo-Pacific policy.

First, President Trump has been unwavering in his opposition to multilateral free trade agreements, which would naturally be in line with freedom and openness, as in the case of the policies of Australia and Japan. This would have also contributed to a competitive strategy towards China. Instead, President Trump withdrew the United States from the Trans-Pacific Partnership and actively encourages U.S. companies to return their manufacturing operations to the United States. Moreover, rather than seeking to raise standards and openness across the region, in the mould of decades of U.S. policy, Trump has instead individually harangued countries with which the United States has a trade deficit.

Second, President Trump has rarely put his personal stamp on his administration's strategy by showing up to key regional meetings, which has led many in the region to question whether he is truly on board with what his officials say. While Trump had hosted numerous leaders in the United States for bilateral meetings early in his presidency and travelled to Vietnam and the

Philippines for the 2017 APEC and East Asia Summit meetings, he ended up leaving Manila before the conclusion of the EAS meeting and did not travel to Asia for the 2018 summits. In Southeast Asia in particular, these absences, as well as the failure to host ASEAN leaders for a summit in the United States along the lines of the 2016 U.S.-ASEAN Sunnylands meeting, have raised questions about U.S. commitment and relevance. The lack of presidential-level endorsement of ASEAN and ASEAN-centric structures has also weakened stated attempts to compete with China.

Third, President Trump's personal scepticism of alliances and his willingness to roil long-standing security partnerships to extract minor economic concessions, such as with South Korea and Canada, has marked a stark departure from longstanding U.S. policy. The result has been increasing uncertainty about the reliability of the United States as a security partner, which ultimately undermines attempts to forge a successful competitive policy vis-à-vis China.

The Result

In sum, the Trump administration's stated approach to the Indo-Pacific is largely a reaffirmation of established policy but adapted to a new era in U.S.-China relations and a return to great power competition. The strategy is also meant to enable the United States to shape the future of the Indo-Pacific based along lines of freedom and openness, in contrast to a Chinese vision, which is cast as predatory and coercive. To support the strategy, the administration has continued a great deal of established lines of policy and programmes while also seeking to be more active in infrastructure financing and to direct U.S. resources to encourage transparency, innovation and other areas of U.S. strength.

However, despite clarity and laudable initiatives from senior officials, President Donald Trump's personal instincts and actions have often undercut his administration's stated policies and undermined his intentions. In particular, his approach to trade, his failure to show up at key meetings and his ingrained scepticism of alliances have muddied the clarity that his administration has sought to construct. Two years in, one of the biggest questions is whether President Trump can get on board with his own administration's strategy.

Notes

1. WOTR staff, "Open Letter on Donald Trump from GOP National Security Leaders", *War on the Rocks*, 2 March 2016 <https://warontherocks.com/2016/03/open-letter-on-donald-trump-from-gop-national-security-leaders/>.

2. "Defining our Relationship with India for the Next Century: An Address by U.S. Secretary of State Rex Tillerson", CSIS, Washington DC, 8 October 2017 <https://www.csis.org/events/defining-our-relationship-india-next-century-address-us-secretary-state-rex-tillerson>.
3. "Remarks by President Trump at APEC CEO Summit, Da Nang Vietnam", 10 November 2017 <https://www.whitehouse.gov/briefings-statements/remarks-president-trump-apec-ceo-summit-da-nang-vietnam/>.
4. *National Security Strategy of the United States of America* (Washington DC: The White House, December 2017) <https://www.whitehouse.gov/wp-content/uploads/2017/12/NSS-Final-12-18-2017-0905.pdf>.
5. "Remarks by Secretary Mattis at Plenary Session of the 2018 Shangri-La Dialogue", Singapore, 2 June 2018 <https://dod.defense.gov/News/Transcripts/Transcript-View/Article/1538599/remarks-by-secretary-mattis-at-plenary-session-of-the-2018-shangri-la-dialogue/>.
6. Michael R. Pompeo, Secretary of State, "Remarks on 'America's Indo-Pacific Vision' ", Washington DC, 30 July 2018 <https://www.state.gov/secretary/remarks/2018/07/284722.htm>.
7. "Prepared Remarks for Vice President Pence at the East Asia Summit Plenary Session", Singapore, 15 November 2018 <https://www.whitehouse.gov/briefings-statements/prepared-remarks-vice-president-pence-east-asia-summit-plenary-session/>.
8. John Lee, *The "Free and Open Indo-Pacific" and Implications for ASEAN*, Trends in Southeast Asia 2018, no. 13 (Singapore: ISEAS – Yusof Ishak Institute, 2018) <https://bookshop.iseas.edu.sg/publication/2325>.

JAPAN'S "FREE AND OPEN INDO-PACIFIC STRATEGY" AND ITS IMPLICATION FOR ASEAN

Tomohiko Satake[1]

In August 2016, Japanese Prime Minister Shinzo Abe announced the "Free and Open Indo-Pacific Strategy" (FOIPs) at the Tokyo International Conference on African Development (TICAD) held in Kenya.[2] Since then, many researchers, journalists and policymakers have discussed what the FOIP Strategy, and the broader concept of a Free and Open Indo-Pacific (FOIP), exactly means.

For some, FOIPs is essentially an exclusive concept that views China as "a hostile existential threat to regional (and global) order, prosperity, and Western interests".[3] Such a view tends to see Abe's FOIPs primarily as a geopolitical strategy aimed at countering Chinese power and influence by creating a maritime coalition with regional democracies, represented by the Quadrilateral Security Cooperation (Quad) between Japan, Australia, India and the United States. The FOIPs is also commonly seen as a competitor or "geoeconomic" strategy against China's Belt and Road Initiative (BRI) by providing the region with alternatives to BRI projects.[4]

For others, however, FOIPs is an inclusive concept that ultimately aims to incorporate China and other powers in an inclusive political and economic system in the Indo-Pacific.[5] Such a view, often stressed by the Japanese government and its officials, tends to dismiss the geopolitical aspect of FOIPs and argues that FOIPs is a comprehensive framework or "vision" for Japanese regional policies, mostly its economic and development cooperation such as infrastructure development and support for regional connectivity.[6] This kind of view also stresses the cooperative, as well as the competitive, aspects of FOIPs by pointing out many overlaps or

---

Tomohiko Satake is Senior Fellow in the Defense Policy Division at the National Institute for Defense Studies (NIDS) in Tokyo.

mutual complementarities, especially in the "third party cooperation", between FOIPs and BRI.[7] According to this line of argument, understanding FOIPs simply as a "counter-China strategy" is a stunted and short-sighted view which ignores the fact that the concept was developed as a response to the long-term shift in the centre of gravity of the global economy from Western Europe to the Pacific and Indian Oceans.[8]

As such, there are almost opposite views over what FOIPs means. Which view explains the reality of FOIPs more accurately? With this question in mind, the chapter first examines why FOIPs has become an important strategic concept for Japan. It then argues that, while FOIPs is undeniably driven by the geopolitical concerns of Japanese policymakers, the reality (or its implementation) of FOIPs can be best described as a "regional order-building strategy", rather than a mere geopolitical or geoeconomic strategy, aimed at establishing a pluralistic and inclusive order incorporating various regional countries under common rules and norms.

As important elements of such a regional order-building strategy, the chapter highlights three aspects — (1) creating a stable (and multiple) power balance; (2) promoting regional resiliency, development and connectivity; and (3) rule-making and norm-setting — that Japan has pursued under the name of FOIPs. After discussing these issues, the chapter examines the implications of FOIPs for ASEAN, and concludes that Japan's cooperation with ASEAN will play a critical role for the success of FOIPs as a regional order-building strategy in order to avoid the emergence of a "new Cold War" in the region.

Why Indo-Pacific?

The term "Indo-Pacific" has become popularly used by the Japanese security community since around 2010.[9] While there are many reasons for this, the most important and fundamental factor is the rise of China and its growing power and influence, especially in the maritime domain. With its constant economic growth, even after the global financial crisis of 2008, China has continued to expand its power and influence in the East China Sea, the South China Sea and the Indian Ocean. Japanese strategic thinkers have been especially worried about China's "grey-zone" tactics, which have gradually undermined the status quo in both the East and South China Seas. They have also been concerned with the "String of Pearls" strategy by China to network its military and commercial facilities in the Indian Ocean. This has significant implications for Japanese security, which is heavily dependent on the Sea Lanes of Communication (SLOCs) running through the Indian and Pacific Oceans.[10]

Such concerns were openly expressed in Prime Minister Abe's personal article titled "Asia's Democratic Security Diamond", published when he became Japanese prime minister in December 2012. While referencing Abe's previous speech in India titled "Confluence of the Two Seas", the article first stresses that "[p]eace, stability, and freedom of navigation in the Pacific Ocean are inseparable from peace, stability, and freedom of navigation in the Indian Ocean". The article then highlights China's growing maritime influence, including its "*fait accompli*" strategy in the East China Sea and the militarization of the South China Sea, which makes the South China Sea "a 'Lake Beijing' ". In order to counter the growing Chinese maritime presence, the article bluntly argues that Australia, India, Japan, and the United States should "form a diamond to safeguard the maritime commons stretching from the Indian Ocean region to the western Pacific".[11]

The Abe administration has actually enhanced Japan's strategic presence and partnerships with Indo-Pacific countries, most notably Australia and India, while maintaining and strengthening the U.S.-Japan alliance. In 2014 the Abe administration upgraded its relations with both Australia and India to a "special strategic partnership" (Australia) and a "special strategic and global partnership" (India). The administration also reinvigorated the Trilateral Strategic Dialogue (TSD), which had not been held at the ministerial level since 2009, and launched the Japan-Australia-India high-level officials' meeting from 2015. In an interview with a Japanese newspaper, moreover, Foreign Minister Taro Kono stated that Japan would pursue quadrilateral strategic dialogue with the United States, Australia and India, which had been suspended since Australia's withdrawal from the Quad in 2008. After Kono's announcement, senior officials of the four countries met in November 2017 and in June and November 2018. Meanwhile, Japanese SDF ships and aircraft have increasingly made port calls or engaged in joint training exercises with Indo-Pacific countries, which has enhanced Japanese presence and partnerships in some vital areas such as the South China Sea and the Indian Ocean.[12]

FOIPs has often been used as political rhetoric to justify Japan's greater military engagement with Indo-Pacific countries. In particular, a central element of the FOIPs involves Japan enhancing its strategic cooperation with India in order to encourage India to adopt a greater role in counterbalancing against China. Behind such a strategy is very geopolitical thinking by Japanese policymakers, such as the deputy secretary general of the National Security Secretariat, Nobukatsu Kanehara, who has evaluated the crucial importance of India in offsetting the growing power and influence of China.[13] Engaging India eastward could also force Beijing to divert some of its resources and attention to the Indian Ocean from the East and South China Seas.[14] In this sense, one can hardly deny that Japan's FOIPs is essentially a geopolitical (or geoeconomic) concept that has developed as a response to geostrategic change in the region due to the rise of China.

This does not necessarily mean, however, that FOIPs is a "containment" strategy against China. While strengthening cooperation with regional democracies on the one hand, Japan has continued and even enhanced its engagement with China on the other.[15] In October 2018, Abe visited China for the first time in seven years as a Japanese prime minister and agreed with Chinese president Xi Jinping that the two countries would promote high-level exchanges, economic cooperation, maritime security and regional and international affairs. Furthermore, Abe and Chinese premier Li Keqiang signed "12 international agreements and memorandums", including cooperation for Maritime Search and Rescue and the establishment of both the "Japan-China Innovation and Cooperation Dialogue" and the "Japan-China Industry Ministers' Dialogue".[16] It was even reported that Abe and Xi agreed on "three principles" — shifting from "competition to collaboration", working together as partners that will not threaten each other, and developing a free and fair trading system — although Tokyo and Beijing seemed to have slightly different understandings of those principles.[17]

Despite the intensification of the U.S.-Sino strategic rivalry, Tokyo wishes to work closely with Beijing on economic, industrial and even political and military issues. Yet such an engagement policy will become increasingly difficult as the power-gap between Japan and China continues to expand. Tensions between Japan and China or the United States and China would inevitably escalate should China continue to re-write the existing order in its favour. To maintain the current constructive relations with China, Japan needs to maintain a stable power balance that can be the backbone of Japan's continuous engagement policy. This is one context from which Japan has expanded its strategic partnership with other like-minded democracies, most notably Australia and India, as well as keeping the U.S. military presence in the region. For Japan, FOIPs is a strategy to maintain, rather than terminate, Japan's continuous and constructive engagement policy with China.

Japan, like Australia and India, also stresses that FOIPs is an "open and inclusive concept, not excluding any country".[18] This means that China is always welcomed to join the FOIPs so long as it respects basic values and principles such as the rule of law, freedom of navigation, openness and free trade. In this sense it may be wrong to see FOIPs simply as a geopolitical or geoeconomic strategy against China. The fundamental emphasis of FOIPs is placed on the establishment of an open, inclusive and pluralistic order where divergent countries, including China, can coexist under common rules and principles.

In this context, FOIPs can be understood as a "regional order-building" strategy, rather than a mere geopolitical or geoeconomic strategy. Unlike a mere geopolitical or geoeconomic strategy that is purely exclusive and competitive, FOIPs as a regional order-building strategy includes both competitive (exclusive) and cooperative (inclusive) elements. Rather than directly targeting China and its BRI projects, FOIPs attempts to build or enhance the regional order per se — it is not "against" something, but "for" something. In fact, the actual policies that the Japanese government has implemented under the name of FOIPs resemble what the author describes as a regional order-building strategy, as will be discussed in the next section.

FOIPs as a Strategy for Building Regional Order: Three Key Elements

There are at least three key elements to FOIPs as a strategy for building regional order. These are: (1) creating a stable (and multiple) power balance; (2) enhancing regional resiliency, development and connectivity; and (3) promoting rule-making and norm-setting.

Creating a Stable (and Multiple) Power Balance

Creating a stable power balance is a top priority of FOIPs, and the U.S.-Japan alliance remains the cornerstone of this. Indeed, one of the most important objectives of FOIPs is to maintain a strong U.S. regional security commitment by expanding the scope of the U.S.-Japan alliance from the Asia-Pacific to the Indo-Pacific.[19] U.S. president Donald Trump's announcement to adopt FOIPs in November 2017 was therefore a clear diplomatic victory for Japan.[20] In fact, Japan has strengthened its cooperation with the United States in the wider Indo-Pacific region in areas such as capacity-building, military exercises/training, and infrastructure investments over the past years.[21]

At the same time, Japan has diversified its strategic partnerships with regional and extra-regional countries, as already discussed. As a former member of the National Security Council of the Trump administration rightly points out, "[o]ne of the little-discussed realities [of] a 'free and open Indo-Pacific' is that the strategy is rooted in the keen recognition that the United States alone will never be capable of achieving and securing the future many states envision for this region".[22] This is the reason why Japan has expanded its strategic partnerships not only with India and Australia but also with other regional and extra-regional countries and bodies such as ASEAN, the United Kingdom and France. Most of these "middle-powers" have recently moved to hike their defence spending in order to respond to more competitive strategic environments. By enhancing strategic partnerships with regional powers, and inviting more non-regional friends and partners to the Indo-Pacific, Japan has tried to create a stable and multipolar power balance to maintain a rules-based order.

Creating a more multiple power balance is essential at a time when the U.S.-Sino strategic rivalry has intensified. As the so-called power-transition theory suggests, conflicts are most likely to occur when the power-gap between a rising power and the existing hegemon narrows.[23] International tensions are expected to become high as the existing hegemon will try to prevent the rising power from replacing its position through all necessary measures — often described as the "Thucydides' trap".[24] Indeed, recent policies by the U.S. government towards China, including imposing high-rate tariffs on imported goods from China and harsh criticism against Chinese foreign and domestic behaviour, seem to endorse such a pessimistic school of thought. To avoid a hegemonic war, and to escape the "Thucydides' trap", one must find broader space that can accommodate both the rising power and the declining hegemon.

Expanding the region from "Asia-Pacific" to "Indo-Pacific", and creating a more multiple power balance by diverse actors, can be understood as an attempt to find and create such a broader strategic space in the region. This may also be good for Beijing, which has sought a more multipolar power balance, rather than the U.S.-dominated world, and advocated "peaceful co-existence" in such a world.[25] While China has not endorsed the concept of the Indo-Pacific (and its government-related media and scholars have criticized the concept), it actually has been one of the most active players in the region.[26] It is also in China's interest to avoid risky competition or conflicts with the United States. In this sense, China, as well as Japan and other regional countries, can benefit from the emergence of a more stable and multipolar Indo-Pacific order.

Promoting Regional Resiliency, Development and Connectivity

Although countries in the Indo-Pacific have developed rapidly, they are still vulnerable to a range of risks and threats, such as terrorism, natural disasters, illegal fishing, transactional crimes, cyber threats and domestic problems such as corruption, economic downturns and political instability. Such vulnerabilities can be easily translated into regional instability or conflicts by undermining the stable governance of regional countries. Reducing the vulnerabilities of regional countries and encouraging their more sustainable and autonomous development is therefore one of the top priorities of FOIPs as a regional order-building strategy.

This is why Japan has recently enhanced capacity-building efforts towards Indo-Pacific countries. Japan's capacity-building efforts cover a wide range of activities, not only maritime security but also humanitarian assistance and disaster relief (HA/DR), counter-terrorism, peacekeeping operations, and cyber or space security. Japan has also expanded its capacity-building assistance from Southeast Asia to the South Pacific, the Indian Ocean, Central Asia and Africa.[27] These capacity-building activities are sometimes conducted in close cooperation with like-minded countries, most notably the United States and Australia.[28]

Japan's defence equipment and technology cooperation with regional countries is also important for enhancing regional resiliency. After introducing the new Three Principles on Transfer of Defense Equipment and Technology in 2014, as well as announcing the new Development Cooperation Charter in 2015, Japan has increasingly promoted cooperation on defence equipment and technology with countries like Australia, India, the Philippines, Vietnam, Thailand, Indonesia, New Zealand, the United Kingdom and France. Unlike the arms exports of some other countries, transfers of defence equipment by Japan are not primarily driven by commercial interests; instead, they are permitted when they contribute to "active promotion of peace contribution and international cooperation" and to the security of Japan.[29] Capacity-building assistance is therefore one of the major objectives of Japan's defence equipment and technology cooperation.

Japan's economic assistance, including its official development assistance (ODA), is another important tool for the regional order-building strategy in the Indo-Pacific. In 2016 the Japanese government allocated more than seventy per cent of its ODA for the Indo-Pacific region, especially for countries identified in FOIPs.[30] Japan has also rapidly increased its investment in the Indo-Pacific region, most notably in India, the Mekong and Africa.[31] Promoting regional connectivity initiatives, such as the Master Plan on ASEAN Connectivity (MPAC), Japan-Mekong Connectivity Initiative and Asia and Africa Growth Corridor, is also important, not only from an economic standpoint but also from political and security perspectives. Without balanced and sustainable economic growth, regional countries cannot achieve political and social stability. In this sense, Japan's economic and development cooperation, including its ODA and hard or soft infrastructure development, plays an important role for FOIPs as a regional order-building strategy to reduce regional vulnerabilities.

As discussed earlier, Japan's connectivity support is often seen as a countermeasure to China's BRI projects. However, Japan supported regional connectivity well before the BRI was announced in 2013.[32] There are, moreover, apparently mutual complementarities between Japan and China in terms of their economic activities in third countries, as demonstrated by the conclusion by Tokyo and Beijing of the "Memorandum on Business Cooperation in Third Countries" in May 2018. It is therefore inaccurate to view Japan's FOIPs only in the context of a strategy to counter China.

Rule making or Norm setting

Finally, Japan has strengthened its efforts for rule making and norm setting in the region. Although sharing universal values, such as the rule of law, is an important objective of FOIPs, Japanese policymakers have been much less vocal to promote those values under the strategy. This is evident when one compares FOIPs to the "Arc of Freedom and Prosperity (AFP)" concept announced by then foreign minister Taro Aso during the first Abe administration in 2007. Although AFP was not necessarily an attempt to contain China, its "value-oriented" approach aroused many concerns and much scepticism that Japan was trying to establish a region that excludes countries with different values and ideologies. Based on this experience, FOIPs stresses rules, norms and principles that can be agreed by all regional countries, rather than values themselves.

Indeed, Japan has enhanced its rule-making and norm-setting efforts. Japan's recent rule-making efforts in trade include the conclusion of the Comprehensive and Progressive Agreement for Trans-Pacific Partnership with other like-minded countries and the Economic Partnership Agreement with the European Union. Japan has also worked hard for the conclusion of the Regional Comprehensive Economic Partnership (RCEP) in order to establish "a free, fair and rule-based market" for the realization of FOIPs.[33] As China is a key player in RCEP, RCEP negotiation would become a touchstone for Tokyo whether or not it can jointly collaborate on regional rule making with Beijing.

Likewise, it was important that Japan and China agreed to launch a Maritime and Air Communication Mechanism (MACM), after long-running negotiations since the late 2000s. The MACM went into operation in June 2018. While the MACM is primarily a crisis-management measure, it also determined that Japan and China will use specific frequencies, signals and abbreviations based on the Code for Unplanned Encounters at Sea (CUES) for their direct communications between vessels and aircraft. Since CUES was adopted at the Western Pacific Naval Symposium in 2014, Japan, with other Western countries, has encouraged China to adopt CUES for its naval activities. It could be argued, therefore, that launching the MACM is part of Japanese efforts to encourage China to be embedded in a mesh of rules and institutions. This is another important aspect of FOIPs as a regional order-building strategy.

ASEAN at the Heart of FOIPs

While some countries, such as Brunei and Cambodia, have officially "welcomed" Japan's FOIPs, ASEAN itself has reservations about endorsing FOIPs, out of concerns that the FOIPs and Quad would marginalize ASEAN's role and centrality. Some ASEAN countries, such as Singapore, worry that pushing FOIPs could divide Asia into two different blocs, which could force some ASEAN countries to have to make "false choices" between the U.S. camp and China.[34] While Indonesia announced its own "Indo-Pacific cooperation concept", the concept is intentionally distinguished from Japan's or the United States' FOIPs by stressing the ASEAN Way of maintaining ASEAN centrality, non-intervention in internal affairs, and consensual decision-making.[35]

ASEAN's concerns are completely reasonable and understandable if one looks at FOIPs simply as a geopolitical or geoeconomic strategy against China. Indeed, there will be a limited role of ASEAN in such a highly competitive environment, or a "new Cold War", where the United States and China respectively create mutually exclusive spheres of influence. If one looks at FOIPs in the context of a regional order-building strategy, however, one may realize that ASEAN is by no means marginalized in FOIPs. Rather, ASEAN is at the heart of Japan's regional order-building efforts under FOIPs.

For instance, ASEAN plays a crucial role in maintaining the multiple power balance in the Indo-Pacific. Although individual ASEAN countries are still weak, a united ASEAN would have a significant impact on the regional power balance, having, combined, the world's third-largest population and fifth-largest economy, a high growth rate and a large working-age population. Geographically, ASEAN is home to the vital SLOCs that link the Indian Ocean and the Pacific.[36] This is part of the reason Japan has consistently supported ASEAN unity, including its integration process, as the association can play a significant role in maintaining stability in the future inclusive and multipolar order in the Indo-Pacific. Japan has also welcomed and supported ASEAN's recent move to a more united and integrated approach to regional security issues, such as the establishment of the ASEAN Defence Industry Collaboration, ASEAN Militaries Ready Group on HA/DR and the ASEAN Center for Military Medicine.[37]

ASEAN is also at the centre of Japan's efforts to enhance regional resiliency, development and connectivity. Nine out of fifteen countries in which Japan's Ministry of Defense (MOD) conducts capacity-building projects are ASEAN member states.[38] Japan has also recently promoted capacity building of ASEAN *as a whole*, as well as for individual ASEAN member states, as demonstrated by the HA/DR seminars for all ASEAN member states conducted in Tokyo in February and March 2018.[39] As MPAC suggests, ASEAN is also the main target of Japan's connectivity projects. ASEAN will also gain greater benefits from its growing connectivity with India, such as through the Mekong-India economic corridor, which Japan has also supported for many years.[40]

Finally, ASEAN is one of the most important partners for Japan's FOIPs in terms of rule making and norm setting. In November 2016, Japanese Defence Minister Tomomi Inada announced the "Vientiane Vision", a guiding principle for Japan's defence cooperation with ASEAN, at the second ASEAN-Japan Defence Ministers' Informal Meeting held in Laos. The vision stressed that "Japan supports ASEAN efforts to uphold principles of international law, especially in the field of maritime and air space".[41] Under this initiative, Japan's MOD has already conducted a number of seminars and projects that facilitate regional rule making and norm setting with ASEAN member states in the maritime and air domains.[42]

Japan and ASEAN also share some important principles or norms, such as support for a free and open, rules-based order, the peaceful resolution of conflicts, complementarity, free trade, ASEAN unity and its centrality, connectivity, and inclusiveness. ASEAN is also vital to the success of RCEP, alongside other Indo-Pacific players such as India, Australia and China. Since this is the case, Japan's cooperation with ASEAN in terms of regional rule making or norm setting under FOIPs will only become more important in the foreseeable future.

Conclusion

While there are certainly geopolitical or geoeconomic elements in Japan's FOIPs, the FOIPs can be best understood essentially as a regional order-building strategy aimed at establishing a pluralistic, inclusive and rules-based regional order. It is therefore possible for Japan to collaborate not only with regional democracies like India and Australia but also with other regional and extra-regional countries, including China. In particular, ASEAN is at the heart of FOIPs as a regional order-building strategy because of its economic and demographic potential as well as its geographical position. This is why Japan has enhanced its cooperation with ASEAN and continues to support its unity and centrality.

At the same time, Japan's FOIPs faces many challenges. Besides its resource limitations, one of the most serious challenges Japan and regional countries face is the rapidly intensifying Sino-U.S. strategic rivalry. As discussed in this chapter, one of the important missions of FOIPs is to create a broader strategic space that can accommodate both the United States and China. If the Sino-U.S. strategic rivalry continues to escalate, however, regional countries, including Japan, may be forced to "choose" between two super-powers. Should such a nightmare materialize, the Indo-Pacific order characterized by open, inclusiveness and transparency would be replaced by a closed, exclusive and non-transparent "new Cold War order". There seems to be many things Japan and regional middle-powers, including ASEAN, can do together to avoid such an undesirable scenario.

Notes

1. The views expressed in this paper are the author's own and do not reflect official viewpoints of NIDS or the Ministry of Defense, Japan.
2. Ministry of Foreign Affairs of Japan, "Address by Prime Minister Shinzo Abe at the Opening Session of the Sixth Tokyo International Conference on African Development (TICAD VI)", 27 August 2016 <https://www.mofa.go.jp/afr/af2/page4e_000496.html>.
3. Michael D. Swaine, "Creating an Unstable Asia: The U.S. 'Free and Open Indo-Pacific' Strategy", Carnegie Endowment for Peace, 2 March 2018 <http://carnegieendowment.org/2018/03/02/creating-unstable-asia-u.s.-free-and-open-indo-pacific-strategy-pub-75720>.
4. See, for instance, Sebastian Maslow, "Japan's 'Pivot to Asia': Tokyo Discovers the Indo-Pacific", *APPS Policy Forum*, 1 August 2018 <https://www.policyforum.net/japans-pivot-asia/>; David Brewster, "A 'Free and Open Indo-Pacific' and What It Means for Australia", *The Interpreter*, 7 March 2018 <https://www.lowyinstitute.org/the-interpreter/free-and-open-indo-pacific-and-what-it-means-australia>; and Axel Berkofsky, "Free and Open Indo-Pacific": Tokyo's Plans and Priorities", 4 June 2018 <https://www.ispionline.it/en/pubblicazione/free-and-open-indo-pacific-tokyos-plans-and-priorities-20690>.
5. Ashish Kumar Sen, "A Free and Open Indo-Pacific", The Atlantic Council, 31 July 2018 <https://www.atlanticcouncil.org/blogs/new-atlanticist/a-free-and-open-indo-pacific>.
6. See, for instance, Ministry of Foreign Affairs of Japan, "Priority Policies for Development Cooperation FY2017", April 2017 <https://www.mofa.go.jp/files/000259285.pdf>.
7. Narushige Michishita, "Cooperate and Compete: Abe's New Approach to China", *Straits Times*, 13 November 2018.
8. Akihiko Tanaka, " 'Jiyu de Hirakareta Indo Taiheiyo Senryaku' no Shatei" [The scope of free and Indo-Pacific strategy], *Gaiko* [Diplomacy] 47 (January/February 2018): 37.
9. Matake Kamiya, "Nihon to 'Indo-Taiheiyo': Kitai to Mondaiten" [Japan and "Indo-Pacific": Expectation and problems], in Japan Institute for International Affairs (JIIA), *Asia ni okeru Anzenhosyo Chichujyo* [Security order in Asia] (Tokyo: JIIA, 2013), p. 29.
10. Matake Kamiya, "Nihon no Ajia Senryaku to "Indo-Taiheiyo" [Japan's Asia strategy

and Indo-Pacific], in JIIA, *Indo-Taiheiyo Jidai no Nihon Gaiko: Suing States he no Taio* [Japan's diplomacy at an era of Indo-Pacific: responses to swing states] (Tokyo: JIIA, 2015), p. 115.

11. Shinzo Abe, "Asia's Democratic Security Diamond", *Project Syndicate*, 27 December 2018 <https://www.project-syndicate.org/commentary/a-strategic-alliance-for-japan-and-india-by-shinzo-abe?barrier=accesspaylog>.
12. Tomohiko Satake, "Chapter 8. Japan: Expanding Strategic Horizon", in *East Asian Strategic Review 2017* (Tokyo: National Institute for Defense Studies, 2017), pp. 237–63.
13. Yoshikatsu Suzuki, *Nihon no Senryaku Gaiko* [Japan's strategic diplomacy] (Tokyo: Chikuma Syobo, 2017), especially chapter 4.
14. Emma Chanlett-Avery, "Japan, the Indo-Pacific, and the 'Quad' ", The Chicago Council on Global Affairs, 14 February 2018 <https://www.thechicagocouncil.org/publication/japan-indo-pacific-and-quad>.
15. For Japan's continuous engagement policy towards China, see Tomohiko Satake, "How to Normalise Sino-Japanese Defence Relations", *East Asia Forum*, 24 August 2015 <http://www.eastasiaforum.org/2015/08/24/how-to-normalise-sino-japanese-defence-relations/>.
16. Ministry of Foreign Affairs of Japan, "Prime Minister Abe Visits China", 26 October 2018 <https://www.mofa.go.jp/a_o/c_m1/cn/page3e_000958.html>.
17. Junnosuke Kobara, "Japan and China See Abe's '3 Principles' Slightly Differently", *Nikkei Asian Review*, 30 October 2018 <https://asia.nikkei.com/Politics/International-Relations/Japan-and-China-see-Abe-s-3-principles-slightly-differently>.
18. Ministry of Foreign Affairs of Japan, "Jiyu de Hirakareta Indo-Taiheiyo ni Mukete" [Toward a free and open Indo-Pacific], September 2018, p. 2 <https://www.mofa.go.jp/mofaj/files/000407642.pdf>.
19. "Nichibei Domei Indo-Taiheiyo ni Kakudai" [Expanding the U.S.-Japan alliance to Indo-Pacific], *Sankei Shinbun*, 12 November 2017.
20. White House, "Remarks by President Trump at APEC CEO Summit", 10 November 2017 <https://www.whitehouse.gov/briefings-statements/remarks-president-trump-apec-ceo-summit-da-nang-vietnam/>.
21. Tomohiko Satake, "Chapter 7 Japan: The US-Japan Alliance Amid Uncertainty", *East Asian Strategic Review* (Tokyo: National Institute for Defense Studies, 2018), pp. 233–36.
22. Abigail Grace, "Beyond Defining a 'Free and Open Indo-Pacific' ", *The Diplomat*, 6 September 2018.
23. A.F.K. Organski and Jacek Kugler, *The War Ledger* (Illinoi: The University of Chicago Press, 1980); Robert Gilpin, *War and Change in World Politics* (London: Cambridge University Press, 1981); Jacek Kugler and Douglas Lemke (eds.), *Parity and War: Evaluations and Extensions of The War Ledger* (Ann Arbor: The University of

Michigan Press, 1996); and Ronald L. Tammen et al., *Power Transitions: Strategies for the 21st Century* (Washington, DC: CQ Press, 2000).

24. Graham Alison, *Destined for War: Can America and China Escape Thucydides's Trap?* (New York: Houghton Mifflin Harcourt, 2017).
25. "Working Together to Build a World of Lasting Peace and Universal Security and a Community with a Shared Future for Mankind", Address by H.E. Yang Jiechi at the Opening Ceremony of the Seventh World Peace Forum, Tsinghua University, 14 July 2018 <https://www.fmprc.gov.cn/mfa_eng/zxxx_662805/t1577242.shtml>.
26. Rory Medcalf, "China and the Indo-Pacific: Multipolarity, Solidarity and Strategic Patience", paper delivered for Grands enjeux stratégiques contemporains — Chaire en Sorbonne Université Paris 1 Panthéon-Sorbonne, 12 March 2018 <https://nsc.crawford.anu.edu.au/sites/default/files/publication/nsc_crawford_anu_edu_au/2018-04/rory_medcalf_sorbonne_indo-pacific_march_2018.pdf>.
27. Ministry of Defense of Japan, "Capacity Building Assistance" <http://www.mod.go.jp/e/d_act/exc/cap_b/ MOD>.
28. See, for instance, the MOD's capacity-building assistance in Timor-Lestle, available at <http://www.mod.go.jp/e/d_act/exc/cap_b/timor_leste/index.html>.
29. Acquisition, Technology and Logistics Agency, "Defense Equipment and Technology Cooperation" <http://www.mod.go.jp/atla/en/policy/defense_equipment.html>.
30. "Japan Shifts its Focus on Indo-Pacific", *Nikkei Asian Review*, 15 August 2018.
31. For a more detailed analysis of Japan's economic approach to the region, see Corey Wallace, "Leaving (North-east) Asia? Japan's Southern Strategy", *International Affairs* 94, no. 4 (2018): 893–904.
32. See, for instance, Ministry of Foreign Affairs of Japan, "14th ASEAN-Japan Summit (Overview)", 18 November 2011 <https://www.mofa.go.jp/announce/jfpu/2011/11/1118-02.html>.
33. Ministry of Foreign Affairs of Japan, "Regional Comprehensive Economic Partnership (RCEP) Summit", 14 November 2018 <https://www.mofa.go.jp/ecm/ep/page25e_000267.html>.
34. Charissa Yong, "Singapore Will Not Join Indo-Pacific Bloc for Now: Vivian", *Straits Times*, 15 May 2018.
35. Jansen Tham, "What's in Indonesia's Indo-Pacific Cooperation Concept?", *The Diplomat*, 16 May 2018 <https://thediplomat.com/2018/05/whats-in-indonesias-indo-pacific-cooperation-concept/>.
36. Prashanth Parameswaran, *ASEAN's Role in a U.S. Indo-Pacific Strategy* (Washington, DC: Wilson Center, 2018), p. 2.
37. U.S. State Department, "Chairman's Statement on the Fourth ASEAN Defence Ministers' Meeting-Plus (4th ADMM-Plus)", 24 October 2017 <https://asean.usmission.gov/chairmans-statement-fourth-asean-defence-ministers-meeting-plus-4th-admm-plus/>.

38. Ministry of Defense of Japan, "Capacity Building Assistance".
39. Ministry of Defense of Japan, "HA/DR" <http://www.mod.go.jp/e/d_act/exc/cap_b/asean/20180226.html>.
40. Economic Research Institute for ASEAN and East Asia, "The Comprehensive Asia Development Plan", October 2010 <http://www.eria.org/publications/the-comprehensive-asia-development-plan/>.
41. Ministry of Defense of Japan, "Vientiane Vision: Japan's Defense Cooperation Initiative with ASEAN", 16 November 2016 <http://www.mod.go.jp/e/d_act/exc/vientianevision/>.
42. Ministry of Defense of Japan, "Achievements of Japan-ASEAN Defense Cooperation Based on the 'Vientiane Vision' ", October 2017 <http://www.mod.go.jp/e/d_act/exc/vientianevision/pdf/achivements_201710_e.pd>.

Brunei Darussalam

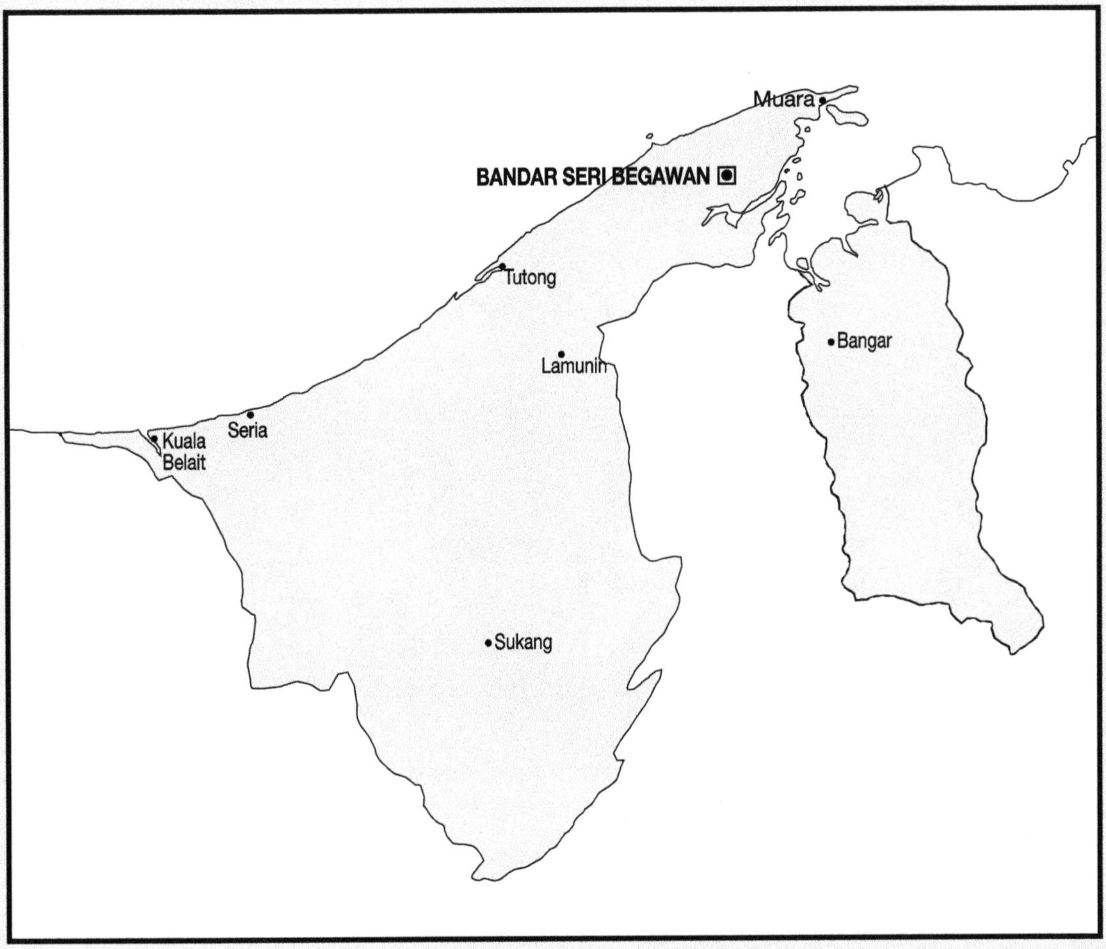

BRUNEI DARUSSALAM: Making Strides with a Renewed Focus on the Future

Mahani Hamdan and Chang-Yau Hoon

Brunei Darussalam, one of the smallest yet richest countries in Southeast Asia with a total population of nearly 450,000, has made remarkable economic progress as a result of its reforms. Some indications of its achievements are presented in this chapter. The 2018 ASEAN+3 Regional Economic Outlook (AREO) projected that Brunei would have strong growth in gross domestic product (GDP), rising from 0.6 per cent in 2017 to 1.6 per cent and 3.4 per cent in 2018 and 2019 respectively. Yet, according to a forecast of the overall growth rate of real GDP among the ten Southeast Asian countries, Brunei experienced the slowest growth rate this decade.[1] The country's average GDP annual growth rate — greatly affected by world prices and the local production of oil and gas — from 2004 to 2018 was 0.13 per cent.

Despite the challenges associated with the decline in energy reserves and falling world oil prices, the Brunei government and industrial players remain optimistic about the future of the country, in view of the rapid development of the global economy and the continual enhancement of the life energy requirement, which in turn increases the global demand for oil and gas. A decade after the 2008 global financial crisis, the casualties of Brunei's near economic downturn are

Mahani Haji Hamdan is Director of the Institute of Policy Studies and Assistant Professor of Accounting at UBD School of Business and Economics, Universiti Brunei Darussalam. She is also a member of the Advisory Committee for Brunei Darussalam Accounting Standards Council.

Chang-Yau Hoon is Director of the Centre for Advanced Research (CARe) and Associate Professor of Anthropology at the Institute of Asian Studies, Universiti Brunei Darussalam. He is also Adjunct Research Fellow at the University of Western Australia.

slowly fading from memory. Oil exploration and drilling activities are actively in progress, with a continued focus on accessing more resources for the development of the overall economy, in line with the country's need for diversification strategies that can deliver sustained, job-intensive and inclusive growth.

Brunei's own experience of sustainable economic growth underscores the importance of economic diversification and broad-based economic development governed by prudent policy and regulation. Economic diversification has been a key theme of Brunei's long-term strategy since the launch of its first development plan, the National Development Plan 1953–1958. While there is reason to be optimistic about the country's future economic prosperity because the government has shown progress in its basic policy of diversifying the economy away from oil and gas, the challenge is how to wean the country off its debt drip without intensifying an economic slowdown.

During the Legislative Council Meeting in March 2018, the second minister of finance and economy indicated that, to promote the country's economic growth, the government will continue to focus on fiscal consolidation and fiscal sustainability policies by emphasizing cost-effectiveness, a pro-business approach and prudent spending, without affecting the level of service, productivity and finances of the government in the long-term. He also highlighted five renewed thrusts for Brunei's fiscal year 2018/19 budget: prudent spending, ease of doing business, enhancing productivity through innovation, creating employment opportunities and capacity-building, and preserving public welfare. This chapter briefly reviews the extent to which Brunei's current economic activities focus on each of these thrusts, along with a discussion on key challenges that stand in the way of these goals being achieved.

Cutting Debts and Deficits by Cutting Spending

Debts and deficits are an expenditure problem. Even if the Brunei government increases its investments to help local businesses and industries, continues social spending and the development of infrastructure, there is more to fiscal prudence than a return to surplus. Through prudent fiscal management, the Brunei government is committed to reducing the country's debt-to-GDP ratio, eliminating deficits and returning to balanced budgets. To date, Brunei's debt-to-GDP ratio is ranked the lowest, by far, among Southeast Asian countries.[2] The government has responded fairly quickly to reducing the nation's debt burden. The country's debt-to-GDP ratio decreased from 2.95 per cent in 2015 to 2.83 per cent in 2017 (Table 1), and it is projected to be approximately 2.40 per cent in 2018.

A higher debt-to-GDP ratio is not necessarily a bad thing, and this indicator has been used to maintain a sustainable financial ecosystem in the country. Debt levels and the nation's spending habits are matters that concern everybody, as these affect investments and the quality of life and contribute towards the betterment of Brunei society as a whole. The government has set out to implement financial reform, including the total debt service ratio (TDSR) policy introduced by the Brunei Monetary Authority (AMBD) in 2015, which seeks to limit personal borrowing to a maximum of 70 per cent of income for loans, as well as the establishment of the Credit Bureau in 2012. These have resulted in lower debt per capita and a lower level of household indebtedness (as measured by personal loans, including credit cards). For the period 2015–16, debt per capita had effectively improved from BN$916 to BN$810, and the level of household indebtedness had been reduced from 19.44 per cent to 17.72 per cent of income.

In recent years the government has been caught between trying to reduce spending and increasing the economic growth rate, as cutting spending may undermine, to some extent, GDP growth. Table 1 shows that Brunei's economy only grew by 0.913 per cent in 2012, amid the sharp fall in oil prices and lower production in the hydrocarbons, oil and gas, mining, and liquefied natural gas (LNG) sectors. This contributed to a negative growth rate for four consecutive

TABLE 1
Key Economic Indicators for Brunei (2008–17)

Year	*GDP at current prices (BN$ millions)*[a]	*GDP growth rate (%)*	*Debt-to-GDP ratio (%)*	*Budget balance to GDP (%)*
2008	–	–1.94	0.94	36.01
2009	–	–1.765	1.11	3.61
2010	–	2.599	1.11	7.61
2011	–	3.745	2.13	25.63
2012	–	0.913	2.10	15.79
2013	–	–2.126	2.21	13.03
2014	21,663.6	–2.35	3.23	3.58
2015	17,778.0	–0.567	2.95	–14.52
2016	15,747.7	–2.466	3.01	–21.68
2017	16,747.7	1.329	2.83	–10.62

Source: https://data.worldbank.org/indicator/NY.GDP.MKTP.KD.ZG?locations=BN.

years, from –2.126 per cent in 2013 to –2.466 per cent in 2016. During the period of low oil prices, Brunei was also exposed to exogenous shocks as a consequence of its greater reliance on hydrocarbon revenues, which were dependent on the strength of the U.S. dollar.

After four years of a negative growth rate (from 2013 to 2016), the country's economy gradually recovered to positive growth of 1.329 per cent in 2017. This was largely attributable to the non–oil and gas sectors,[3] particularly private sector investment in infrastructure and foreign direct investment (FDI) in construction projects. In 2017 there were eleven FDI projects in progress, eleven projects at the implementation phase prior to commencing operations in Brunei, and twenty projects at the initial stage.[4] The economy continued to recover by 2.5 per cent in the first quarter of 2018, and inflation (which had gradually increased from –0.17 per cent in 2017 to 0.4 per cent in 2018) began to feel the impact of the surge in oil and gas production. More than 50 per cent of the country's economic activity is still linked to the oil and gas industry.[5] However, just when expectations were of the economy recovering, economic growth shrank back by 2.8 per cent in the second quarter of 2018, even though oil prices had started to rise. The Department of Economic Planning and Development (JPKE) reported that the economic contraction in the second quarter was due to a decrease in LNG, methanol and oil production, but the reason behind the lowered production was not specified.

The year 2015 marked the start of Brunei's fiscal budget deficits, indicating that government spending outpaced the country's growth rates. The negative budget balance in relation to GDP presented in Table 1 shows a deficit amounting to 14.52 per cent of GDP in 2015 lowering to 10.62 per cent of GDP in 2017. To improve the budget deficit, the government has cut back on expenditure, as evidenced by the consistent fall in national spending and the reduction in national budget allocations over the past five years. Even as the deficit improved by approximately 50 per cent in 2017 (Table 1), there has still been no increase in the budget allocation for fiscal year 2018/19 (Table 2).

Despite the reduction in the budget allocation for Brunei's Five-Year National Development Plan (RKN) from BN$9.5 billion in RKN9 (2007–12) to BN$8.2 billion in RKN10 (2012–17), the government continues to expand initiatives to diversify the economy and increase revenue-generating activities. Nonetheless, a record low in oil prices and the slow government response to diversification efforts are proving disastrous for Brunei's economy, as the effects are still very much being felt today. The annual budget does not vary significantly in size (Table 2), but an inconsistent focus and lack of direction have contributed somewhat to the

TABLE 2
Annual National Budget Allocation, 2014–19

Year	*Annual Budget (BN$ billions)*
2014/15	6.55
2015/16	6.3
2016/17	5.6
2017/18	5.3
2018/19	5.3

economic slowdown (Table 3). Last year, a significant improvement in the budget deficit and debt-to-GDP ratio contributed to a positive GDP growth rate of 1.329 per cent and a further improvement of 2.5 per cent in the first quarter of 2018.

Although the economy suffered a blow in the second quarter of 2018 with a negative growth rate of 2.8 per cent reported by JPKE, overall economic growth performance in this fiscal year remains inconclusive. In fact, the Ministry of Finance predicted that the country's GDP growth rate would double to 3.4 per cent in 2019.

Compared to previous years, the 2018/19 fiscal budget has set goals of developing the skills and marketability of jobseekers and focusing on improving the business environment to increase job creation in the private sector (Table 3). Despite the relative lack of critical attention on stimulating investment from 2016 onwards, a lot of progress has been achieved in boosting Brunei's FDI inflows, both in downstream activities and in economic clusters beyond the oil and gas industry. Taking into account the increase in oil and gas production and the start of downstream production from new energy facilities and gas fields, the foreseeable future for Brunei's economy looks a little more promising. The non–oil and gas sectors will continue to develop, predominantly in water transport because of larger shipments of LNG; in construction, with large-scale projects, including the Temburong Bridge; and in private sector investments supporting diversification into high-tech, agricultural and manufacturing industries and small and medium-sized enterprises.

Easing the Path to Investment and Employment

Brunei Vision 2035 — a long-term national development plan that aims for the country to achieve a high quality of life and a dynamic and sustainable

TABLE 3
Budgetary Focus for Fiscal Year, 2014–19

	2014/15	*2015/16*	*2016/17*	*2017/18*	*2018/19*
Enhance education and training; building capacity and human capital	√	√	√	√	√
Stimulate investment and private sector growth	√	√			
Increase economic productivity through public and private sectors; national productivity through innovation	√	√	√	√	√
Ensure and preserve the welfare of the people	√	√	√	√	√
Prudent spending			√	√	√
Enhance ease of doing business			√	√	√
Creating employment opportunities					√

economy — emphasizes attracting new FDI as one of the main growth drivers to develop the non-energy sectors. It is seen as a strategically important function for the country's industrial and economic development. However, FDI cannot be considered a game changer unless the hurdles to its execution in Brunei are eased. For two consecutive years (2017–18), Brunei has been regarded as "the most improved economy in the world" according to key global rankings of competitiveness. In 2018 the country was ranked 56th out of 190 countries in the World Bank's Report on Doing Business and "was the only high-income economy on the list of top 10 improvers". The country ranked 62nd out of 140 countries in the World Economic Forum's 2018 Global Competitiveness Report, up two places from 2017. These improvements in rankings reflect the government's efforts and commitment towards creating a pro-business environment to enable the further diversification of the economy. These achievements have also been made possible through the introduction of a credit scoring system that allows banks to evaluate lending more efficiently, the streamlining of laws (such as the Business License Act 2016 and the Miscellaneous License Act 2016) and regulations to make it easier and quicker for entrepreneurs and investors to establish businesses, and through systemic changes to improve the ease of doing business, such as dealing with construction permits and electricity. The Department of Electrical Services (DES) has reduced the time taken for buildings and homes to obtain an electrical connection from 36 to 17 days by streamlining their online application process, reducing procedures and tightening the timeframe on external works.

As Brunei's ease of doing business ranking significantly improved from 105th in 2014 to 56th in 2018, FDI inflows and the GDP growth rate are also expected to strengthen. Net inflows of FDI into Brunei, however, have decreased over the years, from BN$1,080.80 million in 2012 to BN$238.2 million in 2015, a figure that is largely derived from the mining and quarrying sector (BN$244.2 million), followed by construction (BN$12.3 million) and financial and insurance activities (BN$5.1 million). To attract FDI, the government is open to other key industrial sectors to create alternative drivers of economic growth other than the oil and gas industry, including investment in business services, downstream oil and gas, halal food, technology, creative industries and tourism. More importantly, many foreign companies have begun to hire more local employees compared to foreign workers. For instance, Western Foods and Packaging (WFP) Sdn Bhd from Turkey currently employs seventy-nine locals, accounting for 96 per cent of the company's workforce in Brunei.[6]

The Prime Minister's Office further reported that nine FDI projects with a total value of more than US$4.7 billion are already in the pipeline (*The Economist*, 2016), including the Western Foods and Packaging Manufacturing Plant and the Hengyi Oil Refinery and Petrochemical Plant Project at Pulau Muara Besar, with total investments, respectively, of US$30 million and over US$15 billion. The intent to increase FDI inflows is commendable, but there is much to be sorted out beneath the surface. Over the past four years the government has implemented a series of reforms — through regulations such as the Brunei Economic Development Act and the Investment Incentive Order, and amendments to the Income Tax Order — to attract FDI and encourage the growth of micro, small and medium enterprises. Entrepreneurs seek relevant, synchronized structural and institutional changes to reduce the procedures, time and cost of doing business.

Although the aforementioned reforms have resulted in fewer procedures and stringent regulation and standards, the prevailing reality of the business environment in Brunei is a lack of effective coordination between government ministries and agencies and local authorities. The regulations underpinning FDI by industrial sector may be different, but the amended laws must still carry the same objective — to make it quicker and easier for entrepreneurs and investors to establish businesses in Brunei. Whilst the Brunei Economic Development Board and Brunei Investment Authority have made efforts to streamline the procedures, the process of reviewing and updating the procedures has been very slow. Thus, there is an urgent need for ministries to be more proactive by improving coordination through the "Whole of Nation" approach at all levels.

New Dimension in Brunei Foreign Policy: Brunei-China Relations

Brunei's foreign policy objectives are to contribute towards the country's peace, security, stability and prosperity, through bilateral and multilateral cooperation on the basis of friendship, mutual respect and peaceful coexistence in the ASEAN region. The country practices a balanced and cautious approach in its foreign policy, and it has come to understand that achieving the strategic objectives of the National Vision 2035 will require the engagement of the international community. The country's foreign policy is largely driven by the goals of economic growth, to increase economic activities and to contribute significantly to economic diversification (away from oil and gas) by promoting a free and open, rules-based and non-discriminatory multilateral trading system. In recent years, Brunei's military, diplomacy, economic activity, trade and investment have expanded far beyond engagement with ASEAN, the OIC (Organisation of Islamic Cooperation) and the Commonwealth. Most obviously, China has been considered as one of Brunei's crucial partners to both diversify and strengthen its fossil fuel based economy and to preserve peace and stability in the Asia-Pacific region.

Sino-Brunei relations existed during the early years of China's Western Han Dynasty, which dates back over two thousand years. But in the modern period, relations were somewhat distant, as Brunei was a British protectorate for most of the last century, until it gained independence in 1984. Given the mutual desire for stability leading to economic growth, Brunei and China have worked hard in recent years to tighten and strengthen people-to-people ties. The last seven years have seen a yet more rapid increase in the number of memoranda of understanding signed between the two countries on trade and economic cooperation in the agriculture, forestry, health and energy sectors, as well as the establishment of sister city relations between Bandar Seri Begawan and Nanjing. The year 2018 also marked the fifth anniversary of the Belt and Road Initiative (BRI). Under this initiative, the Brunei-China Belt and Road Association was formed to facilitate cooperation between the two countries in the fields of investment, trade, culture, education and tourism.

China's relationship-building and large investments may be seen as part of its strategy to create a key partnership with Brunei as it stakes its claims to islets and atolls in the South China Sea, but Brunei has a long tradition of avoiding confrontation and of preferring a low-key approach to deal with contentious issues over the question of the South China Sea. Brunei focuses on multilateral mechanisms for dispute resolution and joint development, rather than insisting on a reference to the dispute. Chinese investments are important to Brunei's strategy of economic diversification, and thus the BRI represents a strategic opportunity to increase FDI inflows and to create market opportunities for the local business community. Brunei's exports to China amounted to $269.1 million, or 4.8 per cent of its overall exports,[7] and its imports from China represented the highest share, at 35.3 per cent.[8]

Bilateral exchanges between China and Brunei are now more frequent than ever. President Xi Jinping's recent visit to Brunei for bilateral talks in November 2018 expressed China's commitment to ramp up cooperation in infrastructure development as part of Beijing's BRI. Today, more than ten major infrastructure projects in Brunei (from the Temburong Bridge and Ulu Tutong Dam to the Telisai–Lumut Highway) are examples of Brunei-China cooperation. Although no new projects or FDI were indicated during President Xi's visit, both countries agreed to push forward cooperation on the Hengyi Industries refinery and petrochemical plant on Pulau Muara Besar. This US$15 billion joint venture, which will start production in 2019 to boost Brunei's export markets, is China's largest investment in the country so far.[9]

To ensure a steady flow of Chinese investment, a Bank of China branch was established in Bandar Seri Begawan in 2016, as part of the BRI strategy to enhance trade along the traditional routes across Eurasia and around Southeast Asia. Huge sums of money have already been invested by Guanxi Ruian Logistic, China State Construction Engineering Corporation, Shenglong New Energy Automobile Co Ltd and Guangxi Zhongli Enterprise Group, to name a few. An increasing number of Chinese companies have also been investing in agriculture, halal food, aquaculture and bio-innovation through the Brunei-Guangxi Economic Corridor. Overall, these projects promise more than ten thousand local jobs. While it may be too early to measure the significant role of knowledge transfer and skills from China in shaping Brunei's development agenda to boost productivity, experiences in other growing economies offer a bright prospect. Moreover, it is not knowledge transfer and skills alone that Brunei will gain from China, but also the technology transfer and the innovation of vital aspects of knowledge diffusion from Chinese firms.

Enhancing Productivity through Innovation

Compared to Singapore and Malaysia, Brunei is still in a weak position in terms of producing new knowledge and technology and in creative outputs. The country lacks an availability of talent, the ability to procure talent, and a supportive environment. Only recently did the country begin to focus on strengthening science, technology and innovation (STI) activities, as reflected in the 2012–17 RKN, which saw an increase in the budget for science and technology and funds for research and development. STI development is not very apparent in the private sector, and is implemented mainly by government organizations. Two main bodies spearhead the country's STI activities. The Ministry of Development focuses on science and technology policy design and development, while the Brunei Research Council coordinates research funding in Brunei and advises the Prime Minister's Office.

To nurture a passion for science and technology among the youth and to foster the nation's progress and economic growth, the Ministry of Education through its National Education System (SPN21) has integrated information and communications technology (ICT) and creativity as one of the core elements in the education curriculum. SPN21 was introduced in 2009, but the ministry made a slow start on the project and it took more time than expected due to lack of strategy implementation, planning and execution capabilities, inadequate support, unexpected resource constraints and incomplete risk assessments as a result of a lack of the right information and forecasts. Although many have expressed positive support for SPN21, the system is expensive to implement because it involves major expenditure on ICT and infrastructure. The government has also set an ambitious target to be reached by 2035 that does not seem to adequately address the current-state gaps and deficiencies or the real challenges to making strategy adjustments when needed.

Continuous training programmes for the growth and education of teachers are necessary to equip them with the necessary skills, competencies and experience for them to use ICTs effectively in their profession. Despite the huge investment in financial and human resources, the government has underestimated the growing need for qualified teachers in the field of science, technology, engineering and mathematics (STEM) to foster intellectual, entrepreneurial and technical talent and design thinking. While there have been several initiatives and government-run programmes — such as The Crown Prince CIPTA Award and UBD Shell

Eco-Marathon Team — to promote and encourage the culture of invention and innovation, more is needed. On a positive note, the country successfully secured investment worth US$14.5 million in 2017 from Japan's MC Biotech to set up Brunei's Bio-Innovation Corridor Industrial Park. This foreign-funded project expects to produce twenty million tonnes of biomass annually. This is one of the sectors identified by the country to have the potential to support the nation's economic diversification efforts and national job creation.

Brunei has also increased the number of joint and bilateral projects it has with other countries, including the Brunei-Guangxi Economic Corridor (BGEC) with China in 2014 (agricultural and industrial park, pharmaceuticals, healthcare industry and logistics), followed by the development of a Fintech ecosystem. Fintech growth in Brunei has generally been slow, yet is progressing. In 2018, Brunei collaborated with South Korea whereby both countries provided US$30 million to set up Islamic Fintech innovation centre. The AMBD also linked up with the Monetary Authority of Singapore to foster innovation and help accelerate Fintech ecosystem development. All these FDI and innovation efforts reveal the country's commitment to open and free trade, as also indicated by improvements in Brunei's Global Innovation Index ranking, moving from 71st in 2017 to 67th globally in 2018, and in its Global Competitiveness Index ranking, improving from 58th in 2016/17 to 46th in 2017/18.

An increase of FDI inflows to Brunei in recent years has also positively contributed to employment generation at the national level. Statistics from the Employees Trust Fund reported that 29,600 new job opportunities in the private sector had been created between 2013 and 2017.[10] In 2017, seventeen FDI firms created 1,321 jobs. This was of course not sufficient to reduce the unemployment rate, which unfortunately continued to increase slightly. Overall, creating wealth through FDI and a greater diversification of the economy is as important as creating jobs for ensuring the stability of Bruneian society and sustainable economic growth.

Job Creation Matters, but So Does Wealth Creation

Young people worldwide are facing an uncertain future of increasing unemployment, skills mismatch, and low-quality employment.[11] Worrying prospects cloud their entry into and participation in the labour market, with implications for their livelihoods and wellbeing and those of their future families.[12] Brunei is to a certain extent facing similar issues. Brunei's unemployment currently stands at 6.9 per cent, which is more than double the ASEAN average of 3.3 per cent.[13] According to a recent study conducted by the Centre for Strategic and Policy Studies in Brunei, almost one in three (29.9 per cent) Bruneian youth between the ages of 15 and 24 are unemployed.[14]

The Brunei Economic Development Board and the Prime Minister's Office have jointly formulated a list of priority industry clusters, including halal products and services, business services, technology and creative industries, tourism, and downstream oil and gas services to diversify the economy and boost future employment.[15] To mitigate youth unemployment, the Ministry of Energy, Manpower and Industry established JobCentre Brunei in 2007, undertook major initiatives to develop vocational training, education retraining and professionalization of manual jobs by establishing the Centre for Capacity Building and the Industry Competency Framework for non-graduates, and introduced the i-Ready Apprenticeship Programme for university graduates.[16] JobCentre Brunei was set up as a "One-Stop Career Centre" that offers up-skilling services to local jobseekers to help improve their employability in the job market. It also provides a platform for private companies in Brunei to recruit local talent.[17]

In the budget for fiscal year 2018/19, the Ministry of Finance and Economy allocated BN$43 million to help create employment for youth through the i-Ready scheme and Centre for Capacity Building (PPK). The PPK is a multi-programme vocational skills training centre that delivers programmes driven by industry demand and certified by industry standards, including re-skilling and up-skilling courses allowing trainees to gain the competencies required by the job market. In January 2018, 619 PPK trainees gained employment at Hengyi Petrochemical Plant at Pulau Muara Besar.[18] The three-year i-Ready Apprenticeship Programme, on the other hand, offers unemployed university graduates the opportunity to gain work experience through on-the-job training. Under the programme, the government will provide a monthly allowance of BN$800 to selected graduates for a maximum period of three years. Throughout the three years, apprentices will be coached and mentored in their job role to ensure their development meets industry needs. Host organizations are expected to permanently employ the apprentices (although not all). The introduction of these initiatives since early 2017 appears to have helped reduce unemployment. For instance, as of 4 March 2017, there were 12,966 registered unemployed Bruneians on the government-led job vacancies website JobCentre Brunei. This figure had dropped to 9,166 by 15 November 2018.[19]

Joining concerted efforts to reduce the worrying level of graduate unemployment has been the Ministry of Education, which, in March 2018, acquired the Labour Management Information System (LMIS) to enable the programmes of higher learning institutions to enhance their skills matching. The LMIS aims to provide data on manpower demands, which will help tertiary institutions make decisions on course offerings to ensure graduates are equipped with the appropriate skills for the jobs needed by the market.[20]

The monarch has also expressed concern over the high number of unemployed youth. Recognizing the social reality of a saturated job market, the sultan has emphasized the need to inculcate a culture of independence and entrepreneurship among Bruneian youth. In his *titah* (royal speech) at the 2018 Eid celebration organized by the Sultan Haji Hassanal Bolkiah Foundation, the monarch reminded graduates to not just look to the government for jobs and urged the public to exercise perseverance and patience when starting a business.[21] A month later, the sultan delivered another *titah* at the 13th National Youth Day celebration to reassure the public that the government is working on revamping and improving the youth entrepreneurship ecosystem to help young people who want to start a business. He instructed national agencies to work closely with young entrepreneurs to offer assistance to the youth to develop and understand business plans. He also encouraged young Bruneians to strengthen their efforts towards penetrating global markets.[22] The sultan's commitment to youth entrepreneurship was further demonstrated by his meeting with thirty-four young entrepreneurs from diverse backgrounds and awarding this year's National Youth Awards to innovative entrepreneurs.

Indeed, considerable efforts have been invested by government agencies as well as private companies in promoting a conducive and supportive ecosystem to grow micro, small and medium enterprises (MSMEs). These include a microcredit financial scheme, co-matching grants, Microbusiness Bootcamps and the Entrepreneurship Open Day initiated by Darussalam Enterprise (DARe) — a statutory body set up to nurture and support local enterprises in collaboration with local banks such as Bank Islam Brunei Darussalam (BIDB) and Bank Usahawan. All these endeavours contributed to a favourable ranking in the recently released 2018 Global Entrepreneurship Index compiled by the U.S.-based Global Entrepreneurship and Development Institute that measures both the quality of entrepreneurship and the extent of support for entrepreneurs. Brunei came in fifth in Asia for the entrepreneurship environment, behind South Korea, Singapore, Japan and China. The 2018 index noted that the abundance of well-educated people with a solid support ecosystem presents vast potential for new business start-ups to thrive in Brunei and beyond.[23]

Preserving Public Welfare a Priority

Preserving public welfare is one of the priorities of the national budget for fiscal year 2018/19. The Ministry of Finance and Economy allocated BN$78 million for health services and supplies, BN$30 million for specialist patient treatment at Pantai Jerudong Specialist Centre and Gleneagles Jerudong Park Medical Centre, BN$21 million to improve public transport, BN$10 million for the National Housing Scheme for lower income citizens, BN$11.5 million for flood management and BN$37.3 million for the maintenance of public amenities and infrastructure.[24]

In May 2018 the Policy Coordination and Strategic Planning Division in the Ministry of Development published the ministry's five-year strategic plan (2018–23), which outlines the steps to realize the Ministry's vision of "Quality Living, Sustainable Development, Prosperous Nation". As the champion for infrastructure development, land use and the environment, the ministry identified key policy directions to be adopted in the next five years that encompass land use, housing, roads, water, drainage, sanitation, the environment, the construction industry and infrastructure financing. The report highlights the current achievements of Brunei in meeting the key performance indicators (KPIs) for a Liveable and Sustainable Nation and those for a Green Nation, and the goals for 2035, as presented in Table 4.[25]

Health is another key priority in Vision 2035. On top of the above-mentioned budget allocated to public welfare related to health services, the Ministry of Health has also been allocated BN$345.18 million for 2018/19, a 7 per cent

TABLE 4
KPIs for Liveable and Sustainable Nation and Green Nation

KPIs for a Liveable and Sustainable Nation	*2017*	*2035*
Home ownership rate (%)	63	85
Access to improved sanitation (%)	94	100
Access to clean drinking water (%)	100	100
Water consumption per capita (litre/capita/day)	380	290
KPIs for a Green Nation	*2017*	*2035*
River quality index	50–69	70–89
Air quality (%)	90	98
Utilization of allocated state land within development plan (%)	66	100
Waste generated per capita (kg/capita/day)	1.28	1.2

increase from the previous year's budget.[26] Some of the key strategies to support the drive for comprehensive healthcare coverage include strengthening basic healthcare through the development of a network of health centres and clinics, implementation of health information management systems through the use of ICT, and the implementation of the Brunei Medicine Policy formulated to ensure safe, quality and effective medicine supplies. In addition, Brunei also supports the World Health Organization (WHO) in its efforts to embed universal health coverage and to ensure that healthcare is accessible to all.[27]

Another main feature of the 2018/19 budget is the amendment to the provision of financial allowances for people with disabilities. Previously such an allowance was only available for people aged 15 and above, but with the amendment this now includes children aged below 15 after obtaining confirmation from a government medical officer.[28] The government is also committed to assisting individuals with special needs in searching for employment or establishing their own businesses. The National Committee of the Ministry of Culture, Youth and Sports is tasked to enhance the welfare and standard of living of these individuals so that they can enjoy equality in terms of job opportunities and quality of life. The committee has also put together enrichment programmes to help allowance recipients be more financially independent.[29]

The contributions to zakat, or tithe, is a major economic means for the promotion of social justice and wealth distribution in Brunei, with the objective of achieving common prosperity and security.[30] It is obligatory for eligible Muslims to contribute to zakat. To facilitate easier zakat payments, Perbadanan Tabung Amanah Islam Brunei and Bank Islam Brunei Darussalam have been appointed by the government as *Amil* representatives to collect zakat. The collection is then distributed by the Brunei Islamic Religious Council under the Ministry of Religious Affairs to the underprivileged and less fortunate individuals and families across the Sultanate.

In a *titah* delivered in conjunction with Nuzul Al-Quran (day commemorating the revelation of the Qur'an) on 1 June 2018, the sultan iterated the importance of zakat in managing the economy and called for the strengthening of zakat management so that the funds can be used to eradicate poverty. He encouraged zakat recipients to use the funds as capital to set up a new business or enterprise in order to break out from the poverty cycle. The monarch wishes to see groups who qualify to receive zakat to eventually become self-sufficient and become givers instead of recipients in the future.[31]

Conclusion

Ever since the 2008 global financial crisis, several reforms and amendments to Bruneian laws and regulations have been introduced and implemented, primarily to improve the way of doing things and prevent the country suffering from the effects of low oil prices. While the latter seems inevitable because Brunei's economy still relies on oil and gas production, there has also been some rapid progress in the non–oil and gas sectors. Rising oil prices and increased efficiencies, which led to growth for Brunei's economy in 2017 and the first quarter of 2018, highlight the government's initiatives in diversifying its energy markets and other industries for private sector growth and FDI. The sudden decrease of the growth rate in the second quarter of 2018 recently published by JPKE, however, is expected to be short-lived. Faced with the possibility of financial difficulties, the resulting efforts to reduce excessive debts and spending have so far been achieved effectively. Although Brunei is still on the road to recovery, the country can be regarded as a politically and economically stable nation. On top of targeting high economic growth, the monarch's concern for people (including their health, welfare, employment and the cost of living) is built into the national agenda to achieve Brunei Vision 2035. Challenges may remain for the country's oil industry, but so do opportunities for innovative solutions. In conclusion, the economic outlook for Brunei in 2018 looks positive, reflecting stronger expansion of activities for greater economic dynamism.

Notes

1. Statista, "Forecasted Growth Rate of the Real Gross Domestic Product (GDP) among Southeast Asian Countries in 2017 and 2018 (Compared to the Previous Year)", 2008 <https://www.statista.com/statistics/621011/forecasted-gross-domestic-product-growth-rate-in-southeast-asia-2017/> (accessed 2 November 2018).
2. A. Salikha, "(Latest) The Rankings of Debt-to-GDP Ratio for Southeast Asian Countries", 2018 <https://seasia.co/2018/09/20/latest-the-rankings-of-debt-to-gdp-ratio-in-southeast-asia> (accessed 15 October 2018).
3. A. Othman, "Brunei Economy Poised for Giant Leap Next Year", *Borneo Bulletin*, 18 May 2018 <https://borneobulletin.com.bn/brunei-economy-poised-for-giant-leap-next-year/> (accessed 16 November 2018).
4. Borneo Bulletin Yearbook 2018, "FDIs an Important Driver of Growth", 1 April 2018 <http://borneobulletinyearbook.com.bn/foreign-direct-investments-fdi/> (accessed 17 October 2018).
5. Aaron Wong, "Brunei Records 2.5% GDP Growth in Q1 2018", *Biz Brunei*, 31 July 2018 <https://www.bizbrunei.com/2018/07/brunei-records-2-5-percent-gdp-growth-in-q1-2018/> (accessed 1 October 2018).

6. H. Hazair, "Gov't Focuses on Improving Business Environment to Boost Job Creation in Private Sector", *The Scoop*, 7 March 2018 <https://thescoop.co/2018/03/07/govt-improving-business-environment-as-private-sector-boon-jobseekers> (accessed 10 October 2018).
7. World's Richest Countries, "Top Brunei Darussalam Exports 2017", 2017 <http://www.worldsrichestcountries.com/top-brunei-darussalam-exports.html>.
8. *Borneo Bulletin*, "Brunei's Total Trade Increases 5.3pc y-o-y in February 2018", 9 May 2018 <https://borneobulletin.com.bn/bruneis-total-trade-increases-5-3pc-y-o-y-in-february-2018/>.
9. Ain Bandial, "Brunei, China Pledge to Ramp Up Infrastructure Development — China's Xi Calls for 'Long-Term, Strategic Partnership' with Brunei, as Two Countries Sign Belt and Road Plan", *The Scoop*, 20 November 2018 <https://thescoop.co/2018/11/20/brunei-china-pledge-to-ramp-up-infrastructure-development/>.
10. H. Hazair, "Gov't Focuses on Improving Business Environment to Boost Job Creation in Private Sector", *The Scoop*, 7 March 2018 <https://thescoop.co/2018/03/07/govt-improving-business-environment-as-private-sector-boon-jobseekers> (accessed 7 March 2018).
11. International Labour Organisation (ILO), *Global Employment Trends for Youth 2013: A Generation at Risk* (Geneva: ILO, 2013).
12. International Labour Organisation (ILO), *World Employment Social Outlook: Trends for Youth 2016* (Geneva: ILO, 2016).
13. James Kon, "Researcher Moots Foresight Approach to Tackle Unemployment", *Borneo Bulletin*, 18 April 2018 <https://borneobulletin.com.bn/researcher-moots-foresight-approach-to-tackle-unemployment/>.
14. "Brunei Darussalam Youth Unemployment and Job Futures", Stakeholder Forum held on 18 October 2018, Centre for Strategic and Policy Studies.
15. Kon, "Researcher Moots Foresight".
16. Danial Norjidi, "2017 Sees a Drop in Unemployment", *Borneo Bulletin*, 8 March 2018 <https://borneobulletin.com.bn/2017-sees-a-drop-in-unemployment/>.
17. <http://www.jobcentrebrunei.gov.bn/>.
18. <http://borneobulletinyearbook.com.bn/employment/>.
19. <http://www.jobcentrebrunei.gov.bn/>.
20. H.H. Azaraimy, "New System to Reduce Graduate Unemployment", *Borneo Bulletin*, 15 March 2018 <https://borneobulletin.com.bn/new-system-to-reduce-graduate-unemployment/>.
21. Rasidah Hj Abu Bakar, "HM Urges Jobseekers to Start Businesses, Be Open to Private Sector Jobs", *The Scoop*, 5 July 2018 <https://thescoop.co/2018/07/05/hm-reiterated-jobseekers-seek-employment-private-sector-engage-entrepreneurship/>.
22. Aaron Wong, "HM: Government Restructuring Youth Entrepreneurship Ecosystem", *BizBrunei*, 1 August 2018 <https://www.bizbrunei.com/2018/08/hm-government-revamping-youth-entrepreneurship-ecosystem-national-youth-day/>.

23. Azlan Othman, "Brunei Ranks Fifth in Entrepreneurship Environment", *Borneo Bulletin*, 24 October 2018 <https://borneobulletin.com.bn/brunei-ranks-fifth-in-entrepreneurship-environment/>.
24. Ain Bandial, "As Deficit Falls by 40%, Gov't Proposes $5.3B Budget for 2018", *The Scoop*, 7 March 2018 <https://thescoop.co/2018/03/07/fiscal-deficit-falls-40-govt-proposes-5-3b-budget-2018/>.
25. Ministry of Development, *Ministry of Development Strategic Plan 2018–2035*, Policy Coordination and Strategic Planning Division, 2018 <http://www.mod.gov.bn/Shared%20Documents/LATEST%20SP%202018%20-%202023.pdf>.
26. Hakim Hayat, "MoH Tables B$345 Million Budget", *Borneo Bulletin*, 18 March 2018 <https://borneobulletin.com.bn/moh-tables-b345-million-budget/>.
27. Rokiah Mahmud, "Brunei Reaffirms Healthcare Commitment", *Borneo Bulletin*, 28 May 2018 <https://borneobulletin.com.bn/brunei-reaffirms-healthcare-commitment/> (accessed 6 September 2018).
28. Rokiah, Mahmud, "Public Welfare a Main Focus of New Budget", *Borneo Bulletin*, 8 March 2018 <https://borneobulletin.com.bn/public-welfare-a-main-focus-of-new-budget/>.
29. Azlan Othman and James Kon, "Welfare of OKUs a Priority", *Borneo Bulletin*, 18 March 2018 <https://borneobulletin.com.bn/welfare-of-okus-a-priority/>.
30. *Borneo Bulletin*, "Purifying Wealth through Zakat", 15 April 2017 <http://borneobulletin.com.bn/purifying-wealth-zakat/>.
31. H. Hayat, "Sultan Calls for Change in Zakat Fund Management", *Borneo Bulletin*, 2 June 2018 <https://borneobulletin.com.bn/streamline-management-of-zakat-sultan-in-titah/>.

Cambodia

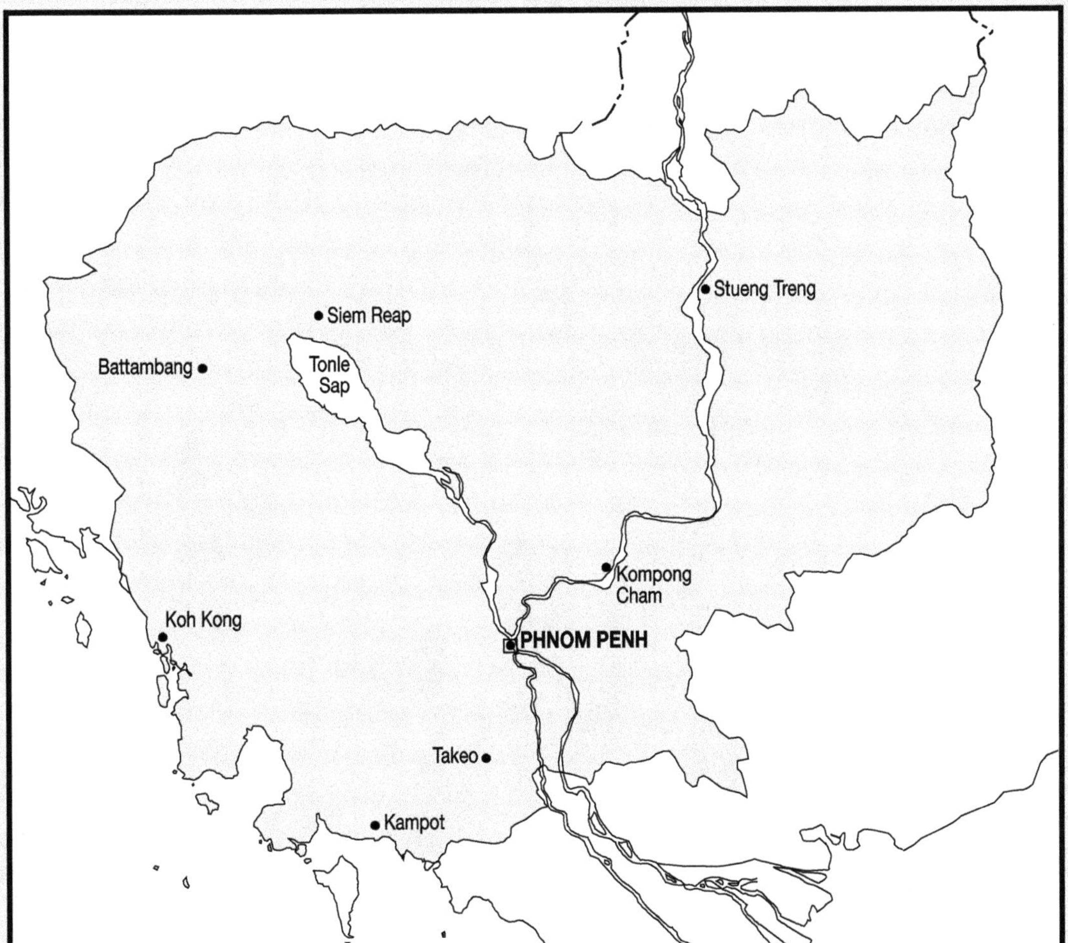
Stueng Treng
Siem Reap
Battambang
Tonle
Sap
Kompong
Cham
Koh Kong
PHNOM PENH
Takeo
Kampot

CAMBODIA IN 2018: A Year of Setbacks and Successes

Sorpong Peou

Cambodia in 2018 was marked by a number of major setbacks in some areas and successes in others. On the political front, the senate and parliamentary elections resulted in the Cambodian People's Party's monopolization of power within the bicameral legislature. Prime Minister Hun Sen continued to tighten his grip on power by taking steps to control state institutions, most notably the armed forces, the judiciary, and the party system. Human rights in the country continued to face an uphill battle, although the CPP government took a few small positive steps towards the end of the year by reversing its tight restrictions on the opposition and political rights. All these negative developments occurred despite positive signs of socio-economic development and international pressure from some major countries on which Cambodia has long depended for economic growth. Developed countries like the United States and those in Europe threatened to impose sanctions on Cambodia because of the election results, but the Hun Sen government did little to address their concerns about the political and human rights situation.

The State and Political Society

The multiparty system that was introduced in Cambodia in 1993 through the 1991 Paris Peace Agreements and the intervention of the United Nations Transitional Authority in Cambodia is now dictated by the CPP, which allows weak and fragile opposition parties to exist without any prospects of them gaining enough seats to form a new government.

SORPONG PEOU is Professor in the Department of Politics and Public Administration at Ryerson University and a member of the Yeates School of Graduate Studies. He is also President of Science for Peace, based at the University of Toronto, and a Member of the Eminent Persons Group at the Asian Political and International Student Association.

The year 2018 was noteworthy in the sense that two major elections for the bicameral legislature — the Senate and the National Assembly — led to the CPP's total dominance, and further marked a move away from a hegemonic-party system to the beginning of a one-party state.[1] The election for the Senate was held on 25 February, after having been postponed from 14 January 2018, and the results left the CPP with all 58 elected seats, taking 12 seats away from the opposition. The CPP also captured all 125 seats in the National Assembly, having collected 4,889,113 votes, leaving the other nineteen political parties without a single seat. Banned in November 2017 by the Supreme Court from competing in the two elections, the Cambodia National Rescue Party (CNRP), which won 55 out of 123 seats in the 2013 elections, was not even among the nineteen parties that competed with the CPP. Also worth noting is the fact that the once-popular royalist party FUNCINPEC, which won the 1993 national election but was forced to form a coalition government with the CPP, once again did not capture even a single seat. FUNCINPEC's political decline began irreversibly when its leader, Prince and First Prime Minister Norodom Ranariddh, was pushed out of power in 1997 after a violent confrontation with the then Second Prime Minister Hun Sen. The royalist party has since been unable to make a comeback.

The CPP's electoral victories since 1998 have come as no real surprise to long-time observers of Cambodian politics. The ruling elite have taken action through control, coercion and co-option to make sure that no opposition parties would be in a position to repeat what took place in the 2013 national election. One of the steps Hun Sen took to tighten his grip on power was through control of the armed forces. In May 2018, Human Rights Watch published a report entitled *Cambodia's Dirty Dozen: A Long History of Rights Abuses by Hun Sen's Generals*, identifying the twelve senior generals and many others in the army, gendarmerie and police on whom Hun Sen has relied to maintain power. The CPP has incorporated military, security and government officials into its Central Committee. According to the report, "If the security forces are not professionalized and key abusers are not appropriately held to account, there is little possibility of democratic reform — or indeed any kind of structural reform — in Cambodia."[2]

While the assessment of Human Rights Watch is compelling, it is worth adding that Hun Sen's rule is far from secure and he is unlikely to give up power anytime soon, as he has kept appointing his family members to top positions of power. Late in 2017 he appointed his third son Hun Manith, the director of intelligence in the Ministry of Defence, as head of a new academy for training spies to combat terrorists and any suspected threat from "colour revolution" forces. Shortly after that he elevated his eldest son, Lieutenant General Hun Manet (a deputy commander of the Royal Armed Forces), to the position of joint chief of staff. He also promoted his son-in-law, Dy Vichea (who formerly led the Ministry of Interior's Central Security Department), to deputy chief of the National Police. This appointment further allowed Hun Sen to tighten his political control over the national police, since his nephew-in-law, General Neth Savoeun, had already been promoted to the position of police chief in 2008.

There may be many reasons explaining Hun Sen's relentless consolidation of power, but his electoral victory in 2018 indicates that he did not want to see the events of the 2013 election repeated. He was more driven by the need to maximize security than enhance his political legitimacy. Recent political developments leading up to the election showed that he was prepared to win at all cost. The imprisonment of the CNRP president, Kem Sokha, in September 2017 based on trumped-up charges of treason, followed by the banning of the CNRP from competing in the 2018 election and the barring of 118 CNRP members from politics for five years, left the electoral process with the full sense of certainty that all traces of democracy had effectively been erased. Inside the country, however, the CNRP sought to boycott the election, making the case that it was "fake" and manipulated. The opposition party regarded the National Election Committee as effectively being under the control of the CPP. It accused the committee of conducting a "fake election" and "artificially inflating voter turnout",[3] told its supporters to ignore the election results and called for action against "CPP dictatorship". Supporters of the CNRP outside Cambodia protested the election results, especially those in the United States, with protestors taking to the streets in New York. During his speech at the UN General Assembly on 28 September 2018, Hun Sen was called a "traitor".

As 2018 was drawing to a close, the CPP took only a few small symbolic steps to give the opposition some breathing space. For instance, the Ministry of Foreign Affairs said in December that it was "reviewing legal provisions to enable individuals who were banned from politics to resume their political activities" and would ease its pressure on civil society, unions and independent media outlets.[4] The National Assembly, whose website said that it took steps to "promote the spirit of national reconciliation as well as strengthening liberal democracy", amended the election laws to allow CNRP members banned from the 2018 election to return to politics.[5]

Overall, 2018 marked another major setback against any hopes of seeing multiparty democracy put back on track. Having consolidated power through tightening control over the armed forces, the legislature and the judicial system,

Hun Sen feels more secure, but he is unlikely to give up power anytime soon. The opposition is no longer in a position to undermine the CPP and is now left without an influential leader capable of mobilizing support to weaken Hun Sen's grip on power, despite the release of CNRP president Kem Sokha after nearly a year in prison. The CNRP's former president, Sam Rainsy, did not even join the protests against the CPP in New York, claiming he had other commitments, such as attending a gathering of liberal parties in South Africa.[6] In spite of condemnations of the election results from democratic states (which will be discussed further later), Hun Sen is unlikely to let the opposition get its own way.

Rule of Law, Human Rights and Justice

Cambodia continues to rank low on the rule of law. The World Justice Project scored the country with a 0.32 on its rule-of-law index (2017–18), placing Cambodia the second-lowest among 113 countries and keeping its standing at the bottom of the list of fifteen countries in East Asia and the Pacific, below Myanmar, the Philippines, China and Vietnam.[7]

While the global and regional ranking of Cambodia's rule of law may not accurately reflect the full realities inside the country in 2018, there is no real evidence to suggest that the country has made real progress in the areas of transparency, accountability and judicial independence. Legal norms and principles such as due process and fair trials are still disregarded and violated. Justice has been carried at the behest of the CPP. The Supreme Court's decision to ban the CNRP from competing in the election was just one glaring example of how the court system is not independent of the executive branch of government. Rhona Smith, the UN Rapporteur for human rights in Cambodia, called on "the Ministry of Justice and judicial institutions to be more transparent in relation to their operations, to take more steps to combat corruption and to strengthen judicial independence and impartiality".[8]

The CPP continues to wage war against political rights and civil liberties. In the Reporters Without Borders' 2018 World Freedom Index, Cambodia ranked 142nd — a drop of ten places compared to 2017.[9] As previously discussed, the CPP's parliamentary victory did not result from a free and fair election, despite the absence of widespread political violence. Not only was the CNRP banned and its members barred from engaging in politics but efforts were also made on the part of the ruling party to put pressure on voters to cast their ballots in its favour. These efforts to intimidate voters prompted Rhona Smith to state that:

> The reports of threats to voters if they did not vote are of particular concern: the ink-stained finger, a sign in the past of hope and freedom, ironically has become a symbol of coercion.[10]

There were signs towards the end of 2018 that the government was becoming less repressive of labour activism. In December 2018, for instance, the Phnom Penh Municipal Court gave only a suspended two-and-a-half-year sentence to each of the six union leaders who had been charged with and found guilty of involvement in violence and property damage during protests in 2014 and 2015. However, the laws adopted to suppress civil liberties, which include the Law on Associations and Non-Governmental Organizations, the Trade Union Law, and a *lèse-majesté* clause in the Penal Code, remain in place.

The overall human rights situation in Cambodia is far from ideal, despite the work done by the donor community, international and national civil society actors, and the Extraordinary Chambers in the Court of Cambodia (ECCC) established to prosecute Khmer Rouge leaders accused of committing the most serious crimes during their reign of terror from 1975 to 1978. The ECCC continued to conduct formal trials against Khmer Rouge leaders. One major development was the conviction of Khieu Samphan (the Khmer Rouge regime's head of state) and Nuon Chea (known as second to Prime Minister Pol Pot), who had been charged with the crime of genocide in addition to other most serious crimes; namely, war crimes and crimes against humanity.

The tribunal faced some setbacks in 2018, after the two ECCC co-investigating judges (one Cambodian and one international) issued two contradictory orders against Oh An, a former Khmer Rouge official who played a role below that of the most senior central command of the regime and was charged with the crime of genocide against the Cham population and crimes against humanity. The Cambodian co-investigating judge, You Bunleng, sought to dismiss the charges, whereas his international counterpart wanted to proceed with the charges to the Trial Chamber.[11] The CPP government then made it clear that it intended to bring to a close the work of the ECCC. According to one report, Deputy Prime Minister Sar Kheng thought that "the tribunal's work had been completed and there would be no more prosecutions for acts committed when the Khmer Rouge was in power".[12]

Whether the ECCC's latest convictions further proved that justice has been served is still a matter of debate among policymakers and pundits, but the fact is clear: only three Khmer Rouge leaders held responsible for the most serious crimes have been convicted, after more than a decade and a cost of at least $300 million.

Whether the hybrid tribunal has helped to deter mass atrocities over the last ten years and brought about peace is a matter of opinion, and it is far from clear whether the ECCC should be adopted as a model of international peace and security through justice. The tribunal was established and came into operation in 2006, long after the disintegration of the Khmer Rouge in the late 1990s. As noted earlier, neither democracy nor the rule of law have since been strengthened. Several top leaders within the CPP, such as Hun Sen and Heng Samrin, are former Khmer Rouge officials who have no wish to see the tribunal succeed beyond punishing a few Khmer Rouge leaders like Nuon Chea and Khieu Samphan.

In short, 2018 was still not a year of real triumph for the rule of law and justice. Not only did democracy suffer another serious setback but the human rights situation also made no headway. Although a number of political leaders were released, and in spite of the ongoing work of the ECCC, political rights and civil liberties were still severely restricted.

Socio-economic Development

The elections and the weak rule of law did not however cause Cambodia to descend into chaos or prevent it from enjoying economic growth, which is an important source of the CPP's performance legitimacy. The average economic growth rate of Cambodia between 1995 and 2017 was 7.7 per cent. Steady economic growth continued in 2018. According to the World Bank, the economy ranked sixth among the world's fastest-growing economies, and it is expected to grow by 7 per cent in 2018 and remain robust in the medium-term.[13] Cambodia is projected to perform better economically than any other country in Southeast Asia: Vietnam (6.9 per cent), Laos (6.6 per cent), Myanmar (6.6 per cent), the Philippines (6.4 per cent), Indonesia (5.2 per cent), Malaysia (5 per cent), Thailand (4.5 per cent), Singapore (3.1 per cent) and Brunei (2 per cent).[14] In 2015, Cambodia attained lower-middle-income status. If the economy continues to grow at the rate of 7 per cent, Cambodia is expected to obtain a high-middle-income status by 2030.

This impressive growth has benefited from low inflation rates and is primarily driven by tourism, foreign aid, trade liberalization, direct foreign investment, and exports. The inflation rate is expected to hover around 3.2 per cent in 2018 and 3.5 per cent in 2019. The tourism industry also did well in 2018. According to the Ministry of Tourism, the country's three international airports in Phnom Penh, Siem Reap and Sihanoukville saw the number of tourist arrivals increase to at least 10 million by the end of 2018, up from 8.8 million in 2017.[15] Official development assistance (ODA) has also been a major factor for economic growth, despite criticism that aid has done Cambodia more harm than good in political terms. Australia, Japan and China were among the major bilateral donors. Australia's ODA remains substantial, standing at $89.1 million in 2017–18 and $83.6 million in 2018–19.[16] In March 2018, Japan pledged more than $90 million in a grant and loan agreement with Cambodia.[17] China has become Cambodia's biggest donor, having given the latter around $4.2 billion worth of grants and soft loans by 2017,[18] with more loans coming in 2018. Multilateral donors also continued to provide development assistance. In April, the World Bank approved $90 million of financing to support Cambodia's higher education sector and research for industrial development.[19] In July, the Asian Development Bank agreed to finance $66 million to build twenty-two roads in Cambodia and "another US$141 million for a climate-friendly agribusiness value chain sector project". In total, Cambodia has received $2.95 billion from the ADB.[20]

Foreign direct investment (FDI) has been another source of economic growth. During the first nine months of 2018, the total amount of FDI flows into Cambodia reached $3.9 billion (compared to $2.8 billion in 2017 and $2.4 billion in 2016). Of the $3.9 billion, the agriculture sector accounted for 9.2 per cent, the industrial sector 17.5 per cent, the services sector 66.5 per cent and the tourism sector 6.8 per cent.[21] Although it declined in the garment and agricultural sectors, the inflow of FDI increased in the banking, real estate, assembly and manufacturing sectors.[22] China has in recent years become the biggest investor in Cambodia, especially after Chinese President Xi Jinping's visit to Phnom Penh in October 2016 (bringing with him more than two hundred Chinese investors as part of his Belt and Road Initiative), and has taken the lead in the real estate sector.[23]

Cambodia's export-led growth can be explained in terms of its access to global markets, especially those in the European Union (EU) and the United States. According to the Ministry of Finance and Economy, the total value of exports in the first nine months of 2018 amounted to $9.63 billion, compared to $17.3 billion in 2017.[24] These exports went to the EU (€2,784 million), the United States ($2,280 million), Great Britain ($887 million), Japan ($805 million), ASEAN ($740 million), and others ($2,143 million). These figures suggest that most of Cambodia's exports have gone to developed countries in the West and that Cambodia has enjoyed trade surpluses. Exports of Cambodian goods to the United States, for instance, reached $3.1 billion in 2017, resulting in a deficit of $2.7 billion for the United States.[25] In contrast, Cambodian exports to China have been small ($634 million from January to November 2017), whereas imports from

China grew to \$4.48 billion in 2017 (from \$4.33 billion in 2016).[26] Cambodia has clearly benefited much more from trade relations with developed countries than with its biggest investor, China.

According to the United Nations Development Program's 2018 statistical update, Cambodia made steady progress in terms of life expectancy at birth, expected years of schooling, mean years of schooling, and gross national income per capita. Cambodia's Human Development Index (HDI) increased to 0.852 (2017) from 0.634 (1990). Life expectancy at birth increased to 69.3 (2017) from 53.6 (1990). Expected years of schooling and mean years of schooling increased to 11.4 and 4.8 (2017) from 6.7 and 2.7 (1990), respectively. However, the country's HDI still ranks 146th out of 189 countries and territories.[27]

In spite of the progress made over the years, Cambodia still faces numerous challenges. Poverty rates — defined as those living on less than \$2 a day — declined to 13.5 per cent (2014) from 47.8 per cent (2007), but a large majority of the population (estimated to be around 70 per cent) still live on less than \$3 a day. Economic growth has been driven by foreign aid, FDI and tourism and remains dependent on exports to developed countries in the West. Overall, the economy is performing well but remains largely vulnerable to external circumstances.

Foreign Relations

Cambodia's relations with international organizations and other states did not change much in 2018, despite the domestic political developments before and after the parliamentary election. Members of the international donor community continued to provide development assistance, as noted earlier, although Cambodia-UN relations were strained due to criticism from senior UN officials about the 2018 elections. During his speech at the UN General Assembly on 28 September 2018, Hun Sen warned against any foreign interference in his country's domestic affairs. In terms of foreign policy direction, Cambodia continued to do more business with China, as the CPP government sought to consolidate political power to the dismay of Western democracies.

The year 2018 began with the high-profile visit of China's Premier Le Keqiang, which saw both countries signing nineteen new memorandums of understanding and other agreements, which include promises by the Chinese to develop infrastructure in Cambodia, such as an expressway connecting Phnom Penh and Sihanoukville at an estimated cost of \$2 billion, two electricity transmission projects, and two new airports in Phnom Penh and Siem Reap. China also committed to the construction of a breeding centre for luxury wood tree species, and a new medical programme called "Love Heart Journey" aimed at providing surgery for heart disease patients in Cambodia.

These new agreements further cemented Cambodia's growing dependence on China, not only for economic development but also for political protection and security. In spite of China's well-known claim about giving aid without any strings attached, the new agreements can be viewed as a foreign policy tool that both countries use to accomplish their political ends. With its growing influence on world and Asian affairs in recent decades, Beijing continues to display an interest in keeping Cambodia as close to China as possible. For his part, Hun Sen treats China as the most credible protector of his regime. Their mutual interest is clearly stated in the joint communiqué, which asserts that the visit "achieved full success and vigorously pushed forward the Cambodia-China Comprehensive Strategic Partnership of Cooperation". The communiqué further made it clear that the "Cambodian side reaffirmed its resolute adherence to the One-China policy, and its support to the Chinese government's efforts to safeguard national sovereignty and territorial integrity".[28] In recent years China has found Cambodia to be a reliable supporter of its territorial claims over the South China Sea. In 2012, Cambodia hosted the annual ASEAN summit and managed to prevent any discussion on the South China Sea, resulting in the regional group's failure to issue a joint communiqué for the first time in its history. In 2016, Cambodia was again seen as being responsible for the omission of any mention of the international arbitration's ruling in favour of the Philippines in its territorial disputes with China in the joint communiqué arising out of the ASEAN summit in Laos.

Cambodia's pro-China foreign policy reaped additional benefits when Beijing rewarded the CPP by defending the 2018 election results. For China, the election was "smooth" and affirming of the Cambodian people's trust in the CPP. Chinese State Councillor Wang Yi made it clear that China "has always resolutely supported Cambodia's efforts to protect its sovereignty, independence and stability, and opposes any foreign country interfering in Cambodia's internal affairs".[29] Chinese president Xi Jinping conveyed his congratulations to Hun Sen, saying his leadership brought about political stability and fast economic growth. According to China's Foreign Ministry, "the Cambodian People's Party will continue to unite and lead the Cambodian people to pursue a development path that suits its own national reality".[30]

Sino-Cambodian relations have also developed with other geopolitical implications. Cambodia's growing dependence on China is also a manifestation of the former's historical distrust of its two more powerful neighbours; namely,

Thailand and Vietnam. What this means is that Cambodia's place in ASEAN is not as positive as it looks or should be. The nineteen newly brokered Cambodia-China deals might have raised more concerns among other ASEAN members, especially those that have competing maritime claims with China. Cambodian-Vietnamese relations, for instance, are no longer as good as they used to be, especially in the 1980s when the Hun Sen regime still depended on Hanoi for military and political support. Concerns about China's growing influence in Cambodia have also been expressed by observers of regional politics. One writer put it this way: "While it cannot be denied that Cambodia's economy faces uncertainty due to the fact of China's growing influence, Cambodia needs to find balance to ensure it remains in control of its own economic future."[31]

The CPP government's growing dependence on China risks alienating Cambodia from other major countries in Asia and around the world. Japan, which has been a major donor in Cambodia, has reason to worry about Cambodia moving closer to its regional rival, China. This explains why Japan continues to support the Hun Sen government by providing foreign aid and democracy assistance, despite the fact that the past elections were unfree and unfair. Before the 2018 election, for instance, Tokyo did what the EU and the United States refused to do, which was to fund Cambodia's National Election Committee, although its assistance fell short of that of China. Japan only provided ten thousand ballot boxes worth $7.5 million, whereas China donated $20 million in equipment, such as computers, laptops and polling booths. Japan, which has tried to form an anti-China alliance of democracies, considered the election "disappointing".[32]

Democratic countries in the West dismissed the election results. Several countries that used to send election observers to Cambodia during its elections chose not to do so in 2018. Tensions between Cambodia and the EU grew after the latter threatened to impose sanctions on the former, although there were signs that the CPP was softening its position on the opposition. The EU pointed to the "lack of genuine electoral competition and the absence of an inclusive political process", which in its view meant "that the 29th July election is not representative of the democratic will of the Cambodian electorate and therefore its outcome lacks credibility".[33] In October 2018 the EU said it would end Cambodia's special access to European markets under the Everything-But-Arms (EBA) preferential trade agreement. The EU threat initially led the CPP government to regard it as an act of "extreme injustice". According to Cambodia's Ministry of Foreign Affairs, "By implementing these withdrawal measures, the European Commission risks negating twenty year's worth of development efforts."[34] By the end of 2018, however, the EU had yet to terminate its EBA agreement with Cambodia.

The United States also played a role in trying to constrain the consolidation of power by the CPP and in deterring it from moving closer to China, but this policy effort appears to have resulted in further straining its bilateral relations with Cambodia. The imprisonment of CNRP president Kem Sokha in September 2017, which resulted from the Hun Sen government's allegation of his collaboration with Washington to overthrow the CPP, led to American politicians making threats to impose sanctions on Cambodia. On 23 October 2017, for instance, Senator Ted Cruz wrote a letter to the Cambodian ambassador to the United States expressing concerns about the political situation in Cambodia and considering the CPP's anti-opposition actions as an "attempt to undermine the Cambodian people's faith in the democratic process". Hun Sen dismissed Cruz's criticism, saying that his country had its own law, that "there is no such thing as international standards when it comes to politics", and that there should be no interference and no need for any legitimization of election outcome from "outsiders".[35] Hun Sen's combative attitude towards the United States may have been emboldened by his belief that the latter had stopped providing ODA to his country since 2016.[36] According to the U.S. Department of State's website dated 15 August 2018, "in 2014, U.S. foreign assistance for programs in health, education, governance, economic growth, and demining of unexploded ordnance totaled over $77.6 million". Assistance after 2014 is not mentioned.[37]

Cambodia's relations with the United States deteriorated further before the 2018 election when Congressman Ted Yoho, chairman of the House Foreign Affairs Subcommittee, introduced a bill known as the Cambodia Democracy Act 2018, which was approved by the House of Representation on 25 July. The bill would impose sanctions on sixteen Cambodian individuals, including Hun Sen, his sons and the head of his bodyguard unit. The Trump administration considered the election to be "neither free nor fair", making it clear that it "failed to represent the will of the Cambodian people" and threatened to take action against the CPP government, "including a significant expansion of the visa restrictions announced on December 6, 2017".[38]

In short, Cambodia's relations with the Western world no longer appear to be where they used to be, as Hun Sen has continued to take steps bringing the country closer to China and further away from the democratic West. Although it is still unclear how far he can go, Hun Sen seems to have learnt from history that he can succeed in playing major powers off against each other in his efforts to maximize security through power consolidation.

Conclusion

The year 2018 witnessed the most serious setback on the political front, despite the fact that the economy performed as well as it had in previous years. For the first time since 1993, the CPP succeeded in politically erasing the remaining traces of democracy by grabbing all possible elected seats in the bicameral legislature. As the CNRP, the country's main opposition party, had been barred from competing in the two elections, other smaller opposition parties were too weak to compete against the CPP and thus failed to win even a single seat. Hun Sen's political success can be attributed to his control of the armed forces and the judicial and party systems, which he has used effectively as coercive means to suppress the opposition. Moreover, the support of China — which has emerged as Cambodia's biggest investor, largest donor and the strongest defender of Hun Sen's authoritarian politics — was another major source of power that he used to counter any threats from developed countries in the West. Cambodia now appears to be emerging as a new site of geopolitical contestation between the democratic West and the authoritarian East led by China, although the security situation is far from being as it was in the 1970s and 1980s when the country was used as a battleground by the rival capitalist and socialist blocs to fight their proxy war. However, Hun Sen's dependence on China may cost his government or himself in the future. Because his political legitimacy is largely tied to economic performance, it becomes an issue that Cambodia's economic growth is both simultaneously dependent on Chinese aid and investment as well as exports to the West. If and when the economy stops performing well, the CPP may end up self-imploding.

Notes

1. Sorpong Peou, "Cambodia's Hegemonic-Party System: How and Why the CPP became Dominant", *Asian Journal of Comparative Politics* (25 July 2018) <https://journals.sagepub.com/doi/abs/10.1177/2057891118788199>.
2. Human Rights Watch, "Cambodia's Dirty Dozen — A Long History of Rights Abuses by Hun Sen's Generals", 27 June 2018, p. 10 <https://www.hrw.org/report/2018/06/27/cambodias-dirty-dozen/long-history-rights-abuses-hun-sens-generals>.
3. Cited in Prak Chan Thul, "Cambodia's CPP Won All Seats: Officials", *The Courier*, 16 August 2018 <https://www.thecourier.com.au/story/5588788/cambodias-cpp-won-all-seats-officials/>.
4. Voice of America, "Cambodia to Ease Restrictions on Opposition as EU Considers Trade Relationship" <https://www.youtube.com/watch?v=zjZLQY3TBd4>.
5. Voice of America, "National Assembly Approves Law Allowing Opposition Officials to Reenter Politics", 14 December 2018 <https://www.voacambodia.com/a/national-

assembly-approves-law-allowing-opposition-officials-to-re-enter-politics/4700865.html>.
6. David Hut, "Cambodia's Domestic Politics in the Spotlight at the United Nations", *The Diplomat*, 28 September 2018 <https://thediplomat.com/2018/09/cambodias-domestic-politics-in-the-spotlight-at-the-united-nations/>.
7. World Justice Project, *Rule of Law Index, 2017–2018* (Washington, DC: World Justice Project, 2018).
8. United Nations in Cambodia, "News Release: Civil Society is Crucial for Sustainable Development in Cambodia <http://kh.one.un.org/content/unct/cambodia/en/home/resource-center/speeche-and-statement/2018/news-release---un-expert--civil-society-is-crucial-for-sustainab.html>.
9. Reporters Without Borders, "Hun Sen's War on Critics" <https://rsf.org/en/cambodia>.
10. United Nations High Commissioner for Human Rights, "Cambodia: UN Expert Questions 'Genuineness' of Ruling Party's Landslide Victory", 26 September 2018 <https://www.ohchr.org/FR/NewsEvents/Pages/DisplayNews.aspx?NewsID=23638&LangID=E>.
11. Open Society Justice Initiative, "Recent Developments at the Extraordinary Chambers in the Courts of Cambodia: Competing Orders in Ao An Investigation". Briefing Paper (New York: Open Society Foundations, September 2018).
12. "Cambodia Reiterates Khmer Rouge Tribunal's Work is Complete", Al Jazeera, 19 November 2018 <https://www.aljazeera.com/news/2018/11/cambodia-reiterates-khmer-rouge-tribunal-work-complete-181119031317329.html>.
13. World Bank, "The World Bank in Cambodia: Overview", 28 September 2018 <https://www.worldbank.org/en/country/cambodia/overview>.
14. Asian Development Bank, *Asian Development Outlook 2018 — Cambodia: Economy* <https://www.adb.org/countries/cambodia/economy>.
15. Tourism of Cambodia, "Cambodian Airports Reach 10 Million Passengers Milestone", 20 December 2018 <https://www.tourismcambodia.com/news/localnews/27128/cambodian-airports-reach-10-million-passengers-milestone.htm>.
16. Australian Government, "Development Assistance in Cambodia" <https://dfat.gov.au/geo/cambodia/development-assistance/Pages/development-assistance-in-cambodia.aspx>.
17. "Cambodia, Japan Sign $90 Million Aid Agreement", Reuters, 8 April 2018 <https://www.reuters.com/article/us-cambodia-japan/japan-cambodia-sign-90-million-aid-agreement-idUSKBN1HF062>.
18. Pheakdey Heng, "Are China's Gift a Blessing or a Curse for Cambodia", *East Asia Forum*, 29 August 2018.
19. World Bank, "New Financing Will Support Cambodia in Improving Higher Education for Industrial Development", 26 April 2018 <https://www.worldbank.org/en/news/press-release/2018/04/26/new-financing-will-support-cambodia-in-improving-higher-education-for-industrial-development>.

20. Cambodia Constructors Associations, "Cambodia Receives Aid from ADB for 22 Rural Roads", 10 July 2018 <https://www.construction-property.com/read-news-1245/>.
21. Interview with Sambath Peou, RADIUS, Phnom Penh, Cambodia, 26 December 2018.
22. Hor Kimsay, "Flow of FDI up in First Half", *Phnom Penh Post*, 23 July 2018.
23. Philip Heijmans, "Chinese Money is Driving One of Asia's Fastest Property Booms, Bloomberg, 10 September 2018 <https://www.bloomberg.com/news/features/2018-09-10/chinese-money-is-driving-a-property-boom-in-cambodia>.
24. Leonie Barrie, "Losing EU Trade Benefits Would Hurt Cambodia Clothing Exports", *Just-style*, 30 October 2018 <https://www.just-style.com/news/losing-eu-trade-benefit-would-hurt-cambodia-clothing-exports_id134878.aspx>.
25. Office of the United States Trade Representative, "Cambodia: U.S.-Cambodia Trade Facts" <https://ustr.gov/countries-regions/southeast-asia-pacific/Cambodia->.
26. May Kunmakara, "Trade with China on the Upswing", *Khmer Times*, 5 January 2018 <https://www.khmertimeskh.com/50100171/trade-china-upswing/>.
27. UNDP, "Human Development Indices and Indicators: 2018 Statistical Update" <http://hdr.undp.org/sites/all/themes/hdr_theme/country-notes/KHM.pdf>.
28. Cited in Kong Meta and Erin Handley, "China Signs 19 New Deals with Cambodia", *Phnom Penh Post*, 11 January 2018.
29. Cited in "China Says Foreigners Should Not Interfere in Cambodia after Election", Reuters, 1 August 2018 <https://www.reuters.com/article/us-asean-singapore-china-cambodia/china-says-foreigners-should-not-interfere-in-cambodia-after-election-idUSKBN1KN034>.
30. Prak Chan Thul, "Cambodia's Ruling Party Won All Seats in July Vote: Election Commission", Reuters <https://www.reuters.com/article/us-cambodia-election/cambodias-ruling-party-won-all-seats-in-july-vote-election-commission-idUSKBN1L01E7>.
31. Cheryl Lim, "Balance Needed in Cambodia-China Relations", *ASEAN Post*, 18 January 2018 <https://theaseanpost.com/article/balance-needed-cambodia-china-relations-0>.
32. Voice of America, "Japanese Gov't Calls Cambodia's Election 'Disappointing' " <https://www.voacambodia.com/a/japanese-govt-calls-cambodias-election-disappointing/4514501.html>.
33. Cited in Prak Chan Thul, "Cambodia to Form New Government after Election that Opposition Calls 'Farce' ", Reuters, 31 July 2018 <https://www.reuters.com/article/us-cambodia-election/cambodia-to-form-new-government-after-election-that-opposition-calls-farce-idUSKBN1KL0MK>.
34. "Cambodia Calls EU Trade Threat 'Extreme Injustice' ", Reuters, 11 October 2018 <https://www.investing.com/news/economy-news/cambodia-calls-eu-trade-threat-extreme-injustice-1639859>.

35. Radio Free Asia, "Cambodia's Hun Sen Dismisses Threats of US Sanctions and Need for International Recognition", 10 November 2017 <https://www.rfa.org/english/news/cambodia/sanctions-11102017162525.html>.
36. "Cambodia Questions US Aid Cut: 'There is No Aid' ", *Al Jazeera News*, 3 March 2018 <https://www.aljazeera.com/news/2018/02/cambodia-questions-aid-cut-aid-180227182024540.html>.
37. US Department of State, "U.S. Relations with Cambodia", 15 August 2018 <https://www.state.gov/r/pa/ei/bgn/2732.htm>.
38. Voice of America, "International Community Condemns Cambodia Elections as 'Setback' to Democracy" <https://www.voacambodia.com/a/international-community-condemns-cambodia-elections-as-setback-to-democracy-/4505764.html>.

Indonesia

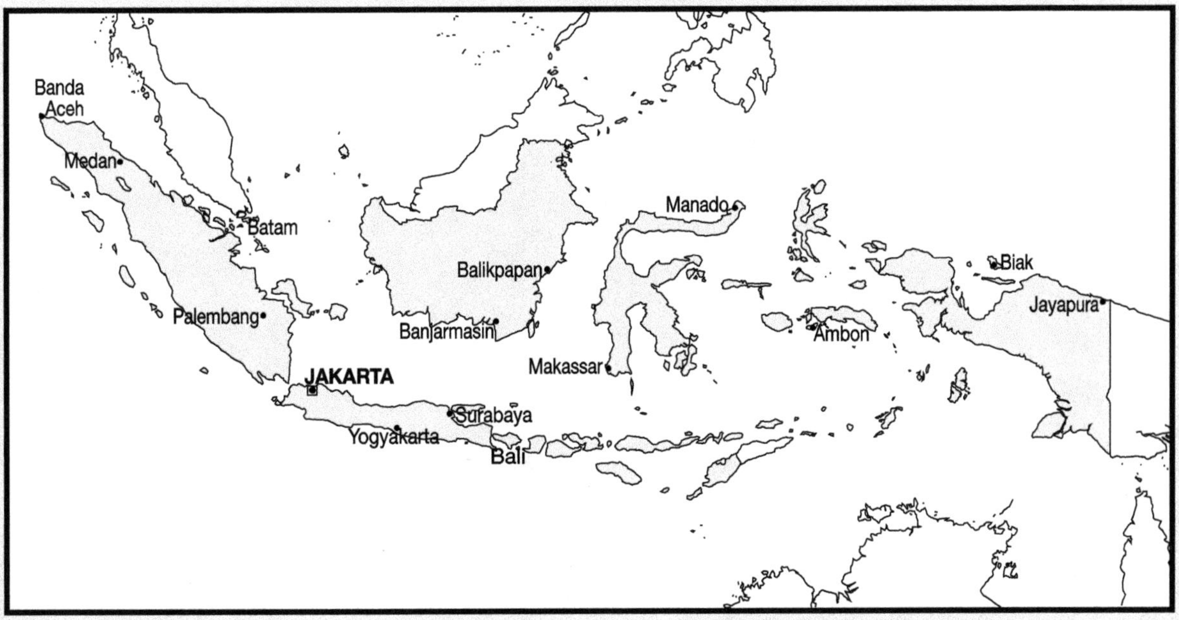
Banda Aceh
Medan
Batam
Palembang
JAKARTA
Yogyakarta
Surabaya
Bali
Balikpapan
Banjarmasin
Makassar
Manado
Ambon
Biak
Jayapura

INDONESIA IN 2018: The Calm before the Election Storm

Natalie Sambhi

The year 2018 marked twenty years since the resignation of Soeharto and the onset of democratic reform in Indonesia. In 1998, Indonesia's leaders faced an ailing economy rife with corruption, domestic instability and student protests, with predictions of "Balkanization" amidst threats of separatism. Today, it is worth reflecting on the state of the country as a relatively consolidated democratic system with a separate police force and vibrant press, particularly when compared to other Southeast Asian states. It is inevitable that today's achievements are weighed against Indonesia's previously dire circumstances, having emerged from the East Asian financial crisis and domestic political turmoil. At the same time, Indonesia's progress is also measured by the hopes and expectations of Indonesians (for those not too cynical) that their new leaders will transcend some of the most odious features of the Soeharto regime. Seen in that light, the country's democratic shine is tarnished by the seemingly never-ending high-profile corruption cases and entrenched money politics.[1] The year saw the jailing of former speaker of the House of Representatives and former Golkar chair Setya Novanto for stealing US$170 million (2.3 trillion rupiah) of public monies.

The year was also a last push for the incumbent president to prove that his programme of national development had made significant gains. In 2018 the key task of President Joko Widodo (Jokowi) was to keep the country on an even keel leading up to the 2019 presidential election. He faced a number of domestic

---

NATALIE SAMBHI is a doctoral student at the Strategic and Defence Studies Centre, Australian National University, focussing on Indonesian military history. Since 2016 she has been Research Fellow at the Perth USAsia Centre, where she has published on Indonesian foreign and defence policy as well as Southeast Asian security.

challenges, from the Surabaya terrorist attacks, which saw children being used in suicide bombings for the first time, to the slew of major natural disasters in the second half of the year. The economy was rocked by volatile oil prices and the fallout from a trade war between the world's largest economies, the United States and China, which led to the precipitous fall of the nation's currency. What follows is an overview of the key trends and major developments that shaped the largest state in Southeast Asia in 2018. The first section discusses the significance of Ma'ruf Amin as Jokowi's running mate and what it reveals about the prevailing political environment. It assesses Jokowi's ability to navigate hosting the Asian Games while providing humanitarian relief to Indonesians affected by severe disasters. The second highlights the impact of the global environment on the economy as well as the Jokowi administration's efforts to shore up trade and investment. The third section covers Indonesia's attempts to promote its vision of the Indo-Pacific region as well as its steps towards leadership in diplomacy. The fourth outlines the major security issues, including the Surabaya terrorist attacks and the legislative changes they spurred, violent incidents such as the events in December 2018 in Nduga Regency, and maritime diplomacy. The final section traces the backsliding of Indonesia's social and religious pluralism, particularly in terms of the impact of the changing demographic of conservative Muslims from lower to higher socioeconomic backgrounds.

Political Developments: Keeping Calm before the Storm

Poignantly, 2018 was also the year immediately before the presidential and legislative elections to be held on 17 April 2019: the calm before the storm. With Prabowo's confirmation as a candidate, 2019 will be a rematch of the 2014 presidential race.

That said, there was significant change, with the announcement of Ma'ruf Amin as Jokowi's vice presidential candidate. Ma'ruf is a well-respected Islamic scholar and a significant figure in Indonesia's religious sphere. Since 2015 he has been the spiritual leader of Nahdlatul Ulama (NU), the nation's largest Muslim organization, as well as head of the Indonesian Ulama Council, the top state-endorsed body that issues rulings on Islamic matters. He is also well known for issuing a "religious opinion" in November 2016 that then Jakarta governor Basuki Tjahaja Purnama (better known as Ahok) had blasphemed against Islam. There is a stark juxtaposition between a president who has gathered significant grass-roots support through young Indonesians and a programme of national development and his seventy-five-year-old running mate, who ostensibly has little in common with millennial voters. Jokowi's favoured candidate had been former Constitutional Court chief justice and ex-defence minister Mahfud MD. The choice of Ma'ruf is seen by political analysts as a move of pure political expediency; not having a political party of his own, Jokowi had been under pressure by coalition partners to pick their preferred candidates. Mahfud was not popular among the coalition and, being sixty-one years old, his potential to run as a presidential candidate in 2024 was seen as a drawback.

The choice of Ma'ruf serves to further boost Jokowi's Islamic credentials. This was particularly important given that NU had threatened to withdraw its support for the president. Drawing on Ma'ruf's religious standing would help avoid sectarian campaigns during and after the election. The selection of Ma'ruf is one of several steps Jokowi has taken over the past year to accommodate political Islamic figures in government. Others include appointing Ali Mochtar Ngabalin — a Golkar politician and former chairman of the Coordinating Body of Indonesian Muslim Preachers who had once urged God to support Prabowo — to the Presidential Staff Office in May to combat fake news,[2] and appointing Din Syamsuddin, the conservative former chairman of Muhammadiyah, as a special envoy for inter-religious and cultural affairs in October 2017. The latter, however, resigned in September.

Ma'ruf's conservatism, which includes suspicion of inter-faith activities and calls for a ban of LGBT activities, is likely to cause concern among Muslim progressives within Indonesia and human rights groups abroad. He is unlikely to bring knowledge of other areas of public policy. It remains to be seen whether Mar'uf will adapt by toning down such rhetoric or whether Jokowi's administration will accommodate more the agenda of political Islam, resulting in the "sacralization" of the Indonesian state.[3] In contrast, Prabowo has selected a younger and more dynamic running mate in the former Jakarta vice-governor Sandiaga Uno. Sandiaga's status as a wealthy and good-looking entrepreneur is more attractive to social-media-savvy millennials. He also brings considerable financial resources to Prabowo's campaign. However, his religious credentials are comparatively not as strong, which may be a weak spot for the opposition slate, although Prabowo's ties to religious groups could make up that shortfall.

By most accounts, the election is Jokowi's to lose. He commands a coalition of nine parties supporting him into the polls, in contrast to Prabowo's five. At the close of 2018, major survey houses found that more than 50 per cent of respondents would vote for Jokowi, compared to just 30 per cent for Prabowo.[4] And these figures have been consistent for much of the year. In order to bridge this gap in electability, Prabowo will have to focus on Jokowi's potential weaknesses, particularly through the issues of the economy and nationalism. There are already signs that Prabowo's campaign will be fiercely populist, as he continues to accuse Jokowi of allowing the country's resources to be plundered by foreign forces.[5] Later in the year, Prabowo had demanded a halt at short notice to the hosting of the IMF and World Bank meetings in Bali, in order to divert funds to natural disaster efforts for Central Sulawesi at the time. There is also disapproval of Jokowi's performance. In March, opposition parties launched the hashtag #2019gantipresiden (#2019changepresident) via social media platforms to consolidate anti-Jokowi sentiments. In some instances, events related to the online movement have led to clashes between supporters on the one side and counter-protesters and security forces on the other. The involvement of both the police and military in dispersing these gatherings exposes Jokowi to criticism that the state security apparatus is not acting impartially. Although the establishment of the anti-Jokowi social media movement pre-dated the confirmation of Prabowo's election bid, it can be easily channelled into support for Prabowo. Social media will thus continue to be an important battleground in the upcoming elections, with the use of disinformation campaigns and bots continuing to increase in elections worldwide.

Jokowi will need to underscore his record of progress since 2014. Although infrastructure continues to be a key pillar of Jokowi's political performance, there was a mixed record of success in 2018. Some of the priority projects slated for operation in 2018 and 2019 have not been completed and some of them have not even begun construction.[6] These include the Makassar–Parepare railway, the Serang–Panimbang toll road and the Probolinggo–Banyuwangi toll road. In terms of successes, the government did construct a light rail transit for Palembang in time for the Asian Games, as well as the Kuala Tanjung international hub port, with further phases for the port planned out to 2023. The circular LRT line planned to service Jakarta, Bogor, Depok and Bekasi, as well as a north-south line in Jakarta, will be operational in 2019. In contrast to transportation, many of the priority projects related to electricity, oil and gas, and water and sanitation are not due to commence until 2019 and beyond, meaning Jokowi will need a second term to fulfil those plans.

The other significant political development in 2018 was the holding of simultaneous local elections across the archipelago on 27 June to elect heads for 17 provinces, 115 regencies and 39 cities. According to the General Elections Commission, 110 million people voted (out of a pool of 152 million eligible voters), a relatively positive sign for democratic participation, although lower than the turnout for the 2017 regional elections. Due to their large populations, the outcomes of gubernatorial elections in the provinces of West Java, Central Java, East Java and North Sumatra were watched carefully. In West Java, the Bandung mayor Ridwan Kamil successfully contested the race. In Central Java, the incumbent Partai Demokrasi Indonesia Perjuangan (PDI-P) governor Ganjar Pranowo won, while in East Java, Khofifah Indar Parawansa, backed by Golkar and the Democrat Party, succeeded in her bid. In North Sumatra, former military general Edy Rahmayadi beat his PDI-P opponent. Some analysts have cautioned against seeing trends in the regional elections as predictive of the presidential race outcome.[7] For instance, the impact of the North Sumatra outcome on the 2019 election remains inconclusive, given that Jokowi had won the majority of the vote in the province in 2014 despite it not traditionally being a PDI-P stronghold.

While natural disasters are common to the archipelago, 2018 was a particularly relentless year, with a string of major disasters. The worst disasters included three earthquakes in Lombok in July and August; an earthquake of 7.5 magnitude, tsunami, land liquefaction and landslides in Palu, Central Sulawesi, in September; and a tsunami in the Sunda Strait caused by the volcano Anak Krakatoa's eruption in December. Each disaster resulted in significant loss of life and displaced communities: 2,256 deaths in Palu and around 80,000 displaced;[8] 563 people killed in Lombok, with 417,000 displaced;[9] and 437 killed, 14,000 injured and 33,700 displaced following the tsunami in the Sunda Strait.[10] Thousands are now living in displacement camps. The Sunda Strait eruption exposed flaws in the government's early warning system, which is designed to detect tsunamis caused by earthquakes but not those generated by undersea landslides or volcanic eruptions. The delivery of aid was made difficult on account of several factors. First, geographical and geological issues hampered efforts; in addition to aftershocks, the remote location of some villages made the provision of clean water to places like Palu challenging. Second, the government prevented international aid organizations from operating directly in the country, forcing them to direct funds through local branches or domestic organizations. The president's critics also argued that Lombok should have been declared a "national disaster", which would have allowed international aid to arrive faster. A National Disaster Agency spokesperson however defended that decision on the grounds that such a declaration would show "weakness of the country".[11] The effective and timely delivery of aid could thus become a point of weakness for the government that Prabowo could use in the run-up to the April elections.

Amidst the humanitarian tragedies, Indonesia basked in the honour of hosting the 18th Asian Games, held in August and September in Jakarta and Palembang,

South Sumatra. Despite the onset of a bitter election campaign, the games were a moment of national unity and pride. A photo of Jokowi and Prabowo group hugging Hanifan Yudani Kusuma, a *pencak silat* athlete who had just won gold for Indonesia, went viral across social media. The Asian Games were another diplomatic coup for Indonesia, since it was the first time the games featured a unified Korean team, with South and North Korean athletes marching under the same flag and competing in events together. Despite issues such as air quality, the Asian Games were generally seen to be a success in promoting Indonesia's international standing and encouraging Indonesians to take an interest in sports. When Indonesia took over Vietnam's role as host at short notice, it was an opportunity to upgrade infrastructure in the capital, particularly given Jakarta's reputation as a congested traffic hub. The games were also highly secure, with intelligence agencies concerned about terrorist attacks, particularly after the Surabaya bomb attacks in May. With Jokowi announcing a bid for the 2032 Olympic Games, it remains to be seen whether such positive nationalist sentiments will be carried over into the election.

Volatile Economic Conditions amidst the U.S.-China Trade War

The major economic event of 2018 was the fall of Indonesia's currency, the rupiah. During 2018, the national currency traded at 15,000 rupiah, its lowest level against the U.S. dollar since the 1998 financial crisis. This was attributed to the U.S.-China trade war — in which both countries imposed tariffs on each other's goods — and very high volatility in oil prices, which had initially seen a strong rise through the first half of 2018. Indonesia remains a net oil-importing country and has one of the largest trade deficits among emerging economies. Jokowi's response was to restrict the import of non-strategic goods while increasing consumption of local products such as biodiesel that use Indonesian-produced palm oil. These conditions have already had a significant impact on Jokowi's infrastructure programme, with several projects that rely on imported materials being temporarily halted.[12] Also, Bank Indonesia raised the interest rate six times between May and year's end, by a total of 175 basis points, in order to defend the rupiah.[13]

Fears about the country descending into violence and riots reminiscent of 1998 were mitigated by the changed conditions in the country. One economist (and former advisor to Soeharto) sees the monetary fundamentals in Indonesia as "quite good", although he blames the Jokowi administration's panicked response for further spooking the markets.[14] Despite the volatility, S&P maintained the country's credit rating at BBB-/stable outlook (investment grade status). Bank Indonesia also changed its governor in May from Agus Martowardojo to Perry Warjiyo. Former finance minister Chatib Basri described the greatest achievement of Martowardojo's five-year tenure as the latter's success in providing greater stability to the economy.[15]

Overall, the economy remains in a good state, with GDP currently growing at 5.1 per cent per year, although this remains lower than what the government needs for its infrastructure plans. Additionally, labour force participation reached a two-decade high in February at 65.7 per cent, with unemployment at 5.1 per cent.[16] Compared to five years ago, the inflation rate has nearly halved, from 6.4 per cent to 3.4 per cent.[17] Due to social assistance programmes and an improved labour market, the poverty rate declined to 9.8 per cent in March 2018, compared to 10.6 per cent in March 2017.[18] Despite this, more than 25.9 million people live below the poverty line, with roughly an additional 20 per cent at risk of poverty.[19] With a growing population, and with a quarter of this population under the age of fourteen, ensuring adequate employment amidst the onset of a fourth industrial revolution will be part of any future president's priorities.

There are also other challenges ahead. As mentioned, infrastructure investment remains a necessary fixation of the Jokowi administration, particularly with the looming election. According to the Ministry of Finance, the government allocated US$28.1 billion (410.7 trillion rupiah) to infrastructure for 2018, the largest amount in Indonesian history. With tax compliance low, the shortfall will have to come from investors outside the country, a point Jokowi's 2019 opponent will capitalize on.

Trade

Indonesia posted its largest trade deficit of US$2.05 billion in November 2018, with its balance of trade swinging wildly between surplus (March, June and September) and deficit throughout the year. Partly this was caused by the rising cost of commodities coupled with the decreased cost of export goods such as palm kernel oil, crude palm oil and coal.

As with previous years, economic diplomacy remained a priority for the Jokowi administration. In response to growing U.S. protectionism under Trump, trade minister Enggartiasto Lukita led a delegation on a week-long visit to the United States in July to defend a programme that helps the growth of developing nations through lower tariffs. That said, as tariffs on Chinese products take greater effect, the World Bank calculates that Indonesia will have an opportunity to increase its exports to the United States at the expense of China.[20] This is however dependent on Indonesia increasing the competitiveness of its economy. In 2018, Indonesia's exports to the United States (totalling US$17.59 billion) fell 12.9 per cent from the previous year, while imports (totalling US$6.96 billion) rose by 1.4 per cent.[21] Meanwhile, trade relations between Indonesia and China continued to grow, with the signing of five contracts worth US$23.3 billion for infrastructure projects in April, including a hydropower plant and a facility to convert coal into dimethyl ether, which can be used as an alternative source of fuel. Indonesia's exports to China (totalling US$14.49 billion) were up 34.7 per cent year-on-year and comprised 15.4 per cent of its total exports, while its imports (totalling US$24.83 billion) increased by 32.0 per cent year-on-year and made up 27.4 per cent of total imports.[22] According to Indonesia's Ministry of Trade, overall trade with China was up by 27.59 per cent from 2017.[23] Despite these gains, Chinese investment slowed in the first half of 2018. Foreign direct investment was also down compared to the previous year.

Indonesia's economic engagement with China is not without hitches. While Chinese investment into Indonesia, particularly for infrastructure, has been welcomed by Jokowi's government, there have been concerns about an influx of Chinese migrants working on infrastructure projects. Addressing these perceptions, Foreign Minister Retno used the occasion of Premier Li Keqiang's state visit in May to state that she wanted to ensure that foreign investments came with transfers of technology that could add value to the domestic labour force.

In 2018, Indonesia continued to enter into trade agreements or related negotiations. For instance, Indonesia and the European Free Trade Association (EFTA) signed a comprehensive economic agreement in December, after eight years of negotiations.[24] The signing of a free trade agreement with Australia that was expected in 2018, however, proved more problematic. The leaders of both countries finalized the terms of the Indonesia-Australia Comprehensive Economic Partnership Agreement (IA-CEPA) in August, but the signing was delayed due to diplomatic tensions. Indonesian leaders, particularly Minister Retno, disapproved of Australia's announcement that it would consider moving its Israeli embassy from Tel Aviv to Jerusalem. Protests against the announcement were held in front of the Australian Embassy in Jakarta and the consulate in Surabaya. The announcement was seen as driven by a desire to match U.S. policy, although it was understood in Australia that the move was motivated by a by-election.[25] At the time of writing, the deal remains unsigned, and — with the rights of Palestinians remaining a sensitive issue in Indonesian domestic politics — Indonesian leaders might have to wait for an appropriate moment for its completion, which will most likely be after the election. The government is also expected to continue to negotiate trade deals in 2019 with Mozambique, Tunisia, Morocco and the European Union, as well as moving forward with the Regional Comprehensive Economic Partnership (RCEP), in order to further expand its exports and help reduce the trade deficit.

Foreign Policy: Indonesia Unveils its Vision of the Indo-Pacific

Indonesia's presence on the global stage was marked by taking greater ownership of shaping the Indo-Pacific construct. Jokowi began the year by articulating Indonesia's vision of the Indo-Pacific's norms and values. During a trip to New Delhi in January, he emphasized the centrality of ASEAN and ASEAN-related mechanisms, as well as the importance of encouraging bilateral and plurilateral cooperation as "building blocks" for the wider region.[26] Foreign Minister Retno elaborated on this vision throughout the year, including at the East Asia Summit foreign ministers' meeting in August, where she described Indonesia's vision of the Indo-Pacific as "open, transparent, inclusive, and respectful to international law."[27] Set against a backdrop of growing U.S.-China rivalry and increased military spending among emerging Indo-Pacific economies, Indonesia's promotion of ASEAN centrality is an attempt to keep the grouping relevant. The "inclusive" vision also openly rejects the language of containment towards China found often in the strategic discourse of the United States and its allies. As mentioned earlier, Indonesia cannot afford to be as openly antagonistic towards China as other states have been. That said, during Premier Li's visit, Retno highlighted the ASEAN Foreign Ministers Retreat statement that rejects the militarization of the South China Sea, which has been construed as indirect criticism of the rapid building of bases by China in the area.[28]

Indonesia has put some of this "building blocks" approach into practice, leading in areas such as cooperation on counterterrorism. In January, six Southeast Asian countries launched the "Our Eyes" intelligence grouping, an initiative of Defense Minister Ryamizard Ryacudu. Loosely based on the U.S.-led "Five Eyes" arrangement, senior defence officials from Indonesia, Malaysia, the Philippines, Thailand, Singapore and Brunei will meet fortnightly to promote information-sharing and intelligence exchange on potential terrorist or militant activities. Intelligence sharing has become more urgent in light of the declaration of a caliphate in Marawi city in the Philippines in 2017 by ISIS-affiliated fighters that included Indonesians and Malaysians. Indonesia, Malaysia and the Philippines have also continued to conduct coordinated maritime patrols in the seas between them to prevent the movement of potential militants between their shores. While Indonesia continues to work with partners such as the United States and Australia, the stepping-up of counterterrorism cooperation among Southeast Asian states, particularly when spearheaded by Indonesia, is a further positive step towards both addressing the threat's transnational nature and overcoming historical distrust between the countries in the region.

Throughout 2018, Indonesia was busy hosting other significant international groupings. First, in keeping with the Jokowi administration's maritime focus, was the 2018 Our Oceans conference on maritime protection and sustainability, which featured six presidents, one vice president, thirty-six ministers and other figures.[29] The conference ended with 305 new commitments, including 278 targets, while Indonesia unveiled an accountability system for tracking progress of the 663 commitments made at past conferences. Another significant event hosted by Indonesia was the 11th Bali Democracy Forum, in December. However, given the shifting political landscape and the gradual move towards authoritarianism in neighbouring countries such as Thailand, the Philippines, Cambodia and Myanmar, some analysts question whether Indonesia's foreign policy would be better served with more specific outcome-driven targets, rather than trying to improve various regional processes.[30]

There were few diplomatic disruptions during the year for Indonesia, save for a few important issues. One has been the country's balancing act between foreign ties and promoting human rights. In October, the Foreign Ministry filed an official protest after Saudi Arabia executed Indonesian domestic worker Tuti Tursilawati without prior notice. Sentenced to death in 2011 for killing her employer, she had claimed her action was an act of self-defence against sexual abuse. The inadequate protection of migrant workers in Saudi Arabia as well as in other parts of the Middle East has been a long-standing thorn in bilateral relations, culminating in a 2015 moratorium banning Indonesian citizens from working in twenty-one countries, mostly in the Middle East. While the protection of overseas Indonesian workers has been a key element of Jokowi's foreign policy, the need to retain good ties with Saudi Arabia — particularly to maintain access to the pilgrimage sites in Mecca and Medina — as well as a focus on domestic politics, means that this is a greater issue for the Foreign Ministry than for the president.

Indonesia also continued to play a role in human rights monitoring in Myanmar in 2018. In September, the Independent International Fact-Finding Mission on

Myanmar released its full report after fifteen months of investigations. The report called for Myanmar's military to be investigated and charged for genocide and human rights abuses against the Rohingya community, notably civilians including women and children.[31] Significant to this mission was the presence of former Indonesian Attorney General and human rights lawyer Marzuki Darusman as the chairperson. Marzuki had previously served as Special Rapporteur on human rights in North Korea. With Marzuki's involvement, Indonesia has a prominent role in the international investigation of human rights abuses of a fellow Southeast Asian country. While this does little to erode ASEAN's long-held norm of non-interference, Indonesia is well positioned to encourage other states to pay more attention to Myanmar's case. This will be bolstered in 2019 with Indonesia assuming its non-permanent seat on the UN Security Council.

However, Myanmar has an important political ally in China, with their burgeoning economic ties forming a key component of the latter's Belt and Road Initiative. With China voting against a briefing on the Myanmar situation in the UN Security Council, Indonesia must carefully navigate intra-ASEAN ties, relations with China, and its commitment to the protection of human rights. Indonesian foreign ministry officials have also conveyed their concerns about China's treatment of Muslims in the Xinjiang province, as more reports about Orwellian-like re-education camps for Uighurs have emerged over the year. Such concerns are partly motivated by the Chinese investment presence in Indonesia, but there have also been efforts by the Chinese government to win over major Islamic groups and political parties.[32] That said, domestic pressure has been mounting for the government to respond, particularly generated by Prabowo's Gerindra, that it remains to be seen whether this will become an election issue.

Security Issues: The Surabaya Bombings that Rocked the Nation

Aside from contending with fears about domestic instability from the fall of the rupiah and a slew of natural disasters, Indonesia experienced several significant security incidents in 2018. According to National Police Chief General Tito Karnavian, there were seventeen incidents of terrorism in 2018, compared to twelve in 2017.[33]

The month of May saw some of the country's deadliest attacks in several years. On 13 May, a series of suicide bombings were carried out at three churches in Indonesia's second-largest city, Surabaya. The perpetrators were a family of six that included two teenage boys and two daughters aged twelve and nine.

The weaponization of children sent shock waves through the country. The same day, three people of one family were killed after a bomb prematurely went off in an East Java apartment complex. The father of the family is believed to have belonged to the same terror cell as the church-bombing perpetrators. The next day, another family, including an eight-year-old child, approached the gates of a police station in Surabaya and detonated two explosive devices, killing the four adult perpetrators and injuring police and civilians. A total of thirty-one people were killed in this series of incidents, with two of the terror attacks being the first time a female suicide bomber and children were involved. The acts were seen as retaliation for the arrests of radical cleric Aman Abdurrahman and Zainal Anshori, who are, respectively, the spiritual leader and the head of the East Java chapter of the Jemaah Ansharut Daulah.

Aside from Christians, the police continued to be the main target of terror attacks in 2018. The Surabaya bombings followed a siege at a high-security prison in Depok, West Java, in which five police officers were held hostage and executed by inmates affiliated with the Islamic State. The siege began on the evening of 8 May when inmates seized weapons and attacked their guards. The rioters were subdued only after two days. The incident resulted in the deaths of five police officers and one inmate, and the transfer of 155 terrorist detainees to a more secure facility. There were two further attacks after the prison riot. One saw the fatal stabbing of a police officer in Depok by a suspect during questioning. Another, on 16 May, was a sword attack on police in Riau province resulting in the death of a police officer and four attackers. The attackers were suspected of belonging to the ISIS-affiliated Negara Islam Indonesia and being linked to the Surabaya bombing cell.[34]

In the wake of the Surabaya attacks, the passing of a number of amendments to Indonesia's 2003 anti-terrorism laws was hastened. The old legislation had been seen by police chief Karnavian as a factor in the state's inability to adequately prevent such attacks.[35] As part of the revision process, extensive consultations were held with religious groups, civil society and academia. Although changes to the law had first been mooted in February 2016, the president's threat to issue an executive order if the bill was not passed before June 2018, as well as the shocking use of children in the Surabaya attacks, proved to be decisive factors in its eventual passage at the end of May.

Significant among the amendments is the new definition of terrorism as an act that has "political and ideological motives and threaten[s] national security".[36] The changes also allow police to hold a suspect for 14 days without charge (increased from 7) and for 290 days after charging a suspect (increased from 180). The military can also be involved at the request of the police chief, thus increasing the scope of domestic security activities that soldiers can be involved in. Other changes included the reactivation of the military's Joint Special Operations Command, which draws personnel from all three services to create an elite counterterrorism team. Some of the amendments have caused consternation among some human rights groups, who argue that a broader, more ambiguous, definition of terrorism could be misused against domestic political groups. Human Rights Watch also objected to the military's involvement because of concerns that their lack of law enforcement training could lead to a sense of impunity.[37]

Aside from terrorism, there have been occasional outbreaks of violence across the archipelago; most notably in December, when separatists killed at least seventeen construction workers in a remote village in Papua's Nduga Regency and a soldier at a military outpost. The National Liberation Army of West Papua, the military wing of the Free Papua Movement (OPM), claimed responsibility for the attack, arguing that the construction of a bridge was to aid military and police movements, and not for the benefit of the people.[38] While the separatists claim that the workers were seen as being part of the military and therefore merely collateral damage, the government has responded that they were civilians employed to build bridges. Previously, the separatist group had also killed three construction workers on the Trans Papua highway, in March 2016. One of Jokowi's priorities has been to increase development in the Papuan provinces, particularly through transport infrastructure such as the Trans Papua highway. Workers from other parts of Indonesia have been employed to do this, further aggravating the Papuans, who have long resisted the deliberate transmigration policies of the Soeharto regime. One Papuan leader has said that development means a loss of land for the people.[39] The subsequent military operation conducted against the perpetrators of the December attacks has terrified locals, with some three hundred of them having fled their villages.[40] Accusations that the military killed four civilians during its operations, questions about the sources of the separatists weapons, corruption and social tensions will add to the unrest that will continue in Papua and West Papua provinces in the near future.

Given the significance of Indonesia's maritime domain, there were relatively few major incidents in the year, compared with 2016 and 2017. Unlike previous years, there were no high-profile collisions, nor were there any provocative policy announcements such as the Indonesian declaration of the North Natuna Sea in 2017. Although Indonesia's military chief unveiled a new naval base in the Natuna Islands in December, this was part of a long-standing plan to consolidate maritime defences, and it did not draw the same kind of public rebuke by Chinese officials as the naming of the North Natuna Sea. As mentioned earlier, there are senior officials in Jokowi's cabinet who are keen to position Indonesia as a bridge between China and the United States.[41] Indonesia's elites appear to be divided on the degree to which China should be courted as a closer partner, which the Foreign Ministry supports, or kept more at arm's length, which the Ministry for Maritime Affairs and Fisheries supports.[42]

In a year of a U.S.-China trade war and tensions with North Korea, Indonesia continued to build ties among its Indo-Pacific security partners. Notably, in the Indian Ocean, ties with India are going from strength to strength. During Prime Minister Narendra Modi's Jakarta visit in May, he announced bilateral relations would be upgraded to a comprehensive strategic partnership. During bilateral talks between the defence ministers in October, Indonesia expressed support for India's involvement in maritime patrols along the Straits of Malacca.[43] The next month, Indonesia and India held the first iteration of a new naval exercise named Samudra Sakti. This is part of a deepening of ties within the Indo-Pacific as U.S. leadership is perceived to further fade under the Trump administration, and with ties to close partners and allies in increasing doubt after the resignation of Defense Secretary James Mattis in December.

Backsliding in Social and Religious Pluralism?

In the year after Ahok's 2017 blasphemy conviction and imprisonment, there was much discussion of whether Indonesia's religious pluralism has degraded during Jokowi's tenure. The Jakarta-based Setara Institute recorded 109 violations between January and July 2018 of the constitutionally guaranteed freedom of religion and belief in 20 out of 34 provinces — an increase of 80 cases over the same period the year before.[44] With the Surabaya church bombings, Christian Indonesians have reported feeling more restricted in religious expression in the country.[45] For Christians of Chinese heritage, their feelings of exclusion are not without justification; a 2017 survey found that non-Chinese Indonesians still harboured prejudice and negative stereotypes against their ethnic-Chinese compatriots, particularly after the Ahok trial.[46] In August, a district court in North Sumatra convicted a Chinese Buddhist women of blasphemy for complaining about the volume of the loudspeaker at a local mosque. December was marked by the desecration of a Catholic grave in Yogyakarta when residents cut the top off a crucifix that was seen as too large and family members were prevented from holding prayers. Residents also argued that the Muslim-majority community would not allow Christians to be buried there in future. Overall, these high-profile cases can further entrench the perceptions of religious intolerance.

However, are such strained inter-religious ties caused by rising conservatism or religious radicalism among Muslims during the Jokowi era? A 2018 study has shown a decline in the levels of religious intolerance or radicalism among Indonesians between 2010 and 2016, but it also revealed a shift in the socio-economic profiles of those who hold more conservative values.[47] In other words, there has been "a shift of the epicentre of conservative-radical attitudes from the lower classes to the middle classes and elites".[48] Further, an absence of Islamic political parties that could cater to the sentiments of this demographic means greater support for more hard-line Islamic organizations such as the Islamic Defenders Front (FPI). This is significant, not only for next year's election but for Indonesia's pluralism in general. Having been instrumental in garnering support for the Action 212 protests, the head of the FPI, Rizieq Shihab, is expected to support Prabowo's campaign. That said, a recent survey found that Action 212 protestors and their alumni preferred the Jokowi-Maaruf slate to Prabowo-Sandiaga.[49] Either way, these potential voters will compel both sets of candidates to pay attention to their more conservative and increasingly hard-line agenda. Therefore, there is every reason to take groups such as FPI seriously.

More broadly, the increased visibility and influence of groups such as FPI has intensified debate as to whether Indonesia is taking an "illiberal" turn. Several significant developments in 2018 support these perceptions. In March, a law known as UU MD3, which criminalizes criticism of public officials, came into effect. Specifically, legal action can be taken against individuals or groups who "degrade the honor of the DPR or DPR members". Without a clear definition for "degradation", this was seen by critics as a backward step in Indonesia's democratic development, arguing that it would be used for silencing criticism of politicians.[50] While the president publicly stated he did not endorse the bill, this act was merely symbolic. The president, or his representative, is constitutionally mandated to have been briefed on the content of the bill, and he is involved in the process of lawmaking. With the support of eight out of ten coalition parties, it is clear that his government supported the amendments through their drafting and passage. Some of the proposed articles, including the one publicly criticized, eventually were struck down unanimously by Indonesia's Constitutional Court in June. Nevertheless, the case demonstrates how willing Indonesia's political parties are to support measures that could erode accountability. This follows last year's parliamentary decision to approve Jokowi's presidential decree on mass organizations, which confers power to the Minister for Law and Human Rights to ban any organization deemed to oppose the official ideology of Pancasila. Critics remain concerned about the misuse of this legislation to silence political opposition in the future.

Amendments to Indonesia's Criminal Code were also debated and were anticipated to pass during the year. Human rights groups, commentators and even some political parties expressed alarm at clauses that could criminalize cohabitation between unmarried couples and homosexual acts, effectively curtailing individual freedoms. If the amendments are not passed before the next election (as is Jokowi's intent), according to the head of the revision team, the discussion will have to begin again.[51] Thus, over the course of 2018, the final full year of Jokowi's presidency, there were lamentable incidents in social and religious pluralism and indeed some worrying legislative developments whose full force will be made known in the years to come.

Conclusion

In his overview of 2017, Priyambudi Sulistiyanto wrote that Jokowi might consider "the politics of accommodation", particularly to address wealth disparity and grievances over majority-minority issues. With the selection of Ma'ruf Amin, it seems as though Jokowi has opted for this strategy in courting political Islam to secure the outcome of the 2019 election. Although his party did not necessarily win in key provinces during the 2018 regional elections, his high polling numbers throughout the year suggest that the election next year remains his to lose. He must continue to underscore his performance in pushing forward his national development agenda and maintaining stable ties with key trade and investment partners. If he can capitalize on successes such as the Asian Games and hold back populist criticism by Prabowo, he will sail to the finish. That said, the opposition will remain poised to exploit a global economic environment that is able to weaken the rupiah and cast sufficient doubt on Jokowi's future prospects. In 2019, Jokowi must be ready to weather the coming storm.

Notes

1. See, for example, Edward Aspinall and Mada Sukmajati, eds. *Electoral Dynamics in Indonesia: Money Politics, Patronage and Clientelism at the Grassroots* (Singapore: NUS Press, 2016).
2. Marguerite Afra Sapiie, "Government is Representation of God on Earth: State Palace Official", *Jakarta Post*, 24 May 2018 <https://www.thejakartapost.com/news/2018/05/24/government-is-representation-of-god-on-earth-state-palace-official.html> (accessed 24 December 2018).

3. Jeremy Menchik, "Crafting Indonesian Democracy: Inclusion-Moderation and the Sacralizing of the Postcolonial State", in *Democratic Transition in the Muslim World: A Global Perspective*, edited by Alfred Stepan (New York: Columbia University Press, 2018).
4. Yohanes Sulaiman, "Incumbent Jokowi versus Prabowo — Who Will Win Indonesia's Presidential Election?", *The Conversation*, 17 December 2018 <https://theconversation.com/incumbent-jokowi-versus-prabowo-who-will-win-indonesias-presidential-election-108338> (accessed 23 December 2018).
5. Karina M. Tehusijarana, "Indonesia Could Go 'Extinct' If I Lose Election: Prabowo", *Jakarta Post*, 18 December 2018 <https://www.thejakartapost.com/news/2018/12/18/indonesia-could-go-extinct-if-i-lose-election-prabowo.html> (accessed 24 December 2018).
6. For a complete list of priority projects and their status, see Committee for Acceleration of Priority Infrastructure, "List of KPPIP Priority Projects", Government of the Republic of Indonesia <https://kppip.go.id/en/priority-projects/> (accessed 5 January 2019).
7. Aisyah Llewellyn, "Indonesia's Elections and the Local Result", *The Interpreter*, 9 July 2018 <https://www.lowyinstitute.org/the-interpreter/indonesia-elections-and-local-result> (accessed 22 December 2018); Deasy Simandjuntak, Eve Warburton and Charlotte Setijadi, "Are Indonesia's Regional Elections a Barometer for 2019?", *East Asia Forum*, 22 June 2018 <http://www.eastasiaforum.org/2018/06/22/are-indonesias-regional-elections-a-barometer-for-2019/> (accessed 22 December 2018).
8. ReliefWeb, "Situation Update No. 12 M 7.4 Earthquake & Tsunami, Sulawesi, Indonesia", 15 October 2018 <https://reliefweb.int/sites/reliefweb.int/files/resources/AHA-Situation_Update-no12-Sulawesi-EQ-rev.pdf> (accessed 4 January 2019).
9. ReliefWeb, "Displacement and Protection Cluster — Earthquake in Lombok 2018 — Narrative Report — 19 September 2018", 19 September 2018 <https://reliefweb.int/report/indonesia/displacement-and-protection-cluster-earthquake-lombok-2018-narrative-report-19> (accessed 4 January 2019).
10. "Number of Injured in Indonesia Tsunami Surges to over 14,000", *The Star Online*, 31 December 2018 <https://www.thestar.com.my/news/regional/2018/12/31/number-of-injured-in-indonesia-tsunami-surges-to-over-14000/> (accessed 4 January 2019); "Indonesia Tsunami: Death Toll from Anak Krakatau Volcano Rises", BBC News, 25 December 2018 <https://www.bbc.com/news/world-asia-46674490> (accessed 4 January 2019); Anne Barker, "Indonesia Tsunami Survivors, Tourists Fear Second Disaster as Anak Krakatau Volcano Continues to Erupt", ABC News, 7 January 2019 <https://www.abc.net.au/news/2019-01-07/indonesia-tsunami-survivors-fear-second-disaster/10688248> (accessed 9 January 2019).
11. David Lipson, "Lombok's Tourist Haven Remains a Scene of Destruction Following Series of Earthquakes", ABC News, 26 August 2018 <https://www.abc.net.au/news/2018-08-26/lomboks-tourist-haven-remains-a-scene-of-destruction/10164980> (accessed 4 January 2019).

12. "Indonesian Rupiah Falls to Record Low amid Rising Pressures", *Straits Times*, 3 October 2018 <https://www.straitstimes.com/asia/se-asia/indonesian-rupiah-falls-to-record-low-amid-rising-pressures> (accessed 2 December 2018).
13. Shotaro Tani, "Bank Indonesia Ends Tumultuous Year on a Silent Note with No Change in Rates", 20 December 2018 <https://asia.nikkei.com/Economy/Bank-Indonesia-ends-tumultuous-year-on-a-silent-note-with-no-change-in-rates> (accessed 28 December 2018).
14. Steve Hanke, "The Fall in the Value of the Indonesian Rupiah — Déjà Vu 1998?", *Forbes*, 17 September 2018 <https://www.forbes.com/sites/stevehanke/2018/09/17/the-fall-in-the-value-of-the-indonesian-rupiah-deja-vu-1998/#10f768446eee> (accessed 2 December 2018).
15. Karlis Salna, "Indonesian Central Bank Governor's Exit is a Déjà Vu", Bloomberg, 15 May 2018 <https://www.bloomberg.com/news/articles/2018-05-15/it-s-deja-vu-for-indonesia-s-central-bank-governor-as-he-exits> (accessed 2 December 2018).
16. World Bank, *Indonesia Economic Quarterly: Urbanization for All*, September 2018, p. 23 <http://documents.worldbank.org/curated/en/498361537371495086/pdf/130014-REVISED-IEQ-Sept-2018-ENG-for-web-revised.pdf>.
17. Department of Foreign Affairs and Trade, "Indonesia Fact Sheet", Government of Australia, December 2018 <https://dfat.gov.au/trade/resources/Documents/indo.pdf> (accessed 2 December 2018).
18. World Bank, *Indonesia Economic Quarterly: Urbanization for All*, p. 27.
19. World Bank, "Indonesia Country Overview", 25 September 2018 <https://www.worldbank.org/en/country/indonesia/overview> (accessed 2 December 2018).
20. World Bank, *Indonesia Economic Quarterly: Strengthening Competitiveness*, December 2018, pp. 33–34 <https://openknowledge.worldbank.org/bitstream/handle/10986/30969/IEQ2018Dec.pdf>.
21. United States Census Bureau, "Trade in Goods with Indonesia" <https://www.census.gov/foreign-trade/balance/c5600.html> (accessed 2 December 2018).
22. Ministry of Commerce, "Statistics on China-Indonesia Trade in January–July, 2018", Government of China, 4 September 2018 <http://english.mofcom.gov.cn/article/statistic/lanmubb/ASEAN/201809/20180902788480.shtml> (accessed 3 December 2018).
23. Ministry of Trade, "Balance of Trade with Trade Partner Country: China", Government of Republic of Indonesia <http://www.kemendag.go.id/en/economic-profile/indonesia-export-import/balance-of-trade-with-trade-partner-country?negara=116> (accessed 3 December 2018).
24. "Indonesia and EFTA Countries Sign Trade Agreement", *Jakarta Post*, 21 December 2018 <https://www.thejakartapost.com/adv/2018/12/21/indonesia-and-efta-countries-sign-trade-agreement.html> (accessed 28 December 2018).
25. David Wroe, "Not One Government Official Was Consulted about Australia's Major Israel Foreign Policy Shift", *Sydney Morning Herald*, 25 October 2018 <https://www.smh.com.au/politics/federal/not-one-government-official-was-consulted-about-australia-

s-major-israel-foreign-policy-shift-20181025-p50bwo.html> (accessed 3 December 2018).

26. Office of Presidential Staff, "Kemitraan ASEAN-India Ciptakan Kestabilan Kawasan Indo-Pasifik" [ASEAN-India partnership creates stability in the Indo-Pacific region], Government of the Republic of Indonesia <http://presidenri.go.id/berita-aktual/kemitraan-asean-india-ciptakan-kestabilan-kawasan-indo-pasifik.html> (accessed 29 November 2018).
27. Ministry of Foreign Affairs, "Introducing the Indo-Pacific Concept, Indonesia Set the Tone at the East Asia Summit", Government of Republic of Indonesia, 6 August 2018 <https://www.kemlu.go.id/en/berita/Pages/Introducing-the-Indo-Pacific-Concept,-Indonesia-Set-the-Tone-at-the-East-Asia-Summit.aspx> (accessed 28 November 2018).
28. "Indonesia to Push for Better Trade Balance with China during Premier Li Keqiang's Visit", *Straits Times*, 5 May 2018 <https://www.straitstimes.com/asia/se-asia/indonesia-to-push-for-better-trade-balance-with-china-during-premier-li-keqiangs-visit> (accessed 29 November 2018).
29. "Susi Wants System to Track Commitments Made in Ocean Conference", *Tempo*, 29 October 2018 <https://en.tempo.co/read/922945/susi-wants-system-to-track-commitments-made-in-ocean-conference/full&view=ok> (accessed 30 November 2018).
30. Evan A. Laksmana, "Indonesian Foreign Policy Needs to Focus More on Impact Than Process", *Jakarta Post*, 15 December 2018 <https://www.thejakartapost.com/academia/2018/12/15/indonesian-foreign-policy-needs-to-focus-more-on-impact-than-process.html> (accessed 28 December 2018).
31. Office of the United Nations High Commissioner for Human Rights, "Myanmar: UN Fact-Finding Mission Releases its Full Account of Massive Violations by Military in Rakhine, Kachin and Shan States", 18 September 2018 <https://www.ohchr.org/EN/NewsEvents/Pages/DisplayNews.aspx?NewsID=23575&LangID=E> (accessed 2 December 2018).
32. Jon Emont, "China Goes All Out to Win Favor with Indonesian Muslims", *Washington Post*, 1 July 2016 <https://www.washingtonpost.com/world/asia_pacific/china-goes-all-out-to-curry-favor-with-indonesian-muslims/2016/06/30/caee52d4-3e08-11e6-9e16-4cf01a41decb_story.html> (accessed 2 December 2018).
33. "'Arrest First, Get Evidence Later': Police Record More Terrorism Cases", *Jakarta Post*, 27 December 2018 <https://www.thejakartapost.com/news/2018/12/27/arrest-first-get-evidence-later-police-record-more-terrorism-cases.html> (accessed 28 December 2018).
34. Audrey Santoso, "Ini Identitas 4 Teroris Penyerang Mapolda Riau" [This is the identity of the Riau police post terrorists], Detik.com, 16 May 2018 <https://news.detik.com/berita/d-4023568/ini-identitas-4-teroris-penyerang-mapolda-riau> (accessed 5 December 2018); Sapto Andika Candra, "Teroris di Pekanbaru Diduga Miliki Jaringan dengan Surabaya" [Terrorists in Pekanbaru suspected of links to Surabaya],

Republika, 16 May 2018 <https://www.republika.co.id/berita/nasional/hukum/18/05/16/p8ttbp430-teroris-di-pekanbaru-diduga-miliki-jaringan-dengan-surabaya> (accessed 5 December 2018).

35. Karnavian notes the inability for police to conduct follow-up investigations under the previous laws: Feri Agus, "Bom Surabaya, Tito Mohon Jokowi Terbitkan Perppu Terorisme" [Surabaya bombing, Tito requests Jokowi to publish terrorism presidential decree], CNN Indonesia, 13 May 2018 <https://www.cnnindonesia.com/nasional/20180513173418-12-297830/bom-surabaya-tito-mohon-jokowi-terbitkan-perppu-terorisme> (accessed 5 December 2018).
36. The full text of the new amendments is available here: Audit Board of Indonesia, "Undang-undang (UU) Nomor 5 Tahun 2018" [Law number 5 of 2018], Government of the Republic of Indonesia <https://peraturan.bpk.go.id/Home/Details/82689/uu-no-5-tahun-2018> (accessed 6 December 2018).
37. "Indonesia: New Counterterrorism Law Imperils Rights", Human Rights Watch, 20 June 2018 <https://www.hrw.org/news/2018/06/20/indonesia-new-counterterrorism-law-imperils-rights> (accessed 6 December 2018).
38. Helen Davidson and agencies, "West Papua: Conflicting Reports Surround Attack that Killed up to 31", *The Guardian*, 5 December 2018 <https://www.theguardian.com/world/2018/dec/05/west-papua-fears-of-spiralling-violence-after-attack-leaves-up-to-31-dead> (accessed 10 December 2018).
39. "Indonesia Attack: Gunmen Kill 24 Construction Workers in Papua", BBC News, 4 December 2018 <https://www.bbc.com/news/world-asia-46446719> (accessed 10 December 2018).
40. "Papua Leaders Demand End to Indonesian Military Operation", BBC News, 21 December 2018 <https://www.bbc.com/news/world-asia-46651420> (accessed 7 January 2018).
41. Luhut B. Pandjaitan, "How Indonesia Could be a Bridge between China and the US in Asia", *South China Morning Post*, 9 April 2018 <http://www.scmp.com/print/comment/insight-opinion/article/2140834/how-indonesia-could-be-bridge-between-china-and-us-asia> (accessed 29 November 2018).
42. Emirza Adi Syailendra, "Indonesia's Elite Divided on China", *East Asia Forum*, 20 April 2018 <http://www.eastasiaforum.org/2018/04/20/indonesias-elite-divided-on-china/> (accessed 28 November 2018).
43. "How Indonesia Could be a Bridge between China and the US in Asia", *Times of India*, 23 October 2018 <https://timesofindia.indiatimes.com/india/india-indonesia-decide-to-boost-maritime-cooperation/articleshow/66337273.cms> (accessed 28 November 2018).
44. Saifulbahri Ismail, "Religious Intolerance on the Rise in Indonesia: Survey | Video", Channel News Asia, 28 September 2018 <https://www.channelnewsasia.com/news/videos/religious-intolerance-on-the-rise-in-indonesia-survey-video-10765606> (accessed 3 January 2019).

45. See, for example, Max Walden, "'We Really Feel Afraid': Indonesia's Religious Pluralism under Threat — Report", *Asian Correspondent*, 2 August 2017 <https://asiancorrespondent.com/2017/08/really-feel-afraid-indonesias-religious-pluralism-threat-report/> (accessed 3 January 2019).
46. Charlotte Setijadi, "Chinese Indonesians in the Eyes of the Pribumi Public", *ISEAS Perspective*, no. 73 (27 September 2017) <https://www.iseas.edu.sg/images/pdf/ISEAS_Perspective_2017_73.pdf>.
47. Marcus Mietzner and Burhanuddin Muhtadi, "Explaining the 2016 Islamist Mobilisation in Indonesia: Religious Intolerance, Militant Groups and the Politics of Accommodation", *Asian Studies Review* 42, no. 3 (3 July 2018): 479–97 <https://doi.org/10.1080/10357823.2018.1473335>.
48. Ibid., p. 484.
49. Ahmad Faiz Ibnu Sani, "Survey Finds Reuni 212 Members Ignoring Rizieq Shihab", *Tempo*, 21 December 2018 <https://en.tempo.co/read/1157549/survey-finds-reuni-212-members-ignoring-rizieq-shihab/full&view=ok> (accessed 3 January 2019).
50. "Indonesian Parliament Accused of Plunging Country into 'Dark Era of Democracy' with New Law Criminalizing its Critics", *Coconuts Jakarta*, 13 February 2018 <https://coconuts.co/jakarta/news/indonesian-parliament-accused-plunging-country-dark-era-democracy-new-law-criminalizing-critics/> (accessed 3 January 2019).
51. Kristian Erdianto, "Presiden Jokowi Ingin Pembahasan RKUHP Dipercepat" [President Jokowi wants to discuss accelerated RKUHP], *Kompas*, 7 March 2018 <https://nasional.kompas.com/read/2018/03/08/17501691/presiden-jokowi-ingin-pembahasan-rkuhp-dipercepat> (accessed 3 January 2019).

INDONESIA-CHINA RELATIONS: Coming Full Circle?

Dewi Fortuna Anwar

The bilateral relations between Indonesia and the People's Republic of China seem to have come full circle. The current state of relations between Jakarta and Beijing brings to mind the earlier period of close bilateral ties during the later years of President Sukarno's presidency until his fall in late 1965. Although President Soeharto had already normalized relations with China in 1990 — after freezing diplomatic ties in 1967 — bilateral relations between Indonesia and China only improved significantly after the fall of Soeharto in mid-1998. Successive Indonesian presidents since the onset of the *Reformasi* era have placed great importance in forging closer relations with China, an increasingly important economic powerhouse as well as a major regional and global player. The momentum for enhanced cooperation between Indonesia and China gathered pace during the Yudhoyono presidency (2004–14) with the signing of the "Strategic Partnership" in 2005, which was then elevated to a "Comprehensive Strategic Partnership" in 2013. Under President Joko Widodo (popularly known as Jokowi), Indonesia-China relations have become even closer, especially in the economic field. China is now Indonesia's most important trading partner and a major source of foreign investment for the government's signature infrastructure projects, while Chinese tourists constitute the largest group of visitors to Indonesia.

The increasingly close economic relations between Indonesia and China, particularly under the Jokowi presidency, and their wider social, political and security ramifications have attracted considerable scholarly attention lately, as

---

DEWI FORTUNA ANWAR is Research Professor at the Research Center for Politics, Indonesian Institute of Sciences and Vice Chairman of the Board of Directors at The Habibie Center in Jakarta.

well as public scrutiny and concern. Many analysts have underlined the fact that domestic dynamics have always been the primary drivers of Indonesia's foreign policy, and that elite as well as public opinions are divided over the current rise of China, which is seen as both a threat and an opportunity.[1] While differences of opinions and competition for power and influence are to be expected in a democracy — and in Indonesia's highly heterogeneous society — some degree of consensus is needed to ensure that a particular policy can be adopted and sustained in the long run. Jakarta-Beijing relations have always, since diplomatic ties were first established in 1950, been complicated. And more than with any other country, relations with China continue to impinge on Indonesian domestic affairs, particularly as a consequence of the significant Chinese-Indonesian population.

The sharp swing in Indonesia's policy from Sukarno's Jakarta-Beijing axis to Soeharto's total freezing of relations with China throughout most of the New Order period was mainly caused by sharp differences in the two leaders' perceptions about threats and priorities and the forces that supported them. With the long period of socio-political control during the New Order era (1966–98), the deep social and ideological cleavages that had characterized Indonesia's early turbulent history had mostly been overcome — but not entirely erased. Political liberalization has opened the path for the re-emergence of identity politics (*aliran* politics), particularly during Indonesia's highly competitive election cycles. While the rapprochement between Indonesia and China is to be welcomed, and should be nurtured, it must be noted that this particular state of relations is being contested. President Joko Widodo has come under increasing criticism for not sufficiently protecting Indonesia's wider national interests in his pursuit of Chinese foreign investment. Great care must therefore be taken to address all of the issues that have arisen. Left unattended they may jeopardize all the gains that have been made, which in turn could risk the return of the darker period of fraught Jakarta-Beijing relations.

From Close Partnership to Long Estrangement

The ups and downs of Indonesia-China relations from the Sukarno to the Soeharto era have been exhaustively analysed by many scholars. In this section, we will skim over the evolution of the bilateral relations during this earlier period to highlight a number of issues that may continue to colour present and future relations between Jakarta and Beijing. While the past should not be allowed to hold the future hostage, forgetting history may condemn us to repeat it.

Indonesia, which declared its independence on 17 August 1945 but only achieved complete independence after the formal transfer of sovereignty from the Dutch colonial government on 27 December 1949, was among the first countries that accorded recognition to the People's Republic of China, soon after the latter's formation on 1 October 1949. Jakarta and Beijing established diplomatic relations on 13 April 1950, while all of the Western developed countries and their allies, under the aegis of the United States, continued to recognize the Republic of China with its capital in Taipei well into the 1970s. This was a clear early manifestation of Indonesia's independent and active foreign policy doctrine, first enunciated by Vice President Mohammad Hatta in 1948. Although Indonesia and the United States had already established diplomatic relations a few months earlier, on the day after Indonesia became fully sovereign,[2] Indonesia had from the very beginning adhered to a "One-China" policy, recognizing Beijing as the capital, a policy that was sustained even when diplomatic relations with China were frozen.

In the decade following its independence, Indonesia tried to forge close relations with both camps in the Cold War; for, despite sharp ideological divisions between the different domestic political factions during the era of parliamentary democracy, the *bebas aktif* ("independent and active") foreign policy doctrine was well accepted by all sides.[3] The high point of Indonesia's diplomatic activism during this period was its hosting of the first Asian-African Conference in Bandung in April 1955, to which China's Prime Minister Chou En-Lai was invited. This was the first international event that the Communist Chinese leader attended, and the visit marked the beginning of closer relations between Jakarta and Beijing. During Chou's visit, Indonesia and China signed the Dual Nationality Treaty on 22 April 1955, which compelled *Tionghoa* (Chinese-Indonesian) residents who held dual nationalities to choose to become the citizen of either China or Indonesia.[4]

The warming of relations between Indonesia and China during this period of the Cold War however alarmed the anti-communist forces in Indonesia, particularly the Islamic parties and the army. President Sukarno, who visited China in mid-1956, was reported to have admired Mao Tse-Tung and Chou En-Lai. Besides state-to-state relations, the Chinese Communist Party also forged party-to-party relations with the Indonesian Communist Party (PKI).[5] The anti-communist forces grew increasingly concerned that the closer Jakarta-Beijing ties would further strengthen the PKI, which then had already been brought into the ruling coalition under Prime Minister Ali Sastroamidjojo of the Indonesian Nationalist Party (PNI) in his first cabinet from July 1953 to July 1955. (The PNI was founded by

Sukarno in 1927.)[6] At Indonesia's first general elections, held on 29 September 1955, the PKI emerged as the party with the fourth-largest number of seats, behind the PNI, the Masyumi (modernist Islamic party) and the Nahdatul Ulama (traditionalist Islamic party).[7]

Widening political divisions at the centre and the grievances of regional military commanders against Jakarta led to the outbreak of PRRI Permesta regional rebellions centred in West Sumatra and North Sulawesi in February 1958.[8] The rebellions were led by anti-communist and U.S.-friendly politicians from Masyumi and the Indonesian Socialist Party (PSI) who had been forced to flee Jakarta due to intimidation from PKI supporters.[9] Among the demands of the rebels were the disbandment of the PKI and the reappointment of Vice President Mohammad Hatta, a West Sumatran who was staunchly anti-communist and had resigned from his position due to increasing differences of opinions with President Sukarno.[10] The regional rebels received covert support from the British in neighbouring Malaya, as well as from the United States, which was then pursuing a policy of containing Communist China and was thus increasingly concerned by Jakarta's tilt towards Beijing.[11] The Indonesian central government was however able to defeat the PRRI Permesta rebellions easily, since the central army leadership, while sympathetic to some of the rebels' demands, could not tolerate any rebellion against the legitimate government.

This history is worth recounting, as the regional rebellions, particularly in West Sumatra, have left a deep scar and deep-seated antipathy towards Sukarno and Sukarnoism, which may explain why in recent times the PDI-P, the successor party of the PNI led by Sukarno's daughter Megawati Sukarnoputri, has never fared well electorally in the region. It may also be of interest that one of the PSI leaders who joined the regional rebellions was the economist Sumitro Djojohadikusumo, the father of the 2014 and 2019 presidential candidate, Prabowo Subianto. In the 2014 presidential election, Jokowi, a PDI-P cadre, obtained only slightly more than twenty per cent of the votes in West Sumatra, while Prabowo swept the rest, which reveals a clear manifestation of the long shadow of history in contemporary Indonesian politics.

In the aftermath, Masyumi and the PSI were banned, which removed the most critical voices against President Sukarno. Subsequently, with the presidential decree of 5 July 1959, Indonesia's first experiment with liberal democracy collapsed, replaced by the so-called Demokrasi Terpimpin ("Guided Democracy") and the restoration of the 1945 constitution, which provides for a strong presidential system. The period of Guided Democracy was dominated by the triangular relations between President Sukarno, the army and the PKI: the PKI needed the protection of President Sukarno against the army that sought to destroy it, while President Sukarno needed the mass support provided by the PKI to counterbalance the powerful army.[12]

During this period, President Sukarno's foreign policy was shaped by his strong opposition to neocolonialism and imperialism, which he regarded as directly threatening Indonesia. The covert support given by the British and the United States to the PRRI Permesta rebels only reinforced Sukarno's threat perception,[13] while the formation of the Malaysian Federation, which included the British North Borneo territories and Singapore, affirmed his suspicions of a British ploy to retain influence in the region and encircle Indonesia. When Sukarno launched a "crush Malaysia" campaign in 1963,[14] China was one of the few countries that supported Indonesia's *Konfrontasi*, or confrontation, against the newly formed Malaysian Federation. This led to the establishment of the Jakarta-Beijing axis (and Sukarno telling the United States "to go to hell with its aid"), which was to last until his fall in 1965.

Meanwhile, the army, which had become increasingly involved in politics under the Guided Democracy,[15] mostly deferred to Sukarno on matters relating to foreign policy. However, the *Konfrontasi* against Malaysia gave plenty of scope to the PKI's mobilization skills and brought Jakarta ever closer to Beijing, and this greatly alarmed the army leadership. The heightened competition between the army and the PKI to succeed the ailing President Sukarno came to a head with the murder of several senior army generals in the late hours of 30 September 1965. The event, which came to be known as the Gestapu affair, was alleged to have been carried out by the PKI with the backing of China in an attempt to seize the initiative against the army. In the counter-coup that followed, President Sukarno was forced out of power by the army under the command of General Soeharto, while the PKI was banned and its followers either killed or jailed.[16] China, whom the army accused of supplying arms to the PKI, was regarded as the primary threat to Indonesian security and political stability due to its subversive activities in supporting the local communists. The army-dominated New Order government froze Indonesia's diplomatic relations with China on 30 October 1967, and this would last for over two decades.[17]

The position and role of the PKI was not the only thorny issue that marred early relations between Jakarta and Beijing. The sizeable presence of the *Tionghoa* community in Indonesia, who have played a critical role in Indonesia's economy since the colonial period, has often attracted the distrust and jealousy of the indigenous population. Efforts by successive governments in Beijing to mobilize support among overseas Chinese had the effect of rendering suspect the latter's loyalty to their respective host countries, including Indonesia. For instance, on 19 March 1956, at the All-Indonesian Congress of National Importers in Surabaya, the keynote speaker, Assaat, a businessman and former leading politician from Masyumi, blamed the ethnic Chinese for many of Indonesia's economic difficulties. He condemned them as a group of opportunists who had helped the Dutch during the colonial period, and who had supported Chiang Kai-shek in China during the period of Kuomintang rule, only to shift their support to the PRC under Mao Tse-tung. He also asserted that it was difficult to distinguish between Chinese who were Indonesian citizens and Chinese foreign nationals. Assaat called for a specific racially based economic policy favouring indigenous Indonesians against Chinese competition in the local economy, a call that drew widespread support throughout the country.[18]

Anti-Chinese sentiments remained high among large sections of the indigenous population, even as Indonesia's relations with China grew increasingly closer during the Guided Democracy era. In 1959, the Indonesian government introduced Government Regulation No. 10 (PP 10), which prohibited aliens from engaging in retail trade in rural areas, effective from 1 January 1960, a move clearly aimed at curtailing the activities of ethnic Chinese in Indonesia. Even more drastically, in 1960, the West Java military commander banned alien Chinese from residing in that area. The PRC government registered strong protests against these discriminatory policies, which ostensibly violated the Dual Nationality Treaty that obligated the Indonesian government to protect the overseas Chinese. Beijing sent ships to repatriate an estimated 102,000 ethnic Chinese who decided to leave Indonesia as the result of these regulations.[19] The PKI often acted as a champion of the *Tionghoa* community against persecution from local officials, and in turn the PKI received material support from important local Chinese groups, thus closely identifying these two groups in the eyes of their opponents. In the chaotic and violent aftermath of the 1965 Gestapu affair, large numbers of *Tionghoa*-owned businesses became targets of looting.

Throughout the New Order period, people of ethnic Chinese descent were forced to assimilate completely to the local culture, which included adopting Indonesian-sounding names and being forbidden from public expression of their Chinese heritage. Direct contact with China was forbidden, while local Chinese schools were closed. The Soeharto government also issued a regulation that replaced the terms *Tiongkok* and *Tionghoa*, the more polite terms referring to China and Chinese descent that had been commonly used in Indonesia, with the term *Tjina*, or *Cina*, which came to have more derogatory connotations.[20] While the *Tionghoa* community suffered various forms of discrimination, such as having their identity cards specially marked and restrictions applied when trying to enter public offices, the New Order government gave special economic privileges to a few major ethnic Chinese conglomerates. These monopolistic practices and crony capitalism under the increasingly corrupt and repressive New Order regime again led to rising anti-Chinese sentiment. Anti-Soeharto demonstrations in the midst of the Asian financial crisis in 1998 were marked by anti-Chinese racial riots in many parts of the country, with the large-scale destruction of businesses owned by ethnic Chinese, as well as reported sexual violence against a significant number of *Tionghoa* women. The 1998 racial riots were only among the latest of periodic violence targeting ethnic Chinese in Indonesia since the beginning of the Dutch presence in the seventeenth century, whose economic activities had attracted large numbers of migrants from mainland China.[21]

From Normalization to Comprehensive Strategic Partnership

Indonesia only resumed full diplomatic relations with the PRC on 8 August 1990, well over a decade after the United States and China established relations on 1 January 1979. The end of the Cold War and the diminished threat of communism, combined with China's modernization policy that had accelerated its economic progress, persuaded the Soeharto government to re-engage with Beijing. The initial push for opening direct contact with Beijing in the mid-1980s came from the business community, who did not want Indonesia to miss out on the opportunity of benefiting from the enormous economic potential that China had to offer. Furthermore, even during the freezing of diplomatic relations, Indonesia and China had continued to trade with each other through third parties, with the latter pocketing most of the profits. Indonesia was keen to tap into China's vast market, especially in the face of rising protectionism in the European Union and North America.[22] Equally important, closer economic cooperation with China was also regarded by some as a means to reduce Indonesia's overt economic dependence on Japan, whose dominant role in the Indonesian economy had unleashed a major anti-Japanese riot during Japanese Prime Minister Tanaka's visit to Jakarta in January 1974, known as the Malari affair, which targeted Japanese business interests.[23]

Strategic considerations also played an important role in Jakarta's drive to resume diplomatic relations with Beijing, since it could not afford to continue to ignore such a large power as China, with its growing influence in regional affairs. The Foreign Ministry supported the resumption of diplomatic relations with China partly as a means to enhance Indonesia's own diplomatic effectiveness, particularly to assist Jakarta's efforts to help mediate the Cambodian conflict, since China was the primary backer of the Khmer Rouge regime that was ousted by the Vietnamese forces in January 1979. For its part, the Indonesian military — which had expressed uneasiness at the ASEAN-China allied opposition to the Vietnamese-backed regime in Cambodia — also supported normalization in the hopes that it might speed up the Cambodian peace settlement and prevent China from further entrenching its influence in the region through a prolonged conflict in Cambodia.[24]

The New Order government's re-embrace of China, however, remained highly cautious. While communist supporters in Indonesia had been decimated, and communism as an ideology banned, the paranoia about the possible rise of communism had not completely disappeared. This was especially true among the security intelligence community and Islamic groups, who continued to have reservations about resuming direct ties with China. Small and medium scale indigenous business groups were also apprehensive that closer economic relations with China would mostly benefit the local ethnic Chinese businesses, at their expense. Euphoria over the move to normalization, however, muted most of this scepticism and criticism.[25] Significantly, despite the resumption of diplomatic relations with China, the Soeharto government did not revoke the various discriminatory policies against the *Tionghoa* community, while people from China wishing to visit Indonesia still faced various restrictions and rigorous vetting processes, including having to travel in organized groups and having to show original invitations from sponsors in Indonesia to obtain visas.

More serious efforts to foster closer cooperation with China began to take place in the post-Soeharto period, which also went hand in hand with the domestic policies of ending the discriminatory practices against the *Tionghoa* community that was part of Indonesia's democratization and commitment to protect the civil and political rights of all its citizens. China's friendly policy towards ASEAN in general, including towards Indonesia, throughout the 1997–98 Asian financial crisis earned the country the goodwill of Jakarta's policymakers. China gave assistance to Indonesia at the height of the latter's economic crisis and provided an alternative source of funding through both bilateral agreements and regional mechanisms, such as the Chiang Mai Initiative between ASEAN and the three Northeast Asian dialogue partners (China, Japan and South Korea). This afforded a measure of relief from the harsh treatment meted to Jakarta by the International Monetary Fund (IMF). With the United States imposing embargoes on the Indonesian military for the violence in East Timor in the wake of the 30 August 1999 referendum — which was eventually won by the pro-independence forces — Indonesia also began to diversify the sources of its imported defence equipment to avoid becoming overly dependent on any one country. With its technological advancement, including in its defence industry, China came to be seen as one of the new important sources for Indonesia's military procurement, a clear indication of the Indonesian military's growing trust towards China. The fact that Beijing's official reaction to the 1998 anti-Chinese riots in Indonesia was relatively muted, regarding them as purely Indonesian domestic affairs, also added to Jakarta's increasingly warmer attitude towards China. Furthermore, Beijing's quick support of Indonesia in the aftermath of the 26 December 2004 tsunami in Aceh further enhanced positive sentiments towards China as a whole.[26]

Indonesia-China bilateral relations began to grow closer under President Abdurrahman Wahid, who was in the post from 20 October 1999 to 23 July 2001. During his state visit to Beijing in December 1999, President Wahid made a point of emphasizing the close cultural and historical ties between China and Indonesia, including the fact that Islam also came to Indonesia through China. Gus Dur, as Wahid was popularly known, was also a strong champion of the rights of minority groups in Indonesia, including the *Tionghoa* community, most of whom are double-minorities, in being both ethnic Chinese and non-Muslim. Gus Dur revoked most of the discriminatory regulations against the ethnic Chinese, and went even further by giving them full cultural recognition, including making the Chinese New Year (Imlek) a national holiday. As the daughter of Sukarno, President Megawati Sukarnoputri was also able to add a more personal touch to Indonesia's bilateral relations with China during her tenure from July 2001 to October 2004. Megawati made a state visit to China in March 2002 and was reported to have been especially warmly received by President Jiang Zemin, with both leaders reminiscing about the earlier close ties between Jakarta and Beijing under President Sukarno. It should be noted, however, that, in their capacity as the newly elected president of Indonesia, both Wahid and Megawati chose to visit Washington first, before their respective visits to Beijing, thus underlining Indonesia's continued adherence to the independent and active foreign policy doctrine and avoiding charges that Indonesia was overly tilting towards China.[27]

Indonesia-China bilateral relations were elevated to an even higher level during President Susilo Bambang Yudhoyono's two-term tenure from 20 October 2004 to 20 October 2014. The two countries signed a strategic partnership in April 2005 during Chinese President Hu Jintao's state visit to Indonesia to attend the 50th anniversary commemoration of the 1955 Bandung Conference. In October 2013, President Yudhoyono and President Xi Jinping, during the latter's state visit to Indonesia prior to attending the 21st APEC Economic Leaders' Meeting in Bali, agreed to elevate Indonesia-China relations to the level of a comprehensive strategic partnership and enhance cooperation on trade and economic development, science and technology, sociocultural areas, the defence industry and in regional and global arenas.[28]

As a result, Indonesia-China relations have flourished at both the government-to-government and people-to-people levels, with significant increases in two-way trade and tourism. Two-way trade increased from a total of US$8.705 billion in 2004, slightly in favour of Indonesia, to US$48.229 billion in 2014, with Indonesia incurring ever-larger deficits, which in 2014 amounted to around US$12.4 billion.[29] China has now replaced Japan as Indonesia's largest trading partner. Indonesia also began to look to China for investment in infrastructure projects, such as for projects to build roads, bridges and power plants. China has provided 45 per cent of the funding for the 5,438-metre-long Suramadu bridge connecting East Java and the island of Madura, while the Chinese company China Communication Construction Group (CCCG) was contracted to complete the project. Construction of the bridge began under President Megawati in August 2003, and the bridge was inaugurated by President Yudhoyono in June 2009. At the level of people-to-people relations, besides visiting China as tourists, increasingly large numbers of Indonesians, not just those of ethnic Chinese descent, have also begun to send their children to study in China. At the same time, with the easing of visa restrictions against individual travellers, tourists from China have started to visit Indonesia in large numbers.

However, despite the increasingly close bilateral relations between Jakarta and Beijing, Indonesia continues to harbour reservations, signifying its deep-seated ambivalence towards China and its care to avoid being too closely identified with China.[30] China's increasingly assertive policy in the South China Sea since 2009 has reinforced concerns about whether China's rise would continue to be peaceful, especially in light of Beijing's perceived role in undermining ASEAN unity. ASEAN's failure to issue a joint communiqué at its summit in Phnom Penh in 2012 for the first time in history, over a disagreement about a statement regarding the South China Sea, was widely known to have been caused by Beijing's influence over Cambodia.

While the government is more concerned about the implications of China's rise on regional security dynamics, members of the wider population have tended to worry more about the impact of China's economic prowess on their livelihoods, especially from the flood of cheap — often illegal — goods from China. Prior to the full implementation of the ASEAN-China Free Trade Area Agreement

(ACFTA) in January 2010, there was pressure on the Indonesian government from the business community and civil society to pull out of the agreement or to renegotiate the terms with Beijing.[31] Indonesia's consistently widening trade deficits with China, as well as concerns about de-industrialization and the loss of jobs, became more acute, reinforcing general scepticism about the benefits of the ACFTA for the Indonesian economy.

Although the Indonesian public blamed the government for not sufficiently informing them about the ACFTA and for not protecting Indonesian producers from the influx of cheap Chinese products, throughout the Yudhoyono period, Indonesia's economic relations with China had not been a divisive political issue. Nor was Yudhoyono, better known for his "one million friends and zero enemies" foreign policy, seen as being too pro-China. Continuing improvements in interracial relations in Indonesia also gathered pace as the country continued to consolidate its democracy, thus opening the space for people from the *Tionghoa* community to run for public office, with greater acceptance from the wider public. Furthermore, President Yudhoyono revoked the last remnant of the New Order's discriminatory policy by restoring usage of the earlier terms *Tiongkok* and *Tionghoa* to replace *Tjina/Cina*, along with its negative connotation.[32]

Growing Criticisms of China's Economic Roles in Indonesia

However, there has been an apparent marked change in public attitudes towards Indonesia's ever-closer economic relations with China since Jokowi took office in October 2014. Growing criticisms about the various negative impacts of China's economic roles in Indonesia are now often accompanied by charges against Jokowi himself. While most of the criticisms from foreign policy observers have focused on the wider security implications of Indonesia's increasing dependence on Chinese investments, particularly on the constraint this has imposed on Indonesia's ability to respond more decisively to developments in the South China Sea,[33] the general public have increasingly raised concerns about the extent and nature of China's penetration of the Indonesian economy. In this section, the focus will be on the latter, since it has a more direct bearing on Indonesian domestic political contests.

Jokowi made infrastructural development one of the key priorities of his presidential campaign, and he has pursued this in earnest since taking office. Insufficient infrastructure has long been a problem for the country, reducing Indonesia's economic competitiveness and widening the socio-economic gap between the more developed western part of Indonesia and the eastern outlying regions of the country. Since state coffers are not sufficient to fund Jokowi's massive infrastructure projects, the government has had to look for alternative sources of funding, especially from overseas. It is important to note that traditional donor countries prefer to provide concessional loans for attaining Millennium Development Goals (MDGs) in areas such as health, education and the development of civil society. In contrast, China's foreign aid and concessional loans are mostly aimed at infrastructural development projects, and mostly as commercial loans provided by China's state-owned banks, rather than as government-to-government grants.[34] China has therefore become a favoured source of funding for the Jokowi government's ambitious infrastructural development, even though Indonesia was initially hesitant to participate in China's Belt and Road Initiative (BRI) on the possibility that it could conflict with Jokowi's vision of transforming Indonesia into a Global Maritime Fulcrum. Indonesia has also joined the China-led Asian Investment Infrastructure Bank (AIIB) and designated a number of areas as being part of the BRI. This is not to say that Indonesia has neglected other sources of funding, with Singapore and Japan remaining as the top two foreign investors in Indonesia.

Projects funded by loans from China are usually built by Chinese firms, employing large numbers of workers brought in from China, mostly for reasons of efficiency. Boosting the tourism industry is another priority of the Jokowi government, which it has tried to achieve by, among other steps, granting free visas to the nationals of 169 countries, including the PRC. Jokowi has expressed a wish to see the number of tourists from China reaching ten million people annually. These two factors in recent years have become a source of controversy and confusion, becoming fodder for negative campaigns against the government in general and Jokowi in particular. For instance, in the run-up to the 2017 Jakarta gubernatorial election, a hoax proliferated on social media about the influx of up to ten million Chinese nationals illegally entering Indonesia, allegedly to vote for the ethnic Chinese incumbent governor, Basuki Tjahaja Purnama (Ahok), who had served as vice governor when Jokowi was the governor of Jakarta, and was thus closely identified with the latter.

While the social media rumour could easily be shown to be fabricated, concerns about the large numbers of blue-collar Chinese workers employed by the Chinese companies, both officially registered and unregistered, have also been raised by the mainstream media. For example, on 15 November 2017 the *Jakarta Post* published a series of reports about the development of an industrial park in Morowali, Central Sulawesi, which was managed by a Chinese joint venture, PT Indonesia Morowali Industrial Park (IMIP). The titles of the articles — which include "Morowali: A Tale of China's Grip on Rich Region" and "Anti-Chinese

Spectre Raises Head in C. Sulawesi Regency" — speak for themselves. The first of these two articles highlights the disaffection Indonesian workers felt due to their perception of not being treated as well as their Chinese counterparts, as well as the cultural problems encountered, such as the one portrayed in a viral video of a Chinese foreman refusing to allow Indonesian workers to perform their Friday prayers. The second article noted that local residents believed that "thousands" of workers from China were employed by the IMIP, and, although unseen, "it has not averted growing anti-Chinese sentiment and rallies in the past year". Periodic media reports about the presence of both legal and illegal workers from China in different parts of the country have kept these issues alive.

In "Public Perceptions of China in Indonesia: The Indonesian National Survey", Herlijanto noted that the findings reveal that Indonesians generally believe that close economic relations with China will bring benefits. Hence, "unlike the negative views circulating on Indonesian social media, there are degrees of acceptance of Chinese migrant workers and of Chinese investment in Indonesia".[35] In a public release of a survey on perceptions of external threats to Indonesia carried out by *Median* in late 2017, however, China emerged as the country seen to be the greatest threat (22.7 per cent), followed by the United States (14.7 per cent). The survey noted that the generally negative sentiment towards China was mostly caused by economic factors, particularly the perceptions of Chinese domination of the economy, particularly in terms of the influx of China-made products and Chinese nationals coming into the country.[36] More disconcertingly, concerns about foreign Chinese and the *Tionghoa* community have become blurred in the public perception, such that the growing anti-Chinese sentiment has also evolved into anti-*Tionghoa* sentiment. A survey by the Wahid Foundation in 2017 revealed that 59.9 per cent of respondents disliked particular groups, with the ethnic Chinese being cited by the majority. These facts have naturally raised alarms, given the history of periodic violence against this community.[37]

At the same time, public perceptions about these issues have become increasingly divided by partisan politics in which facts have often been blurred by the proliferation of hoax or fake news. Herliyanto noted that concerns about the Chinese role in the Indonesian economy and China's assertive behaviour in the South China Sea are most apparent among the *pribumi* elite, who are either opposed to or are neutral towards the Jokowi government.[38] The rise in identity politics, which gathered momentum during the gubernatorial electoral campaign in Jakarta in late 2016 when the popular incumbent, Ahok, an ethnic Chinese Christian, was the target of large-scale demonstrations by Islamic groups who accused him of blasphemy against Islam, have again to a certain extent conflated

Indonesia-China relations with domestic political competition for power. In the run-up to the forthcoming presidential election in April 2019, Jokowi has become the target of a massive black campaign on social media that accuses him of being a handmaiden of both China's and local *Tionghoa*'s interests.[39] Although so far Jokowi's popularity has not been too affected by the various allegations made against him, including the patently false rumours that his family were members of the PKI and are of Chinese descent, there are real concerns that in the increasingly charged political climate the rise in anti-Chinese sentiment could again be manipulated for political purposes.

Leo Suryadinata has highlighted five issues that may affect Indonesia-China relations negatively in the future. These are the issues of Chinese workers in joint projects, the rise of *pribumi*-ism in Indonesia, domestic anti-Chinese sentiments, problems relating to Indonesia's Exclusive Economic Zone to the north of the Natunas, and changes in China's policy on overseas Chinese.[40] The first three issues are related, and while they may pose dangers to future Indonesia-China bilateral relations, an even more serious consequence is the widening of Indonesia's social-political cleavage that may endanger the racial harmony that Indonesia has slowly rebuilt after the 1998 racial riots. The onus is on both the Indonesian and Chinese governments to address the fundamental concerns that have soured to some extent the earlier mostly positive sentiment towards re-engaging China in Indonesia.

Conclusion

Bilateral relations between Indonesia and China have many complicating factors, and they will need to be handled carefully if they are to be sustainable. While recognizing the growing importance of China as a rising major power, particularly in the economic field, Indonesians have generally continued to express ambivalence towards China. In recent years, especially since President Jokowi's overt courting of Chinese investment in Indonesia's infrastructure projects, there has been mounting domestic criticism against China's business practices and Indonesia's increasing economic dependence on China. Although it has been shown to be widely exaggerated, the reported influx of large numbers of Chinese nationals entering Indonesia to work either legally or illegally have raised real concerns among Indonesians.

Foreign investments are usually expected to yield multiplier effects, including in the forms of technology transfer, know-how and employment for the local communities where development projects are being carried out. By bringing in most of the workers from China — not just the top personnel and experts, as is the usual practice among American, European or Japanese companies — Chinese investments in Indonesia's massive infrastructural projects have, therefore, come under fire for their lack of multiplier benefits, especially for denying greater work opportunities to local low-skilled workers. The Jokowi government has also been criticized for accepting Chinese foreign investments and loans for infrastructural projects under these terms, since they are not in line with Indonesia's quite restrictive employment law, which only allows expatriates with special skills that Indonesia still lacks to work in the country.

To prevent more damaging pushbacks against China's involvement in Indonesia's development projects, which may also trigger anti-Chinese sentiments, both the Chinese and Indonesian governments will need to change the ways that projects are carried out, to ensure that they provide multiplier benefits to the local communities. Moreover, Indonesia cannot ignore rising international concerns about China's "predatory" investment practices under its BRI ventures, which have trapped a number of countries with heavy debt burdens that they cannot repay, thereby forcing them to cede control of strategic assets to China through a long lease or allow Beijing to exert political influence. While it is in Indonesia's interest to remain open to Chinese investment and other opportunities that an advanced China has to offer, it is also critical that Jakarta continues to diversify its sources of investment and loans and avoid becoming too dependent on any one country. Allowing China to become too dominant and visible in the Indonesian economy may incur serious risks, as demonstrated by the anti-Tanaka riot against perceived Japanese domination of the Indonesian economy in 1974.

Notes

1. See Johanes Herlijanto, "How the Indonesian Elite Regards Relations with China", *ISEAS Perspective* 2017, no. 8 (10 February 2017).
2. Anak Agung Gde Agung, *Twenty Years Indonesian Foreign Policy, 1945–1965* (The Hague: Mouton, 1973).
3. For an explanation of the "*bebas aktif*" foreign policy doctrine, see Mohammad Hatta, "An Independent Active Foreign Policy", in *Indonesian Political Thinking, 1945–1965*, edited by Herbert Feith and Lance Castles (Ithaca: Cornell University Press, 1970).
4. Herbert Feith, *The Decline of Constitutional Democracy in Indonesia* (Ithaca: Cornell University Press, 1978), pp. 384–94.
5. See David Mozingo, *Chinese Policy toward Indonesia, 1947–1967* (Ithaca: Cornell University Press, 1976).

6. George McTurnan Kahin, *Nationalism and Revolution in Indonesia* (Ithaca: Cornell University Press, 1970), p. 90.
7. Feith, *The Decline of Constitutional Democracy*, pp. 434–35.
8. PRRI/Permesta was short for Pemerintah Revolusioner Republik Indonesia/Piagam Perjuangan Semesta, or Indonesia's Revolutionary Government/Charter for Universal Struggle.
9. Feith, *The Decline of Constitutional Democracy*, pp. 586–88.
10. R.Z. Leirisa, *PRRI Permesta: Strategi Membangun Indonesia tanpa Komunis* [Strategy for developing Indonesia without the Communists] (Jakarta: Pustaka Utama Grafiti, 1991).
11. Audrey R. Kahin and George McT. Kahin, *Subversion as Foreign Policy: The Secret Eisenhower and Dulles Debacle in Indonesia* (New York: The New York Press, 1995).
12. Herbert Feith, "Dynamics of Guided Democracy", in *Indonesia*, edited by Ruth T. McVey, pp. 309–409 (New Haven: Human Relations Area File Press, 1963).
13. See John Legge, *Sukarno: A Political Biography* (London: Penguin, 1972).
14. J.A.C. Mackie, *Konfrontasi: The Indonesia-Malaysia Dispute, 1963–1966* (Kuala Lumpur: Oxford University Press, 1974).
15. See Harold Crouch, *The Army and Politics in Indonesia* (Ithaca: Cornell University Press, 1978).
16. This episode of Indonesian history has continued to generate great controversy, with a number of scholars arguing that the Gestapu affair was an internal army affair, not one masterminded by the PKI, with others supporting the official New Order version of the event. Since the fall of Soeharto, a number of Indonesian scholars have also published their research on the subject, but the question of who was ultimately responsible for the killings of the army generals and the subsequent bloody reprisals against PKI members and sympathizers has continued to be a very divisive and touchy subject in Indonesia.
17. Sheldon W. Simon, *The Broken Triangle: Peking, Jakarta and the PKI* (Baltimore: John Hopkins Press, 1969).
18. Feith, *The Decline of Constitutional Democracy*, pp. 481–87.
19. Leo Suryadinata, *China and the ASEAN States: The Ethnic Chinese Dimension* (Singapore: Singapore University Press, 1985), pp. 35–36.
20. Surat Edaran Presidium Kabinet Ampera Nomor SE-06/Pred.Kab/6/1967.
21. See M.C. Ricklefs, *A History of Modern Indonesia Since c. 1300* (London: Macmillan, 1993), pp. 90–91, 115–16.
22. Dewi Fortuna Anwar, *Indonesia and the Security of Southeast Asia* (Jakarta: CSIS, 1992), pp. 41–43.
23. Ibid., pp. 36–37.
24. Ibid., p. 62.
25. Ibid., pp. 43–45.

26. See Rizal Sukma, "Indonesia-China Relations: The Politics of Re-Engagement", *Asian Survey* 49, no. 4 (July/August 2009), pp. 591–608.
27. Dewi Fortuna Anwar, "Megawati's Search for an Effective Foreign Policy", in *Governance in Indonesia: Challenges Facing the Megawati Presidency*, edited by Hadi Soesatro, Anthony L. Smith and Han Hui Ling (Singapore: Institute of Southeast Asian Studies, 2002), pp. 70–90.
28. Document on "Future Direction of Indonesia-China Comprehensive Strategic Partnership", issued in Jakarta, 2 October 2013.
29. "Indonesia-China Balance of Trade", data compilation of Statistics Indonesia/BPS and Ministry of Trade 2018.
30. See Evi Fitrini, "Indonesian Perceptions of the Rise of China: Dare You, Dare You Not", *Pacific Review*, 2018 <https://doi.org/10.1080/09512748.2018.1428677>.
31. Alexandra C. Chandra and Lucky A. Lontoh, "Indonesia-China Trade Relations: The Deepening of Economic Integration amid Uncertainty?", Trade Knowledge Network (tkn), International Institute for Sustainable Development (iisd), 2011.
32. Keputusan Presiden (Keppres) No. 12 Tahun 2014 mencabut Surat Edaran Presidium Kabinet Ampera Nomor SE-06/Pred.Kab/6/1967.
33. See Emirza Adi Syailendra, "Indonesia's Elite Divided on China", *East Asia Forum*, 20 April 2018; and Evan A. Laksmana, "The Domestic Politics of Indonesia's Approach to the Tribunal Ruling and the South China Sea", *Contemporary Southeast Asia* 38, no. 3 (2016): 382–88.
34. Pierre van der Eng, "Why Does Indonesia Seem to Prefer Foreign Aid from China?", *East Asia Forum*, 2 December 2017.
35. Johannes Herliyanto, "Public Perceptions of China in Indonesia: The Indonesia National Survey", *ISEAS Perspective* 2017, no. 89 (4 December 2017).
36. "Survei Median: Cina Paling 'Mengancam' Indonesia", Republica.co.id, 15 November 2017.
37. Munawir Aziz, "Tionghoa, Antara Sasaran Kebencian dan Ketimpangan Sosial", Kompas.com, 22 February 2018.
38. Herlijanto, "How the Indonesian Elite".
39. Fajar Riza Ul Haq, "Jokowi dan Tionghoa", *Kompas*, 7 July 2018.
40. Leo Suryadinata, *The Growing 'Strategic Partnership' between Indonesia and China Faces Difficult Challenges*, Trends in Southeast Asia 2017, no. 15 (Singapore: ISEAS – Yusof Ishak Institute, 2017).

Laos

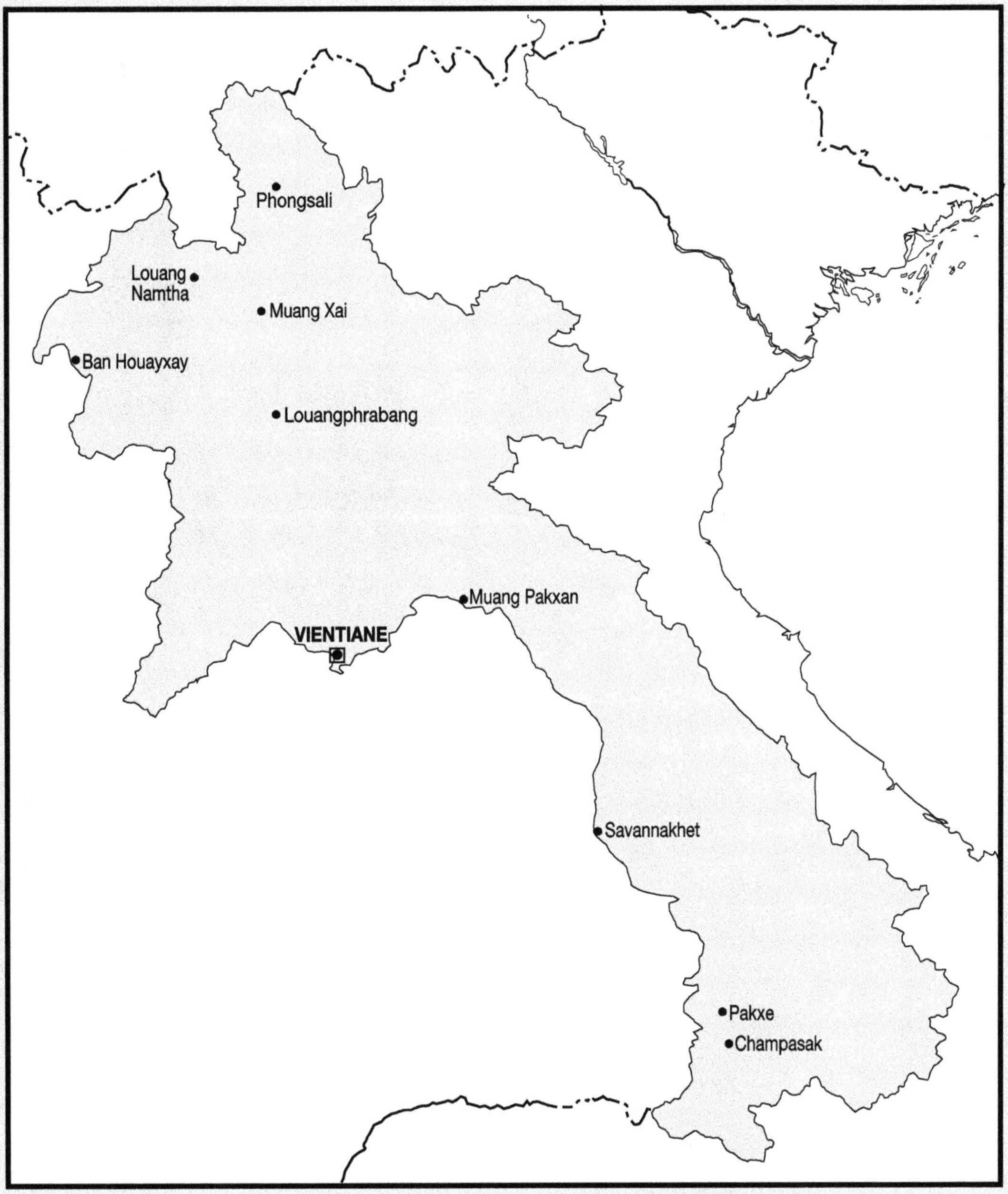
Phongsali
Louang Namtha
Muang Xai
Ban Houayxay
Louangphrabang
Muang Pakxan
VIENTIANE
Savannakhet
Pakxe
Champasak

LAOS ON THE PATH TO SOCIALISM?

Boike Rehbein

The government of Prime Minister Thongloun Sisoulith has strengthened the position of the Lao People's Revolutionary Party (LPRP) and tightened its grip on society. At the same time, socialist terminology has become fashionable again. Observers wonder whether the government is actually returning to a socialist agenda. Or is the shift that occurred with the Party Congress in 2016 linked to the increasing influence of China? Yet another hypothesis refers to the fact that Lao society has become too complex, fragmented and unequal to be controlled under the conditions of economic liberalization. This chapter explores the three scenarios and argues that each of them tells part of the story. The first section situates Laos in the current geopolitical configuration. The second section looks at the economic situation, while the remaining three sections are devoted to Lao society. The third deals with civil society, the fourth with inequality and the fifth with consumer culture and capitalism.

Is Everything About China?

Laos is a small landlocked country located at the southern border of China. Add the fact that the country has plenty of natural resources and a per-capita GDP of around US$2,400, the story emerges without difficulty: China is seeking to control Laos. The strategy pursued by China is similar to other cases. The Chinese carry out large infrastructure projects that are financed by loans extended to the country's government and which are to be paid back at some point. For this service, the Chinese demand nothing except the lease of the infrastructure for a certain period of time, while being able to hold the government hostage until the debt is paid back.

BOIKE REHBEIN is Professor for Society and Transformation in Asia and Africa at the Humboldt University of Berlin.

In the case of Laos, the largest project is a high-speed train from the Chinese-Lao border to Vientiane (and then linking it to the Thai railway network). Part of China's Belt and Road Initiative, the project is expected to cost more than US$6 billion and to be completed before 2022.[1] In late 2018, the completion rate was at a reported 30 per cent. The cost of the project is equivalent to almost a third of the annual GDP of Laos. One wonders how the country will ever be able to raise even a significant fraction of that sum. In addition, Laos has had to cede a corridor of land along the railway tracks to the Chinese.[2]

Apart from this mega-project, China is present in Laos through many other enterprises. Several dams generating electricity for China have been and are being constructed in northern Laos, mostly by Chinese labourers working for Chinese companies. The Chinese are also running rubber plants in most parts of the country, while again drawing much of the labour from China. Furthermore, Chinese farmers have settled in many districts of Northern Laos. Moreover, most of the largest businesses in the small Laotian economy belong to Chinese entrepreneurs and/or investors. While it would be an exaggeration to say that Laos is already owned by China, it is difficult to state the opposite with any confidence.

The important question arising in this configuration concerns the position of the Lao government towards China. Western donors and NGOs have been complaining for years that their working environment keeps deteriorating. At the same time, the LPRP has returned to a socialist rhetoric, which obviously does not cater to the West.[3] It is evident that Western powers no longer play a relevant role in Laos. Relations with neighbouring Thailand had been improving from the 1990s into the early 2000s, but it is now no longer the priority for the Lao government. The socialist rhetoric is quite clearly not aimed at the Thai government. We thus have to look towards the two other big neighbours of Laos to understand its return to socialist rhetoric.

Both China and Vietnam are nominally one-party socialist states whose relations have not been the best for many periods in history. But since the breakdown of the Soviet Union they are the only nominally socialist nation states remaining, apart from a few medium-sized countries such as Cuba or North Korea and a handful of small countries such as Laos. Once again, Laos is in the position of not having much of a choice in its foreign policy. It has to turn either to Vietnam or to China. Or does turning to one mean turning to the other as well?

Since the revolution of 1975, Vietnam has been considered to be the "big brother" of Laos, with some commentators even going as far as to describe the LPRP as a branch of the Vietnamese Communist Party.[4] Since Vietnam has successfully defied the Chinese on several occasions, the obvious thing for the Lao leadership to offset Chinese influence is to form a close alliance with Vietnam. This actually seems to be the case. However, given how Sino-Vietnam relations have improved over the past decades, it is not clear whether an alliance with Vietnam can offset Chinese influence. To be more precise, as long as China and Vietnam get along, Laos does not have much leverage against China.

To regard Laos as China's puppet, however, would be too simple. From the Chinese perspective, Laos is not merely another country to be exploited and dominated. Laos is one of China's few real allies, since it is one of the few countries that adopts the same form of nominal socialism — a capitalist market economy ruled by a single party adhering to a socialist ideology (or rhetoric). The Lao leadership is entirely aware of the amount of independence this entails. The decision to return to a socialist rhetoric is related to China's influence, but not caused by it. China, Vietnam and Laos have all moved towards the simultaneous tightening of civil society and the strengthening of the ruling party's position in the state. This has pushed the three countries closer together and strengthened them both internationally and domestically. It is precisely to this degree that China is dependent on Laos — and not only the other way around.

The Lao Economy in 2018

The position of Laos in the international configuration has certainly played a role in its decision to return to a socialist rhetoric, but the domestic situation has been far more important. In order to understand the domestic situation, a brief look at the economy is necessary. The macro-economic framework itself was not a major factor in the return to a socialist rhetoric, but it is relevant for its relations to China and the dynamics in domestic politics.

Economic growth has been consistently high over the past decade, but national capital stock and consumer spending are still comparatively low. Foreign aid and investment, as well as the export of raw materials, continue to be the drivers of economic growth, which stood at 6.8 per cent in 2017, just like in the year before.[5] Per-capita income has increased tenfold since 2000 and GDP stands at around US$16 billion. Consumers also profited from a further drop in the rate of inflation to 0.8 per cent in 2017, which is likely to have increased again in 2018.[6] The industrial base keeps expanding as well — in contrast to many lower-income countries. Furthermore, general conditions for economic activity have improved. The time it takes to start a business was halved between 2003 and 2017.[7] Finally, Laos has almost reached its goal of advancing beyond the status of a "least developed country".

As in many other economies in a similar situation, productivity is reaching a glass ceiling due to the relatively low level of skills in the workforce. Laos is now hosting its first electronics, IT and even aircraft component factories, distinguishing the Lao economy from other comparatively poor countries around the world. However, finding more skilled labour beyond those already employed in these industries is proving difficult.[8] This is also true for the services sector and especially high-end production. The primary sector remains as the pillar of the Lao economy, including the immediate exploitation of raw materials such as gold, timber and water power.

The Lao political economy has taken an interesting turn since 2016, with Prime Minister Thongloun's struggle against corruption.[9] The State Inspection Agency, which is in charge of prosecuting corruption, had previously not been very successful in carrying out its mandate. However, ever since this new initiative began, hardly a week has passed without some officials being exposed. Millions of U.S. dollars in black money have been seized or returned to the state. In 2017, almost a thousand individuals were exposed for corruption.[10] Even though this agenda can also be interpreted as a purge aimed at political opponents, it has certainly changed the general atmosphere. Whereas corruption had been normalized prior to 2016, it is currently no longer taken for granted or considered as an integral or unavoidable part of doing business in Laos. This also implies that high officials cannot rely on corruption as their major source of income anymore. Furthermore, while the struggle against corruption can be understood as an attempt to improve the market economy, it is also worthwhile to understand it as a step towards socialism, which helps to contextualize the return of socialist rhetoric since 2016.

Socialism and Civil Society

After three decades of market liberalization, the LPRP has returned to a socialist rhetoric. The Party Congress in 2016 made official the tendency that observers had detected in the preceding years. At the 2016 Congress, the old socialist guard with strong ties to Vietnam assumed power again and proclaimed the return to the socialist agenda with the long-term goal of becoming a communist state. Prime Minister Thongloun Sisoulith and President Bounnhang Vorachith became the faces of the return to a socialist rhetoric. The key question to be asked about Laos in 2018 is whether this rhetorical shift also means the return to a socialist agenda, which according to Marx would first entail developing a capitalist mode of production before the transition to a socialist mode of production and government can be undertaken.

Together with the proclamation of socialist precepts, the government has also tightened its grip on civil society. Decree 115, which allows civil society organizations to officially register, was revised in 2016/17. Each registered organization now has to seek approval from the government on a yearly basis. This level of control is far higher than at any other point during the past two decades. In 1975, non-governmental organizations were basically replaced by communist mass organizations. However, an increasing number of international organizations had been allowed into the country in the following years. In the same period, there were also many international experts in Laos working for organizations that can be interpreted as International NGOs (INGOs). A Lao civil society, however, only began to emerge after economic liberalization from 1986, with civil society organizations, legally termed as "non-profit associations" (NPA), only officially recognized from 2009.

From the perspective of the Lao government, a civil society in the Western sense is not necessary in a socialist country. The LPRP entertains several mass organizations (youth, women, senior citizens and trade unions), which are supposed to represent the interests of these groups. Apart from them, the party itself is the platform for the discussion of public issues. Given the overlap between the party structure and the government administration, the input of citizens within the party is supposed to have immediate political repercussions. Indeed, the LPRP itself can be considered as originating from civil society, since it was part of the anti-colonial independence movement. Today, however, only around 200,000 citizens, or 3 per cent of the population, are party members.

From the perspective of the Lao leadership, the LPRP and the mass organizations constitute civil society, since the population can voice its concerns within the party framework. In spite of the low level of party membership, ordinary citizens can gain access to decision-making processes to a rather high level within the party and its associated organizations relative to Western societies. However, these institutions are much more tightly controlled and regulated in Laos, and it is the party leadership that ultimately decides on the legitimacy of citizens' concerns.

Apart from the mass organizations, rural associations, which are traditional forms of community self-organization, form the backbone of civil society in Laos. The social space for civic engagement in the country has, for many centuries, been the village. The village continues to be a somewhat democratic organ, even though the village headman and his assistants are usually party members (and male). Their task is to mediate between the population and the government, or, more precisely, to report to the higher levels in the party structure and to disseminate the official party policies to the village population. In theory, the headman is also supposed to represent grass-roots concerns to the higher levels, though in practice this has meant information gathering for the higher levels rather than interest representation.

A Western-style civil society has begun to develop in the new urban middle class, which comprises only around 20 per cent of the population. This development is of concern to the Lao leadership, particularly in the context of the transformation of the Lao social structure. The return to a socialist rhetoric and the tightened control of civil society organizations are directed against this new urban middle class, which no longer fully accepts the leadership of the LPRP and no longer functions in the framework of village politics. Social inequality and the rise of a capitalist consumer culture feed into the tension between the middle class on the one hand and the peasants and elites on the other.

Increasing Inequality

An interesting side effect of Thongloun's struggle against corruption is the exposure of the incredible level of wealth accumulation among Lao elites. While wealth accumulation has existed and has generally been known about since the early 2000s, the State Inspection Agency now publishes numbers for public consumption.[11] These numbers bear witness to an exploding level of inequality, which is the exact opposite of a socialist ideal. This level of inequality clearly shows that Laos has deviated from the socialist economy and society of the 1970s and 1980s. However, the LPRP simply denies the problem of inequality, claiming to focus on poverty instead. The claim is however not very convincing, since Laos has not even significantly reduced poverty rates in past years. As a consequence, Oxfam has identified Laos as one of the countries least committed to the fight against inequality.[12]

The high level of socio-economic inequality is partly a result of the transition to a market economy, which I refer to as a "capitalist transformation".[13] In all societies, the capitalist transformation appears to generate a hierarchy of social classes that are rooted in earlier hierarchies. These hierarchies partly persist and partly transform into social classes. I call the persisting hierarchies "sociocultures".[14] A socioculture is a prior historical social structure that still informs contemporary structures. Social classes in a capitalist society do not emerge out of the blue, but are rooted in earlier hierarchies. Each socioculture comprises a hierarchy of strata or levels that connect over time to form a hierarchy of "tradition lines". The younger generations tends to remain on the same level of the hierarchy as their parents, even if they grow into a new socioculture, since they usually receive education and resources from their parents. Therefore, they share a lot with members of the former generation, especially their parents, often more so than with people on another hierarchical level in the same socioculture.

A study of Laos reveals that the emerging hierarchy of social classes is rooted in hierarchies that existed in and before the socialist period. At the same time, the pre-socialist and socialist hierarchies still persist, since only a minority of Lao citizens have actually converted to a capitalist economy and lifestyle. The pre-socialist hierarchy was basically identical with the "mandala" social structure, a polity of levels of loyalty ranging from the village to the urban centre to a princely court.[15] The nation state of Laos comprises several mandala structures, which were united under colonial rule. It consists of ethnic minority villages that are not integrated into the mandala, the peasants, the urban population and the nobility. The mandala structure basically persisted under colonial rule and during the civil wars from 1893 to 1975. It was then superseded by a socialist hierarchy that consists of rank differentiation within the party structure: village cadres, administration, and party leadership. The capitalist hierarchy that began to emerge from 1986 comprises the marginalized class (unemployed, beggars, day labourers), the working class, a rural middle class (commercial farmers and traders), the new urban middle class, and the capitalists. This means that each stratum in society consists of three different sociocultures (Table 1). These three types of hierarchy coexist, but the capitalist structure will gradually expand while the other two sociocultures will slowly decrease.

With time, the hierarchy of social classes will become more rigid and inflexible. Social mobility is more difficult in a society that has not seen any major social change for a long period of time. In Laos, the capitalist transformation began in 1986. A lot of social mobility occurred in the following decades. This window of

TABLE 1
Sociocultures in Laos

Pre-socialist	*Socialist*	*Capitalist*
	Dominant class	
Patrimonial elites	Party cadres	Urban middle class
	Administration	Commercial farmers
Peasants	Rural party	Labourers
Minorities		Marginalized

mobility has however begun to close in recent years. Certain social classes have expanded, especially the new urban middle class, but this expansion has been due to a general transformation towards a capitalist class structure (or a mobility of socioculture from left to right in Table 1) rather than upward social mobility. While the transition to a market economy has opened up business opportunities and the prospect of social mobility, most of the new members of the capitalist class have however been drawn from the old and new elites, as well as businesspeople from neighbouring countries.

We can also observe that the relative social positions are largely reproduced from one generation to the next. In contemporary Laos, the fathers of most of the current crop of peasants were similarly peasants, while almost half of the current batch of state employees had a father who was a state employee.[16] Only two per cent of current peasants reported that their grandfather was not a peasant. Likewise, if a grandfather was a private employee, trader, businessperson or administrator, it is likely that his grandchildren would be in a profession unrelated to agriculture. Furthermore, members of the next generation tend to remain in the same professional group. The reproduction of relative social position is also visible as far as education is concerned. If the father occupied a high social position, his children will invariably receive a high level of education. In contrast, almost all those with primary education or less are children from a rural or lower-class background. However, there is also a significant number of people who are either marginalized, working, or part of the new urban middle class whose parents were peasants. This is a symptom of the capitalist transformation — people are integrated into capitalism and thereby into social classes.

Due to the rapid capitalist transformation, the Lao population has been experiencing a rapid transformation of its lives and livelihoods. By and large, people migrate from the left to the right columns in Table 1, both physically and socially, while remaining on the same level of the social hierarchy. Marginalized peasants, especially from ethnic minorities, become unskilled labourers or beggars. Subsistence peasants with good land become commercial farmers; those with relatively poor land are likely to become labourers. The urban groups of the colonial and pre-colonial periods have become the core of the new urban middle class. Also, in a pattern reminiscent of colonial times, there are Vietnam nationals coming into Laos as petty traders and entrepreneurs and Chinese entering as businesspeople, while immigrants from both countries are also working in Laos as farmers and labourers.

The group that has begun to form a rather integrated class or stratum in the social hierarchy is the dominant class or elite. The leaders of the LPRP are marrying members of the pre-socialist elites and successful entrepreneurs. At the same time, some party leaders and many members of pre-socialist noble families engage in business ventures themselves. A network has emerged reminiscent of the pre-socialist elite, including some of the same family names, complemented by the leading socialist families.

This new dominant class has been expanding for decades, just like the other social classes. In past years it has become too large to accommodate everyone. A struggle for pieces of the cake in terms of money and power has developed. The replacement of high officials and ministers is an expression of this struggle. The reshuffling of the central committee and the shift to a socialist rhetoric cannot be reduced merely to this intra-elite struggle, but it is definitely connected. The group of party leaders that took part in the revolutionary fight and that is closely linked to the Vietnamese leadership has re-emerged as the dominant force within the LPRP.[17] It has never been out of power, but it has previously had to deal with groups with closer links to China and Thailand, which now take a back seat.

Increasing Consumerism

Capitalism is not only structuring social hierarchies in Laos but it is also becoming the dominant culture. Capitalist culture presents two problems for the Lao leadership. First, the social base of the LPRP loses its high social standing to the new urban middle class. Second, consumerism becomes more attractive than socialist ideology to a large part of the population. The strength of the LPRP's grip on society is closely related to finding answers to these two problems.

The differentiation in attitudes towards socialism expresses the development of capitalism and a corresponding culture. Even though the new urban middle class is clearly gaining ground, its members are unhappy with political restrictions (such as one-party rule and state control of civil society), corruption, clientelism and the slow pace of development. Almost every member of the new urban middle class shares negative opinions about the current state of affairs in Laos, which they link to their own lives.

However, while there is too much socialism for the new urban middle class, there is too little for the disadvantaged farmers and peasants. These groups are economically poor and defined as underdeveloped and backward by the various poverty-eradication programmes sponsored by the Lao government and INGOs. This classification is however not acknowledged by the economically privileged factions of the rural population, who instead repeat the socialist discourse on the

Lao peasant; namely, that the peasant incorporates the ideal Lao and produces the national food, which is rice. However, the absolutely poor peasants settling in remote areas and mountainous regions, who mostly belong to ethnic minorities, have realized they are the "losers" of the capitalist transformation. This is also the case for those peasants who live close to urban areas who consider themselves poor, even if they are sufficiently well off, since they are integrated into the money economy and can assess their relative poverty.

The rice-growing peasant has been lionized as the hero of socialist Laos and they are still seen to epitomize the spirit of the nation. These peasants also support the current socialist agenda, since it raises their status and calls for socio-economic equality. In contrast, the urban population and international organizations demonstrate disrespect for their way of life, indicating how the capitalist socioculture is dismissive of the peasantry. More than 90 per cent of all adolescents and almost 100 per cent of young people in the cities have declared that they do not want to be peasants or farmers.[18] Furthermore, the majority of peasants who regard themselves as poor prefer to seek a different source of income and a different way of life. The younger generation also no longer wants to engage in agriculture,[19] with this dismissal of farming increasing with the level of education.

The peasants who have come to regard themselves as poor literally live in a different historical period, or, rather, in a different socioculture. Their mentality was formed under conditions that no longer exist, which can be described as an "untimely habitus".[20] Because it was formed in a different social environment, the untimely habitus is not adapted to the current conditions. The untimely habitus invokes insecurity and fear, and this insecurity leads to a demand for order. Order, along with more respect for the peasant in general, is promised and provided for in Laos by the socialist agenda. The LPRP's return to socialist rhetoric has thus been popular among the ranks of peasantry, thus further strengthening its support base.

However, the younger generation also experiences insecurity, albeit of a different type. Adolescents in Laos are aware that they form the first generation in Lao history who cannot be fully prepared for life by their parents, and that they are the first generation to have turned away from the homes and customs of their parents. Especially in the urban areas, Western lifestyle choices are becoming increasingly attractive to the younger generation. This is clearly visible in the clothing, music and language preferences of Lao adolescents. Lao youths largely reproduce their parents' social position without replicating their forms of life or their ideas. As the youth form a significant part of the Lao population, the fact that these adolescents are clearly moving towards the capitalist socioculture suggests that the socialist rhetoric is losing ground to consumerism and Western lifestyles.

Conclusion

The peasantry is still a significant faction in the Lao population. Together with the party apparatus and the socialist elites, they are, at least to a certain degree, opposed to fully fledged capitalism. Together, these groups can be united behind the socialist rhetoric. They however face a rapidly growing capitalist socioculture, which comprises the new urban middle class, labourers and adolescents. The Lao leadership has realized that the capitalist transformation has got out of its control and it seeks to turn the wheel back. From an orthodox Marxist perspective, this backward turn can be interpreted as a step forward to socialism. The majority of Lao citizens would however not be convinced by this argument. It is unclear to what degree the Lao leadership actually believes it, but for them to hold on to power it is certainly worthwhile to attempt to convince those social groups that remain in the socialist socioculture and the peasants. For the time being, these groups form the majority of the Lao population.

It certainly helps that China and Vietnam have embarked on a similar course of policy and ideology. This configuration has clearly strengthened the old guard of revolutionaries associated with the Vietnamese leadership. Having taken over at the party congress in 2016, the old guard now seeks to gain control of civil society, capitalism and the elite network itself. At the same time, it is also attempting to de-globalize Lao society, in a similar manner to how many Western societies are at present doing this — albeit against a very different background.

Notes

1. Peter Janssen, "China Train Project Runs Roughshod over Laos", *Asia Times*, 18 August 2018 <http://www.atimes.com/article/china-train-project-runs-roughshod-over-laos/> (accessed 3 December 2018).
2. Ibid.
3. Boike Rehbein, "Laos in 2017: Socialist Rhetoric and Increasing Inequality", in *Asian Survey* 58, no. 1 (2018): 201–5.
4. Martin Stuart-Fox, *Buddhist Kingdom, Marxist State: The Making of Modern Laos* (Boulder, CO, 1996), pp. 192–97.
5. Asian Development Bank, *Asian Development Outlook 2018* (Manila, 2018), p. 260.
6. Ibid., p. 261.
7. World Bank 2018 <https://data.worldbank.org/indicator/IC.REG.DURS> (accessed 3 December 2018).

8. Dexanourath Senedouangdeth, *Special Economic Zone — The Way to Development in Laos*, Vientiane 2016.
9. Oliver Tappe, "On the Right Track? The Lao People's Democratic Republic in 2017", in *Southeast Asian Affairs 2018*, edited by Malcom Cook and Daljit Singh (Singapore: ISEAS – Yusof Ishak Institute, 2018), pp. 167–83.
10. David Hutt, "Is Laos Really Launching a New Corruption Crackdown?", *The Diplomat*, 16 May 2018 <https://thediplomat.com/2018/05/is-laos-really-launching-a-new-corruption-crackdown/> (accessed 3 December 2018).
11. Tappe, "On the Right Track?", p. 172.
12. Oxfam, *Commitment to Reducing Inequality Index* (London, 2018), p. 53 <https://oxfamilibrary.openrepository.com/bitstream/handle/10546/620553/rr-commitment-reducing-inequality-index-2018-091018-en.pdf> (accessed 3 December 2018).
13. Boike Rehbein, *Society in Contemporary Laos* (London, 2017).
14. Boike Rehbein, *Globalization, Culture and Society in Laos* (London, 2007).
15. Oliver W. Wolters, *History, Culture, and Region in Southeast Asian Perspectives* (Singapore, 1999).
16. Rehbein, *Society in Contemporary Laos*, p. 69.
17. Martin Rathie, "The History and Evolution of the Lao People's Revolutionary Party", in *Changing Lives in Laos — Society, Politics, and Culture in a Post-Socialist State*, edited by Vanina Bouté and Vatthana Pholsena (Singapore, 2017), pp. 19–55.
18. Rehbein, *Society in Contemporary Laos*, p. 101.
19. Phout Simmalavong, *Rice Rituals in Laos* (New Delhi, 2010), p. 114.
20. Rehbein, *Globalization, Culture and Society*, p. 70.

RENT CAPITALISM AND SHIFTING PLANTATIONS IN THE MEKONG BORDERLANDS

Yos Santasombat

This chapter documents the impact of Chinese capitalism on the Mekong region's agricultural sector in Laos based on a survey of the Chinese-owned banana plantations near the Laotian border town of Houy Xai.[1] It will demonstrate how the high demand for bananas in China and unregulated rent capitalism have made it possible for small and medium Chinese banana plantations operating in the Thai-Lao border areas to compete successfully with larger companies. However, the small-scale and short-term land acquisitions and the practice of shifting plantation by the Chinese companies have resulted in large-scale, long-term environmental and health impacts on local lives and livelihoods.[2]

The "Shifting Plantation" System

In her study of the banana industry in the Caribbean, Barbara Welch divides the global banana trade into four independent subsystems, in the North Atlantic, the Western Pacific, Southern Africa and Southeastern South America.[3] In terms of production, however, there are three identifiable forms: the large plantation system, the family farm, and the small shifting plantation system.

The banana is highly perishable, with a short period of time between its edible maturation and time of spoilage. While most major markets lie in the

---

Yos Santasombat is Professor of Anthropology, Department of Sociology and Anthropology, Faculty of Social Sciences, Chiang Mai University, and Senior Research Scholar, Thailand Research Fund. He was a Visiting Senior Fellow in the Thailand Studies Programme of the ISEAS – Yusof Ishak Institute in 2017.

temperate zones, cultivation is confined to tropical areas. The banana industry — in terms of production, logistics and marketing — requires high levels of efficient business organization. The geography of the banana industry contributed to the emergence of the large plantation system in Latin America or what James Wiley calls the "Banana Empire".[4] This type of organization began with the founding of the United Fruit Company in 1899. Since then, the banana industry in Latin America has been controlled by trans-national companies such as United Fruit, Del Monte, Dole, and Chiquita, among others. From the beginning, land acquisition was one of the paramount goals of these companies. The empire-building task of setting up plantations required huge investments in forest clearing, irrigation techniques, labour management and logistics. During the industry's incipient stage, the capital required to accomplish these herculean tasks was only available in the North. Consequently, control over the banana industry — land, railroad and shipping — resided in the consuming regions rather than the producing regions.

The "family farm" banana production system used in the Caribbean is different from the large plantations in Latin America. It differs in scale, landscape, land-tenure systems and the labour that tends to the farms. This type of production system is based on independent smallholders who are members of cooperative associations. The banana growers associations (BGAs) purchase bananas directly from their members and perform shipping arrangements. Inputs including fertilizers, pesticides, herbicides, fungicides, blue vinyl covers, boxes, and other items are sold to members on credit and deducted from the payments due to the farmers once their fruit has been delivered. Small-scale family farms are however vulnerable to weather, disease and price fluctuations, over which farmers have very little control. Nevertheless, they can be relatively assured of being able to generate a regular income each year.

The Chinese-owned banana plantations in the Mekong region, however, represent a new form of banana production system unique to the region. In this "shifting plantation" production system, plots of land are cultivated temporarily through the short-term rental of land. Small and medium-sized Chinese fruit enterprises have adopted this form of agricultural production and become migratory. After six to ten years of producing a particular fruit on a rented farm plot, the company usually abandons it for another plot once soil depletion and pest infestation begin to lower the yield. This is especially true of banana production, which requires large amounts of pesticides and chemicals to keep the bananas beautiful and uniform looking. With the high level of contamination and waste, it is not unusual that the productivity of yield decreases over time.

The shifting plantation system allows smaller companies to compete with larger competitors. Since production is invested on a smaller scale and is highly mobile, the entire production process from cultivation to packing and transportation can be done entirely in the field, without having to set up an elaborate workers' camp or an on-site refrigerated warehouse. The strategy of "shifting" plantations also enables these companies to avoid bearing any accountability for land contamination or the disruption of local livelihoods.

Banana Production and Consumer Demand in China

China is one of the major producers of banana. The crop has been cultivated there for more than two thousand years, and in the last two decades it has become one of the most important fruit crops in the country. With an output of 8,042,702 tons over an area of 311,106 hectares in 2008, banana production came in fourth after apples, citrus fruits and pears.[5] As demand for bananas in China is high, domestic production can only meet 90 per cent of demand, with the other 10 per cent needing to be imported. Major banana cultivation regions include Guangdong, Guangxi, Hainan, Fujian and Yunnan, with Guangdong leading in terms of cultivated area and production capacity. The banana industry in China has also evolved rapidly over the past two decades. Many high-yielding and quality-enhancing production techniques have been widely adopted by banana growers, such as micro-propagated plantlets, water-saving irrigation, fertilization, and bunch-management techniques. Since 2003, the industrialization of banana production has been promoted through the implementation of the "Banana Industrial Upgrading Plan" developed by the Agricultural Ministry.[6] However, Chinese banana production still faces many challenges such as pests and disease, adverse weather conditions and insufficient industrialization. In order to promote healthy and sustainable development of the banana industry, the National Industry System of Bananas was initiated by the National Agricultural Ministry in 2008. Through this initiative, scientists have been organized to tackle key issues in breeding, cultivation technology, harvesting and processing, and marketing and trade. Nonetheless, the increasing consumer demand coupled with challenges facing domestic production have compelled many Chinese banana investors to search for other places to develop their plantations, including in the Laotian borderland areas in the Mekong region. This became even more urgent after China banned the import of bananas from the Philippines in 2012 as a result of the dispute over ownership of the Spratly Islands in the South China Sea, thus pressuring Chinese companies to seek alternative supply chains for the fruit.

Rent Capitalism and Land Acquisition in Northern Laos

Over the past decades, Laos has gradually embraced economic globalization and market neoliberalism, implementing a national strategy of "turning resources into capital".[7] The country's economy has grown rapidly as the government has begun to decentralize control and encourage private investment. However, despite rapid economic growth averaging 7–8 per cent annually, Laos remains one of the least developed and poorest countries in Southeast Asia. The disparity in income between the urban and rural populations is widening. The majority of rural households remain under or close to the poverty line, while the natural resources vital to their livelihoods are increasingly threatened by trans-national mega-projects designed to exploit natural wealth for corporate profit.

In recent years, China has surpassed Thailand, Vietnam and South Korea to become the biggest investor in Laos. China is also the biggest donor to Laos and its second-largest trading partner. Economic cooperation between China and Laos is continuously increasing. Chinese private and stated-owned enterprises (SOEs) have penetrated into the various provinces of Laos to build dams, casinos, hotel complexes and mining operations. Given the country's desperate need for foreign investment, the Laotian elites have not been troubled by this increasing dependence on China, believing that the economic advantages of the close Sino-Laos relationship far outweigh any drawbacks of "commodifying sovereignty".[8] Consequently, large-scale land concessions in the form of special economic zones have been granted to Chinese investors. What thus emerges is a form of "rent-seeking" capitalist economy in which the Laotian government obtains income and capital from land and other natural resources without having to make any genuine contribution to productivity.[9]

Houy Xai is the capital of the Laotian province of Bokeo. In earlier times, Houy Xai served as a trading centre at the crossroads of Yunnan, Chiang Saen and Nan. Presently, it is a vibrant border town with a dozen guesthouses and hotels catering to young Western tourists making their way to the old capital of Luang Prabang to the northeast. The Bokeo province was officially split from its northern counterpart Luang Namtha in 1983. It is one of the smallest provinces in Laos, covering an area of 6,196 square kilometres with a reported population of 179,300 in 2015.

Over the past few years, Houy Xai's economy has grown rapidly as its farmlands, particularly those located on the banks of the Mekong, have proved attractive to Chinese banana investors. The increasing migration of overland Chinese entrepreneurs[10] and the commercialization of agriculture in northern Laos is heavily driven by its close proximity to China and the access facilitated by the R3A Highway linking Boharn in Sipsong Panna, Yunnan and Boten in Luang Namtha, Laos. The Chinese entrepreneurs have been investing in a multitude of businesses, from hotels and guesthouses, restaurants, automobile and motorcycle shops, mobile phones, tools and machinery to agricultural production in export crops such as rubber, watermelons and maize. The presence of Chinese investment is most visible in the gigantic banana plantations sprawling over most of Bokeo province and parts of Udomxai and Luang Namtha, which have displaced much of the traditional small-scale farming.

The 2014 field research by Cecilie Friis in the Long district of Luang Namtha reveals how the rapid growth of Chinese banana plantations since 2008 was achieved by renting agricultural land in the easily accessible and fertile lowland areas directly from villagers.[11] Arrangements for this often took the form of loose contractual agreements between local Laotian farmers and Chinese investors, which circumvented the prohibition by provincial authorities against large-scale acquisition in the form of land concessions. A focus on the network of actors involved in bringing about these banana investments and the strategies employed by Chinese investors for land acquisitions sheds new light on how the Chinese entrepreneurs have established a network of village headmen to function as local land brokers able to leverage on their personal relationships with the farmers to facilitate negotiations over the rental of land. By connecting small parcels of rented farmland together through snowballing techniques and personal persuasion, the Chinese investors could gain access to almost all the farmland available in the local villages. Hence, what appears at first as piecemeal and small-scale land acquisitions eventually results in Chinese control over large swathes of agricultural land. This obviously has significant implications for access to resources such as farmland, water and animal grazing ground for local communities. In recent years, many provinces of northern Laos have witnessed the rapid expansion of banana plantations through such "small-scale land acquisitions", which, when taken in aggregate, can amount to a powerful force of "exclusion" against local villagers.[12]

Banana Plantations in Houy Xai, Bokeo

Boon Ngern wakes up at dawn every morning to tend to his cattle and garden. He still resides in the house that he was born in, one that his father built in Ban Phu Wan fifty years ago. Aged forty-four years, Boon Ngern has been a peasant for most of his adult life, although he also now serves as the deputy headman of his native village. Over the past few years, however, his fellow villagers no longer work in their rice fields. Since the Chinese banana investors arrived in Houy Xai in 2014, the village headman and Boon Ngern were able to persuade most, if not all, of the 158 Phu Wan households to rent their farmland to Jianda, a Chinese company from Guangxi, on a short ten-year contract for 5,000 baht per rai[13] annually. In subsequent years, the effective promotional efforts and communication among the network of headmen and brokers led to a snowballing of interest among the villagers in Houy Xai about the rental income they could get from the Chinese investors for their farmland. At the time, Boon Ngern thought the rent income was very lucrative. Furthermore, in addition to the income from the rental of land, a number of villagers were also able to work in the banana plantations for daily wages of 300–400 baht.

For the Chinese investors, Laos presented a good opportunity for banana production, given the availability of fertile land, the favourable climate, the abundance of water resources and easy access to the R3A Highway, which provides a convenient and direct transportation link to China. Ai Liu, a Lue-Chinese from Sipsong Panna who has been managing banana plantations in Houy Xai for three years, said:

> Our company is a small one. We came here because the demands for the fruits are high. It is easy to make a good profit. The land in Bokeo is fertile with plenty of water and rent is not so expensive. The weather is suitable for banana growing. We can produce the fruits all year round. … The demand [in China] is rising every year and the supply is still low. Plantations in China are facing a serious problem with the fungus and the production is uncertain.[14]

In general, the Chinese banana companies in Laos not only plant and care for the fruit but are also responsible for processing, packaging and transporting their products from the plantations to the markets in Sichuan, Yunnan, Guangxi and elsewhere in China. The Chinese banana plantations employ an intensive agricultural technique that requires clearing all native vegetation from tracts of land, followed by densely planting and fertilizing the banana plants. This intensive technique produces the highest yield of fruit per hectare, but it also introduces the risk of chemical contamination to the local environment and poses health risks to the plantation workers. Depending on the companies and the scope of the operation, a plantation in northern Laos may vary between 20 and 200 hectares and recruit hundreds of local workers on monthly and/or daily wages. Prior to the harvesting of the bananas, the production process includes cultivating, fertilizing, grass-cutting and pest-mitigating. Once harvested, the picked banana bunches need to be transported to the packing line where a number of workers will do the sorting, washing, and packing of the fruits into a waiting 18-wheeler.

The life of a banana plantation worker is not easy. Boon Ngern shared that Lao farmers were accustomed to a slow relaxing life of subsistence farming. However, plantation workers have to work long hours, especially during the harvesting period. The process of planting to bunch emergence takes from six to nine months, during which workers have to apply fertilizers and pesticides, while getting rid of weeds and grass underneath the growing plant. From bunch emergence, it takes the bananas another three to four months before being ready for harvest. The process of harvesting and packing is carried out non-stop from dawn to midnight until the truck is fully loaded for its trip to China.

For many Chinese investors, banana growing is a significant profit-generating engine because it requires mostly cheap labour, thus delivering a relatively quick return on effort and investment. Furthermore, this lucrative investment provides income for the villagers all year round. In the beginning, the deal was a win-win situation and favourable for everyone: the local villagers received a lot of money in exchange for renting out their land, while the Chinese investors gained a new source of banana production and a great deal of profit. However, it was not long before the unexpected side effects began to outweigh the economic advantages of the banana plantations.

Impact of Banana Plantations on Local Villagers

Alongside the economic benefits, the process of land acquisitions by the Chinese and the transformation of paddy fields into banana farms have had three major repercussions on local livelihoods in Laos: social tensions, environmental degradation, and health issues. When we asked the villagers of Ban Phu Wan about the biggest impact of the plantations on their livelihoods, the villagers highlighted the lack of grazing ground for their cattle. This particularly affects those landless villagers who make a living from raising cattle. The land previously used for a combination of paddy rice, sugarcane, vegetable gardens and animal grazing was cleared after the land-rental contracts with the Chinese investors were signed. Cattle that previously roamed the village freely were prohibited from entering the plantation once the banana seedlings were planted. Cattle owners thus have to watch over their animals carefully to prevent them from trespassing into the plantation for fear of having to pay a heavy fine to the banana company as a result of damages caused by their cattle. Water competition during the dry season has also become an issue of tension in the village.

More significantly, the banana plantations have had adverse impacts on the environment and the health of the local population. The Chinese investors have drenched the land with fertilizers, pesticides, anti-fungus agents and other chemicals which have polluted the air and contaminated the water that the villagers rely on for washing and drinking. In the area bordering the plantations, one can see discarded bright blue plastic sheets, empty chemical containers, rotten banana bunches and other agricultural waste strewn over the land. Parts of irrigation channels have been filled to construct a road for transportation of the bananas, while the water in other irrigation channels is polluted and without any sign of life. Many farmers have also shown their concern about the destruction of land markers previously used by villagers to recognize boundaries between plots and about converting the land back to paddy cultivation upon the expiry of the contract. Furthermore, the banana plantations account for a huge amount of water use and contamination. Since bananas require a constant level of moisture, the fields are interlaced with channels for irrigation and drainage, which vastly increases soil erosion and delivers agrochemicals into the nearby waterways. In plantations located along the Mekong River and its tributaries, this kind of runoff may affect fish populations and water sources.

The intensive use of chemicals has led to serious health issues among local villagers. Since 2014, three villagers in Ban Phu Wan have died from illnesses that local residents believe are related to heavy exposure to chemicals. Many others have fallen ill with fever, nausea, fatigue and body rashes. The health hazards are more acute for the workers in the plantations, where vast quantities of pesticides, herbicides and fungicides are required to maintain monoculture production. A study by the Laos National Agriculture and Forestry Institute indicated that a staggering 63 per cent of workers in the banana plantations have reported falling ill over a six-month period.[15]

Since 2015, the health hazards of these Chinese banana plantations have received attention in national and international media. An excerpt from a *Southeast Asia Globe* report of the thirty-odd Lao and Khmu workers living in a camp located inside a Ton Pheung banana plantation in Bokeo reveals the extent of the problem:

> "We all have headaches, although we're wearing masks when we spray pesticides", says Sith, an ethnic Khmu from the mountains of neighbouring Xayaburi province.

> "My son doesn't eat anymore. He always feels like vomiting," he adds, pointing out a teenager with patches of severe skin rash.
>
> A few meters away a man is squatting in a hut, his head bowed. "His six-month-old baby died two weeks ago" explains a trader who comes daily to sell food and drink in the camp. "The child went yellow and began to vomit blood. The doctor said it was a liver problem."
>
> At a hospital next to the plantation, a doctor, who gave his name as Bounkhong, confirms that the massive use of pesticides is a clear health risk. "Most of our patients are workers from the plantations, particularly their children. Tests show that their lungs are affected", he says.[16]

A study in the five provinces of Phongsaly, Udomxay, Luang Namtha and Salavan, jointly undertaken by the National Agriculture and Forestry Research Institute and the National University of Laos, concluded that while the banana plantation investments have created incomes and working opportunities for local villagers and improved local infrastructure, they have also led to significant negative impacts on health and the environment.[17] The study found many troubling issues related to the use of chemicals throughout the production process. For instance, it is estimated that between 105 and 140 different chemical substances are used in the process, which when mixed together can increase the degree of harm. Based on this study, the provincial government of Bokeo issued a ban in 2017 on the development of any new banana plantations, adding that upon their expiry the existing contracts with the Chinese investors would not be renewed. The government also encouraged workers to stop working in the plantations immediately to prevent further risk to their health.

The rapid spread of banana plantations also has repercussions on food security. Food security is a key policy of the government of Laos, and many Northern provinces are identified as strategic rice producing areas. The taking over of land by the banana plantations, especially in the lower-lying areas and river valleys, has had the effect of reducing rice production. Furthermore, it is unclear whether this situation will be resolved once the land-rental contracts expire, with villagers expressing worries about whether the Chinese investors will assume responsibility for cleaning up the land and restoring it for rice cultivation.

The many detrimental effects of banana plantations on workers and the environment have however been regularly overlooked and dismissed by the Chinese investors fixated on making a profit. Plantation manager Ai Liu expressed his frustration and anger at the government officials. He argued that the use of chemicals was necessary, while denying that workers were falling ill due to exposure to chemicals. According to him, "If you want to grow bananas, you have to apply fertilizers and pesticides." He also said that "we paid the officials", claiming that "they just wanted more money". Furthermore, Ai Liu shared that as a result of the ban, other Chinese investors have instead moved to Myanmar and Cambodia, adding that "we are also moving to Attapeu province on the border with Cambodia".[18]

Migrant Workers and Remittance Economies

In recent years the rental income from the leasing of land and the associated health risks have prompted a number of villagers to decline to take on jobs in the banana plantations. With many lowland villagers no longer willing to work in the plantations, many Chinese investors have instead begun to employ migrant highlanders from various provinces.[19] Consequently, a thriving internal migrant labour market has developed. These highlanders are victims of the "sedentarization" process in which subsistent slash-and-burn cultivation is prohibited and highland villagers have been relocated closer to roads and highways for easy surveillance by state officials.[20] Sedentarization is designed to control people by firmly freezing them in space, permitting the state to tax, count and supervise them. It also permits the state to educate people and make them "modern".[21] In many Chinese-owned banana plantations, including Ai Liu's, there are increasing numbers of Hmong who have left their homes to seek a better future in the banana industry. Many of the Hmong couples are circular or seasonal migrants who come to seek employment for up to ten months each year.

The banana industry is merely the most recent iteration of the social networks of internal rural migrants in Laos, which have previously been formed over the years through the production of other "boom crops" such as coffee and rubber. The Hmong migrant networks are based upon kinship and clan relationships.[22] Through these networks, the numbers of Hmong worker-couples have increased. From the 2014 statistics on income generated by the plantations in Bokeo, wage payments to contract labourer/Hmong couples accounted for a considerable 49 per cent, while land rental to Lao farmers came second and accounted for only 27 per cent. Since 2014, new banana plantations have sprung up in Bokeo and the total banana growing area increased almost five times from 2,961 hectares in January 2014 to 11,266 hectares in September 2015.[23]

For the Hmong migrants, the lack of farmland and job opportunities back home and the high wages earned from Chinese plantations were reasons to migrate to Bokeo. The average net annual household income of Hmong migrants working in banana plantations during the seven to ten months of the banana season was 72,091 baht, while the average remittance by the Hmong migrants amounted to 23,097 baht annually per person.[24] The Chinese banana plantations have thus attracted thousands of migrant workers from the highlands, although the majority remain subjected to demeaning working conditions, high exposure to chemicals, and crowded housing conditions.

Extending the "Shifting Plantation" to Other Countries in Southeast Asia

The ban by the Laotian government on new banana plantations in its northern provinces has not dampened the ambitions of Chinese investors. Instead, they have re-doubled their efforts to expand to other neighbouring regions in Southeast Asia. Several of the companies have already prepared to move their banana farmlands to alternative sites. Some investors revealed that they were moving to Kachin State in northern Myanmar in an area under the control of the Kachin Independence Army. A few companies are investing in land along the Ayeyarwady River upstream of Chibwe Township, about sixty miles from Myitkyina, the capital of Kachin State. In recent years the rice fields in Waimaw Township have been transformed into banana farmlands as Chinese investors have extended their plantations through a similar method (as in Laos) of renting or purchasing land in Myanmar territory. This has provoked similar local concerns about the Chinese acquisition of thousands of acres of land along the Ayeyarwady River, which includes a mixture of pastoral, vacant and forest-reserved land, as well as virgin forests. Furthermore, the prospect of Chinese investment has prompted several reported instances of Kachin villagers seizing land from protected forests in order to sell it for US$367 an acre. A farmer in Tarlawgyi village claimed that:

> Chinese proprietors buy and lease land from legitimate owners at first. Since the village is near the protected forest, some villagers have fenced the land in the forests to claim it. Some supposed forestry officials come and ask for about Ks200,000 from every land deal. Many areas in Malawi forest have been occupied with banana plantations. Forests are thinning [and mingling with human settlements]. The residents have started invading the Aranama forest. I think thousands of acres in Tarlawgyi are going to be covered with Chinese bananas. Trees are being bulldozed.[25]

Similarly, over the past few years there has been increasing interest among Thai farmers to grow Cavendish bananas for export, aided by the promotional efforts undertaken by the networks of Chinese investors and their Thai nominees. In addition to leasing farmland to the Chinese banana plantations, many northern Thai farmers are also keen to grow their own bananas on their land in contract-farming arrangements with banana "brokers" who actively promote the Cavendish banana as a new miracle cash crop. In such contract-farming arrangements, the broker provides his clients (*Luk Suan*) with tissue-culture banana seedlings and the technical know-how of banana planting. At the end of the season, all "standardized" bananas produced will then be bought by the broker at an agreed-upon price. The presence of the Chinese banana plantations has also ruffled local feathers. In 2015 the *Hongta International*, a Chinese banana company from Yunnan, developed a huge plantation on 2,700 rai (432 hectares) of rented land in the Phya Mengrai district of Chiang Rai. A conflict over water usage between local residents and the Chinese company soon erupted. Local farmers accused the banana company of pumping excessive water from the public creek. The newly established banana plantation, in need of a huge amount of water to irrigate the newly planted banana seedlings, caused the creek to dry up, thus depriving local farmers of their traditional source of water.

The Chinese banana investors also have Cambodia in their sights. The *Phnom Penh Post* reported in August 2016 that Jinsui, a Chinese banana company based in Guangdong, had extended an invitation to Heng Samrin, the president of the National Assembly, to visit their plantation, while proposing the establishment of a banana plantation in Cambodia.

Conclusion

This chapter has documented the impact of unregulated rent capitalism on the agricultural sector in a Mekong border region. The central contention is that these apparently small-scale, short-term, land acquisitions and the practice of shifting plantations can have large-scale, long-term environmental and health impacts on local lives and livelihoods. Shifting plantation practices have turned the Mekong borderlands into neoliberal agricultural frontiers where the intensified process of export-oriented resource extraction motivated by the Chinese-driven banana boom and rent capitalism continues to damage the region. In sum, these shifting plantation practices should present a growing concern for the governments around the Mekong, especially given their lack of national and regional forms of "land governance" to adequately deal with the challenges of resource grabbing, promoting sustainable agricultural development, and protecting the security of land tenure for small farmers.[26] For the Chinese government, there is reason to be concerned about whether the business activities of Chinese banana investors in Southeast Asia are engendering a supportive image of China as a benign and collaborative regional leader. The case of Chinese banana plantations in Laos is a striking negative example of the challenges posed by Beijing's increasing economic involvement with Southeast Asia.

Notes

1. Also commonly spelled as Houayxay, Huoeisay, Houei Sai or Huay Xai.
2. The data and findings presented in this chapter are derived from field research conducted in the Thai-Lao border areas — especially in Ban Phu Wan, Huay Xai district in Bokaew, Laos and Phya Meng Rai district, Chiang Rai, Thailand — and supported by The Thailand Research Fund and Newton Fund. The fieldwork in Huay Xai was carried out between September 2016 and May 2017. However, due to unusual circumstances, fieldwork in Laos was characterized by short visits lasting days to document the changing ecological conditions and carry out in-depth interviews with local villagers, Lao officials, Chinese investors and plantation managers.
3. Barbara Welch, *Survival by Association: Supply Management Landscapes of the Eastern Caribbean* (Mona, Jamaica: University of the West Indies Press, 1996), pp. 22–23.
4. James Wiley, *The Banana: Empires, Trade Wars, and Globalization* (Lincoln: University of Nebraska Press, 2008), p. 15.
5. C.Y. Li, Y.R. Wei, Y.L. Wu, B.Z. Huang and G.J. Yi, "Status, Challenges, and Trends of Chinese Banana Industry", *Acta Hortic* 897 (2011): 31.
6. Ibid., pp. 32–33.
7. Ian Baird, "Turning Land into Capital, Turning People into Labour: Primitive Accumulation and the Arrival of Large-Scale Economic Land Concessions in the Lao People's Democratic Republic", *New Proposals: Journal of Marxism and Interdisciplinary Inquiry* 5, no. 4 (2011): 10.
8. Laungaramsri Pinkaew, "Commodifying Sovereignty: Special Economic Zones and the Neoliberalization of the Lao Frontier", in *Impact of China's Rise on the Mekong Region*, edited by Yos Santasombat (New York: Palgrave MacMillan, 2015), p. 117.
9. Gordon Tullock, "Efficient Rent-seeking", in *Toward a Theory of the Rent-seeking Society*, edited by J. Buchanan, R. Tollison and G. Tullock (College Station: Texas A&M University Press, 1980), pp. 99–102.

10. Aranya Siriphon, "*Xinyimin*, New Chinese Migrants, and the Influence of the PRC and Taiwan on the Northern Thai Border", in *Impact of China's Rise on the Mekong Region*, edited by Yos Santasombat (New York: Palgrave MacMillan, 2015), p. 148.
11. Cecilie Friis, "Small-scale Land Acquisitions, Large-scale Implications", in *Land Grabbing, Conflict, and Agrarian-Environmental Transformations: Perspectives from East and Southeast Asia, BRICS Initiatives for Critical Agrarian Studies (BICAS)* (2015).
12. Derek Hall, Philip Hirsch and Tania Murray Li, *Powers of Exclusion: Land Dilemmas in Southeast Asia* (Honolulu: University of Hawai'i Press, 2011), p. 3.
13. 1 hectare = 6.25 rai.
14. Interviewed on 8 September 2016.
15. Prasanth Paramesvaran, "What's Behind Laos' China Banana Ban?", *The Diplomat*, 14 April 2017.
16. Arnaud Dubus, "The True Cost of Lao's Banana Plantations", *Southeast Asian Globe*, 10 February 2016.
17. *Vientiane Times*, 4 April 2016.
18. Interviewed on 29 May 2017.
19. Many Chinese investors say that the highlanders have better working habits and qualities than the lowland Laos. They are considered more diligent, motivated and hard-working.
20. Oscar Salemink, "Sedentarization and Selective Preservation among the Montagnards in the Vietnamese Central Highlands", in *Turbulent Times and Enduring Peoples: Mountain Minorities in the South-East Asian Massif*, edited by Jean Michaud (Richmond, Surrey: Curzon, 2000), p. 124.
21. Jonathan Rigg, "Roads, Marketization and Social Exclusion in Southeast Asia: What Do Roads Do to People?", *Bijdragen tot de Taal-, Land- en Volkenkunde* 158, no. 4 (2002): 620.
22. Prasit Leepreecha, "Hmong across Borders or Borders across Hmong? Social and Political Influences upon Hmong People", *Hmong Studies Journal* 15, no. 2 (2013): 1–12.
23. Stuart Ling, "The Use of Remittances by Circular Hmong Migrants to Chinese Banana Plantations in Bokeo, Lao PDR" (Master's dissertation, University of New England, 2015), pp. 43–45.
24. Ibid., p. 62.
25. *The Nation*, "Banana Plantation in Myanmar Breaches Forests", 18 March 2017 <http://www.nationmultimedia.com/news/aec/asean_plus/30309495> (accessed 4 August 2017).
26. Philip Hirsch and Natalia Scurrah, in *The Political Economy of Land Governance in the Mekong Region* (2015), define land governance succinctly as follows: "Land

governance consists of the means by which authority is wielded and collective action applied in order to achieve particular social and economic outcomes through land use, distribution, access and security. Land governance is concerned with processes, institutions, laws, practices and structures of power involving a diverse range of public and private actors."

Malaysia

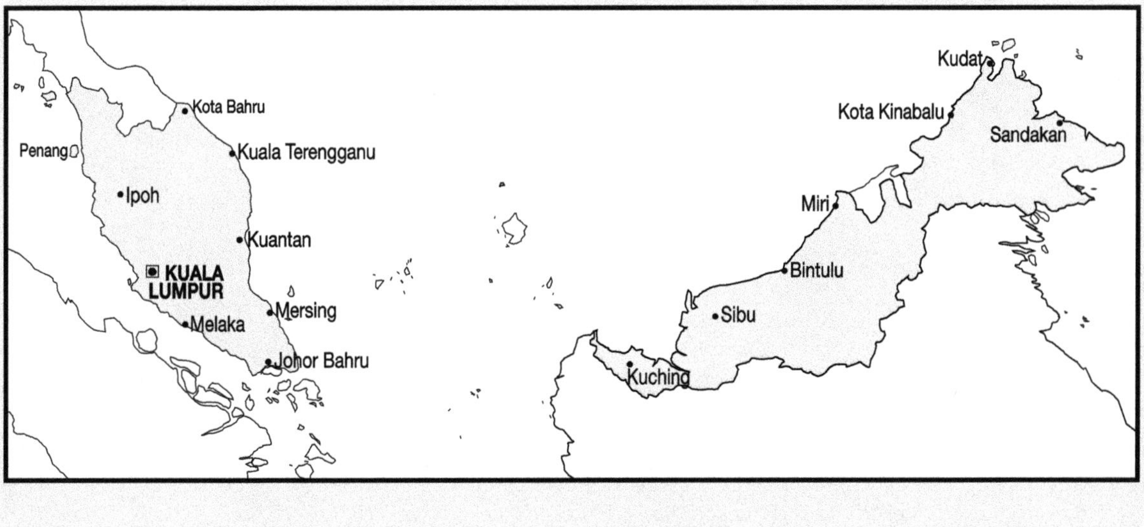

Kota Bahru
Kuala Terengganu
Penang
Ipoh
Kuantan
KUALA LUMPUR
Mersing
Melaka
Johor Bahru
Kudat
Kota Kinabalu
Sandakan
Miri
Bintulu
Sibu
Kuching

MALAYSIA IN 2018: The Year of Voting Dangerously

Geoffrey K. Pakiam

> And when I went in the room with all these thoughts of, okay, what I do next might actually change the nation, I started to shake.
>
> – Jean Vaneisha[1]

If a week is a long time in politics, what of an entire year? Malaysians embarking on an extended holiday at the beginning of 2018 would have returned to a deeply disorienting socio-political landscape at year's end. They would have had to absorb the fact that the once-mighty Barisan Nasional political alliance now lay in tatters, with former prime minister Najib Razak facing thirty-eight criminal charges of fraud, corruption and money laundering related to the 1Malaysia Development Berhad (1MDB) scandal. They would be reading newspapers filled with daily pronouncements from nonagenarian Mahathir Mohamad, Malaysia's now-returned premier, supported by a cast of political players mostly unused to wielding federal power. Their shopping and dining receipts would be marked by the conspicuous absence of the goods and services tax (GST). Their friends, families and colleagues might speak of new expectations, whether in terms of future livelihoods, educational opportunities, inter-ethnic relations, or the rule of law. This chapter will discuss how this situation came to be, as well as its deeper significance for Malaysians and their neighbours.

Politics: A Glass Half Full?

The road to Malaysia's political upset arguably began in September 2016, when Mahathir cemented his break with the United Malays National Organisation (UMNO) by founding Parti Pribumi Bersatu Malaysia (Bersatu) on the 8th of the

Geoffrey K. Pakiam is Fellow at the ISEAS – Yusof Ishak Institute.

month, before literally joining hands with former political arch-rival Anwar Ibrahim the following day.[2] Drawing in several disaffected Malay political heavyweights, including former deputy prime minister Muhyiddin Yassin, former Kedah chief minister Mukhriz Mahathir and former Negri Sembilan chief minister Rais Yatim, Bersatu acquired further mainstream credibility in March 2017 when the Pakatan Harapan coalition — with Anwar Ibrahim's approval — formally accepted Bersatu into its fold. Reconciliation was reinforced in July 2017 when Pakatan's leadership agreed on having Mahathir as its prime ministerial candidate, with Anwar as Pakatan's de facto leader and Mahathir's eventual political successor.

Notwithstanding these remarkable events, many Malaysians entered 2018 with little clarity regarding which party they should support at the ballot box. Each option had its drawbacks and potential dangers. Casting a winning vote for a Barisan Nasional component party could allow Najib and his allies to consolidate power, preside over deepening corruption, and even spell the end of cohesive political opposition in Malaysia.[3] In contrast, a winning vote for a candidate affiliated with Pakatan Harapan — whether from Parti Keadilan Rakyat (Keadilan), the Democratic Action Party (DAP), Parti Amanah Negara (Amanah) or Bersatu — might lead to a new dawn in politics, excising Barisan from federal power for the first time since 1973 (or 1957, if former incarnation the Alliance Party is counted). A sticking point in previous elections — the lack of a strong opposition leader to champion Malay-Muslim issues — was seemingly addressed by Bersatu's incorporation into Pakatan, with Mahathir at the helm.

Yet Malaysians nursing memories of authoritarian rule under Mahathir's first premiership often saw the purported rapprochement between Mahathir and his former enemies — including Anwar, then Penang chief minister Lim Guan Eng and former DAP party leader Lim Kit Siang — as a deeply opportunistic arrangement geared at wresting power from Najib and transferring it back to Mahathir's own family and friends, with little hope for longer-term reforms in the public interest.[4] Even those less sceptical of Mahathir's motives were concerned about how a future Pakatan government would be able to effectively govern, let alone restructure a system moulded to one dominant coalition's benefit for the past six decades.[5]

Such dilemmas bolstered the incumbent government's confidence of winning the general election in the months leading up to GE14, and even recapturing the parliamentary supermajority lost in 2008. For every critic pointing to the likelihood that the 1MDB corruption allegations surrounding Najib Razak would cost Barisan future votes, it could be countered that many voters were more concerned with daily living costs, and whether Barisan would provide sufficiently generous handouts and benefits linked to votes.[6] Suspicions that most Malay voters would continue to support UMNO were deepened at the onset of 2018: Parti Islam Se-Malaysia (PAS), having left the Pakatan coalition in 2015, announced that it would contest an unprecedented 130 parliamentary seats across the peninsula, threatening to split the Malay anti-establishment vote further.[7] Fuelled by what was seen as Mahathir's hijacking of the *Reformasi* platform, political apathy among Malaysia's younger voters appeared to reach new heights in early 2018 — as symbolized by the #UndiRosak vote-spoiling campaign — possibly jeopardizing Pakatan Harapan's electoral prospects.[8] In the run-up to May, most pollsters predicted a victory for Barisan, only differing by the expected winning margin.

Seen in this light, the electoral results of 9 May were simply stunning. From controlling 132 (out of 222) parliamentary seats before GE14, Barisan lost control of the Dewan Rakyat for the first time in history, trailing Pakatan's 113 seats by an eye-popping 34 constituencies. The capture of Putrajaya by Pakatan was further consolidated by the electoral haul at both the federal and state seat levels of ally Parti Warisan Sabah (Warisan). Where Barisan had previously presided over ten (out of thirteen) state governments, they were now left clinging to the support of a mere three (Pahang, Sarawak and Perlis), with Pakatan now in charge of seven states (Johor, Kedah, Malacca, Negeri Sembilan, Penang, Perak and Selangor), PAS two (Kelantan and Trengganu) and Warisan one (Sabah). From a low of 47 per cent in GE13, Barisan's popular vote dropped to just 33 per cent in GE14. PAS, confounding predictions of its imminent political irrelevance, managed to capture one-sixth of the popular vote. As electoral observers soon realized, most Malay voters had simply decided not to vote for Barisan politicians (60–65 per cent of Malays, according to Merdeka Centre), Chinese voters had continued to favour Pakatan candidates, and East Malaysians had deserted Barisan in droves.[9]

The enormity of this political shift was encapsulated in Malaysia's slimmed-down cabinet two months later, comprised of twenty-eight full ministers and twenty-seven deputy ministers drawn overwhelmingly from Pakatan's ranks. The federal leadership now contained a mere three individuals with previous ministerial experience (Mahathir, Muhyiddin Yassin and Saifuddin Abdullah). It also harboured eleven members who had no experience of electoral contestation prior to 2018, including those now helming the ministries of Education, Tourism, Entrepreneurship, Rural Development, Youth and Sports, and National Unity and Social Well-being.

The deeper reasons behind Pakatan's victory will be debated for years to come. Several tentative explanations have already been advanced, grouped into short-, medium- and long-term perspectives. Analysts have noted how electoral campaigning may have fostered a "late surge" in support for Pakatan and its allies. Unlike previous opposition-led rallies in 2008 and 2013, Mahathir was now present, accompanied by a bevy of Malay political veterans, injecting public gatherings and *ceramah* with energy, wit and charisma. Perhaps most importantly, Mahathir was able to render the 1MDB saga easily digestible for less-educated voters, and, regardless of accuracy, linking the apparent venality of the Najib administration with rising day-to-day living costs, not least the federal government's decision to pass the consumption-oriented GST, a highly visible and potentially regressive tax instrument.

Moreover, Barisan Nasional — and Najib in particular — purportedly alienated many fence-sitting voters by introducing new measures to influence electoral outcomes unfairly. The Barisan-dominated parliament gazetted an Anti-Fake News Act on 11 April. The new law was then used by UMNO-linked groups to probe Mahathir's claim of transport sabotage three weeks later.[10] Worse still, a month before Election Day, Mahathir's Bersatu was threatened with permanent dissolution on technical grounds by the Registrar of Societies. The Electoral Commission's unusual decision to hold GE14 in the middle of the week was also generally viewed as an underhanded way to stop Pakatan-friendly voters working in urban areas from casting their votes in distant hometowns, triggering popular movements to organize efforts to get voters and votes to their ballot boxes in time (#BalikUndi, #PulangMengundi, #CarpoolGE14). With mobile network coverage having expanded to cover most rural areas since GE13, Pakatan's propaganda machinery was able to harness these campaign dynamics to their own benefit through growing numbers of followers on Twitter, Facebook and WhatsApp.[11]

No less important were historical legacies weighing down Barisan's popularity. Since at least 2015, not only was Najib (as well as his family and friends) widely suspected of overseeing billions of dollars' worth of money-laundering through the 1MDB but Malaysia's then premier deepened suspicions the following year by quashing local investigations and ejecting political colleagues for daring to question his actions. In helming GE14 while dogged by scandal, Najib and his remaining associates thus contributed to a yawning "trust deficit" between Barisan and the public, making a prospective Mahathir-Anwar combination under Pakatan look relatively more acceptable — even to Malaysians concerned about a return to "Mahathirism".[12]

Barisan's eclipse, nevertheless, predates both Najib's machinations and Mahathir's return. Neither was directly responsible for the coalition's historic loss of its two-thirds parliamentary majority in 2008. Much credit, as others have noted, is due to activists and opposition politicians who had been contesting Barisan's hegemony since at least the late 1990s. This group of middle-class Malaysians, now expecting more from political leaders than old promises to uphold Malay rights and privileges, was itself a product of long-term economic growth and mass education.[13] Running parallel to this demographic shift was the gradual consolidation of popular support for PAS in north Malaysia, underwritten by the party's painstaking cultivation of party loyalists through its extensive network of educational and religious institutions since the 1980s, if not earlier.[14]

Under Pakatan, select areas of federal governance have already seen rapid change in 2018. In keeping with manifesto promises, the new administration eliminated the GST and stabilized petrol prices shortly after emerging victorious, introduced a modicum of Employees Provident Fund contributions for housewives, began restructuring National Higher Education tertiary education loans, re-opened investigations into 1MDB, launched new enquiries into misconduct within the Federal Land Development Authority, Majlis Amanah Rakyat and Lembaga Tabung Haji, and cancelled or suspended several Najib-era megaprojects, including the East Coast Rail Link and Kuala Lumpur–Singapore high-speed rail line. By 1 July, over three-quarters of the eighty-plus government agencies previously under the Prime Minister's Department had been merged, transferred out or scrapped, heralding a new era of institutional independence for government offices in charge of anti-graft efforts, electoral oversight, judicial appointments and human rights governance.

Yet, despite its remarkably non-violent character, the formal transfer of federal power has re-opened old socio-political fault lines running through Malaysia's population, complicating Pakatan's post-electoral reformist agenda. In November 2018, the new government failed a major test of political will when it abandoned a highly publicized plan to ratify the International Convention on the Elimination of All Forms of Racial Discrimination (ICERD). Leaders flinched in the face of protests organized by the youth wings of UMNO and PAS and prominent Malay-Muslim non-governmental organizations. Dissenters, including UMNO's Khairy Jamaluddin, alleged that ratification would violate Article 153 of the Federal Constitution, which assigns responsibilities to safeguard the "special position" of Malays and other natives to the King of Malaysia. Before this politicized and contentious assertion could be qualified by legal experts or the King of Malaysia, Mahathir himself effectively handed his political opponents a major win on 18 November by proclaiming that assimilating ICERD would necessitate constitutional amendments, making its ratification virtually impossible.[15] Mahathir's tendency to prize political expediency over considered consultation was hardly new; in a bid to outflank an ascendant PAS in 2001, he once proclaimed in parliament that Malaysia was a "fundamentalist Islamic state".[16] As in the past, the elder statesman's public assertions drew highly articulate counter-arguments from senior government officials and civil society actors. But the damage had already been done. Leaders of UMNO and PAS spearheaded a victory rally on 8 December, having re-asserted their respective parties' *raison d'être* as guardians of Malay-Muslim rights, successfully reinvigorating the notion that the Federal Constitution somehow legitimized Malay supremacy in perpetuity. In doing so, the ICERD episode effectively rendered tentative efforts to roll back bumiputra quotas in higher education and public procurement — arguably the most visible and entrenched aspects of the race-based preferential system — even harder than before.

Race and religion aside, a large number of long-awaited institutional reforms are likely to take longer than expected to materialize because of their technical and legal intricacies. As a result, structural modifications to make elections fairer by lowering the minimum voting age to eighteen, reforming political party funding legislation and changing the way political parties are registered are all still being studied by the new government. A future electoral boundary re-delineation exercise to redress gross malapportionment and gerrymandering — an old bugbear of urban voters — is only permissible under current constitutional law in 2025.[17]

In the field of criminal law, Pakatan has been labouring to repeal the much-criticized Emergency-era Sedition Act, as well as the death penalty, by year's end. Nevertheless the legal reforms promised within the coalition's manifesto may take as long as a decade to fulfil, owing to their sheer number.[18] Even the apparently simple repeal of the unpopular Anti-Fake News Act by the lower house (Dewan Rakyat) in August 2018 was delayed for an additional year after being rejected by the upper house (Dewan Negara), still controlled by Barisan, a month later.

Meanwhile, criminal proceedings against Najib Razak, his wife Rosmah Mansor, fugitive businessman Low Taek Jho, former 1MDB CEO Arul Kanda, and closely linked political associates like Zahid Hamidi and Musa Aman are gathering pace. Yet the scale and complexity of the corruption charges levelled against these elites, coupled with the new government's need to be seen to be adhering to the rule of law, mean that the trials will only take place in 2019 at the earliest, and be protracted affairs, allowing the defendants ample space in the meantime to defend themselves in the court of public opinion.

Age-old questions regarding political autonomy and oil royalty payments for the East Malaysian states — themselves hinging on how the provisions of the MA63 Agreement and 1974 Petroleum Development Act are interpreted by stakeholders — remain unresolved. Any progress on these matters is only likely to arise in mid-2019, when a recently formed MA63 committee, headed by Mahathir himself, will table its report and recommendations.[19]

Fears of authoritarian rule under Mahathir continue to persist. Critics have argued that several swiftly enacted reforms — the creation of a Minister of Economic Affairs post for Azmin Ali, the establishment and perpetuation of the Council of Eminent Persons past its initially mooted one-hundred-day lifespan, and the replacement of key personnel in various government agencies and government-linked companies — open the way for Mahathir to replenish the corridors of power with old and new cronies who can perpetuate his wishes, shielded from public scrutiny. These concerns have been accentuated by the Barisan coalition's increasingly likely dissolution, and UMNO's steady loss of key party members to Bersatu, with Mahathir ultimately deciding who can come aboard.[20] More sanguine interpretations see an ageing premier who is genuinely interested in restoring the rule of law, requiring experienced and powerful allies to help secure this long-term goal.[21] Pakatan's absorption of former UMNO members of parliament would also help it move closer to locking in a two-thirds parliamentary majority needed to initiate constitutional reforms.[22]

The pressing question of when Anwar — now fully absolved from past sodomy charges and currently Port Dickson's new parliamentary representative — will succeed Mahathir as prime minister, or if he will even do so, also remains unresolved. While in other situations a leader's increasing willingness to stay on beyond a self-imposed two-year timeline might be a non-issue, such dynamics within the Mahathir-Anwar situation spark understandable worry and rumour-mongering.[23] Mahathir's track record of managing leadership successions since the 1980s does not inspire much confidence, and any possible falling out between the two political titans could quickly fracture the Pakatan coalition once more, paving the way for political instability, state decay, social upheaval and further economic stagnation. Only time will tell if the sceptics and pessimists are right.

A Year of Economic Transitions

Compared to the recent political drama, 2018 was a relatively quiet year for the Malaysian economy. Gross domestic product (GDP) growth was weaker than previously forecast, dropping to 4.4 per cent year-on-year in the third quarter of 2018. Real annual GDP growth is likely to round off at 4.7 per cent for 2018, while the International Monetary Fund forecasts 4.5 to 5.0 per cent growth for 2019.[24] Economists pinned the unforeseen slowdown on both domestic and external factors. Internally, the suspensions/cancellations of several infrastructure projects by the Pakatan administration, including the RM81 billion East Coast Rail Link and RM4 billion Trans-Sabah Gas Pipeline projects, were believed to have deflated the construction sector somewhat. Slowing international demand for Malaysian exports and heightened global financial market volatility were also blamed.[25] At the same time, the U.S.-China trade war appeared to have spurred foreign direct investment into Malaysia, which rebounded from RM14 billion in January–September 2017 to RM48.2 billion during the same period in 2018, with Chinese firms leading the way.[26]

That being said, the Malaysian economy was now also operating under genuinely unprecedented constraints. In late May, the new finance minister Lim Guan Eng revealed that Malaysia's national debt was actually 40 per cent higher than previous official figures, exceeding an unprecedented RM1 trillion. He blamed this state of affairs on the secretive behaviour and shoddy accounting practices of the Najib administration. Following this news, the Malaysian ringgit, already declining in value since April, slid below RM4 to the U.S. dollar. It continued to drift downward in reaction to trade tensions between the United States and China and the lack of a clear growth strategy by Malaysia for most of the year.[27] While most public debt load is ringgit-denominated, thus reducing capital flight risks, Malaysia's revised debt situation has nonetheless coloured every fiscal initiative that has followed the debt revelations.

Nowhere was this more apparent than in the new government's reviews of high-profile infrastructure projects. Prasarana Malaysia Berhad's thirty-seven-kilometre-long Light Rail Transit 3 project for Kuala Lumpur was only allowed to continue development in July after the state-owned transport company conceived a plan to cut total project costs by almost half, resulting in RM15 billion worth of savings.[28] Similarly, the Pakatan leadership only permitted the restarting of the MRT2 line project connecting Sungei Buloh to Putrajaya after infrastructure company MMC-Gamuda brought down overall project costs by RM10 billion in October.[29] The Pan-Borneo highway continues to face cost reduction pressures, with new works minister Baru Bian promising to appoint an independent consultant to conduct a project review.[30]

Conversely, early attempts by the Mahathir administration to escape Malaysia's current middle-income trap by revitalizing domestic manufacturing are also being crimped by economic constraints. In the case of automotive manufacturing, political pressures have compounded fiscal ones. Members of the public have expressed much unhappiness with plans that first surfaced in June for a new national car project. Concerns were grounded in unhappy memories of the massive subsidies meted out to Proton and other vehicle manufacturing joint ventures during the

1980s and 1990s under Mahathir. The sheer vehemence of these objections appeared to catch the new government off guard, prompting senior officials to assure the public that the new project, still *in utero*, would be "fully driven by the private sector" and would focus on technological upgrading and economic spill-overs.[31] Mahathir then rounded off the year by launching the Proton X70, a sports utility vehicle fitted with a Geely 1.5 litre turbocharged engine.[32]

Whatever their differences, the new administration and the broader public appear united by concerns about deteriorating living standards. Although headline unemployment rates for Malaysia up until September 2018 held steady at between 3.3 and 3.4 per cent, unemployment rates among youth (15–24 years of age) remained well over three times higher, hovering between 10.4 and 11.6 per cent during the same interval.[33] Anxieties over worsening structural unemployment have been compounded by growing economic inequality, reinforced by a study released by Khazanah Research Institute in October 2018 that highlighted how relative poverty has risen by over 50 per cent to three million households from 1995 to the present day. Of Malaysia's 6.9 million households, 43 per cent can at present be considered impoverished, with a large proportion concentrated in the states of East Malaysia and northern Peninsular Malaysia.[34]

Malaysia's new economic administrators were thus compelled to walk a tightrope, tempering structural transformation goals with budgetary limitations and welfare priorities. The elimination of GST and fuel subsidies after May helped rein in inflation, which rose only 0.2 per cent year-on-year in August, the lowest amount in forty-two months.[35] Inflation, however, rebounded slightly in the months that followed, led by hikes in utilities costs.[36] The degree to which the sales and services tax (SST) — re-introduced from 1 September onwards — has been responsible for rising living costs remains to be fully seen. The federal government, conscious of the need to yoke revenue recovery to progressive taxation, granted SST exemptions on a battery of items believed to disproportionately affect lower-income households, including even the plastic packaging used to contain rice for retail distribution.[37] With eventual SST collections projected to be less than half of GST revenues for 2017, other taxes such as a new sugar tax (to be introduced in April 2019) may go some way to address revenue shortfalls in the longer-term, and perhaps even combat Malaysia's notoriously high obesity rate.[38]

Capping the year's proceedings was the Mahathir administration's budget for 2019, confirming a major break in governance with previous Barisan-led federal governments. Overseen by Finance Minister Lim Guan Eng, RM56.7 billion was allocated towards development expenditures, nearly one-fifth more than the Najib administration's 2018 election-geared budget. The Prime Minister's Department saw its 2019 funding slashed by 70 cent of the roughly RM12.2 billion/year witnessed during Najib's second term as premier, with correspondingly scaled-up fiscal transfers to the ministries of Public Works, Economic Affairs, Transport, Home Affairs, Housing and Local Government, and others.[39] Education expenditures remained high, while the defence budget was cut by a tenth.

The new government also pleasantly surprised many businesses expecting an austerity budget or one including wealth taxes by adopting an expansionary approach, coupled with moderately tightened corporate taxes. The fiscal deficit for 2019 was projected to rise to 3.4 per cent of GDP, up from 2.8 per cent in 2018. Petronas dividends would be used to cover the costs of GST refunds, as well as numerous tax credits for small and medium enterprises. In lieu of a capital gains tax, property taxes were moderately hiked, and balanced with measures to make home ownership more affordable. Rural community leaders, including Orang Asli representatives, welcomed new allocations for rural development, hoping that dedicated funds to repair creaking infrastructure and expand social amenities would not get held up by excessive red tape. Overall, the Budget put flesh on the bones of the Mahathir administration's previously stated intentions to reinvigorate the principles of federal governance while promoting inclusive growth.

A Return to Middle Power Diplomacy

Thanks to the electoral upset, 2018 proved to be a rather topsy-turvy year for those operating within Malaysia's sphere of influence. In past years, the Najib administration had been associated with increasingly close ties to China, Saudi Arabia and Singapore, as well as to the United States under President Trump. With Barisan's electoral defeat, previous deals and alliances with foreign entities came under heavy scrutiny by the new Mahathir-led administration, in line with campaign promises to review Najib-era international mega-investment agreements for signs of lopsided benefits. Despite media-accentuated fears that these reviews would cause all such deals to fold, recalibration, rather than rejection, has been the main outcome to date. Mahathir's return to power also marked a pronounced shift back towards middle-power diplomacy, including a more assertive stance on South China Sea disputes, relations with major powers, as well as the future of multilateral trade agreements — if not in actual policy, at least in rhetoric.

Relations with Singapore were characterized by a number of major developments following Pakatan's victory. The RM60 billion Kuala Lumpur–Singapore high-speed rail project — first unveiled in February 2013 and already in preliminary stages of implementation by early 2018 — was initially threatened with abandonment by the Pakatan government in May on cost-cutting grounds. Three months later, Malaysian and Singaporean government representatives formally agreed to postpone the project until May 2020, with Singapore to receive S$15 million in initial reimbursement costs from the Malaysian authorities.[40] The Mahathir administration's May 2018 decision to discontinue Malaysia's challenge to an International Court of Justice ruling favouring Singapore's sovereignty over Pedra Branca helped keep relations on an even keel,[41] as did cooperation between Singapore's and Malaysia's 1MDB Special Task Forces to repatriate assets associated with the development fund.[42] Negotiations regarding the RM4 billion Johor Baru–Singapore Rapid Transit System Link, aimed at reducing Causeway congestion, also proceeded relatively smoothly, with Malaysia's new transport czar Anthony Loke reaffirming his ministry's commitment to the project by May's end.[43] In the second half of 2018, the Johor authorities themselves continued to push for ways to improve cross-Strait infrastructure, tabling various proposals for a third bridge to Singapore. Overshadowing these proceedings, however, was Mahathir's purported interest in reviving a previously cancelled "crooked bridge" to replace the Malaysian half of the Causeway.[44] Resurrected disputes over the price of raw water sold to Singapore, shared airspace, and territorial waters also look likely to persist into 2019, clouding relations further.[45]

Bilateral relations with Malaysia's other immediate neighbour, Indonesia, grew visibly warm and constructive by the year's end. Following Pakatan's shock win, both Mahathir and new foreign minister Saifuddin Abdullah made official introductory visits to Jakarta in June and July respectively, each reiterating Malaysia's intentions to cooperate with Indonesian counterparts to promote palm oil product exports, manage illegal fishing, alleviate the mistreatment of Indonesian migrant workers and expand educational opportunities for children of Indonesian labourers in East Malaysia.[46] October and November saw both sides meet to sign memorandums of understanding (MoUs) to resolve select international boundary disputes in Borneo's terrestrial areas and maritime locales in the Straits of Malacca and the vicinity of Sulawesi.[47] Both meetings also facilitated preparations for further boundary settlements in Borneo, as well as another MoU on the protection of migrant workers in Malaysia, to be signed when Indonesia's President Joko Widodo visits Kuala Lumpur in January 2019.[48]

As with Singapore, the Mahathir administration's dealings with China were marked by renewed assertiveness. The logic behind the shift had less to do with antagonizing foreign powers than with trying to erase the Najib administration's footprint in foreign relations, particularly with China — a major flashpoint during

2018's election campaign. Two Najib-era China-backed oil and gas pipeline projects in mainland Malaysia and Borneo, as well as a pipeline linking Malacca to a petrochemical plant in Johor, were first suspended in July, before being officially cancelled in September. The 688-kilometre East Coast Rail Link project — already facing criticism from non-partisan observers for its questionable economic viability and heavy reliance on loans from China's Export-Import Bank — still hovers on the brink of cancellation, pending further reviews by the new government. The Chinese-dominated Forest City township project in Johor, which Mahathir with his trademark acid humour once suggested should become a real forest, inhabited by baboons and monkeys, is now likely to focus on constructing lower-cost housing to make it more politically acceptable to middle-class Malaysian voters.[49] Yet Chinese investment in services and manufacturing continued to pour into Malaysia in the months following Pakatan's victory, encouraged by the new administration's openly stated intentions to court foreign investors through tax incentives in value-added activities.[50] Even if many of these initiatives targeted Japanese investors as part of a broader strategy to court East Asian investments, Chinese businesses were still being welcomed.[51]

Malaysia under Mahathir also saw a return to the outspoken nationalistic posturing associated with the premier's first term of office. While frequently courting more foreign investment for Malaysia, Mahathir warned Chinese and U.S. leaders in August and November respectively that unfair trade practices with smaller countries could be construed as neo-colonialism. The same messages were reinforced during Malaysia's interactions within the ASEAN grouping at year's end, with Mahathir offering to take a leading role in expressing concerns over rising global trade tensions and protectionism on behalf of all members.[52] On several occasions in the second half of 2018, the premier also attempted to de-escalate international tensions over the South China Sea by suggesting that "small patrol boats" should replace "big warships".[53] In line with this more neutral stance, the new administration also began to cool relations with Saudi Arabia, initiating moves to withdraw Malaysian troops from Saudi territory from late June onwards, shortly before closing down a Saudi-backed anti-terrorism think tank first launched in Kuala Lumpur in March 2017. In other areas, such as Malaysia's public condemnation of the persecution of Rohingya communities in Myanmar, the Mahathir administration was already following a precedent set by the Najib administration since at least 2016. But whether the new government, in line with campaign promises, will expand Najib-era initiatives on integrating refugees into a comprehensive refugee policy for all asylum seekers (many of whom are Rohingya) remains to be seen.[54]

Final Remarks

On the surface at least, 2018 was an incredibly dramatic year for Malaysia. The country saw a charismatic ninety-three-year-old ex-premier spearhead the electoral destruction of the alliance he once championed, made possible in turn by reconciliation with his former political nemesis Anwar Ibrahim. The Mahathir administration then spent the rest of the year trying to reconcile two conflicting priorities. The first involved setting the wheels of *Reformasi* into motion and beginning to fulfil the long list of promises made in the run-up to elections. The second required the new government to perform damage control and reassure conservative voters, investors and foreign governments that little in Malaysia had fundamentally changed. The vote that gave rise to this balancing act will undoubtedly go down as a turning point in Malaysia's history. But what that turning point implies, and its long-term impact on Malaysians and the region, remains largely an enigma to date.

Notes

1. R.AGE, "The People Speak. The Incredible Story of Malaysia's 14th General Elections", video <https://www.youtube.com/watch?v=jyJIrbPblQo> (accessed 9 November 2018).
2. Jami Blakkarly, "Malaysia's Former PM Mahathir Mohamad Unites with Enemy Anwar Ibrahim in Bid to Oust Najib Razak", ABC News, 9 September 2016.
3. Faizal S. Hazis, "Malaysia in 2017: Strong Economic Growth amidst Intense Power Struggle", in *Southeast Asian Affairs 2018*, edited by Malcolm Cook and Daljit Singh (Singapore: ISEAS – Yusof Ishak Institute, 2018), p. 214.
4. Kua Kia Soong, "Mahathir Must State What He is Sorry For", *Free Malaysia Today*, 2 January 2018.
5. Faizal Hazis, "Malaysia in 2017", p. 214.
6. Eileen Ng, "Looking ahead to 2018: Do or Die Battle for Najib and BN in 'Father of All Elections'", *Today*, 31 December 2017.
7. Rosli Zakaria, "PAS to Contest At Least 130 Parliamentary Seats: Hadi", *New Straits Times*, 31 December 2017.
8. Reuters, "Angry Malaysian Youths Push Protest Vote Campaign", 26 January 2018.
9. Faizal S. Hazis, "GE14: The Political Earthquake That Ended BN's 60-Year Rule", in *Regime Change in Malaysia: GE14 and the End of UMNO-BN's 60-Year Rule*, edited by Francis Loh and Anil Netto (Petaling Jaya/Penang: SIRD/Aliran, 2018), pp. 273–78.
10. *The Star*, "Dr M under Fake News Probe", 3 May 2018.
11. Khor Yu Leng, "Malaysia: The Political Economy of Social Media in GE14", *Khor Reports*, 21 April 2018 <https://www.khor-reports.com/data-analysis/2018/4/21/

malaysia-the-political-economy-of-social-media-in-ge14> (accessed 23 November 2018).

12. Chandra Muzaffar, "The Trust Deficit and the BN Defeat", *Sun Daily*, 15 May 2018; Syed Jaymal Zahiid, "Study Shows Youth Suspicious of Pakatan, Dr M Despite Voting for Them", *Malay Mail*, 30 August 2018.
13. Iskandar Hasan Tan Abdullah, "Dilema Melayu Baharu", *Sinar Harian*, 2 July 2018; Dan Slater, "Malaysia's Modernisation Tsunami", *East Asia Forum*, 20 May 2018.
14. Mohamad Nawab Mohamed Osman, "Why PAS Surpassed Expectations in Malaysia's GE and is New Forbearer of Malay Politics", *Today*, 18 May 2018.
15. Zuraimi Abdullah, "PM: Almost Impossible for Malaysia to Implement ICERD", *New Straits Times*, 18 November 2018; Amy Dodds, "ICERD: Debates and Protests as Malaysia Looks to Ratify Human Rights Treaty", *Southeast Asian Globe*, 5 November 2018.
16. Barry Wain, *Malaysian Maverick. Mahathir Mohamad in Turbulent Times*, 2nd ed. (Houndmills: Palgrave Macmillan, 2012), p. 210.
17. *The Star*, "No Redelineation, At Least Not Until 2025", 1 November 2018.
18. *Malaysiakini*, "AG Wants Ministries, Stakeholders to Help Speed Up Law Reforms", 20 September 2018.
19. Bernama, "MA63: Steering Committee Headed by PM with 16 Members", 11 October 2018.
20. *The Star*, "Ramkarpal: Umno Reps Switching Allegiance to Dr. M is a 'Dangerous Development' ", 13 December 2018.
21. Shamsul Amri Baharuddin, "Status Majlis Penasihat Kerajaan", *Utusan Malaysia*, 26 August 2018.
22. Martin Cavalho, "Pakatan Inches Closer to Majority", *The Star*, 13 December 2018.
23. Joceline Tan, "Lots of Shadow-boxing Going On", *The Star*, 2 November 2018.
24. International Monetary Fund, "IMF Staff Completes 2019 Article IV Consultation to Malaysia", 12 December 2018.
25. Minderjeet Kaur, "Economist: Recession on the Cards If US-China Trade War Continues", *Free Malaysia Today*, 23 August 2018; Tan Xue Ying, "World Bank Cuts Malaysia's 2018 GDP Growth Forecast to 4.9%", *The Edge Financial Daily*, 5 October 2018.
26. Emmanuel Santa Maria Chin, "FDIs Spiked 250pc in 2018, Says Finance Minister", *Malay Mail*, 3 December 2018.
27. Takashi Nakano, "Mahathir's Economic Vision a Hard Sell for Investors", *Nikkei Asian Review*, 10 July 2018.
28. Debra Chong, "Cabinet Greenlights LRT3 after Prasarana Slashes Cost to RM16.63b", *Malay Mail*, 12 July 2018.
29. *The Star*, "Cabinet Accepts MMC-Gamuda Offer", 27 October 2018.

30. Natasha Joibi, "Government Committed to Completing Pan Borneo Highway, Says Works Minister", *The Star*, 14 October 2018.
31. *Malay Mail*, "Govt Received 14 Proposals on New National Car Project, Says Miti", 17 October 2018.
32. Tashny Sukumaran, "Proton X70: An SUV, or a Sign China-Malaysia Ties Are Shifting Up a Gear?", *South China Morning Post*, 13 December 2018.
33. Department of Statistics Malaysia, *Laporan Survei Tenaga Buruh. Suku Tahun Ketiga* (Putrajaya: Department of Statistics Malaysia, 2018), p. 33.
34. Shannon Teoh, "Study Shows Malaysia's Income Gap Has Doubled in Two Decades", *Straits Times*, 16 October 2018.
35. "Malaysia's CPI Rises 0.2% in August", *The Star*, 19 September 2018.
36. Department of Statistics Malaysia, "Press Release. Consumer Price Index Malaysia October 2018", 2018.
37. "Plastic Bags for Rice to be Exempted from SST", *Malay Mail*, 9 September 2018.
38. Justin Lim and Arjuna Chandran Shankar, "F&N Braces for Negative Sugar Tax Impact", *The Edge Financial Daily*, 13 November 2018.
39. Darshan Joshi, "Key Changes to Development Expenditure in Malaysia's Budget 2019", *Penang Institute ISSUES*, 30 November 2018.
40. Cynthia Choo, "KL-Singapore HSR Project Officially Deferred to May 2020", *Today*, 5 September 2018.
41. "Malaysia Drops Challenge to ICJ Ruling on Pedra Branca", *Today*, 30 May 2018.
42. Chester Tay, "Singapore to Return Stolen 1MDB Money", *The Edge Financial Daily*, 1 June 2018.
43. "JB-S'pore Rapid Transit System Rail Link Still On", *Free Malaysia Today*, 30 May 2018.
44. Ben Tan, "Johor's New Crossing to Singapore Nothing to Do with Causeway, State Official Clarifies", *Malay Mail*, 20 November 2018.
45. Bhavan Jaipragas, "Water War Brews as Malaysia's Mahathir Wants Singapore to Cough Up More", *South China Morning Post*, 2 September 2018; Faris Mohktar, "Singapore Protests as Malaysia Expands Port Limits, Vessels Intrude Territorial Waters off Tuas", *Today*, 4 December 2018.
46. Marguerite Afra Sapiie, "Jokowi, Mahathir Discuss Migrant Worker Protection, Border Settlement", *Jakarta Post*, 29 June 2018.
47. Bernama, "Malaysia and Indonesia Ink MoU to Resolve Boundary Issues", 11 October 2018.
48. "Malaysia to Sign MOU to Protect Indonesian Migrants", *Asia Times*, 22 November 2018; "Malaysia, Indonesia Achieve Breakthrough in Territorial Disputes", Bernama, 22 November 2018.
49. "Forest City to Have Affordable Homes", *The Star*, 23 October 2018.
50. "P.M.: Malaysia Could Extend Tax Breaks for Key Foreign Investors", Reuters,

20 June 2018; Adam Aziz, "Malaysia Received RM26.5b FDI in 1H18, China Top Contributor, Says MITI", *The Edge Markets*, 19 November 2018.

51. "Dr M in Japan Says Malaysian Govt Will Remove Obstacles to Doing Business", *Malay Mail*, 6 November 2018.
52. Amir Yusof, "Not Time for ASEAN Countries to Adopt Trade Protectionist Measures: Mahathir", Channel NewsAsia, 13 November 2018.
53. Liew Chin Tong, "The Mahathir Doctrine: A New Deal between Malaysia and China", *Free Malaysia Today*, 13 July 2018; "No Warships in ASEAN Waters, Mahathir Tells United States", Bernama, 15 November 2018.
54. Melissa Goh, "Rohingya Refugees to Be Allowed to Work in Malaysia from March", Channel NewsAsia, 2 February 2017; "Malaysia Needs to Empower Refugees, says Santiago", *The Star*, 1 October 2018.

GE14 IN EAST MALAYSIA: MA63 and Marching to a Different Drum

James Chin

While most scholars argued that 1MDB, Najib and kleptocracy, and the reputation of the United Malays National Organisation (UMNO) were key factors in the historical defeat of UMNO and the Barisan Nasional (BN) in the 2018 general elections, a key part of the shock election outcome has received scant attention: Sabah and Sarawak. If there is one single issue in East Malaysia that rallied the polity, it is the issue of the 1963 Malaysia Agreement (MA63) and the rise of state nationalism. In this chapter, I seek to explain how the MA63 issue became the mainstay of political debate and was the source of historical grievances and the political upheavals caused by the 2018 GE.

In Sabah, the opposition led by the combined Parti Warisan Sabah (Warisan or Sabah Heritage Party) and Pakatan Harapan (PH) won the parliamentary elections convincingly when it took 15 of 25 seats. At the state level, the Warisan-Pakatan alliance won 29 of 60 seats. These are outstanding results for a two-year-old party. In Sarawak, the opposition managed to win 12 of the state's 31 parliamentary seats. (There was no state election, as Sarawak holds their state elections separately.) In the 2013 general elections, the opposition only managed to win 3 parliamentary seats in Sabah and 6 in Sarawak. The opposition thus made major inroads in East Malaysia this round. They managed to replace the Barisan-led state government in Sabah, while laying the foundations for a real challenge to the incumbent in Sarawak when the next state election, due in 2021, comes around. In both Sabah and Sarawak, state nationalism, autonomy and MA63 were key themes used by all sides.

James Chin is the Director of the Asia Institute at the University of Tasmania.

What is MA63

The controversy over MA63 can be summed up in two words: historical grievances. Simply put, the peoples of East Malaysia feel that they have been marginalized in the Malaysian Federation, despite the fact that they were one of the three founding entities (Malaya, Singapore, North Borneo/Sarawak) that came together to establish a new federation in the region. They feel strongly that the spirit of the agreement, safeguards and special privileges promised in the 1963 Malaysia Agreement (MA63) have for the past half-century mostly not been kept by the federal government.

What are the key parts of the historical grievances?[1] They can be broken down into three broad parts, all interrelated: the special position of Sabah and Sarawak, the issue of consent and the role of the British, and federal intervention and the transfer of the UMNO model to Sabah and Sarawak.

The Special Position of Sabah and Sarawak

When East Malaysians speak of their "special position", it refers to the set of political safeguards commonly called "The Twenty Points". These twenty points were political safeguards requested by the Borneo leaders as preconditions for accepting the federation proposed by Tunku Abdul Rahman. The main parts of the safeguards are summarized below:

- Islam's status as a national religion was not to be applicable to Sarawak nor Sabah. While there was no objection to Islam being the religion of the federation, there will be no state religion in either Sabah or Sarawak.
- Immigration control was to be vested in Sabah and Sarawak, allowing them to deny entry even to other Malaysian citizens residing outside the two states.
- Complete the Borneanization of the civil service as quickly as possible, promoting Borneo natives to fill the senior positions then held by British expatriates.
- No right of secession from the federation.
- The "special position" of the Malays in the new Malaysian Constitution will apply to the indigenous peoples of the Borneo states.
- Sabah and Sarawak were to be given a high degree of autonomy over their civil service, financial affairs, local government, education and health.
- No modification of these safeguards by the federal government without the consent of Sabah and Sarawak.

While there is debate among East Malaysians over these key areas, there is general consensus that the federal government has not kept its promise in any of these areas, save for perhaps immigration control.

The "special position" also refers to what the East Malaysians regard as disrespect for history. They are unhappy that Hari Merdeka (Independence Day) is celebrated on 31 August. While 31 August 1957 is the date of independence for Malaya, the Federation of Malaysia actually came into being on 16 September 1963. Many entities, including government departments, date the number of years of independence from 1957 rather than 1963. The official school history textbook concentrates on the role of UMNO in the road to Malayan independence in 1957, rather than the road to the formation of the federation in 1963.

Another insult, according to many East Malaysians, is the purposeful downgrading of Sabah and Sarawak's position in the Federal Constitution. In the original Federal Constitution adopted on 16 September 1963, Article 1(2) states that:

> The States of the Federation shall be-
> (a) The States of Malaya, namely, Johore, Kedah, Kelantan, Malacca, Negeri Sembilan, Pahang, Penang, Perak, Perlis, Selangor and Terengganu.
> (b) the Borneo States, namely, Sabah and Sarawak; and
> (c) the State of Singapore.

In 1976, however, there was a constitutional amendment, leading to a new Article 1(2), which states that:

> The States of the Federation shall be Johore, Kedah, Kelantan, Malacca, Negeri Sembilan, Pahang, Penang, Perak, Perlis, Sabah, Sarawak, Selangor and Terengganu.

For many East Malaysians, this represented total disrespect for history and an attempt to "downgrade" the two Borneo states as being of equal status to the other Malayan states.

Another issue often raised was the promise of development. Part of the reason why Sabah and Sarawak were "special" was due to their relative underdevelopment back in the 1960s. Malayan and Singapore leaders made clear promises that if the Borneo states merged into the federation they would be developed at a much faster pace. Half a century later, Sabah remains one of the states with the highest levels of poverty, and there are still no roads into many parts of the interior of Sabah or Sarawak. The unhappiness is compounded by the fact that Sabah and

Sarawak are leading oil and gas producers in the country. Unfortunately, under the Petroleum Development Act (PDA1974), all oil and gas resources belong to the federal government, while states are only entitled to a five per cent royalty. The public perception is that most of the major infrastructure projects in Malaysia — such as the highways, ports and airport and the iconic Petronas Twin Towers — were built with the oil and gas revenues from East Malaysia, at the expense of the development of Sabah and Sarawak. Hence, the popular narrative is that Peninsular Malaysia "stole" the oil and gas from East Malaysia to fund its own development. They also believe that if Sabah and Sarawak were independent, this would not have happened.

The Issue of Consent and the Role of the British

There is widespread belief among East Malaysians that the formation of the federation was "fixed" by the British, and that the peoples of North Borneo (as Sabah was called before 1963) and Sarawak were not consulted. On paper, there was extensive consultation, including the Malaysian Solidarity Consultative Committee (MSCC) and the Cobbold Commission. Between 24 August 1961 and 1 February 1962, the MSCC held four meetings, in Jesselton (now Kota Kinabalu), Kuching, Kuala Lumpur and Singapore, where the local political leaders from Malaya, Singapore, North Borneo and Sarawak met to discuss the proposed federation.[2] This led a formal Malayan/UK commission, called the Cobbold Commission, to ascertain the views of the peoples of Sarawak and North Borneo. In the processes of both the MSCC and the Cobbold Commission, the British played a key role in mobilizing support for the Tunku's proposal. Finally, there was the Inter-Governmental Committee (IGC), formed to plan the legislative framework of the Malaysia Agreement. Lord Lansdowne represented the United Kingdom, while Tun Abdul Razak represented Malaya. The IGC held meetings from August to December 1962. It was divided into five sub-committees: constitutional, fiscal, legal and judicial, public service, and departmental organization. The final IGC report was published in February 1963, which contained the safeguards requested.[3]

Prior to the MSCC process, the most senior British officials in Southeast Asia — Sir Alexander Waddell (the governor of Sarawak), Sir William Goode (the governor of North Borneo), Mr D.C. White (the high commissioner of Brunei), Lord Selkirk (the commissioner-general for the United Kingdom in Southeast Asia) — had met secretly in July 1961 to coordinate the support of the civil service in the territories for the proposal. Moreover, not one of the five members of the Cobbold Commission was an independent actor — Lord

Cobbold, Sir Anthony Abell and David Watherston were representatives of the Colonial Office, while Wong Pow Nee and Ghazali Shafie represented the Malayan government, and both the British and Malayan governments were proponents of the federation proposal.

The key findings of the Cobbold Commission were that one-third of the peoples in North Borneo and Sarawak supported the formation of Malaysia without conditions, another third supported Malaysia with safeguards, while the remaining third were against it. Thus, the British and Malayan governments argued that, as long as the safeguards were put in place, two-thirds of the population could be considered as being in favour of the proposed federation. However, another way of reading the results is that two-thirds of the population did not agree to Malaysia. Furthermore, it was clear that the indigenous population had no idea what the new federation or merger with Malaya and Singapore would entail, since the majority of the indigenous population were illiterate and did not fully grasp the concept of a new sovereign nation.

The hidden hand on the part of the British in ensuring the creation of Malaysia was further evidenced during the United Nations Malaysia Mission in 1963,[4] which came to the exact conclusion as the Cobbold Commission. Prior to the UN Mission, the British UN delegation telegrammed the Foreign and Commonwealth Offices to give the assurance that "the assessment teams will be hand-picked to produce the right results from our point of view".[5]

The role played by the British is not lost on the present generation. In the past five years, two petitions have been handed to Buckingham Palace asking the queen to review the MA63 agreement. In both cases the petitioners received a polite reply from the palace stating that MA63 was a domestic matter for Malaysia.[6]

Federal Intervention and the Transfer of the UMNO Model to Sabah and Sarawak

Since 1963, the UMNO-led federal government has taken an active interest in the domestic politics of the two East Malaysian states. UMNO appears to seek two objectives. It wants Sabah and Sarawak to replicate the Barisan Nasional model, where Malay/Muslims are first among equals and Islam takes a leading role, often referred to as *Ketuanan Melayu* (Malay Supremacy) and *Ketuanan Islam* (Islamic Supremacy).[7] In practice, this means the federal government will intervene, whenever possible, to ensure that the post of chief minister is held by a Malay, or at least a Muslim, and the state government remains pro-Barisan and aligned with the federal government. This is insisted upon, even though indigenous Muslims are a minority in both states, while the largest indigenous groups in Sarawak (the Dayaks) and Sabah (the Kadazandusun Murut, or KDM) are largely non-Muslims or Christians.

In 1966, 1970 and 1987, the federal government played a decisive role in ensuring that the Melanau Muslims took power at the expense of the Dayak community in Sarawak. In Sabah, in 1965, 1967, 1976, 1985/86 and 1994, UMNO tried its best to install a Muslim-led state government each time.[8] When the KDM community rebelled against the political dominance of Islam in the 1980s, the federal government established a secret "Project IC" to make Sabah a Muslim-majority state.[9] Project IC involved giving citizenship illicitly to Muslim immigrants from Mindanao (Southern Philippines) and Indonesia. By the early 1990s, Sabah had become a Muslim-majority state.

UMNO's success at keeping Muslims in power in East Malaysia means that the indigenous majority of Sabah and Sarawak have been prevented from becoming the chief minister unless they convert to Islam. This leaves the indigenous population feeling as though they are "second class bumiputra" compared to Malay-Muslims, contrary to the MA63 promise that they will be treated as equals to Malays. The common theme in Sabah and Sarawak is the marginalization that the indigenous people have endured over the past half-century, especially in comparison to the benefits accrued by the Muslim communities in both states.[10]

The issue of *Ketuanan Islam* is highly sensitive in both states. The Barisan state government in Sabah has changed its state constitution to elevate Islam as the official religion, although Sarawak has not. A significant number of indigenous people in both states are Christians, leading them to feel discriminated against when the federal government openly restricts the Christian faith. The Kalimah Allah issue is a case in point. Even before 1963, Christians had used the word "Allah" in worship and print in many indigenous churches throughout Sabah and Sarawak. Hence, they could not understand the federal government's move to stop them from using the word in their churches at present. Furthermore, attempts to ban Bahasa Indonesia and Iban-language bibles for use by the indigenous Christian congregations is another sore point. Resentment is growing at efforts, ongoing since the 1970s, to convert as many indigenous groups as possible to Islam to secure a Muslim-majority, often with rewards and promise of aid.[11]

Post-GE14: Rebranding in Sarawak

The moment the component parties in the Sarawak Barisan coalition realized that UMNO and the Barisan Nasional had lost power at the federal level, they decided to exit the coalition. Although the same parties were still in power at the state level, the change at the federal level gave an unmistakable signal that the Barisan coalition was no longer electable and faces certain defeat at the next state election in 2021. Unlike in Sabah, the four parties in the Sarawak Barisan coalition — Parti Pesaka Bumiputra Bersatu (PBB), Parti Rakyat Sarawak (PRS), Sarawak United People's Party (SUPP) and Progressive Democratic Party (PDP) — remained intact. The governor of Sarawak, Taib Mahmud, the real power behind PBB, flew to Kuala Lumpur to meet up with Mahathir. Taib tried to get Mahathir to accommodate the four Sarawak parties within the Pakatan Harapan coalition, but Mahathir refused to commit himself.[12] Without an agreement with Mahathir, Sarawak chief minister Abang Johari announced that the Sarawak Barisan would rebrand itself as Gabugan Parti Sarawak (GPS). GPS would only accept Sarawak-based parties and pursue a "Sarawak-First" policy. The number one priority for GPS was to "reclaim" the MA63 rights lost over the past fifty years.[13]

In a remarkable move, Abang Johari also blamed UMNO and the federal government for taking away Sarawak's special autonomy. However, the breathtaking hypocrisy of the GPS could not hide the fact that it was during the period of Taib Mahmud's iron rule in Sarawak, lasting over three decades, that the federal government eroded the state's rights and autonomy. The component parties of GPS were the very same parties that had worked with UMNO. In fact, Taib Mahmud was a strong political ally of Mahathir when the latter was the head of UMNO, and it was also Taib who strongly supported the PDA (1974) that transferred all of Sarawak's oil and gas resources to Petronas. If it was Mahathir who had centralized too much power in the federal government during his twenty-two years as prime minister, then it was Taib Mahmud on the Sarawak side that did not resist. Taib, for one, certainly did not mention anything about MA63 "rights" during his tenure as chief minister. In fact, if anything, Taib's stranglehold on Sarawak politics allowed him, allegedly, to siphon off billions.[14]

The GPS strategy is unpretentious: it believes that the use of MA63 nationalism can help it to win over all ethnic groups in Sarawak. By claiming to be the "real" MA63 champion, it positions itself as the umbrella for all Sarawak-based parties, and thus against the peninsular-based Pakatan parties such as Parti Pribumi Bersatu Malaysia (Bersatu), the Democratic Action Party (DAP), Parti Keadilan Rakyat (PKR) and Amanah. Mahathir's Bersatu expanded its reach into Sarawak in December 2018 to challenge PBB directly for the Muslim vote, leaving DAP and PKR to spearhead the challenge against SUPP, PDP and PRS for the non-Muslim vote.[15]

Post-GE14: Collapse of Sabah BN

Although the Warisan-Pakatan alliance secured twenty-nine state seats, it was still short of a simple majority in the sixty-seat state assembly and had to rely on defections, a common occurrence in Sabah politics.[16] The first to leave the Sabah Barisan coalition was the United Pasokmomogun Kadazandusun Murut Organisation (UPKO), with UPKO announcing on election night (9 May) itself that five of its state assemblymen would defect to the Warisan-Pakatan alliance, giving the latter a clear majority.

At almost the same time, Musa Aman, the incumbent chief minister and leader of Sabah UMNO, persuaded the state governor to swear him in as chief minister again, claiming that he had the support of two assemblymen from Parti Solidariti Tanah Airku Rakyat Sabah (STAR, or the Homeland Solidarity Party), a small opposition party. He further claimed that other than the president of UPKO, the remaining four UPKO assemblymen had not defected to the Warisan-Pakatan alliance. A day later, however, the governor filed a police report alleging that Musa had "intimidated" him into holding the swearing-in ceremony.[17] Two days later, on the 12 May, Shafie Apdal of Warisan was sworn in as chief minister.[18]

This also coincided with developments on 11 and 12 May. On 11 May, the Chinese-based Liberal Democratic Party (LDP) announced that it was leaving the Barisan coalition. A day later, the KDM-based Parti Bersatu Rakyat Sabah (PBRS, or United Sabah People's Party) and Parti Bersatu Sabah (PBS, or United Sabah Party) announced that they would also be leaving Barisan.

With the collapse of Sabah Barisan, the now-former chief minister Musa Aman suddenly left for London and did not return to Malaysia until 21 August. In early November he was charged with corruption.[19] Barely a month later, Sabah UMNO imploded when almost its entire slate of elected members of parliament and state assemblymen resigned en masse from the party, leaving it with a single MP and one state assemblyman.[20]

Rise of State Nationalism

Although there has always been a minority of peoples in East Malaysia who were unhappy with the federation, it only became a mass movement after the 2008 general elections. The results of the 2008 general elections changed the entire tone of Putrajaya–East Malaysia relations. In that particular election, Barisan lost its two-thirds majority in the Federal Parliament for the first time in half a century. The BN won 140 seats to the opposition Pakatan Rakyat's 82. The same occurred in the 2013 general elections, with Barisan winning 133 to Pakatan's 89 seats. What changed the relationship was the number of East Malaysian federal parliamentarians that made up Barisan's national count. In 2008, East Malaysia provided 55 Barisan MPs; in 2013 it provided 47. Barisan had a parliamentary majority of 28 seats in 2008, which was reduced to 21 seats in 2013. In other words, without the component parties of East Malaysia, UMNO and Barisan would have lost power in 2008 and 2013. It is no coincidence that then prime minister Najib Razak declared an additional public holiday on 16 September as "Malaysia Day", as a nod to East Malaysia. From then on, activists from Sabah and Sarawak have used social media to mobilize support for complete autonomy from the federal government, i.e., MA63. The more it was discussed, the more it became apparent that there was a deep well of resentment against the federal government and the peninsular states over MA63 and marginalization over the nearly half-century of the federation.

Going forward, state nationalism centred on MA63 grievances will take centre stage in East Malaysian politics for some time to come. Politicians from all sides now claim to be the true champions of MA63, including those who had previously collaborated closely with UMNO, such as the GPS in Sarawak. Anifah Aman, one of Sabah UMNO's most senior leaders, has announced he was leaving UMNO to form a new political party that will stand on a single issue: MA63.[21]

The new Pakatan administration is aware of the potency of MA63, and has moved quickly to try to defuse anti-federal sentiments in East Malaysia.[22] In July, barely two months in power, the Pakatan federal government announced that it was setting up a federal, cabinet-level committee to deal with issues relating to MA63 and decentralizing power back to East Malaysia.[23] Its first priority is to amend Article 1(2) of the Federal Constitution to return it to its original wording to ensure that Sarawak and Sarawak are listed separately from the Malayan states.[24]

The greatest fear for the federal government is secession or the growth of an independence movement in Sabah and Sarawak. In the past decade, nascent secessionist movements have emerged in both states, mobilized primarily through social media. Groups based outside Malaysia, such as Sabah Sarawak Keluar Malaysia (SSKM) in the United Kingdom and Sabah Sarawak Rights Australia New Zealand (SSRANZ), openly advocate for secession as the only option, given the extensive breaches of MA63 by the federal government.[25] Secessionist movements physically located in East Malaysia are more discreet about promoting secession, for fear of arrest. Advocating secession falls under the crime of sedition in Malaysia. They thus couch their rhetoric in terms of state nationalism, such as "Sabah for Sabahans" and "Sarawak for Sarawakians". Some however argue that it is not a crime to talk about secession, given that the Federal Constitution is silent on secession.[26] Others believe that the best way to break away from Malaysia is to hold a referendum on this issue.[27] The political reality is that the federal government will not allow Sabah or Sarawak to break up the federation, either now or for the foreseeable future, without bloodshed. The Malay leadership in Kuala Lumpur is still sore about the exit of Singapore from the federation in 1965. The Malay elite in Malaysia saw that as a grave political mistake that must never be repeated. Another political barrier is precedence: the Malay establishment is worried that other constituent states with strong state identities such as Johor or Kelantan may break away if Sabah and Sarawak were allowed to leave. There is also the economic argument: there are still massive untapped natural resources in addition to oil and gas found in East Malaysia. There is no reason to think that the Malay leadership in Putrajaya are not interested in these resources.

The next big political test for MA63 will be the Sarawak state election, due by 2021 but likely to be held in 2020. As mentioned above, the GPS is standing solely on the issue of MA63 state nationalism and nothing else. The Pakatan opposition in Sarawak is also standing on MA63 state nationalism, but with a twist: the Sarawak Pakatan is telling Sarawakians that if they want the full MA63 autonomy and the return of state powers, they must replace the ruling GPS with Pakatan, since the federal Pakatan administration would only devolve power to an ally. The point here is that no matter which side wins, MA63 will still be the driving force of East Malaysian politics for some time to come.

Notes

1. James Chin, "Federal-East Malaysia Relations: Primus-Inter-Pares?", in *50 Years of Malaysia: Federalism Revisited*, edited by Andrew Harding and James Chin (Singapore: Marshall Cavendish, 2014), pp. 152–85.
2. Brunei initially took part in the MSCC but dropped out when the sultan decided not to join the proposed federation.
3. The three most important documents, including the actual Malaysia Agreement, were compiled and published as a single book by one of the signatories from Sarawak. See James Kim Min Wong, *The Birth of Malaysia: A Reprint of the Cobbold Report, the I.G.C. Report and the Malaysia Agreement* (Sweet & Maxwell Asia, 2008).
4. The Philippines and Indonesia were against the Malaysia proposal, and they pressured the Tunku to agree to a UN survey team being sent to Sabah and Sarawak to, like the Cobbold Commission, ascertain the wishes of the peoples.
5. Matthew Jones, *Conflict and Confrontation in South East Asia, 1961–1965: Britain,*

the *United States, Indonesia and the Creation of Malaysia* (Cambridge University Press, 2001), p. 84.

6. Personal communication from people involved with the petition. One group came from Sarawak and the other group from Sabah.
7. James Chin, "Exporting the BN/UMNO Model: Politics in Sabah and Sarawak", in *Routledge Handbook of Contemporary Malaysia*, edited by M. Weiss (London: Routledge 2015), pp. 83–92.
8. James Chin, "Politics of Federal Intervention in Malaysia, with reference to Kelantan, Sarawak and Sabah", *Journal of Commonwealth and Comparative Politics* 35, no. 2 (July 1997): 96–120; Audrey Kahin, "Crisis on the Periphery: The Rift between Kuala Lumpur and Sabah", *Pacific Affairs* 65, no. 1 (1992): 30–49.
9. Kamal Sadiq, "Redefining Citizenship: Illegal Immigrants as Voters in India and Malaysia" (PhD thesis, University of Chicago, Department of Political Science, 2003). See also the Report of Royal Commission of Inquiry on Immigrants in Sabah (Government of Malaysia 2014).
10. In Malaysia, being classified as a bumiputra brings significant benefits, such as special business licences, bank loans, easier access to scholarships and entry to public universities, jobs in the public sector and discounts for buying new houses. The non-Muslim indigenous bumiputra in East Malaysia argued that the Malays and other Muslims are the main beneficiaries. See James Chin, " 'Malay Muslim First': The Politics of Bumiputeraism in East Malaysia", in *Illusions of Democracy: Malaysian Politics and People*, edited by Sophie Lemiere (Selangor: Strategic Information and Research Development Centre, 2017), pp. 201–20.
11. "Don't Threaten Borneo Christians, Sarawak Lawmaker Warns 'Islamisation Champs' ", *Malay Mail* online, 30 June 2015. For a first-hand account of how Kuala Lumpur tries to convert indigenous leaders in Sabah to Islam by promising rewards and persecuting priests, see Bernard Sta Maria, *Peter J. Mojuntin, the Golden Son of the Kadazan* (1978). This book was banned by the federal government in 1978 and remains banned to this day.
12. "Report of Dr M-Taib Meeting Sparks Speculation about Shift in S'wak", *The Star*, 11 May 2018.
13. " 'Sarawak First' among Main Struggle of GPS — Abang Johari", *Borneo Post*, 25 November 2018.
14. Lukas Straumann, *Money Logging: On the Trail of the Asian Timber Mafia* (Basel: Bergli Books, 2014). There have been extensive and credible investigations by NGOs into Taib's ill-gotten wealth, but to this day he has been able to escape all form of sanction. He is so powerful politically that locals call him the new "White Rajah" of Sarawak.
15. "Dr Mahathir Launches Sarawak PPBM", *Malay Mail* online, 1 December 2018.
16. James Chin, "A Regime Change Glanced Askance", *New Mandala*, 22 June 2018.

17. "Police Seek Musa Aman over 'Intimidation' of Governor", *Malaysiakini*, 24 May 2018.
18. Musa Aman went to court claiming he was the rightful chief minister but he lost the case. See "Shafie Apdal, Not Musa Aman, is Legitimate Sabah Chief Minister, Court Rules", *Straits Times*, 7 November 2018.
19. "Former Sabah Chief Minister Musa Aman Pleads Not Guilty to 35 Graft Charges Involving S$87m", *Straits Times*, 5 November 2018.
20. "Sabah UMNO Exodus Sees Nine of 10 Aduns, Five of Six MPs Leave", *The Star*, 12 December 2018.
21. "Anifah Prepared to Form New Party, Focus on MA63", *Malaysiakini*, 14 December 2018.
22. James Chin, "Why New Malaysian Govt Must Heed MA63 Rallying Cry", *Straits Times*, 31 May 2018.
23. Andrew Harding, "Devolution of Powers in Sarawak: A Dynamic Process of Redesigning Territorial Governance in a Federal System", *Asian Journal of Comparative Law* 12, no. 2 (2017): 257–79.
24. "KL Set to Elevate Status of Sabah, Sarawak as PH Shores Up Support", *Straits Times*, 18 December 2018.
25. Some members of SSKM and SSRANZ have been harassed by the Malaysian police for advocating secession. A few of them applied for political refugee status in Australia.
26. No secession was part of the "20 Points" but it was left out in the final draft of the 1963 federal constitution.
27. "Soo: Grant a Referendum to People of Sarawak, Sabah", *Borneo Post*, 1 October 2018.

Myanmar

Myitkyina
Mandalay
Taunggyi
NAYPYITAW
Pyinmana
Yangon
Pathein

MYANMAR IN 2018: New Democracy Hangs in the Balance

Morten B. Pedersen

The National League for Democracy (NLD) government has struggled to deliver on its promise of "change" since it swept into office with a landslide victory in the 2015 elections. The year 2018 saw a new push for reform, especially in the socio-economic arena. However, criticism of the government's handling of the peace process and the Rohingya crisis only grew in volume during the year, and business confidence remained subdued. For the majority of people in the country, there was little improvement in their daily lives.

The danger of persistent underperformance was brought home by the NLD's relatively poor showing in the November by-elections. The NLD won seven of the thirteen seats contested but lost three seats that it previously held to the Union Solidarity and Development Party (USDP) and another one to the Chin League for Democracy, suggesting that its hold on power may be weakening as the 2020 elections loom ever larger on the horizon. Meanwhile, broader systemic threats to Myanmar's new democracy are growing, both internally and externally.

A Push for Reform

While the majority of assessments of the NLD government continued to be overwhelmingly negative,[1] it did take some important steps to strengthen governance and accelerate socio-economic reform. Through their first two years in office, government leaders had seemed largely dismissive of criticism, routinely insisting

MORTEN B. PEDERSEN is Senior Lecturer in International and Political Studies at the University of New South Wales Canberra (Australian Defence Force Academy) and a former senior analyst for the International Crisis Group in Myanmar.

that they were focusing on long-term, structural issues and needed time to deliver. However, with the 2020 elections fast approaching, there appeared to be a growing recognition that new initiatives would be needed for the NLD to maintain voter support and consolidate civilian, democratic government.

The first major change came in March with the retirement of President Htin Kyaw and the subsequent election of former lower house speaker U Win Myint as the new head of state. Although State Counsellor Aung San Suu Kyi remained the de facto leader of the government, observers universally saw the choice of Win Myint as an important step, pointing to his reputation as a more decisive leader than his predecessor. At the same time as his election as president, Win Myint was also appointed as new vice-chairman (1) of the NLD, thus seemingly positioning him as the successor of Aung San Suu Kyi. The party billed this as a rejuvenation of the party leadership, which also included the appointment of Mandalay Region chief minister U Zaw Myint as vice-chairman (2). Although both men are in their sixties, they are considered part of the second generation of NLD leaders.[2]

Another significant restructuring of the government followed in June when the long-embattled minister of finance and planning U Kyaw Win was removed amidst accusations of poor leadership and corruption and was replaced by U Soe Win. Although the seventy-three-year-old former head of Deloitte Myanmar was hardly a youthful addition to an already ageing cabinet, he came to the post with unrivalled experience in both finance and business and, importantly, was seen as much more capable than his predecessor. The parallel appointment of former national security adviser and minister of the Union Government U Thaung Tun, initially as chairman of the Myanmar Investment Commission and later also as the head of a new Ministry of Investment and Foreign Economic Relations, completed the formation of a more high-profile and proactive economic team.

With a new line-up of key leaders and, by all accounts, much improved internal decision-making structures, the government made a renewed push for reform. In twin speeches following his inauguration, the new president and the state counsellor both emphasized the need to step up efforts to improve the socio-economic lives of the people, seemingly signalling a change in priorities from political to economic issues.[3] A few weeks later, in his New Year address, Win Myint further fleshed out what this would mean, laying out an eleven-point reform plan that included, among other things, tackling corruption, creating an independent and impartial judiciary and returning confiscated land to its rightful owners.[4] Although it was never said explicitly, it soon became apparent that the new president would take a more active leadership role than his predecessor, with a particular focus on improving governance. During his first months in office, he seemed to be focussing especially on marshalling the civil service behind the government's reform drive and reinforcing its signature anti-corruption drive.

While the new president focused on improving public administration, the new economics team got down to the business of realizing a number of long-planned economic reforms, which had been held back by bureaucratic inertia and opposition from vested business interests. In August, the government finally revealed the Myanmar Sustainable Development Plan 2018–2030 (MSDP), which brings together the country's myriad of sectoral, ministerial and sub-national plans under the aegis of a single national strategy.[5] Aside from expressing an overall national development vision, the MSDP will be linked to a Project Bank of priority public investment projects that have already been scrutinized and approved by the government.[6] It was followed two months later by a new Myanmar Investment Promotion Plan, which aims to dramatically expand public investments over the next twenty years.[7] Crucially, each of these plans highlights the importance of promoting responsible investments in support of sustainable, broad-based growth and increased equality, thus establishing a firm value-basis for the country's economic policy going forward.

Beyond broad economic plans (but in line with them), the year also saw further liberalization of the retail and wholesale, banking and insurance sectors, which were opened to foreign participation. These steps had faced strong opposition from powerful domestic business interests. As such, although the openings remained partial, they revealed a government that was getting bolder in asserting its priorities. A new assertiveness was evident also in the government's negotiations with China around major investment projects, such as the China-Myanmar Economic Corridor and the Kyaukphyu Special Economic Zone, which were concluded on terms that were more favourable to Myanmar than originally proposed.[8]

Finally, a few days before the end of the year, in its boldest move yet to increase civilian democratic space, the government announced that the General Affairs Department (GAD) would be transferred from the Ministry of Home Affairs to the Ministry of the Office of the Union Government and thus brought more fully under civilian control. This was a highly significant move, since the GAD forms the primary link between the national and lower levels of government and therefore is key to ensuring that national-level reforms filter through to and benefit local communities. Under the 2008 constitution, the department has direct control of district and township authorities, the country's key administrative institutions, with wide-ranging responsibilities to uphold security, enforce laws and regulations, collect taxes and manage public services. According to government officials, the transfer was necessary to bring the GAD under control of the regional and state chief ministers — which under the existing system were often circumvented by GAD officials reporting directly back to the minister of home affairs — and prepare the country for a federal system.[9] It will be a challenge for the NLD government to reform a department that has long been under military control and whose senior staff are overwhelmingly from the military. However, it appears to have made a deliberate effort to "soften" the transition by appointing two ex-military officers, U Min Thu and U Tin Myint as, respectively, the new minister and deputy minister of the Office of the Union Government.[10] The former reportedly has been playing a key role in communications between the civilian and military sides of government even before his promotion, and, as such, would seem to be well positioned to mediate the inevitable clash of administrative cultures and institutional interests.[11]

The Quest for Peace

While the year saw some important governance reforms, the peace process seemed to be going nowhere fast. Peace was to have been an easy win for Aung San Suu Kyi, whose father, General Aung San, is credited with bringing the different ethnic groups together at independence in 1948 to form the Union of Burma. However, the popular democracy leader who is used to having her way in her own party and government always seemed out of her element in the rough-and-tumble of the peace negotiations, and perhaps therefore has fallen back on a tightly scripted and formalistic process that has demonstrably failed to overcome the deep-rooted trust deficit between the Burman-dominated government and the ethnic armed organizations (EAOs). It has not helped that she appears to have gradually ceded leadership of the process to the military.

There was a small breakthrough in February when the New Mon State Party and Lahu Democratic Union, after much coaxing — and facing the prospect of losing out on new development funding going into the Southeast — signed the National Ceasefire Agreement (NCA), thus increasing the total number of EAO signatories from eight to ten. Despite frequent suggestions by government peace negotiators that a deal was near to bring in the much larger ethnic armies in the Northeast, including the United Wa State Party (UWSP) and the Kachin Independence Organisation (KIO), the count however stayed at ten. Instead, in late October, in a now-familiar pattern of one-step forward, two-steps back, the two leading signatories, the Karen National Union (KNU) and the Restoration Council of Shan State (RCSS), both suspended their participation in parts of the

NCA-based peace process, which thus seemed to have hit its lowest point since it began in 2011.

There are many reasons why the EAOs remain reluctant to join the NCA process, which the government insists is the "only game in town", but the main one is the lack of progress in the national political dialogue, which is supposed to produce a national peace accord by 2020. The government and the participating EAOs have been at a deadlock since the second 21st Century Panglong Conference held in May 2017. On the face of it, the main point of contention is the insistence by the military that in return for being granted self-determination and individual state constitutions under a new federal system, EAOs must pledge not to secede from the union and accept that there can only be one army in the country. But the deeper problem appears to be the continued priority given by many of the armed groups, including the Tatmadaw and key EAOs, to short-term, military strategic objectives over longer-term political goals (which in turn reflects the aforementioned lack of trust between the parties).

The third 21st Century Panglong Conference — originally scheduled for January 2018 — was delayed several times and went ahead only after agreement was reached to postpone discussion of the above-mentioned political principles, which continued to divide the parties. Thus, when it was finally held in mid-July, agreement was reached only on fourteen "soft" issues, mainly related to generic human rights commitments that are already guaranteed in the 2008 constitution. To most intents and purposes it was a non-event. In an attempt to break the deadlock, an unprecedented leaders' meeting was held in mid-October, bringing together all the top leaders from the EAOs and the government. But, again, little was achieved other than a vague agreement to revisit the framework for political dialogue. Commander-in-Chief Min Aung Hlaing reportedly left soon after delivering his opening address, which EAO leaders saw as further evidence of military intransigence, and the meeting closed a day early.[12] Having faced yet another disappointment and with internal disagreements coming to a head over the best way forward, the KNU announced it would suspend its participation in the formal peace process, although it would continue informal negotiations with the government.[13] The RCSS followed suit by withdrawing from the Joint Monitoring Committee, which is the main mechanism for resolving conflicts and disagreements between the parties to the NCA process.[14]

In the absence of any meaningful breakthroughs in the peace negotiations, armed conflict continued in several areas across the country, involving a mix of large-scale strategic battles for control of territory and smaller skirmishes mostly caused by localized disagreements over troop movements and economic activities.

The largest conflagrations continued to be in Kachin and Northern Shan states, where fighting between the Tatmadaw and the Kachin Independence Army and Ta'ang National Liberation Army (TNLA), respectively, as well as between the Shan State Army-South and the TNLA, continued to cause large-scale loss of life and displacement of civilian populations. However, from the perspective of the peace process, the eruption of two new "fronts" was perhaps of even greater concern. In the Southeast, the Tatmadaw and the Karen National Liberation Army's 5th Brigade clashed in both March and October in the worst fighting seen in the area since the government-KNU ceasefire in January 2012. Although both sides sought to avoid further escalation, there is little doubt that these developments added to growing unease within the KNU about the NCA process and contributed to its decision later in the year to suspend formal peace talks.

Even more ominously, fighting between the Tatmadaw and the Arakan Army (AA) in Northern Rakhine State escalated dramatically from the beginning of December. The AA has traditionally been based in Kachin State, where it was formed in 2009 as the military wing of the United League of Arakan (ULA) with help from the KIO and has been fighting with the Northern Alliance. Since 2015, however, it has been infiltrating in ever-greater numbers into the mountainous northern townships of Rakhine State and has been strengthening its call for an autonomous Arakan (Rakhine) State. The escalation of fighting appears to have resulted from a concerted effort by the Tatmadaw to dislodge the AA before it was able to establish more permanent bases and control, but the AA evidently was already present in significant force. On 4 January 2019, it thus took the fight to the government by overrunning four border guard police posts in Buthidaung township, causing the President's Office to denounce the group as "terrorists" and instructing the Tatmadaw to "crush" it.[15] As a result, the Tatmadaw, which already had the Arakan Rohingya Salvation Army (ARSA) to contend with, now faces two new liberation armies in Rakhine State, representing, respectively, the Rohingya Muslim and Rakhine Buddhist populations — and both are active in the same small area in the north to which hundreds of thousands of Rohingya refugees are supposed to be repatriated over the coming months and years (see further below).

The last month of the year did see some more positive developments. On 13 December, the government Peace Commission announced that it would start negotiations with three EAOs in the Northeast — Palaung State Liberation Front, Myanmar National Democratic Alliance Army (MNDAA) and ULA — which had previously been excluded from the peace process. Their exclusion had been a major point of contention since 2015, when it supposedly was one of the main reasons why several other EAOs refused to sign the NCA. A week later, on 21 December, the Tatmadaw took everyone by surprise by declaring a unilateral ceasefire across the Northeast, which it said would be used by the government to conduct further negotiations with EAOs that had not yet signed the NCA, including presumably the UWSP and KIO, as well as the PLSF, MNDAA and ULA. The implications of these steps though remain unclear. If it is merely a tactical move, as some critics have speculated, to buy the Tatmadaw some breathing space while it contends with ARSA and AA in the Northwest, then little may come of it. If, on the other hand, it is part of a deal-in-the-making with the powerful EAOs in the Northeast, facilitated by China, it could then be a significant breakthrough. Government peace negotiators generally expressed optimism about the new developments,[16] while some ethnic armed leaders were less sanguine. The chief of the AA, Tun Myat Naing, was the most pessimistic, telling the *Irrawaddy* in an interview in January 2019 that "peace is nowhere in sight".[17]

The Rohingya Crisis

One of the reasons for the deterioration of the peace process over the course of the year was the government's increasing preoccupation with the Rohingya crisis.

As evidence mounted of atrocities committed by the Myanmar army during its "area clearance operations" in Northern Rakhine State in 2017, increasingly strong international demands for justice followed. In a major report in June, Amnesty International concluded that "these crimes amount to crimes against humanity under international law, as they were perpetrated as part of a widespread and systematic attack against the Rohingya population".[18] The game changer, however, was another report by the Independent International Fact-Finding Mission (IIFFM) in August, which called on the United Nations Security Council (UNSC) to refer five named senior Myanmar military officers, including the commander-in-chief Senior General Min Aung Hlaing, to the International Criminal Court (ICC) to be investigated and prosecuted for genocide.[19] Having conducted a detailed eighteen-month investigation, including 875 interviews with victims and eyewitnesses, the mission concluded that the "crimes in Rakhine State, and the manner in which they were perpetrated, are similar in nature, gravity and scope to those that have allowed genocidal intent to be established in other contexts". It highlighted the shared responsibility of the civilian government, which "through their acts and omissions … have contributed to the commission of atrocity crimes", but limited its calls for criminal prosecution and other punitive measures to the military.

With both China and Russia implacably opposed to any punitive action against Myanmar, a UNSC referral to the ICC was a non-starter. However, with an authoritative, if still tentative, determination of genocide, actions followed quickly by other elements of the international human rights community, which will likely frame international responses not only to the Rohingya crisis but also to Myanmar more generally for years to come. Just three weeks after the release of the IIFFM report, the prosecutor of the International Criminal Court, Mrs Fatou Bensouda, announced that she was launching preliminary investigations into the alleged deportation of 700,000 Rohingya Muslims from Myanmar to Bangladesh as a possible crime against humanity; a few days later, the United Nations Human Rights Council voted by an overwhelming majority to establish an ongoing independent mechanism to collect evidence for future legal proceedings, whether under the ICC, as an independent tribunal, or as a domestic mechanism. Bilateral punitive measures remained limited to targeted sanctions on senior Myanmar military officers. However, with pressure building on governments to ensure that they are seen to be on the right side of justice, it seems just a matter of time before broader economic and aid sanctions will follow. Moreover, Aung San Suu Kyi was personally subjected to censure by a number of local political and private bodies, which withdrew awards previously bestowed upon her for her struggle for democracy and human rights.

Initially, the Myanmar government seemed to respond to the growing pressure by stepping up cooperation with the international community. Having previously refused access to the country for the IIFFM, it agreed to receive a UNSC mission, which visited Naypyitaw and Northern Rakhine State in late April. In a statement after the visit, Aung San Suu Kyi described it as a "turning point" in Myanmar's relations with the UN, and soon after the government announced that it would be setting up an independent commission of inquiry, with international participation, to investigate alleged human rights violations in Northern Rakhine State; it also signed a memorandum of understanding with the United Nations High Commission for Refugees and United Nations Development Programme to work together to ensure the voluntary, safe, dignified and sustainable repatriation of refugees from Bangladesh, and announced it was working on a strategy for closing down the camps for internally displaced persons in Central Rakhine State, which had been in place since the communal violence of 2012. The contrasting reactions to these measures internationally and domestically, however, served only to emphasize the difficulty of the government's political position. While the international human rights community mostly dismissed these statements as lacking credibility and substance, inside Myanmar they were met with strong criticism from the military, opposition parties and other nationalists who saw them as a threat to Myanmar's sovereignty and national interests. And as the year progressed it became clear that the government was ultimately less responsive to international pressure than to the imperatives of domestic politics.

There are three related but distinct aspects of the Rohingya crisis, none of which showed much sign of being resolved in 2018. First is the issue of accountability. The Myanmar government has flatly rejected all efforts by the international community to investigate the alleged human rights violations or pursue criminal prosecution of the perpetrators, instead presenting its own Independent Commission of Inquiry as a more appropriate alternative. The purpose of this commission however does not appear to be accountability per se, certainly not of a legal or retributive nature. According to its chair, Philippine diplomat Rosario Malano, it "will not blame or finger-point at anyone but seek to cooperate for peace in the region".[20] This is in line with a long-standing position of the NLD regarding human rights violations, which is to prioritize national reconciliation over retribution, thus highlighting the limitations of the commission as an alternative to the ICC. The most that it would seem to be able to deliver is some measure of truth seeking, and perhaps reparations for victims.

The Tatmadaw itself, meanwhile, took some limited steps in 2018 towards accountability, by sacking, reassigning or, in a few cases, prosecuting soldiers and police involved in the violence. It has also established a new training programme in international human rights and humanitarian law, which all officers must attend before promotion.[21] In a speech to army cadets in April, commander-in-chief Min Aung Hlaing warned them that they "must abide by the military codes of conduct and international laws and conventions", referring to the prosecution and sentencing of seven soldiers to ten years in prison with hard labour for killing ten Rohingya men in the village of Inn Din in Maungdaw township in September 2017.[22] None of this will have provided much comfort to the victims or their families, but it may indicate an opening for longer-term socialization of the Tatmadaw into international norms.

The second issue concerns the security, welfare and rights of the Muslim population in Rakhine State. While international attention is naturally focused on the recent violence and mass exodus, Rohingya Muslims have been fleeing Northern Rakhine State for decades. At times they have left in floods, usually in response to major military security operations; at other times they have left in trickles as a result of the cumulative stresses of everyday state repression, discrimination and poverty. But they have never been "safe". After past mass exoduses in 1978 and 1991, the majority of refugees were pushed back to Myanmar, but in the absence of any real improvements in the security situation there, the cycle of displacement continued unabated. To simply return them offers no resolution to the present crisis either, unless there are major changes first in official attitudes, policies and practices.

Efforts in this area have focused on implementation of the recommendations of the Advisory Commission on Rakhine State, headed by the late former secretary-general of the United Nations Kofi Annan, which elicited broad commitments of support from both the government and the international community. In a meeting in Copenhagen in June to assess progress on this issue, a senior government official claimed that they were working on implementing eighty-one of the eight-eight recommendations.[23] However, this excluded key recommendations regarding, for example, a review of the 1982 Citizenship Law. And even the government's own records, which are presented in regular reports by the Committee for Implementation of the Recommendations on Rakhine State, served mainly to highlight how little was being achieved in many other areas.[24] Meanwhile, Northern Rakhine State remained highly militarized, and hundreds of Rohingya who had stayed behind after the violence of 2017 continued to leave every month for the refugee camps in Bangladesh. In interviews with international media, many explained that they simply could no longer survive in their home villages because of continuing harassment by security forces and restrictions on movement, livelihood activities and social services, including humanitarian aid.[25] Given the Tatmadaw's long-standing counter-insurgency doctrine, which emphasizes the use of military force over winning hearts and minds, along with the persistent threat from ARSA and now also AA, there is little prospect that any of this will change for the foreseeable future.

Finally, there is the issue of repatriation of the hundreds of thousands of refugees currently languishing in camps around Cox's Bazar. The Myanmar government has been adamant since the crisis first erupted that it is willing to take back any bona fide refugees, and in November 2017 signed a bilateral agreement with Bangladesh to this effect. It has also taken steps to establish the formal process and physical infrastructure for repatriation. However, as 2018 wore on, it became increasingly clear that this would be a very long process. The date for starting repatriation was repeatedly postponed as Myanmar and Bangladesh traded accusations of obstruction, and when the two countries finally seemed ready to go ahead in mid-November, the 2,200 Rohingya selected simply refused to go. Many reportedly fled the camps they were residing in to avoid being forced to return, although to the credit of the relevant authorities, no attempt was ultimately made to compel them to do so. So, at the end of the year, there were more Rohingya refugees in Bangladesh than there had been at the beginning of the year, not less, and most of those who did leave did so illegally, risking their lives on rickety boats to seek refuge in Malaysia, Indonesia or further afield. The numbers remained relatively small — hundreds, or perhaps a few thousand — but will invariably grow over time as a sense of hopelessness sets in among the camp population, unless the relevant governments and international agencies find ways to assure the refugees that there is a viable alternative for them.

It may be a cliché, but when it comes to the Rohingya, Myanmar's elected government is truly "stuck between a rock and a hard place". Although a number of individuals and organizations made valiant efforts throughout the year to find a way forward, the gap between what the international community and Rohingya leaders have demanded and what was possible in the local context was simply too large to be bridged. If anything, the escalation in international pressure had the effect of aggravating nationalist sensitivities and forcing the government to turn increasingly inwards to focus on its own initiatives and programmes, with support from friendly countries in the region. Some of those neighbours, meanwhile, were too quick to accept simplistic representations of the crisis as a development problem, which fits with their own national interests but will do little to resolve the crisis, and could well make it worse by increasing both economic and political divisions among the different communities in Rakhine State.

The Economy

As noted at the start of this chapter, the NLD government seemed to be hoping that a renewed focus on the economy could help improve its political "balance sheet", and perhaps even contribute to the resolution of the peace process and the Rohingya crisis. However, if that plan is to succeed, it will take time (and the party will probably have to weather the 2020 elections by other means). The government may have paid greater attention to economic planning and policy in its third year in office, but neither international investors nor the majority of ordinary people in Myanmar seem to have felt much improvement in their position.

The overall economic picture in 2018 was less than rosy. According to the World Bank, overall economic growth slowed from 6.8 per cent in 2017/18 to an estimated 6.2 per cent in 2018/19 — sound by global or regional standards but significantly below the country's potential. Foreign direct investment (FDI) commitments declined by over 50 per cent in the first half of 2018/19 compared to the same period in 2017/18, indicating that FDI flows would start declining too in the second half of 2018/19 (although extrapolating from FDI approvals to FDI flows is difficult). Moreover, inflation was expected to accelerate from 5.5 per cent in 2017/18 to 8.8 per cent in 2018/19, in large part due to the depreciation of the kyat against the U.S. dollar.[26]

At the level of individual businesses, things looked even worse. According to a survey published by the European Chamber of Commerce in Myanmar in October 2018, 81 per cent of the European companies rated the Myanmar business environment as "poor" or "needs improvement" compared to 76 per cent in 2017 and 67 per cent in 2016; 45 per cent of the companies responded that in the last twelve months the overall business environment "decreased" or "greatly decreased" compared to 30 per cent in 2017 and 18 per cent in 2016; and only 37 per cent of the surveyed companies were able to report a profit in 2018 against 41 per cent in 2017 and 50 per cent in 2016.[27]

As for the general population, the evidence is largely anecdotal but many people were complaining, citing stagnant income opportunities and rising prices, especially for daily necessities such as transport and food. Although some commented more positively on improvements in social services, mainly in education and health, the majority of households seemed to have not yet benefitted significantly from the transition to a (more) democratic government.

A key reason for the depressed economy was undoubtedly that economics cannot be divorced from politics. For Western investors in particular, the Rohingya crisis has greatly increased the political risks. Even with limited formal sanctions in place, the image of Myanmar has changed in just a year from "last frontier market" to another "failing state" riven by conflict and human rights violations. Another problem, however, is a continuing gap between national policy and realities on the ground. Despite new and improved investment and company laws, and a frequently stated commitment by the government to improve the ease of doing business, the economy was still hampered by a myriad of economic controls. This was confirmed by the World Bank's "Doing Business 2019" index, which ranked Myanmar 171st out of 190 economies (tied with Iraq) and as the least favourable ASEAN member country in which to conduct business.[28]

Prospects for the NLD Government, and the Country's New Democracy

The most urgent concern of the NLD government at this point may be to stay in power long enough to be able to (more fully) implement its new vision for the country. If there is one thing that is working in Myanmar's young democracy, it is the horizontal accountability imposed by free and fair national elections. Although the 2020 elections are still almost two years away, they are already having a major impact on the country's politics and governmental policies. The failure by the government to deal effectively with any of the major national issues — the peace process, the Rohingya crisis and the economy — leaves it vulnerable to challenges from both the former ruling party, the Union Solidarity and Development Party (USDP), and ethnic political parties, especially in conflict-affected areas. Elections in Myanmar, however, are decided by the votes of the large Burman-Buddhist rural population, most of whom by all accounts continue to support, and even adore, Aung San Suu Kyi, *for now at least.* Short of a military coup or another cataclysmic event, it is therefore likely that the NLD will still be in government after 2020. At worst it should be able to form a coalition government with key ethnic political parties that share at least part of its policy agenda and are more likely to side with the NLD than a USDP-military coalition.

While the NLD may still govern Myanmar for some years to come, there are however two emerging issues that should be of serious concern to anyone who wants the country's new democracy to deepen and its people to prosper. The first is the rise of nationalism as the defining fault line in Myanmar politics. It was both notable and worrying to see in 2018 how blatantly, and almost singularly, political challengers to the NLD government framed their challenges in the language of national security and national sovereignty. This was not only the case for the military, as one would expect, but also the USDP, which made a point of questioning or openly criticizing almost any step the government made towards cooperation with foreign countries or international agencies, clearly seeing this as the best opportunity for luring voters away from the NLD. As the chairman of the USDP U Than Htay said in an interview with the *Irrawaddy* in March, "Every citizen must protect his religion, race and faith. We are not liberal. You can label us as nationalist."[29] This approach has not turned overly "nasty" in mainstream politics yet. However, the vitriol spewed by nationalist extremists in more informal contexts and on social media, coupled with the existence of a large, disempowered and impoverished, increasingly urban underclass should warn against any complacency about the potential for nationalism to disrupt any further growth of a more liberal politics in Myanmar.

The second, less direct but perhaps no less serious, threat to Myanmar's new democracy is the rise of China, and in particular the return of Chinese influence of Myanmar's politics. China over the past year has made the most of the opportunity created by the damage done by the Rohingya crisis to Myanmar's relationships with Western countries and international organizations such as the UN and World Bank and is now well and truly back in a position as the dominant international influence in the country. The NLD government has seemed relatively comfortable with this so far and has openly courted Beijing, seeking not only protection in the UN Security Council but also support for the peace process and much-needed investments. However, it is far from clear that Myanmar's and China's interests coincide in any of these areas, and even if Chinese intentions were relatively benevolent, there is a great risk that its growing political and economic influence and physical presence could provoke anti-Chinese sentiment, both in the Tatmadaw and in the general population. To avoid this, any Myanmar government will have to ensure that it not only carefully evaluates the costs and benefits of the new China-Myanmar Economic Corridor and other large-scale Chinese investment projects but that it also does its utmost to balance overall relations with China by strengthening cooperation with Japan, India and key ASEAN countries such as Singapore and Indonesia, all of which have more to offer an emerging democracy with a commitment to good governance and responsible investments than China does.

None of this is to suggest that Myanmar's new democracy is doomed, but it is certainly a long way from being consolidated. To ensure that it survives, the NLD government will have to do a lot more to improve its performance, including its leadership on key political issues. Greater economic growth will not be enough, and indeed could be a negative factor if it does not support improved equality and social welfare.

Notes

1. See, for example, International Crisis Group, *Myanmar's Stalled Transition*, Asia Briefing no. 151 (28 August 2018).
2. There was growing speculation during the year, including from sources close to the State Counsellor, that she might be tiring under the onslaught of criticism and be looking to hand over some of her responsibilities.
3. The full text of the speech delivered by President U Win Myint at the ceremony to take the oath of office at the Pyidaungsu Hluttaw, 30 March 2018 <www.president-office.com.mm/en> (accessed 12 December 2018); State Counsellor Daw Aung San Suu Kyi's speech on the second anniversary of the NLD government, *Global New Light of Myanmar*, 2 April 2018.
4. "Myanmar New Year Greetings of President U Win Myint", 18 April 2018 <http://www.president-office.gov.mm/en/?q=briefing-room/news/2018/04/18/id-8680> (accessed 19 April 2018).

5. Myanmar Ministry of Planning and Finance, *Myanmar Sustainable Development Plan (2018–2030)*, August 2018 <http://themimu.info/sites/themimu.info/files/documents/Core_Doc_Myanmar_Sustainable_Development_Plan_2018_-_2030_Aug2018.pdf> (accessed 15 December 2018).
6. Thiha Ko Ko, "Project Bank to Facilitate Infrastructure Development Established", *Myanmar Times*, 5 December 2018.
7. Myanmar Investment Commission, *Myanmar Investment Promotion Plan 2016/17–2035/36*, 2018 <https://www.dica.gov.mm/sites/dica.gov.mm/files/news-files/mipp_english_version_with_cover_pages.pdf> (accessed 15 December 2018).
8. Interview by author, government economic adviser, Yangon, 6 October 2018. See also Chan Mya Htwe, "Myanmar Successfully Renegotiates Debt, Ownership Terms for Kyaukphyu", *Myanmar Times*, 1 October 2018.
9. Interview by author, Yangon, 6 January 2019. See also "Government Announces Transfer of Military-Controlled Department to Civilian Ministry", *The Irrawaddy*, 21 December 2018.
10. U Min Thu, an ex-colonel and former air force pilot, previously served as deputy minister in the same ministry. U Tin Myint, a former army captain, came from GAD, where he served as director-general.
11. Interview by author, government official, Yangon, 6 January 2019.
12. Sai Wansai, "Burma's Peace Process: From Stagnation to Drawback?", Shan Herald Agency for News, 12 November 2018 <https://english.shannews.org/archives/18326> (accessed 13 November 2018).
13. Karen National Union, "Statement on the 6th Central Standing Committee Emergency Meeting", 10 November 2018 <https://www.burmalink.org/statement-on-the-6th-central-standing-committee-emergency-meeting/> (accessed 11 November 2018).
14. Restoration Council of Shan State, "Statement of Central Executive Committee of RCSS Emergency Meeting", 12 November 2018 <http://www.taifreedom.com/english/images/stories/2018/November/multimedia/statement_en.pdf> (accessed 13 November 2018).
15. "Myanmar's Civilian, Military Leaders Meet, Vow to 'Crush' Rakhine Rebels", Reuters, 8 January 2019 <https://www.reuters.com/article/us-myanmar-politics/myanmars-civilian-military-leaders-meet-vow-to-crush-rakhine-rebels-idUSKCN1P118S> (accessed 9 January 2019).
16. See, for example, Nyein Nyein, "Latest Peace Talks with EAOs 'Quite Successful': Gov't Spokesman", *The Irrawaddy*, 16 January 2019 <https://www.irrawaddy.com/in-person/interview/latest-peace-talks-eaos-quite-successful-govt-spokesman.html> (accessed 18 January 2019).
17. Nan Lwin Hnin Pwint, "Arakan Army Chief Promises Myanmar Government Eye for an Eye", *The Irrawaddy*, 17 January 2019 <https://www.irrawaddy.com/in-person/arakan-army-chief-promises-myanmar-military-govt-eye-eye.html> (accessed 18 January 2019).

18. Amnesty International, *"We Will Destroy Everything": Military Responsibility for Crimes against Humanity in Rakhine State, Myanmar*, June 2018.
19. A/HRC/39/64, *Report of the Independent International Fact-finding Mission on Myanmar*, 27 August 2018.
20. Quoted in Nyein Nyein, "Commission of Inquiry for Rakhine to Report to President within a Year", *The Irrawaddy*, 16 August 2018 <https://www.irrawaddy.com/news/burma/commission-enquiry-rakhine-report-president-within-year.html> (accessed 8 September 2018).
21. Interview by author, government official, Yangon, 6 January 2018. It is unclear whether this was done before or after the tragic events of 2017.
22. Quoted in "Citing Rohingya Massacre, Myanmar Army Chief Urges Soldiers to Obey the Law", Reuters <https://www.reuters.com/article/myanmar-rohingya-military/citing-rohingya-massacre-myanmar-army-chief-urges-soldiers-to-obey-law-idUSL3N1RW41M> (accessed 3 December 2018).
23. "Myanmar Rejects Citizenship Reform at Private Rohingya Talks", Reuters, 27 June 2018 <https://www.reuters.com/article/us-myanmar-rohingya-meeting-exclusive/exclusive-myanmar-rejects-citizenship-reform-at-private-rohingya-talks-idUSKBN1JN0D7> (accessed 10 June 2018).
24. See "Report to the People on the Progress of the Implementation of Recommendations on Rakhine State (January to April 2018), n.d. <https://reliefweb.int/sites/reliefweb.int/files/resources/Report-to-the-People-on-the-Progress-of-the-Implementation-of-Recommendations-on-Rakhine-State-_January-to-April-2018_.pdf> (accessed 10 January 2019). There is also a report for April to December 2017, but apparently none for the later period.
25. "A Year on, Rohingya Still Fleeing Myanmar for Crowded Camps", Reuters, 23 August 2018 <https://www.reuters.com/article/us-myanmar-rohingya-anniversary/a-year-on-rohingya-still-fleeing-myanmar-for-crowded-camps-idUSKCN1L802H> (accessed 8 September 2018).
26. World Bank, *Myanmar Economic Monitor*, December 2018.
27. EuroCham Myanmar, *Business Confidence Survey 2018, October 2018* <https://eurocham-myanmar.org/uploads/37584-business-confidence-survey-2018-web-.pdf> (accessed 8 January 2019). These findings echoed an earlier survey by the Union of Myanmar Federation of Chambers of Commerce and Industry (UMFCCI) published in December 2017, which showed that short-term positive business sentiment among Myanmar companies had fallen from 73 per cent in 2016 to 49 per cent in 2017, with a majority of businesspeople citing the lack of clear economic policy. See UMFFCI, *Myanmar Business Sentiments Survey* (in Burmese) <https://www.facebook.com/UMFCCI/videos/findings-of-the-myanmar-business-sentiment-survey-2018/1167488656725306/> (accessed 8 January 2019).
28. World Bank, *Doing Business 2019*, October 2018 <http://www.worldbank.org/content/

dam/doingBusiness/media/Annual-Reports/English/DB2019-report_web-version.pdf> (accessed 8 January 2019).

29. U Than Htay continued: “We never betray [the national interest]. Liberal democracy preaches co-existence, but we cannot allow the loss of our sovereignty because of it.” Quoted in Htet Naing Zaw, “‘You Can Label Us as Nationalist’, USDP Chairman Says”, *The Irrawaddy*, 21 March 2018 <https://www.irrawaddy.com/news/can-label-us-nationalist-usdp-chairman-says.html> (accessed 3 December 2018).

ETHNICITY, CITIZENSHIP AND IDENTITY IN POST-2016 MYANMAR

Moe Thuzar and Darren Cheong

Myanmar has been experiencing less peaks than troughs in its transformation after Aung San Suu Kyi's National League for Democracy (NLD), which won a landslide victory in the November 2015 polls, took office in 2016. The NLD inherited deep-seated legacies and prejudices, as well as a unique blend of political identity entrenched over seventy years of civil war. From 2016's promise of being an *annus mirabilis* under a democratically elected government, Myanmar's fledgling democracy experienced several challenges, particularly in getting the economy back on track amidst ongoing negotiations on power- and resource-sharing with ethnic armed organizations (EAOs), with whom the NLD's predecessor administration had engaged in a nationwide ceasefire process.

The years 2017 and 2018 were something of *anni horribiles* for the country. Foremost among the litany of disappointments decried by critics has been the NLD government's — and particularly Daw Suu's — reluctance to explicitly condemn violence against the Rohingya in the wake of a disproportionate response by Myanmar's armed forces, the Tatmadaw, to an armed insurgency in August 2017. The Tatmadaw's operations in the northern part of Myanmar's Rakhine State bordering Bangladesh were reported to have included rape, torture, and burning of villages, causing the largest exodus to date of some 700,000 Rohingya residing in Myanmar across the border to Bangladesh. Domestic support for Daw Suu

MOE THUZAR is Co-coordinator of the Myanmar Studies Programme at the ISEAS – Yusof Ishak Institute.

DARREN CHEONG is studying Political Science at the National University of Singapore, and interned with the ISEAS Myanmar Studies Programme in 2018. The authors wish to acknowledge with appreciation the valuable advice of Dr Tin Maung Maung Than, Associate Fellow at ISEAS, on this essay.

strengthened in proportion to the mounting international advocacy for human rights and humanitarian principles towards a community with whom many people in Myanmar feel no affinity. Within Myanmar, the Tatmadaw wields a constitutional veto as well as a considerable functional dominance in defence, home affairs and border affairs. The Tatmadaw, with Senior General Min Aung Hlaing at its helm, is reportedly unhappy with this insinuated scapegoat role.[1] Daw Suu and her cabinet members have continued the emphasis on national security when discussing the issue at home and abroad.

The NLD government has also acknowledged the effects of the international response on the country's economy. Speaking at the Myanmar Investment Forum organized by the Singapore Institute for International Affairs in September 2018, Aung Naing Oo, the head of Myanmar's Department for Investments and Company Administration, frankly admitted having "totally underestimated" the economic impact of the Rohingya issue, and that foreign direct investment (FDI) had declined in the two years since November 2016 when the crisis first erupted.[2]

Business confidence in the country's economic prospects also seems to have weakened. The *Myanmar Insider*'s quarterly Myanmar Economic Confidence Index (2018 Q3) found that over 60 per cent of the survey respondents viewed the economy as "very bad" and expected it to worsen. There is a high degree of reluctance to make further investments in the economy, with 40 per cent indicating that they would be unlikely to do so and another 40 per cent unsure. *Myanmar Insider* also reported that most businesspersons surveyed were negative about the country's economic prospects, and that this lack of confidence would have a contagion effect on FDI.[3]

Hope for a change in this situation is now placed on the Myanmar Sustainable Development Plan,[4] launched in June 2018 and made available to the public in August 2018. The objectives and principles of the plan highlight an acknowledgement that the various sectoral plans and priorities needed stronger policy coherence and transparency, and that bold measures were necessary to "reinvigorate reform".

Since assuming office in 2015, the main focus of the NLD government has been on navigating peace negotiations with the numerous EAOs representing the myriad interests of the different ethnic nationalities, as well as entertaining other stakeholder inputs to the process. This was one of the main performance legitimacy targets by the Union Solidarity and Development Party (USDP) administration led by President Thein Sein. The Nationwide Ceasefire Agreement (NCA) process started by the USDP led to eight out of sixteen major EAOs signing the NCA in October 2015. The NLD government recast the NCA negotiations as the 21st

Century Panglong Conference, invoking the spirit of the 1947 Panglong meeting between Aung San — Daw Suu's father and the leader of Burma's independence movement — and several ethnic leaders. The NLD also recast the semi-independent Myanmar Peace Center, which had served as the secretariat for the peace talks in the USDP administration, as the National Reconciliation and Peace Center, with more government oversight and new chief negotiators. Daw Suu appointed her personal physician and long-time confidant Dr Tin Myo Win to the post of chief negotiator.[5] The NLD government also created an ethnic affairs ministry,[6] appointing a Mon political veteran as minister for ethnic affairs in May 2016,[7] with a view to allay doubts among the various ethnic groups about equality and participation. The ministry does not have a mandate for peace and reconciliation,[8] and focuses on promoting ethnic rights and ethnic languages and culture.

Building trust continues to be the paramount issue in the peace negotiations, as insiders to this process since the Thein Sein administration years have noted. The legacy of broken trust harks back to the days of the past military governments, even as the chief negotiators on both sides of the table could reach some level of mutual personal trust.[9]

Two years and three sessions later, the 21st Century Panglong process has welcomed two more EAOs to the NCA.[10] However, fighting between the Tatmadaw and significant EAOs continued in Kachin and northern Shan States, which resulted in more forced displacements of civilians in the conflict areas. In October 2018, the Karen National Union (KNU), a key EAO in the NCA process, announced that it was suspending participation in future peace talks,[11] and it recently reiterated its disagreement with the current process.[12] As things stand at the time of writing, significant EAOs such as the United Wa State Army (UWSA) and the Kachin Independence Organisation (KIO) have yet to sign on to the NCA. Several NCA signatories have called the current process "a deviation from the path they had envisioned".[13]

Parallel to these developments at the NCA negotiations, ethnic political parties have also started flexing their legislative potential in the various regions and states. Two Kaya parties in Kayah State merged into a single party in 2017, and three Karen parties in Karen State did likewise in 2018. Two Mon parties, four Kachin parties, and some Chin parties are also starting merger processes in preparation for the 2020 elections.[14]

Analysts monitoring Myanmar's transition note the importance of "sequencing" the wide-ranging, myriad and multiple challenges the NLD government is expected to tackle simultaneously. These analyses place first getting the economy back on track as a performance legitimacy indicator for the now looming 2020 elections, which in turn might give the NLD a better negotiating position with the EAOs on resource- and power-sharing.[15] Decentralizing power and governance in the conflict-affected areas will also need to take into account existing administrative and justice systems in these areas.[16]

There is merit in triaging Myanmar's pressing priorities. This triage — and all stakeholders and partners within and outside Myanmar who are engaging in it — may need to take a fresh look at the issues of ethnicity, citizenship and identity that have beset the country's contemporary politics. Three perennial realities may help in both assessing and clarifying the most challenging obstacles to Myanmar's continued transformation.

The centrifugal forces in the country are not new to scholars and students of Myanmar or to Burma/Myanmar watchers. Recent scholarship on issues of ethnicity, citizenship and identity in Myanmar have produced multidisciplinary (if not yet interdisciplinary) approaches to understanding these complex and multiple strands of tension and conflict. Ashley South and Marie Lall's edited volume on *Citizenship in Myanmar: Ways of Being in and from Burma* (2018) stands out as the first comprehensive attempt to address issues of ethnicity, citizenship and identity in post-2016 Myanmar.

Scholars of Burma/Myanmar studies such as David Steinberg, Robert H. Taylor, Tin Maung Maung Than, Kyaw Yin Hlaing, Martin Smith, Andrew Selth and Maung Aung Myoe have discussed at length the politics of ethnicity/race and it implications for the peace negotiations that authoritarian, military, quasi-civilian and the current democratic administrations have all attempted to tackle. Ian Holliday and Nick Cheesman have also written extensively on Myanmar's citizenship crisis and the implications of the Rohingya tragedy. Andrew Selth, Maung Aung Myoe and Mary Callahan in particular have discussed the Tatmadaw's enmeshment of national defence and state-building.[17]

These scholarly assessments have provided much-needed insights into context and agency in addressing these issues. This is important, as the country's current situation and the "quick-read" narratives that abound signal a need for reviewing inherited (and thus immanent) assumptions about Myanmar in policy circles, not least in the country itself. This is perhaps easier said than done.

Ethnic Relations Determine Politics and Identity in Myanmar

The official narrative emphasizes Myanmar as a multicultural, multiracial and multireligious society. In 1989 the military junta listed 135 ethnic nationalities under the eight major nationality groups of Kachin, Kayah, Kayin (formerly Karen), Chin, Bamar, Mon, Rakhine and Shan. This number of 135 is presumably based on figures derived from the last published British census of Burma taken in 1931.[18] Many in Myanmar continue to cite this figure today. The 1983 census estimated that the Bamar population constituted about 60 per cent of the population.[19] The 2014 census, carried out after a hiatus of more than three decades, included a question on "*lumyo*", which translates to ethnicity (or race, or nationality). However, the data on *lumyo* was not included in the census reports, nor has it been subsequently released. Mary Callahan observes that the 2014 census information on ethnicity "came to be viewed as destabilising to the political reform and peace process". Dissecting the layered nuances of *lumyo* (which is closer to the English concept of race) and *taingyinthar* (which translates as "ethnic"), she further states that "any census question about race asked during a period of civil wars fought in terms of identity, during a nascent and tenuous transition away from fifty years of authoritarian rule, and during a fragile peace process was bound to invite controversy and its results to be highly contentious".[20]

Many of Myanmar's minority ethnic populations have long perceived themselves as victims of discrimination by the Bamar-dominated central government. Many of these EAOs were initially formed with the intent to seek autonomy and self-determination, resorting to armed struggle to challenge the idea of the unitary state advocated by the central government. Myanmar nationalists among the Bamar majority have consistently placed the blame on the British colonial administration for their decision to administer the "frontier regions" separately from the Bamar-dominated central regions.[21]

Tense ethnic relations have thus been a key characteristic of politics in Myanmar since the country emerged from British colonial rule in 1948 and found itself almost immediately plunged into armed conflict and insurgencies. For the past seven decades the Tatmadaw has been engaged in fighting the different EAOs, and continues to do so today in Kachin and Shan States. An offshoot of these tense relations, particularly in areas along Myanmar's shared border with China, is that successive governments have also had to balance an uneasy modus vivendi with China. China's larger-than-life proximity has influenced how Burma under socialism and Myanmar under military dictatorship balanced relations with its large neighbour to the north. Even today, China plays a different role from other external interlocutors engaged with Myanmar in the peace process as well as in dealing with the credibility fallout in the aftermath of the 2017 Rohingya exodus.

While trust issues in the peace negotiations have again come to the fore, with an increasing number of EAOs seeking political assurances from the government in

Naypyitaw, the inclusion of non-signatories in the dialogue process also continues to be a major sticking point. A recent analysis shows that non-signatory EAOs constitute a larger fighting force with more recent combat experience compared to signatory EAOs.[22] From these non-signatory EAOs, the Federal Political Negotiation and Consultative Committee (FPNCC), comprising seven EAOs, emerged.[23] The FPNCC is at best mistrustful and at worst opposed to the current stance of the NLD government and Tatmadaw, who require that all EAOs lay down their arms under the NCA framework before embarking on peace negotiations. For the FPNCC, the condition of disarmament constitutes a de facto surrender. The FPNCC's proposal for negotiations based on their own framework is equally a non-starter in the eyes of the NLD government and the Tatmadaw.[24] In the three meetings of the 21st Century Panglong held thus far, there have been attempts to include FPNCC members. However, the UWSA had famously walked out in the first meeting, citing unhappiness regarding its status as an observer (as opposed to a fully fledged participant) at the conference.[25] FPNCC members such as the KIO are locked in conflict with the Tatmadaw.[26] More recently, on 4 January 2019, the seventy-first anniversary of Myanmar's independence, the Arakan Army (AA) mounted attacks on border security posts,[27] killing thirteen police officers, and occasioning a military crackdown and censure for damaging national reconciliation and the peace process.[28]

Myanmar's ethnic conflicts and the mutual blame game thus continue to beset the country's politics. The AA is the latest to add to this, taking advantage of the aspirations of Rakhine youth and the continuing mistrust in Rakhine towards the political dominance of the Bamar. This is invoked in a YouTube video posted by the Tribal Action Group, entitled "Arakan Army: The Way to Rakhita", celebrating the young men and women joining the AA as "laying the groundwork for defence of their people and nation" and identifying the Myanmar armed forces as invaders.[29]

At the 3rd Panglong Conference in June 2018, Senior General Min Aung Hlaing blamed NCA non-signatories for prolonging the conflict, adding that the NCA was a non-negotiable part of the peace process, and as such it was imperative for the FPNCC to sign on to it if any peace is to be made. After three rounds of meetings, and a special retreat summit in October 2018, optimism surrounding the 21st Century Panglong is waning, as there seems to be no meeting of minds over longstanding issues surrounding demands by the EAOs for self-determination (under a federal framework) and ethnic equality. Trust issues aside, there is no other (better) alternative for dialogue in which all three stakeholders — the NLD government, the Tatmadaw and the EAOs — could agree to engage. At the very least, the 21st Century Panglong has not completely broken down, and that is perhaps the best news for the peace process. To make further sense of why the 21st Century Panglong has been unable to make any substantial progress, it may be necessary to delve deeper into the legacies of mistrust between an authoritarian state largely dominated by Bamars and the diverse ethnic nationalities.

The Politics of Ethnicity Compounds Issues of Citizenship and Identity

Burma at independence in 1948 allowed automatic citizenship to persons who could trace their families' residence in the country prior to 1823. Interestingly, this is the year before the First Anglo-Burmese War started in 1824. When that war ended with Burmese defeat in 1826, the British annexed Arakan (now Rakhine) and the southern part of Tennasarim (now Tanintharyi). Precedence of citizenship rights went to those who were members of one of the eight "major" ethnic groups, which the Constitution of the Union of Burma (1947) lists as Kachin, Kayah, Karen (now Kayin), Chin, Bamar, Mon, Rakhine and Shan. Though initially referred to as ethnic nationalities, the years of socialist rule entrenched the somewhat confusing appellation of "national races" to these groups. The Union Citizenship Law (1948) allowed persons who were not part of any of the ethnic groups but whose ancestors had settled in then Burma after 1823 to register and apply for citizenship. However, the political uncertainties of post-independence Burma, where multiple outbreaks of armed rebellion across the country posed a threat to the nascent state's stability, meant that many residents living within the country, including members of the ethnic groups, were in legal limbo.

Robert H. Taylor observes that

> the post-independence governments of Myanmar, primarily concerned with suppressing various internal rebellions, most in the name of indigenous ethnicity, did not make it either obvious or easy for such persons to apply and be recognized as citizens. This remains the case and while the 1948 citizenship law has been superseded by a much criticised 1982 citizenship law, the problem of both pieces of legislation is not in the laws themselves but in the failure to implement their provisions.[30]

Compounding the problem was the politicization of ethnicity and race, which became a negotiating tool for the survival and control of political leaders. Taylor acknowledges that the "military socialist regime of General Ne Win failed to depoliticise the ethnicity/race issue" and that the 2008 Constitution further perpetuated the centrality of ethnicity/race in Myanmar politics. This continues in Myanmar today. There is an ethnic affairs minister at the union level as well as in each of the fourteen state/regional governments.

The Rohingya issue must be contextualized against this complex and complicated backdrop.[31] It has been a conflict situation of a recurrent or cyclical nature since 1948, with the level of conflict and tensions ebbing in between the periodic clashes. The narrative surrounding the situation has been entrenched over the decades with security and ethno-nationalist underpinnings.

Prior to 2017, periodic clashes in Rakhine State caused two large-scale exoduses of Rohingya communities to Bangladesh that required bilateral negotiations with Dhaka and the monitoring of international observers. For decades, many Rohingya have also sought to leave the country by boat. In 2009, Thailand's reluctance to host a boatload of Rohingya refugees brought the issue to both ASEAN and international attention. The then foreign minister of Myanmar U Nyan Win informed his ASEAN counterparts that the Rohingya were of Bengali origin and not part of Myanmar's ethnic make-up.[32] This refrain continued through the USDP administration to the present, making the term "Rohingya" one of the most controversial words in Myanmar politics today.[33] The 2012 communal clashes between Rohingyas and Rakhines, and the 2015 migrant crisis at sea, caused more international attention and reporting to be focused on the humanitarian situation of the Rohingyas, creating a sense of victimhood in Rakhine communities. In fact, the AA is framing the planned repatriation of the Rohingya as a Bamar "divide and rule" tactic against the Rakhine people.[34]

Beyond the name by which they identify themselves, the Rohingya's citizenship status is also contested. The military junta had courted Rohingya votes for the 2010 elections, issuing temporary identification documents known as "white cards" and promising their replacement with updated national registration cards. This did not happen, and in February 2015 the USDP government bowed to pressure from nationalist groups and announced the expiry of the white cards on 31 March 2015. Elections were to take place in November 2015.[35] The Rohingya community was not the only one to be issued white cards. Ethnic groups such as the Wa have also been issued white cards as a prelude to citizenship.[36]

Discussions related to the Rohingya or the EAOs are often treated separately, but the two issues share similar contextual origins: the entrenchment of Bamar ethnic nationalism that saw the marginalization of Myanmar's minority ethnic populace.

The Rohingya issue has polarized perceptions and debate, much of it fuelling and fuelled by the immediacy of information via social media networks. At the same time, international criticism of the government's — particularly Daw Suu's

— reluctance to deal with the Rohingya issue in accordance with humanitarian principles and recommendations has not abated. This has resulted in a solidifying of support for her among Myanmar citizens and nationals at home and abroad, against what they perceive as biased reporting and pre-judged conclusions. The reactions around the sentencing of the two Reuters journalists Wa Lone and Kyaw Soe Oo in July 2018 highlight the wide gaps between domestic and external narratives in the Rohingya case. Wa Lone and Kyaw Soe Oo were charged with violating the Official Secrets Act over their investigation into the murder of ten Rohingya men in In-Dinn village in Rakhine State. Their sentencing sent shockwaves through the media community in Myanmar and abroad as it signalled a harsher line taken towards media freedom in Myanmar under a democratically elected government.[37] Yet, public reaction in Myanmar to their sentencing took on a condemnatory tone towards the two journalists, who were seen as working for foreign interests.

The NLD government is trying to emphasize a civilian-led role in coordinating responses to humanitarian needs in Rakhine State. The Union Enterprise on Humanitarian Assistance, Resettlement and Development in Rakhine was launched under the aegis of the State Counsellor's Office on 17 October 2017. Myanmar's emphasis on the Union Enterprise initiative, and the government's insistence on working things out bilaterally, provide a glimpse into Daw Suu's preference to deal directly in a bilateral (or at most a mini-lateral) setting.

This reflects the recognition among policymakers dealing with this issue that "do-nothing" is not an option. Yet, some tension remains. According to the "State of Southeast Asia: 2019" regional survey conducted by the ASEAN Studies Centre at the ISEAS – Yusof Ishak Institute, close to 60 per cent of the Myanmar respondents indicated a preference for ASEAN to undertake a mediation role between the Myanmar government and other stakeholders. At the same time, a relatively large segment (41.4 per cent) of Myanmar respondents view this issue as Myanmar's domestic affair, and only a few (7.1 per cent) of the respondents seemed to prefer diplomatic pressure on Myanmar. Regionally, the most preferred option for working with Myanmar on this issue is mediation (66.5 per cent). The second most preferred option regionally is humanitarian assistance (50.9 per cent), followed by diplomatic pressure (38 per cent).[38]

Myanmar has kept the door open for regional organizations such as ASEAN to work with Myanmar for humanitarian assistance. However, the deployment of an ASEAN-coordinated needs assessment team for the repatriation process has been delayed[39] as a result of the repatriation process itself being delayed.

The secretary-general of ASEAN had visited Myanmar in December 2018 to discuss ASEAN's role in helping Myanmar address repatriation and other concerns related to the issue, including a needs assessment team to visit Rakhine.[40] Repatriation, if and when it takes place, will be under the framework of the November 2017 agreement between Myanmar and Bangladesh for "the Return of Displaced Persons in Rakhine State". This has been stalled amidst finger-pointing (between the authorities on both sides) and fear (by the Rohingya refugees slated for repatriation),[41] and a renewed attempt to start repatriation in November 2018 was not successful. Here, again, trust (or the lack of it) is a key factor.

For as long as the Rohingya continue to live in limbo in refugee camps in Bangladesh and other Southeast Asian countries, the foreign policy actions and pronouncements of the NLD government will continue to be viewed (and judged) through the prism of the Rohingya crisis. Bilateral relations between Myanmar and Bangladesh are at an all-time low, although there are ongoing low-profile mediation efforts to bridge this trust deficit and find practical pathways to restoring relations.

The Past is Still a Guide, However Inadequate, to the Present

Present-day analyses of Myanmar's crisis of community cannot ignore or dismiss the historical spirals of Buddhism and nationalism in Myanmar's long history. The complexity of ethnic relations and identity in Myanmar results from the conflation of race and religion that took place during the Burmese nationalist movements from the 1920s to 1940s. Burmese nationalists felt that their country was twice colonized, first by the British and secondly by South Asians. Governed as a province of British India until 1937, Burmans witnessed South Asian immigrants and capital flowing freely into the country. This phenomenon added much to the growing nationalism in the 1930s. This has been described as a "crisis in masculinity", where Burmese men were marginalized in the workplace, the marketplace and in social settings, and where foreign competition caused the feelings of disempowerment that led to nationalist attitudes.[42] Consequently, Buddhism was perceived as being under threat, particularly from the rapid growth of the South Asian Hindu and Muslim populations. The separate administration of the "frontier" regions from those with a preponderance of the Burman population also added to the sense of grievance and fanned the flames of nationalism.

Furthermore, although there is a ban prohibiting members of the (mainly Buddhist) religious order from voting or standing for election, there remain some grey areas allowing for the political activism and participation of Buddhist monks in Myanmar. Indeed, monks have been involved in anti-colonial, anti-communist and anti-military politics since colonial times to the present.[43] Following the 2012 communal clashes in Rakhine, the controversial Ma Ba Tha, or the Organization for the Protection of Race and Religion, stepped up its anti-Muslim rhetoric. The Ma Ba Tha, which was declared an illegal organization by the NLD government in May 2017, has drawn international attention to what is being termed "militant Buddhism", drowning out more moderate views from the wider clergy. It was the Ma Ba Tha that first proposed the four laws on race and religion[44] that were eventually passed in September 2015.[45] These laws, which were justified on the grounds of "protecting Burmese Buddhist women from abuse and violence",[46] were understood to be a response to the perceived spread of Islam in Myanmar, as it sought to impose strict restrictions on non-Buddhists marrying Buddhist women, "birth spacing" intervals, bigamy/polygamy, and religious conversion (or adopting a new religion).[47]

Thus, a powerful theme from Burma's nationalist past — race, or ethnicity, compounded by religion — is being repeated today. Taylor suggests that depoliticizing ethnicity and race may provide a solution towards maintaining political order and "reasoned politics", and observes that the confusion of human rights with group aspirations in modern discourse will only add to the difficulties.[48]

Studying the challenges of a community in crisis from the perspective of history may help alleviate or bridge the polarizing sentiments. As Aung-Thwin and Aung-Thwin have suggested, "in the end, Myanmar's future will be shaped by its own past", which itself will "continue to remain an indelible part of its present".[49] Throughout this past, a steadfast devotion to Theravada Buddhism, encouraged and led by the state, and the nationalist streak informing initiatives to build a national identity transcending ethnicity (but still celebrating a strong Buddhist heritage and cultural traditions) have added to the tensions. From time to time, these tensions have erupted in crises, dividing and polarizing communities living within the country.

If assertions of historical patterns in a country or region can inform analyses of current events, then a fresh look at existing scholarship on the themes of religion, nationalism and the crisis of community that cyclically beset Myanmar should trigger a renewed analysis into the links between these important themes, and their impact on concepts of ethnicity, citizenship and identity in Myanmar.

Will peace and stability still elude Myanmar? The siege mentality is now strong in the NLD government in Naypyitaw,[50] throwing up historical parallels of U Nu's Anti-Fascist People's Freedom League government facing similar challenges as "the Rangoon Government".[51] Facing another situation of a dichotomy between optimism and despair,[52] Myanmar post-2016 seems to have come full circle from its post-1948 dilemma. The rhetoric, and even the reactions of the government authorities, seems to rhyme across seventy years of civil war. Ethnic groups still challenge the state. The process of making peace is still fraught with dissent and defiance, while external interlocutors still seek to impose a better way of doing things. It is time to construct a new narrative for Myanmar if the country and the people who reside in it are to finally come in from the cold. This new narrative will need to highlight both the pitfalls of historical parallels and the promises of new beginnings.

Notes

1. Moe Thuzar's personal conversations with Myanmar researchers and former military officers in December 2018 and January 2019.
2. John Geddie, "Myanmar Official Says 'Totally Underestimated' Economic Impact of Rohingya Crisis", Reuters, 5 September 2018 <https://www.reuters.com/article/us-myanmar-rohingya-investment/myanmar-official-says-totally-underestimated-economic-impact-of-rohingya-crisis-idUSKCN1LL1QZ> (accessed 30 November 2018).
3. *Myanmar Insider* 5, no. 61 (December 2018): 24.
4. Government of the Union of Myanmar, Ministry of Planning and Finance, "Myanmar Sustainable Development Plan 2018–2030", 2018 <http://themimu.info/sites/themimu.info/files/documents/Core_Doc_Myanmar_Sustainable_Development_Plan_2018_-_2030_Aug2018.pdf> (accessed 14 January 2019).
5. Narayanan Ganesan, "Changing Dynamics in Myanmar's Ethnic Peace Process and the Growing Role of China", *Asian Journal of Peacebuilding* 5, no. 2 (2017): 329.
6. "Ministry for Ethnic Affairs Brings Hope for Peace to Myanmar's Minorities", *AsiaNews.it*, 15 July 2016 <http://www.asianews.it/news-en/Ministry-for-Ethnic-Affairs-brings-hope-for-peace-to-Myanmar%E2%80%99s-minorities-38053.html> (accessed 14 January 2019).
7. "Ethnic Affairs Minister: The Mandate and its Executive Power from the Lady's Lips", BNI Multimedia Group, 16 May 2016 <https://www.bnionline.net/en/opinion/op-ed/item/1690-ethnic-affairs-minister-the-mandate-and-its-executive-power-from-the-lady-s-lips.html> (accessed 14 January 2019).
8. Hein Ko Soe, "The State of Ethnic Affairs", *Frontier Myanmar*, 14 July 2016 <https://frontiermyanmar.net/en/the-state-of-ethnic-affairs> (accessed 14 January 2019).
9. Myanmar Forum 2016, 20 May 2016, Singapore. Organized by the ISEAS – Yusof Ishak Institute.
10. The New Mon State Party and Lahu Democratic Union signed the NCA on 13 February 2018. Ye Mon, "Two Steps Closer to Peace? Mon, Lahu Ethnic Armed Groups Sign NCA", Democratic Voice of Burma, 13 February 2018, available at <https://reliefweb.

int/report/myanmar/two-steps-closer-peace-mon-lahu-ethnic-armed-groups-sign-nca> (accessed 15 February 2018).

11. Nyein Nyein, "Analysis: Why Did the KNU Temporarily Leave Peace Talks?", *Irrawaddy*, 29 October 2018 <https://www.irrawaddy.com/factiva/analysis-knu-temporarily-leave-peace-talks.html>.
12. "KNU Slams Government's Peace Process", Mizzima, 4 January 2019 <http://mizzima.com/article/knu-slams-governments-peace-process>.
13. Nyein Nyein, "NCA Signatories Recommend Review of Peace Path", *Irrawaddy*, 4 July 2017 <https://www.irrawaddy.com/news/burma/nca-signatories-recommend-review-peace-path.html> (accessed 21 June 2018).
14. Aung Aung, "Myanmar's Current Politics: Implications for 2020 General Elections", *ISEAS Perspective* 2018, no. 61 (5 October 2018) <https://www.iseas.edu.sg/images/pdf/ISEAS_Perspective_2018_61@50.pdf> (accessed 5 October 2018).
15. Min Zin, speaking on the political and economic outlook for Myanmar at the Regional Outlook Forum 2019, organized by the ISEAS – Yusof Ishak Institute in Singapore on 9 January 2019.
16. Brian McCartan and Kim Jolliffe, *Ethnic Armed Actors and Justice Provision in Myanmar* (Yangon: The Asia Foundation, October 2016).
17. Maung Aung Myoe, *Building the Tatmadaw: Myanmar Armed Forces since 1948* (Singapore: Institute of Southeast Asian Studies, 2008); Andrew Selth, *Burma's Armed Forces: Power without Glory* (Norwalk, CO: EastBridge, 2002); Mary Callahan, *Making Enemies: War and State-Building in Burma* (Cornell University Press, 2005).
18. Robert Taylor, "Refighting Old Battles, Compounding Misconceptions: The Politics of Ethnicity in Myanmar Today", *ISEAS Perspective* 2015, no. 12 (2 March 2015), p. 8.
19. Tin Maung Maung Than, "Ethnic Insurgencies and Peacemaking in Myanmar", *ISEAS Perspective Selections 2012–2013*, edited by Ooi Kee Beng (Singapore: ISEAS – Yusof Ishak Institute, 2013), pp. 103–15. See also *The Newsletter*, no. 66 (Winter 2013) of the International Institute of Asian Studies (IIAS) <https://iias.asia/sites/default/files/IIAS_NL66_37.pdf>.
20. Mary Callahan, "Distorted, Dangerous Data? *Lumyo* in the 2014 Myanmar Population and Housing Census", *SOJOURN: Journal of Social Issues in Southeast Asia* 32, no. 2 (July 2017), pp. 452–78.
21. Tin Maung Maung Than, "Ethnic Insurgencies".
22. Bobby Anderson, "Stalemate and Suspicion: An Appraisal of the Myanmar Peace Process", *Tea Circle Oxford*, 6 June 2018 <https://teacircleoxford.com/2018/06/06/stalemate-and-suspicion-an-appraisal-of-the-myanmar-peace-process/#_ftn> (accessed 15 June 2018).
23. The FNPCC consists of the Arakan Army (AA), the Kachin Independence Organisation (KIO), the Myanmar National Democratic Alliance Army (MNDAA), the Ta'ang

National Liberation Army (TNLA), the Shan State Progress Party (SSPA), the Shan State East National Democratic Alliance Association (NDAA) and the United Wa State Army (UWSA). They have an estimated fighting force of 92,000 soldiers, including reserves.

24. Federal Political Negotiation and Consultative Committee (FNPCC), "The General Principles and Specific Proposition of Revolutionary Armed Organisations of All Nationalities upon the Political Negotiation", 19 April 2017 <http://fpncc.org/fpnccprinciple.pdf> (accessed 21 June 2018).
25. Ei Ei Toe Lwin, "Panglong Fractures with UWSA Delegation's Indignant Exit", *Myanmar Times*, 2 September 2016 <https://www.mmtimes.com/national-news/nay-pyi-taw/22298-panglong-fractures-with-uwsa-delegation-s-indignant-exit.html> (accessed 21 June 2018).
26. Helen Regan, "What Future Do We Have? Caught in the Crossfire of Myanmar's Northern Conflict, Civilians See Little Hope", *Time*, 3 May 2018 <http://time.com/5263930/myanmar-kachin-fighting-displaced-humanitarian-aid/>.
27. "Rakhine Rebels Kill 13 in Independence Day Attack on Myanmar Police Posts", Channel NewsAsia, 4 January 2019 <https://www.channelnewsasia.com/news/asia/rakhine-buddhist-myanmar-police-security-clash-rohingya-11086486> (accessed 5 January 2019).
28. Htoo Thant and Nyan Lynn Aung, "Govt Orders Crackdown on Arakan Army", *Myanmar Times*, 21 January 2019 <https://www.mmtimes.com/news/govt-orders-crackdown-arakan-army.html> (accessed 21 January 2019).
29. Tribal Action Group, "Arakan Army: The Way to Rakhita", YouTube, 14 January 2018 <https://www.youtube.com/watch?v=0zQGZ8VE1PY>.
30. Robert Taylor, "The Politics of Ethnicity in Myanmar: Forward to the Past", *ASEANFocus* 2018, no. 2 (March/April 2018): 14–15 <https://www.iseas.edu.sg/images/pdf/ASEANFocus%20Mar-Apr.pdf> (accessed 26 October 2017).
31. Ibid.
32. Wai Moe, "Burma Insists Rohingyas are Bengalis", *Irrawaddy*, 27 February 2009 <http://www2.irrawaddy.com/article.php?art_id=15209> (accessed 21 January 2019).
33. "Analysis: Using the Term Rohingya", *Irrawaddy*, 21 September 2017 <https://www.irrawaddy.com/news/burma/analysis-using-term-rohingya.html> (accessed 21 January 2019). See also <https://www.voanews.com/a/nyanmar-government-wont-negociate-with-rohingya-insurgents/4043062.html>.
34. Gerard McCarthy, "Rakhine State Politics a Major Barrier to Rohingya Return", ISEAS – Yusof Ishak Insitute, 20 December 2018 <https://www.iseas.edu.sg/medias/commentaries/item/8739-rakhine-state-politics-a-major-barrier-to-rohingya-return-by-gerard-mccarthy> (accessed 20 December 2018).
35. Nehginpao Kipgen, "Lived in Rakhine for Generations, yet Rohingya Muslims 'Do Not Belong in Myanmar'", Channels NewsAsia, 27 September 2017 <https://

www.channelnewsasia.com/news/asia/commentary-lived-in-rakhine-for-generations-yet-rohingya-muslims-9251580> (accessed 21 January 2019). See also <https://www.mmtimes.com/national-news/16158-courting-of-rohingya-in-2010-comes-back-to-haunt-usdp.html>.

36. Moe Thuzar's personal conversation with a former military officer, December 2018.
37. Reuters has detailed the story in a special report published in September 2018: <https://www.reuters.com/article/us-myanmar-journalists-trial-specialrepo/special-report-how-myanmar-punished-two-reporters-for-uncovering-an-atrocity-idUSKCN1LJ167> (accessed 5 December 2018).
38. *The State of Southeast Asia: 2019 Survey Report* (Singapore: ASEAN Studies Centre, ISEAS – Yusof Ishak Institute, 2019) <https://www.iseas.edu.sg/images/pdf/TheStateofSEASurveyReport_2019.pdf> (accessed 29 January 2019). See also, "Survey Report — State of Southeast Asia: 2019", *ASEANFocus* 2019, no. 1 (January 2019) <https://www.iseas.edu.sg/images/pdf/ASEANFocus%20FINAL_Jan19.pdf> (accessed 7 January 2019).
39. The deployment was initially planned for 21–26 January 2019. See Apornrath Phoonphongphiphat, "Date of Rohingya Repatriation Unclear after ASEAN Ministerial Meeting", *Nikkei Asian Review*, 18 January 2019 <https://asia.nikkei.com/Politics/International-Relations/Date-of-Rohingya-repatriation-unclear-after-ASEAN-ministerial-meeting> (accessed 18 January 2019).
40. Ibid.
41. "Bangladesh, Myanmar Agree to Start Repatriation of Rohingya in November", *Straits Times*, 30 October 2018 <https://www.straitstimes.com/asia/se-asia/bangladesh-myanmar-to-start-returning-rohingya-in-november> (accessed 18 January 2019).
42. Chie Ikeya, "The Modern Burmese Woman and the Politics of Fashion in Colonial Burma", *Journal of Asian Studies* 67, no. 4 (2008): 1277–1308.
43. Nyi Nyi Kayw, "Who Set the Parameters of Monastic Politics in Myanmar?", ISEAS – Yusof Ishak Institute, 31 January 2019 <https://www.iseas.edu.sg/medias/commentaries/item/9005-who-set-the-parameters-of-monastic-politics-in-myanmar-by-nyi-nyi-kyaw> (accessed 31 January 2019).
44. Nyein Nyein, "Ma Ba Tha Resists Reforms to Race and Religion Laws", *Irrawaddy*, 27 January 2017 <https://www.irrawaddy.com/news/burma/ma-ba-tha-resists-reforms-to-race-and-religion-laws.html> (accessed 31 January 2019).
45. United States Library of Congress Law Library, "Burma: Four 'Race and Religion Protection' Laws Adopted", *Global Legal Monitor*, 14 September 2015 <http://www.loc.gov/law/foreign-news/article/burma-four-race-and-religion-protection-laws-adopted/>.
46. Ibid.
47. "Scrap 'Race and Religion' Laws that Could Fuel Discrimination and Violence", Amnesty International, 3 March 2015 <https://www.amnesty.org/en/latest/news/2015/03/myanmar-race-and-religion-laws/> (accessed 1 February 2019).

48. Robert H. Taylor, "Refighting Old Battles, Compounding Misconceptions: The Politics of Ethnicity in Myanmar Today", *ISEAS Perspective* 2015, no. 12 (2 March 2015).
49. Michael Aung-Thwin and Maitrii Aung-Thwin, *A History of Myanmar since Ancient Times* (Reaktion Books, 2013).
50. Nicholas Farrelly, "Explaining Naypyitaw under the National League for Democracy", in *Myanmar Transformed: People, Places and Politics*, edited by Justine Chambers, Gerard McCarthy, Nicholas Farrelly and Chit Win (Singapore: ISEAS – Yusof Ishak Institute, 2018).
51. Frank Trager, "The Failure of U Nu and the Return of the Armed Forces in Burma", *Review of Politics* 25, no. 3 (July 1963): 309–28.
52. Gerard McCarthy referring to his analysis of the situation in Myanmar today, at the book launch discussion of *Myanmar Transformed* at the ISEAS – Yusof Ishak Institute on 27 November 2018.

Philippines

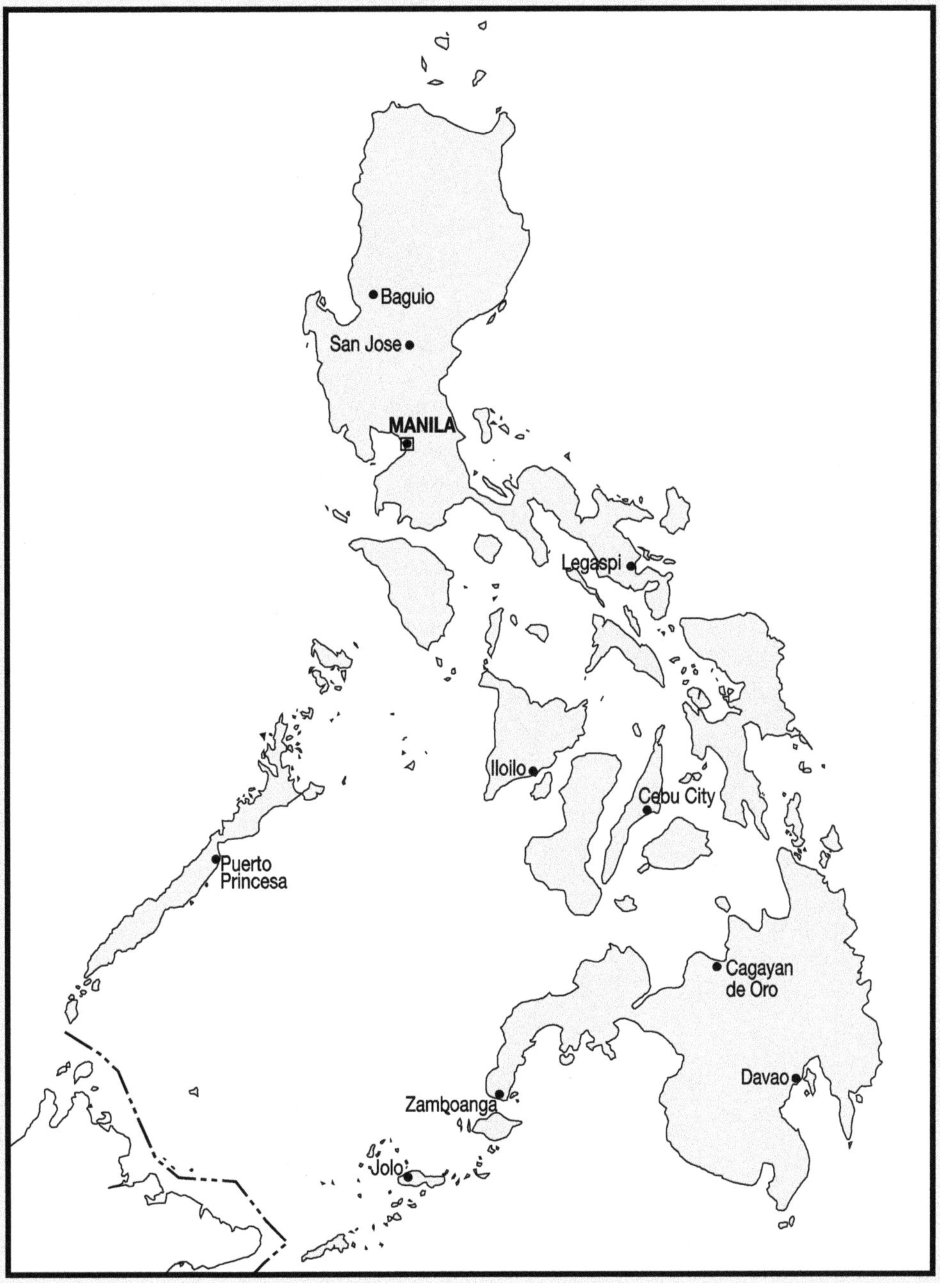

TOXIC DEMOCRACY? THE PHILIPPINES IN 2018

Nicole Curato

Toxic is the *Oxford English Dictionary*'s word of the year for 2018. It is a word that captures the mood of our time, evidenced by the 45 per cent spike in frequency of people who looked up the term.[1] Used in tandem with the word *masculinity*, toxic has served as descriptor to emphasize the physical harm, emotional damage and lethal effects of patriarchal power.

The same word can summarize the year 2018 for the Philippines. Beyond President Rodrigo Duterte's overt displays of toxic masculinity is a discernible pattern of his administration's aggressive attacks against the integrity of democratic institutions. From attempting to jail opposition figures to forging controversial deals with China that place the Philippines' sovereignty at risk, the regime has demonstrated the extent to which it is willing to breach the boundaries of state power while evading accountability.

This chapter analyses the Philippines in 2018 around the three themes of toxic politics, toxic policies and toxic deals. Each of these themes focuses on specific issues that will draw attention to broader patterns of Duterte's rule, which, as this chapter argues, has assumed a toxic quality for democratic life. Toxic politics focuses on issues of press freedom and the ouster of the Supreme Court chief justice Maria Lourdes Sereno. Toxic policies examines how Duterte's iron-fisted approach to governance shaped the conduct of the Boracay island shutdown and Marawi rehabilitation. Finally, toxic deals focuses on Chinese investment and new tax laws.

NICOLE CURATO is Senior Research Fellow at the Centre for Deliberative Democracy and Global Governance at the University of Canberra. She is the editor of *A Duterte Reader: Critical Essays on Rodrigo Duterte's Early Presidency* (2017).

By identifying these issues, this chapter does not intend to portray a bleak future for Philippine democracy. The final part of the chapter demonstrates how the public has responded to this political trajectory, and prompts reflection on where the nation may be headed.

Democracy's Autoimmune Disease

There has always been a danger that the populist President Duterte would have a toxic effect on Philippine democracy.[2] Populism, as political theorist Simon Tormey puts it, is a *pharmakon*, "a powerful substance intended to make someone better, but which might end up killing him or her".[3] There is no way to know the outcome in advance, he argues, for the toxicity of populism "depends on the dosage and receptivity of the body".[4]

In the first two years of Duterte's six-year term there was reason to think that the foul-mouthed mayor from Davao City infused just the right amount of populism to enliven Philippine democracy. His campaign may have unleashed a toxic online culture through his army of "trolls", but it also invigorated citizens who have long felt alienated from elite democracy to start actively taking part in grass-roots electoral campaigning.[5] Beyond the disparaging comments about Duterte's political style are hopeful remarks about how the first president from Mindanao gives voice to the suffering of the people in the country's most war-torn region. The man who has lived through conflict can solve conflict, the story goes, as many pinned hopes on his administration's peace deals with rebel fighters.[6] Shifting the country's unitary system of government to a federal one was pitched as "our last card to attain peace and order in this country".[7] *PHederalism* — the Philippine version of federalism — was discussed among elite circles of government, business and academia, down to over 42,000 *barangays* (villages), whose leaders were encouraged to pass a resolution supporting this agenda.[8]

There is of course a dark side to these developments. The brutal anti-narcotics campaign has, according to official police figures, cost the lives of over five thousand people. These victims — often young male breadwinners from poor families — are dismissed as "collateral damage" of a war meant to keep the streets safe. Senator Leila de Lima, one of the president's most vocal critics, was jailed on bogus charges. The burial of the former dictator Ferdinand Marcos at the Cemetery of Heroes sparked a series of protests. The Islamic City of Marawi was devastated by months of air strikes by government forces to liberate the city from ISIS-inspired fighters.

Despite (or because of) all this, Duterte continued to enjoy very good trust ratings. It is apparent that the Philippines has entered into a new social contract with a strongman who expresses little regard for civil liberties but who holds the promise of delivering peace and prosperity to all.

The trajectory of Duterte's populism took a definitive turn in 2018. Populism in the Philippines, it turns out, is not a *pharmakon* but democracy's autoimmune disease.[9] Duterte's toxic rhetoric were not empty threats. They resulted in attacks against power-scrutinizing institutions necessary for democracy's survival, from the judiciary to the media, the International Criminal Court to activist organizations. The year 2018 was also the time when the regime tested the boundaries of state power. It extended — and requested for a further extension of — Martial Law in Mindanao; imposed a state of national emergency in the Bicol region, Samar, and Negros Oriental and Negros Occidental; and ordered the shutdown of an entire island, with little consultation with local government units. Meanwhile, the federalism agenda has fizzled out, such that the plebiscite initially planned to coincide with the 2019 midterm election will likely not materialize.

These developments are instantiations of toxic democracy — a situation where the state uses the vocabulary of democracy to facilitate its own demise. It has features of "sophisticated authoritarianism", where states use some repression to maintain control but primarily manipulates the political realm to create subtle ways of challenging its rule.[10] The third year of Duterte's presidency has been marked by lethal blows to democratic institutions using a combination of brute force and political intimidation, and legitimized using the language of the rule of law and popular rule. These patterns of behaviour are evident in the way the regime conducts politics, forms policies and strikes deals, all of which embody a toxic quality. Such an approach to governance, however, has not gone uncontested. Alongside attempts to consolidate state power has been a consistent pushback from an increasingly critical public about the terms of the strongman rule.

Toxic Politics

The Philippines has one of the most vibrant media landscapes in the region, but it is also one of the most dangerous places to practice journalism. Long before Duterte threatened the media, the Philippines had witnessed some of the highest incidences of journalists being killed in the world.[11] Journalism in the Philippines is a dangerous enterprise, made even more toxic by a president who sees journalists as the enemy.[12]

The year 2018 started with an attack on free press, manifested by a series of cases filed against *Rappler*. *Rappler* is an online news organization which published investigative pieces that exposed Duterte's online troll army, questionable procurement deals and impunity in the drug war. Since he took office, Duterte has been persistent in accusing *Rappler* of violating the constitutional requirement for mass media organizations to have a hundred per cent Filipino ownership. *Rappler* is American-owned, Duterte claims, is backed by the CIA, and out to destabilize his administration. *Rappler* denies this claim.

On 15 January 2018, the Securities and Exchange Commission revoked *Rappler*'s licence to operate, for violating the Foreign Equity Restriction of the Philippine Constitution. A month later, *Rappler*'s Malacañang correspondent Pia Ranada was banned indefinitely from covering the president. The six-year-old media start-up also found itself facing a cyber-libel complaint and five charges of tax evasion, together with unrelenting online death threats to its journalists.

The National Union of Journalists, together with the editors of foreign media organizations, has condemned these moves as a clear form of harassment. According to Maria Ressa, the chief executive of *Rappler*, this is the government "weaponizing the rule of law".[13] *Rappler* has appealed to the courts as it continues its daily operations. Ressa is out on bail after being indicted for tax evasion. Duterte, meanwhile, has remained belligerent and has warned the media about the limits of press freedom. "It's a privilege in a democratic state", he said. "You have overused and abused that privilege."[14]

The harassment of *Rappler* has had a chilling effect on media organizations in the Philippines. And it is not only *Rappler* that has been the object of the president's ire. Duterte has shamed the *Philippine Daily Inquirer* and ABS-CBN News as "rude" in his speeches. "See how they slant", he complained. "I'm not scaring them, but someday, karma will come." Observers read this as a clear threat to two of the country's biggest media organizations. The ABS-CBN franchise is up for renewal in 2020. The president has said that if it were up to him he would not renew it. The *Inquirer*, meanwhile, felt "bullied", according to insiders.[15] Duterte said the broadsheet has gone "too far in your nonsense" for keeping a "Kill List" of people who died in the drug war.

The Supreme Court also had a challenging year. Chief Justice Maria Lourdes Sereno was ousted from her position, with lawyers' groups describing the development as the "final nail in the coffin of judicial independence".[16] The first female chief justice had a tense relationship with the macho president. Early in Duterte's term, Sereno reminded Duterte that only the judiciary had the right to discipline judges, after he had publicly accused a number of them of being part of the drugs trade. As in the case of *Rappler*, Duterte threatened Sereno not to create a crisis, "because I will order everybody in the executive department not to honor you".[17]

These threats became even harsher in 2018. Duterte put Sereno "on notice" that "I am your enemy and you have to be out of the Supreme Court". Duterte demanded that Congress fast-track Sereno's impeachment, and to this Congress dutifully acted. What ensued was a spectacle of associate justices breaking tradition to testify against one of their own in congressional hearings. "Ganging up" was how some described the testimonies, with Sereno's colleagues exposing petty jealousies and personal gripes against the chief magistrate.[18]

Parallel to the impeachment proceedings in Congress has been a case filed by Solicitor General Jose Calida to consider Sereno's appointment void from the beginning. Sereno was accused of failing to accurately declare her wealth in her Statement of Assets, Liabilities and Net Worth when she applied for the post of chief justice. This, according to the solicitor general, effectively questions her integrity, thereby disqualifying her from holding public office. With a vote of eight against six, the Supreme Court made history by removing its own chief.

The implications of this development are worrisome. Many have expressed concerns over the way the chief justice was ousted, for the constitution is clear that a chief justice may only be removed from power through an impeachment proceeding, not through a trial by the same peers who testified against her in Congress.[19] In his dissent to the ruling, Associate Justice Marvic Leonen warned that the judgment undermines the security of tenure of justices who express opinions that are contrary to the executive's wishes.[20] Before the end of 2018, Duterte appointed Lucas Bersamin as the chief justice, a man whose voting record was noted to lean towards the executive, including in the acquittal of former president Gloria Macapagal-Arroyo (who appointed him to the Supreme Court) and former senator Jinggoy Estrada for plunder.

The experiences of *Rappler* and the Supreme Court are not isolated episodes of political drama, but are part of a broader pattern of the Duterte administration's strategy of injuring institutions that scrutinize state power. Other developments in the year consistent with this pattern have been the threatened arrest of opposition senator Antonio Trillanes III, the detention of militant lawmakers Satur Ocampo and France Castro and the deportation of the Australian activist nun Patricia Fox. All these forms of intimidation have been justified using legal terms, whether it was Trillanes' failing to comply with the requirements of his amnesty for launching a military coup, accusations of human trafficking against leftist politicians, or violating the terms of a missionary visa. What is clear from these patterns is the increasing cost of political dissent and the state's capacity to use democratic institutions to subvert democratic practice.

Toxic Policy

"A cesspool" was how the president described the island of Boracay in a business forum in February 2018 in Davao City. The tourist hotspot known for its gentle coastlines, powder-white sand and Instagram-worthy sunsets is at risk of environmental destruction as establishments dump sewage directly into the sea. In the same forum, Duterte ordered the island's closure, putting at risk the livelihoods of over seventeen thousand hotel and restaurant workers and tour operators and revenues of up to a billion U.S. dollars. Duterte declared a state of calamity in three *barangays* and temporarily closed the island to tourists for six months.

The Boracay shutdown, while drastic, is not surprising. Political scientist Mark Thompson found the way Duterte dealt with the island's environmental problems to be within the character he portrays of himself, as a strongman defending the nation from corrupt officials and businessmen.

> [Duterte] invokes graphic images to justify drastic decisions. He portrayed Boracay as a 'cesspool' that must be closed. His 2016 presidential campaign was largely run on the narrative that drugs have been ruining people's lives and threatening to destroy the nation, with Duterte urging Filipinos to murder users and dealers whose dead bodies would fill Manila Bay until the fish grew fat. When rage is sufficiently aroused, extreme solutions become acceptable, even if the cost is lost jobs or even extrajudicial killings.[21]

Residents decried the heavy-handed approach to the island's rehabilitation. Notices of eviction were served in the presence of fully camouflaged military personnel. Policemen conducted drills in full riot gear in preparation for violent confrontations with protesters. Over six hundred policemen, Navy Seals and a patrolling gunboat were seen at the island — a scale of deployment typically reserved for battle zones or disaster operations. There was little consultation about the conduct of the rehabilitation with the scientific community, environmental movements or the island's residents. There is, as one journalist put it, "an undeclared Martial Law in Boracay".[22]

The island partially reopened in October. Many celebrated it as a demonstration of Duterte's political will in cleaning the country of social ills. A survey found that more than 60 per cent of Filipinos supported the shutdown to protect the natural environment. Meanwhile, Duterte continued his attacks against unscrupulous businesses that had damaged the island's natural resource. The president insisted that it is the *Ati* — the original inhabitants of the island — who should have rights to the place, which led to him distributing certificates of ownership of over 274 hectares of land to the indigenous population.

Boracay is not the first instance of such a policy. Before Boracay there was Marawi — the war-torn city devastated after five months of air strikes and ground combat between government forces and ISIS-inspired fighters. Like Boracay, there was little resistance to the government's swift and forceful response to the crisis. Despite 62 per cent of Filipinos finding no need to extend martial law in Mindanao,[23] lawmakers overwhelmingly voted (240 to 27) to continue martial law until the end of 2018. In practice, martial law in Mindanao means warrantless arrests can be made. Human rights group Karapatan reports at least 49 cases of extra-judicial killings, 22 cases of torture and 89 victims of illegal arrest and detention since martial law in Mindanao was declared on 23 May 2017.

Like Boracay, the rehabilitation of Marawi is being conducted without public consultation, with internally displaced people left in the dark. A series of peace rallies took place to commemorate the siege and liberation of the city. Marawi's residents marched to the main battle area where their homes once stood only to be blocked by security forces. Anxieties run deep as reports have surfaced of a consortium of Chinese and Filipino firms bagging government contracts to build "the new Marawi". Residents are concerned that the government's rehabilitation plan is not suited to Maranao faith and culture.[24] Interfaith network Duyog Marawi reported that those who presented rehabilitation plans "dismissed our comments, recommendations, and protestations as though we knew nothing and have no business getting involved in rebuilding our very own city".[25] While Marawi's residents support the construction of better facilities, they fear that the government would take over their land to build a military camp and cause further displacement.[26]

The International Crisis Group has also warned of the implications of getting Marawi's rehabilitation wrong:

> Mishandling Marawi's reconstruction, notably by carrying it out in a manner that angers inhabitants, also risks amplifying the idea, pushed by the Maute Group and its allies, that Islam is under attack in Mindanao. A botched reconstruction could also impugn the autonomy-centric political

> stance of mainstream groups such as the MILF, potentially driving more of its younger members toward jihadism.[27]

Indeed, the top-down approach to Marawi's rehabilitation goes against the ethos of the Bangsamoro Organic Law that Duterte signed in July 2018. There may be a legal framework for creating a new autonomous region in Muslim Mindanao, but, if Marawi's reconstruction gives any indication, there are no guarantees that Moro voices and interests will be genuinely heard, especially in times of crisis. Marawi is a defining issue for the Duterte regime. It will be a crucial test case on whether the first president from the South can meaningfully respond to historical and contemporary grievances.

What do the cases of Boracay and Marawi say about the kind of policies advanced by the Duterte regime? In both cases one can see how policies are defined by a politics of shortcuts. Duterte's populist style of naming the enemy and invoking a crisis in order to take decisive action comes at the expense of thoughtful procedures that can listen to, respond to and empower communities in shaping decisions that directly affect their lives. In 2018 the Duterte regime's template for governance revealed clearly that political will can make things happen, but making things happen for whom remains an open question.

Toxic Deals

When Duterte assumed power in 2016, he inherited a fast-growing economy that outperformed all countries in the region. The six years of Benigno S. Aquino's administration recorded an average of 6.3 per cent growth, upgraded credit ratings and a deficit of less than 1 per cent of GDP. Observers credit this to Aquino's good governance agenda of institutionalizing transparency coupled with fiscal and budgetary reforms.

The Duterte administration took a slight shift from this trajectory. While attracting foreign investment remained a cornerstone of the economic agenda, the shift took place as far as priorities are concerned. Duterte's economic ministers committed to accelerate infrastructure spending and to avoid bottlenecks in implementation. This was a departure from the policy of the Aquino administration, which was criticized for underspending, partly due to the hurdles caused by complex procurement procedures.[28]

With the Duterte administration's multi-trillion-peso flagship "Build, Build, Build" programme, the National Economic and Development Authority envisions that the Philippines will be a high-middle-income country by the end of Duterte's term. Government spending was up 42 per cent in the first half of 2018 compared to the same period in 2017, mostly going into road, rail and airport projects.

Duterte is hedging his bets on Chinese investments to finance his economic vision. While the Aquino administration took a proactive approach against China in pursuing territorial claims, Duterte took a pragmatic route, preferring bilateral negotiations and the joint development of resources.[29] Since 2016, Duterte has been courting China's support. He announced his own "separation from the United States" in a 2016 speech in Beijing. Before he left for China in April 2018, he publicly declared his "love" for Xi Jinping. Xi's highly anticipated state visit took place in November, with twenty-nine deals signed. The most controversial of these deals is a memorandum of understanding covering the joint exploration of oil resources in the South China Sea.

Are these deals worth it? Are they not toxic deals — a debt-trap in which China secures influence by "bankrupting its partners and bending them to its will?"[30] One can only speculate, as these deals are shrouded in mystery. It took a leaked document for the public to find out the terms of the draft deal on sea exploration. This document is silent on the 60:40 split of revenues between the two countries, as mandated by the Philippine Constitution. Some senators expressed concern over Chinese loans for big-ticket items. Senator Ralph Recto questioned China's prerogative to hire its own consultants, conduct feasibility studies, execute the projects and lend the money.[31] Early in Duterte's term, red flags had been raised about the contractors that bagged government projects. At least one of them from China had been blacklisted by the World Bank. Meanwhile, the Filipino counterpart companies have poor track records of implementing projects of this scale. "We know startlingly little about these firms", argues sociologist Kenneth Cardenas in a report filed for the Philippine Centre for Investigative Journalism. "Many do not have a substantial public profile. Some have never been covered by the Philippine media; neither have they disclosed anything publicly about their ownership, management, or their past deals."[32] Who, indeed, is building Duterte's Philippines?

The scepticism regarding China resonates with the public. A survey conducted by the Social Weather Stations found that 84 per cent of Filipinos do not approve of the government's "do nothing policy" on the West Philippine Sea.[33] China is at the bottom of the chart when it comes to trust ratings of other countries. Unlike the United States and Japan — which registered increases of 59 per cent and 28 per cent trust, respectively — China registered a reduction of 16 per cent net trust. Xi's November visit was met with protests all over Manila demanding that China get out of Philippine waters. While it remains to be seen how these deals will help to realize the administration's promised prosperity, there are enough reasons to demand transparency in their implementation.

Aside from making deals with China, the Duterte administration is also financing its infrastructure programme through a new deal with businesses and the people through new tax laws. On the first day of 2018, the Tax Reform for Acceleration and Inclusion (TRAIN) Law took effect. The main goals of the reform are to "enhance the productivity of the tax system" and "improve levels of disposable income", which can stimulate economic activity. Its key features include decreasing tax on personal incomes whilst increasing tariffs on passive incomes.[34]

TRAIN also imposes an excise tax on sweetened beverages, automobiles, cigarettes and petroleum products. The impact of the excise tax was acutely felt in everyday life. Coupled with the spike in world oil prices and the weakening of the peso against the U.S. dollar, the increase in the cost of petroleum affected the rest of the economy, causing inflation across the board. Inflation hit a nine-year high of 6.7 per cent in September 2018. Consumers experienced a nearly 20 per cent spike in the cost of vegetables, 12 per cent for fish and 7 per cent for meat.[35] According to the Finance Secretary Carlos Dominguez, rice has been one of the major drivers of inflation in 2018, leading the president to issue an administrative order removing restrictions on the importation of agricultural products.[36] While the connection between inflation and TRAIN is debatable among economists, one could argue that the new tax measure provided opportunistic traders the chance to impose unwarranted price increases and reap above-normal profits.[37]

These two examples — investment deals with China and a new tax deal with the people — are critical issues that warrant monitoring in the coming years, as both are tied to the urgent national concerns of the public. In a Pulse Asia poll conducted in September, controlling inflation topped all issues across the country and socio-economic class. This was followed by the need to increase the pay of workers and to reduce the poverty of many Filipinos. While defending territorial integrity remains among the least of their concerns, second only to changing the constitution, the promised deals with China may address these everyday concerns, or they could exacerbate them. The reports of Chinese nationals taking Filipino jobs has become one of the increasingly politicized issues advanced by Duterte's critics, such as the jailed Senator De Lima who protested against the "immigration surge" that "steals jobs away from ordinary Filipinos".[38]

A note of caution, however, is necessary. Despite the wide coverage about Chinese investments in local and foreign media, it is worth recognizing that the actual investments by and trade with China have not been "dramatically higher", except in tourism, gambling and real estate.[39] Economists warn that the investment gains from the pivot to China have been "minor" compared to net equity capital from the European Union, Singapore, the United States, Taiwan and Japan. The scorecard of China's influence in the country will have to be examined in the years to come.

Surviving a Toxic Time

The third year of the Duterte administration has revealed the character of this regime. It has demonstrated how the state is able to flex its political muscle when it comes to putting pressure on opposition figures or passing tax legislation, but it also finds weakness in pursuing the bigger agendas of federalism and the peace process. The year 2019 will be a pivotal one. The midterm elections can be viewed as a referendum on the president's mandate, or it could also expose the general indifference of the political system to the president's wishes. Old names from political dynasties continue to top senatorial polls, who will survive with or without Duterte. Protests in the streets continue, while resistance in the digital public sphere takes ever more creative forms. Predicting the Philippines is always a difficult enterprise, but if history provides any clue, one could surmise that Philippine democracy, with all its imperfections and capacity to surprise, will survive a toxic time.

Notes

1. Oxford Dictionaries, "The Word of the Year 2018 is ...", 2018 <https://en.oxforddictionaries.com/word-of-the-year/word-of-the-year-2018> (accessed 12 December 2018).
2. Randy David, "Dutertismo", *Philippine Daily Inquirer*, 1 May 2016 <https://opinion.inquirer.net/94530/dutertismo> (accessed 12 December 2018); Mark Thompson, "Bloodied Democracy: Duterte and the Death of Liberal Reformism in the Philippines", *Journal of Current Southeast Asian Affairs* 35, no. 3 (2017): 39–68.
3. Simon Tormey, "Populism: Democracy's *Pharmakon*", *Political Studies* 39, no. 3 (2018): 261.
4. Ibid.
5. Jonathan Corpus Ong and Jason Vincent A. Cabañes, *Architects of Networked Disinformation: Behind the Scenes of Roll Accounts and Fake News Production in the Philippines* <http://newtontechfordev.com/wp-content/uploads/2018/02/ARCHITECTS-OF-NETWORKED-DISINFORMATION-FULL-REPORT.pdf> (accessed 12 December 2018); Walden Bello, "Spider Spins His Web: Rodrigo Duterte's Ascent to Power", *Philippine Sociological Review* 65, no. 1 (2017): 19–48.
6. Bilveer Singh, "Duterte: Delivering the Promised Peace to Mindanao", *RSIS*

Commentaries, no. 112 <https://www.rsis.edu.sg/wp-content/uploads/2016/05/CO16112.pdf> (accessed 12 December 2018).

7. Miriam Grace Go, "DILG Mobilizes 42,000 Barangays for Federalism Campaign", *Rappler*, 24 March 2017 <https://www.rappler.com/nation/165139-dilg-march-25-barangay-assemblies-support-federalism> (accessed 12 December 2018).
8. Ibid.
9. See John Keane, "The Pathologies of Populism", *The Conversation*, 29 September 2017 <https://theconversation.com/the-pathologies-of-populism-82593> (accessed 12 December 2018).
10. Rachel Vanderhill, *Promoting Authoritarianism Abroad* (Boulder, CO: Rienner, 2013).
11. See Paul D. Hutchcroft, "The Arroyo Imbroglio in the Philippines", *Journal of Democracy* 19, no. 1 (2008): 141–55; also see Lisa Brooten, "Media, Militarization, and Human Rights: Comparing Media Reform in the Philippines and Burma", *Communication, Culture & Critique* 4, no. 3 (2011): 229–49.
12. See Committee to Protect Journalists, 2018 <https://cpj.org/asia/philippines/> (accessed 12 December 2018).
13. Hannah Ellis-Petersen, "Philippines Editor Accuses Duterte of 'Weaponizing' Rule of Law", *The Guardian*, 12 November 2018 <https://www.theguardian.com/world/2018/nov/12/maria-ressa-rappler-philippines-duterte-outcry-tax-charges> (accessed 12 December 2018).
14. Leila B. Salaverria, "Duterte, Rappler Clash over Fake News, Press Freedom", *Philippine Daily Inquirer*, 18 January 2018 <https://newsinfo.inquirer.net/961414/duterte-rappler-clash-over-fake-news-press-freedom> (accessed 12 December 2018).
15. *Rappler*, "Duterte's Target: The Philippine Daily Inquirer", 16 August 2017 <https://www.rappler.com/newsbreak/in-depth/178715-duterte-target-philippine-daily-inquirer> (accessed 12 December 2018).
16. See statement by FLAG (Free Legal Assistance Group), "Final Nail in the Coffin of Judicial Independence, 12 May 2018 <http://www.mindanews.com/statements/2018/05/flag-statement-final-nail-in-the-coffin-of-judicial-independence/> (accessed 12 December 2018).
17. Nicole Lorena, "Timeline: The Many Times Duterte and Sereno Clashed", *Rappler*, 20 May 2018 <https://www.rappler.com/newsbreak/iq/202763-timeline-maria-lourdes-sereno-rodrigo-duterte-clashes> (accessed 12 December 2018).
18. Maricel Cruz, "Three SC Justices Gang up on Sereno at House Hearing", *Manila Standard*, 17 January 2018 <http://manilastandard.net/news/top-stories/256485/three-sc-justices-gang-up-on-sereno-at-house-hearing.html> (accessed 12 December 2018); Elizabeth Angsioco, "A Tarnished Supreme Court", *Manila Standard*, 3 March 2018 <http://manilastandard.net/opinion/columns/power-point-by-elizabeth-angsioco/260009/a-tarnished-supreme-court.html> (accessed 12 December 2018).
19. See Gabriel Pabico Lalu, "Law Profs, Deans: Ousting Sereno Not by Impeachment is

'Unconstitutional' ", *Philippine Daily Inquirer*, 10 May 2018 <https://newsinfo.inquirer.net/989069/law-profs-deans-ousting-sereno-not-by-impeachment-is-unconstitutional> (accessed 12 December 2018).

20. Marvic Leonen, "Dissenting Opinion, G.R. No. 237428, Republic of the Philippines v. Maria Lourdes P.A. Sereno", available at <https://www.rappler.com/nation/202342-document-supreme-court-justice-marvic-leonen-dissenting-opinion-sereno-quo-warranto> (accessed 12 December 2018).
21. Mark Thompson, "Is There More to President Rodrigo Duterte's Boracay Closure and Drug War Than Meets the Eye?", *South China Morning Post*, 1 May 2018 <https://www.scmp.com/comment/insight-opinion/article/2144058/there-more-dutertes-boracay-closure-and-drug-war-meets-eye> (accessed 12 December 2018).
22. Raisa Robles, "In Locking down Boracay, President Duterte is Turning to the Phrase that Destroyed a Republic", 26 April 2018 <https://www.raissarobles.com/2018/04/26/in-closinglocking-down-boracay-president-duterte-is-turning-to-the-phrase-that-destroyed-a-republic/> (accessed 12 December 2018).
23. See Julius N. Leonen, "62% Oppose Martial Law Extension in Mindanao — SWS", *Philippine Daily Inquirer*, 22 December 2017 <https://newsinfo.inquirer.net/954489/62-oppose-martial-law-extension-in-mindanao-sws> (accessed 12 December 2018).
24. Carolyn O. Arguillas, "Displaced Marawi Residents: 'The World Now Knows about Our Plight' ", *MindaNews*, 31 March 2018 <https://www.newmandala.org/first-tragedy-farce-unlearned-lessons-reconstructing-ravaged-cities/> (accessed 12 December 2018).
25. See Duyog Marawi <https://www.duyogmarawi.org/> (accessed 12 December 2018).
26. Dakila Yee, "First as Tragedy, Then as Farce: Unlearned Lessons of Reconstructing Ravaged Cities", *New Mandala*, 23 May 2018 <https://www.newmandala.org/first-tragedy-farce-unlearned-lessons-reconstructing-ravaged-cities/> (accessed 12 December 2018).
27. Joseph Franco, "Philippines: Addressing Islamist Militancy after the Battle of Marawi", *International Crisis Group*, 17 July 2018 <https://www.crisisgroup.org/asia/south-east-asia/philippines/philippines-addressing-islamist-militancy-after-battle-marawi> (accessed 12 December 2018).
28. Gerard Lim, "SONA 2015: Aquino Gov't Continues to Underspend", *Rappler*, 26 July 2015 <https://www.rappler.com/nation/special-coverage/sona/2015/100542-aquino-administration-underspending-fiscal-performance> (accessed 12 December 2018).
29. Aileen Baviera, "President Duterte's Foreign Policy Challenges", *Contemporary Southeast Asia* 38, no. 2 (2016): 202–8.
30. John Pomfret, "China's Debt Traps around the World are a Trademark of its Imperialist Ambitions", *Washington Post*, 27 August 2018 <https://www.washingtonpost.com/news/global-opinions/wp/2018/08/27/chinas-debt-traps-around-the-world-are-a-trademark-of-its-imperialist-ambitions/?utm_term=.5c8a22d14d00> (accessed 12 December 2018).
31. Quoted in Paolo Romero, "Senate to Review Deals with China", *Philippine Star*,

22 November 2018 <https://www.philstar.com/headlines/2018/11/22/1870706/senate-review-deals-china> (accessed 12 December 2018).

32. Kenneth Cardenas, "Duterte's China Deals, Dissected", Philippine Center for Investigative Journalism, 8 May 2017 <http://pcij.org/stories/dutertes-china-deals-dissected/> (accessed 12 December 2018).
33. Social Weather Stations, "Third Quarter 2018 Social Weather Survey: Pinoys Maintain Anti-Chinese Stance on West Philippine Sea Issue", 20 November 2018 <https://www.sws.org.ph/swsmain/artcldisppage/?artcsyscode=ART-20181119235355> (accessed 12 December 2018).
34. See Dennis Dimaguiba and Kristine Anne Mercado-Tamayo, "INSIGHT: Philippines Tax Reform Continues in 2019", Bloomberg, 21 August 2018 <https://www.bna.com/insight-philippines-tax-n73014481879/> (accessed 12 December 2018).
35. See Aurora Almendral, "Duterte's Luster Dulls as Rice Prices Soar in Philippines", *New York Times*, 10 October 2018 <https://www.nytimes.com/2018/10/10/world/asia/duterte-philippines-inflation-rice.html> (accessed 12 December 2018).
36. Mary Grace Padin, "Rice Multiplies Inflation Weight 10-fold", *Philippine Star*, 12 October 2018 <https://www.philstar.com/business/2018/10/12/1859261/rice-multiplies-inflation-weight-10-fold> (accessed 12 December 2018).
37. J.C. Punongbayan, "Higher inflation: Is TRAIN to blame?", *Rappler*, 2 June 2018 <https://www.rappler.com/thought-leaders/203964-higher-inflation-is-train-to-blame-part-1> (accessed 12 December 2018).
38. Rambo Talabong, "De Lima: Probe 'Influx of Chinese Nationals' in Philippines", *Rappler*, 3 June 2018 <https://www.rappler.com/nation/203986-de-lima-senate-investigate-influx-chinese-nationals-philippines> (accessed 12 December 2018).
39. Ronald U. Mendoza and Miann S. Banaag, "Is the Philippines' Pro-China Policy Working?", *The Diplomat*, 14 November 2018 <https://thediplomat.com/2018/11/is-the-philippines-pro-china-policy-working/> (accessed 12 December 2018).

THE RISE OF CHINA, NEW IMMIGRANTS AND CHANGING POLICIES ON CHINESE OVERSEAS: Impact on the Philippines

Teresita Ang See and Carmelea Ang See

The year 2018 marked forty years since the economic reforms in China were ushered in by Deng Xiaopeng. China and the overseas Chinese community commemorated the anniversary with conferences, forums, exhibits and other celebratory activities worldwide to share China's achievements and the phenomenal success of its economic reforms and developmental model.

China's rise to become the world's second-biggest economy has benefitted both the Philippines and the region. For the Philippines, China's capital (through loans or grants) and expertise in building infrastructure and boosting agricultural production would be key in stimulating Philippine economic growth and development. This has also been accompanied by new migration patterns and business overtures to the Philippines, especially under the Belt and Road Initiative. The past decade has seen a sharp rise in the number of new immigrants from China, particularly in the past two years since the election of President Rodrigo R. Duterte in 2016. They continue to pour into the Philippines, some seeking residency legally through investment and retirement visas or special working permits.

The presence of the new Chinese immigrants has caused some tensions and complications in the Philippines, especially among the local ethnic Chinese community. The Chinese-Filipinos, or Tsinoys, sometimes find themselves embroiled in the popular discontent against China and Chinese immigrants. This

TERESITA ANG SEE is Executive Trustee at the Kaisa Heritage Center in the Philippines.

CARMELEA ANG SEE is Faculty at the College of Education, De La Salle University.

is further complicated by China's recent outreach efforts to the Chinese diaspora, which has been characterized by a relative lack of careful consideration about the distinction between Chinese nationals abroad and foreign nationals of ethnic Chinese descent.

The first section of this chapter will discuss the state-to-state relationship between China and the Philippines, especially the burgeoning cooperation in infrastructural developments in the Philippines. It will also describe why Chinese-backed projects have not been popularly received in the Philippines, although sometimes through no fault of China. The second section will cover the contemporary wave of Chinese immigrants into the Philippines as well as highlight the tensions and problems associated with the migrants. The third section will explore the recent policies of the Overseas Chinese Affairs Bureau, which risks alienating many citizens of Southeast Asia who are of Chinese descent, including those in the Philippines.

China and the Philippines

Although the Philippines established diplomatic relations with the People's Republic of China on 9 June 1975, it remained the bastion of Taiwan's Kuomintang (KMT) influence, with the ethnic Chinese community in the Philippines being largely pro-Taiwan, at least up to 1999.[1] From 1945 to 1975, Chinese schools and community organizations in the Philippines were supervised by the Taiwan-KMT embassy. One such organization was the Federation of Filipino-Chinese Chambers of Commerce and Industry, Inc. (FFCCCII), which only switched its sympathy in 1999 with an official visit of Chinese-Filipino businessmen to China.

The establishment of diplomatic relations in 1975 was, however, still significant, since it occurred with the recognition that the Chinese diaspora in Southeast Asia were not a separate sovereign group owing allegiance to a Chinese motherland, but rather an ethnic minority who would have to determine their political future in concert with the indigenous counterparts in their respective countries.[2] This meant that China had to dispel the belief that it was exploiting the overseas Chinese community for its own political purposes and against the interests of their countries of residence, in part to neutralize hostility towards overseas Chinese.[3] As Wang Gungwu wrote, the situation was such that it "was no longer acceptable for Southeast Asian Chinese in the new nation-states to hang on to the status of being temporarily resident in their adopted country", and neither was it acceptable "for the governments in Beijing and Taipei to continue calling them *huaqiao* or sojourners".[4]

In September 1954, Chinese premier Zhou Enlai acknowledged this so-called "overseas Chinese problem" in his remarks during the 1st National People's Congress (NPC). For the first time, the Chinese Communist Party (CCP) had to weigh the usefulness of demanding the loyalties of the overseas Chinese against the need to establish peaceful coexistence with the governments of Southeast Asia, where most of the overseas Chinese resided. This led to the passage of the National Law during the 5th NPC in September 1980, which stated that "the People's Republic of China does not recognize dual nationality for any Chinese national". The law also codified Zhou's policy that any Chinese national who resides in a foreign country and voluntarily acquires foreign citizenship would thus be forfeiting his Chinese citizenship.

Thus, in return for formalizing relations, the Philippines received Chinese assurances that it would neither interfere in the internal affairs of the host countries of the Chinese overseas nor seek to export the communist revolution. The latter meant China would stop supporting the Communist Party of the Philippines (CPP).[5] This particular promise was essential in the context of the Philippines, given the Communist Party of the Philippines' history of arms procurements from China in the 1970s and the foiled shipment of arms in 1972. In that incident, a shipment of 1,400 rifles from Fujian was intercepted by the Philippine military off the waters of Isabela Province, which became a pretext for former president Ferdinand Marcos to declare martial law in order to neutralize the communist insurgency.[6]

China's Growing Economic Role in the Philippines

The rise of China as an economic powerhouse has meant that, at the state-to-state level, the bilateral relationship has proven to be an economic boon for the Philippines.[7] In 2017, total trade volume amounted to US$50 billion, while Chinese investment into the Philippines reached US$53.84 million, representing a year-on-year increase of 67 per cent. China is now the Philippines' top trading partner and source of imports. As of August 2018 China was also the top export market for the Philippines. Various infrastructural projects in the Philippines have been mooted and pursued, such as the New Centennial Water Source — Kaliwa Dam Project, the Philippine National Railways South Long Haul, and the Safe Philippines and Chinese Industrial Park. The infrastructural boom has been taking place as China has sought to synergize its Belt and Road Initiative (BRI) with the Philippines' development plan *Ambisyon Natin 2040*, as well as Duterte's "Build, Build, Build" programme, an ambitious undertaking to build bridges, new roads, subways, ports and airports as a means of pump-priming economic development.

Implementation Challenges

Many of these cooperative ventures between China and the Philippines are, however, yet to materialize, as they have been beset by various delays. China has borne the brunt of criticism for the sluggish development, even though the delays have often been due to a lack of proper preparation on the part of the Philippines. Many of the proposed ventures were tabled without proper due diligence, feasibility analysis or public consultation. Thus, once announced, affected stakeholders would usually erupt in protest against the project, leading to its delay. These ventures are also affected by administrative bottlenecks arising from weak absorbative capacity and difficulties in securing the necessary right of way for public works like railways.

For instance, in August 2017 the Philippines National Economic and Development Authority (NEDA) established a Joint Economic and Trade Cooperation Commission with China to implement an infrastructure development programme from 2017 to 2022. Among the twenty-nine priority projects of the programme are plans for twelve bridges along the Pasig River and its tributaries. Under the agreement, China will provide a grant for two bridges while extending soft loans for an additional five, and the Philippines has the choice of identifying the two bridges that will be built under the grant. NEDA elected to build the Binondo-Intramuros Bridge under the grant, but progress has been hampered by concerns from heritage conservationist groups and the Chamber of Commerce of the Philippine Islands (CCPI) about possible adverse effects of the bridge on the heritage value of Intramuros, particularly given the proximity of construction works to the San Agustin Church, a UNESCO World Heritage Site.[8] In particular, the CCPI has suggested that either the Del Pan Bridge — located only 150 metres away from the proposed bridge — be expanded or a new bridge built beside it in order to alleviate the traffic congestion caused by the passage of cargo trucks between North and South Harbours, which has a knock-on effect on the similarly congested port operations in the area.[9] These criticisms highlight the failure of local agencies such as the Department of Public Works and Highways as well as NEDA to undertake due diligence and to consult with stakeholders before moving ahead with their proposals under the Chinese grant.

There are other China-backed projects that, while perhaps well-intentioned at the outset, are now frowned upon by various sectors in the Philippines. Again, these projects often end up mired in controversy because of the failure to conduct prior consultations with and seek local endorsement of the relevant stakeholders, or even the local government agencies that are meant to benefit from these projects. Examples include the rebuilding of houses and infrastructure in devastated Marawi City and the construction of the Kaliwa Dam to support the new Centennial Water

Source. In November 2017, the Chinese premier Li Keqiang pledged a sum of 1.1 billion pesos towards the rehabilitation of Marawi. The rebuilding efforts have however been greeted with suspicion, especially among local leaders in Marawi who are concerned about how the redevelopment of the region will affect their Muslim faith and tribal traditions. Part of their worries arise from the fact that the consortium that secured government approval to direct the reconstruction of Marawi is composed of five Chinese companies (one of which was found to have been blacklisted by international funding agencies) and three domestic companies with little to no track record of fulfilling public contracts in the Philippines.[10] Similarly, progress on the Kaliwa Dam has stalled due to the vehement opposition of local communities despite plans having been drawn up since the Aquino administration. The plan for the dam was resurrected in 2017, but with a change in the funding stream: instead of the initial public-private partnership scheme, the dam was to be financed through a soft loan of 10 billion pesos under China's Overseas Development Assistance. The involvement of Chinese ODA has only heightened objections, with even the Catholic Bishops' Conference formally articulating their protest against the dam project.[11]

A further example is the ten-thousand-bed drug rehabilitation centre established in an eleven-hectare compound in Nueva Ecija, a province in Central Luzon. The rehabilitation centre was inaugurated with great fanfare but remains underutilized. The centre was proposed to complement President Duterte's anti-drugs campaign, and was financed through a donation from Chinese business tycoon Huang Rulun. Two years after its opening, however, there are fewer than three hundred patients, because of the lack of budget, manpower and expertise and its isolated location. The centre is now a white elephant, as addicts are not able to afford the cost of rehabilitation, while the local government lacks the budget to admit them for treatment. Moreover, Huang has been accused of financing the centre only out of self-serving interests, as he was keen to ingratiate himself with the Duterte administration.[12]

The Philippines in the Belt and Road Initiative

China's BRI offers the Philippines an opportunity to rectify its decades-old infrastructural deficit. Potentially, if handled well, the Philippines stands to benefit greatly from the BRI and Chinese development assistance. China can indeed be a potential transformative development partner. Hence, even though people in the Philippines are cautious about Chinese investment, they are cognizant of the need for further infrastructural development, especially in terms of overcoming existing traffic and logistical constraints.

However, these cooperative ventures also provoke certain doubts about the capability of public officials in the Philippines to handle such projects. There also remains the strong possibility of corruption and huge kickbacks arising from the infrastructural development undertaken through China's loans. The financial sector in the Philippines is also concerned about the lack of feasible long-term plans to sustain the huge infrastructure spending. This is especially so since the recent tax reform package under the Tax Reform for Acceleration and Inclusion (TRAIN) law — which imposed an excise tax in order to increase tax revenue — has had the inadvertent effect of contributing to inflation, as the prices of products such as fuel, automobiles and sugar-sweetened beverages increased. Moreover, there also remain significant doubts about whether any projected increase in tax revenue will be sufficient to repay the Chinese loans that are financing these infrastructural projects.[13]

Hence, the Philippine government has to remain vigilant and properly assess whether the Chinese partnership is in accordance with the national laws, priorities and interests of the Philippines. Transparency and accountability are necessary to avoid the fiasco that transpired from two of the biggest deals the Philippines signed with China: the North Rail project and the agreement between the National Broadband Network (NBN) and ZTE Corporation. The North Rail project, designed to link the northern part of Metro Manila and Clark International Airport in Pampanga, was overpriced at $421 million and subsequently aborted. In the NBN-ZTE deal, controversy erupted when ZTE was awarded a $329 million contract to develop a nationwide broadband infrastructure to improve communications among government facilities. Accusations of graft and scrutiny by the Senate and the judiciary eventually led to the cancellation of the contract.[14]

Public Opinion of China

The strong economic relationship between China and the Philippines belies increasing public distrust of China among Filipinos, especially due to Chinese activities in the South China Sea. For instance, in a June 2018 survey of adult Filipinos, 81 per cent of respondents stated that it is not right for the Philippine government to be passive about China's intrusions in disputed waters, while 80 per cent demanded that the military, particularly the navy, be strengthened.[15] Furthermore, the respondents reported an overall negative net trust in China by a margin of 35 points: while 53 per cent indicated that they had *little trust* in China, only 18 per cent registered *much trust* in China, with a further 27 per cent undecided. Even among Filipinos who were satisfied with President Duterte, the net trust in China was negative by a margin of 32 points. As the next section will reveal, China's standing in the Philippines has not been helped by the influx of Chinese immigrants.

The New Chinese Immigrants in the Philippines

With the burgeoning economic relations and flurry of Chinese-led construction projects, it is no surprise that the Philippines plays host to a significant number of Chinese immigrants. Historically, there have been Chinese immigrants to the Philippines since the era of Spanish colonial rule. However, the contemporary influx of Chinese immigrants into the Philippines started in the 1970s, especially after the establishment of diplomatic relations with China in 1975. It escalated in the 1980s with the market reforms instituted by Deng Xiaoping and the opening up of China to foreign markets. This influx increased even more considerably in the two years after President Duterte was elected in 2016.

The academic term for the current generation of Chinese immigrants (both legal and illegal residents) is *xinyimin* (新移民), although they are more popularly known in the Philippines as *xinqiao* (新僑). The *xinqiao*, also sometimes referred to as *zhongguoren* (中國人), comprise the gamut of Chinese tourists, temporary visitors, individuals with fake papers, permanent residents and Philippine passport holders who arrived in the country from the 1990s to the present. The *jiuqiao* (舊僑), on the other hand, are an older generation of overstaying Chinese aliens who arrived in the Philippines via Hong Kong during the 1950s to 1980s. As long-time residents in the Philippines, most of the *jiuqiao* were able to legalize their residency status in the 1990s. Lastly, there is also the *lao qiao* (老僑), which refers to an even earlier generation of Chinese migrants who came to the Philippines before the Second World War.

In contrast to these migrant Chinese Filipinos, there is also a distinct generation of younger Chinese Filipinos (*Tsinoy* or *Tsinong Pinoy*) who were born and bred in the Philippines. This group includes the children of the so-called *jiuqiao* or *xinqiao*. Given their upbringing in the Philippines, the younger Tsinoys often adopt an identity and orientation that differs from their migrant parents. Having been educated in local Philippine schools, their first languages are Filipino and English, while Hokkien or Mandarin is something that they might pick up later. Rooted to Philippine soil, they often identify themselves as Filipino citizens first rather than with their ethnic identity, with an estimated 90 per cent of them also professing the Christian faith.[16]

The Size of Chinese Migration into the Philippines

The actual size of the current Chinese migrant population in the Philippines requires some educated guesswork. According to a presidential press release, "the tally of Chinese tourists to the Philippines in the first three quarters of 2018 has exceeded the full-year total in 2017, reaching over 972,000".[17] Other than tourist arrivals, Chinese nationals are also allowed to come to the Philippines via investor visas, retirement visas, or special working permits (SWP). The Bureau of Immigration reported that 3.12 million Chinese citizens arrived in the Philippines as tourists, investors, students and professionals from January 2016 to May 2018. Of these, 2.4 million hail from the mainland, while the rest are from Hong Kong, Macau and Taiwan. Government figures also revealed that there were 1.38 million Chinese arrivals in 2017 and 1.02 million in 2016.[18]

There was likewise a sharp increase in the number of Chinese nationals applying for SWPs, which allow a foreigner to work temporarily in the Philippines for up to six months. The figure rose from a five-year average of 1,051 SWP applicants in 2008–12 to a five-year average of 14,895 in 2013–17. The increase was first observed in 2016, the year Duterte was elected to office. The number of applicants rose to 14,775, which is double the figure of 7,200 for 2015. As of September 2018, the number of applicants for SWPs had reached 70,121.[19] While holding a SWP, migrants can apply for a separate Alien Employment Permit (AEP) from the Department of Labor and Employment (DOLE), which is more expensive but enables the permit holder to work in the Philippines for a longer period of up to five years. The DOLE reports that it has issued AEPs to 53,111 Chinese nationals for the period January 2016 to May 2018.

Taken together, the official figures suggest that there are a total of 123,232 Chinese nationals in the Philippines on AEPs and SWPs. However, the DOLE has warned that there are around 150,000 Chinese nationals who have failed to obtain a permit from them, including those who have overstayed or violated the terms of their visas. Such Chinese nationals become illegal residents and further violate the laws by either working without permits or engaging in retail trading, which contravenes the Philippine Retail Trade Nationalization Law.[20]

There is hence no accurate figure about the size of the *xinqiao*. A reasonable estimate from an extrapolation of immigration figures and enrolment numbers in Chinese-medium schools, however, would suggest a maximum of 200,000 Chinese nationals in the Philippines, a figure which includes overstaying migrants. In contrast, the number of Filipino citizens who happen to be ethnic Chinese is not more than 1.2 million, or 1.2 per cent of the total population of the Philippines.

The Xinqiao *Community in the Philippines*

The new Chinese immigrants bring the benefit of revitalizing the ethnic Chinese community in the Philippines, particularly through sustaining institutions such as schools, the Chinese language press, and community organizations.

Chinese-medium schools in the Philippines are currently facing the threat of decline due to the lack of both students and teachers. It is also the children of *xinqiao* families who are often the winners of Chinese declamation or essay-writing contests. Many organizations have contributed funds to the FFCCCII to support their efforts to halt the falling enrolment rates of Tsinoy children in the Chinese-medium schools. Many of these schools are also offering scholarships for their students to study in China in order to return to the Philippines and replace the ageing local teachers. Currently, around a third of the teachers in Chinese-medium schools are volunteers from the mainland, with some coming from Taiwan.

The *xinqiao* have also contributed to the longevity of the local Chinese language dailies. The local readership is often composed of people aged sixty-five and above, whose subscriptions are usually cancelled upon their death. Furthermore, there are currently very few Filipinos of Chinese descent who have editorial or columnist roles in the papers. The *xinqiao* community has however helped the Chinese dailies to remain viable, functioning as a source of new readership and investment, as well as supplying workers familiar with typesetting, proofreading and publishing in Chinese.

There has also been a proliferation of new Chinese community organizations in recent years, such as the Philippines-China Friendship Foundation in 2017 and the Fujian Province Overseas Association in 2018. New municipality-based hometown organizations and hometown-associated chambers of commerce have also been created, partly in an effort to provide the new Chinese immigrants with community leadership opportunities.[21] Significantly, these community organizations consider their members as not merely distinct from mainstream Philippine society but also separate from the local Tsinoy community itself. In the past decade, most of the new members of these organizations have been enlisted from among the *xinqiao*. Furthermore, older members are not being replaced by their children, who are often born and raised in the Philippines. This leaves the community organizations and their members detached from the wider Philippine society and incapable of exerting any significant influence beyond the immediate circles of new immigrants.

Social Tensions and Negative Perceptions

The lack of integration between new Chinese immigrants and the local Filipino population has created social tensions. This partly manifests in charges of chauvinism against the Chinese nationals, with Filipinos complaining that they "look down on Filipinos", particularly when "they refuse to learn and [instead] complain a lot about the country and its people".[22] Chinese immigrants have also been chastised for a lack of social graces in their interactions with Filipinos in public spaces, especially in trying to dismiss complaints about their poor behaviour through monetary payments.

This resentment against the Chinese has also been stoked by accusations that these migrants are taking jobs away from local workers. The Senate convened an investigation in November about the supposed rise in the numbers of illegal workers in the country. Leading the inquiry was Joel Villanueva, who is also the head of the Senate Committee on Labor. He made the observation that "along with the rising number of Chinese workers is the rising number of unemployed Filipinos".[23] However, there is no concrete data to show that Chinese immigrants are competing against and displacing Filipino workers. While the DOLE admits that there is a large contingent of Chinese workers employed in online gambling operations, this is not an industry in which local Filipinos compete, since the migrants are hired for their ability to speak in Chinese. However, the DOLE did observe that there is an increasing number of workers in technical fields and construction projects funded by China, which has prompted economists and legislators to question whether Chinese investments are effective in creating job opportunities for local Filipinos.[24]

The negative impression about the Chinese presence is further exacerbated by news of Chinese nationals being involved in crime. In November 2018, within a span of eight days the mainstream media reported on the rape of a Chinese girl by nine Chinese nationals,[25] as well as a case of four Chinese nationals murdering and mutilating a Chinese woman.[26] The Chinese immigrants are also burdened by the image of China as the main source of illegal drugs, especially given Duterte's harsh anti-drug policy and the alleged use of extrajudicial killings against traffickers, who are often poor, low-level couriers wearing only "*sando at tsinelas*" (undershirt and slippers).[27] There have been numerous reports of major drug busts involving Chinese nationals over the course of the year.[28] Furthermore, in the aftermath of raids on Chinese-run drugs laboratories in the Philippines, the drugs are now shipped from China. A recent shipment of drugs placed in thick steel magnetic lifters was successfully intercepted, although the Philippine Drugs

Enforcement Agency believes that many more have slipped into the country as a result of corrupt officials at the Bureau of Customs.[29]

The Chinese are also associated with cybercrime, particularly with bank fraud, fake documentation and fake investment opportunities. In WeChat, a popular messaging platform, there are frequent advertisements offering Chinese nationals a variety of services such as facilitating immigration entry, securing government permits and obtaining bank cards, credit cards and credit lines. These services also purportedly offer the possibility of rescinding immigration court orders, with fees quoted for removing one's name from the immigration watch list (100,000 pesos) and reversing a hold departure order (300,000 pesos). Although directed at the new Chinese immigrants, these advertisements affect the local Tsinoy community, who are disquieted by the insinuated aspersions on the professionalism and integrity of Filipino civil servants.

Anti-Chinese Racism

Geopolitical developments also aggravate the unfriendly sentiment against the Chinese. China's actions in the South China Sea, particularly its infrastructural projects on features located in disputed waters, have given rise to an anti-Chinese backlash, especially in the wake of President Xi's state visit in November 2018.

This backlash can often take the form of indiscriminate anti-Chinese racism. For instance, three days after Xi's visit, columnist Solita Monsod penned an article in the *Philippine Daily Inquirer* about "Why Filipinos Distrust China".[30] In the article, she expressed her doubts about the loyalty of the Chinese Filipinos, accusing them of being the country's most hated employers, and being averse to marrying Filipinos. But in doing so, she conflated the Chinese government, the Chinese people, the Chinese immigrants in the Philippines, and Filipinos of ethnic Chinese descent. Her column generated much[31] criticism,[32] particularly against her questioning of the Tsinoy allegiance to the Philippines, her failure to differentiate between the various Chinese sub-groups, and her generalization about "Chinese" billionaires being bad employers.

According to Carmelea See, the undercurrent of anti-Chinese racism, having lain dormant for some time, has perhaps become more visible due to the popular perceptions that the Duterte administration is mishandling the dispute with China over the South China Sea. She suggests that Filipinos, in lacking opportunities to effectively resist the government's actions, have instead channelled their frustrations against the Chinese in general, including Chinese Filipinos. She thus emphasized the need to remove ethnic origins from the equation, such as avoiding the temptation to generalize individual instances of misdemeanours or misbehaviour into a racial problem.[33]

The Blurring of Distinction and the Return of the Overseas Chinese "Problem"

Complicating the current position of the ethnic Chinese in the Philippines (as well as those in Southeast Asia) are China's recent moves at reaching out to the Chinese diaspora, which have the effect of obscuring the distinction between Chinese nationals who are overseas and foreign nationals who are ethnic Chinese. This has, in effect, recapitulated the so-called "overseas Chinese problem" that Zhou sought to address in 1954.

Leo Suryadinata described how

> As China grows in political and economic power, its policy towards the overseas Chinese also changed. It has gradually abandoned its earlier practice of differentiating between *huaqiao* (Chinese nationals overseas) and *huaren* (foreign citizens of Chinese descent).[34]

Recent policy pronouncements, especially from the Overseas Chinese Affairs Bureau, suggests that the Chinese government is adopting an expansive view of the *huaqiao* to include all ethnic Chinese residing overseas, even though as Wang Gungwu has argued, in today's context, "the *huaqiao* no longer includes those who have become foreign nationals since most Chinese living in foreign countries have adopted local nationalities".[35] There is an increasing tendency amongst the Chinese leadership to generalize about the diverse Chinese communities residing and living outside China, thus conflating the local-born *huaren* who have integrated into their respective societies and the *huaqiao* who are Chinese nationals studying or working abroad. Hence, China's attempt to regard the overseas Chinese as a homogeneous group which functions as a policy asset of China's strategic growth have provoked much concern amongst the *huaren*, who value their identity as Southeast Asian Chinese (rather than merely ethnic Chinese who happen to live in Southeast Asia). This tension is becoming more pronounced with the regular commentary of Chinese officials in forums and conferences about how "the strength or power of the Chinese overseas cannot be neglected in our BRI strategy".

The Outreach Efforts of the Overseas Chinese Affairs Bureau

The Overseas Chinese Affairs Bureau, or *qiaoban*, has been at the forefront of such efforts to reach out to and consolidate the "worldwide network of overseas

Chinese". Testifying to the increasing importance of the bureau, it was reorganized and placed under the supervision of the United Front Work Department of the Central Committee of the Chinese Communist Party in 2018.

During the 19th People's Congress, the deputy head of the bureau, Xu Yu Seng, reported that "the overseas Chinese are helping to realize China's dream". However, Xu did not elaborate or clarify the composition of the *huaqiao*, or the overseas Chinese, that he was referring to. Such rhetoric is especially disconcerting, especially as China has sought to boost its domestic talent pool by appealing to the overseas Chinese — regardless of nationality or passport — to return and help "the motherland", with perks such as residency permits.[36] Furthermore, in the Philippines the Chinese Embassy has requested, through community organizations close to China, for a list of outstanding university graduates and skilled professionals who are of Chinese descent.

These policy movements, especially under the auspices of the United Front Work Department, have contributed to the suspicion that not only is China blurring the distinction between the *huaqiao* and *huaren* but also all overseas Chinese — whether by nationality or ethnicity — are now considered as strategic resources to be exploited for China's interests. Academic sentiment in China does not allay this view. For instance, Zhuang Guotu, head of Southeast Asian Studies at Xiamen University, has described "the Chinese overseas" as "Xi Jin Ping's secret economic weapon".[37] He further explained that:

> The number of Chinese immigrants, including those who have changed their nationalities, is estimated at about 60 million. The number continues to rise as more people study abroad. In terms of population, 60 million is nearly equivalent to the world's 25th-largest country. As a whole, they hold the eighth-largest amount of assets in the world, meaning they can exert the same amount of influence as a developed country. We estimate they own more than $2.5 trillion in assets.[38]

Similar claims were advanced by Li Qirong in a 2016 conference paper, although Li valued the assets of the overseas Chinese to be worth US$4 trillion.[39] However, the figure of sixty million overseas Chinese (海外僑胞) merits scepticism. There is no explanation of whether the Chinese in Hong Kong, Taiwan and Macau are included in this figure, and it fails to distinguish between the *huayi* (華裔, or Chinese descendants), *huashang* (華商, or Chinese merchants), *huaren* (華人, or ethnic Chinese), and *huaqiao* (華僑, or sojourners).[40] More significantly, the figure subsumes foreign nationals into the Chinese polity on the mere basis of their ethnicity, even if they have no identification with or allegiance to China.

Furthermore, the valuation of the assets owned by the overseas Chinese brings to mind Edmund Terence Gomez's caution about "the sensational claims made about ethnic Chinese business".[41] Here, the dollar value of the assets matter less than the implication that these assets are somehow collectively owned by the overseas Chinese as a singular public unit, to be appropriated, harnessed or distributed by the Chinese government as it deems fit in its pursuit of development and progress.

Southeast Asian scholars have highlighted the dangers of such misrepresentations and blurring of distinctions by the Chinese. Leo Suryadinata argued that the "habit of not differentiating between *huaqiao* and *huaren* is worrying", especially when senior Chinese officials refer to

> *huashang* (foreign businessmen of Chinese descent) as *qiaoshang* (China's businessmen overseas), ignoring their citizenship. They also referred to *haiwai huaren* (Chinese overseas) as *haiwai qiaobao* (overseas compatriots), attempting to return to their past practice.[42]

Furthermore, pronouncements claiming that the "Chinese overseas is China's most potent secret weapon" or the "worldwide network of *huaqiao* is helping realize [the] Chinese Dream" serve to augment the sense of "yellow peril" that results in books such as Clive Hamilton's *The Silent Invasion*.[43] Moreover, the current trajectory of China's diasporic policy not only provokes suspicion about its motives and intent but also rekindles popular mistrust in Southeast Asia of the ethnic Chinese as a fifth column.

The Chinese in the Philippines

The expectation that the overseas Chinese community — including foreign nationals of Chinese descent — is to function as a strategic resource for China's development has also led to well-intended but ultimately misguided efforts by the Chinese to strengthen the position of overseas compatriots in their host countries. For example, a Chinese scholar associated with the Guangxi *qiaoban* argued that the status of the Chinese in the Philippines will remain weak as long as the community lacks a political party to mobilize behind.[44] This illustrates how the Overseas Chinese Affairs Bureau still lacks understanding and sensitivity about the circumstances of the ethnic Chinese, especially those in Southeast Asia. For the Chinese Filipinos, a Chinese-based political party would be ill advised. Such a party in the Philippines would only have the effect of marginalizing the Tsinoys from mainstream Philippine society and creating a social divide between

Chinese and Philippine identities. While the Tsinoys may recognize and take pride in their ethnic cultural heritage, they are simultaneously assimilated into all aspects of Philippine socio-economic and political life. For the Tsinoys, their loyalty is first and foremost to the Philippines. This sentiment is best encapsulated in the credo of a Chinese-Filipino NGO which states that "Our blood may be Chinese, but our roots are deep in Philippine soil and our bonds are with the Filipino people".

Conclusion

Bilateral relations between China and the Philippines at the state-to-state level are currently at their most robust, especially following the election of President Duterte. However, public sentiment remains against China, with many distrustful of its motives and intentions. President Duterte's decisions to set aside the Philippines' legal victory against China at the Hague Tribunal under UNCLOS and to downplay the maritime disputes in favour of joint Sino-Filipino exploration of petroleum resources have proven unpopular with Filipinos. These accommodationist policies have been greeted with much public disapproval, and much needs to be done to mitigate the resulting distrust and suspicion.

Furthermore, beyond maritime disputes, China must address the tensions that its immigrants are causing in the Philippines, especially since they not only reflect badly on China but also affect the reputation of other law-abiding immigrants and tourists as well as local-born ethnic Chinese Filipinos. For one, China can be more proactive and vigorous in confronting the issue of Chinese criminal activities in the Philippines. The joint agreement between the two countries to fight crime is a positive development towards this end.

Furthermore, China has to be sensitive in its outreach to the overseas Chinese community. The Chinese diaspora is diverse, and it includes a significant proportion of foreign nationals of ethnic Chinese descent who have acculturated and integrated into the mainstream of their respective countries. To treat these people as *huiqiao*, or consider them as "assets" or "secret weapons" of China, risks not only stoking their resentment at the forced co-optation but may also revive Cold War–era anxieties about their loyalties and allegiances. China must learn from its Cold War experience, in which its every move was viewed with suspicion and scepticism. While such a situation might not be entirely China's fault, it does however require China to be more nuanced and sensitive in its public diplomacy. China thus has to make the effort to convince its neighbours, especially the Philippines, of its peaceful intentions to help the region develop and prosper.

Notes

1. Theresa Chong Cariño, *Chinese Big Business in the Philippines: Political Leadership and Change* (Singapore: Times Academic Press, 1998), pp. 33–55.
2. Stephen Fitzgerald, *China and the Overseas Chinese: A Study of Peking's Changing Policy 1949–1970* (Cambridge: Cambridge University Press, 1972), pp. 74–75.
3. Ibid., pp. 103–4.
4. Wang Gungwu, "Sojourning: The Chinese Experience in Southeast Asia", in *Sojourners and Settlers: Histories of Southeast Asia and the Chinese*, edited by Anthony Reid (University of Hawai'i Press, 1996), pp. 1–14. See also, "The Origins of Hua-Chiao", in *Community and Nation: China, Southeast Asia and Australia*, edited by Wang Gungwu (North Sydney: Asian Studies Association of Australia in association with Allen & Unwin, 1992), pp. 1–10.
5. Richard J. Kessler, *Rebellion and Repression in the Philippines* (Yale University Press, 1989), p. 100. See also Leo Suryadinata, *The Rise of China and the Chinese Overseas* (Singapore: ISEAS – Yusof Ishak Institute, 2017), pp. 114–19.
6. "The NPA Arms Landing that Convinced Marcos to Declare Martial Law" <https://news.abs-cbn.com/ancx/culture/spotlight/12/12/18/the-npa-arms-landing-that-convinced-marcos-to-declare-martial-law>.
7. Dharel Placido, "China-funded Pasig River Bridges Break Ground", *ABS-CBN News Online*, 17 July 2018 <https://news.abs-cbn.com/news/07/17/18/china-funded-pasig-river-bridges-break-ground> (accessed 4 December 2018); Xi Jinping, "Open up a New Future Together for China-Philippine Relations", *Manila Bulletin Online*, 19 November 2018 <https://news.mb.com.ph/2018/11/19/open-up-a-new-future-together-for-china-philippine-relations/> (4 December 2018).
8. Edgar Allan Sembrano, "UNESCO Advisory Group Warns against Planned Binondo-Intramuros Bridge", *Inquirer.net*, 30 July 2018 <https://lifestyle.inquirer.net/301461/unesco-advisory-group-warns-vs-planned-binondo-intramuros-bridge/> (accessed 4 December 2018).
9. "Chamber Rejects Intramuros-Binondo Bridge" <https://www.manilatimes.net/chamber-rejects-binondo-intramuros-bridge/437799/>.
10. "A Year after Siege Marawi Rehab Mired in Multiple Problem" <https://www.gmanetwork.com/news/news/specialreports/654198/a-year-after-siege-marawi-rehab-mired-in-multiple-problems/story/>.
11. "Bishops Oppose P18 Billion Quezon Dam Project", *CBCP News*, 10 August 2018 <http://cbcpnews.net/cbcpnews/bishops-oppose-p18-billion-quezon-dam-project/> (accessed 4 December 2018).
12. "Mega Drugs Rehab Center a Mistake", *ABS-CBN News Online*, 1 November 2017 <https://news.abs-cbn.com/news/11/01/17/mega-drug-rehab-center-in-n-ecija-a-mistake-ddb-chiefg> (accessed 4 December 2018).
13. "Higher Inflation — is TRAIN to Blame?" <https://www.rappler.com/thought-leaders/203966-higher-inflation-is-train-to-blame-part-2>.

14. Javier J. Ismael, "Remember Northrail-NBN-ZTE Says Drilon on 29 Deals with China", *Manila Times*, 22 November 2018 <https://www.manilatimes.net/remember-northrail-nbn-zte-says-drilon-on-29-deals-with-china/471758/>.
15. "Second Quarter 2018 Social Weather Survey: 4 out of 5 Pinoys Repudiate Government's Policy of Allowing Chinese Intrusion in the West Philippine Sea", *Social Weather Stations Online*, 14 July 2018 <https://www.sws.org.ph/swsmain/artcldisppage/?artcsyscode=ART-20180714202446> (accessed 4 December 2018).
16. This author has written several articles on the problems of integration and identity in the five volumes of *The Chinese in the Philippines: Problems and Perspectives* (Kaisa Para Sa Kaunlaran, 1997). See, in particular, "The Ethnic Chinese as Filipinos", in *The Chinese in the Philippines*, vol. 2, pp. 24–68; and "Integration and Identity: Social Change in the Post-WWII Philippine Chinese Community", *The Chinese in the Philippines*, vol. 1, pp. 1–19.
17. Li Xia, ed., "Interview: Xi's Visit Expected to Boost China-Philippines Relations: Duterte", *XinhuaNet*, 18 November 2018 <http://www.xinhuanet.com/english/2018-11/18/c_137615662.htm> (accessed 26 November 2018).
18. From an official response of the Bureau of Immigration to this author's written request, dated 24 September 2018 and signed by Immigration Commissioner Jaime H. Morente.
19. Ibid.
20. "Influx of New Chinese Immigrants to the Philippines: Problems and Challenges", in See, ed., *The Chinese in the Philippines*, vol. 5, pp. 200–35; Tetch Torres-Tupaz, "2 Chinese Nationals Ordered Deported over Illegal Retail Trade", *Inquirer.net*, 27 February 2013 <https://newsinfo.inquirer.net/365889/2-chinese-nationals-ordered-deported-over-illegal-retail-trade> (accessed 4 December 2018); Raul J. Palabrica, "Threat to Filipino Retailers", *Inquirer.net*, 16 October 2017 <https://business.inquirer.net/238701/threat-filipino-retailers> (accessed 4 December 2018).
21. Chinben See, "Chinese Clanship in the Philippine Setting", in *The Chinese Immigrants, Selected Writings of Prof. Chinben See*, edited by Teresita Ang See (Manila: Kaisa Para Sa Kaunlaran and Chinese Studies Program, De La Salle University, 1992), pp. 91–118.
22. Teresita Ang See, "The Rise of China and Changing Policies on Chinese Overseas: Impact on the Philippines and the Tsinoy Community: An Exploratory Study", presented at the focus group discussion on "The Rise of China: New Overseas Chinese Policies, Impact on the Philippines and Tsinoy Community", held at Xaiver School, Greenhills, San Juan City, 4 September 2018.
23. "Senate Probes Rise of Illegal Foreign Workers in PH", *ABS-CBN News Online*, 26 November 2018 <https://news.abs-cbn.com/news/11/26/18/senate-probes-rise-of-illegal-foreign-workers-in-ph> (accessed 4 December 2018).
24. Ronald U. Mendoza and Miann S. Banaag, "Is the Philippines' Pro-China Policy

Working?" *The Diplomat*, 14 November 2018 <https://thediplomat.com/2018/11/is-the-philippines-pro-china-policy-working/>.

25. Joel E. Zurbano, "Police Nab 5 Chinese Accused of Gang Rape", *manilastandard.net*, 16 November 2018 <http://manilastandard.net/news/national/280693/police-nab-5-chinese-accused-of-gang-rape.html> (accessed 28 November 2018).
26. Robertson Ramirez, "Chinese Woman's Mutilated Body Found in Makati City Condo", *PhilStar Global*, 28 November 2018 <https://www.philstar.com/nation/2018/11/24/1871188/chinese-womans-mutilated-body-found-makati-city-condo> (access 28 November 2018).
27. Rambo Talabong, "Kian and Carl: What the Deaths of Two Boys Have in Common", *Rappler*, 4 September 2017 <https://www.rappler.com/newsbreak/iq/181093-kian-delos-santos-carl-angelo-arnaiz-similarities-differences-explainer> (accessed 28 November 2018); "Philippines: Events of 2016", World Report 2017: Philippines, Human Rights Watch <https://www.hrw.org/world-report/2017/country-chapters/philippines> (accessed 28 November 2018).
28. Maricar Cinco, "Shabu' Lab Raided; 4 Chinese Nationals Arrested", *Inquirer.net*, 13 April 2018 <https://newsinfo.inquirer.net/982105/shabu-lab-raided-4-chinese-nationals-arrested> (accessed 28 November 2018); Ria Fernandez, "P136-M Shabu Seized from a Chinese National in Manila Drug Bust", *Inquirer.net*, 24 September 2018 <https://news.mb.com.ph/2018/09/24/p136-m-shabu-seized-from-a-chinese-national-in-manila-drug-bust/> (accessed 28 November 2018).
29. Center for Media Freedom and Responsibility, "The Drugs That Got Away: Questions Linger on Multibillion-peso Drug Shipment", 28 November 2018 <http://cmfr-phil.org/media-ethics-responsibility/journalism-review/the-drugs-that-got-away-questions-linger-on-multibillion-peso-drug-shipment/> (accessed 28 November 2018); "P4.3-B Shabu Shipment Intercepted by Customs", *GMA News Online*, 7 August 2018 <https://www.gmanetwork.com/news/news/nation/663310/p3-4-b-shabu-shipment-intercepted-by-customs/story/> (accessed 28 November 2018).
30. Solita Collas-Monsod, "Why Filipinos Distrust China", *Inquirer.net*, 24 November 2018 <https://opinion.inquirer.net/117681/why-filipinos-distrust-china?fbclid=IwAR3m7YFC8HxxMV02GbUdoqhFMrri3KKqISja-1zsvoEpBZ3Nh-2NQ9MrGB4> (accessed 4 December 2018).
31. Richard T. Chu, "On Being Chinese Filipino (with 'Filipino' First)", *Esquire Online*, 28 November 2018 <https://www.esquiremag.ph/politics/opinion/chinese-filipino-opinion-a2260-20181127> (accessed 4 December 2018).
32. Caroline Hau, "Why I Distrust Solita Monsod's 'Why Filipinos Distrust China' ", *Ikangablog*, 27 November 2018 <https://ikangablog.wordpress.com/2018/11/27/why-i-distrust-solita-monsods-why-filipinos-distrust-china/> (accessed 4 December 2018).
33. Gaea Katreena Cabico, "Frustration over Sea Dispute No Reason to Hate Chinese People", *PhilStar Global*, 26 November 2018 <https://www.philstar.com/

headlines/2018/11/26/1871913/frustration-over-sea-dispute-no-reason-hate-chinese-people> (accessed 4 December 2018).

34. Suryadinata, *The Rise of China*, p. 9.
35. Wang Gung Wu, *Don't Leave Home: Migration and the Chinese* (Singapore: Times Academic Press, 2001), p. 88.
36. 許又聲. "國務院僑務辦公室主任國務院關於華僑權益保護工作情況的報告(全文). —— 2018年4月25日在第十三届全国人民代表大会常务委员会第二次会议上 [Xu Yu Seng. "Report of the State Council Overseas Chinese Affairs Office of the State Council on the Protection of Overseas Chinese Rights and Interests (Full Text)". Beijing: Second meeting, of the Standing Committee of the 13th National People's Congress, 25 April 2018], Overseas Chinese Affairs Office of the State Council, 26 April 2018 <http://www.gqb.gov.cn/news/2018/0426/44797.shtml> (accessed 6 December 2018).
37. "Xi's Secret Economic Weapon: Overseas Chinese: Scholar Says Today's 'New Immigrants' Can Boost China-US ties", *Nikkei Asian Review*, 3 April 2017 <https://asia.nikkei.com/Economy/Xi-s-secret-economic-weapon-Overseas-Chinese> (accessed 5 December 2018).
38. Ibid.
39. 李其荣. "華僑華人與 '一帶一路' 人文交流." 2016年5月7–8日，台北海外華人研究學會年會暨國際研討會在台北市立大學召開。李其榮教授應邀出席，並分別擔任分場討論的主持人和點評人。本次會議主題是："接觸場域：海外華人聚落研究的新視野與新方向"。主辦單位是台北市立大學歷史與地理系、台北海外華人研究學會、台灣師範大學海外華人研究中心 [Li Qirong, "Huaqiao Chinese and the 'Belt and Road' Cultural Exchanges", paper delivered at the Taipei Overseas Chinese Studies Society Annual Conference and International Symposium on "Contact Field: New Vision and New Direction of Overseas Chinese Settlement Research", organized by the Department of History and Geography of Taipei City University, the Taipei Overseas Chinese Research Association, and the Overseas Chinese Research Center of Taiwan Normal University and held at Taipei City University, Taipei, Taiwan, 7–8 May 2016] <http://history.ccnu.edu.cn/info/1073/9338.htm>.
40. Wang Gungwu has written extensively on the definitions and nuances behind the different terms for Chinese overseas like *huaqiao* and *huaren*. See in particular Wang Gungwu, "The Origins of Hua-Chiao", in *Community and Nation: China, Southeast Asia and Australia*, edited by Wang Gungwu (North Sydney: Asian Studies Association of Australia in association with Allen & Unwin, 1992), pp. 1–10.
41. Edmund Terence Gomez, "Ethnic Enterprise, Economic Development and Identity Formation: Chinese Business in Malaya", in *The State, Economic Development and Ethnic Co-Existence in Malaysia and New Zealand*, edited by Edmund Terence Gomez and Robert Stephens (Kuala Lumpur: Centre for Economic Development and Ethnic Relations, University of Malaya, 2003), pp. 121–45.
42. Suryadinata, *The Rise of China*, p. 162.

43. Clive Hamilton, *Silent Invasion: China's Influence in Australia* (Hardie Grant, 2018).
44. Yang Jinglin, "Filipino-Chinese Community and the Territory Dispute of South China Sea between China and the Philippines" (in Chinese), paper presented at the international conference on "Chinese Diasporas in the Contemporary Era of China's Rise: Migration, Settlement and Transnational Linkages", organized by ISSCO (International Society for the Study of Chinese Overseas) and held at the University of Melbourne, Australia, 25–26 October 2018.

Singapore

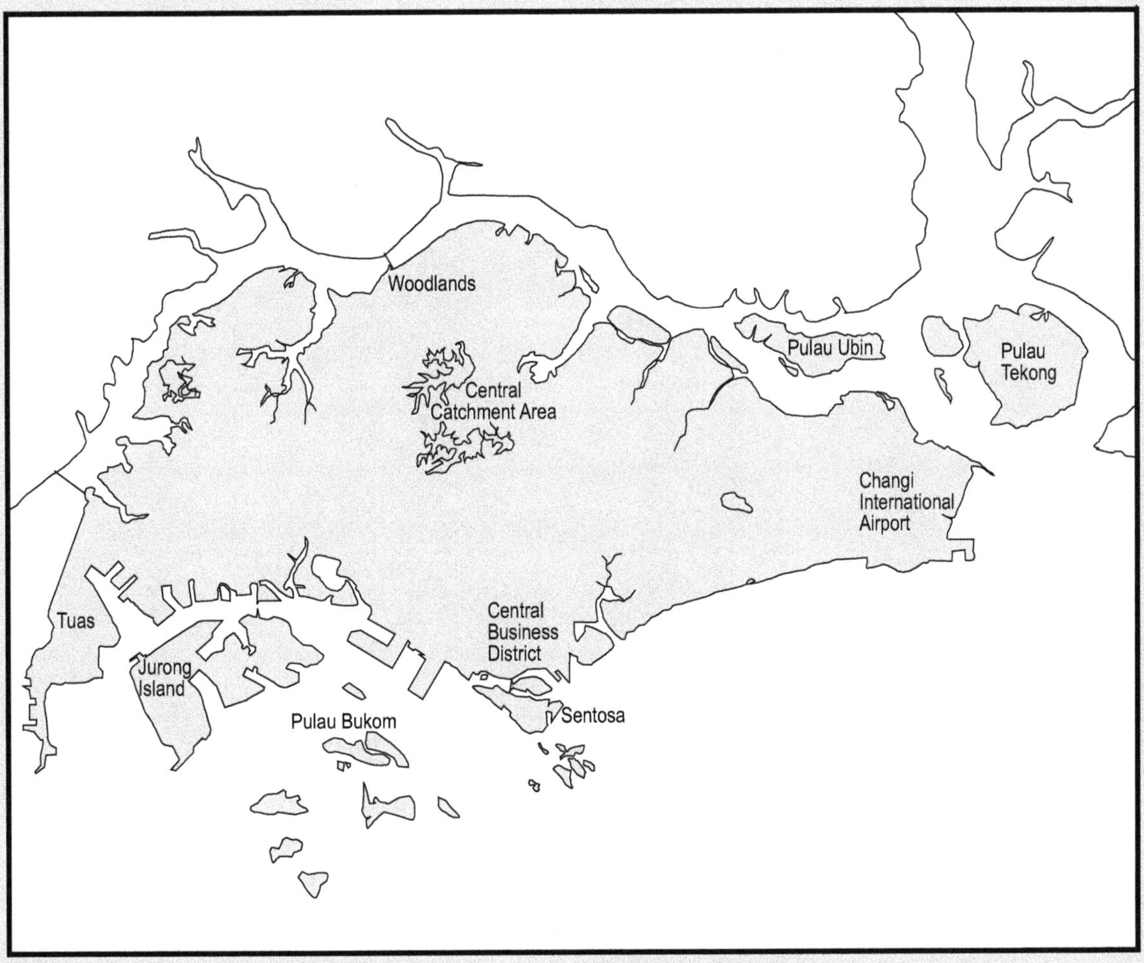
Woodlands
Central Catchment Area
Pulau Ubin
Pulau Tekong
Changi International Airport
Tuas
Jurong Island
Central Business District
Sentosa
Pulau Bukom

SINGAPORE IN 2018: Between Uncharted Waters and Old Ghosts

George Wong and Woo Jun Jie

For the city state of Singapore, 2018 was a year of many firsts. It marked the midpoint of the 13th Parliament of Singapore within a manifestly post–Lee Kuan Yew era. The incumbent government of the People's Action Party (PAP) began the year with the pleasant surprise that economic growth in 2017 had reached 3.6 per cent. This exceeded the modest expectations of 1.5 to 3.5 per cent.[1] But despite the positive start, 2018 was to be filled with headwinds for Singapore, both new and familiar. Top of the list was the revival of tensions with Malaysia, as well as a newly elected PAP Central Executive Committee, marking a crucial occasion of fourth-generation leadership transition for the world's third-longest ruling political party. On the international front it was the year of summits, with Singapore hosting two major events: the North Korea–United States Summit — the "Trump-Kim summit" — and the 33rd ASEAN Summit, both amidst the trade war between China and the United States. Meanwhile, in local politics, other notable firsts included the formation of the Select Committee on deliberate online falsehoods and the convening of its public hearings, as well as a cyberattack on SingHealth, Singapore's largest healthcare provider, resulting in the records of about 1.5 million patients being compromised. On the ground, *inequality* took the crown as buzzword of the year in the public consciousness as Singapore

George Wong is a doctoral candidate with the Sociology Department of Nanyang Technological University. He received his Master's Degree in Sociology from the same institution and his Bachelor's of Social Science in Political Science and Sociology from the Singapore Management University.

Woo Jun Jie is Assistant Professor in the Department of Asian and Policy Studies, the Education University of Hong Kong.

grappled with various encounters, propelling the otherwise academic term into the limelight. On the policy side, the introduction of the Merdeka Generation Package set a new bar for the government's commitment to reducing the healthcare costs of elderly Singaporeans.

4G Leadership Transition of the PAP

In 2018, political leadership successions and renewal went into high gear both for major political parties and the government. It began with a joint-statement in January by a self-identified fourth-generation (dubbed 4G) team consisting of sixteen ministerial leaders under the ruling People's Action Party, as part of the party's commitment to pick a leader "in good time".[2] The statement came barely a week after a social media post made by Emeritus Senior Minister Goh Chok Tong urging the current cohort of the political leadership to consolidate its succession challenge, including choosing a designate from among them for the post of prime minister. The lingering question of the PAP's leadership transition was further satiated in the latter part of the year during the party's election of its 35th Central Executive Committee (CEC). The party held its 2018 biennial CEC elections on 11 November, which bore witness to major but much anticipated overhauls. Notable changes included the stepping down from the CEC of prominent political heavyweights such as Lim Swee Say, Khaw Boon Wan, Tharman Shanmugaratnam, Teo Chee Hean and Yaacob Ibrahim, albeit retaining their cabinet positions. Succeeding them were Heng Swee Keat, Chan Chun Seng, Ong Ye Kung, Masagos Zulkifli and Grace Fu. The CEC also saw two new elected faces, Ng Chee Meng and Indranee Rajah, reflecting the party's confidence in the wider circle of leadership stock. The committee also co-opted six more members — Josephine Teo, Ng Eng Hen, Lawrence Wong, Desmond Lee, Sitoh Yih Pin and Christopher de Souza — bringing the total tally to eighteen and cementing an unmistakably 4G presence at the party's apex.

The climax of the transition was the confirmation of Heng Swee Keat and Chan Chun Sing as the 1st and 2nd assistant secretaries-general, respectively, with the former being touted as a strong forerunner for the role of prime minister. This news however did not come as a major surprise, since news from ground sources had already identified Heng's ascension days before the selection. Furthermore, reiterating the current narrative of political transition, Heng emphasized that the confirmation was aligned with the PAP's commitment to provide a team-centred transition of continuity and stability for Singapore.[3] The cabinet reshuffle earlier in April was also a strong signal of the government's commitment of preparing the 4G leaders to assume key ministerial positions, with numerous ministerial successions and reappointments suggesting a desire to give the new blood greater autonomy in their ministerial portfolios.[4] All the events leading up to the CEC elections suggested that little had changed in the PAP's leadership transition narrative, where its core principles lie in establishing confidence and stability through collegiality and predictability. However, this was also the party's first leadership transition since the passing of Lee Kuan Yew, the party's co-founder and paramount leader, a factor that the succession planners obviously had no control over. However, despite remarkable changes to both the party leadership and the government, Prime Minister Lee has announced that he will lead the party in the next general elections, although it is expected that the 4G leaders will take a greater role.[5] The elections must be held at the latest by April 2021, although ground sentiments suggest a much earlier schedule. All these hint at the ruling party's stance of not throwing caution to the wind in expecting an easy transition in the upcoming ballots, a reasonable judgment considering the possibility of a return of the "new normal" electoral politics scenario of 2011.

Leadership Renewal of the Workers' Party

Renewal fever in 2018 was not constrained to the ruling party. The Workers' Party, fresh out of its sixtieth anniversary celebrations of the year before, saw Low Thia Kiang, after seventeen years at the helm, being succeeded by Pritam Singh as secretary-general and de facto leader of the opposition. Other than that, the party's leadership remained relatively unchanged, with Sylvia Lim continuing as chair and all but two of the previous members being returned to the party's leadership.[6] All eyes are on whether Singh can fill the shoes of his predecessor, whose stellar track record includes six consecutive electoral victories and securing the opposition's first ever win in a group representative constituency (GRC). The start of the Aljunied-Hougang Town Council (AHTC) trials, with hearings commencing on 5 October, added to the pressures faced by the new leadership. The trial saw a total of eight defendants: Sylvia Lim, Low Thia Khiang and Pritam Singh (all three currently parliamentarians); AHTC town councillors Kenneth Foo and Chua Zhi Hon; and former managing agents of AHTC How Weng Fan and the late Danny Loh. They are accused by AHTC and Pasir Ris–Punggol Town Council (PRPTC) of breaching their fiduciary duties, on the back of audit reports by KPMG and PricewaterhouseCoopers.[7] The hearing lasted an eventful seventeen days, bringing intriguing case details to light, including the transcript of a phone call between Ms Ho and an employee of the audit firm KPMG which revealed the former's lack of confidence in Ms Lim in her role of town council chairperson,[8] as well as Ms Lim conceding that she had failed to disclose the prevailing rates charged by the town council's previous managing agent when she sought to waive the tender process for a new managing agent.[9] Albeit in the doldrums of the trial hearings, a silver lining came in the form of public support pouring in for Mr Low, Ms Lim and Mr Singh when their personal appeal for donations to defray their legal expenses ended up raising more than S$1 million from the public over three days.

Swearing-in of New Nominated Members of Parliament

Beyond party-related renewals, 2018 also saw the ushering in of nine new Nominated Members of Parliament (NMPs). The nine were selected, from among forty-eight nominations, to represent non-partisan views from various sectors of civil society. The NMP scheme was introduced in 1990 with the expressed aim of promoting a greater diversity of opinions in the House from independent and non-partisan voices.[10] Drawing from the fields of the arts, sciences, business, community sector and labour unions, NMPs are either nominated by the respective lead organizations or are self-nominated. After being assessed and appointed through a Parliamentary Select Committee, NMPs serve a term of two and half years and are vested with the power to vote on bills and motions not concerning constitutional amendments, public budget, and confidence in the government.[11]

The new slate of NMPs for 2018 also included two members below the age of 30, with Yip Pin Xiu (26) and Abbas Ali Mohamed Irshad (29) touted to provide a voice for younger Singaporeans. Other notable members include Associate Professor Walter Edgar Theseira and Arasu Duraisamy, who will be representing the science sector and labour unions, respectively. The nominations of NMPs were however not without event, as seen in the attempts by the arts community to seek a worthy successor to Kok Heng Leun, the outgoing Arts NMP, who was regarded during his stint as a successful mediator between the government and the arts and culture sector.[12] A town hall session was set up on the 24 July to identify nominations for the Arts NMP, with two candidates, Dr Woo Tien Wei and Dr Felicia Low, receiving mixed support from attendees.[13] The subsequent nomination however fell to Ho Wee San, managing director of the Singapore Chinese Orchestra. This development saw the breaking of a practice, upheld since 2009, of the Arts NMP being nominated with the explicit endorsement of the arts community.[14] Speculation on the ground suggested that the lack of confidence stemming from the town hall session may have played a role in this.

Singapore-Malaysia Tensions

Disquiet over leadership succession also seized the minds of Singaporeans when in neighbouring Malaysia the Pakatan Harapan coalition defeated the Barisan Nasional, which had ruled for sixty-one years, ushering in a new chapter in Malaysian politics, with Mahathir Mohamad returning for a second time as prime minister of the new government. Part of the anxiety stemmed from a reminder of the testy bilateral relations and cross-straits disputes between Singapore and Malaysia that characterized the ninety-three-year-old political veteran's previous tenure as premier between 1981 and 2003. The question in the minds of the Singapore public was whether the return of Mahathir would reignite old tensions in cross-straits relations.[15] These apprehensions were confirmed when Mahathir made two controversial moves within the first hundred days of the Pakatan government. The first was a unilateral announcement in May to scrap — and later, in July, to defer — the KL–Singapore High-Speed Rail project.[16] The second was his suggestion in a June interview for renegotiation of the terms of the 1962 Water Agreement,[17] a statement seen by the Singapore government as an affront to the premises of Singapore's sovereignty.[18] The uneasy bilateral ties were further strained in a diplomatic double whammy in the form of a maritime confrontation off Singapore's northwestern coast and an airspace dispute in southern Johor. The maritime dispute was sparked by the announcement on 25 October by the Malaysian federal government of an extension to Johor's port limit, which was met a week later by a strong formal protest by Singapore on the grounds of sovereignty. Tensions escalated in the contested waters following multiple near-altercations between security vessels of the two states in late November and early December.[19] Meanwhile, disagreements over the impact of the Instrument Landing System at Singapore's Seletar Airport and airspace arrangements over southern Johor saw the Malaysian government declaring the area as restricted airspace on Christmas Day.[20] The restriction means planes need to make additional manoeuvres in order to land at Seletar Airport.

Despite calls for resolution[21] and planned reconciliatory meetings,[22] these tensions will be unlikely to abate any time soon if past episodes are any indicator.[23] A recent move saw consideration by Malaysia to limit the export of eggs during the Christmas and Lunar New Year festive season, sending Singaporean suppliers scrambling for alternative sources to meet local demand.[24] On the rhetorical front, Dr Rais Hussin, a leader in Mahathir's party, added controversy to the maritime dispute when he warned that Singapore will get "only pain by a thousand cuts" if it continued with its current stance against Malaysia.[25] Furthermore, the elephant in the room is the question of Malaysia's own political succession, with the crowning of Dr Anwar Ibrahim as Malaysia's prime-minister-in-waiting,[26] a moniker bestowed by Mahathir himself,[27] as well as growing concerns over infighting within and between parties of the new but fragile governing Pakatan coalition.[28] These factors add to the challenge of deciphering cross-straits relations and expectations. For Singapore, any suggestion of a quick fix is unlikely.[29] Meanwhile, this growing enigma of a neighbour will test the limits of Singapore's existing bilateral strategies. And only time will tell whether the city-state's continued reliance on conventional Track One diplomatic measures will prove to be as effective a posture as it has in the past.

What Does Inequality Look Like?

On 19 February a seemingly unembellished book was published that has since rolled out an otherwise sociological term into the public lexicon.[30] *This Is What Inequality Looks Like*, by sociologist Teo You Yenn, topped the local book charts as one of Singapore's best-selling non-fiction titles of 2018,[31] selling over twenty thousand copies to date.[32] Inequality and its synonym — social stratification — have both taken their spots as buzzwords of 2018 in public conversations about government policies and public narratives regarding poverty, welfare and social mobility. In more ways than one, the book was a timely gift for a public seeking a narrative to articulate mounting proof of social inequality.[33] Moreover, the critically acclaimed movie *Crazy Rich Asians*, which featured Singapore prominently as a home of wealthy Asians (or more accurately, Straits Chinese), has also helped to steer conversations on the prevailing divide between the ostensibly wealthy and their poorer counterparts.[34] In her opening speech of the second session of the 13th Parliament, President Halimah Yaccob similarly brought the topic of inequality and social stratification to the fore by emphasizing its importance in maintaining the social compact that could make or break society.[35]

The conversations on inequality and social stratification centred on three local episodes. First were the volleys of commentaries in response to an article by Dr Teo that captured the essence of her book after it had surfaced into public discourse.[36] The first salvo was an op-ed by Dr Sudha Nair, a familiar face in the social work sector, which questioned Dr Teo's privileging of dignity over getting low-income families to face up to their problems.[37] Dr Nair's commentary itself faced criticism in the form of a letter by forty social service practitioners that echoed Dr Teo's argument about the importance of tackling structural conditions that engender poverty. The debate finally received government attention, with

Dr Maliki Osman responding in an op-ed that reiterated Dr Nair's stance of tough love and intervention, while celebrating the resilience of social workers in Singapore.[38] While the exchange died down soon after, the release of Oxfam's Commitment to Reducing Inequality Index in October, which placed Singapore in the bottom ten, reignited the debate.[39] The Oxfam report received harsh rebuttals from the government — first from Minister for Social and Family Development Desmond Lee[40] and later from Finance Minister Heng Swee Keat[41] — for being too fixated on certain narrowly defined indicators and inputs at the cost of neglecting outcomes. And last but not least, a TV documentary called "Regardless of Class", which aired on 24 September, generated considerable buzz on account of the controversial but honest sharing by participants in the programme.[42] One revelation indicated that about half of the 1,046 citizens surveyed cited social class as the most likely factor of social divide in Singapore, compared to about 20 per cent who cited race.[43] The documentary also drew criticism, with one commentary castigating the conclusions drawn by the film as reproducing the problematic narrative of "a crusade against snobbery ... and a question of people behaving badly by 'judging' others as low class and refusing to mix", the very narratives Dr Teo aimed to unravel in the first place.[44] Others saw the documentary as a good starting point for furthering conversations on inequality, but urged for deeper and more inclusive dialogues.[45] The current headway with these local encounters suggests that inequality and social stratification might not pass from the minds of the public any time soon, with political leaders seeking new ways to engage this newfound public consciousness.[46]

Cyberattack on SingHealth

On 4 July 2018, Integrated Health Information Systems detected an unauthorized breach in one of SingHealth's patient databases. A subsequent investigation confirmed the breach as a cyberattack that resulted in the records of about 1.5 million patients — including those of Prime Minister Lee and other political leaders — being accessed and copied between 27 June and 4 July. The cyberattack came just a year after the May 2017 deadline to delink public Internet services from public sector agencies, a cybersecurity measure imposed by GovTech, the government's new digital services office.[47] It was also the first ever cyberattack of such magnitude on Singapore soil.[48] In the aftermath of the attack, notifications were sent to the affected patients to allay public alarm and an inquiry was carried out to investigate the incident. Investigations later revealed that the breach occurred at a front-end workstation[49] and that the pattern of the attack suggested possible state-sponsored involvement, though none were named.[50] Key findings in the report further emphasized that the attack was facilitated by lapses in protocols among employees and monitoring systems.[51] The incident was a rude wake-up call for Singapore's cybersecurity measures as the city-state advances its Smart Nation initiatives,[52] and all eyes are now on how the government will seek to restore public confidence in maintaining a credible cybersecurity posture in a landscape of growing cyberthreats.[53] Taken as a cautionary tale, the cyberattack however may also be seen as an unexpected boon,[54] as it provides cybersecurity actors a valuable opportunity for scenario analysis, especially in identifying organizational weaknesses in cyber-hygiene. It also sends a stern reminder to policymakers that shoring up defences against cybersecurity threats requires more than just unplugging public systems from the public Internet; it also requires a deeper understanding of human factors, such as the habits of digital users and the loopholes that are facilitated by human lapses.

Select Committee on Deliberate Online Falsehoods

The other significant threat came in the form of deliberate online falsehoods, colloquially known as "fake news". A parliamentary select committee was tasked with examining the extent of the threat in order to make recommendations to mitigate its effects in Singapore. The impetus for this committee was driven by a call from Home Affairs and Law Minister K. Shanmugam in response to a series of online articles that was seen as contributing to public misinformation in 2017. Recognizing the seriousness and prevalence of fake news in light of the current limits of existing legal frameworks, the minister urged for more reviews into the matter.[55] Following a unanimous vote in Parliament in 2018, a committee comprising eight PAP MPs, one opposition MP and one NMP was formed.[56] The committee conducted a public hearing over eight sessions in March[57] and saw fifty-five oral submissions from a span of political, corporate and civil society actors as well as members of the public.[58] The hearings were not without notable exchanges, one of which included a three-hour grilling of Facebook's top representative Simon Milner by Shanmugam. The hearing probed into Facebook's involvement with Cambridge Analytica, the data leak and the U.S. presidential elections in 2016.[59] Only one other exchange trumped the former in both duration and content, and that was the six-hour debate between Shanmugam and history scholar Dr Thum Pin Tjin. The exchange covered a wide span of agendas, including Thum's earlier works on Operation Coldstore, the accusations made by Thum about the PAP's use of fake news to arrest political opponents,[60] and a constant attack on Thum's credibility as a historian by focusing on alleged ambiguities of his academic affiliations.[61] The Shanmugam-Thum exchange was met with both online and offline speculation. Furthermore, the spate continued even after the hearings had concluded, with a letter from Oxford sent to the Select Committee confirming Thum's credentials,[62] as well as a damning statement from the committee chair and PAP MP Charles Chong accusing Thum of working with foreign actors "to try to influence and subvert our parliamentary processes".[63]

The subsequent Select Committee report was presented to Parliament in September; it concluded with twenty-two recommendations. These included reinforcing public education and social cohesion, tackling structural conditions that promote the production and dissemination of fake news, and having protocols to deal with deliberate attacks made by state-sponsored actors.[64] While it is not certain how these recommendations will shape existing policies, experts warn against an overreliance on policy measures to deal with the issue of fake news, a sentiment also shared by the committee.[65] Similarly, there are concerns over the extent that new legislation aimed at tackling fake news might take, with lingering questions over safeguards to prevent an abuse of power and the applicability of these laws to a wide slew of digital domains and devices. On the other hand, a survey by Ipsos in September revealed that over 90 per cent of Singaporeans experienced difficulty in recognizing fake news, which drew concern to the prevalence of the issue and the susceptibility of Singaporeans in falling for fake news.[66] The survey highlighted the urgency for a more effective solution beyond fancy acronyms or AI-driven measures that have yet to yield considerable results.[67] Furthermore, with the proliferation of social-media platforms such as Whatsapp, the problem of "dark social" platforms[68] poses new complications for media laws focused on traditional digital platforms such as the Internet. With an estimated social media penetration rate of 83 per cent (with most users active on Whatsapp, Youtube and Facebook), the problem is an extremely pertinent one for Singapore.[69] In light of the role of social media in previous elections,[70] it would not be such a great surprise if we were to see new measures introduced to address such concerns as the deadline for the next general election looms.

Trump-Kim Summit 2018

On the international scene, Singapore entered the history books on 12 June 2018 as having played host to the first-ever meeting between the leaders of the United States and North Korea. The historical meeting was the culmination of events beginning with the testing by North Korea of its first intercontinental ballistic missile. In response to the test, Trump retorted that any North Korean aggression towards U.S. interests would "be met with fire, fury and frankly power, the likes of which the world has never seen before".[71] This was followed by a series of escalations on the parts of both countries before reconciliatory measures began emerging in early 2018, with meetings between North and South Korean delegates aimed at de-escalating tensions between the two states. These meetings were successful and subsequently led to the historic meeting between South Korea's President Moon Jae-in and North Korea's Kim Jong Un at the third Inter-Korean Summit in April 2018.[72] The meetings also yielded the surprise invitation, relayed by South Korean counterparts, to Kim Jong Un for a meeting with Donald Trump. The invitation was accepted and marked the start of the North Korea–United States summit. Singapore was touted as a possible location for the summit,[73] and it was eventually held at Capella Singapore on the city-state's island of Sentosa.[74]

Analysts and political leaders touted the hosting of the summit by Singapore as testimony of the nation's standing in the international community,[75] although the $16.3 million expenditure incurred by the government initially received some public criticism. Almost half of the bill was due to security provisions, for what were reportedly Singapore's most significant security operations for an international event of this scale.[76] Analysts have however forecast that the benefits and publicity reaped by Singapore for this historical milestone will definitely pay off, with estimates of $150 million in media value.[77] Experts have suggested that the branding potential of the summit will also see positive payoffs in the tourism and investment sectors, since it burnishes Singapore's image as a safe city for travel and for business opportunities.[78] Internally, the summit also allowed for Singapore's local security forces to demonstrate their security capabilities, with the Singapore Armed Forces receiving high praise from Defence Minister Dr Ng Eng Hen.[79]

ASEAN Summit 2018

The year 2018 also coincided with Singapore assuming the chair of the ASEAN summit after the Philippines. The tagline of the 2018 summit was "resilient and innovative", capturing the goal of promoting a forward-looking ASEAN in the face of global uncertainties. The biennial meetings of ASEAN's apex policymaking body in April and November saw the ten member states and their global partners and counterparts looking into the main concerns of the region.

Of these, three key agendas stood out. The first was securing regional stability by establishing and furthering joint measures to tackle traditional and non-traditional security issues such as terrorism and climate change. The highlights to these commitments included a symposium on counterterrorism aimed at addressing the issues of militarized terrorism, de-radicalization efforts and strengthening community support in resisting recruitment efforts from terrorist groups. The "Resilience, Response and Recovery" framework for counterterrorism cooperation was introduced in response to the growing complexity in the prevention and recovery from terrorist activities.[80] The collective framework serves to enhance cooperation through increased information sharing and joint training exercises against an evolving landscape of threats by new and existing terrorist groups.[81] Furthermore, recognizing the urgency for a coordinated cybersecurity effort in ASEAN, this year's summit also saw the adoption of the ASEAN Leaders' Statement on Cybersecurity Cooperation. The statement is the first of a planned series of coordinated exchanges among the public agencies of ASEAN members to identify and recommend a list of protocols and solutions for an ASEAN norm towards cybersecurity threats. Other cybersecurity measures include improving the standards of safeguards among ASEAN financial sector authorities by promoting the sharing of best practices, and the formation of an ASEAN-Singapore Cybersecurity Centre of Excellence to support ASEAN states in enhancing their cybersecurity systems.[82] The threat of climate change also featured as a major concern for ASEAN, with a Special ASEAN Ministerial Meeting on Climate Change convened. The meeting sought to bolster climate action efforts and reaffirm the commitment of ASEAN member states to the Paris Agreement, with Singapore launching the Climate Action Package to grow the region's capacity towards the long-term management of risks related to climate change.[83] Traditional security measures were not neglected either, with the first ever ASEAN-China maritime exercise conducted in October in a show of ASEAN's commitment to maritime security and coordination in the waters of the region.[84]

Reinforcing connectivity between the region's economies was also a major agenda of the summit. More specifically, expediting trade, services and capital flows with the introduction of shared clearance systems and by improving the ASEAN self-certification scheme were top of this year's economic efforts.[85] These schemes are set to further open up the opportunities of a regional market comprising over 640 million people, with little sign of it slowing down any time soon.[86] Last but not least, this year's summit saw Singapore's Smart Nation project extended into the ASEAN Smart Cities Framework, which is aimed at identifying and resolving contemporary urban challenges in Southeast Asia. The framework saw twenty-six cities nominated for its pilot project — which will run from 2018 to 2025 — and a consensus on the standards for "Smart Cities".[87]

The impact of Singapore's chairing of ASEAN in 2018 can be seen in two lights. The first is positive, which attests to Singapore's capabilities in steering ASEAN's interests in the midst of the rivalry and ongoing trade war between China and the United States, including some headway in the issue of the South China Sea with an agreement for a Code of Conduct promised as early as 2019.[88] Relations between ASEAN and China have also steadily improved, with a new ASEAN-China Strategic Partnership Vision 2030 announced.[89] ASEAN-U.S. relations, on the other hand, began with speculation regarding the absence of President Trump from the summits and controversy over the term "Indo-Pacific", suggesting a slight against the significance of the region to the United States.[90] Despite reassurance that ASEAN-U.S. relations were "healthy",[91] Prime Minister Lee warned that ongoing Sino-American tensions may compel Southeast Asian states into a situation where they are forced to choose between the United States or China.[92] On the other hand, this year's summit did little to provide respite to the region's failure to handle the conspicuous issue of the Rohingya crisis in Myanmar. Despite the humanitarian crisis becoming a major talking point during a summit between ASEAN and Australia, ASEAN's non-interventionism blunts the pressure it can exert on Myanmar's government to provide a satisfactory resolution to the situation in Rakhine.[93]

For Singapore, its chairmanship in 2018 reinforces its ardent commitment to the development of ASEAN member states by extending its national initiatives on a regional scale. Locally, despite reiteration of the mutual tangible and intangible benefits between ASEAN and Singapore,[94] more could be done to translate these partnerships into narratives conceivable for Singaporeans. Experts suggest that Singapore could, for instance, focus on communicating such benefits by weaving them into Singapore's educational discourses and in equipping language and cultural skills to prepare Singaporeans for a Southeast Asian future.[95]

Policies at a Glance

Public Order and Safety (Special Powers) Act

In the context of increased concerns about the threat of terrorism, certain laws were tightened on security grounds. The Public Order and Safety (Special Powers) Act, which was passed in March and came into force two months later, grants the police "wide-ranging new powers" in dealing with "major security incidents".[96]

The special powers introduced by the act include a "communication stop order" (CSO), which allows the police to "prevent the public and media from taking videos, pictures, audio recordings, or text messages that could compromise ongoing security operations".[97] Those caught violating the order may face imprisonment of up to two years and/or fines amounting to $20,000. According to the government, the CSO, which can be issued by the commissioner of police once the minister of home affairs activates the act, is meant to "minimise terrorists' access to information".[98] However, some parliamentarians raised concerns that the act may be too broad and could be extended to apply to "a sit-down peaceful protest that grows in size". PAP MP Louis Ng argued that the threat of fines and imprisonment for non-compliance can "seem excessive".[99] Civil society groups also articulated their misgivings about the inclusion of protests as a "serious incident".[100]

Administration of Justice (Protection) Act

Meanwhile, the PAP government continued to act vigorously in response to what it regarded as unfounded charges of corruption in government and slurs against the country's judiciary. In October, a civil society activist and opposition politician were both found guilty of impugning the integrity and impartiality of the judiciary with their Facebook posts suggesting that "Singapore's courts are not as independent as Malaysia's on cases with political implications". These were the first convictions under the Administration of Justice (Protection) Act that came into operation in October 2017.[101] Li Shengwu, an assistant professor in economics at Harvard and the nephew of the prime minister, was also involved in contempt of court proceedings for allegedly describing in a July 2017 Facebook post that Singapore has a "pliant court system" and that the Singapore government was "very litigious".[102] Li is currently contesting the decision that allowed the attorney general to serve papers on him outside Singapore. The court action against Li began while his father and aunt, Lee Hsien Yang and Lee Wee Ling, were involved in a public spat with the prime minister over the fate of the Oxley Road family home of their late father and founding prime minister Lee Kuan Yew. The online media scene was also affected by legal proceedings on similar issues. In December the editor of the long-running *The Online Citizen* was the subject of a criminal defamation charge for publishing an article that alleged "we have seen multiple policy and foreign screw-ups, tampering of the Constitution, corruption at the highest echelons and apparent lack of respect from foreign powers ever since the demise of founding father Lee Kuan Yew".[103] The author of the article was also similarly charged.

Merdeka Generation

At 2018's National Day Rally, PM Lee Hsien Loong introduced the Merdeka Generation Package (MGP) as part of the government's appreciation of Singaporeans born between 1950 and 1959 for their contributions to Singapore's nation building efforts.[104] Continuing its stance from the highly popular Pioneer Generation Package, the government responded with the MGP in recognition of some half a million Singaporeans who will enjoy a range of healthcare subsidies and payouts over the long term. While the details of the MGP will only be made known in 2019, the policy reaffirms the government's promise of keeping healthcare costs manageable for elderly Singaporeans in their twilight years. However, with Singapore's healthcare costs rising faster than those of its regional counterparts,[105] the MGP may be seen as a double-edged sword. It is simultaneously a popular but also a challenging promise — not for what it offers but for inculcating the expectation that there will be future packages waiting for succeeding generations. Nevertheless, the MGP is seen as a welcome policy by Singaporeans from all walks of life, and will certainly be a major topic of conversion favouring the incumbent government as elections draw near.

Educational Assessment Changes

In a bid to de-emphasize examination anxiety and allow students more time to explore subjects in their formative educational stages, the minister of education Ong Ye Kung announced the removal of school-based mid-year examinations at certain levels of both primary and secondary schools, as well as the removal of level and class positions of students in academic reports.[106] This announcement comes as part of the ministry's efforts to tone down examinations,[107] a significant feature of Singapore's educational system that partly fuels a tuition industry worth over a billion dollars annually.[108] These announcements received mixed responses, with some applauding the ministry for taking gradual but bold steps in tackling an educational system that has traditionally favoured examination results over other forms of achievement.[109] Others also lauded the move but commented that tackling more significant examination milestones such as the Primary School Leaving Examination (PSLE) — usually taken by students at the age of twelve — would deliver a far more impactful and convincing message to parents and students alike.[110] On the other hand, some parents were unsure whether the lack of assessment indicators to track academic progress might affect students' development. Testifying to the durability of the exam-oriented culture in Singapore, tuition centres have sought to allay parents' concerns about the changes by introducing their own private assessment schemes, much to the chagrin of the education minister.[111] This episode illustrates the deep-seated problems within the education-tuition-parents complex in Singapore, in which the tuition industry and parents have to play equally important roles in making positive reforms in the education systems a reality. Moving away from an emphasis on examinations provides opportunities for Singapore's educational system to tune into other forms of educational pathways better equipped to respond to the contemporary global demands for nurturing talents in creativity, adaptability and leadership. However, if parents and private educational practitioners are reluctant or, worse, hostile to giving up their comfortable but inadequate preconceptions of student development, it would ultimately affect the courage of policymakers to make necessary but unpopular decisions.[112]

Economy

Singapore's economic performance in 2018 followed its momentum of the previous year, continuing its performance of 3.3 per cent growth amidst pessimistic global outlooks from the ongoing U.S.-China tariff tussles and market uncertainties. The overall positive performance however did not overshadow the growing trends that seek to usurp Singapore's regional competitiveness. For instance, the region recently saw new competition to challenge Singapore's position as the leading financial hub. The city-state recently lost its place to Vietnam as the largest initial public offering (IPO) fundraiser in the ASEAN region, with $2.6 billion raised by the latter at the onset of its drive towards privatization.[113] Notwithstanding these IPO hiccups, however, Singapore stands among the world's top four major financial centres, behind Hong Kong, New York and London.[114]

With regard to Singapore's labour outlook, the city snagged another laurel as it topped the World Bank's human capital rankings, which measure the future productivity and earning potential of citizens through health, education and mortality indicators.[115] For employees, employment rates in the first half of the year saw a slight increase owing to growth in the services sector, while the resident unemployment rate rose to 2.9 per cent, a 0.1 per cent increase from the previous year that was brought on by new job seekers entering the workforce.[116] Meanwhile, the Adapt and Grow initiative under Workforce Singapore saw an estimated 30,000 job seekers matched through its programme, a positive sign for the national efforts at managing mid-career transitions among job-seekers displaced by disruption and retrenchment.[117] Beyond traditional indicators, a workforce study published in 2018 also captured a snapshot of Singapore's freelancing population, with over 82 per cent of freelancers reporting that they are doing so by choice, and 67 per cent of them indicating it as their primary occupation.[118] These numbers support the receptivity amongst Singaporeans towards the gig economy, thus posing opportunities and risks for employees and employers alike. For employees, while the greater flexibility may offer the temporary freedoms especially sought by younger demographics of Singaporeans, work in the gig economy lacks benefits such as health insurance and income consistency, thus leaving them exposed to income risks.

Disruption was also an oft-cited word in conversations on Singapore's economic future. In the manufacturing sector, disruption is expected to make or break the current gloom, with Minister of Trade and Industry Chan Chun Seng highlighting the urgency in setting up a rigorous intellectual property protection regime and the continued promotion of research and development. These initiatives aim to bolster the confidence of foreign investors in Singapore's viability as a high-quality manufacturing hub. In the food and agricultural sector, disruption took the form of import restrictions of key staples such as eggs and of food availability being subject to increasingly uncertain climate factors.[119] Despite glowing indicators in relative food affordability, logistics and safety, the challenge lies in Singapore's ability to ramp up its food security based on multiple "doomsday scenarios" of food disruptions, and to mitigate these risks beyond the nation's current thresholds. This means exploring options to establish food security while tapping on technological innovations and new social compacts to diversify the country's urban spaces beyond the conventional utility.

Conclusion

With major hurdles and uncertainties expected from both local and regional events, 2019 is set to be a rather challenging year for Singapore. With hints of the possibility of a general election, the year will be one of much anticipation. With the prime ministerial succession race given some closure, analysts will look to how the leadership transition continues to unfold for the rest of the 4G leaders in the next Cabinet reshuffle, slated to take place after February's Budget debate.[120] This however does not preclude a possible change to the succession line-up, though such an attempt would be atypical of the PAP's methodical and calculated treatment of the transition thus far. Meanwhile, observers have been curious as to whether the familiar team with a new leader at the Workers' Party will carve out any new political headway, or whether they will hunker down in preparation for what lies ahead with the AHTC trials. Furthermore, with the recently announced return of Tan Cheng Bock to politics,[121] the upcoming elections are set to filled with both new adversaries and old opponents. As public consciousness towards social stratification lingers, policy initiatives aimed at explicitly reducing inequality will be considered far more favourably. And with further details of the Merdeka Generation Package slated to be revealed during the next Budget, people are eager to see whether the new set of government policies will help to meet their expectations in a climate of economic uncertainties. On the external front, with the U.S.-China trade war raging on with few positive signs, the long-expected adversities are expected to dampen Singapore's economy.

Notes

1. Tan See Kit, "Singapore Economy Clocks Faster-than-Expected Growth of 3.6% in 2017", Channel NewsAsia, 14 February 2018 <https://www.channelnewsasia.com/news/singapore/singapore-economy-clocks-faster-than-expected-growth-of-3-6-in-9958302>.
2. Ng Jun Sen, "16 'Younger Ministers' Sign Statement", *Straits Times*, 5 January 2018 <https://www.straitstimes.com/politics/16-younger-ministers-sign-statement>.
3. Faris Mokhtar, "Heng Swee Keat to be PAP's 1st Assistant Secretary General, and Next PM: Party Sources", 22 November 2018 <https://www.todayonline.com/singapore/heng-swee-keat-be-pap-1st-assistant-secretary-general-and-next-pm-party-sources>.
4. Prime Minister Office, "Changes to Cabinet and Other Appointments (Apr 2018)", 24 April 2018 <https://www.pmo.gov.sg/newsroom/changes-cabinet-and-other-appointments-apr-2018>.
5. Afifah Ariffin, "PM Lee Says Will Lead PAP in Next Election, but 4G Leaders Will Be 'In the Thick of Things'", Channel NewsAsia, 3 December 2018 <https://www.channelnewsasia.com/news/singapore/pm-lee-will-lead-pap-in-next-election-4g-leaders-10992420>.
6. "Pritnam Singh Elected New WP Chief: Current Phase of Leadership Renewal Completed, Says Low Thia Khiang", *Straits Times*, 8 April 2018 <https://www.straitstimes.com/politics/pritam-singh-elected-unopposed-as-leader-of-wp>.
7. Lydia Lim, "AHTC, PRPTC Lawsuits against Workers' Party MPs to Go To Trial on Friday", Channel NewsAsia, 4 October 2018 <https://www.channelnewsasia.com/news/singapore/ahtc-prptc-lawsuits-against-workers-party-mps-to-go-to-trial-on-10755682>.
8. Lim and Chia, "AHTC Trial Wraps Up after 17 Days, with Last Defence Witnesses at the Stand", Channel NewsAsia, 30 October 2018 <https://www.channelnewsasia.com/news/singapore/ahtc-trial-wraps-up-court-defence-workers-party-10879696>.
9. Wong Pei Ting, "WP's Sylvia Lim Concedes She and Fellow MPs Breached Duties by Not Disclosing CPG Rates to Town Council", *Today*, 23 October 2018 <https://www.todayonline.com/singapore/wps-sylvia-lim-concedes-she-and-fellow-mps-breached-duties-not-disclosing-cpg-rates-town>.

10. Factually, "What Exactly Does a Nominated Member of Parliament Do?", 12 August 2014 <https://www.gov.sg/factually/content/what-exactly-does-a-nominated-member-of-parliament-do>.
11. Lim Puay Ling, "Nominated Member of Parliament Scheme", *Singapore Infopedia 2016* <http://eresources.nlb.gov.sg/infopedia/articles/SIP_1016_2010-12-24.html>.
12. Jo Tan, "At Unique Sessions, NMP Kok Heng Leun Seeks Input from Artists", *Today*, 22 September 2016 <https://www.todayonline.com/entertainment/arts/nominated-member-parliament-kok-heng-leun-forking-out-own-time-and-money-hold>.
13. Benjamin Lim, "As Long As the Arts Community Remains Fragmented, We'll Never Progress", RiceMedia, 29 June 2018 <http://ricemedia.co/current-affairs-commentary-arts-community-remains-fragmented-well-never-progress/>.
14. Matthias Ang and Martino Tan, "New NMP Ho Wee San is the First Arts NMP to Not Be Elected or Nominated by the Arts Community since 2009", *Mothership*, 27 September 2018 <https://mothership.sg/2018/09/nmp-ho-wee-san-arts-yip-pin-xiu/>.
15. Sean Lim, "How Long Will Mahathir Mohamad Hold These Grudges against Singapore?", *South China Morning Post*, 15 December 2018 <https://www.scmp.com/comment/letters/article/2177938/how-long-will-mahathir-mohamad-hold-those-grudges-against-singapore>.
16. "Mahathir Confirms Malaysia Will Scrap KL-Singapore HSR Project", Channel NewsAsia, 28 May 2018 <https://www.channelnewsasia.com/news/singapore/mahathir-mohamad-confirms-malaysia-pulls-out-of-kl-singapore-hsr-10284144>.
17. Sumisha Naidu, "Exclusive: Price of Water Sold to Singapore 'Ridiculous'; Malaysia to Renegotiate Deal, Says Mahathir", Channel NewsAsia, 25 June 2018 <https://www.channelnewsasia.com/news/singapore/mahathir-water-singapore-malaysia-price-ridiculous-10466780>.
18. Yasmine Yahya, "Parliament: S'pore Will Honour 1962 Water Agreement and Expects Malaysia to Do the Same, Says Vivian Balakrishnan", *Straits Times*, 9 July 2018 <https://www.straitstimes.com/politics/parliament-spore-will-honour-1962-water-agreement-expects-malaysia-to-do-the-same-vivian>.
19. "Singapore, Malaysia Maritime Dispute: A Timeline", Channel NewsAsia, 6 December 2018 <https://www.channelnewsasia.com/news/singapore/singapore-malaysia-maritime-dispute-port-limits-timeline-11006762>.
20. "Singapore, Malaysia Airspace Dispute: What We Know and Timeline", Channel NewsAsia, 5 December 2018 <https://www.channelnewsasia.com/news/singapore/singapore-malaysia-southern-johor-airspace-seletar-airport-10997022>.
21. "Malaysians Want Both Countries to Settle Dispute Quickly", *Straits Times*, 11 December 2018 <https://www.straitstimes.com/asia/se-asia/malaysians-want-both-countries-to-settle-dispute-quickly>.
22. "Foreign Minister: Malaysia, Singapore to Discuss Airspace Dispute on Jan 8", *Malay Mail*, 1 January 2019 <https://www.malaymail.com/s/1708075/foreign-minister-malaysia-singapore-to-discuss-airspace-dispute-on-jan-8>.

23. Charrissa Yong, "Singapore-Malaysia Ties Face Uncertain Times: Panellists at ST Global Briefing", *Straits Times*, 13 August 2018 <https://www.straitstimes.com/singapore/singapore-malaysia-ties-face-uncertain-times-panellists-at-st-global-briefing>.
24. "Malaysia Egg Shortage Leaves Importer Singapore Scrambling for Alternatives", *New Straits Times*, 16 December 2018 <https://www.nst.com.my/world/2018/12/441226/malaysia-egg-shortage-leaves-importer-singapore-scrambling-alternatives>.
25. "Senior Member of Mahathir's Party Warns S'pore of 'Pain by a Thousand Cuts' for its Stance on Maritime Dispute", *Today*, 9 December 2018 <https://www.todayonline.com/world/senior-member-mahathirs-party-warns-singapore-thousand-cuts>.
26. Tashny Sukumaran and Bhavan Jaipragas, "Malaysian PM-in-Waiting Anwar Ibrahim Insists No Timeline on Taking Power as He Makes Official Return to Politics", *South China Morning Post*, 15 October 2018 <https://www.scmp.com/week-asia/politics/article/2168652/malaysian-pm-waiting-anwar-ibrahim-makes-official-return-politics>.
27. "Mahathir: 'Anwar Ibrahim Will Be the Next Prime Minister'", Al Jazeera, 16 July 2018 <https://www.aljazeera.com/indepth/features/mahathir-anwar-ibrahim-prime-minister-180716091759735.html>.
28. Tashny Sukumaran, "If You Thought Malaysia's Bitter Leadership Battles Were Over…", *South China Morning Post*, 28 October 2018 <https://www.scmp.com/week-asia/politics/article/2170282/if-you-thought-malaysias-bitter-leadership-battles-were-over>.
29. Bhavan Jaipragas, "Diplomatic Rift with Malaysia Unlikely to Be over Soon: Singapore Foreign Minister", *South China Morning Post*, 14 January 2019 <https://www.scmp.com/week-asia/politics/article/2182024/diplomatic-rift-malaysia-unlikely-be-over-soon-singapore-foreign>.
30. Chua Mui Hoong, "Inequality is a Threat — Name It, and Face It", *Straits Times*, 18 February 2018 <https://www.straitstimes.com/singapore/inequality-is-a-threat-name-it-and-face-it>.
31. Olivia Ho, "Best-Selling Non-Fiction Titles of the Year", *Straits Times*, 11 December 2018 <https://www.straitstimes.com/lifestyle/arts/best-selling-non-fiction-titles-of-the-year>.
32. Ibid.
33. For example, see Chua, "Inequality is a Threat" and Catherine J. Smith, *A Handbook on Inequality, Poverty and Unmet Social Needs in Singapore* (Singapore: Lien Centre for Social Innovation) <https://lcsi.smu.edu.sg/sites/lcsi.smu.edu.sg/files/publications/A-Handbook-on-Inequality-Poverty-Unmet-Needs-in-Singapore.pdf>.
34. Kok Xing Hui, "Behind Crazy Rich Singapore's Mask, A Growing Class Divide", *South China Morning Post*, 20 October 2018 <https://www.scmp.com/week-asia/people/article/2169438/behind-crazy-rich-singapores-mask-growing-class-divide>.
35. Office of the President of the Republic of Singapore, "Address by President Halimah

Yacob for Second Session of the Thirteenth Parliament", 7 May 2018 <https://www.istana.gov.sg/Newsroom/Speeches/2018/05/HY-for-Second-Session-of-the-Thirteenth-Parliament>.

36. Bertha Henson, "COMMENT: Opening Salvos in the Poverty Debate", *Yahoo News*, 27 June 2018 <https://sg.news.yahoo.com/comment-opening-salvos-poverty-debate-083905260.html>.
37. Sudha Nair, "$500 a Month on Cable TV and Cigarettes and this Family Still Wants Aid?", *Straits Times*, 23 June 2018 <https://www.straitstimes.com/opinion/helping-families-find-hope-and-courage-to-change>.
38. Maliki Osman, "This is What Helping Families Look Like", *Straits Times*, 27 June 2018 <https://www.straitstimes.com/opinion/this-is-what-helping-families-looks-like>.
39. "Singapore in Bottom 10 of Oxfam Index on Efforts to Tackle Inequality", Channel NewsAsia, 9 October 2018 <https://www.channelnewsasia.com/news/singapore/singapore-inequality-oxfam-index-10806026>.
40. "Oxfam Inequality Index: Singapore Achieves Real Outcomes Rather Than Satisfies Indicators, Says Desmond Lee", Channel NewsAsia, 9 October 2018 <https://www.channelnewsasia.com/news/singapore/oxfam-inequality-index-singapore-achieves-real-outcomes-rather-10808172>.
41. Amir Yusof, "Oxfam Inequality Index a 'Completely Wrong Analysis': Heng Swee Keat", Channel NewsAsia, 12 October 2018 <https://www.channelnewsasia.com/news/singapore/heng-swee-keat-oxfam-inequality-index-completely-wrong-analysis-10821672>.
42. Grace Yeoh, "CNA's 'Regardless of Class' Seemed Too Perfect. So We Dug Deeper", Rice Media, 20 October 2018 <http://ricemedia.co/current-affairs-features-cna-regardless-of-class-too-perfect-dug-deeper/>.
43. Derrick A. Paulo and Low Minmin, "Class — Not Race nor Religion — Is Potentially Singapore's Most Divisive Fault Line", Channel NewsAsia, 1 October 2018 <https://www.channelnewsasia.com/news/cnainsider/regardless-class-race-religion-survey-singapore-income-divide-10774682>.
44. Pan Jie, "CNA's 'Regardless of Class' is Everything That's Wrong with Singapore's Inequality Debate", Rice Media, 3 October 2018 <http://ricemedia.co/current-affairs-cna-regardless-class-everything-thats-wrong-singapores-inequality-debate/>.
45 Kok Xinghui, "Behind Crazy Rich Singapore's Mask.
46. Jalelah Abu Baker, " 'Keep the Escalator Moving Up': DPM Tharman Urges Singapore to Maintain Social Mobility", Channel NewsAsia, 26 October 2018 <https://www.channelnewsasia.com/news/singapore/keep-the-escalator-moving-up-dpm-tharman-ips-anniversary-10865146>.
47. Irene Than, "Some Government Agencies Delink Net Access ahead of Deadline", *Straits Times*, 15 March 2017 <https://www.straitstimes.com/singapore/some-govt-agencies-delink-net-access-ahead-of-deadline>.

48. "Timeline of Attack on SingHealth's IT Systems and Other Notable Cyber Breaches in Singapore", *Today*, 20 July 2018 <https://www.todayonline.com/singapore/timeline-stolen-singhealth-patient-records-and-other-notable-cyber-attacks-singapore>.
49. Ibid.
50. Vincent Cheng, "Style of SingHealth Cyber Attack, Info Targeted Point to State-backed Hackers, Say Experts", *Straits Times*, 22 July 2018 <https://www.straitstimes.com/singapore/style-of attack-info-targeted-point-to-state-backed-hackers-say-experts>.
51. Cynthia Choo, "SingHealth Cyber Attack a Result of Human Lapses, IT System Weaknesses: COI Report", *Today*, 10 January 2019 <https://www.todayonline.com/singapore/singhealth-cyber-attack-result-human-lapses-it-system-weaknesses-coi-report>.
52. Irene Tham, "SingHealth Cyber Attack: Pause on Smart Nation Projects Lifted; 11 Critical Sectors Told to Review Untrusted External Connections", *Straits Times*, 3 August 2018 <https://www.straitstimes.com/singapore/singhealth-cyber-attack-pause-on-smart-nation-projects-lifted-11-critical-sectors-told-to>.
53. Microsoft Singapore News Centre, "Cybersecurity Threats to Cost Organisations in Singapore US$17.7 Billion in Economic Losses", 18 May 2018 <https://news.microsoft.com/en-sg/2018/05/18/cybersecurity-threats-to-cost-organisations-in-singapore-us17-7-billion-in-economic-losses/>.
54. Irene Tham, "SingHealth Cyber Attack: Benefits and Risks of Smart Nation Projects in Pipeline", *Straits Times*, 24 July 2018 <https://www.sgsme.sg/news/singhealth-cyber-attack-benefits-and-risks-smart-nation-projects-pipeline>.
55. "Government 'Seriously Considering' How to Deal with Fake News: Shanmugam", Channel NewsAsia, 3 April 2017 <https://www.channelnewsasia.com/news/singapore/government--seriously-considering--how-to-deal-with-fake-news-sh-8712436>.
56. Kamini Devadass, "Select Committee Formed to Study Deliberate Online Falsehoods", Channel NewsAsia, 11 January 2018 <https://www.channelnewsasia.com/news/singapore/select-committee-formed-to-study-deliberate-online-falsehoods-9851096>.
57. "Select Committee on Deliberate Online Falsehoods to Hold Public Hearings in March", Channel NewsAsia, 5 March 2018 <https://www.channelnewsasia.com/news/singapore/select-committee-on-deliberate-online-falsehoods-public-hearings-10013840>.
58. Singapore Parliament. Report of the Select Committee on Deliberate Online Falsehoods — Causes, Consequences and Countermeasure, 19 September 2018 <https://sprs.parl.gov.sg/selectcommittee/selectcommittee/download?id=1&type=subReport>.
59. Belmont Lay, "Minister Shanmugam Grills Facebook Representative for 3 Hours at Parliamentary Hearing", Mothership, 22 March 2018 <https://mothership.sg/2018/03/shanmugam-questions-facebook-select-committee/>.
60. Yasmine Yahya, "Minister K. Shanmugam Grills Research Fellow Thum Ping Tjin and Says He is Not an Objective Historian", *Straits Times*, 29 March 2018 <https://

www.straitstimes.com/politics/shanmugam-grills-research-fellow-and-says-he-is-not-an-objective-historian>.

61. Lianna Chia, "Thum Ping Tjin had 'Clearly Lied' about Academic Credentials, no Weight Given to his Views: Select Committee", Channel NewsAsia, 20 September 2018 <https://www.channelnewsasia.com/news/singapore/thum-ping-tjin-lied-academic-credentials-select-committee-10739894>.
62. Tham Yeun-C, "Oxford Academics say Thum is and Remains a Trained Historian", *New Paper*, 3 May 2018 <https://www.tnp.sg/news/singapore/oxford-academics-say-thum-and-remains-trained-historian>.
63. "Charles Chong Says Historian Thum 'Engineered' Support for Himself, Part of 'Coordinated Attempt' to Subvert Parliamentary Process", *Today*, 1 May 2018 <https://www.todayonline.com/singapore/historian-thum-appears-have-engineered-support-himself-says-charles-chong-pointing>.
64. Royston Sim, "Select Committee Releases 22 Proposals to Combat Fake News", *Straits Times*, 21 September 2018 <https://www.straitstimes.com/singapore/select-committee-releases-22-proposals-to-combat-fake-news>.
65. Faris Mokhar, "Countering Fake News is More Than Just about Having New Laws, Experts Say", *Today*, 20 September 2018 <https://www.todayonline.com/singapore/countering-fake-news-more-just-about-having-new-laws-experts-say>.
66. Ng Huiwen, "4 in 5 Singaporeans Confident in Spotting Fake News but 90 per cent Wrong When Put to the Test: Survey", *Straits Times*, 27 September 2018 <https://www.straitstimes.com/singapore/4-in-5-singaporeans-confident-in-spotting-fake-news-but-90-per-cent-wrong-when-put-to-the>.
67. Gary Marcus and Ernest Davis, "No, AI Won't Solve the Fake News Problem", *Straits Times*, 22 October 2018 <https://www.straitstimes.com/opinion/no-ai-wont-solve-the-fake-news-problem>.
68. Nicole Rigillo, "WhatsApp Can Be Dangerous", *Washington Post*, 26 September 2018 <https://www.washingtonpost.com/news/theworldpost/wp/2018/09/26/whatsapp/?noredirect=on&utm_term=.1e2b615a2af9>.
69. "4.83 Million Singaporeans Are Now Online", *Singapore Business Review*, 30 January 2018 <https://sbr.com.sg/information-technology/news/483-million-singaporeans-are-now-online>.
70. Lau Geok Theng, "The General Election in a Social Media Age", *Business Times*, 28 August 2015 <https://www.businesstimes.com.sg/opinion/singapore-general-election/the-general-election-in-a-social-media-age>.
71. Jacob Pramuk, "Trump Warns North Korea Threats 'Will be Met with Fire and Fury' ", CNBC, 8 August 2017 <https://www.cnbc.com/2017/08/08/trump-warns-north-korea-threats-will-be-met-with-fire-and-fury.html>.
72. Rick Noack and Joyce Lee, "The Historic Kim-Moon Meeting as It Unfolded", *Washington Post*, 27 April 2018 <https://www.washingtonpost.com/news/worldviews/

wp/2018/04/27/the-historic-kim-moon-meeting-as-it-unfolded/?utm_term=.d4549adedbcb>.

73. David Tweed, "Here Are Nine Potential Locations for the Trump-Kim Jong Un Summit", BloomBerg, 18 April 2018 <https://www.bloomberg.com/news/articles/2018-04-18/here-are-nine-potential-locations-for-the-trump-kim-summit>.
74. Jeremy Diamond, "Trump-Kim Singapore Summit Venue is Set", CNN, 6 June 2018 <https://edition.cnn.com/2018/06/05/politics/singapore-capella-hotel-trump-kim/index.html>.
75. Amir Yusof, "Hosting Trump-Kim Summit Says Something about Singapore's Standing Internationally, says PM Lee", Channel NewsAsia, 10 June 2018 <https://www.channelnewsasia.com/news/singapore/hosting-trump-kim-summit-says-something-about-singapore-s-10415386>.
76. "Trump-Kim Summit the 'Most Significant Security Operation' in Singapore: Vivian Balakrishnan", Channel NewsAsia, 11 June 2018 <https://www.channelnewsasia.com/news/singapore/trump-kim-summit-most-significant-security-operation-singapore-10420062>.
77. Dean Carroll, "Trump-Kim Summit Cost $20m, but Could be Worth $150m in Earned Media for Singapore", *Mumbrella Asia*, 13 June 2018 <https://www.mumbrella.asia/2018/06/trump-kim-summit-cost-20m-but-could-be-worth-150m-in-earned-media-for-singapore>.
78. Lianna Chia, "Trump-Kim Summit a Priceless Branding Opportunity for Singapore, Sentosa and Hotels Involved, say Industry Experts", Channel NewsAsia, 9 June 2018 <https://www.channelnewsasia.com/news/singapore/trump-kim-summit-a-priceless-branding-opportunity-for-singapore-10410420>.
79. Aqil Haqiz Mahmud, "Short of Real War, Trump-Kim Summit Was a Test that Proved SAF's Capabilities: Ng Eng Hen", Channel NewsAsia, 30 June 2018 <https://www.channelnewsasia.com/news/singapore/trump-kim-summit-test-proved-saf-capabilities-10485780>.
80. Mohamad Maliki Bin Osman, "A Collective Regional Approach to Fight Terrorism Threat", *Business Times*, 13 November 2018 <https://www.businesstimes.com.sg/hub/asean-singapore-2018/a-collective-regional-approach-to-fight-terrorism-threat>.
81. Ibid.
82. "Singapore to Pump in S$30m for New Regional Cybersecurity Training Centre", Channel NewsAsia, 19 September 2018 <https://www.channelnewsasia.com/news/singapore/singapore-to-pump-in-s-30m-for-new-regional-cybersecurity-10735308>.
83. National Climate Change Secretariat, "Special Asean Ministerial Meeting on Climate Action (Samca) and Expanded-Samca (E-Samca)", 11 July 2018 <https://www.nccs.gov.sg/news/articles/detail/special-asean-ministerial-meeting-on-climate-action-(samca)-and-expanded-samca-(e-samca)>.

84. Linette Lim, "ASEAN, China Kick Off First Maritime Exercise", Channel NewsAsia, 22 October 2018 <https://www.channelnewsasia.com/news/asia/asean-china-kicks-off-first-maritime-exercise-10852692>.
85. Janice Heng, "Asean Services Providers, Exporters to Gain from Two Accords Signed at Asean Economic Ministers Meeting", *Business Times*, 29 August 2018 <https://www.enterprisesg.gov.sg/media-centre/news/2018/august/asean-services-providers-and-exporters-to-gain-from-two-accords-signed-at-asean-economic-ministers-meeting>.
86. Sanchita Basu Das, "Commentary: The Rebirth of the ASEAN Miracle Growth Model", Channel NewsAsia, 4 November 2018 <https://www.channelnewsasia.com/news/commentary/asean-economic-community-connectivity-rebirth-growth-model-10879030>.
87. Lianna Chua, "26 Cities to Pilot ASEAN Smart Cities Network", Channel NewsAsia, 28 April 2018 <https://www.channelnewsasia.com/news/singapore/26-cities-to-pilot-asean-smart-cities-network-10183550>.
88. Tan Dawn Wei, "Asean, China Agree on Early Completion of Sea Code", *Straits Times*, 15 November 2018 <https://www.straitstimes.com/singapore/asean-china-agree-on-early-completion-of-sea-code>.
89. ASEAN, "ASEAN, China Reaffirm Strategic Partnership", 9 June 2018 <https://asean.org/aseanchina-reaffirm-strategic-partnership/>.
90. Bhagyashree Garekar, "Trump's No-show at Summit, Indo-Pacific Vision Churn up Debate", *Straits Times*, 14 November 2018. <https://www.straitstimes.com/singapore/trumps-no-show-at-summit-indo-pacific-vision-churn-up-debate>.
91. Jalelah Abu Baker, "ASEAN-US Ties 'Healthy', But Need to be Seen in Backdrop of US-China Relationship: PM Lee", Channel NewsAsia, 15 November 2018 <https://www.channelnewsasia.com/news/asean2018/asean-us-ties-healthy-but-need-to-be-seen-in-backdrop-of-us-10933206>.
92. Michelle Jamrisko, Jason Koutsoukis and Toluse Olorunnipa, "Singapore PM Says Asean May Need to Choose between U.S. and China", Bloomberg, 16 November 2018 <https://www.bloomberg.com/news/articles/2018-11-15/singapore-fears-asean-may-need-to-choose-between-u-s-china>.
93. "Myanmar's Suu Kyi Pressed on Rohingya Crisis at ASEAN Summit", Channel NewsAsia, 18 March 2018 <https://www.channelnewsasia.com/news/asia/myanmar-s-suu-kyi-pressed-on-rohingya-crisis-at-asean-summit-10054104>.
94. Tommy Koh, "Why Asean is Good for Singapore", *Straits Times*, 9 January 2019 <https://www.straitstimes.com/opinion/why-asean-is-good-for-singapore>.
95. "How Singapore can Prepare for its Southeast Asian Future: Linda Lim", *Business Times*, 30 May 2018 <https://www.businesstimes.com.sg/asean-business/how-singapore-can-prepare-for-its-southeast-asian-future-linda-lim>.
96. "Police Gain Sweeping New Powers amid Changing Technologies, Security", *Today*, 21 March 2018 <https://www.todayonline.com/singapore/safeguards-place-new-police-special-powers-can-be-used-josephine-teo>.

97. "Law Granting Police Special Powers in Serious Incidents Takes Effect on Wednesday", *Today*, 15 May 2018 <https://www.todayonline.com/singapore/law-granting-police-special-powers-serious-incidents-takes-effect-Wednesday>.
98. "Parliament Passes Law Banning Photos, Videos of Security Operations during a Terror Attack", Channel NewsAsia, 21 March 2018 <https://www.channelnewsasia.com/news/singapore/ban-photos-videos-messages-terrorist-posspa-10062836>.
99. "How 'Serious' Must an Incident Be for Singapore to Invoke New Special Powers Act? MPs Debate", Channel NewsAsia, 21 March 2018 <https://www.channelnewsasia.com/news/singapore/serious-incident-singapore-special-powers-posspa-10063766>.
100. "Civil Society Groups Express Concerns over Breadth of Public Order Bill", AWARE, 14 March 2018 <https://www.aware.org.sg/2018/03/civil-society-groups-express-concerns-over-breadth-of-public-order-bill/>.
101. "Jolovan Wham and John Tan Found Guilty of Scandalising the Singapore Judiciary, First Convictions under Administration of Justice (Protection) Act 2016", Attorney-General's Chambers, 9 October 2018 <https://www.agc.gov.sg/newsroom/newsitem2temp/jolovan-wham-and-john-tan-found-guilty-of-scandalising-the-singapore-judiciary-first-convictions-under-administration-of-justice-(protection)-act-2016>.
102. "Court of Appeal Allows Li Shengwu to Appeal in Contempt of Court Case", Channel NewsAsia, 3 September 2018 <https://www.channelnewsasia.com/news/singapore/li-shengwu-contempt-of-court-appeal-can-proceed-10679186>.
103. "The Online Citizen Editor Charged with Criminal Defamation, Along with Author of Article", Channel NewsAsia, 13 December 2018 <https://www.channelnewsasia.com/news/singapore/online-citizen-toc-editor-terry-xu-charged-criminal-defamation-11025326>.
104. "Merdeka Package", 2018 <https://www.gov.sg/microsites/ndr2018/merdeka-generation>.
105. Jalelah Abu Baker, "Singapore Ranks High in Report on Medical Inflation in Asia", 7 April 2018 <https://www.channelnewsasia.com/news/singapore/medical-hospital-costs-singapore-inflation-aon-10112896>.
106. Lianne Chia, "Fewer Exams, Assessments in Schools to Reduce Emphasis on Academic results: MOE", Channel NewsAsia, 28 September 2018 <https://www.channelnewsasia.com/news/singapore/exams-assessments-scrap-mid-year-primary-secondary-schools-10767370>.
107. Kevin Kwang, "Addenda to President's Address: MOE Will Continue to 'Dial Back Overemphasis' on Exam Results", Channel NewsAsia, 10 May 2018 <https://www.channelnewsasia.com/news/singapore/addenda-to-president-address-moe-exam-results-overemphasis-10221638?cid=h3_referral_inarticlelinks_24082018_cna>.
108. Amelia Teng, "Tuition Industry Worth over $1b a Year", *Straits Times*, 25 December 2016 <https://www.straitstimes.com/singapore/education/tuition-industry-worth-over-1b-a-year>.

109. R. Sinnakaruppan, "Why Singapore's Education System Needs an Overhaul", *Today*, 27 March 2017 <https://www.todayonline.com/daily-focus/education/why-spores-education-system-needs-overhaul>.
110. Jason Boon, "Commentary: With Less Focus on Grades, is PSLE Still a Necessary Checkpoint?", Channel NewsAsia, 28 November 2017 <https://www.channelnewsasia.com/news/singapore/commentary-with-less-focus-on-grades-is-psle-still-a-necessary-9444772?cid=h3_referral_inarticlelinks_24082018_cna>.
111. Jolene Ang, "Tuition Centres Should Not Prey on Parents' Anxieties over Removal of Exams: Ong Ye Kung", *Straits Times*, 3 October 2018 <https://www.straitstimes.com/singapore/education/tuition-centres-should-not-prey-on-parents-anxieties-over-removal-of-exams-ong>.
112. Adrian W.J. Kuah, "Why Move to Reduce Examinations and Emphasis on Grades is Disconcerting, but Necessary", LKY School of Public Policy, 1 October 2018 <https://lkyspp.nus.edu.sg/gia/article/why-move-to-reduce-examinations-and-emphasis-on-grades-is-disconcerting-but-necessary>.
113. Yen Nee Lee, "Vietnam Unseats Singapore as Largest IPO Fundraiser in Southeast Asia", CNBC, 26 December 2018 <https://www.cnbc.com/2018/12/27/vietnam-unseats-singapore-as-largest-ipo-fundraiser-in-southeast-asia.html>.
114. "Here's Why Singapore Can't Beat Hong Kong's Financial Centre Ratings", *Singapore Business Review*, 13 September 2018 <https://sbr.com.sg/financial-services/news/heres-why-singapore-cant-beat-hong-kongs-financial-centre-ratings>.
115. "Singapore Tops World Bank 'Human Capital' Rankings based on Health, Education", Channel NewsAsia, 11 October 2018 <https://www.channelnewsasia.com/news/singapore-tops-world-bank-human-capital-rankings-based-on-health-10814282>.
116. Seow Bei Yi, "More Singaporeans Find Jobs, but Long-term Unemployment Rate Rises: MOM", *Straits Times*, 13 September 2018 <https://www.straitstimes.com/singapore/more-singaporeans-find-jobs-but-long-term-unemployment-rate-rises-mom>.
117. Tang See Kit, "About 30,000 Workers Found Jobs through Adapt and Grow Initiative in 2018: PM Lee", Channel NewsAsia, 11 January 2019 <https://www.channelnewsasia.com/news/singapore/workers-found-jobs-through-adapt-and-grow-pm-lee-11111640>.
118. Augustine Lee, "Trends and Shifts in Employment: Singapore's Workforce", Civil Service College, 12 January 2018 <https://www.csc.gov.sg/articles/trends-and-shifts-in-employment-singapore-s-workforce>.
119. Paul Teng, "Commentary: That Singapore Must Cope with Food Disruption and Vulnerability is Our Reality", Channel NewsAsia, 23 December 2018 <https://www.channelnewsasia.com/news/commentary/singapore-eggs-fish-shrimp-shortage-malaysia-curbs-11053228>.
120. Charissa Yong, "Cabinet Reshuffle to Take Place after Budget 2019: PM", *Straits Times*, 4 December 2018 <https://www.straitstimes.com/world/americas/cabinet-reshuffle-to-take-place-after-budget-2019-pm>.

121. "Tan Cheng Bock Files Application to Form New Political Party", *Today*, 18 January 2019 <https://www.channelnewsasia.com/news/singapore/tan-cheng-bock-new-political-party-progress-singapore-11138530>.

Thailand

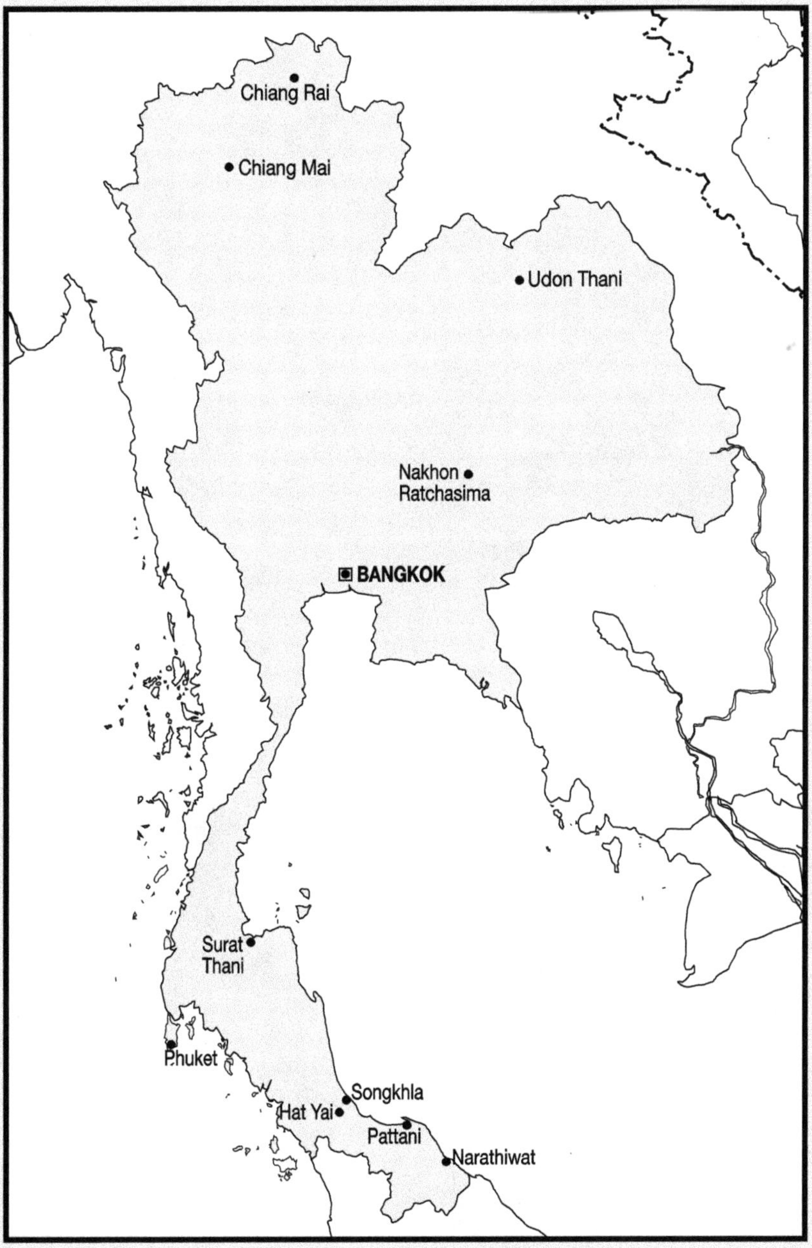
Chiang Rai
Chiang Mai
Udon Thani
Nakhon Ratchasima
BANGKOK
Surat Thani
Phuket
Songkhla
Hat Yai
Pattani
Narathiwat

THAILAND IN 2018: Military Dictatorship under Royal Command

Eugénie Mérieau

On 22 May 2014, Thai army chief General Prayuth Chan-ocha staged a military coup — two days earlier he had declared martial law for the entire territory of the kingdom. The junta, renamed the National Council for Peace and Order (NCPO), abolished the 2007 constitution and replaced it with an interim constitution banning political parties and elections. In April 2015 it lifted martial law only to replace it with NCPO Order 3/2015 prohibiting gatherings of more than five people.

Upon seizing power the NCPO had promised to return the country to democracy according to a roadmap stipulating for the drafting of a new constitution and the organization of elections. Following a referendum in August 2016, the newly crowned King Vajiralongkorn, who had ascended to the throne in December 2016, promulgated a new "permanent" constitution in April 2017. Elections were then planned for November 2018, which were later delayed to February then March 2019. In 2018, in preparation for the upcoming election, the military government lifted some of its restrictions on political activities. It allowed the registration of political parties in March and lifted the ban on political gatherings in December, after more than four years under martial law and NCPO Order 3/2015. In both cases, Prayuth used his absolute powers under Article 44 of the 2014 interim constitution to lift his previous orders.

The general election planned for 2019 will certainly not "return" democracy to Thailand. The planning and organization of elections following a military takeover

---

EUGÉNIE MÉRIEAU is Postdoctoral Fellow at the Chair of Comparative Constitutionalism, University of Goettingen.

is part of a regular pattern in Thailand, and has been called the "vicious cycle of Thai politics" (*wongchon ubat*).[1] Each cycle starts and ends in a military coup. First a coup is staged, with martial law declared and the constitution abolished. A short interim constitution banning both political parties and elections is promulgated instead. The interim constitution is in turn followed by a permanent constitution providing for elections, only to lead to a further crisis and a military or judicial-military coup, installing a military government. In 2006, the democratically elected leader Thaksin Shinawatra was ousted by a military coup, the 1997 constitution abolished and replaced with the 2006 interim constitution, followed by the permanent 2007 constitution adopted by referendum. Elections were held in December 2007, only for the subsequent government of Samak Sundaravej to be dismissed by the Constitutional Court in 2008. After years of mass mobilization of the red-shirts calling for new elections to be held, Yingluck Shinawatra, the sister of Thaksin, was eventually elected in 2011, but she faced disqualification by the Supreme Administrative Court in 2014. Her government was finally overthrown in the military coup staged by the NCPO.

This regular pattern exhibits continuity beyond the apparent political and constitutional instability. The military and the monarchy remain powerful actors, even at times when there are regular elections and an alternation of civilian governments, suggesting that Thailand is a tutelary democracy. A tutelary democracy, according to Adam Przeworski, is "a regime which has competitive, formally democratic institutions, but in which the power apparatus, typically reduced to the armed forces, retains the capacity to intervene to correct undesirable states of affairs".[2]

In Thailand, the tutelary powers, identified as the monarchy and the army, can veto decisions of elected politicians whenever needed, while allowing some degree of electoral politics to play out. The nature and dynamics of the relationship between the two tutelary powers are two of the most contentious questions in the academic field of Thai studies. Several analysts have tried to conceptualize this relationship as an alliance, either in functional-structural terms (deep state,[3] parallel state[4]) or in agent-focused types of analysis (network monarchy[5]).

Adopting a historical-institutional approach, this chapter analyses the Thai regime in terms of tutelary democracy, where tutelary powers as well as the mechanisms used by tutelary powers to veto decisions of elected politicians are entrenched through the constitution, laws and administrative structures created by laws. In that regard, the year 2018 was instrumental in setting the structures of continued military rule under royal command, buttressed on a system of flawed electoral democracy — for decades to come.

Thailand's Tutelary Democracy as Devised by the 2017 Constitution and 2018 Organic Acts

The 2017 constitution must be understood as a corrective to the 2007 constitution, the aims of which were to establish a tutelary democracy, whereby entrenched elites — the military and the monarchy — could retain their power and status whenever threatened by democratization and the rise of elected leaders. The endeavour ultimately failed with the election of Samak Sundaravej in late 2007 and Yingluck Shinawatra in 2011, both close allies of Thaksin. The 2017 constitution, adopted by referendum in August 2016, aimed to entrench tutelary democracy further by refining provisions regarding the Constitutional Court, the Senate and independent constitutional organs, as well as through the creation of a National Strategic Committee and a National Reform Committee. Like its predecessor the 2007 constitution, but with more assertiveness, the 2017 text organizes a system of *elite self-interested hegemonic preservation* that will be able to insulate the policy preferences of tutelary powers from the vicissitudes of electoral politics and gives them the means to overthrow elected leaders.[6] Meanwhile, constitutional revision is made highly difficult, with broad and vague eternity clauses[7] and a procedure involving the Senate and the Constitutional Court, two bodies placed under the control of the military.

According to the 2017 constitution and its organic acts, especially the 2017 Political Party Act and the 2018 Act on the Election of Members of the House of Representatives, the Constitutional Court has, with the help of independent organs such as the Election Commission and the National Anti-Corruption Commission, the means to overthrow elected leaders and dissolve political parties. These powers are not mere constraints: they are powers to be used. In 2006 and 2014, the Constitutional Court was instrumental in paving the way for the military coups that ousted Yingluck Shinawatra and Thaksin Shinawatra by voiding elections that would have confirmed them into power and thus creating a political vacuum which allowed the military to step in. Thaksin's political party was also dissolved twice, in 2007 and 2008.

Yet the 2017 constitution does not state that the Constitutional Court can dissolve parties as it did in 2007. Such provisions are now "hidden" in the Political Party Act. The new Political Party Act, adopted in September 2017, lists in its Article 92 the acts for which a political party shall face dissolution by the Constitutional Court. The 2018 Act on the Election of Members of the House of Representatives complements this list with a few others. Many of the defined offences are broad and unclear, such as "failure to act according to the Democracy with the King as Head of State". The types of actions that can lead to dissolution by the Constitutional Court are so numerous that the Electoral Commission (EC) has prepared a hundred-page document summarizing dissolution grounds for distribution to party leaders — listing thirteen of them.[8] In the name of prohibiting vote buying and the rise of undemocratic parties, the tools of *militant democracy* are here used to thwart democratization. In practice, the Constitutional Court can almost initiate a case of party dissolution *suo motu*: the constitution provides for an individual with the unfiltered right of petition before the Court and no *locus standi* is required.[9] On top of this, it can also veto legislation before and after promulgation, and void constitutional amendments on both formal and substantial grounds.[10] Furthermore, proposing an "unconstitutional" amendment could also be interpreted by the Constitutional Court as an act of malfeasance and lead to cabinet dismissal. In 2014 the Constitutional Court dismissed Yingluck on the grounds that one of her administrative acts had been found by the Supreme Administrative Court to be illegal. This entire framework has been devised to protect the hegemony of the military. To ensure they remain under the control of the military, Constitutional Court judges must, according to the 2017 constitution, be approved by the Senate, which is fully appointed by the military.[11]

According to the "transitory provisions" of the 2017 constitution, the Senate will initially be a body of 250 members fully appointed by the military junta for a five-year term. Of these 250 members, six are ex-officio: the permanent secretary of the Ministry of Defense, the supreme commander, the commander-in-chief of the Royal Thai Army, the commander-in-chief of the Royal Thai Navy, the commander-in-chief of the Royal Thai Air Force, and the commissioner-general of the Royal Thai Police. The powers of the Senate are very broad: it participates in the appointment of the prime minister, who does not need to be an elected member of parliament.[12] Moreover, it can impeach elected politicians. Lastly, the Senate is also tasked with monitoring the implementation of the National Strategy Plan,[13] which is legally binding on the government.

The constitution provides for a National Strategy Committee composed of thirty-four people appointed by the junta to write and monitor the twenty-year National Strategy Plan. Half the members of the National Strategy Committee are ex-officio members, including the prime minister, speakers of the Houses and the Senate, a deputy prime minister or minister, the Defence permanent secretary, the chiefs of the armed forces, army, navy, air force and police, the secretary general of the National Security Council, the chairman of the National Economic and Social Development Board, and the heads of the Board of Trade,

Federation of Thai Industries, Tourism Council of Thailand and Thai Bankers Association (seventeen members). The remaining members were appointed by the NCPO in July 2017. The twenty-year National Strategy Plan was adopted unanimously in July 2018.

Working under the umbrella of the National Strategy Committee is the National Reform Committee. The National Reform Act, adopted in 2017 to complete the constitution, created eleven subcommittees comprised of approximately ten members each, tasked with writing reform plans and monitoring their implementation by the government and government agencies: about 150 people, many of them members of the military, were appointed in August 2017 to form such subcommittees. Policies of the government must conform to the National Strategy.[14] Failure to follow the National Strategy can lead to dismissal from office.

Meanwhile, similar to the 2007 constitution, an array of other judicial and quasi-judicial bodies can easily remove and initiate both criminal prosecution and civil cases against elected leaders, as was the case with Thaksin Shinawatra and his sister Yingluck Shinawatra, both sentenced to prison terms according to special procedures. For instance, the National Anti-Corruption Commission can petition against the elected government in the Supreme Court for the latter's failure to implement the National Strategy. The EC and the Ombudsmen can petition the Constitutional Court to request for the dissolution of a political party. The EC can also petition the Supreme Court to revoke a politician's right to stand for elections for ten years, which is a doubling of the penalties provided for under the 2007 constitution.[15]

Under the new constitution, extra-constitutional military coups are no longer needed, as the military can stage coups through constitutional means — just as the Constitutional Court no longer needs to twist the constitution to stage judicial coups, as it has been empowered to dissolve political parties and dismiss elected governments on a wide spectrum of legal grounds.

The Militarization of the Thai State

In 2018, the NCPO and King Vajiralongkorn militarized the Thai State by appointing military officers to key positions.

In its four years of rule, the NCPO has militarized the Thai state through hundreds of long-lasting appointments. This process was accelerated in 2018, under the constraint of the prospect of the upcoming election. As of late 2018, according to Thai Lawyers for Human Rights, the NCPO and its advisors consist of about 40 members, of which more than 30 are military officers.[16] Military officers have been appointed to positions in all major ministries, on top of forming the majority of members of the National Legislative Assembly (200 members), the National Reform Committee and its Subcommittees (150) and the National Strategy Committee (34). In addition, in late 2018 a draft bill was tabled for consideration to make generals eligible for appointments in independent constitutional organizations such as the Ombudsman, the National Anti-Corruption Commission or the EC.[17]

In 2018, appointments to the Privy Council and the Crown Property Bureau also showed a pattern of militarization. The king appointed three new privy councillors: Ampon Kittiampon, Chalermchai Sitthisad and Chom Rungswang. The latter two come from the army, increasing the ratio of army generals in the Privy Council. Meanwhile, two privy councilors, Wirat Chinwinichakul and Tirachai Nakwanit, were dismissed only a few months after their appointment by the king. Significantly, Air Chief Marshal Satitpong Sukvimol, a close aide to the king, was appointed in March 2018 as director-general of the Crown Property Bureau.

A few months later, in October, Apirat Kongsompong, freshly appointed as new army chief, was named board member of the Crown Property Bureau. He is the son of the general who overthrew Chatichai Choonhavan in 1991, and, in line with his father's legacy, did not rule out a coup in the future. Unlike his immediate predecessors, who hailed from the Queen's Guard, he comes from the King's Guard, a unit in which the king himself had served in his youth. The same month, the king appointed another close aide as board member: Privy Councillor Ampon Kittiampon. The Crown Property Bureau now comprises 11 men, most of whom are members of the military and police and close to King Vajiralongkorn. Only one member maintained his position from the previous reign.

Since coming to power, the king has sought to gain, through the revision of key legislation, direct control over organs previously under some, or at least formal, control of the elected government, such as the Crown Property Bureau and the Buddhist Supreme Patriarch. These moves highlight a return to the conditions of the 1960s, when King Bhumibol built his power through an alliance with military dictator Sarit Thanarat.

In November 2018 the Crown Property Act was amended, redefining the king's possessions to include what the monarchy had "accumulated under ancient royal traditions". According to Article 5 of the act, any disputes over what assets are considered Crown property under the ancient royal traditions are to be decided by the king himself. The Crown Property Act had already been amended in 2017, allowing the king discretion to appoint members of the committee managing the

Crown property. The Crown Property Bureau, which has more than sixty square kilometres under its oversight, has reclaimed plots of land in the vicinity of the Palace, notably at Dusit Zoo, the horse-racing track, Ananta Samakhom Throne Hall and the current parliament buildings.

In July 2018, the Sangha Act was amended to give the king the power to appoint and dismiss all twenty members of the Sangha Council. The act had already been amended in 2017 to grant the king the power to appoint the supreme patriarch. He had used this power of appointment in February 2017 to select Amborn Prasatthaphong, a representative of the Thammayut sect, which has close relations with the Palace, bypassing the nominee for supreme patriarch proposed by the Supreme Council. The Supreme Council nominee, Somdet Chuang, is associated with the Dhammakaya sect, usually considered close to Thaksin. Likewise, in May 2018, Vajiralongkorn used discretionary powers to dismiss three members of the Supreme Council following their arrests on grounds of corruption.

A more punitive and expeditious approach to law and order under the guidance of the monarchy could also be observed by the resumption of the death penalty in Thailand in June 2018. In what was the country's first execution since August 2009, a twenty-six-year-old man convicted for murder was executed by lethal injection. The death penalty in Thailand is closely connected with the institution of the monarchy, through the institutionalized practice of royal pardon — only after a royal pardon has been rejected can an execution be carried out. A remarkable development in 2018 though concerns the use of the *lèse-majesté* law. The number of cases significantly dropped in 2018, reversing a trend of its skyrocketing use since the 2014 coup and the 2016 death of King Bhumibol. According to Thai Lawyers for Human Rights, no new cases were prosecuted in 2018.[18] Several high-profile cases were either entirely dropped or convicted under other charges. In September, young people who had set fire to portraits of Kings Vajiralongkorn and Bhumibol were not convicted of *lèse-majesté* but instead charged with damaging public property. Prominent social critic Sulak Sirivaksa (who himself faced charges in early 2018) reported, following an audience with the king, that such a drastic change could be explained by a royal order towards "mercy".[19]

Towards Elections?

The year 2018 was marked by preparations for the coming elections. In September, two organic laws were promulgated: the Act on the Election of Members of the House of Representatives and the Act on the Recruitment of Senators. Meanwhile, the Political Party Act that was adopted in September 2017 went into effect.

According to the version modified by an order issued in September 2018, political parties must meet the following requirements: to possess funds of at least a million baht, have branches in different parts of the country, and have at least five hundred members. In December, using its sweeping powers of Article 44, the military amended the Political Party Act to lift the ban on political activities and confirmed that the election would take place on 24 February 2019, the election decree issued on 2 January 2019, the official announcement by the Election Commission made on 4 January, and applications to be filed between 14 and 18 January in order for the official announcement to be released on 25 January. The stated aim is that parliament could convene in early May (after the appointment of senators). Yet, the decree was not issued on 2 January 2019, and the possibility that the election will be delayed looms large.

According to the Organic Act on the Election of Members of the House of Representatives, the House shall be composed of 500 members divided into 350 constituency seats and 150 party-list seats. Unlike the situation under the 2007 constitution, eligible voters can only cast a single vote each, which counts for a specific candidate as well as for that candidate's party. This electoral reform fragments the vote, making electoral majorities more unlikely and leading to unstable coalition governments. Small parties failing to obtain many constituency members of parliament will receive additional party-list seats, while those scoring well in constituencies will be allocated a reduced number of party-list seats, following a mechanism of "inverted" majority bonus or minority bonus. The targeted party is the Pheua Thai Party, which will see its number of seats reduced. However, the Pheua Thai Party had anticipated the manoeuver and had created sister parties to increase its chances under the complicated system: the Thai Raksa Chat (Thais Safeguard the Nation), the "Pheua Tham" ("for justice") and "Pheua Chart" ("for the nation"). Having sister parties might also prove critical if Pheua Thai were to be dissolved by the Constitutional Court.

In March, political parties began to register for the election. More than 30 parties registered immediately, followed by almost 50 more to date. A pro-military party was formed to support Prayuth in the upcoming election: the Palang Pracharat Party. Uttama Savanayana, the current minister for industry, is the official leader, while other Cabinet members have also joined the party. It was also reported that more than 150 former MPs, senators, ministers and famous figures have defected from their parties to join the pro-military party. Other like-minded parties have also registered, such as the party created by Suthep Taugsuban, former member of the Democrat Party and leader of the PDRC, together with Anek Laothamatas, an academic close to the Democrat Party, called Phalang Prachachat Thai. A third party supporting the army, Prachachon Patirup, was founded by Paiboon Nittitawan. Other than the three pro-military parties, it remains unclear whether the traditional Phuea Thai parties, led by Sudarat Keyuraphan and Chatchat Sittipunt, and the Democrat Party, led by Abhisit Vejjajiva, would entertain the possibility of an alliance with the military.

New anti-military forces have also emerged, such as the Future Forward Party and the Party of the Common People. The Future Forward Party is led by Thanathorn Jeungrungruangkit, a Thai billionaire known for his political antipathy towards the military and the conservative elites. The Future Forward Party has "vowed to cut the military budget and reduce the number of generals in the army". The Party of the Common People is led by Tanaporn Sriyakorn, a former member of Thaksin's original Thai Rak Thai party banned from politics after the 2006 coup. Both parties share a common platform aimed at reducing inequalities, decentralizing power, solving the conflict in the South by promising more autonomy, promoting freedom of expression and association, and demilitarizing Thailand.

On 7 December the army organized a meeting of the NCPO, the EC and representatives of seventy-five political parties to discuss preparations for the elections. The meeting was however boycotted by the major political parties, including Phuea Thai, the Democrat Party and the Future Forward Party.

Delays in the organization of the election have created rifts in the EC. In March, the chair of the EC, Somchai Srisutthiyakorn, critical of the military's handling of the election, was dismissed by Prayuth through Article 44. In July, the NLA endorsed five new EC members and the EC picked Ittiporn Boonpracong as its chairman. In November, Prayuth once again invoked Article 44 to allow the EC to redraw the electoral constituencies to disadvantage the larger parties, Phuea Thai and the Democrat Party. Meanwhile, other measures and mechanisms were put in place to monitor, on behalf of the army, the implementation of the election, such as the setting up of election monitors appointed under the supervision of the military. The military-dominated ISOC will also play a role in such monitoring throughout the entire territory during the time of the electoral campaign. In November 2017, Prayuth Chan-ocha had used Article 44 to amend the Internal Security Act to add "domestic threats" as part of the mandate of the Internal Security Operations Command, a body under direct command of the military.[20] In sum, the entire constitutional, legal, and administrative framework is designed to make Prayuth the next premier. He himself hinted at this calculation by declaring: "I talked to the legal team: I don't need to be a member or anything [to become premier]".[21] Indeed, provided all 250 Senators support him, Prayuth needs only

126 members of parliament (out of 500) to vote for him in order to command a majority in parliament (376 out of 750).

Meanwhile, the repression of protesters calling for elections continued unabated. The "We want elections" protesters led by prominent activist Nuttaa Mahattana have been arrested repeatedly by the army. Academics who held a banner bearing the slogan "An Academic Conference is Not a Military Barracks" in July 2017 were prosecuted; the trial is still ongoing. Meanwhile, censorship of the press, TV and the Internet has continued, with the use of the Computer Cybercrime Act as amended in 2016 and NCPO orders. An unprecedented opening, however, surprisingly occurred with the dissemination on YouTube of a rap song entitled "What My Country's Got" (*prathet ku mi*). The music video achieved ten million views within a couple of weeks and passed fifty million by the end of 2018. The song, written and performed by a collective of rappers known as "Rap Against Dictatorship", or RAD, denounces the meddling of the army in politics, corruption and the repression of dissent. The clip is a tribute to the events of October 1976, when students were massacred in Bangkok by the military and police forces. The military at first issued a summons for the rappers but then backed down.

Economy and Foreign Policy

In preparing for the upcoming elections, the Thai military has engaged in the massive distribution of cash handouts to eligible voters. The military government has been replicating Thaksin's policies of benefitting the poor in the hope of getting their votes. These policies have included a three-year moratorium on farmers' debts, monthly cash handouts of 200 to 500 baht per person for people of low incomes, free Internet SIM cards, cheap loans to first-home buyers, and funds for small and medium-sized enterprises. This has amounted to hundreds of billions of baht in public spending under the Palang Pracharath scheme.

Following the scandal of the luxury watches seen on the wrist of deputy chairman of the junta and deputy prime minister Prawit Wongsuwan, the National Anti-Corruption Commission announced in December that it was "finalizing its investigation", although no member of the military junta has been prosecuted so far. Other scandals of corruption tainting the military government have been silenced. It has been reported that inequalities have grown since the military took power. In 2016, the 1 per cent richest Thais (500,000 people) owned 58.0 per cent of the country's wealth, while in 2018 they controlled 66.9 per cent.[22] Meanwhile, economic growth stagnated at 4 per cent, while it had averaged 7 per cent under Yingluck's elected government.

In order to get out of the middle-income trap, the military announced a plan entitled Thailand 4.0, which includes megaprojects such as developing U-Tapao, a former American base, into a full airport to make Thailand an airport hub in Southeast Asia, and high-speed trains to China through Laos which would connect Isan to Bangkok. In July 2018 the National Legislative Assembly voted unanimously to approve the National Strategy, with binding effect over the next twenty years and penalties for non-compliance. The six strategic areas were security, competitiveness, human resources, social equality, green growth and public sector development.

In the field of foreign policy, since the coup there has been a clear shift towards China, accompanied by a reinforcement of cooperation with authoritarian governments while Thailand prepares to assume the chairmanship of ASEAN in 2019. The 2014 coup harmed U.S.-Thai relations and prompted Thailand's turn to China for the sake of political legitimation. The Thai military has purchased Chinese submarines and is planning to buy Chinese tanks, while discussing advancing military cooperation with China. The high-speed railway project with China as part of the Belt and Road Initiative was agreed to hastily through the use of Article 44, and construction is set to start in early 2019. The Chinese influence can also be seen in the admiration Prayuth has never concealed for Chinese President Xi Jinping.

Meanwhile, the Thai military has also sought legitimation from democratic governments. Following the government's promise of a general election, European governments softened their stance towards the ruling generals. The European Union expressed interest in restarting negotiations for a free-trade agreement with Thailand, which had been frozen since the military takeover. Prayuth was keen on getting legitimation from democratic governments in order to boost his legitimacy at home. Prayuth toured Europe in June, meeting Emmanuel Macron in Paris and Theresa May in England. In July he was featured on the cover of the Asia edition of *Time* magazine with the subtitle "Democrat. Dictator. Which path will Thailand's Prayuth Chan-ocha choose?" Although the cover treatment upset him, in several speeches he mentioned his international recognition and the trust given to him by the governments of Germany, the United States, Australia, the United Kingdom and France. This enterprise of legitimation is important, as Thailand is set to assume the chairmanship of ASEAN in 2019 — several op-eds, including some in the *Jakarta Post*, have urged ASEAN to refuse Thailand's chairmanship due to its lack of legitimacy.

Thailand has not only deepened its cooperation with China but also with other authoritarian governments, most notably in Southeast Asia, but also elsewhere. The first area of cooperation has been the return of political fugitives to their countries of origin, including those with refugee status. In 2015 Thailand returned several Uighurs to China. This year it vowed to return Cambodian fugitives in exchange for the return of Thais hidden in Cambodia. In January the dead bodies of Thai dissidents exiled in Laos were found floating in the Mekong River.

Conclusion

The current apparent liberalization of Thai politics in 2018, as part of preparations for the coming elections, should not mask Thailand's sophistication of authoritarianism since the coup, an increased authoritarianism that has been noted by international think tanks on freedom and democracy. The almost five hundred pieces of legislation enacted, either as NCPO orders or laws passed by the National Legislative Assembly, will remain in force after a government is sworn in and they will continue to repress dissent and constrain the political system. Moreover, it is likely that the elections will further militarize the state by giving a stamp of legitimacy to Prayuth Chan-ocha, who is very likely to be appointed premier by the parliament. The 2017 constitution has entrenched Thailand's "Deep State" even further than the 2007 constitution did, embedding the 2014 post-coup interim charter (very short and authoritarian, giving full power to the army) into its democratic-liberal framework (a long document beginning with a catalogue of rights, providing for elections, legislatures, political parties and governments, as well as watchdog bodies). The set of laws issued and appointments made during 2018 highlight the reinforcement and deepening of the institutionalization of the alliance between the military and the monarchy.

Notes

1. Chai-Anan Samudavanija, *Thailand's Young Turks* (Singapore: Institute of Southeast Asian Studies, 1982), p. 1.
2. Adam Przeworski, "Democracy as a Contingent Outcome of Conflicts", in *Constitutionalism and Democracy*, edited by Jon Elster and Rune Slagstad (Cambridge University Press, 1988).
3. Eugénie Mérieau, "Thailand's Deep State, Royal Power and the Constitutional Court", *Journal of Contemporary Asia* 46 (2016): 445–66.
4. Paul Chambers and Napisa Waitoolkiat, "The Resilience of Monarchised Military in Thailand", *Journal of Contemporary Asia* 46 (2016): 425–44.
5. Duncan McCargo, "Network Monarchy and Legitimacy Crises in Thailand", *Pacific Review* 18 (2005): 499–519.

6. Ran Hirschl, *Towards Juristocracy* (Harvard University Press, 2004).
7. Section 255. An amendment to the Constitution which amounts to changing the democratic regime of government with the King as Head of State or changing the form of the State shall be prohibited.
8. Election Commission, *Khwampit le attar thot tam kotmai thi kiaokap kanlueaktang lae phak kanmueang* (December 2016).
9. Section 49. No person shall exercise the rights or liberties to overthrow the democratic regime of government with the King as Head of State. Any person who has knowledge of an act under paragraph one shall have the right to petition to the Attorney-General to submit a motion to the Constitutional Court for an order to cease such act. In the case where the Attorney-General orders a refusal to proceed as petitioned or fails to proceed within fifteen days as from the date of receiving the petition, the person making the petition may submit the petition directly to the Constitutional Court. The action under this section shall not prejudice the criminal prosecution against the person committing an act under paragraph one.
10. According to Section 256, an amendment to Chapter I General Provisions, Chapter II The King or Chapter XV Amendment to the Constitution, or a matter relating to qualifications and prohibitions of persons holding the positions under the Constitution, or a matter relating to duties or powers of the Court or an Independent Organ, or a matter which renders the Court or an Independent Organ unable to act in accordance with its duties or powers, shall involve a referendum and can be reviewed by the Constitutional Court subject to a petition filed by at least one-tenth of the members of both houses.
11. Section 204. A person who is elected or selected to hold the position of judge of the Constitutional Court must obtain the approval of the Senate with the votes of not less than one-half of the total number of the existing members of the Senate. In the case where the Senate disapproves any selected or elected person, a new person shall be selected or elected and thereafter submitted to the Senate for approval.
12. This particular disposition was approved by referendum in August 2016. It was the object of an additional question: "To solve the crisis, should the Senate participate in the nomination of the prime minister?"
13. Section 270. Apart from the duties and powers provided in the Constitution, the Senate under section 269 shall have the duty and power to monitor, recommend and accelerate national reform in order to achieve the objectives under Chapter XVI National Reform, and the preparation and implementation of the National Strategy. In this regard, the Council of Ministers shall report the progress of implementing the national reform plan to the National Assembly every three months.
14. Section 162. The Council of Ministers which will assume the administration of the State affairs must, within fifteen days as from the date it takes office, state its policies to the National Assembly, which must be consistent with the duties of the

State, directive principles of State policies and National Strategy, and declares the sources of incomes which will be expended in the implementation of the policies, with respect to which no vote of confidence shall be passed.

15. Section 226. When proceedings under section 225 are undertaken, or after announcing the result of an election or selection, if there appears evidence to reasonably believe that a candidate of the election or selection has committed a dishonest act in the election or selection or has connived at such act of other persons, the Election Commission shall submit a petition to the Supreme Court for an order to revoke the right to stand for election or the right to vote of such person. The consideration of the Supreme Court under paragraph one shall be based upon the file of the investigation or inquiry of the Election Commission, and in the interest of justice, the Court shall have the power to order an inquiry for additional facts or evidence. In the case where the Supreme Court has rendered a judgment deciding that the person under paragraph one has committed an offence as petitioned, the Supreme Court shall order the revocation of the right to stand for election or the right to vote of such person for a period of ten years, in accordance with the Organic Act on the Election of Members of the House of Representatives, or the Organic Act on Installation of Senators, as the case may be.
16. Thai Lawyers for Human Rights, *Collapsed Rule of Law: The Consequences of Four Years under the National Council for Peace and Order for Human Rights and Thai Society* (2018), p. 6.
17. Ibid., p. 7.
18. Thai Lawyers for Human Rights, "Changes in Thailand's lèse majesté Prosecutions in 2018" (2019) <https://www.tlhr2014.com/?p=10431>.
19. Shawn Crispin, "A Lighter Royal Touch for Thailand", *Asia Times*, 16 October 2018.
20. See Puanthong Pawapakan, *The Central Role of Thailand's Internal Security Operations Command in the Post-Counter Insurgency Period*, Trends in Southeast Asia 2017, no. 17 (Singapore: ISEAS – Yusof Ishak Institute, 2017).
21. Quoted in "Thai PM Prayuth Keeps Options Open", *Straits Times*, 27 November 2018.
22. "Report: Thailand Most Unequal Country in 2018", *Bangkok Post*, 6 December 2018 <https://www.bangkokpost.com/business/news/1588786/report-thailand-most-unequal-country-in-2018>.

COMPETING LOGICS: Between Thai Sovereignty and the China Model in 2018

Gregory V. Raymond

In September 2018 a quarrel between a Thai border guard and a tourist from the People's Republic of China at Bangkok's Don Mueang Airport turned violent. The argument took place after the Chinese visitor was denied entry on the grounds that he could not produce evidence that he would return to China after his trip to Thailand.[1] The incident should be worrying for Thailand, given the country's increasing reliance on the growing numbers of Chinese tourists since the coup of 2014. Yet this incident is also symbolic of the internal pressure generated within the Thai state as a result of having to manage China's encroachments on Thai sovereignty.

In 2018 the Thai military government struggled to maintain a balance between two opposing policy logics. On the one hand, China has become not just a critical economic partner but also a potential model of governance; on the other, Thailand's resilient strategic culture and national identity each emphasize sovereignty and independence, requiring judicious diplomacy with the great powers as the primary tool to achieve these ends. Clearly, there is a tension here: while Thailand may find the stability of authoritarian capitalism attractive, it no more wants coercion from China than it does from the United States.

In this chapter I assess the extent to which 2018 may have seen the high-water mark of Thailand's embrace of China and its adoption of the China

---

GREGORY RAYMOND is Research Fellow in the Strategic and Defence Studies Centre, Australian National University. Prior to joining ANU he was a policy advisor in the Australian Government, including in the strategic and international policy areas of the Department of Defence and the Australian Embassy in Bangkok.

model. I argue that while permanent traces of this connection will remain in the form of more repressive domestic security policies and the goal of greater mainland Southeast Asian economic connectivity, warming relations with the United States will balance Thailand's strong tilt to China over the past five years. The article proceeds in five parts. I begin by examining Thailand's domestic political situation, highlighting how, since 2014, the junta's need for legitimacy has increasingly relied on the Thai elites who fear the rise of a mass movement capable of urban disruption. In the second section, I contend that Thailand is seeing the development of a protection pact between elites, such that they are prepared to sacrifice political liberties for increased security. Here, I document the rise of the Internal Security Operations Command over the past five years. In the third section, I look at Thailand's partial embrace of the China model of governance, which is both the consequence of the protection pact among the elites and the Chinese influence as an authoritarian centre of gravity. In the fourth section, I appraise the obstacles preventing Thailand's full transition to a China model, which can be explained by the widespread local preference for democracy and Thailand's strategic culture. I also examine indications that Thailand is beginning to limit its accommodation of China's interests and to turn back instead towards the United States. In the fifth section, I survey what 2018 has meant for the Thai military, including in terms of posture, procurement, budget and great power relations.

The Legitimacy Deficit

Like all unelected military governments, Prime Minister General Prayuth Chan-ocha's regime suffers from a legitimacy deficit. While there was some justification for a strong hand at the tiller to oversee the royal transition in the months following the passing of the beloved King Bhumipol Adulyadej in October 2016, there have however been no signs that the change has provoked additional instability in the Thai body politic. On the contrary, the new monarch has settled in rapidly, making a series of changes to increase the autonomy and financial security of the palace.[2]

One alternative path to legitimacy consists of competent economic management and delivering strong sustained growth. In this regard the junta has been placing significant hope in increased border trade and seeking to push forward with infrastructure projects. For example, the junta expects that the Eastern Economic Corridor will generate sufficient economic growth to help Thailand escape the middle-income trap by raising per capita income from US$6,500 to US$20,000 within twenty years.[3] The Eastern Economic Corridor, comprising transport links including high-speed rail and airports (Suvarnabhumi, Don Mueang and Utapao), is supposed to help Thailand grow its automobile, electronics and IT industries through linkages with China via the Belt and Road Initiative and by placing the Southeast Asian region within an hour's reach by plane.[4] However, the current reality is that weaker global growth in the post–global financial crisis period and a slowing Chinese economy have constrained Thailand's GDP growth to no more than 3 to 4 per cent since the coup.[5] Inevitably, the relatively weaker growth record of the junta compared to those of the Thaksin-affiliated regimes remains a political thorn in its side.[6]

Another path to legitimacy is to anoint authoritarianism with the optics of an election. At the time of writing, an election looked more likely than not, since the monarch signed into law an election bill in September, thus necessitating an election to be held between February and May 2019.[7] The Prayuth regime has given many indications that it will seek to allow a non-elected prime minister — presumably from the military — to form the government. One clear signal was the constitutional referendum in 2016 which asked voters whether they would accept an unelected prime minister, a question that received muted support of 58 per cent.[8] The constitution promulgated the following year included Article 272, which specifies that any new prime minister would need to command half the votes of a joint sitting of the 750-member legislative assembly. Assuming that the 250 junta-appointed Senate seats would lean towards a candidate from the military, he would then require only an additional 126 votes from the lower house to achieve a majority. Article 272 further specified that if no candidate within the parliament could be found, an unelected person could be chosen to fill the role. This year Prayuth has admitted to an interest in politics and commenced publicity efforts on social media, while his colleagues have sought to recruit former Pheu Thai party members to join a new party, Phalang Pracharat, which supports the appointment of a prime minister with a military background.[9]

The junta's fourth path to legitimacy is through emphasizing its role as a bulwark against the chaos, violence and instability of recent years. Some eight years ago, political division saw Bangkok paralysed, businesses burnt, and both protesters and soldiers shot. Almost from the day he assumed office, Prayuth has issued warnings that violence or chaos would delay a return to elections.[10] This particular path to legitimacy has been aided by a shift in sentiment away from democracy amongst some Thai elites, including some influential Sino-Thais, who fear a return to unrest and are hence becoming attracted to the China model of authoritarian capitalism.

Protection Pact

In his book *Ordering Power*, Dan Slater argued that Southeast Asian authoritarianism occurs when contested politics, especially urban-based movements, threaten the interests of elites. In these circumstances the elites are prepared to sacrifice freedoms and fund the expansion of the security apparatus of the state.[11] For Slater, Singapore and Malaysia were the strongest examples of authoritarian leviathans in Southeast Asia. In comparison, Thailand did not develop a strong internal security state. He argued that the forms of Cold War rural unrest in Thailand, with the communist insurgency confined to the outer provinces, did not catalyse an elite protection pact. Competition between elite factions, rather than mass insurgency movements, were the primary driver of Thailand's contested politics. Slater's research was however conducted before the unrest of Thailand's Red Shirts reached its crescendo. I propose here that there is a prima facie case that the Red Shirts' unrest of 2010 may have contributed to the development of an elite consensus on a protection pact.

Between March and May 2010, Thailand experienced severe unrest in its capital Bangkok, with significant levels of lethal violence. Hundreds of thousands of people from Thailand's Red Shirts movement seized and occupied large portions of Bangkok's governmental and commercial districts, chanting that they were *phrae* (commoners) ready to fight against the *ammat* (elites).[12] The leaders of the Red Shirts also frequently threatened and sponsored violence.[13] Amongst the protesters were black-shirted militants armed with assault rifles and M-79 grenade launchers, some of whom attacked and killed members of the security forces.[14] The occupation ended with a savage military crackdown on the protestors on 21 May 2010, resulting in the deaths of some ninety-one individuals at a Buddhist temple.[15] In the wake of the crackdown, shopping malls and department stores at the Ratchaprasong commercial district were set alight, causing billions of dollars of damage. In the view of scholar Serhat Unaldi, the Red Shirts movement was,

> … laying claim to an area whose development had been initiated by the monarchy and pursued by the monarchy and pursued further in close cooperation with Sino-Thai entrepreneurs, bureaucrats, and military dictators — a symbiotic royal commercial complex that the Red Shirts had identified as their main target.[16]

The Red Shirts movement was arguably a clearer and more serious challenge to the existing social order than in the previous periods of protests in 1973, 1976 and 1992. This time the protestors were more prepared to use violence to achieve their aims. Importantly, this uprising took place in the nation's capital city and urban centre. This raises the possibility that it is only now that Thailand is beginning to exhibit the development of a *protection pact* amongst its elites, who are prepared to support authoritarianism because of their shared fears of popular unrest. Two key pieces of evidence support this view. The first is the enhancement and enlargement of the Internal Security Operations Command (ISOC) as a tool for strengthening Thailand's internal security, while the second is the open discussion of the merits of Thailand adopting a "China model".

Repressive security is not new to Thailand, which has violently suppressed protest movements on many occasions, most notably in relation to the student protests of 1976 and 1992. However, the role of internal security agencies is becoming more pervasive and constant. In particular, the ISOC — an institutional legacy of the Cold War, previously responsible for coordinating Thailand's anti-communist operations — is currently being retooled and rearmed to become a central pillar of the Thai security state. In the post–Cold War period, ISOC's main role was limited to coordinating between the various agencies involved in overcoming the insurgency in Southern Thailand. However, in the last five years ISOC has been given a new lease of life. Soon after the 2014 coup, while the arrests and detentions of opponents of the coup were ongoing, Prayuth ordered the ISOC to use its provincial apparatus to establish reconciliation centres in every province. The ISOC also assumed authority over cyber-surveillance,[17] bypassing the police and the judiciary to shut down hundreds of websites and thousands of URLs deemed anti-royalist.

The status of the ISOC, which administratively sits within the Office of the Prime Minister and hence reports directly to the prime minister, is also being elevated through legislation. In 2017 Prayuth invoked Article 44 of the interim constitution to amend the security law regulating the ISOC. The amendment had the effect of placing an ISOC official above other non-military officials from different agencies, including the Justice and the Interior Ministries, under a unified structure at the national, regional and provincial levels.[18] To assist with its expanding remit, ISOC's budget, which declined under the Yingluck government, has been steadily increasing since the 2014 coup (Figure 1). The ISOC is increasingly becoming a general troubleshooting agency, assigned to all manner of tasks, from running polls on the popularity of the Pheu Thai Party to improving tour boat safety in Phuket.

Increasingly pervasive surveillance also points to the strengthening of Thailand's internal security apparatus. In line with global trends, Thailand has increased its surveillance of public spaces, installing a nationwide array of

FIGURE 1
Internal Security Operations Command Budget 2010–17

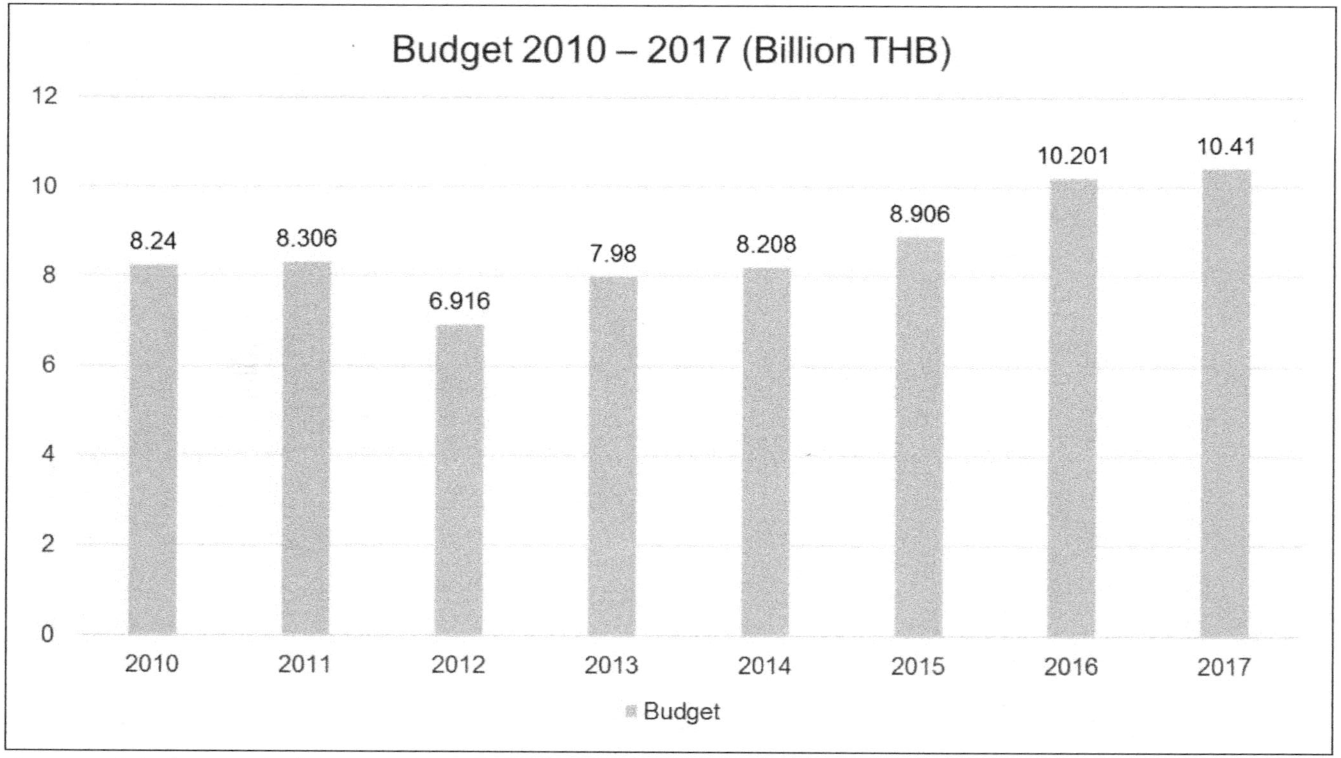

Sources: Data from budget documents available in Thai and English from the Thai Budget Bureau at <http://www.bb.go.th/en/topic3.php?gid=709&mid=456> and <http://www.bb.go.th/topic3.php?catID=1151&gid=862&mid=545> (accessed 18 October 2018).

surveillance cameras.[19] This year Thailand moved in a direction similar to China by introducing facial recognition technology into Phuket.[20] More recently the junta-appointed legislative assembly has been considering a Cyber Security and Safety Bill that would allow the monitoring of electronic communications and the seizures of computers without a warrant.[21]

The China Model

That Thailand's elites are coalescing around a protection pact is also suggested by the way which Thai elites in the political, military and banking circles have become more positive towards the idea of Thailand adopting the China model of authoritarian capitalism.[22] While China is indeed becoming more confident of its capacity to become a model for others, China does not appear to be actively promoting its model of governance to Thailand. The Thai elites will frankly admit that China does not care, such as when former prime minister Thaksin Shinawatra attested that "Whoever becomes the government, [the Chinese] do business with them. They are like entrepreneurs, they do business, they don't do politics."[23] Here, China's influence, rather than being that of a regional hegemon, may be more akin to the "authoritarian gravity centre" model posited by scholars Kneuer and Demmelhuber.[24] The analogy to gravity is deliberate; just as physical proximity matters to the strength of a gravitational force, so does its effects on the extent of authoritarian influence. Kneuer and Demmelhuber argue that authoritarian centres of gravity can exert influence, even unintentionally, on a regional basis as a result of (i) the quantity of interactions, (ii) the existence of networks and (iii) the similarities of outlook.

The shared continental geography of Southern China and mainland Southeast Asia gives rise to an increased frequency of interactions between Thailand and China. Generally speaking, ASEAN leaders interact with their Chinese counterparts through several multilateral forums, such as the ASEAN Plus Three, the ASEAN Defence Ministers Meeting Plus, the ASEAN Regional Forum, the East Asian Summit, and the Asia Pacific Economic Cooperation (APEC), to name a few. However, Thai and other mainland Southeast Asian leaders are also likely to meet with Chinese leaders, including officials from the province of Yunnan, more frequently. This is due to the many joint infrastructure projects, including road, rail and electrical networks, which are meant to link mainland Southeast Asia with Yunnan. There are also a number of sub-regional arrangements, such as the Greater Mekong Sub-region programme and Lancang Mekong Cooperation summit, which do not have similar counterparts in maritime Southeast Asia.

The special economic zones straddling the border regions are another source of interactions.

There are also networks. In Thailand's case the role of Sino-Thais in building Thailand's economic links with China has been well documented. The story of Charoen Pokhphand Group (CP), under the stewardship of Sino-Thai Dhanin Chearavanon, leading the first large foreign investment into Deng Xiaopeng's post-1979 China is popular legend. Under Dhanin, whose father emigrated from Guangdong in 1921, CP became the world's single-largest investor in China during the 1980s. The role of Sino-Thais in promoting the China model is a more recent phenomenon. Paisal Puechmongkol, a lawyer and an aide to Deputy Prime Minister Prawit Wongsuwan following the 2014 coup, is an example of a Sino-Thai who has pushed for Thailand to reorient its security and foreign policy away from the West and towards Russia and China.[25] According to scholar Kasit Tejapira, the turn of some Sino-Thais to China is not a matter of ethnic identification; rather, in the face of the West's antagonism towards Thailand's royalist-nationalist conservativism, some have started to see a China-centred order as preferable.

Finally, there have also been some similarities in outlooks towards the West. Both the Thais and Chinese perceive the West as manipulative, crusading and hypocritical. Western missteps, such as its response to the 1997 Asian financial crisis and the 2003 invasion of Iraq, have caused some disquiet. Larry Diamond recently pinpointed 2005 as the beginning of a global democracy recession.[26] The 2003 Iraq invasion may have contributed to this, Diamond suggests, because it linked the promotion of democracy with the use of military force. This resonates with the view that retired academic Thai Kien Theervit advanced in 2017:

> The United States is believed to be the champion of democracy but there isn't any other country that has done more harm to innocent people around the world. Who was the leader that deposed Saddam Hussein in Iraq, who toppled the government of Gaddaffi in Libya? Causing both these countries to fall into civil war until today. There is still Afghanistan, Syria and others. So Thais shouldn't lose themselves in a desire for democracy.[27]

Thai elites also have an abiding recollection of U.S. arrogance and disinterest in Thailand during the 1997 financial crisis. In late 1997, Dr Veerapong Ramangkura, then deputy prime minister for economic affairs, met Dr Stanley Fischer, the managing director of the International Monetary Fund (IMF). Veerapong requested for Fischer to work together with him to review the IMF-Thai deal that was then being worked out. Fischer declined, with the excuse that he had too many countries to look after. When Veerapong argued that a single formula should not be applied to every country, given their different economic and political cultures, Fischer reportedly replied, "Don't worry. The single formula can be applied all over."[28] Till today, senior Thai officials express weariness at the West's "suffocating hold" on key global organizations such as the IMF.[29]

Competing Logic: Sovereignty and Thailand's Strategic Culture

However, any serious move towards a full embrace of the China model faces large obstacles. While the movement that toppled the Yingluck government in 2014 may despise elections and view a "good society" as one in which the non-democratic institutions of the monarchy and the military are powerful,[30] the Thai population still overwhelmingly holds democracy to be the best system of government. From a sample of 1,200 Thais across the country, the 2013 World Values Survey found that 68 per cent viewed democracy as a "very good system", while 24 per cent saw it as a "good system". Army rule, on the other hand, was described as "very bad" by 30 per cent and "fairly bad" by 35 per cent. (A significant minority of 24 per cent did, however, describe the army ruling as "fairly good", while another 11 per cent described it as "very good".)[31]

Although the protection pact and the China model might have taken hold among the Thai elites, there is a stronger, older and more enduring set of security antibodies that mitigates Thailand's drift into a vassal state relationship with China. Deep in the DNA of the Thai elites is the belief that King Chulalongkorn Rama V (1868–1910) preserved Thailand's independence through his agile diplomacy, particularly through his willingness to find friends amongst many great powers. Much as the Thai elites have resented the United States for what was seen as, at best, hypocritical hectoring and, at worst, possible indications of plans for regime change, there is also quiet resolve to limit China's encroachments on Thai sovereignty. One indication is the decision to resist the offer of Chinese loans and to instead internally finance the high-speed railway connecting Nong Khai and Bangkok.[32] Thailand's bureaucrats are allergic to debt, which was one of the reasons why Yingluck's rice-pledging scheme was so detested.[33]

The reversal on improving the Mekong's navigability is another example. In 2016 the Thai Cabinet agreed to a plan to develop Mekong navigability. Subsequently, Laos, Thailand, Myanmar and China agreed to improve navigability in the Mekong to allow the passage of ships greater than five hundred tonnes. But a study conducted by some Thais in the Chiang Rai province between October

2017 and May 2018 revealed strong concerns about the removal of obstacles to improve navigability, especially in terms of its impact on the environment and the livelihoods of affected locals.[34] As a result the Thai foreign minister Don Pramudwinay announced in late January 2018 that China had agreed to halt the blasting programme. While this decision may have been prompted by environmental concerns, it may also have been motivated by the trepidation at having large Chinese vessels moving freely down the Mekong into Thai territory.

That Thailand is content with overlapping and potentially competing Mekong forums is another manifestation of the way in which Thailand pluralizes and diversifies — in other words, hedges — in order to diffuse Chinese dominance. While China would like to see the Lancang Mekong Cooperation initiative become *the* forum for developing mainland Southeast Asia and Southern China, neither Thailand nor the other members of the Mekong River Commission — Laos, Vietnam and Cambodia — have shown any indication of relinquishing the non-China Mekong forums. This year the countries used the Mekong Forum to praise the 1995 Mekong Agreement's "prior consultation process", which seeks inputs from all stakeholders before commencing any major project.[35] Together with the Cambodian prime minister Hun Sen and the other leaders, Prayuth also used the occasion to raise concerns about disaster management and the sustainability and environmental challenges facing the Mekong, including climate change and development. While the Mekong River Commission, where China is merely an observer, has minimal legal or physical leverage on China, it may still be valued for its normative potential.[36]

Then there is the proposed canal across the Isthmus of Kra in southern Thailand — a project attractive to China because it would alleviate its "Malacca Dilemma" of relying too heavily on the sea-routed trade passing through the thin strait between Malaysia and Singapore. The project is often framed as another litmus test of Thailand's accommodation of China. In 2015 there was an awkward Sino-Thai exchange when Chinese media sources announced an

TABLE 1
Mekong Region Organizations

Mekong Region Organizations without China	*Mekong Region Organizations with China*
Ayeyawady–Chao Phraya–Mekong Economic Cooperation Strategy	Greater Mekong Subregion
Mekong River Commission	Lancang Mekong Cooperation Initiative
	Safe Mekong Initiative

agreement on the project, reports which were subsequently denied strongly by the Thai government. At that time the Thai media interpreted this as China *yohn hǐn tǎam taang* — floating a test balloon to gauge Thai levels of support.[37] This year the Thai government appeared to accommodate China's interest in ordering a feasibility study.[38] Here, however, caution is warranted, since there have been more than twenty-five similar feasibility studies, without the project commencing.[39] Despite backing from well-connected groups such as the Thai Canal Association and the Thai-Chinese Culture and Economy Association, each staffed by former generals and high-profile Sino-Thais, senior Thais from General Prayuth to the former foreign minister Surakiart Sathirathai have emphasized the perception that a canal would endanger Thailand's territorial integrity by dividing the country in two.[40] It remains possible that Thailand may eventually proceed with the canal, but given these concerns, the lack of any direct economic interest, and the sensitive geopolitical ramifications, Thailand may continue to stall while avoiding a blunt rejection to China's overtures.

Finally, there are signs that the U.S.-Thai relationship is on the mend. The end of 2017 and the beginning of 2018 saw a flurry of high-level meetings, including between Prayuth and U.S. president Trump in December 2017, and the state visits to Thailand by U.S. defence secretary James Mattis, the chairman of the Joints Chiefs of Staff General Joe Dunford and the Indo-Pacific commander Harry Harris. This year's Cobra Gold exercise was also restored to full scale, with the participation of 6,800 U.S. personnel.[41] And, in an encouraging sign for future U.S.-Thai relations, the new Thai Chief of Army, General Apirat Kongsongpom, received his education and training in the United States and is reported to be pro–United States in his orientation.[42]

Defence Relations and Underbalancing

The Chulalongkorn-inspired approach of pursuing equidistance in relations with the great powers has influenced Thailand's defence policy. This leads to an underbalancing with regard to Thai military capability. Historically, and in the context of external security, Thailand has tended to rely on its military power as a diplomatic tool, rather than seeking to develop a force capable of destroying or inflicting unacceptably high costs on an adversary.[43] There is nothing in recent years to suggest that this fundamental approach has changed. While the Thai defence budget has grown following the 2014 coup, emulating a broad historical pattern in Thailand of military governments increasing defence spending, there is little to suggest that Thai military planners are perceiving increased levels of military threat. If anything, the Prayuth government has been relatively restrained, with its increases of 4.3 per cent in 2015 and 5.1 per cent in 2016, lower than those of the Surayud government, which lifted defence spending by 30.6 per cent in the first year following the 2006 coup and by 18.7 and 18.3 per cent in the subsequent two years.[44] Defence as a share of government spending in recent years has been less than a third of the figures recorded during the final decade of the Cold War, when Thailand was greatly concerned about Vietnam's occupation of neighbouring Cambodia.[45]

Furthermore, the Thai elites still see relatively little prospect of direct military threat in the current era. Between 2015 and 2017, Professor John Blaxland and I found that Thai military officers rated non-state forms of threat as more serious than state-based threats, and that they felt high levels of security with regard to external military threats.[46] They are also ambivalent with regards to China. On one hand, China's growing power is viewed with concern; on the other, China is viewed as a potential protector.[47] The memory of military cooperation which Thailand pursued with China against Vietnam in the last decade of the Cold War still shapes perceptions.

In 2018 the outcome has been the continuation of the recent trend of gradually increasing defence engagement with China, but not at the expense of maintaining military ties with the United States. Thailand's procurement of Chinese submarines reached a significant milestone in 2018 with the laying of a submarine keel in Wuhan, the capital of the Wuhan province in China.[48] This followed the announcement of plans for a jointly funded Chinese-built weapons maintenance centre in the northeastern Thai province of Khon Kaen, as well as a warehouse for spare parts of Chinese-made military equipment in the nearby province of Nakhon Ratchasima, in September 2017.[49] The progress of in-country materiel cooperation follows other recent advances such as the commencement of joint air exercises in 2015. Thailand is also procuring Chinese tanks alongside its Ukrainian ones. However, the policy of procuring from China is as much, if not more, about affordability as it is about geopolitical alignment. If judged through the lens of quantity and quality of joint exercises, the United States continues to be Thailand's primary defence partner, with upwards of fifty defence exercises annually.

The absence of pressure for reform, or even accountability, of the military, especially under a military government, is another factor contributing to underbalancing. In 2018 the defence minister General Pravit Wongsawan defended the army's demonstrable incompetence in acquiring the fake GT200 bomb-detection device, stating that "there are no lessons to be learned".[50] With internal stability, and the situation in Southern Thailand the pre-eminent security concern amongst the leadership, there is little evidence that the Thai military is undertaking any serious reform or shifting its strategic posture vis-à-vis the changing geopolitical and military balances of power in the Asia-Pacific region. Thailand has not issued a defence White Paper since 2005, and little effort has been paid towards defence transparency since the 2006 coup. Furthermore, if past experience was of any guide, the ten-year modernization plan announced in late 2017 is more likely to have been an exercise in which each service presented their desired shopping lists, rather than any rigorous analysis of future capability needs based on plausible operational scenarios.[51] Thailand's weak central control over the services means the army, navy and air force have their own independent procurement processes which have little regard for maximizing total operational capacity. That said, Thailand's defence budget is large enough for it to maintain a large, mostly well-equipped defence force, including having one of the best-equipped air forces in Southeast Asia.

Overall, it is too early to say how the rising geopolitical and geoeconomic competition between China and the United States will play out in Thailand and the region. Thailand remains seized by ASEAN's vision for a "seamlessly and comprehensively connected and integrated ASEAN that will promote competitiveness, inclusiveness, and a greater sense of Community".[52] However, the United States under the Trump administration is beginning to reject the values of liberalization, globalization, connectivity and integration, especially when it comes to China. Along with transactionalism, the United States is articulating a geoeconomic vision that seeks to exclude countries it deems to not be "genuine market economies". The dangers of great power competition are however not new to Thai calculation. Indeed, Thailand could be said to have long practised a form of geoeconomics in its use of foreign advisers from multiple countries, particularly when it sought to develop itself into a modern state at the zenith of colonialism in Southeast Asia in the late nineteenth and early twentieth centuries. The urge to "balance" — not in the sense of building stronger forces or alliances in order to counterbalance a clear and apparent threat but in terms of ensuring that great powers compete for influence in a way that prevents any one from achieving dominance — remains strong amongst Thailand's foreign policy establishment.

Conclusion

Over the past five years, the imperatives of increased trade and maintaining internal stability have opened a path for China's influence, including an embrace of the

China model of marrying political authoritarianism with free-market liberalism. But flirting with the dragon has its limits. In 2018, older and more cautious voices of foreign policy reasserted themselves. Thailand, always protective of its sovereignty and its freedom to manoeuvre, started to limit its accommodation of China's interests and began to strengthen relations with other great power partners that are able to balance the Chinese influence. While military reform and significantly increased defence spending are not on the immediate horizon, the Mekong has emerged as the locus for geopolitical shifts and as a test case for managing China's dominance. In this respect, the pragmatism of the Trump administration's foreign policy has offered a welcome opportunity to move on from the rancour that marked the U.S.-Thai relationship in the aftermath of the May 2014 coup. What are the implications for the Thai military? The shift to a more repressive authoritarian model of statehood means the Thai military leadership is becoming increasingly entangled in internal security, especially through the growing role of ISOC. Moreover, with the military's continuing hold on the levers of power, it remains shielded from pressures to reform. While China's steady growth in military power may cause some concerns among Thai military planners, their long-term tendency to underbalance should remain.

Notes

1. "Airport Guard's Assault Attempt on Chinese Tourist Worries Prayut", *Bangkok Post*, 30 September 2018 <https://www.bangkokpost.com/news/general/1549490/airport-guards-assault-attempt-on-chinese-tourist-worries-prayut>.
2. See, for example, "Thai King Maha Vajiralongkorn Granted Full Ownership of Crown Billions, *Straits Times*, 16 June 2018 <https://www.straitstimes.com/asia/se-asia/thai-king-maha-vajiralongkorn-granted-full-ownership-of-crown-billions> (accessed 17 June 2018).
3. เศรษฐกิจกับผลเลือกตั้ง? [The economy and the election results?], editorial, *Thai Rath*, 18 August 2018 <https://www.thairath.co.th/content/1356409> (accessed 3 September 2018).
4. ชู "อีอีซี" เชื่อมศก.ไทย-จีน หอฯหนุนพัฒนาเมืองรอง" [Uphold the EEC, connect Thai and Chinese industry — China Thai Trade Council supports developing secondary cities], *Matichon*, 17 March 2018, p. 9.
5. Thitinan Pongsudhirak, "Thai Politics under a New Reign", *East Asia Forum*, 4 September 2018 <http://www.eastasiaforum.org/2018/09/04/thai-politics-under-a-new-reign/> (accessed 18 October 2018).
6. "Poor Economy on Top of Public Complaints: Suan Dusit Poll", *Bangkok Post*, 3 June 2018 <https://www.bangkokpost.com/news/general/1478025/poor-economy-heads-public-complaints-suan-dusit-pollon> (accessed 4 June 2018).

7. "Election Bill Enacted, Paving Way for 2019 Poll", *Khaosod English*, 12 September 2018 <http://www.khaosodenglish.com/politics/2018/09/12/election-bill-enacted-paving-way-for-2019-poll/> (14 September 2018).
8. Duncan McCargo, Saowanee T. Alexander and Petra Desatova, "Ordering Peace: Thailand's 2016 Constitutional Referendum", *Contemporary Southeast Asia* 39, no. 1 (April 2017): 81.
9. "Ministers Tipped to Join 'Regime Party' ", *Bangkok Post*, 22 September 2018 <https://www.bangkokpost.com/news/general/1544382/ministers-tipped-to-join-regime-party> (accessed 23 September 2018).
10. "Attacks Could Delay Election, PM Says", *Bangkok Post*, 24 May 2017 <https://www.pressreader.com/thailand/bangkok-post/20170524/281479276357521> (26 October 2018).
11. Dan Slater, *Ordering Power: Contentious Politics and Authoritarian Leviathans in Southeast Asia* (New York: Cambridge University Press, 2010).
12. Anonymous, "Anti-Royalism in Thailand Since 2006: Ideological Shifts and Resistance", *Journal of Contemporary Asia* 48, no. 3 (2018) 363–94 <https://doi.org/ 10.1080/00472336.2018.1427021>.
13. Human Rights Watch, "Descent into Chaos: Thailand's 2010 Red Shirt Protests and the Government Crackdown" (New York: Human Rights Watch, 2011).
14. "Q+A: Who are Thailand's Mysterious Black-Clad Gunmen?", Reuters, 27 April 2010 <https://www.reuters.com/article/us-thailand-politics-gunmen/qa-who-are-thailands-mysterious-black-clad-gunmen-idUSTRE63Q1F220100427> (18 October 2018).
15. "Hundreds in Bangkok Mark the Anniversary of Army Crackdown", Reuters, 20 May 2019 <https://www.reuters.com/article/us-thailand-politics/hundreds-in-bangkok-mark-anniversary-of-army-crackdown-idUSKCN1IK0JT> (22 October 2018).
16. Serhat Unaldi S., *Working Towards the Monarchy: The Politics of Space in Downtown Bangkok* (Honolulu: University of Hawai'i Press, 2016), p. 137.
17. Puangthong R. Pawakapan, *The Central Role of Thailand's Internal Security Operations Command in the Post-Counter-insurgency Period*, Trends in Southeast Asia 2017, no. 17 (Singapore: ISEAS – Yusof Ishak Institute, 2017), p. 5.
18. "Thailand: Sinister Motive Seen in Move to Empower Isoc", *Asia News*, 23 November 2017 <http://annx.asianews.network/content/thailand-sinister-motive-seen-move-empower-isoc-61697> (10 October 2018).
19. "Govt to Link 367,000 Spy Cameras Nationwide", *Bangkok Post*, 12 January 2018 <https://www.bangkokpost.com/news/security/1394766/govt-to-link-367-000-spy-cameras-nationwide>.
20. "Thailand to Use Facial Recognition in Safe City Project", *EGov Innovation*, 1 January 2018 <https://www.enterpriseinnovation.net/article/thailand-use-facial-recognition-safe-city-project-1275110759?utm_source=addthis&utm_medium=website&utm_campaign=SocialMedia#.Wkr7V_F-XQ0.twitter> (accessed 8 October 2018).

21. ต้องไม่ขัดกฎหมายสูงสุด [Must not contravene the highest law], *Thai Rath*, 19 October 2018 <https://www.thairath.co.th/content/1398862> (accessed 22 October 2018).
22. Benjamin Zawacki, *Thailand Shifting Ground between the US and a Rising China* (London: Zed Books, 2017), pp. 297–99.
23. Ibid., p. 299.
24. Marianne Kneuer and Thomas Demmelhuber, "Gravity Centres of Authoritarian Rule: A Conceptual Approach", *Democratization* 23, no. 5 (2016) 775–96 <https://doi.org/10.1080/13510347.2015.1018898>.
25. Kasian Tejapira, "The Sino-Thais' Right Turn towards China", *Critical Asian Studies* 49, no. 4 (October 2017). This is far from a uniform leaning. My research with John Blaxland suggests that the strong socialization of the military homogenizes differences between Sino-Thai and non-Sino-Thai military officers when it comes to attitudes on foreign and defence policy, including towards the great powers. John Blaxland and Greg Raymond, "Tipping the Balance in Southeast Asia? Thailand, the United States and China", Centre of Gravity Series (Strategic & Defence Studies Centre, ANU College of Asia & the Pacific, November 2017), pp. 12–13.
26. Larry Diamond, "The Future of Democracy: What It Means for China, the West and the Rest' A Dream Thailand", public lecture and panel discussion, 23 August 2018, Chulalongkorn University <https://www.youtube.com/watch?v=ayV70usUvTY&feature=youtu.be> (accessed 20 September 2018).
27. Khien Teerawit, "Nayok khonnok pen khonthai reu plao?" [Is an outsider PM a Thai or not?]. *Thaipost*, 23 August 2016, as cited in Kasian, "The Sino-Thais' ", p. 9.
28. Kasian, "The Sino-Thais' ", p. 5.
29. "Prescriptions for ASEAN and Thailand: Better Governance, Stronger Institutions", *Nikkei Asian Review*, 28 August 2018 <https://asia.nikkei.com/Economy/Korn-Chatikavanij-Prescriptions-for-Asean-and-Thailand-Better-governance-stronger-institutions> (accessed 20 April 2018).
30. Max Grömping and Aim Sinpeng, "The 'Crowd-factor' in Connective Action: Comparing Protest Communication Styles of Thai Facebook Pages", *Journal of Information Technology & Politics* 15, no. 3 (2018): 202 <https://doi.org/10.1080/19331681.2018.1483857>.
31. R. Inglehart, C. Haerpfer, A. Moreno, C. Welzel, K. Kizilova, J. Diez-Medrano, M. Lagos, et al., eds., "World Values Survey: Round Six — Country-Pooled Datafile Version" (Madrid: JD Systems Institute, 2014), p. 12 <http://www.worldvaluessurvey.org/WVSDocumentationWV6.jsp>.
32. Pongphisoot Busbarat, "Thailand in 2017: Stability without Certainties", in *Southeast Asian Affairs 2018*, edited by Malcolm Cook and Daljit Singh (Singapore: ISEAS – Yusof Ishak Institute, 2018), p. 356.
33. William J. Siffin, *The Thai Bureaucracy: Institutional Change and Development* (Honolulu: East-West Center Press, 1966).

34. รมค้านระเบดแก่งเปิดเดินเรือน้ำโขง [Opposition to blasting rapids to open passage of ships in Mekong], *Post Today*, 6 March 2018, p. B12.
35. "Pact Calls for Talks before Major Mekong Projects", *The Nation*, 6 April 2018, p. 5A.
36. "Mekong River Conference Hears of Determination to Work with LMC", *The Nation*, 3 April 2018, p. 5A.
37. จีนรุกไทยขุดคอคอดกระเพิ่มอำนาจมั่นคงมั่งคั่ง [China invades Thailand to build the Kra Canal to increase power security and prosperity], *Manager Weekly*, 10 October 2015, p. 8.
38. "Kra Phoenix Rises Again", *Bangkok Post*, 13 February 2018 <https://www.bangkokpost.com/opinion/opinion/1411502/kra-phoenix-rises-again>.
39. Zawacki, "Thailand Shifting Ground", p. 313.
40. Surakiart, quoted in ibid.; จิ๋โต้ไม่เกี่ยวคอคอดกระ [Chaovalit rejects involvement in Isthmus of Kra Project], *Khao Sot*, 23 May 2015, p. 9.
41. "Pentagon Steps up its Diplomacy in Thailand", *Asia Times*, 8 February <http://www.atimes.com/article/pentagon-steps-diplomacy-thailand/> (accessed 20 September 2018).
42. เปิดประวัติ "พล.อ.อภิรัชต์ คงสมพงษ์" ผบ.ทบ.คนล่าสุด [Biography of General Apirat Kongsongpom, latest army commander], *Manager Online* <https://mgronline.com/onlinesection/detail/9610000103838> (accessed 19 October 2018); "Thailand Mends US Military Ties, Rebalance after China Tilt, Most Probable New Thai Army Chief Staunchly pro-American", *Nikkei Asian Review*, 30 July 2018 <https://asia.nikkei.com/Politics/International-Relations/Thailand-mends-US-military-ties-rebalance-after-China-tilt>.
43. For elaboration of this argument, see Gregory V. Raymond, *Thai Military Power: A Culture of Strategic Accommodation* (Copenhagen: NIAS Press, 2018).
44. Defence Intelligence Organisation, *Defence Economic Trends in the Asia Pacific 2017* (Canberra: Commonwealth of Australia, 2017), p. 24. All figures are real growth rates.
45. Raymond, *Thai Military Power*, p. 217.
46. John Blaxland and Greg Raymond, "Tipping the Balance in Southeast Asia? Thailand, the United States and China", Centre of Gravity Series, Strategic & Defence Studies Centre, ANU College of Asia & the Pacific, November 2017, pp. 7–8.
47. Ibid., pp. 6, 12.
48. "Chinese Shipbuilder Starts Work on US$411 Million Submarine for Thai Navy", *South China Morning Post*, 5 September 2018 <https://www.scmp.com/news/china/military/article/2162944/chinese-shipbuilder-starts-work-us411-million-submarine-thai> (accessed 23 October 2018). Thailand contracted for a single submarine in May 2017 for US$411 million.
49. "Russia Courts Southeast Asian Partners with Authoritarian Streaks, Putin Looks to

Capitalize on Wariness of China and the West", *Nikkei Asian Review*, 16 January 2018 <https://asia.nikkei.com/Politics-Economy/International-Relations/Russia-courts-Southeast-Asian-partners-with-authoritarian-streaks?n_cid=NARAN012> (accessed 20 September 2018).

50. Tweet by *Bangkok Post* journalist @wassanaNanuam, 26 September 2018, 8:55 p.m. (accessed 26 October 2018).
51. "Thailand's Expanding Military Capability Advances Modernisation Programme", *Asian Military Review*, 1 November 2017 <https://asianmilitaryreview.com/2017/11/thailands-expanding-military-capability-advances-modernisation-programme/> (24 October 2018).
52. ASEAN Secretariat, "Master Plan on ASEAN Connectivity 2025", ASEAN Secretariat, Jakarta, November 2016, p. 39.

Timor-Leste

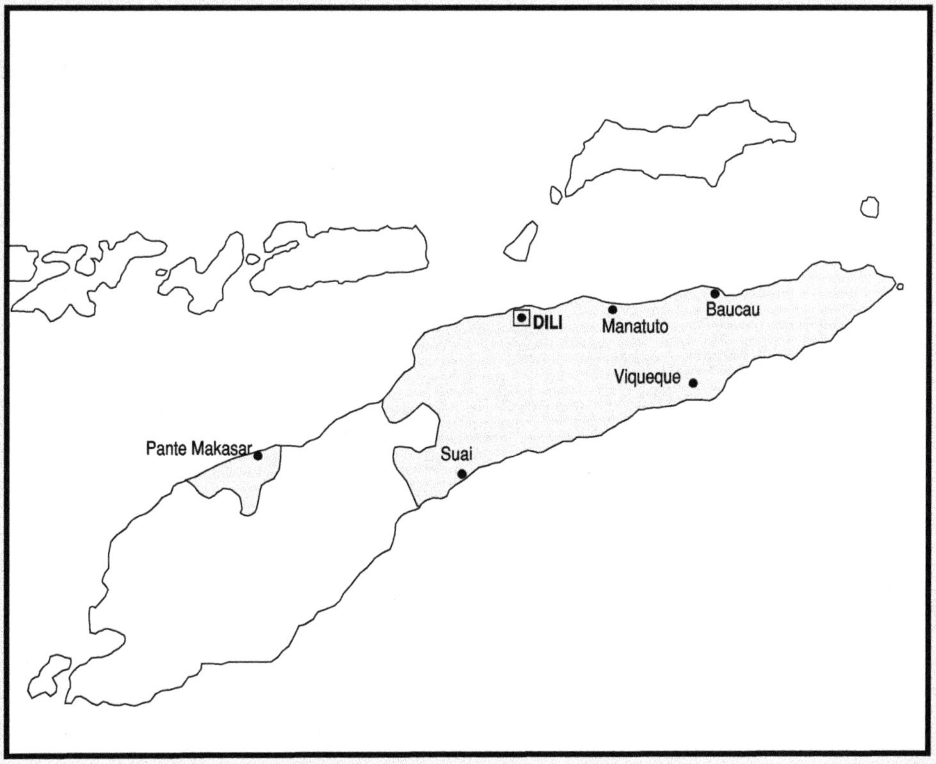

TIMOR-LESTE IN 2018: An Eventful Year Ends in Tension

Michael Leach

From 25 January, when the president announced an early election for 12 May, it was clear 2018 would prove an eventful political year in Timor-Leste. The May election followed a nine-month Fretilin-led minority government that proved unable to steer its programme and budget through parliament, as the opposition parties formed a majority bloc a month after the government was installed. The election brought the Xanana Gusmão–led Alliance for Change and Progress (AMP) coalition back into office. Having taken power, the new government soon found itself mired in a standoff over ministerial appointments with the president, Fretilin's Francisco Guterres, in the first genuine experience of cohabitation under Timor-Leste's semi-presidential system. The year also saw an historic agreement between Timor-Leste and Australia that fixed maritime boundaries at the median line in the Timor Sea,[1] thus ending a long-running dispute between the two nations. The year was capped off by the government outlining its bold vision for resource sovereignty, and its plan to purchase a majority share in the Greater Sunrise joint venture in order to advance its ambitious vision of downstream processing of oil and gas on the East Timorese south coast.

The End of the Minority Government

The 2017 election saw the opposition Fretilin party emerge narrowly ahead of the CNRT on seats but unable to form a majority alliance. With no alternative majority coalition then being proposed, in September President Guterres appointed the first

---

MICHAEL LEACH is Professor of Politics and International Relations at Swinburne University of Technology, Melbourne, Australia. He has researched and published widely on the politics and history of Timor-Leste and is the author of *Nation Building and National Identity in Timor-Leste* (2016). He is co-founder of the Timor-Leste Studies Association (www.tlstudies.org/).

minority government in Timor-Leste's short constitutional history: a thirty-seat minority coalition with the Democratic Party. But events moved rapidly and a political stand-off emerged in October when three opposition parties, the National Congress for Timorese Reconstruction (CNRT), the Popular Liberation Party (PLP) and Kmanek Haburas Unidade Nasional Timor Oan (KHUNTO), together controlling thirty-five of parliament's sixty-five seats, rejected the government's programme.

Having failed to pass a budget rectification measure needed to fund new ministries and programmes, the state reverted to a "duodecimal" system based on monthly allocation of the previous year's budget. This extended use of this reserve budget system lasted until a new budget was passed in September 2018, depressing the economy, which remains heavily reliant on government-led expenditure. Rather than installing the opposition AMP alliance as the government, President Guterres announced a new election, with the Fretilin–Democratic Party executive acting as a caretaker government in the meantime.

Maritime Boundary Negotiations with Australia

Meanwhile, in the realm of international relations, maritime boundary negotiations with Australia continued, under the aegis of a UN Convention on the Law of the Sea (UNCLOS) compulsory conciliation process, triggered by Timor-Leste. Following twelve months of negotiations that saw "confidence-building measures" enacted, including the termination of the CMATS treaty (which purported to delay maritime boundary determination for fifty years) and Timor-Leste's cessation of a separate espionage case against Australia, Timor-Leste and Australia jointly declared they had reached an agreement on "central aspects" of a maritime-boundary determination in late 2017.[2]

Revealed on 6 March 2018, the agreement, when ratified by both parties, will create permanent maritime boundaries and revised resource-sharing arrangements in the yet-to-be-developed Greater Sunrise oil and gas field.[3] Timor-Leste also secured a median-line boundary in the Timor Gap, creating a permanent maritime boundary for the first time. The median-line boundary will place 100 per cent of the existing Joint Petroleum Development Area (JDPA) in Timor-Leste's waters, whereas current treaties divided the revenue 90-to-10 in its favour. As these fields are nearing the end of their life, far more financially significant is the renegotiated revenue split over the as-yet-untapped Greater Sunrise field, worth in excess of $40 billion, which straddles the eastern lateral (or side) boundary of the JDPA.

The renegotiated agreement saw a substantial increase in Timor-Leste's share of the future Greater Sunrise revenues from 50 per cent to 70 or 80 per cent, pending resolution of the final contested issue of whether the pipeline for downstream processing will land in Australia or Timor-Leste. The higher revenue figure would operate in the event that Timor-Leste does not achieve its goal of sending the pipeline to the southern cost of Timor.

Despite these successes, which vindicated the East Timorese use of the UN Convention on the Law of the Sea conciliation process, chief negotiator Xanana Gusmão remained unhappy at the failure to secure a pipeline to the East Timorese coast, a development vision he had championed for years. Advancing the government vision for "downstream processing" remained a key focus of the government throughout 2018. Despite this aspect of the issue remaining unresolved, the historic treaty marked the end of a key stumbling block in the Australia–Timor-Leste relationship, opening the way for a major resetting of the troubled bilateral relationship, and ministerial visits soon resumed — the first in five years.

2018 Parliamentary Elections

Unlike the 2017 elections, parliamentary elections in 2018 delivered a decisive result. The AMP, by now a coalition of three parties combining CNRT, PLP and KHUNTO, won 49.6 per cent of the national vote, delivering thirty-four out of sixty-five seats and winning a narrow majority in its own right. In Timor-Leste's proportional system, where outright majorities are uncommon, this was a strong vindication of the decision to combine the forces of Gusmão's CNRT with Taur Matan Ruak's PLP and the smaller, youth-focused party, KHUNTO, in a formal pre-election coalition.

While the AMP achieved a swing of 3.1 per cent on its collective 2017 results, the entry of a new, smaller coalition, the Democratic Development Forum (FDD), saw the AMP's collective tally of seats fall by one from the previous sitting. Fretilin received 34.2 per cent of the national vote, and twenty-three seats, maintaining its 2017 seat tally. This represented a substantial swing of 4.5 per cent, the first major swing towards the party since 2007, though it proved insufficient to overcome the formidable AMP coalition. The Democratic Party was also back in parliament with five seats (down from seven in 2017), and the new FDD coalition secured three — though this smaller alliance soon split, with one of its MPs clearly more favourable to the Fretilin opposition. This left the government with a simple majority in its own right, but without the two-thirds "supermajority" necessary for the reversal of certain presidential vetoes.

The 2018 campaign was marked by a high level of polarization and by the resurgence of the "history wars", the ongoing clashes between the two wings of the East Timorese resistance active during the Indonesian occupation. The AMP reunited Xanana Gusmão and his CNRT with former president Taur Matan Ruak's Popular Liberation Party, both of which were at loggerheads during the 2017 election. Both were former leaders of the armed resistance Falintil. The 2018 campaign was frequently depicted as a contest between the military front and members of the diplomatic front, who were outside the country during the occupation, including Prime Minister Alkatiri and key diplomatic figure Jose Ramos-Horta, who had thrown his weight behind the Fretilin campaign. A series of campaign attacks sought to diminish the contribution of those who struggled for independence in the international arena, instead emphasizing the greater suffering endured by those within the territory during the occupation.

This division over resistance history lent an unpleasant air to a campaign also marked by exchanges of personal slurs between the major party leaders, including some outbursts of anti-Muslim sentiment directed at the Fretilin leader Mari Alkatiri and fractious personal debates on Facebook. Civil society called for a new focus on policies rather than personalities and for parties to refrain from personal attacks.[4]

Election day passed without major incident, though comments from Gusmão on the day that he "would not accept the result if it was not fair" were unhelpful; these built on a series of complaints from the AMP in the campaign that were not backed by strong evidence. In its preliminary report, the largest observer mission referred to the "injudicious and inappropriate language of some political representatives" and noted that allegations about the election process are "serious in character and, if made, need to be supported by evidence".[5] After the ballot, Fretilin raised similar concerns over the vote in Oecusse, the only district in which its vote had dropped, again without immediately offering compelling evidence. This outcome was particularly interesting as Fretilin had been in charge of the Special Zones of Social Market Economy project: a major national development project in the East Timorese enclave of Oecusse. Despite these complaints, Timor-Leste's two electoral agencies again did an excellent job in the face of the pressure of the re-run campaign and limited budgets.

Cohabitation Tensions

Despite leading a smaller party, Ruak was appointed prime minister in June, with the CNRT leader Gusmão proposed as minister of state advising the prime minister. The decisive result of the May elections and the AMP's clear majority looked set to provide for stability and a much-needed budget.

However, the first experience of genuine "cohabitation" in the semi-presidential system between a Fretilin president and an AMP government disrupted these early projections, revealing the extent of presidential power in Timor-Leste's system, and causing problems for the governing coalition.

Tensions first came to a head in June as President Guterres refused the appointments of twelve of the forty-one proposed ministers in the new government, citing judicial inquiries into misconduct or "poor moral standing", including two current court processes.[6] The sole nominee associated with the PLP was a strictly bureaucratic matter requiring a resignation from the military, and was soon resolved, reducing the list to eleven. The remainder of the refused ministerial nominees were dominated by CNRT figures, while two were from KHUNTO.

Though Gusmão was not among them, the CNRT leader boycotted the swearing-in ceremony in protest, accusing the president of "unprecedented, unusual, seditious and politicized" behaviour by not swearing in the full suite of government members.[7] Another ministerial nominee boycotted the ceremony, though not all CNRT ministers did. President Guterres stated that he had asked the prime minister to review the names in light of the evidence provided, arguing that such nominations might undermine public faith in the government. Gusmão responded by releasing a statement signed by a judge that nine of the impugned nominees had no current charges pending, and agreed to replace the two nominees facing current court processes. This was a reasonable step, which distinguished between actual and potential charges, but had the unfortunate political side effect of adding detail to the nature of accusations against the would-be ministers, though some involved matters unrelated to corruption. Soon after, the parliament denied the president permission to travel on a scheduled state visit to Portugal. While it was argued that business of state made the trip untimely, it was another clear sign of cohabitation tensions. Seizing on the politics of the moment, Fretilin reintroduced a 2014 anti-corruption bill into parliament on 10 July.

The CNRT then threatened action against the president if he did not install the ministers within ten days. But, with Timor-Leste's equivalent of impeachment also requiring a two-thirds majority vote of parliament, it remained unclear how this would be done. No such action was ultimately taken. In a further development, the president refused to immediately pass emergency budget measures to draw US$140 million from the Petroleum fund to top up state coffers for July and August, referring the matter to the Court of Appeal to test its constitutionality. The government argued this measure was necessary to address slowdown in the economy as a result of emergency budget measures in place since early 2017, and the court ultimately approved the withdrawal.

By the end of the year, the institutional standoff, primarily involving CNRT members, was in its sixth month. Some former ministers have instead been working as senior advisers, and parliament has responded to the president's action by repeatedly denying his travel requests. The standoff gave the new government a curiously dual character. On the one hand, its normal business was being carried on by an incomplete ministry over-represented by figures from the minor alliance parties, PLP and KHUNTO. On the other, a powerful group of CNRT figures without formal portfolios, led by Gusmão, has been primarily concerned with advancing the Greater Sunrise project.

Presidential Power

These events cast new light on presidential power in Timor-Leste, which has frequently been underestimated, and has to some degree remained latent until this present situation of formal cohabitation, owing to the election of non-partisan presidents in previous years. Though former presidents have used their veto powers, and have been highly critical of government agendas, this was the first time the two major parties have faced off in this way. While presidential vetoes of legislation are reversible by parliament (vetoes of executive decree laws are absolute), many substantive policy areas require a two-thirds parliamentary majority for reversal, making the power far more substantial than it appears at first blush. While former president Ruak was often highly critical of the former national unity government from 2015 to 2017, which integrated ministers from Fretilin into the CNRT-dominated government, he faced a parliament controlling more than two-thirds of the seats, thus limiting his veto capacity. However, despite losing government, Fretilin's twenty-three seats proved just enough to deny the rest of the parliament a two-thirds majority. This means the possibility of a presidential veto in many areas would be an ongoing reality for the new AMP government.

While it is possible that Timor-Leste's Court of Appeal could one day review Guterres' actions over ministerial appointments, it appears more likely they will remain as unreviewable political decisions,[8] ones for which the president is ultimately accountable for at elections, and which can only be resolved through discussions with the prime minister. As to the wider politics of the stand-off, it was notable that there was little public clamour in support of the rejected ministerial nominees. Even some military veterans traditionally supportive of Gusmão argued that investigations can take time to get to court, and formal charges should not therefore be needed to disqualify certain nominees from senior positions of public trust. Clearly, Guterres was not afraid to exercise such powers as the president possesses, and regarded his own role as the guarantor of national institutions, a position for which there is some constitutional support in Articles 74 and 107. He also justified his position as one which protects the judicial system by preventing ministerial immunity for impugned nominees. The government countered that this violates the presumption of innocence and the separation of powers. By the end of the year, this latter view would receive unexpected support from former president Ramos-Horta.[9]

Whatever the outcome of the president's actions, it was clear by June 2018 that Gusmão's support of Guterres in 2017 — the final expression of major party cooperation from the "national unity government" era — had been a major political miscalculation. The appointment of Ruak as prime minister was a popular one, which solidified the alliance, but also meant the president had no ongoing constitutional obligation to talk to the CNRT's leader.

The AMP in Power

Despite this standoff, the government had important wins. Its budget for the remainder of 2018 passed through parliament in early September, ending the recurrent "twelfths" system, which had contributed to a flattening of the economy. The Court of Appeal also found the government's withdrawal from the petroleum fund — which kicked off this process — to be constitutional. The AMP's return to the new school curriculum, which prioritizes Tetun literacy in the early school years and introduces Portuguese language later, was also broadly welcomed, after this move had been briefly reversed by the Fretilin government. This approach accords more strongly with the educational evidence, which strongly suggests this staging is more likely to produce improved fluency in both official languages.

But the government also faced renewed student protests over MPs' new Prado cars in late 2018, with such vehicles being a common focus of grass-roots concern over waste and inequality. Associated protests by the University Students Movement were met with heavy-handed policing from a force that was already under a cloud after an off-duty policeman killed three and wounded others at a party.[10] The incident highlighted the lax enforcement of rules prohibiting the possession of guns when off-duty, which must be addressed.

Above all, 2018 saw the AMP government focus its energies on advancing Gusmão's ambitious plan to bring oil and gas from the Greater Sunrise field to

Timor for downstream processing. The government believes this will maximize the economic and social returns from the project: above and beyond the country's increased share of Greater Sunrise revenues, which has risen from 50 per cent to at least 70 per cent since the deal was struck with Australia. Planned major infrastructure projects along the south coast, collectively known as Tasi Mane, are still at an early stage.

As such, despite the commitment of the PLP to greater spending on education and health, the 2018 budget was still largely focussed on infrastructure spending. This focus on resource processing was also reflected in the government's proposed US$2.1 billion budget for 2019, passed by parliament in December. More than a third of the 2019 budget was devoted to Tasi Mane infrastructure works and joint venture acquisition costs. Key items include the proposed purchase of Conoco Philips's stake in Greater Sunrise Joint Venture for US$350 million, along with the buyout of Shell Australia's share for US$300 million. If these purchases are ultimately approved, Timor-Leste would have a 56 per cent stake in the joint venture. The plan is controversial among sectors of East Timorese civil society worried that the costs will outweigh the benefits.[11] But the government predicts greatly increased returns, and appears to be having some success in stirring nationalist support for its vision of increased resource sovereignty.

As a preliminary step, the government made changes to the Petroleum Activities Law to lift the legislated 20 per cent limit on state ownership. A presidential veto challenged that move in December, though Guterres' justification focused primarily on the financial sustainability of the nation's petroleum fund, and he objected also to some retrospective measures in the legislation. Some local non-governmental organizations (NGOs) believe that the 20 per cent limit was unenforceable anyway, and that the recent changes to the law were instead aimed at reducing the capacity of Timor-Leste's Audit Court to review large contracts — an accusation the government denies.[12] The Audit Court has certainly proved the most active and able of the East Timorese watchdogs, previously overturning a contested US$720 million contract for constructing the supply base in Suai.

Parliament successfully reversed this veto on 10 January 2019, as Fretilin staged a parliamentary walkout: allowing the government a rare opportunity to assemble two-thirds of those present (and rendering moot the question of whether a supermajority was in fact needed for this legislation). Opposition members of parliament later referred the reaffirmed Petroleum Activities Law legislation to the Court of Appeal to test its constitutionality. The court was still considering this decision at the time of writing.

In the meantime, President Guterres vetoed the 2019 budget on 23 January, arguing that it was "gravely" unsustainable and drew too heavily on the principal reserves of Timor-Leste's sovereign wealth fund. This action potentially placed the Greater Sunrise joint venture payments in jeopardy, as Fretilin could deny the government the parliamentary supermajority needed to reverse the budget veto. This potential for a presidential block to a major government agenda therefore left a central tension brewing in the political system. However, this tension was soon resolved, at least for the short term, when parliament revised the budget down to US$1.4 billion on 31 January, by removing the $650 million joint venture payment. The government did this as it now appeared confident it could use the Petroleum Fund itself as the source of the payment, having altered the fund's investment rules in the recent Petroleum Activities Law amendments. If however the court finds those amendments unconstitutional, the government will be without the means to pay for the purchases and could face penalty contract charges.

Resource Sovereignty

More positively for the government, the politics of this issue appeared to be travelling broadly in its favour, with all parties offering in-principle backing for a pipeline to Timor-Leste. Fretilin maintained that it supports the downstream processing vision but opposes alterations to petroleum fund governance and wants the cost-benefit analysis made public. Some NGOs strongly question the wisdom of the megaproject, and fear the sovereign wealth fund of US$17 billion could be depleted even sooner than projected. The balance, they point out, dropped a record US$680 million in October.[13]

A presentation by Xanana Gusmão in December outlined the broad strokes of this vision. He revealed government modelling which estimated costs in the order of US$10.5 billion, 80 per cent of which would be sourced from joint venture partners, loans or other financing. Claimed returns from the project under government modelling are in the order of US$28 billion to US$54 billion above the return from a simple revenue split, depending on capital and operational expenditures and oil and gas prices. East Timorese NGOs countered that the government's investment could instead cost up to US$14 billion and that price assumptions and external financing are uncertain. They are also worried that the project will rapidly deplete the petroleum fund, the interest from which is intended to subsidize annual budgets into the future.

Where the majority of funds for the massive Tasi Mane project will come from is now an even more critical question. As NGOs have pointed out, becoming a joint-venture partner exposes Timor-Leste to an equivalent share of the massive capital development costs. The government counters that the joint venture partnership will also bring new income streams beyond the revenue split negotiated between the countries, including extra tax revenue and returns on capital expenditure. These form the basis of the government's revenue projections.

While Fretilin leader Mari Alkatiri and President Guterres were notable absences from the presentation in December, the vision drew support from José Ramos-Horta (though he expressed concern over amending the petroleum activities law). Ramos-Horta also tactfully urged dialogue between the government, president and opposition. While the president appeared to get the best of the furore over ministerial appointments, the government was having more success in framing the oil and gas issue as one of national pride and resource sovereignty, which complicates the terrain for critics of the Tasi Mane megaproject.

While the revised 2019 budget was promulgated by the president on 7 February 2019, he remained openly critical of the relatively low expenditures on basic development indicators. Here the government had some vulnerability, as the 2019 budget proposed a modest increase of just $11 million in education spending, with health and agriculture spending remaining essentially static,[14] despite being declared "budget priorities" by the government. This suggests that the PLP has had relatively little success pushing its policy agenda within the coalition, despite holding the prime ministership. On the other hand, business groups remain deeply concerned about the economic impact of a return to a recurrent budget system, as the economy remains heavily dependent on government expenditures of oil and gas revenues.[15] This factor clearly placed additional pressure on the president to pass the budget.

The wider politics of the East Timorese government's vision of resource sovereignty are significant. It rejects the presumption that downstream processing is the natural preserve of more developed countries — a powerful argument capable of recruiting strong nationalist support. Gusmão already has a strong track record in promoting international organizations like the G7-Plus, which call for developing countries to lead their own development strategies and recruit donor support on that basis.

Beyond its bold forecast of greatly increased returns, the government's vision of resource sovereignty is also a potent potential nationalist motif to mobilize political support, including for future election campaigns. Likewise, it may see longer-term political benefits in providing jobs and training in Tasi Mane, even if projected returns from resources projects are lower than anticipated. In contrast to the civil society focus on bottom line costs to the economy and Petroleum Fund, the calculus may not be a simple economic one for the government.

For Timor-Leste's neighbours, the larger question concerns the likely partners to fund the majority of the project. The prospect of China's involvement obviously raises great concerns in Canberra, and while there is no hard evidence of Chinese interest, the question of how the government would finance the remaining 80 per cent remains unclear. Notably, the contract for a new digital television network went to a Chinese company in December.[16]

As 2018 drew to a close, political tensions were rising again in Dili. The ongoing clash between a determined government agenda and presidential veto powers suggested that a new election in 2019 could not be ruled out, especially if government Petroleum Law amendments were found unconstitutional. For the government, the prospect of winning one more seat and removing Fretilin's block on a parliamentary supermajority, weakening President Guterres' veto power, may prove appealing if the Greater Sunrise vision were somehow thwarted. Though elections are formally in the president's hands, any protracted institutional standoff over this agenda may leave few other solutions. However, given the uncertainty that any new election would resolve the institutional standoff, a compromise over ministerial appointments and dialogue between the parties might prove the real solution, something former president Ramos-Horta, who openly supported Fretilin and the Democratic Party in 2018, called for as the year ended.[17]

Notes

1. Michael Leach, "Timor-Leste: Architect of its Own Sunrise", *Inside Story*, 8 March 2018 <https://insidestory.org.au/timor-leste-architect-of-its-own-sunrise/>.
2. Permanent Court of Arbitration, "Conciliation between the Democratic Republic of Timor-Leste and the Commonwealth of Australia", press release, 1 September 2017 <https://pcacases.com/web/sendAttach/2230>.
3. Permanent Court of Arbitration, "Timor-Leste and Australia Sign New Maritime Boundaries Treaty", press release, 8 March 2018 <https://pcacases.com/web/sendAttach/2230>.
4. Fundasaun Mahein, "Policies over Personalities", 5 April 2018 <http://www.fundasaunmahein.org/2018/04/05/policies-over-personalities/>.
5. Australia Timor-Leste Election Observer Mission, "Australia Timor-Leste Election Observer Mission 2018 Report", 17 May 2018 <https://blogs.deakin.edu.au/deakin-speaking/2018/05/17/australia-timor-leste-election-observer-mission-2018-report/>.
6. Jose Belo, "New Timor-Leste Govt Beset with Problems as Gusmão Walks Away,

La Croix International, 27 July 2018 <https://international.la-croix.com/news/new-timor-leste-govt-beset-with-problems-as-gusmao-walks-away/8158>.

7. Lusa, "Xanana Gusmão Criticizes East Timor President for Government Appointment Criteria", 23 June 2018 <https://www.plataformamedia.com/en-uk/news/politics/interior/xanana-gusmao-criticizes-east-timor-president-for-government-appointment-criteria-9497191.html>.
8. Rui Graça Feijó, "Timor-Leste — 'Belligerent Cohabitation' at Work", 25 July 2018 <https://presidential-power.com/?p=8491>.
9. "Eis PM Ramos-Horta: Rai ida ne'e labele moris ho veta", GMN TV, 19 December 2018 <http://gmntv.tl/en/politika/2018/12/eis-pr-ramos-horta-rai-ida-nee-labele-moris-ho-veta/>.
10. Helen Davidson, "Timor Leste: Drunk Police Officer's Alleged Killing of Three Teenagers Sparks Protests", 20 November 2018 <https://www.theguardian.com/world/2018/nov/20/timor-leste-drunk-police-officers-alleged-killing-of-three-teenagers-sparks-protests>.
11. La'o Hamutuk, "Timor-Leste Buys into the Sunrise Oil and Gas Project", 30 October 2018 <https://www.laohamutuk.org/Oil/Sunrise/18SunriseBuyout.htm>.
12. Ibid.
13. La'o Hamutuk, "Timor-Leste Petroleum Fund / Fundu Petroliferu", 23 November 2018 <http://www.laohamutuk.org/Oil/PetFund/05PFIndex.htm#2018>.
14. La'o Hamutuk, "Submission to Committee C, RDTL National Parliament about the Proposed General State Budget for 2019", 29 November 2018 <http://www.laohamutuk.org/econ/OGE19/LHSubPNOJE2019-29Nov18en.pdf>.
15. Lusa, "East Timor: Foreign Businessmen Fear Economic Worsening in Timor-Leste", 15 January 2019 <http://www.macaubusiness.com/east-timor-foreign-businessmen-fear-economic-worsening-in-timor-leste/>.
16. Telecompaper, "Timorese Government Greenlights DTT Contract with China", 7 December 2018 <https://www.telecompaper.com/news/timorese-government-greenlights-dtt-contract-with-china--1272406>.
17. "Eis PM Ramos-Horta", GMN TV, 2018.

Vietnam

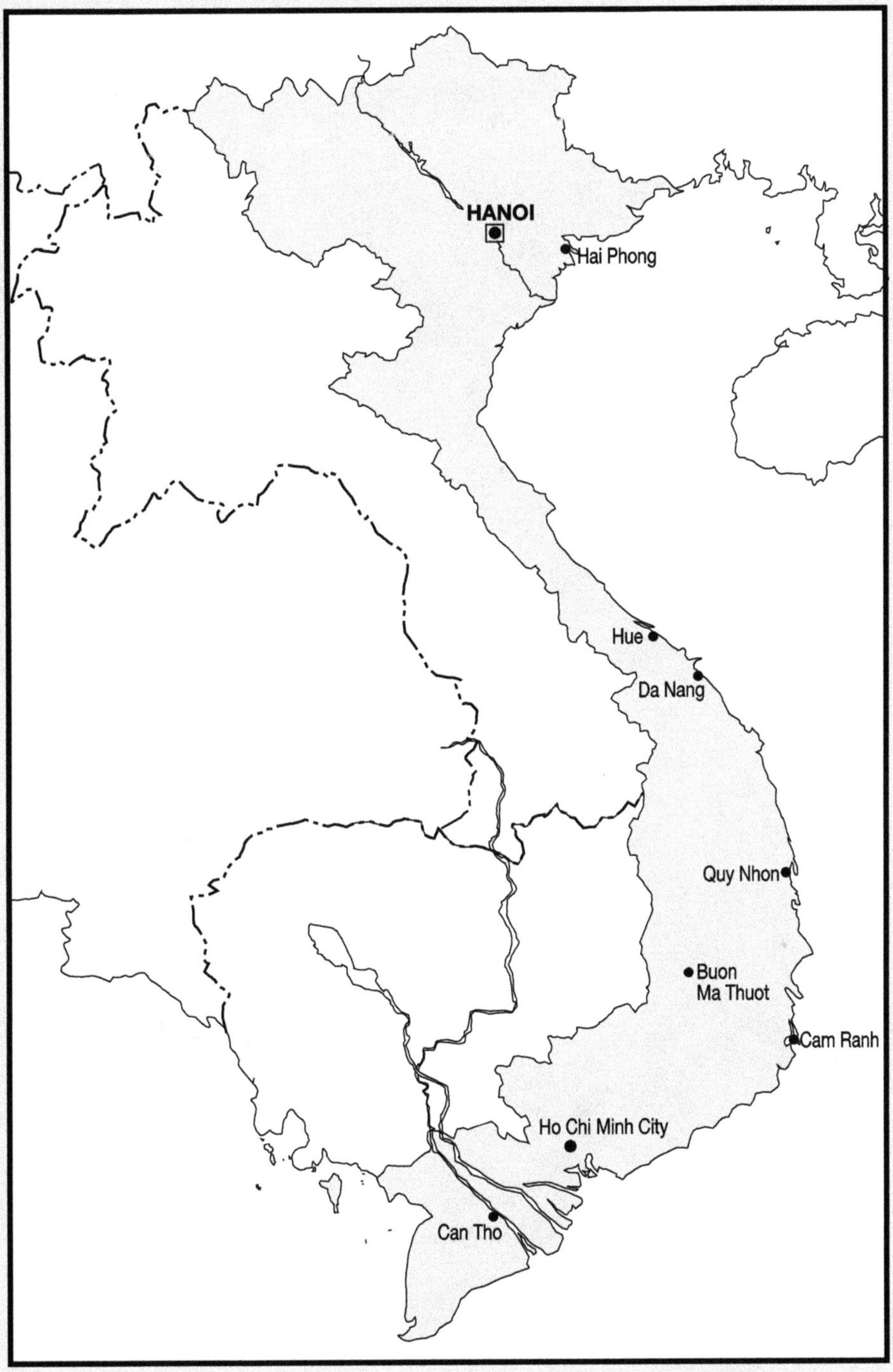
HANOI
Hai Phong
Hue
Da Nang
Quy Nhon
Buon
Ma Thuot
Cam Ranh
Ho Chi Minh City
Can Tho

VIETNAM IN 2018: A Rent-Seeking State on Correction Course

Alexander L. Vuving

The Evolution of Vietnamese Politics

The state of Vietnamese politics since the reunification of the country in 1975 has been evolving as the triumph, crisis, and course correction of first a totalitarian state and then a rent-seeking state. During the period from 1975 to 1986, the triumphant Communist Party of Vietnam (CPV) imposed a totalitarian state that planned everything and forced its programmes on the population. The totalitarian state, however, failed miserably to motivate people to work and soon plunged into a severe crisis. The death of party chief Le Duan and the election of Truong Chinh as general secretary of the CPV in 1986 paved the way for a sweeping correction of the totalitarian state. Known as *doi moi*, or "renovation", this correction course was focused on economic reform while delaying political reform, which was watered down to mere "administrative reform". *Doi moi* mainly consisted of the gradual introduction of the free market and the selective loosening of totalitarian politics. By the mid-1990s, this hybrid had succeeded in bringing the country out of the grave economic crisis and putting it on a rapid growth path, while maintaining CPV rule and breaking out of international isolation.

As this triple success made *doi moi* a long-term principle of Vietnamese politics, the hybrid also changed the nature of the Vietnamese state. Whereas the mixture of authoritarianism and capitalism in the "Asian tigers" gave rise to developmental states, the marriage of totalitarianism and commercialism in Vietnam resulted in a rent-seeking state. While the developmental state intervenes to enhance the country's competitiveness in the global market, the rent-seeking

---

Alexander L. Vuving is Professor at the Daniel K. Inouye Asia-Pacific Center for Security Studies. The views expressed in this chapter are the author's own.

state focuses on extracting payments from society. After two decades of *doi moi*, rent-seeking emerged in the mid-2000s as Vietnam's most powerful policy current, more than regime preservation and national modernization.[1]

When Nguyen Tan Dung was elected as Prime Minister in 2006, rent-seekers achieved primacy in the Vietnamese leadership. Dung pursued an economic policy that relied on high investment and state-owned conglomerates. He appointed cronies regardless of their competence in business and management to lead these "dinosaurs", turning them into money-extracting devices for the rent-seekers. In early 2008, months ahead of the global financial turmoil that started the same year, Vietnam fell into a prolonged period of economic slowdown. During Dung's first term in power (2006–11), several of the state-owned conglomerates either went bankrupt or technically defaulted, causing an estimated loss of more than US$10 billion, which was about 10 per cent of Vietnam's GDP in a year.[2]

Dung's second term in office (2011–16) was marked by the rent-seekers' continued campaign to control the business world and the ruling class, the continued crisis of the rent-seeking state, and a growing anti-corruption drive spearheaded by CPV general secretary Nguyen Phu Trong. At the 12th National Congress of the CPV in January 2016, Dung was forced to retired, while Trong was granted an exception to stay in power despite exceeding the age limit.[3] As *doi moi* entered its fourth decade, the rent-seeking state was put on a correction course. Where will this path lead? To assess the country's trajectory, this chapter will examine the major developments in Vietnam's domestic politics, economic life and foreign relations that occurred in 2018.

Attacks on the Political-Business Complex

The most important political development in 2018 was the attack on the "Big Four" of the rent-seeking networks. Three decades of *doi moi* has given rise to a political-business complex that commercializes the state's ownership of land, policy, firms and funds for private interests. As all land in the country belongs to the communist state, leaders of local government and state-owned companies are virtually owners of the best real estate, which they can take from one user and sell to another, while pocketing the large difference in the buying and selling prices of land. Absent any effective mechanism of punishment, many government officials often favour their family members and cronies in their decisions. Also, businesspeople with good connections to policymakers can easily influence policies. Such political-business complexes exist at most local and central government agencies, but four particular rent-seeking networks, often called "*nhóm lợi ích*" in Vietnamese (literally: interest groups), have emerged as the country's biggest.

The largest and most influential of the Big Four was centred on former PM Nguyen Tan Dung. During his premiership, Dung built a private empire with two major wings in the industrial and financial sectors, along with multiple tentacles in the provinces, the police and the military. One of his key allies in the industrial wing was Dinh La Thang, who was chief executive and chairman of PetroVietnam, the national oil and gas company, from 2005 to 2011, and Minister of Transportation from 2011 to 2016. Thang became a Politburo member at the 12th CPV Congress, but was arrested on 8 December 2017 and, after an unusually rapid process, sentenced to thirty years in prison. In late November 2018, Tran Bac Ha, who was dubbed the "second prime minister" under Dung for his power and role in the Dung empire, was arrested in Laos and extradited to Vietnam. Ha had been under investigation for years, but the final decision to prosecute him was not made until the summer of 2018. From 2003 to 2016, Ha was first the chief executive officer and then the chairman of the Bank of Investment and Development of Vietnam (BIDV). As the boss of the country's largest investment bank, Ha was able to move billions of U.S. dollars and determine winners and losers in the business world. In one instance, with the support of then state bank governor Nguyen Van Binh (currently a Politburo member and head of the Party Central Economics Department), Ha and Nguyen Duc Kien (chairman of the then-largest private bank, Asia Commercial Bank) lent billions of dollars to Tram Be, whose Southern Bank was technically in default, in order to gain a majority of shares and then take over the best-performing Sacombank. Sacombank was then chaired by Dang Van Thanh, a close friend of the then deputy prime minister (and current prime minister) Nguyen Xuan Phuc. While Kien was jailed back in 2012, Be was arrested only in late July 2017.

The same CPV Central Inspection Committee statement that denounced Ha in late May 2018 also declared that "grave violations" were committed in the purchase of the private television firm AVG by the state-owned telecom giant MobiFone. By inflating the value of the television firm and arguing that national security considerations called for a purchase by a state-owned company in order to prevent foreign ownership, the officials involved caused a loss of roughly VND 8 trillion (US$360 million). For their responsibilities in the deal, Minister of Information and Communication Truong Minh Tuan lost his seat in July 2018, while his predecessor, Nguyen Bac Son, a former secretary of former president Le Duc Anh (a Dung ally), was stripped of his former title. The two would be arrested in February 2019. Several other officials were also punished, including not only the culprits but also those who were actually against the deal but were pressured to sign supporting documents, such as then CEO of MobiFone Cao Duy Hai and then minister of planning and investment Bui Quang Vinh. At the same time, however, more senior officials who had approved the deal, including Dung and President Tran Dai Quang (who was former minister of public security), remained untouched.[4]

As it gained momentum in 2017, the fight against corruption launched its first major attacks on the rent-seeking groups in the military and the police, which had thus far remained nearly untouchable due to their privilege as "states within a state". Five days before Dinh La Thang was detained, the military arrested leaders of Thai Son Company, including Dinh Ngoc He, better known by his nickname "Ut troc", and Phung Danh Tham, a relative of former minister of defense Phung Quang Thanh. Thai Son was in fact He's private company, but with Tham's help it was able to use its name as a Ministry of Defense unit and to employ the ministry's assets for its own business.[5] More than two weeks later, an arrest warrant was issued against Phan Van Anh Vu, better known by his nickname "Vu nhom", who led two front companies of the Ministry of Public Security's intelligence agency, Bac Nam 79 and Nova Bac Nam 79. Vu fled to Singapore but was extradited to Vietnam in January 2018. These men would be brought to court on 30 July and charged for corruption. In December 2018, two police generals involved in the "Vu nhom" case, Tran Viet Tan and Bui Van Thanh, were also detained. Tan was the intelligence chief from 2009 to 2012 and a deputy minister of public security from 2011 to 2016, while Thanh had served as a deputy minister of public security from 2014 until his dismissal in August 2018.[6] In another case, two police generals, the former head of the Hi-Tech Crime Police Department Nguyen Thanh Hoa and former chief police investigator of the Ministry of Public Security Phan Van Vinh, were sentenced to ten and nine years in prison, respectively, for using an online gambling company as a front of the ministry's cybersecurity watchdog and collecting huge protection fees from it.[7]

By the autumn the anti-corruption campaign had spread to the fourth of the Big Four, the group around Le Thanh Hai, who governed Ho Chi Minh City from 2001 until 2015, first as mayor and then as party secretary. Hai is estimated to be Vietnam's second-richest man after former prime minister Dung. Each of the two is said to have amassed a fortune that far exceeds that of Vingroup chairman Pham Nhat Vuong, who, with US$7 billion, is the richest person in Vietnam according to Forbes. Within three months from mid-September, the heat was felt by three of Hai's acolytes, who were all former vice-mayors of Ho Chi Minh City. Nguyen Huu Tin was prosecuted on 18 September; Tat Thanh Cang was declared a wrongdoer by the Party on 15 November and stripped of membership in the

Central Committee and dismissed as first deputy party secretary of Ho Chi Minh City on 26 December; and Nguyen Thanh Tai was arrested on 8 December. Their major wrongdoings were related to the mismanagement of lands in downtown Saigon, Nha Be and Thu Thiem, where huge differences in land prices can be created with a single administrative decision. Their massive land grab at Thu Thiem, a district selected more than two decades ago for development into an international financial hub, was the cause of one of the largest popular agitations in the year. The front companies of the police were among their clients in the land transfers (one of Hai's sons is said to be on the police intelligence service's payroll), but their major partners in the political-business complex include several of Vietnam's richest tycoons, most notably the ethnic Chinese real estate developer Truong My Lan, who was revealed in a 2014 court hearing to have once given the then chief police investigator US$1 million in bribes. However, Lan has so far avoided investigation.

A Battle on Two Fronts

Although much intensified than before, the anti-graft drive still remains limited in strength. Former prime minister Dung and former Ho Chi Minh City party boss Hai, the "godfathers" of the two biggest rent-seeking empires in Vietnam, along with General Thanh, who built a powerful rent-seeking group during his ten-year tenure as minister of defence, all remain untouched. Moreover, former governor of the state bank Binh and former deputy prime minister Hoang Trung Hai, two of Dung's close associates who were behind many of the corruption scandals, continue to sit on the Politburo. This indicates the rent-seekers' continued strength, but it also reflects party chief Trong's cautious approach, which favours selective attacks over sweeping battles. Trong has famously stressed that the anti-graft drive must "not break the vase when beating the rats", indicating that the higher goal of the campaign is to maintain political stability.[8]

In fact, Trong has been fighting a battle on two fronts against both corruption and political liberalism. He launched the anti-graft drive under the broader agenda of cleansing the party from both corruption and ideological paganism, which in party parlance is described as "political opportunism" (*cơ hội chính trị*), "self-evolution" (*tự diễn biến*) and "self-transformation" (*tự chuyển hoá*). While lamenting that "corruption is threatening the survival of the regime", Trong believes that "political decadence is even more dangerous", as he explained the purge of the retired deputy minister of science and technology Chu Hao.[9]

In late October the party announced its intention to reprimand Hao, who quickly responded by renouncing his party membership, thus prompting the party to dismiss him altogether. A reform advocate, Hao has pioneered a publishing house promoting liberal thought. In August 2009 his publishing house received the first party inspection, but the second was not made until October 2016, after the 12th CPV Congress. The third and fourth inspections took place in 2018.[10] According to the party, Hao's "violations" of party principles started in 2005, when he established the Knowledge Publishing House, which published books containing "wrongful ideas", "inflating the limits of socialism and the democratic values of capitalism" and "spreading views contrary to the party line". One of Hao's "highly grave violations" was advocating a multiparty system and a military free from ideological and party control.[11]

Popular Protests

Driving the attacks on the Big Four rent-seeking groups and on Chu Hao was the dual motive of deterring corruption and liberalism, while demonstrating the party's commitment to fight them. Meanwhile, the public remained largely discontented with the quality of governance and the continued strength of the rent-seeking apparatus. Increasingly disgruntled, people have resorted to more vigorous whistle-blowing, petitioning, protests and civil disobedience.

In one innovative form of protest, truckers started to pay for tolls with small change when they felt they were charged unfair tolls, inducing the operators to lift tolls to mitigate traffic jams. The toll gates for these roads, called "BOT" in Vietnamese after the "build-operate-transfer" scheme under which they were built, were so arranged as to force even toll-free road users to pay. This, and the ease of inflating toll prices, made the BOT roads into a goldmine for corrupt businesses and an excellent pool of kickbacks for leaders in the transportation ministry to use as bribes to powerful people. With the help of transportation officers like Thang and Nguyen Van The, who is currently the minister of transportation, family members and close associates of many party, military and police leaders (such as former party chief Nong Duc Manh, former CPV Central Inspection Committee chair Ngo Van Du, former minister of defence Thanh, and President Quang) have gained the best of the toll roads.[12] Recognizing the injustice and fearing the spillover effect of the protests, the government has refrained from quelling the protests with force, instead choosing to temporarily lift the tolls while trying to find solutions to the problem. Meanwhile, protests continue to persist at several toll gates: there are occasions when drivers and local residents peacefully took over the gates, while in some instances truckers have simply knocked the barriers down.[13]

While the land grabs, excessive taxes, unfair tolls and pollution were major causes of popular agitation throughout 2018, what triggered the year's largest protests was the fear of China's peaceful invasion through special economic zones. From 9 to 11 June, a hundred thousand Vietnamese took to the streets at several locations throughout the country to oppose the two draft laws on special administrative-economic zones and cybersecurity, with the largest gathering comprising factory workers in Ho Chi Minh City. While the demonstrations were generally peaceful in most cities, protesters stormed government buildings, burned vehicles and fought with police in Binh Thuan province. (By November 2018, more than 120 protesters had been imprisoned.) Agitation over the bills had been brewing for more than a week on social media before the protests broke out on the streets, even after the National Assembly postponed the passage of the Special Zone Act. Feeling intense pressure from the population, the Politburo decided, at the very last minute, to postpone the vote in the parliament on the bill, previously scheduled for 9 June. On 9 June, the National Assembly voted to delay the law's passage to the next session in October, only to have it postponed again to 2019 in August. However, the parliament went ahead to pass the Cybersecurity Law on 12 June, which, according to Reporters Without Borders, is "largely a copy-and-paste version" of China's.[14] The central cause of anger that sparked the protests was a provision in the Special Zone Act that would allow ninety-nine-year leases of land to foreign investors. Although the law did not specify any particular country, it was widely believed that China, with its deep pockets and close proximity, would dominate investments in these special zones and turn them into de facto Chinese territories.[15] Spearheaded by Pham Minh Chinh, but opposed by most leading experts for various reasons, the Special Zone Act was originally a product of Chinh, who is now personnel czar in the Politburo, and Dung, the then prime minister, who needed the act to facilitate the flow of money, not least from casino visitors, to their favourite islands Van Don and Phu Quoc, respectively.[16] Besides Chinh on the Politburo, National Assembly chairwoman Nguyen Thi Kim Ngan and Deputy Prime Minister Vuong Dinh Hue were reportedly the main supporters of the project, while party chief Trong, CPV executive secretary Tran Quoc Vuong and Prime Minister Phuc were reportedly more hesitant.

Leadership Selection

Although the 12th CPV Congress put an end to the primacy of rent-seekers at the top echelons, it did not terminate the dominance of rent-seekers in the system. The cadre of policymakers that was installed at the Congress has remained unaffected by Dung's last-minute defeat in his bid for the top job in the party. This cadre continues to remain largely intact despite the spectacular anti-corruption campaign of the last two years. Only three members have so far been removed from the 200-strong CPV Central Committee (two others died). During 2018, the party introduced new schemes for leadership selection. It established a new cadre strategy at the Seventh Plenum of the Central Committee in May, and, in a new practice, screened new candidates for the next Central Committee at the extraordinary Ninth Plenum in December. In the new schemes of leadership selection, more powers are devolved to the lower levels, with the procedures made more transparent and apparently more democratic, but the controlling role remains in the hands of the incumbent leadership.[17] Of note, most of this leadership in 2018 had been arranged before the 12th Congress and bore the mark of the primacy of rent-seekers.[18] Perhaps to compensate for this deficit, the party created a new body called the Steering Committee on Strategic-level Cadre Planning for the Term 2021–2026, headed by party chief Trong, which would play a key role in the screening and vetting of candidates.[19]

When General Secretary Trong was re-elected with an exemption to the age limit at the 12th CPV Congress, the informal bargain foresaw a leadership transition in the midterm with either CPV executive secretary Dinh The Huynh or President Quang to succeed him as party chief. These two options however fell off the table in 2018, the midterm year. On sick leave since June 2017, Huynh was formally relieved from the second-highest position in the party apparatus in March 2018, and CPV Central Inspection Committee chair Tran Quoc Vuong, who had performed Huynh's job since August 2017, became officially the party's new executive secretary. On 21 September, Quang passed away after having fallen sick periodically since July 2017. At its 30 September meeting, the Politburo overwhelmingly nominated Trong to fill Quang's post; the only dissenting vote was from Trong himself, who had instead nominated National Assembly vice-chairwoman Tong Thi Phong. The traditional separation of the two top positions in the party-state hence ceased to exist on 23 October, when the National Assembly elected Trong as state president.

While unusual, this is not the first time that a CPV leader has worn both hats. From 1951 to 1969 and during the latter half of 1986, Ho Chi Minh and Truong Chinh were respectively party chief–cum–head of state. What is unprecedented, though, is that Trong is the first party chief to sit on both the Central Military Commission and the Central Party Commission for Public Security, the two party bodies that lead the military, police and security forces (Trong joined the Central Party Commission for Public Security on 21 September 2016). With such a concentration of power, it is tempting to describe Trong as Vietnam's Xi Jinping, but a comparison to the Chinese strongman would be misleading. While Xi's dream is to make China great again (and himself greater than Mao), Trong's ambition is to save the CPV from decay. While Xi is willing to take risks, Trong is extremely risk-averse. And while there is no time limit to Xi's hold on power, the party constitution rules out Trong's re-election as party chief in 2021. The nomination of Trong for president was initiated by Pham Minh Chinh, head of the CPV Central Organization Commission. A front-runner for the top job at the next party congress, Chinh has reason to hope for inheriting the dual hat when Trong retires in a little over two years. Still, based on nomenclature, Executive Secretary Vuong is better positioned to succeed Trong, while Trong sees his dual position as a temporary solution borne out of exigencies rather than a permanent unification (*nhất thể hóa*).[20]

Drivers of Economic Growth

While General Secretary Trong entered his second term with an agenda to consolidate the Communist Party, combat corruption and maintain stability, Prime Minister Nguyen Xuan Phuc took up the helm of government with a vision to build a development-enabling state (*nhà nước kiến tạo phát triển*), remove the major barriers to development and promote new drivers of economic growth. Based on a consensus formed during the last decades, the government vowed to advance substantial reform in the areas of institutions, infrastructure and human resources, as these were viewed as the key drivers but also the major bottlenecks of the economy. In 2018, backed by a CPV Central Committee resolution on promoting private economy (10-NQ/TW of 3 June 2017) and realizing that the fourth industrial revolution provides a "historic opportunity" for Vietnam to play catch-up with the advanced industrial countries, the government endorsed the private sector and the innovation and application of high-technology as two additional key drivers of growth, vigorously pledging to promote these areas.[21]

Institutional reform was focused on cutting red tape and reforming state-owned enterprises. The year 2018 marked a turning point as the representation of state ownership in nineteen state-owned conglomerates was transferred from the line ministries to a "super commission" (*siêu ủy ban*) called the Commission for the Management of State Capital at Enterprises (CMSC), which was modelled upon China's State-owned Assets Supervision and Administration Commission of the State Council (SASAC) and Singapore's Temasek Holdings. Data from 2017 show that CMSC would manage a total asset of more than VND 2,300 trillion (US$100 billion), or two-thirds of the state sector in the economy by value.[22] Furthermore, drastically reducing regulations and paperwork and eliminating unreasonable requirements have been identified as a major measure to improve the business environment. While the government's Central Institute for Economic Management advised to eliminate three quarters of the existing 5,700 requirements, the government set the target of 50 per cent by the end of October. The result, however, was a mere 13 per cent, with only 30 per cent of the eliminated requirements being of real significance.[23] Vietnam's "ease of doing business" rank, according to the World Bank, improved from 82 in 2016 to 68 in 2017 but worsened to 69 in 2018.[24]

Infrastructure development remained a realm of rampant rent-seeking. Expensive but shoddy roads continued to make headlines. The high-profile controversy over Ho Chi Minh City's Tan Son Nhat Airport is a good example of how the government dealt with infrastructure development. Increased demand for air transportation and chronic traffic jams in the southern vicinity of the airport required an extension of the airport to the north, where land reserved for national defence has been leased by the military to a private company for a golf course. Under pressure from the public, the Ministry of Defence agreed to return the golf course land to the airport whenever the government so demands. In the end, although an expert panel authorized by Ho Chi Minh City party secretary Nguyen Thien Nhan proposed a north extension, Prime Minister Phuc decided to pick the Ministry of Transportation's preferred option that would keep the airport facing south, thus leaving the golf course in place until 2025.[25]

Education did not fare better. While Minister of Transportation Nguyen Van The is reportedly an ally of Prime Minister Phuc, Minister of Education Phung Xuan Nha is said to be close to party chief Trong. There was a plan in the summer to promote Nha to deputy prime minister but it never materialized because scandals of fraud, violence and corruption in the education field made public opinion turn against him. In a confidence vote held in the National Assembly in late October, Nha received the most number of "low confidence" votes among all cabinet members. This was perhaps what prompted Trong to say in early November that "our education field has never been as good as today".[26]

The silver lining for Vietnam appears to come from the private sector and the digital economy. The year 2018 marked the first time that a domestic private company, Vingroup, appeared among the top ten largest companies in Vietnam. Vingroup ranked sixth, while Samsung Electronics retained the top spot for the second year running. According to a government report, the ratio of domestic private investment in the country's total increased steadily to 42.4 per cent in 2018 from 40.5 per cent in 2017, 38.9 per cent in 2016, and an average of 38.3 per cent during 2011–15.[27]

As for the digital economy, the lawsuit initiated by the traditional taxi company Vinasun against the app-based ride-hailing firm Grab, which lasted throughout the year, and the concurrent drafting of a related regulatory decree, exemplify the dilemma the government faces and the way it has responded to the challenges and opportunities provided by the fourth industrial revolution. The government has been torn between two tendencies: one supports new modes of business created by the digital economy, the other sticks to the old way and prefers control and overregulation. The battle between the two views see-sawed throughout the year, which ended with Grab losing its case, partially due to its evasion of rules and taxes, although the new welcoming attitude to the digital economy appears to prevail, also partially, in the new regulation.[28]

In July, Truong Minh Tuan's fall in the AVG scandal led to Nguyen Manh Hung, chairman of the military's tech giant Viettel, becoming the minister of information and communication. A successful entrepreneur, Hung brought in a new thinking on almost everything. He said that he would let new business models develop freely and apply a regulatory "sandbox" as testing grounds for the emerging models. He viewed the fourth industrial revolution as essentially a revolution of policy rather than one of technology, thus emphasizing the need for flexible and adaptive policies. Eager to reap the first-mover advantage, he vowed to make Vietnam one of the first countries to have a commercial 5G network,

TABLE 1
Vietnam: Macro-economic Trends

	2011–15 average	*2016*	*2017*	*2018*
GDP growth (%)	5.91	6.21	6.81	7.08
TFP growth's contribution to GDP growth (%)	33.58	40.68	45.19	43.50
Labour productivity growth (%)	4.6	5.29	6.02	5.93
ICOR	6.25	6.42	6.11	5.97

Notes: TFP is total factor productivity. ICOR is incremental capital output ratio, which measures the inefficiency of investment. Data are from General Statistics Office, Government of Vietnam. GDP figures are based on the supply side and might be about 3 percentage points less if based on the demand side. TFP figures may be inflated by around 10 percentage points.

which will be indispensable for the next wave of industrialization and likely to boost the country's nascent but vibrant tech start-up ecosystem.[29]

Navigating the Geopolitical Torrents

Vietnam's correction course takes place amidst epochal changes in the international environment. The post–Cold War era began to end when China embarked on its Belt and Road Initiative (BRI), imposed an "air defense identification zone" in the East China Sea, and commenced the building of artificial islands in the South China Sea, all in 2013. In 2018, the Trump administration launched a trade war against China, effectively starting a new period characterized by U.S.-China strategic competition. Vietnam endeavours to strike a dynamic balance between China and the United States in which its relationship with Washington is overall just a few degrees warmer than with Beijing, because Vietnam's strategic interests are more in conflict with China's. At the same time, Vietnam tries to insure this balancing act by strengthening ties with other major powers, primarily India, Russia and Japan, and insisting on ASEAN's centrality in the regional architecture.

Vietnam responds to China's epoch-making BRI by paying lip service to it while trying to find ways to placate Beijing without increasing its dependence on China. What makes Vietnamese government officials reluctant to accept the offer of Chinese aid money is the double worry about a debt trap and the ire of the public. Unlike in many other countries that have endorsed BRI, nearly all major infrastructure projects using Chinese money in Vietnam are dated from the pre-2016 period. The Special Zone Act was reportedly meant to be an arrow to kill two birds: to replicate the success of Shenzhen and to accommodate but contain China's BRI. However, it was opposed by most leading experts and unleashed strong waves of protest. In late August 2018, when the State Bank of Vietnam allowed the use of Chinese renminbi as a medium of exchange in the provinces bordering China, it provoked a large controversy among the public as well as in the parliament.

In late September, party chief Trong was reported by Xinhua — but not by Vietnam's state-sanctioned press — as telling a senior visiting Chinese Communist Party leader that Vietnam-China relations were at the best time in history.[30] Trong's statement reflects the "warm outside but cool inside" state of the relationship. In March, under Chinese pressure, Vietnam had ordered Spanish energy firm Repsol to halt a major oil drilling project in the South China Sea called *Ca Rong Do* (Red Emperor) in Block 07/03, which is adjacent to Block 136/03 where another project by Repsol was similarly cancelled after a month of drilling in

July 2017 due to Chinese complaints.[31] But in mid-September, Vietnam decided to resume the Blue Whale project with ExxonMobil in Block 118, which it had previously put on hold in November 2017 due to Chinese objection. It seems apparent that some modus vivendi was reached with China during the annual meeting of the China-Vietnam Steering Committee for Bilateral Relations on 16 September. This might also explain Trong's odd September statement about the state of Sino-Vietnam relations. However, the "best time of Vietnam-China relations" did not seem to last long. In December, Vietnamese press, citing a reputed Chinese website, reported of a field exercise held by the Chinese military near the Vietnamese border that simulated a military confrontation with a "neighboring country X".[32]

While China-Vietnam ties remained cool on the inside though they appear to be warm outside, U.S.-Vietnam relations continue to get warmer. In October, Secretary of Defense James Mattis paid a second visit to Vietnam in a year, after the first in January. This visit was unprecedented in that it broke the previous rule of having a U.S. chief of defence visit once every three years. Also unprecedentedly, in March, the USS *Carl Vinson* visited Da Nang, becoming the first U.S. aircraft carrier ever to make a port call in communist Vietnam. In the summer, Vietnamese military participated for the first time in the U.S.-led RIMPAC exercise, albeit without any vessels and only in humanitarian assistance and disaster relief. The years 2017–18 have also witnessed at least thirteen U.S. Navy ship visits to Vietnam, despite the rule of one visit per year for any foreign country. The Trump administration has also invited CPV chief Trong, well before his assumption of the presidency, to visit the United States. Meanwhile, key agencies in Vietnam deliberated the official upgrading of the "comprehensive partnership" to a "strategic partnership", which might be announced when Trong meets with Trump in 2019. In April, Minister of Investment and Planning Nguyen Chi Dung travelled to the United States to study how Americans dealt with the fourth industrial revolution.[33] In June, Deputy Prime Minister Vuong Dinh Hue paid an official visit, and over November and December, Truong Thi Mai, a Politburo member and head of the CPV Mass Mobilization Commission, went on a working visit to the United States during which they discussed a wide range of issues from strengthening bilateral relations to trade, aid and the South China Sea dispute. Mai also suggested cooperation on revising the law to comply with international labour standards.[34]

In November, the National Assembly unanimously ratified the Comprehensive and Progressive Trans-Pacific Partnership (CPTPP), the new version of the Trans-Pacific Partnership that proceeds without U.S. participation. Vietnam joined the

TPP in 2008 at the invitation of the United States in the hope that it would provide a huge market for Vietnamese goods, external pressure for economic reform and a geopolitical counterweight to China. The asymmetry of trade with China and the American turn towards protectionism has pushed Vietnam farther on the free trade path. In October, Prime Minister Phuc used his trip to attend the Asia-Europe Meeting Summit in Brussels to lobby for the EU-Vietnam Free Trade Agreement (EVFTA), which then was passed from the European Commission to the European Parliament for ratification. One of the major concessions the CPV made in the CPTPP and the EVFTA is the commitment to international labour standards, including the rights of workers to form independent labour unions.

Given the rapidity and unpredictability of changes in the international environment, Vietnam has developed its own concept of "forward defence" (*giữ nước từ xa*), which gears its defence efforts towards preventing danger to its security ahead of time (*giữ nước từ khi nước chưa nguy*). A key aspect of Vietnam's forward defence is, as party chief Trong noted, Vietnam's defence and security relations with Russia and India. Trong also said that defence and security were the top priority in relations with these two countries.[35] In early September, Trong paid official visits to Russia and Hungary. His trip to Hungary, the first by a CPV General Secretary to Eastern Europe in three decades, witnessed the designation of Hungarian-Vietnamese relations as a "comprehensive partnership". The EVFTA, the Free Trade Agreement between Vietnam and the Eurasian Union, and joint oil explorations with Russia in the South China Sea were among the major agenda items of Trong's trip to Hungary and Russia respectively.[36] Defence and trade were also the focus of Trong's official trip to France in March. With India, the year 2018 saw a state visit by President Quang in March, a state visit by Indian President Ram Nath Kovind in November, a visit by Prime Minister Phuc in January, and the visits by Indian Minister of Defence Nirmala Sitharaman in June and Minister of External Affairs Sushma Swaraj in August. In March, a formal "strategic partnership" with Australia, which Vietnam had for years lobbied for, was finally announced during a trip by Prime Minister Phuc to Canberra. In 2018 alone, Defence Minister Ngo Xuan Lich signed four joint vision statements on defence cooperation with the defence ministries of Japan, South Korea, France and Australia during his visits to these countries.

The Rhyme of History

In 2018, Vietnam's economy grew at the highest rate in a decade amidst a steady improvement of investment efficiency. Not accidentally, the year was also the best in more than a decade in terms of combating corruption. Vietnam appears to be on the way out of the period of slowdown that followed the ascent of the rent-seekers. Three years into a full course of correction, the results remain mixed at best. Little has been done structurally to keep rent-seeking in check. The correction course risks fading if a new leader less inclined to fight rent-seeking replaces Nguyen Phu Trong at the 13th CPV Congress in 2021. Yet anti-corruption, as well as *doi moi*, has become a cultural trait and a systemic tendency that will not go away easily.

Like three decades ago when the first years of *doi moi* coincided with the last phase of the Cold War, Vietnam entered its second correction course simultaneously with the ending of the post–Cold War era. But whereas *doi moi* took place when cooperation among the great powers largely prevailed over their rivalry, this second course of correction is accompanied by heightened competition between the United States and China, the region's two biggest powers. During 1989–90, *doi moi* reversed course partially but consequentially when party chief Nguyen Van Linh and his conservative colleagues, shocked by the collapse of communism in Eastern Europe and imagining a menace of regime change coming from the West, placed Vietnamese foreign policy on a course that veered more towards China than the West. This China-tilt has indirectly contributed to the rise of rent-seeking in the decades that followed, which rendered them "lost decades" on the path to development and completely shattered Vietnam's dream, set at the 9th CPV Congress in 2001, of becoming an industrialized country by 2020. Today, unlike then, Vietnam's preferred position is one step farther from China than from the United States. This and the U.S.-China rivalry may help keep Vietnam's correction course intact in the years to come.

Notes

1. Alexander L. Vuving, "Vietnam: A Tale of Four Players", in *Southeast Asian Affairs 2010*, edited by Daljit Singh (Singapore: Institute of Southeast Asian Studies, 2010), pp. 36–91; Alexander L. Vuving, "Vietnam in 2012: A Rent-Seeking State on the Verge of a Crisis", in *Southeast Asian Affairs 2013*, edited by Daljit Singh and Pushpa Thambipillai (Singapore: Institute of Southeast Asian Studies, 2013), pp. 325–47.
2. Alexander L. Vuving, "Vietnam's Search for Stability", *Diplomat*, 25 October 2012; Vuving, "Vietnam in 2012", pp. 326–28.
3. Alexander L. Vuving, "The 2016 Leadership Change in Vietnam and Its Long-term Implications", in *Southeast Asian Affairs 2017*, edited by Daljit Singh and Malcolm Cook (Singapore: ISEAS – Yusof Ishak Institute, 2017), pp. 421–35.
4. See Dương Vũ, "Ai đã làm khánh kiệt đất nước (Phần 13): Con cá mập AVG đã

nuốt MobiFone như thế nào?", *Dân Luận*, 14 March 2017 <https://www.danluan.org/tin-tuc/20170313/ai-dang-lam-khanh-kiet-dat-nuoc-phan-13-con-ca-map-avg-da-nuot-mobifone-nhu-the-nao>; and the series by "Nguyễn Văn Tung", pseudonym of a group of MobiFone employees, titled "Đại án tham nhũng Mobifone mua AVG" on *Dân Luận* from February 2016 to May 2018, especially part 28, 18 May 2018 <https://www.danluan.org/tin-tuc/20180518/dai-an-tham-nhung-mobifone-mua-avg-phai-xu-ly-nghiem-cac-ca-nhan-sai-pham-ky-28>.

5. Nam Nam, "Út 'trọc', Phùng Danh Thắm hầu toà", *Nhà đầu tư*, 30 July 2018 <https://nhadautu.vn/ut-troc-phung-danh-tham-hau-toa-d11987.html>.
6. For documents on these front companies, see the four-part series by Công Lý, titled "Tư liệu tuyệt mlocalt" on danluan.org from 6 to 10 May 2017 <https://www.danluan.org/tin-tuc/20170506/tu-lieu-tuyet-mat-ky-1-thu-truong-cong-an-tran-viet-tan-da-tang-av75-phan-van-anh> <https://www.danluan.org/tin-tuc/20170506/tu-lieu-tuyet-mat-ky-2-tuong-an-tap-bui-van-thanh-da-tang-gi-cho-av75-phan-van-anh> <https://www.danluan.org/tin-tuc/20170508/tu-lieu-tuyet-mat-ky-3-tuong-tinh-bao-phan-huu-tuan-tuong-hau-can-ksor-nham-tiep> <https://www.danluan.org/tin-tuc/20170509/tu-lieu-tuyet-mat-ky-3-ngoai-cac-ong-tuong-tinh-bao-tuong-hau-can-con-nhung-ai-noi>; and Công Lý, "Giải mã bí ẩn thân thế của đại thiếu gia tập đoàn Novaland", *Dân Luận*, 28 April 2017 <https://www.danluan.org/tin-tuc/20170427/giai-ma-bi-an-than-the-cua-dai-thieu-gia-tap-doan-novaland>.
7. "Vì sao Phan Văn Vĩnh, Nguyễn Thanh Hoá lĩnh án cao hơn mức đề nghị?", Zing.vn, 3 December 2018 <https://baomoi.com/vi-sao-phan-van-vinh-nguyen-thanh-hoa-linh-an-cao-hon-muc-de-nghi/c/28834486.epi>.
8. "Tổng bí thư: Diệt chuột đừng để vỡ bình", *VietNamNet*, 6 November 2018 <http://vietnamnet.vn/vn/thoi-su/tong-bi-thu-diet-chuot-dung-de-vo-binh-200746.html>.
9. "Tổng Bí thư, Chủ tịch Nước nói về việc kỷ luật ông Chu Hảo", *VnExpress*, 24 November 2018 <https://vnexpress.net/thoi-su/tong-bi-thu-chu-tich-nuoc-noi-ve-viec-ky-luat-ong-chu-hao-3844097.html>.
10. "TS Chu Hảo tuyên bố từ bỏ Đảng Cộng sản Việt Nam", *Bauxite Việt Nam*, 29 October 2018 <https://boxitvn.blogspot.com/2018/10/ts-chu-hao-tuyen-bo-tu-bo-ang-cong-san.html>.
11. Phạm Đức Tiến, "Vi phạm của đồng chí Chu Hảo — đảng viên trí thức có biểu hiện suy thoái, 'tự diễn biến', 'tự chuyển hoá' rất nghiêm trọng", website of the CPV Central Inspection Committee, 31 October 2018 <http://ubkttw.vn/nghien-cuu-trao-doi/-/asset_publisher/bHGXXiPdpxRC/content/vi-pham-cua-ong-chi-chu-hao-ang-vien-tri-thuc-co-bieu-hien-suy-thoai-tu-dien-bien-tu-chuyen-hoa-rat-nghiem-trong>.
12. Dương Vũ, "Ai đã làm khánh kiệt đất nước (Phần 11), *Dân Luận*, 8 November 2014 <https://www.danluan.org/tin-tuc/20141108/duong-vu-ai-dang-lam-khanh-kiet-dat-nuoc-phan-11>; Phạm Chí Dũng, "Hải, Thăng, Thể, Dụ, Thắng, Tâm: Ai ăn BOT khiến Phúc đổ vỏ?", VOA blog, 15 December 2017 <https://www.voatiengviet.com/a/bot-cai-lay-tham-nhung-dau-thau/4165307.html>.

13. "Vì sao trạm thu phí Cai Lậy 'thất thủ'?", *Công Luận*, 8 October 2018 <https://baomoi.com/vi-sao-tram-thu-phi-cai-lay-that-thu/c/28063739.epi>; "Vì sao người dân phản đối tại trạm thu phí BOT Tân Đệ?", *Việt Nam Mới*, 3 July 2018 <https://vietnammoi.vn/vi-sao-nguoi-dan-phan-doi-tai-tram-thu-phi-bot-tan-de-115470.html>; "Xoá sổ BOT Tân Đệ, Tasco xây trạm thu phí mới", *VietNamNet*, 21 December 2018 <http://vietnamnet.vn/vn/thoi-su/an-toan-giao-thong/xoa-so-bot-tan-de-tasco-xay-tram-thu-phi-moi-495883.html>; "Vẫn 'dậm chân tại chỗ' các tồn đọng của các trạm BOT giao thông", VOV.VN, 21 December 2018 <https://vov.vn/xa-hoi/van-dam-chan-tai-cho-cac-ton-dong-cua-cac-tram-bot-giao-thong-854223.vov>; "Tài xế quây BOT Bắc Thăng Long-Nội Bài, Bộ GTVT chỉ đạo khẩn", *VietNamNet*, 21 December 2018 <http://vietnamnet.vn/vn/thoi-su/an-toan-giao-thong/tai-xe-quay-bot-bac-thang-long-noi-bai-bo-gtvt-chi-dao-khan-495851.html>; "Nhiều người bám trụ trạm BOT Bắc thăng Long để phản đối thu phí", *VietNamNet*, 21 December 2018 <https://vnexpress.net/thoi-su/nhieu-nguoi-bam-tru-tram-bot-bac-thang-long-de-phan-doi-thu-phi-3857724.html>.
14. "RSF Calls for Repeal of Vietnam's New Cybersecurity Law", Reporters Without Borders, 15 June 2018 <https://rsf.org/en/news/rsf-calls-repeal-vietnams-new-cybersecurity-law>.
15. Bennett Murray, "Vietnamese See Special Economic Zones as Assault from China", *South China Morning Post*, 7 June 2018; "Anti-China Protests: Dozens Arrested as Vietnam Patriotism Spirals into Unrest", *South China Morning Post*, 11 June 2018; Trân Văn, "Việt Nam, từ khuya 9 tháng Sáu đến 10 tháng 6", VOA Vietnamese, 10 June 2018 <https://www.voatiengviet.com/a/bieu-tinh-chong-luat-dac-khu-va-an-ninh-mang/4432515.html>; "Ai sẽ hưởng lợi từ các cuộc biểu tình ở Việt Nam?", *Việt Nam Thời Báo*, 25 June 2018 <http://www.vietnamthoibao.org/2018/06/vntb-ai-se-huong-loi-tu-cac-cuoc-bieu.html>; "Chùm bài cả nước xuống đường 10-6-2018", *Bauxite Việt Nam*, 11 June 2018.
16. Huỳnh Phan, "Đặc khu kinh tế ở Việt Nam: Những thử nghiệm và thất bại", *Người đô thị*, 4 June 2018 <https://nguoidothi.net.vn/dac-khu-kinh-te-o-viet-nam-nhung-thu-nghiem-va-that-bai-13907.html>; "Quảng Ninh đã chuẩn bị Đặc khu Vân Đồn ra sao", BBC Vietnamese, 27 June 2018 <https://www.bbc.com/vietnamese/vietnam-44610484>.
17. "Dành tỷ lệ lớn cho cán bộ có thể làm đủ 2 nhiệm kỳ", *Zing.vn*, 25 December 2018 <https://news.zing.vn/danh-ty-le-lon-cho-can-bo-co-the-lam-du-2-nhiem-ky-post902827.html>; "Nhiều nơi đã chốt cán bộ quy hoạch Trung ương khoá XIII", *Pháp luật Thành phố Hồ Chí Minh*, 6 December 2018 <http://plo.vn/thoi-su/nhieu-noi-da-chot-can-bo-quy-hoach-trung-uong-khoa-xiii-806519.html>; "Sáng nay khai mạc Hội nghị Trung ương 9, khoá XII", *VnExpress*, 25 December 2018 <https://vnexpress.net/thoi-su/sang-nay-khai-mac-hoi-nghi-trung-uong-9-khoa-xii-3858462.html>; "Những điểm mới trong đề án xây dựng cán bộ cấp chiến lược", *VnExpress*, 5 May 2018 <https://vnexpress.net/tin-tuc/thoi-su/nhung-diem-moi-trong-de-an-xay-dung-can-bo-cap-chien-luoc-3745305.html>; "Bà Bùi Thị An: Công khai người giới thiệu để tránh kẻ cơ hội chui sâu leo cao", *Giáo dục Việt Nam*, 5 December 2018

<http://giaoduc.net.vn/Xa-hoi/Ba-Bui-Thi-An-Cong-khai-nguoi-gioi-thieu-de-tranh-ke-co-hoi-chui-sau-leo-cao-post193463.gd>.

18. Trương Huy San, "Thế hệ thứ ba", Facebook, 26 December 2018 <http://www.viet-studies.net/kinhte/HuyDuc_TheHeThuBa.html>.
19. "Tổng Bí thư, Chủ tịch nước làm Trưởng Ban Chỉ đạo xây dựng quy hoạch cán bộ cấp chiến lược", *Người lao động*, 4 November 2018 <https://nld.com.vn/thoi-su/tong-bi-thu-chu-tich-nuoc-lam-truong-ban-chi-dao-xay-dung-quy-hoach-can-bo-cap-chien-luoc-20181104172846407.htm>.
20. "Tổng bí thư được giới thiệu ứng cử Chủ tịch nước 'không phải nhất thể hoá' ", *VnExpress*, 8 October 2018 <https://vnexpress.net/thoi-su/tong-bi-thu-duoc-gioi-thieu-ung-cu-chu-tich-nuoc-khong-phai-nhat-the-hoa-3820639.html>.
21. "Thủ tướng Nguyễn Xuân Phúc: Thực hiện 3 đột phá chiến lược và 2 động lực tăng trưởng kinh tế", *Công Thương*, 5 December 2018 <https://congthuong.vn/thu-tuong-nguyen-xuan-phuc-thuc-hien-3-dot-pha-chien-luoc-va-2-dong-luc-tang-truong-kinh-te-112915.html>.
22. " 'Siêu Uỷ ban' ra mắt: Thủ tướng yêu cầu tránh kẽ hở tham nhũng, thất thoát", *Dân trí*, 30 September 2018 <https://dantri.com.vn/kinh-doanh/sieu-uy-ban-ra-mat-thu-tuong-yeu-cau-tranh-ke-ho-tham-nhung-that-thoat-20180930175619361.htm>.
23. Trâm Anh, "Cắt giảm điều kiện kinh doanh: Còn đối phó, không thực chất", *Kinh tế và Đô thị*, 15 November 2018 <http://kinhtedothi.vn/cat-giam-dieu-kien-kinh-doanh-con-doi-pho-khong-thuc-chat-329859.html>.
24. Trần Thuỷ, "Cải cách rất nhiều nhưng thiếu đột phá: Còn xa mới bằng Thái Lan", *VietNamNet*, 24 December 2018 <http://vietnamnet.vn/vn/kinh-doanh/dau-tu/moi-truong-kinh-doanh-nhieu-cai-cach-nhung-thieu-dot-pha-495540.html>.
25. "Thủ tướng quyết định mở rộng sân bay Tân Sơn Nhất về phía nam", *Tuổi Trẻ*, 28 March 2018 <https://tuoitre.vn/thu-tuong-quyet-dinh-mo-rong-san-bay-tan-son-nhat-ve-phia-nam-20180328171655472.htm>; "Đề xuất mở rộng Tân Sơn Nhất của ADPi được cho là không phù hợp", *VnExpress*, 1 March 2018 <https://vnexpress.net/thoi-su/de-xuat-mo-rong-tan-son-nhat-cua-adpi-bi-cho-la-khong-phu-hop-3716730.html>.
26. " 'Giáo dục của chúng ta chưa bao giờ được như bây giờ' ", *Giáo dục Việt Nam*, 4 November 2018 <http://giaoduc.net.vn/Giao-duc-24h/Giao-duc-cua-chung-ta-chua-bao-gio-duoc-nhu-bay-gio-post192455.gd>; "Kết quả lấy phiếu tín nhiệm của các thành viên Chính phủ", *VietNamNet*, 25 October 2018 <http://vietnamnet.vn/vn/thoi-su/quoc-hoi/ket-qua-lay-phieu-tin-nhiem-cac-thanh-vien-chinh-phu-485142.html>.
27. "Nền kinh tế duy trì đà chuyển biến tích cực", *Doanh Nghiệp*, 22 October 2018 <https://baomoi.com/nen-kinh-te-duy-tri-da-chuyen-bien-tich-cuc/c/28262192.epi>.
28. "Toà tuyên buộc Grab bồi thường cho Vinasun gần 5 tỷ đồng", VOV.VN, 28 December 2018 <https://vov.vn/vu-an/toa-tuyen-buoc-grab-boi-thuong-cho-vinasun-gan-5-ty-dong-857362.vov>; Phương Loan, "Vinasun kiện Grab: VKS bất ngờ thay đổi quan điểm", *Pháp luật Thành phố Hồ Chí Minh*, 28 December 2018 <https://baomoi.

com/vinasun-kien-grab-vks-bat-ngo-thay-doi-quan-diem/c/29161514.epi>; Hiếu Công, "Chính phủ có cách tiếp cận mới về 'siêu ứng dụng' như Grab", Zing.vn, 8 December 2018 <https://news.zing.vn/chinh-phu-co-cach-tiep-can-moi-ve-sieu-ung-dung-nhu-grab-post898683.html>; Thục Quyên, "Grab & Vinasun nên tự hoà giải, để kinh tế chia sẻ tự phát triển", *Tiền Phong*, 18 November 2018 <https://www.tienphong.vn/kinh-te/grab-vinasun-nen-tu-hoa-giai-de-kinh-te-chia-se-tu-phat-trien-1346449.tpo>; Hiếu Công, "Vì sao Bộ GTVT đổi chiều coi xe công nghệ giống taxi truyền thống?", Zing.vn, 25 October 2018 <https://news.zing.vn/vi-sao-bo-gtvt-doi-chieu-coi-xe-cong-nghe-giong-taxi-truyen-thong-post887147.html>.

29. "Phát biểu của Bộ trưởng TT&TT Nguyễn Mạnh Hùng tại Smart IoT Vietnam 2018", *VietNamNet*, 25 October 2018 <http://vietnamnet.vn/vn/thong-tin-truyen-thong/phat-bieu-cua-bo-truong-tt-tt-nguyen-manh-hung-tai-smart-iot-vietnam-2018-485096.html>.
30. "Tổng bí thư Trọng ca ngợi quan hệ với Trung Quốc đang tốt đẹp nhất", *Người Việt*, 30 September 2018 <https://www.nguoi-viet.com/viet-nam/tong-bi-thu-trong-ca-ngoi-quan-voi-trung-quoc-dang-tot-dep-nhat/>.
31. "Vietnam Halts South China Sea Oil Drilling Project under Pressure from China", Reuters, 22 March 2018 <https://www.reuters.com/article/us-southchinasea-vietnam/vietnam-halts-south-china-sea-oil-drilling-project-under-pressure-from-beijing-idUSKBN1GZ0JN>.
32. "Trung Quốc tập trận gần biên giới Việt Nam, xe tăng kiểu mới Type-15 lần đầu lộ diện", *VietTimes*, 20 December 2018 <https://viettimes.vn/trung-quoc-tap-tran-gan-bien-gioi-viet-nam-xe-tang-kieu-moi-type15-lan-dau-lo-dien-311487.html>.
33. Lan Anh and Tư Giang, "Vé để lên ngay con tàu 4.0", *VietNamNet*, 12 August 2018 <http://vietnamnet.vn/vn/tuanvietnam/tieudiem/ve-de-len-ngay-con-tau-4-0-469219.html>.
34. "Phó Thủ tướng Chính phủ Vương Đình Huệ thăm chính thức Hoa Kỳ", VOV.VN, 26 June 2018 <https://vov.vn/chinh-tri/pho-thu-tuong-chinh-phu-vuong-dinh-hue-tham-chinh-thuc-hoa-ky-779513.vov>; "Trưởng Ban Dân vận TƯ Trương Thị Mai thăm và làm việc tại Hoa Kỳ", VOV.VN, 1 December 2018 <https://vov.vn/chinh-tri/truong-ban-dan-van-tu-truong-thi-mai-tham-va-lam-viec-tai-hoa-ky-845790.vov>.
35. "Tổng Bí thư, Chủ tịch nước nói lý do kỷ luật ông Chu Hảo", *VietNamNet*, 24 November 2018 <http://vietnamnet.vn/vn/thoi-su/quoc-hoi/tong-bi-thu-chu-tich-nuoc-nguyen-phu-trong-noi-ly-do-ky-luat-ong-chu-hao-490715.html>.
36. "Chuyến thăm Nga, Hungary của Tổng Bí thư đạt nhiều kết quả quan trọng", VOV.VN, 12 September 2018 <https://vov.vn/chinh-tri/chuyen-tham-nga-hungary-cua-tong-bi-thu-dat-nhieu-ket-qua-quan-trong-811833.vov>.

VIETNAM AND MEKONG COOPERATIVE MECHANISMS

To Minh Thu and Le Dinh Tinh

Regional cooperation in the Mekong Basin has become increasingly dynamic in recent years with the emergence of new mechanisms and the reshuffling of existing ones. During the 1990s, Mekong cooperative efforts were primarily confined to the riparian countries. However, over the past ten years, as a result of its strategic location and growth potential, the Mekong Basin region has attracted the attention of major powers and developmental partners, including the United States, China, Japan, India and the European Union. The cooperative mechanisms both among riparian countries and with external partners have provided platforms for discussion of regional issues, especially water resource management, economic development and integration into the regional and global markets, regional connectivity, and addressing common challenges.

In 2018, a series of summits related to the Mekong region took place. In January, Cambodia hosted the 2nd Mekong-Lancang Cooperation (MLC) Summit. In March, Vietnam held the 6th Greater Mekong Subregion (GMS) Summit and the 10th Cambodia-Laos-Vietnam (CLV) Development Triangle Area Summit. In April, the 3rd Mekong River Commission Summit took place in Cambodia. This was followed by the 8th Ayeyawady–Chao Phraya–Mekong Economic Cooperation Strategy (ACMECS) Summit in Thailand in June and the 10th Mekong-Japan Summit in October. In addition, a number of Ministerial-level meetings were held,

---

TO MINH THU is Director of the Center for Security and Development, Institute for Foreign Policy and Strategic Studies in the Diplomatic Academy of Vietnam.

LE DINH TINH is Deputy Director General of the Institute for Foreign Policy and Strategic Studies, Diplomatic Academy of Vietnam. This chapter benefits from the contribution of Dr Le Hai Binh's discussion of the various Mekong cooperative mechanisms published in the June 2018 issue of the *Communist Review*.

laying the ground for further cooperation as well as the restructuring of many of the major cooperative frameworks. Vietnam has made significant contributions to the success of these summits, particularly through hosting the GMS Summit and the CLV Development Triangle Area Summit, and its active participation in others. This chapter will review the development of these major cooperative frameworks in the Mekong Basin and Vietnam's proactive and comprehensive approach to these mechanisms, including the newly established MLC framework.

Diversity and Mixture of Cooperative Mechanisms

At present there exist more than ten cooperative mechanisms in the Mekong Basin Region. Some involve only the riparian countries while others are between the countries along the Mekong and its external partners. The following section briefly explains the formation and recent development of these mechanisms.

Cooperative Mechanisms between Riparian Countries

The Mekong River Commission (MRC): In April 1995, Cambodia, Laos, Thailand and Vietnam signed "The Mekong Agreement for Cooperation for the Sustainable Development of the Mekong River Basin", which established the Mekong River Commission.

Among the many existing cooperative mechanisms in the Mekong basin, the MRC is the only organization that was formed based on an international agreement, with a well-established operating structure serving as a recognized knowledge hub and platform for water diplomacy in the region. With the Mekong Agreement, the MRC is also the sole organization that has the function of setting legal frameworks for water resource management, with specific and strict regulations on water use. However, the absence of China and Myanmar means that these countries are not bound by decisions and consultation made by the MRC. In addition, despite having a series of procedures designed to provide a systematic and uniform process for implementing the agreement and a large number of expert reports for consultation by member countries, the MRC has been criticized for lacking legally binding authority over its members.[1] Some donors have also cut their funding to the commission, accusing it of financial mismanagement. As a result, the MRC has recently undergone major reforms to transfer ownership of the commission from foreign donors to the member countries, including a new funding mechanism in which member countries will gradually increase their contributions to the MRC, with the goal of achieving financial independence by 2030.[2]

Amid criticism of its efficiency and authority, the 3rd MRC Summit in Siem Reap in April 2018 issued the Phnom Penh Declaration, which "reiterates the MRC member countries' highest-level political commitment to the 1995 Mekong Agreement and the primary and unique role of the MRC in cooperating on sustainable development of water and related resources in the Mekong River Basin". Furthermore, the declaration articulates the expectation for "the MRC to foster joint efforts and partnerships to optimize any development opportunities and to address challenges and risks through a basin-wide, integrated, gender-sensitive and inclusive multi-disciplinary process". According to the Commission's Chief Executive Officer, Dr Pham Tuan Phan, the summit "confirms the MRC as the premier intergovernmental body … set to lead sustainable development of the Mekong River Basin".[3]

Greater Mekong Subregion Cooperation (GMS): The GMS was established in 1992 at the initiative of the Asian Development Bank (ADB), comprising Cambodia, China (represented by Yunnan Province and Guangxi Zhuang Autonomous Region), Laos, Myanmar, Thailand and Vietnam. The GMS agenda focuses on infrastructural connectivity along the three landmark economic corridors: the North-South Economic Corridor, the East-West Economic Corridor and the Southern Economic Corridor. In addition it identifies other priority areas, including transportation, energy, the environment, tourism, telecommunications, trade, investment, human resource development, agricultural and rural development, and urban development in the economic corridors. Over the past three decades, GMS projects have helped to promote regional connectivity and production networks in the region. Since its establishment, more than $20 billion in investments have been directly channelled through the programme. These investments have helped the GMS countries to diversify, strengthen and integrate their economies.[4]

The 6th GMS Summit was held in Hanoi in March 2018 and saw the approval of the Regional Investment Framework 2022, with a list of 227 specific projects worth approximately US$66 billion,[5] the adoption of the Joint Declaration of the Summit, the Hanoi Plan of Action 2018–2022, and a number of documents guiding key areas and measures for cooperation over the next five years, including expanding the current economic corridors. It was also the first time that a GMS Business Summit was held. This was an initiative of the Vietnamese host to strengthen dialogues between private enterprises and governments and connect businesses in the region and the world, while encouraging resources from the private sector for the GMS programmes.

The Ayeyawady–Chao Phraya–Mekong Economic Cooperation Strategy (ACMECS): ACMECS is the framework for economic cooperation among Cambodia, Laos, Myanmar, Thailand and Vietnam, established in November 2003 at the initiative of Thailand during the Bagan Summit. ACMECS focuses on seven areas of cooperation through its working groups on trade and investment, agriculture, industry, energy, transport, tourism, human resource development and healthcare.

The recent 8th Summit in Thailand this year marked a turning point for this mechanism. At this summit, the leaders agreed on the ACMECS Master Plan 2019–2023, which provides guidelines for ACMECS over the next five years. The ACMECS Master Plan focuses on multidimensional connectivity and highlights a people-centred approach. It aims to complement the Master Plan on ASEAN Connectivity 2025 and other regional and global development efforts. The ACMECS Master Plan is expected to help the subregion "integrate into the global value and supply chains through the application of knowledge and innovation, access to digital technology, and public-private partnerships".[6]

To help finance projects under the ACMECS Master Plan, Thailand has proposed the establishment of an ACMECS Fund, which received support from both riparian countries and its development partners. The ACMECS Fund has attracted interest from regional observers, who view it as a step to reduce dependence on investment from major powers.[7]

Mekong-Lancang Cooperation (MLC): Thailand first proposed the idea of Mekong-Lancang cooperation between Vietnam, Cambodia, Laos, Myanmar, Thailand and China in 2012. The initiative, at that time, however, did not attract much attention. Later, at the November 2014 ASEAN-China Summit in Myanmar, China's Premier Li Keqiang expressed support for the initiative and proposed establishing the Mekong-Lancang cooperation and dialogue mechanism. With the strong support of China, the MLC was formally established on 23 March 2016 with the adoption of the Sanya Declaration on Mekong-Lancang Cooperation, which defines the "3+5" cooperation framework. The "3+5" framework represents the three cooperation pillars (political and security, economic and social, sustainable development and humanities) and five key priority areas (connectivity, production capacity, cross-border economic cooperation, water resources, agriculture and poverty reduction) of the MLC.[8]

In the space of two years, the MLC has achieved substantial results in terms of institution building and project implementation. Regarding institutional capacity, the MLC has created a multi-level meeting mechanism, from biennial summits, the annual ministerial meetings and the Senior Officials Meeting, to the specialized working groups on various areas such as water resources, poverty reduction, connectivity, and cooperation in production capacity. The MLC has also established two regional cooperation centres, the Environmental Cooperation Center in Phnom Penh and Water Resources Cooperation in Beijing. Member countries of the MLC have established a secretariat or national coordination unit for the MLC under their respective ministries of foreign affairs. In addition, cooperation at the sectoral and local levels and among scholars and businesses has been conducted. Furthermore, the MLC's Special Fund has supported 132 projects (including 49 projects of Mekong countries), adopted the list of 45 "early harvest" projects, and implemented many other initiatives from 2016 to 2018. Financially, China has committed $11.54 billion in preferential loans and credit, of which $1.54 billion is in yuan.

The 2nd MLC Summit in Phnom Penh on 10 January 2018 adopted two important documents, the Phnom Penh Joint Declaration and the Plan of Action on the Lancang-Mekong Cooperation (2018–2022). The documents affirm that 2018 and 2019 are for foundation laying, which means emphasis should be focused on strengthening sectoral cooperation as well as planning and implementing small- and medium-sized cooperation projects. From 2020 to 2022, the MLC will embark on the consolidation and expansion stage, in which member countries will further strengthen their cooperation in the five priority areas and may explore new areas of cooperation. The meeting also noted a list of 214 project proposals and reports from six specialized working groups.

The rapid development of the MLC has primarily been due to the efforts and activeness of China. Although the Mekong countries have some doubts about China's agenda, they continue to support the MLC out of political calculation, as well as shared interests and goals.

In addition to the above-mentioned mechanisms the Mekong Basin is also home to several others; such as the Cambodia-Laos-Vietnam Development Triangle, the Cambodia-Laos-Myanmar-Vietnam Cooperation, and the ASEAN Mekong Basin Development Cooperation, which focuses on closing development gaps among countries in the region.

Regional Cooperative Mechanisms with External Partners

Mekong-Japan Cooperation: The Mekong-Japan Cooperation Framework was launched in 2007, covering a wide range of areas of cooperation such as socio-economic development and the implementation of the Millennium Development Goals, infrastructure construction, environmental protection, and water security in the Mekong. Some noteworthy collaborations include "The Japan-Mekong Plan of Action for 63 Joint Programs", focusing on the Green Mekong Initiative and the Mekong-Japan Economic and Industrial Cooperation Initiative. The Green Mekong Initiative seeks to promote biodiversity, cooperation on the management of water resources and to urgently address environmental issues relating to regional development. For the period 2016 to 2018, Japan has also pledged to increase its official development assistance to ¥750 billion (which constitutes an additional ¥150 billion relative to the previous cycle) to promote sustainable development in the four pillars of development of industrial infrastructure, industrial resources, sustainable development and policy coordination with stakeholders.[9]

The year 2018 also marked a new stage for Mekong-Japanese cooperation. At the 10th Mekong-Japan Summit in October, leaders adopted the "Tokyo Strategy 2018 for Mekong-Japan Cooperation", together with annexes on "Mekong-Japan Cooperation Projects for promoting SDGs", "Mekong-Japan Cooperation Projects in Synergy with Japan's policy to realize a free and open Indo-Pacific" and "Japan's Ongoing or Possible Cooperation Projects related to ACMECS Master Plan". These documents are to set the course for future Japan-Mekong cooperation, with higher commitment in terms of financial resources and a deeper cooperation agenda.

Lower Mekong Initiative and Friends of the Mekong: The year 2009 saw the United States' return to the Mekong region[10] with the Lower Mekong Initiative (LMI) signed between the United States, Cambodia, Laos, Thailand and Vietnam (Myanmar would join later in 2012). The countries agreed to enhance cooperation in areas of the environment, health, education and infrastructure development. To date, the LMI has been carrying out a number of outstanding initiatives and collaborative activities. The Mekong River Commission and the Mississippi River Commission have recently signed a "sister-river" agreement to exchange experience and cooperation. The "Forecast Mekong" programme aims to build an automatic observatory to monitor climate change in the subregion.

The LMI "takes a forward-looking vision which promote[s] women's empowerment across all lines of effort, and tak[es] an integrated approach to enhancing water, energy, food security, and addressing environmental challenges in the region".[11] In 2018, at the 11th LMI Ministerial Meeting, the U.S. secretary of state and the foreign ministers approved a new organizing structure for the LMI to be

> more dynamic in responding to the sub-region's needs by combining previous work streams into two inclusive pillars: 1) the Water, Energy, Food, and Environment Nexus; and 2) Human Development and Connectivity

> (which will include but is not limited to activities related to connectivity, health, and education). Member countries will integrate the themes of gender equality and women's empowerment, connectivity, and public-private partnership across all LMI activities.[12]

The United States also provided US$2 million in support of the Mekong Water Data Initiative to strengthen water data management and information sharing in the lower Mekong. The results of the 2018 LMI Ministerial Meeting can be seen as a sign of more concrete American commitment in the region.

In addition to the LMI, the countries have also established the Friends of the Lower Mekong (FLM), a cooperative mechanism between the LMI countries and its development partners, with the first FLM Ministerial Meeting held in July 2011 with the participation of LMI countries, Australia, Japan, South Korea, New Zealand, the European Union, the ADB and the World Bank.

It can be said that regional cooperation in the Mekong Basin has been undergoing tremendous change in both quality and quantity. Through these mechanisms, riparian countries have attracted more resources to improve their infrastructures, transport connectivity, sustainable management of water resources, and people's livelihoods. The programmes and projects under the various cooperative frameworks have helped to protect and sustainably develop the water resources of the Mekong in the interests of the over sixty million people living in the basin, thus contributing to poverty reduction in one of the poorest regions in the world. Furthermore, connectivity projects also help the Mekong countries to integrate with the vibrant economic centres of the wider Asia-Pacific region.

However, subregional cooperation also faces various challenges. It is easy to see that the countries in the region, with the exception of China, have limited economic capacity to invest in regional programmes and thus rely on external support. Mekong countries lack ownership over the funding and sometimes even control of the development projects. This form of cooperation leaves little room for them to assert their own regional and national interests vis-à-vis the geopolitical agenda of their development partners.[13] In addition, the involvement of and competition between regional powers in recent years have made it even more challenging for Mekong countries to manage the cooperation agenda or even follow the new initiatives by external partners.

Moreover, despite the existence of more than ten cooperative mechanisms, cooperation on water management in the Mekong falls far below expectations. Dams have been built on the river mainstream without notification or consultation with relevant countries, causing irreversible and long-term environmental and economic impacts for the countries in the Lower Mekong Delta, such as a lack of water, loss of sediment and unexpected changes in the ecosystem.

Furthermore, the presence of the large number of cooperative mechanisms in a subregion of six countries inevitably leads to overlap and duplication of cooperative efforts. Thus, there remains a great deal of room for the Mekong countries to play a more proactive role in setting cooperation agenda and synchronizing the areas of focus, which can help to harness these mechanisms more effectively for national and regional development.

Vietnam's Proactive and Comprehensive Approach to the Mekong Cooperative Mechanisms

As the lowest-lying country in the Mekong Delta, Vietnam has the greatest urgency in wanting to promote trans-border cooperation. In fact, Mekong cooperative mechanisms have enabled Vietnam to "boost growth and regional connectivity, particularly in border areas".[14]

Security and Development Challenges

In the words of Vietnam's Prime Minister Nguyen Xuan Phuc, the Mekong subregion is the space of "both security and development" which directly affects Vietnam.[15] The water of the Mekong plays a critical role in the lives of nearly eighteen million Vietnamese people, which is equivalent to twenty per cent of the country's population. Half of Vietnam's rice production comes from the Mekong Delta. Paradoxically, while the delta is the granary of the country, it remains the poorest area. Culturally, the Vietnamese are proud of what they call "Nine-Dragons delta". Unfortunately, due to both natural and man-made reasons, two of the "Nine-dragons" are no longer there to ascend. The river mouths of Ba Lai and Bat Sac are already dead and unnavigable. Infrastructure in the delta remains lacklustre, while educational levels are below average for the country. Furthermore, the water security challenges of the Mekong delta are aggravated by climate change and the rising sea level.

It has become a well-known fact that although the Xayaburi and Don Sahong dam projects in Laos have not begun to store water, the Mekong Delta already lacks water for cultivation as a result of salinization and landslides. The situation will only become worse as more dams are being built or planned upstream, particularly further north towards China. The livelihoods of the people in the Mekong Delta will depend not only on assurances of food, fish, water and transportation but also the ability to respond to related non-traditional security challenges such as climate change, environmental degradation and natural disasters.[16] Scientists have forecast that if these challenges are not dealt with properly, the Mekong Delta will be wiped off the map by the end of the century.[17]

Several commentators have argued that the issue of security and development challenges in the Mekong is the "new South China Sea issue" for Vietnam.[18] In fact, the Mekong's water security challenges affect the daily livelihoods of millions who are tied to the fortunes of the river.

Prior to the Xayaburi dam project, Vietnam was not especially vocal about the Mekong issue at regional fora or even in bilateral settings. The advancement of the project however caught many in the policymaking and scholarly circles of Vietnam by surprise. Initially, Vietnam did not see the project as helpful to the economic development and sustainability of the basin or for Vietnam-Laos relations. Later, as the issue unfolded, the understanding that the decision by Laos was based on that country's national interests gained more ground in Vietnam, first and foremost among academia. It is, however, difficult to arrive at that perception, because the water issue is by its nature transboundary and, more importantly, Vietnam is the lowest Mekong country.

Therefore, after Xayaburi, Vietnam became more vocal about its concerns and began to seek new ways to more effectively safeguard Mekong water security. The Ministry of Foreign Affairs, which is responsible for coordinating line agencies on the subject matter at regional fora, began to issue documents that prioritize the Mekong issue in the national agenda. One example is the issuance of a significant document titled "Vietnam International Integration Strategy" in 2015, which was among the first documents that "securitize" the water issue in the country. Traditionally, water was considered as a "resource" issue, and thus had mostly been under the ambit of the Ministry of Agriculture and Rural Development and the Ministry of National Resources and Environment. These days, the water issue of the Mekong is an ongoing concern among line agencies and the Communist Party leadership. In addition to being a resource, water has officially become a security issue in Vietnam.[19]

The securitization of water takes place against the background of fragile peace and stability in Southeast Asia. A report by the Stimson Center argues that the Mekong issue should be approached with sensitivity due to the "hard-won peace and stability" of this region.[20] Given that war in the jungles and deltas of Southeast Asia still remains a recent memory, along with the skirmishes between Thailand and Cambodia over the Preah Vihear Temple, the border tensions between

Cambodia and Laos, the crisis in Rakhine State, terrorism in different parts of the region, and the disputes in the South China Sea, peace and stability in the region should not be taken for granted.

Preferred Approaches and Measures

Vietnam adopts a proactive and comprehensive approach to the Mekong issue. This is reflected in Vietnam's hosting of a number of related international meetings and summits. The latest example is the 6th Greater Mekong Subregion Summit organized in March 2018 in Hanoi, where, under the auspices of Vietnam, many ideas were proposed to the regional audience. Vietnam was also the host of the 8th Cambodia-Laos-Myanmar-Vietnam Cooperation Summit, the 7th ACMES Summit in October 2016, and the 2nd Mekong-Japan Summit in 2010. In a similar fashion, Vietnam tries to raise its concerns and priorities and look for mutual shared interests through the other cooperative mechanisms.

At the 3rd Summit of the Mekong River Commission in Cambodia on 18 April 2018, Prime Minister Nguyen Xuan Phuc proposed that the MRC should focus on "fair, appropriate, and sustainable" use of the Mekong water resources and other resources,[21] the effective and full implementation of the 1995 Mekong Agreement and other related procedures, and the promotion of its monitoring and coordinating role among the MRC member states.[22]

Similarly, within the framework of the Mekong-Lancang Cooperation, Vietnam emphasizes the management and sustainable utilization of water resources for the sake of "balance of interests and responsibilities" among the riparian countries.[23] For Vietnam, ensuring water resource security and enhancing cooperation in trans-border river management are its highest priorities in the MLC.[24]

In being proactive, Vietnam not only reacts to partners' proposals but also comes forward with its own. For instance, at the GMS in March 2018, Prime Minister Nguyen Xuan Phuc stated as follows:

> As one of three pillars of GMS, the Government of Viet Nam currently prioritizes investing and attracting investment in the vital transport routes. In addition to already funded expressways such as Ho Chi Minh City–Can Tho–Ca Mau, Ha Noi–Hai Phong, Ha Noi–Lao Cai (connecting to Kunming), Ha Noi–Lang Son (connecting to Nanjing), we also work to connect the "two corridors, one economic belt" framework with the Belt and Road Initiative. Viet Nam is actively promoting investment in transport infrastructure on the East-West, North-South, and Southern economic corridors.[25]

Vietnamese enthusiasm for Mekong development means that it has become a favourite partner and recipient country of major external donors. Although it was Thailand that initiated the MLC, Vietnam is not shying away from working with China, the biggest country and donor in the basin. Vietnam has actively participated in the MLC since the early days. Furthermore, the projects proposed by Vietnam match the MLC's specific priorities, such as flood and drought management and harmonization of criteria and procedures.[26] As for the GMS, by December 2017, connectivity projects in Vietnam had been valued around US$6 billion, accounting for 30 per cent of the GMS's mobilized capital.[27]

Vietnam's engagement is not just limited to attracting inbound investments and assistance; the government and businesses of Vietnam are also committed to going outbound. For instance, Vietnam has supported Laos and Cambodia in building expressways to connect border localities and border markets. Furthermore, Vietnamese enterprises have invested in a hundred projects in the CLV, with total registered capital of more than US$3.8 billion.[28]

Another example of Vietnam's activism is in Track II diplomacy. In 2017, the Vietnam Center for Mekong Studies was established in the Diplomatic Academy of Vietnam (DAV), as part of the MLC's network of Global Centers for Mekong Studies, to share information and improve management capability. It is noteworthy that the DAV is one of the first academic institutions in Vietnam to have suggested the inclusion of security in research and policy recommendations to the government. Vietnamese scholars took part in all of the series of meetings of the Council for Security Co-operation in the Asia-Pacific, which produced memorandums of understanding on enhancing water security in the region.[29]

The approach that Vietnam adopts vis-à-vis the Mekong issue is also comprehensive. The case of Xayaburi shows that Vietnam does not separate the dam project from the overall Vietnam-Laos relationship. Vietnam raises the issue in ASEAN in a cautious manner for fear of causing disunity within the association.[30] This fear is grounded on two premises. One is the fact that the Mekong does not physically run through all the ASEAN countries. The other is due to the association's packed agenda, which may not be able to cope with the addition of another contentious matter. This is similar to Vietnam's approach to the South China Sea disputes. Vietnam's goal for the South China Sea within the ASEAN framework is twofold: solving the issue (peacefully) and maintaining the association's solidarity. In the ideal scenario, Vietnam wants to make a case for mutual inclusion, not exclusion.

Vietnam's delicate approach to the Mekong originates from the country's foreign policy of keeping a balanced relationship with regional major powers —

namely, the United States, China, Japan and India — who have recently sought to engage more in the subregion. The propensity for major powers to have conflicting interests is predictable. Their rivalries continue to play in the background of the Mekong cooperative mechanisms, with China declining to become a member of the Mekong River Commission while the United States is not part of the Greater Mekong Subregion Cooperation.

In proposing a "balance of interests and responsibilities", Vietnam is aware of the fact that the goals of the LMI do not contradict those of the MLC. However, these are two starkly different processes led by two different sponsors. The LMI has strategic significance for the United States, which is evidenced by the smooth transition of the initiative from the Obama administration to its successor Republican administration, which might have been expected not to prioritize any undertaking relating to the environment. Unfortunately, the LMI has not been free of criticism. One major complaint is that the LMI is underfinanced, suggesting that it is more symbolic than substantive. This is in contrast to the MLC, which came into being much later but grew rapidly under Chinese supervision. However, the MLC is constrained by the ongoing anxieties of the other riparian states about China, since China's physical presence in the greater Mekong subregion may impair its objectivity and impartiality.

The different goals and approaches taken by the United States and China make a country like Vietnam more cautious. The Trump administration has labelled China "a strategic competitor" and "revisionist" country. The rivalry has resulted, inter alia, in the unfolding trade war between the two countries. Vietnam is mindful of this dynamic and thus tries to tap into the strengths of each mechanism. This hedging is reflected in a recent statement by the deputy minister of national defence, Lieutenant General Nguyen Chi Vinh, that Vietnam does not wish to "get caught in the spiral of competition between the United States and China".[31]

Inclusion, openness, transparency, consultation and ASEAN's centrality remain Vietnam's top governing principles in the construction of regional regimes and regulations when it comes to issues such as security architecture or transboundary water issues.

In terms of inclusion, Hanoi has, on multiple occasions, tried to convince China to join the MRC. For example, at the 2nd MRC summit in Ho Chi Minh City in April 2014, member states, including Vietnam, expressed their hope that China and Myanmar would join the institution.[32] The decision-making process, according to the Vietnamese government, should involve all the stakeholders. Furthermore, Vietnam invited around two thousand businesses from around the world for the March 2018 GMS in order to help governments and businesses interact and learn from each other.

As for openness, the discussions among policymakers and scholars show that Vietnam does not expect any cooperative mechanism in the Mekong basin to conform to any exclusionary way of thinking and grouping. Openness is helpful for enhancing connectivity.[33] Besides, the problem of the overlapping cooperative mechanisms in the Mekong Basin could be tackled if they were to supplement and complement each other. Ideally, these mechanisms could work in harmony towards the same goals, but only if they are open and inclusive in nature.

With regard to transparency, Vietnam's viewpoint is that upstream nations should disclose information about the operational regimes of their dams. Sharing information and data is key to ensuring water security in the basin.[34] Transparency is not only technical but also political. Of the various groupings that the country has membership in, Vietnam has made clear that it does not intend to use them to gang up on any country. This is demonstrated in Vietnam's engagement with the mechanisms led by Mekong countries, the U.S.-led initiative and the China-sponsored frameworks. Political friction, if any, from Vietnam's partaking in these mechanisms is an unfortunate side effect rather than the ultimate goal of the country.

On the role of consultation and information sharing, Pham Binh Minh, deputy prime minister and foreign minister has said,

> Close consultation and mutual learning are two of MLC's key features. Yet we notice that information sharing on project implementation has not been given due attention. Therefore, it is imperative that we strengthen the communication channel among member countries to ensure that information on the implementation of MLC projects is shared and member countries are given opportunities to involve in the process as they wish. This is particularly relevant as the number of projects under MLC framework is going very fast.[35]

Lastly, in light of ASEAN centrality, Vietnam has brought the Mekong issue to the discussions among members with the expectation that ASEAN should be at the helm of any security concern that might affect the region.[36] The initiatives by major powers are welcome by ASEAN as long as they do not impair ASEAN's central role. Being a "proactive and responsible" member of the association, Vietnam strictly follows this rule of the game. Vietnam's promotion of ASEAN's centrality can be seen during Vietnam's single chairmanship in 2010 and likely again in 2020. Sharing the approach taken by other members with regard to the

United States' Free and Open Indo-Pacific Strategy and China's Belt and Road Initiative, Vietnam would like to discuss these grand schemes within the ASEAN framework. The reason behind this motive of Vietnam's to keep ASEAN centrality is that the United States and China could well dominate the regional discourse of cooperation and competition with their predominant ideas and resources. The Mekong issue is part of the enhanced engagement of the region by the United States and China, and thus Vietnam looks at it no differently than at any issue of a similar nature. That means any cooperation regimes for the Mekong should be designed and promoted in a way that could work in tandem with the ASEAN-led mechanisms.

Conclusion

The year 2018 passed with a series of high-level events, marking a milestone in major Mekong regional cooperative frameworks. Both riparian countries and external partners have demonstrated greater commitment in making each and every mechanism more relevant and responsive to the development needs of the region in a more efficient and sustainable way. Vietnam's contribution to regional development has been well received, highlighted by its successful hosting of the 6th GMS Summit and the 10th CLV Summit in Hanoi, as well as its active participation in all of the regional frameworks.

Given all the challenges and in line with the country's foreign policy direction, Vietnam's targets for the Mekong issue include the promotion of regional cooperation on water resource management, connectivity, sustainability and security. Vietnam's preferred approach stems from widely adopted rules of the game such as fair and rational use of water resources, inclusion, transparency, openness, consultation and respect for regional cooperative mechanisms, with ASEAN being at the centre. In the meantime, due to the strategic and difficult nature of the issue, Vietnam has shown that it is responsive to new ideas and institutions, of which the Mekong-Lancang Cooperation is one, as long as they meet the high standards of sustainability, ensure security for all the stakeholders, and observe the rules of the game. Whether the reality would correspond to Vietnam's wishes would depend also on how other partners act.

Notes

1. Gabriella Neusner, "Why the Mekong River Commission Matters", *The Diplomat*, 7 December 2016 <https://thediplomat.com/2016/12/why-the-mekong-river-commission-matters/>.

2. Luke Hunt, "Mekong River Commission Faces Radical Change", *The Diplomat*, 22 January 2016 <https://thediplomat.com/2016/01/mekong-river-commission-faces-radical-change/>.
3. <http://www.mrcmekong.org/news-and-events/news/media-release-mekong-leaders-reaffirm-the-mekong-river-commissions-primary-and-unique-role-in-sustainable-development-of-the-mekong-river-basin/>.
4. ADB, *Greater Mekong Subregion: Twenty-Five Years of Partnership* (Asian Development Bank, 2018).
5. <https://greatermekong.org/gms-regional-investment-framework-2022>.
6. <http://www.mfa.go.th/main/en/information/8151/90577-Press-Statement-by-His-Excellency-General-Prayut-Chan-o-cha-(Ret.)-Prime-Minister-of-the-Kingdom-of-Thailand-at-the-Press-Conference-on-Outcome-Documents-of-the-8th-Ayeyawady-Chao-Phraya-Mekong-Economic-Cooperation-Strategy-(ACMECS)-Summit.html>.
7. Yukako Ono, "Thailand Plans Regional Infrastructure Fund to Reduce China Dependence", *Nikkei Asian Review*, 4 June 2018 <https://asia.nikkei.com/Politics/International-Relations/Thailand-plans-regional-infrastructure-fund-to-reduce-China-dependence>.
8. "Sanya Declaration" <http://www.fmprc.gov.cn/mfa_eng/wjdt_665385/2649_665393/t1350039.shtml>.
9. New Tokyo Strategy 2015 for Mekong – Japan Cooperation (MJC2015).
10. Chheang Vannarith, "An Introduction to Greater Mekong Subregional Cooperation", CICP working paper no. 34 (Cambodia Institute for Cooperation and Peace, 2010).
11. <https://www.state.gov/r/pa/prs/ps/2018/08/284928.htm>.
12. 11th LMI Ministerial Joint Statement <https://www.lowermekong.org/news/11th-lmi-ministerial-joint-statement>.
13. Doung Bosba, "Dynamics of Cooperation Mechanisms in the Mekong", *Khmer Times*, 23 October 2018 <https://www.khmertimeskh.com/50543025/dynamics-of-cooperation-mechanisms-in-the-mekong/>.
14. "PM: Mekong – River of Cooperation and Development", *Voice of Vietnam*, 29 March 2018 <https://english.vov.vn/politics/pm-mekong-river-of-cooperation-and-development-371595.vov> (accessed 1 November 2018).
15. "PM Writes about VN's Contributions to GMS, CLV", *VGPNews* <http://news.chinhphu.vn/Home/PM-writes-about-VNs-contributions-to-GMS-CLV/20183/33475.vgp> (accessed 15 November 2018).
16. See, for example, Nguyen Ngoc Tran, "Dong bang song Cuu Long: Nhung thach thuc hien nay va ngay mai" [The Mekong Delta: Current and future challenges], *Tia Sang*, 4 April 2016 <http://tiasang.com.vn/-dien-dan/dong-bang-song-cuu-long-nhung-thach-thuc-hien-nay-va-ngay-mai-9531> (accessed 9 November 2018).
17. For instance, forecasts made by scientists at the 2017 Greater Mekong Forum on Water, Food, and Energy, Yangoon, Myanmar. Further information is available at <https://wle-mekong.cgiar.org/event/2017-greater-mekong-forum/>.

18. See, for example, Richard Heyderian, “Proactive Diplomacy in the Mekong Dispute Only Way to Resolve Brewing Conflict”, *South China Morning Post*, 14 January 2018 <https://www.scmp.com/news/china/policies-politics/article/2128079/proactive-diplomacy-mekong-river-dispute-only-way> (accessed 28 October 2018).
19. See, for example, the Central Executive Committee of the Communist Party of Vietnam, *Resolution of the Poliburo on International Integration (Resolution No. 22)*, 10 April 2013.
20. Richard P. Cronin and Timothy Hamlin, *Mekong Turning Point: Shared River for a Shared Future* (Washington, DC: The Stimson Center, 2012).
21. “April 2–8: PM Nguyen Xuan Phuc Attends Third MRC Summit in Cambodia”, *Nhan Dan Online*, 9 April 2018 <http://en.nhandan.com.vn/week_review/item/6020602-april-2-%E2%80%93-8-pm-nguyen-xuan-phuc-attends-third-mrc-summit-in-cambodia.html> (accessed 7 November 2018).
22. “PM Attends Third Mekong River Commission Summit”, *Viet Nam News*, 6 April 2018.
23. Le Hai Binh (2018), “Cooperation Mechanisms in the Mekong Region and Vietnam’s Participation”, *Communist Party Review*, 27 July 2018 <http://english.tapchicongsan.org.vn/Home/Foreign-Relations-and-International-Intergration/2018/1141/Cooperation-Mechanisms-in-the-Mekong-Region-and-Vietnams-participation.aspx> (accessed 8 November 2018).
24. To Minh Thu, “Hợp tác Mê Công – Lan Thương: Những nhân tố tác động và triển vọng phát triển” [Mekong-Lancang Cooperation: Key factors and prospect], *Nghien cuu Quoc te*, no. 3 (114) (September 2018): 64–82; “Thủ tướng kết thúc tham dự Hội nghị cấp cao Hợp tác Mekong – Lan Thương” [Prime minister concluded his attendance at Mekong-Lancang Cooperation Summit] <http://thutuong.chinhphu.vn/Home/Thu-tuong-ket-thuc-tham-du-Hoi-nghi-cap-cao-Hop-tac-MekongLan-Thuong/20181/27555.vgp> (accessed 12 November 2018).
25. Speech by Prime Minister Nguyen Xuan Phuc at the GMS Business Summit <http://news.chinhphu.vn/Home/Speech-by-Prime-Minister-Nguyen-Xuan-Phuc-at-GMS-Business-Summit/20183/33506.vgp> (accessed 15 November 2018).
26. “Mekong-Lancang Cooperation for Peace, Sustainable Development”, *Voice of Vietnam (VOV)*, 1 October 2018 <https://english.vov.vn/politics/mekonglancang-cooperation-for-peace-sustainable-development-366427.vov> (accessed 13 November 2018).
27. “PM Writes about VN’s Contributions to GMS, CLV”, *VGPNews* <http://news.chinhphu.vn/Home/PM-writes-about-VNs-contributions-to-GMS-CLV/20183/33475.vgp> (accessed 15 November 2018).
28. “Ibid.
29. See, for example, Le Dinh Tinh, “Troubled Water: Seeking Co-operation along the Mekong”, *Global Asia* 7, no. 3 (2012): 95–99.
30. See, for example, Le Dinh Tinh, “Enhancing Water Security in Southeast Asia”,

Non-Traditional Security Challenge in Asia: Approaches and Responses, edited by Shebonti and Uttam Kumar Sinha (New Delhi: Routledge, 2015), pp. 175–205.

31. "Vietnam khong de bi cuon vao cuoc canh tranh My-Trung" [Not to let Vietnam get caught in the spiral of competition between the United States and China], *VnExpress*, 28 November 2018 <https://vnexpress.net/tin-tuc/thoi-su/viet-nam-khong-de-bi-loi-cuon-vao-cuoc-canh-tranh-my-trung-3845743.html> (accessed 28 November 2018).
32. Vietnam's Consulate General in Savanakhet-Laos, *MRC Wants China and Myanmar Joined* <https://vnconsulate-savanakhet.mofa.gov.vn/en-us/About%20Vietnam/General%20Information/Economic/Pages/MRC-wants-China-and-Myanmar-joined.aspx?p=3> (accessed 29 October 2018).
33. See, for example, "Remarks by Deputy Prime Minister, Foreign Minister Pham Binh Minh at the 3rd Indian Ocean Conference", 27 August 2018 <http://news.chinhphu.vn/Home/Remarks-by-Deputy-PM-FM-Pham-Binh-Minh-at-3rd-Indian-Ocean-Conference/20188/34510.vgp> (accessed 29 October 2018).
34. Remarks by Deputy Prime Minister, Foreign Minister Pham Binh Minh at the 3rd Mekong-Lancang Cooperation Ministerial Meeting, 15 December 2017, Yunan, China.
35. Ibid.
36. See, for example, "Remarks by Deputy Prime Minister, Foreign Minister Pham Binh Minh at the 3rd Indian Ocean Conference", 27 August 2018.

www.ingramcontent.com/pod-product-compliance
Lightning Source LLC
Chambersburg PA
CBHW061831260326
41914CB00005B/954